MANDE MUSIC

MANDE
MUSIC

Traditional and Modern Music of the Maninka

and Mandinka of Western Africa

Eric Charry

Chicago and London
The University of Chicago Press

Eric Charry is associate professor of music at Wesleyan University.

The University of Chicago Press, Chicago 60637
The University of Chicago Press, Ltd., London
© 2000 by The University of Chicago
All rights reserved. Published 2000
Printed in the United States of America
09 08 07 06 05 04 03 02 01 00 1 2 3 4 5

ISBN: 0-226-10161-4 (cloth)
ISBN: 0-226-10162-2 (paper)

Library of Congress Cataloging-in-Publication Data

Charry, Eric S.
    Mande music : traditional and modern music of the Maninka and Mandinka of
Western Africa / Eric Charry.
        p. cm. — (Chicago studies in ethnomusicology)
    Discography: p.
    Videography: p.
    Includes bibliographical references (p.) and index.
    ISBN 0-226-10161-4 (alk. paper).—ISBN 0-226-10162-2 (pbk.: alk. paper)
    1. Mandingo (African people)—Music—History and criticism. 2. Music—
Africa, West—History and criticism. I. Title. II. Series.
ML3760.C38 2000
781.62'9634 21—dc21

                                                                    99-046011

In memory of my parents, Lawrence and Hannah Charry
For Sandra, Hannah, Priya, and Miriam

CONTENTS

ILLUSTRATIONS

Figures

Maps

Transcriptions

TABLES

ACKNOWLEDGMENTS

I owe my first and deepest debt of gratitude to my family for their patience and understanding. Traveling through the villages and cities of four West African countries with my wife, Sandra, and our daughter Hannah was a great joy and a never-ending source of inspiration. Along with our other children, Priya and Miriam, they provided an atmosphere that made it possible for me to complete this book.

African hospitality knows no limits, and the warmth with which my family and I were received wherever we went, usually unannounced, made for a real education in human kindness. I thank all our hosts and friends in Africa for their unconditional acceptance of strangers. Although my motives as an American student of African music may have puzzled many of those I met, there was never the slightest hesitation in respecting the remarkable obligations of African hospitality, startling to one raised in the United States.

My initial interest in the kora was sparked and nurtured in America by my first kora teacher, Djimo Kouyate, and my first trip to Africa and continued growth would not have occurred without his expert and long-term guidance. My other African teachers are mentioned in the text, but I must single out those closest to me: Amadu Bansang Jobarteh, my principal kora teacher in Africa, and Bala Dounbouya, my principal bala teacher. I thank them for their generosity and teaching. I also benefited greatly from lessons and close contact with Sidiki Diabate, Dembo Konte, Lamin Konte, and Mamadou Kouyate on the kora, Fode Doumbia and Siriman Kouyate on the bala, Moussa Kouyate on the koni, Serang Kanoute on the dundun, Drissa Kone on the jembe, Omar Camara and Babanding Sanyang on kutiro drums, and "Salikene" Jemori Kouyate (my host in Niagassola) on the guitar. Toumani Diabate was extremely helpful and inspiring during my stays in Bamako. The bulk of my knowledge comes from these masters of their music, and I thank them dearly.

I have profited immensely from my contact with a community of scholars in the United States and abroad, and I appreciate their interest and help. The nucleus of this book was guided by two people: my principal dissertation adviser, Harold Powers, whose scholarly thoroughness and breadth have been a model not just for me but for countless others; and my outside reader, Roderic Knight, whose pioneering dissertation and other writings continue to inform my work. I held extended discussions about my dissertation with Judit Frigyesi and Charles Bird, and in more limited areas with John Ralph Willis, Sue Carole DeVale, and Philip Schuyler. My colleagues in the Mande Studies Association (MANSA), an exemplary interdisciplinary organization, have provided me with a perspective both broad and deep, and I have especially benefited from long discussions with David Conrad, Cheick M. Cherif Keita, Lansiné Kaba, Rainer Polak, and Clemens Zoebel and more limited discussions with Peter Mark and Valentine Vydrine. Both Namankoumba Kouyate, with whom I have played bala and guitar on three continents, and Lucy Durán, whose trails I followed from The Gambia to Mali, have been inspiring and helpful with my work. John Chernoff and David Conrad provided detailed, insightful comments on a nearly complete manuscript and continued discussions with me afterward. I gratefully acknowledge the active participation of all these scholars in my writing, and they are largely responsible for clarity of presentation. I also wish to thank three earlier teachers of mine: Peter Row and Ran Blake, who have greatly influenced how I think about and hear music, and David Locke, who first introduced me to African drumming.

My research in Africa would not have been possible without the expert linguistic, cultural, social, and day-to-day guidance of Gibril Bah in The Gambia and Kabine Kante in Conakry. I thank those African musicians and music lovers who shared their knowledge with me in lessons, interviews, or informal conversations: in The Gambia, Bakanding Camara, Samba Dansa, Ibrahima Jobarteh, and Salimu Kouyate; in Guinea, Kabine Diabate, Kerfala "Papa" Diabate, Sekou "Docteur" Diabate, Sekou "Bembeya" Diabate, Abraham Doukoure, Mohamed "Hombre" Doumbia, Fatoumata Kamissoko, Manfila "Dabadou" Kante, "Soba" Manfila Kante, Kemo Kouyate, Pivi Moriba, Balla Onivogui, Momo "Wandel" Soumah, and Jean Baptiste Williams; in Mali, Bakari Diabate, Djeli Mady Diabate, Kemogo Diabate, Moussa Diabate, Kasse Mady Diabate, Lansana Diabate (the surviving one of the Lafiabougou twins), Bala Djimba Diakite, Madou Diakite, Batrou Sekou Kouyate, Samba Kouyate, Bouba Sacko, Siaka Sidibe, and Djeli Mady Tounkara; in Senegal, Babou Diabate, Bakary Diedhiou, Lucky Diop, Abdoulaye Kanoute, Mory Kouyate, Soriba Kouyate, and Abdoulaye Ndiaye; and in France, Papa Diabate, Djessou Mory Kante, Manfila Kante, Salif Keita, and Kabine "Tagus" Traore.

Discographical research was greatly aided by Günter Gretz and his magnificent Archives of Popular African Music, Leo Sarkisian of the Africa section of Voice of America, and the private collections of Djimo Kouyate and Filipe Tejeda. In working directly with Arabic script I was aided by Mona Zaki.

The support and help of my former colleagues and students at the University of North Carolina at Greensboro and my new colleagues and students at Wesleyan University is much appreciated, and I thank them for their faith. I have also gained from contact with students in the first three Summer Jembe Institutes at UNCG, as well as with the faculty: Papa Ladji Camara, Sidi Mohammed "Joh" Camara, Mohamed Da Costa, Madou Dembele, Papus Diabate, Abdoul Doumbia, Djimo Kouyate, and Lansana Kouyate. For their help in various ways I also thank Akya Kouyate, Sandy Blocker, Daouda "le Sentimental" Toukone, John Elmore, Ingrid Monson, and Michael Veal.

I thank the following individuals and their institutions for their kind assistance: Daouda Gaye of the Archives Culturelles (Dakar); Kemoko Sano and Italo Zambo of Les Ballets Africains (Conakry); Ntchi Diakite and Djeli Mady Kouyate of the Ballet National du Mali (Bamako); the Bibliothèque Nationale de France (Paris); Abdrhamane Diop of the Conservatoire National de Musique (Dakar), Bakary Sidibe and B. K. Sagnia of the National Council for Arts and Culture (Banjul), Kenneth Moore of the Metropolitan Museum of Art (New York), Trân Van Khê, Gilbert Rouget, and Hugo Zemp of the Musée de l'Homme (Paris), Samuel Sidibé and Salia Malé of the Musée National du Mali (Bamako), Nicolas Meeus of the Musée Instrumental (Brussels), and Bamboun Kaba and Yaye Haby Barry Diallo of Radiotelevisiondiffusion Guinée (Conakry). The excerpts from Levtzion and Hopkins (1981) in appendix A, © University of Ghana, International Academic Union, Cambridge University Press 1981, are reprinted with the permission of Cambridge University Press. I also thank David Brent, Alice Bennett, and Martin Hertzel of the University of Chicago Press for their expertise in the realization of this book.

Research in Africa from mid-1988 to mid-1990 was made possible by a grant from the International Doctoral Research Fellowship Program for Africa of the American Council of Learned Societies and the Social Science Research Council. Additional funding was provided by the Council on Regional Studies at Princeton University. An American Philosophical Society Research Grant let me return to Guinea and Europe during the summer of 1994. A New Faculty Research Grant (1993), Excellence Foundation Summer Research Fellowship (1995), Research Leave (fall 1996), and Kohler Fund Travel Grant to Bamako (1997), all awarded by the University of North Carolina at Greensboro, enabled me to complete the research and finish writing the manuscript. A Wesleyan University Project Grant helped defray certain production expenses. I gratefully acknowledge the financial support provided by all these agencies.

Technical Notes

Varying use of Mande-derived terms has led to a confusing array of references (see Vydrine 1995–96) that demands I clarify my own usage at the outset (see table 1). Africans speaking local languages use the dialect variants *mande, manden, mandeng,* or *manding* with one principal meaning: a homeland situated in its narrowest sense between the upper Niger River and its tributary the Sankarani in the vicinity of the Mali-Guinea border, but usually understood to include the larger stretch of the Niger (and to the west) roughly between Kouroussa (Guinea) and Bamako (Mali). Throughout this book I use the following forms to refer to this larger area: Manden; the Mande heartland or homeland; Old Mande; and Old Mali. I refer to the vast territories that came under the political dominion of the *mansa*s (kings) who ruled from Old Mande from the thirteenth to the sixteenth century as either the Mande empire or the Mali empire.

To refer to a person from the Mande homeland or one who claims origins in this homeland, the suffix *-ka* or *-nka* (in western dialects) is attached to the place-name, similar to the suffix *-n* in English (e.g., America and American). This yields Mandenka, which will be used here as a convenient way to group together peoples who refer to themselves as Maninka (in Guinea and Mali) and Mandinka (in the Senegambia). "Mandenka" may not be a very widespread pronunciation, but it appears to have some currency among jelis in Kita (Kele Monson Diabate in Moser 1974:208, 210; Kandia Kouyate 1999-disc: *Mandenkalou*) and other Malians (C. Keita 1995b).

Linguists have used the term "Mande" over the past century in grand classification schemes to refer to a major Niger-Congo language branch spoken by peoples in perhaps a dozen or more countries (see chapter 1). Linguist Charles Bird (1970, 1982) has labeled one of the northern Mande languages Mandekan (literally "Mande language"), the primary language within the scope of this book. An alternative spelling, Mandenkan, has currency in some linguistic circles (e.g., Séminaire-atelier 1994:7) and as the title of a journal. Native speakers, however, attach the word *kan* (neck, throat, sound, language) to the *-ka* (person from) suffix, theoretically yielding Mandenkakan (Balde 1980–81:3), which may not be current in any dialects. Native speakers refer to the two major dialects used in this book as Maninkakan (Guinea and Mali) and Mandinkakango (Senegambia).

Table 1 Mande-Derived Terms

References to a homeland

Mande	North American usage. Limited distribution within Mali and upper Guinea.
Manden	Growing international usage. Wide distribution in Mali and upper Guinea.
Mandeng	French usage (in the form of Mandingue). Limited distribution in Mali and upper Guinea.
Manding	British usage. Wide distribution in the Senegambia.
Mali	A corruption one or more of the terms above that became standardized in European writing.

References to people

Maninka	Those who remain geographically near the homeland (Mali and Guinea).
Mandinka (Mandinko)	Those farther west in the Senegambia.
Mandenka	A cover term for Maninka and Mandinka.

Linguistic references

Mande	A major branch of the Niger-Congo language family, comprising northern, southeastern, and southwestern subgroups.
Mandekan (Mandenkan)	A northern Mande language including (from the Senegambian coastline to the Mali-Burkina Faso border): Mandinka, Xasonka (Khassonka), Maninka, Bamana, Jula, and Dafin.
Maninkakan	The language of the Maninka.
Mandinkakango	The language of the Mandinka.

I also use Mande to modify "music" and "musicians," or simply as a noun referring to a broad spectrum of people, in an unresolvably and purposely ambiguous way. Readers can narrowly interpret this as a shorthand reference to a Mandenka (Maninka and Mandinka) core, but often the boundaries can be expanded to include other northern Mande speakers such as Xasonka, Soninke, and Susu peoples. Occasionally Mande can be expanded further to peoples of the more distant southern branches. In some cases I simply do not know the geographic and ethnic extent to which my statements apply. Although some working definitions are helpful for establishing a comprehensible discourse, fluid local concepts of group identity that can enlarge and contract according to the situation suggest that any further demarcation could be counterproductive.

Two major Mandekan dialects are used here: Maninka or Maninkakan (from Guinea and Mali) and Mandinka or Mandinkakango (from The Gambia and southern Senegal). When appropriate, dialect variants will be given in Maninka (Mn:), Mandinka (Md:), or Bamana (Bm:). Arabic terms (Ar:) and alternative French spellings (Fr:) are occasionally given. In addition to Bird (1982), language materials I have drawn on include Gregoire (1986),

Séminaire-atelier (1994), and Spears (1973) for Maninka; Gamble (1987a, 1987b) for Mandinka; and Bird, Hutchison, and Kante (1977) and Bird and Kante (1976) for Bamana. Quotations are given in the dialect in which they were spoken. Throughout the text I use the dialect spelling relevant to the geographic region being discussed, most noticeably in my alternation between *jali* or *jalo* (Senegambian Mandinka) and *jeli* (Guinean and Malian Maninka). Owing to the complexity of working in several different dialects, I have simplified transliterations, which have been done phonetically following general standards adopted by the host countries. Consonants follow their pronunciation in English with the exception of the following.

c	*ch* as in check
r	should be rolled
x or *kh*	pronounced as a velar fricative, as if clearing one's throat

A grave accent is used to indicate a short vowel, yielding the following possibilities with sample English pronunciations.

a	bond
è	bet
e	clay
ì	bin
i	bee
ò	bought
o	bone
u	dune

Following Gamble (1987b: vi), long vowels in Gambian Mandinka are written as *ee* (clay), *ii* (bee), and *oo* (bone). Nasalized consonants, such as *ng* and *ny,* should be pronounced as such, instead of as "en" plus the second consonant.

To indicate plurals I use the Maninka/Mandinka plural suffix *-lu* or *-nu* (after nasals). To improve readability I have occasionally left words in the singular or used the English *-s* plural marker. I also occasionally use the Bamana plural suffix *-w* when relying on research with a marked Bamana bias. Tonal markers are omitted for easier reading. Action nouns are formed by adding the suffix *-li* or *-ri* to the verb in Mandinka, Maninka, and Bamana. In Mandinka, word-final nasals are usually velar nasals, represented here as *-ng,* and the suffix *-o* represents the definite article. For example, *fen* in Maninka is *fengo* in Mandinka. Mandinka terms can often be recognized by this *-ngo* ending. Nasals before bilabials become bilabial nasals, therefore the *n* in *kun* becomes *m* in *kumben.* Prenasals have been lost in the Maninka spoken in the Mande heartland (Bird 1982: 269–70), so I use the Maninka term *koni* here when referring in general to the lute known as *kontingo* in

Mandinka and *ngoni* in Bamana. In the Mandinka dialect *jali* is commonly used with its definite article, yielding *jalo,* with a plural of *jalolu.* Three other distinctions between Bamana and Mandinka should be noted. The Bamana *e* and *è* sounds are sometimes *ì* in Mandinka, yielding *den* and *dìng* (child), and *jèmbe* and *jìmbe* in Bamana and Mandinka, respectively. Consequently "Mande" and "Manden" may be heard in Bamana or Maninka, but "Manding" in Mandinka. Intervocalic velars drop out in Mandinka, yielding *mogo* and *moo* (person) in Bamana and Mandinka, respectively. Occasionally there is an alternation between an intervocalic *r* (Bamana) and *l* (Mandinka), yielding *juru* in Bamana and *julu* (or *julo*) in Mandinka.

The phrase "western Africa" is used to limit generalizations to the area south of the Sahara from the Atlantic Ocean to the Niger bend around Timbuktu or Gao (see Brooks 1993:1–8). The description "western sahel and savanna" is used to further limit generalizations by eliminating the southern coastal forest regions (Liberia and Côte d'Ivoire).

Citations may be found in one of four places: the bibliography; the discography if -disc is appended to the date; the videography if -vid is appended; or the listing of my own personal recordings (including interviews, lessons, and video or audio recordings) if -per is appended. The bibliography is divided into two sections: references from before the twentieth century (listed chronologically rather than alphabetically), and twentieth-century references (listed alphabetically). The discography and videography are divided into sections according to country: Burkina Faso, Côte d'Ivoire, The Gambia, Guinea, Guinea-Bissau (not in the videography), Mali, Senegal, and Miscellaneous (multicountry recordings or other countries). If the country of the artist is not clear from the context, readers will have to search the various sections. References to quotations from sleeve notes to recordings are keyed to the discography. Roman numerals and letters after interview dates refer to the tape number and side, respectively, in my own collection; page numbers refer to my unpublished transcriptions and translations. The bibliography and personal recordings listing contain only references cited in the text and appendixes; the discography and videography contain references cited as well as many additional items.

Where contemporary works have been translated into English not long after their initial publication, only the date of the English translation is given in the text (e.g., Niane 1965). References to Arabic writings concerning West Africa are keyed to Levtzion and Hopkins (1981), and further bibliographic details may be found there.

Unless otherwise specified, the maps, photographs, musical transcriptions, figures, and English translations of interviews and French published sources are my own. Mandinka interviews with Amadu Bansang Jobarteh and Sidiki Diabate were initially transcribed and translated into English by Djibril Bah, after which I arrived at a final translation. I made my personal recordings either in the home of the person named or at my own home in the town or city where the person was living. Wherever possible I have used published English translations of writings originally published in foreign languages. When I quote published sources, all parentheses are from the original and all brackets are my own unless specifically noted.

The following conventions regarding names apply throughout, although readers will occasionally find a lapse in consistency dictated by context. Names of musicians are spelled according to how they themselves spell them or how they appear on their passports, but I have omitted the French accents. Where I lacked that information they are spelled phonetically. Although Diabate, Dioubate, Dyubate, and Dibate all refer to the same family name in Guinea, I use Diabate, except for Oumou Dioubate, who has released CDs with this spelling. Although the order of Guinean names is usually reversed in French publications (and on some recordings) and the names are listed that way in library catalogs, I follow the convention of writing the given name followed by the family name. Fodeba Keita and Laye Camara, therefore, are usually listed in catalogs with their names reversed as Keita Fodeba and Camara Laye. This French practice of reversing names is not usually done with Malian or Senegalese names. In general, French versus phonetic spelling of other names is dictated by the historical context (e.g., the modern town of Segou and the eighteenth-century Segu kingdom).

I use footnotes extensively for significant sources, other sources for further information, and Mandekan language quotations from which translations were made. To conserve space I have not included original French texts from published sources. I have tried to accommodate those interested in music but with little experience in Africa as well as those interested in Africa but with little experience in music by the liberal use of parenthetical translations or definitions. I hope they do not bog down the reading.

Some common abbreviations are:

(Mn:)	Maninka
(Md:)	Mandinka
(Bm:)	Bamana
(Ar:)	Arabic
(Fr:)	French
(pl.)	plural form
B.P.	before the present
C.E.	Common Era, same as A.D.
B.C.E.	Before the Common Era, same as B.C.

"central Sahara" refers to a location in between the northern Sahara and the
southern Sahara.

"Central Sahara" refers to a location in between East Africa and West Africa.

"Niger" refers to the modern nation.

"the Niger" refers to the river.

"Sudan" refers to the modern East African nation.

"The Sudan" refers to West Africa south of the Sahara.

Some common grammatical suffixes in Maninka/Mandinka/Bamana
are:

-ya	creates an abstract noun (-ness or -hood)
-ba	big or very big
-ni (nin)	little
-w	plural marker in Bamana
-lu or *-nu*	plural marker in Mandinka and Maninka
-ke	male
-muso	female
-ka/nka	person from, as in Manden-ka
-tigi/tii	owner, or the one responsible for
-la/laa	creates an agentive noun, one who does (like -er in worker)

Some common French spellings and their British equivalents:

French	British
dia (dialy)	ja (jali)
die (diely)	je (jeli)
dj	j
ou (Doundounba)	u (Dundunba)
Diabate (Mali)	Jobateh
or Dioubate (Guinea)	or Jobarteh

Transcription, or the translation of musical sound into written symbols, involves fundamental decisions about the nature of the music and how best to communicate it. Notions of a uniquely African rhythmic sensibility and appropriate methods of transcribing music from Africa have been the subject of intense scrutiny since the writings of Ward (1927) and von Hornbostel (1928). Critical surveys discussing technical aspects of the notation of rhythmic aspects of music from Africa include those of David Locke (1979, 1:300–316; 1982), Robert Kauffman (1980), and Alan Merriam (1982).

Although it may be futile to search in Africa for direct equivalents of the word "rhythm," an understanding of its etymology "to flow," from the Greek *rhein,* entering into English by way of the Greek *rhythmos* to Latin *rhythmus* to French *rythme* (Simpson and Weiner 1989, 13:873–76), helps to define differences in perspective. The closest term my teachers used to refer to the flow of events over time, such as the sequence of strings plucked on a guitar or kora, or of strokes on a xylophone, is *ben* (to meet, agree). *Ben* entails the idea of coming together rather than flowing forward. This conception may help readers appreciate the issues involved in the notation here of polyrhythm (sometimes called cross-rhythm) and in the indication of a starting point in a cycle.

Polyrhythm, a fundamental rhythmic feature found in much of Africa south of the Sahara, is exhibited in Mande music as a play of two or four equally spaced beats in the same durational space as three equally spaced beats (or vice versa), often resulting in an ambiguity of a single overriding beat sequence (meter). This ambiguity—being able to feel a particular performance in more than one meter—is creatively exploited by African musicians in performance and is one of the most difficult aspects of music in Africa for non-Africans to grasp. A similar effect may also take place on a micro level, where the spacing of strokes between each beat may be inflected one way or another toward a binary or ternary interpretation (see chapters 2 and 4 below and Polak 1996b, 1998). A little-known account (among musicologists, at least) by a late nineteenth-century French colonial army officer in Mali may have been the first to technically detail the practice of two simultaneous rhythms or beat sequences in West African music. The French term *s'entrecroisent* (intersect, intertwine) was used.

> The tam-tams (generally two, sometimes three [probably referring to jembe
> drums]) each have a different sound, and they execute drum strokes more or
> less spaced out, more or less closer together [sped up], which punctuate, so to
> speak, the gestures of the female dancer . . . of the head, the arms, and the
> body. . . . It is not the least bit curious that these two rhythms that cross each
> other [*s'entrecroisent*] move away [*s'éloignent*] from one another, meet up
> again two or three measures later, and then diverge anew. (Tellier 1898 : 176)

In the transcriptions here I have taken cues to arrive at a rhythmic notation that follows the path of least resistance—a fundamental meter comprising a fixed number of beats (and pulses making up those beats) that is
simplest for me to feel and that usually does not change during the course
of a single piece. The cues are based on study of the instruments with African teachers and, in the drumming transcriptions, on the dance steps and
clapping by those in the dance circle. Whether the performer feels it in the
same way is a separate issue that I do not directly address, although in most
cases I believe our perceptions of rhythmic frames of reference converge.
A century ago Tellier also understood one of the functions of hand clapping:

> As for the musical rhythm, it is supported by the hand clapping of the women
> and young girls; one could notate it perfectly with eighth notes and sixteenth
> notes, etc.; it [the clapping] very much makes one feel the strong and weak
> beats. (Tellier 1898 : 177)

The apparent lack of a definitive starting point in a cycle is also difficult
for non-Africans to grasp and presents serious notational problems. One of
the most common questions that American jembe students ask of their African teachers is Where is one? This question does not make sense from a
local African point of view. Pieces might best be thought of as starting up
rather than starting at a specific point in time. The verb used to direct someone to start up a piece is *wuli,* "to stand up" or "to prepare," as in preparing tea by first boiling water. The image of boiling is apt; one moves into a
piece rather than starting it cold. In the transcriptions, I have chosen starting points according to what is the simplest for me to feel. This choice also
should not be confused with how the African performer may feel it, although
our perceptions here too probably converge most of the time.

The transcription method adopted here is the same for each of the instruments and is based on a concept, formulated by Western scholars rather
than by the African musicians I studied with, of a fastest regularly occurring unit of time, called a pulse. Pulses group together into larger units called
beats. A single cycle of an accompaniment pattern then may comprise a certain number of beats (usually four, eight, or twelve), each in turn composed
of a certain number of pulses (usually two, three, or four). Within a single
cycle of an accompaniment pattern the number of pulses per beat normally

does not vary. Occasionally two simultaneous series of beats made up of different numbers of pulses will be notated to show polyrhythms between two hands (in the case of the bala). A twenty-four-pulse accompaniment pattern may consist of eight beats of three pulses each, twelve beats of two pulses each, or both simultaneously (e.g., one rhythm in each hand—see *Kulanjan*, transcription 12). Beats consisting of two pulses each are called binary; those with three pulses, ternary; and those with four pulses, quaternary. In all the transcriptions each line (one staff) shows one full cycle of a piece. Metronome markings should be taken only as a general guide; the tempo at which any piece may be played can vary greatly. The simbi, kora, bala, and koni transcriptions were transposed to F as the tonic pitch to make comparison easier. Traditionally there is no concept of a fixed pitch on these instruments, but those who play with guitars, brass, or keyboard instruments may be aware of the convention. The guitar transcriptions were left in the key in which they were recorded.

None of the African musicians I have spoken with have ever verbalized references to pulses, grouping pulses into beats, or counting beats within a cycle. However, I (and many others before me) have found this to be the most effective way to get readers to grasp certain technical aspects of the rhythms of the pieces discussed and to be able to hear and play them.

The look of the notation for all the instruments is based on Roderic Knight's (1971, 1972a, 1973a) transcriptions for the kora, a method that has the advantage of showing every pulse by a stem rather than using additional abstract symbols for rests. Rests, meaning that nothing is played on that pulse, are notated by stems with no notehead attached. Beats are indicated by beams connecting the stems. Binary beats are shown as two stems connected by a beam, ternary beats by three stems connected by a beam, and quaternary beats by four stems connected by a beam. Only attacks are indicated, not durations. Whether stems point up or down is arbitrarily based on ease of reading the transcription.

Square noteheads (my own addition to Knight's method) show that the note is played by the left hand (on the jembe or bala) or left index finger or thumb (on the kora). Oval noteheads indicate the right hand (on the jembe or bala) or right index finger or thumb (on the kora). In the guitar transcriptions square noteheads mean the thumb is plucking, and oval noteheads indicate the index finger. Hollow oval noteheads indicate alternative choices that could be played instead of the solid noteheads. Hollow diamond noteheads are used in transcription 20 (*Dundunba*) to indicate an alternative to the hollow oval noteheads and in figure 11 (kora kumbengo examples) to indicate an accidentally struck string. Noteheads in the shape of an *X* (rather than an oval or a square) indicate dampened strokes or presses (on the bala, simbi, dundun, and kutiro drums), ghost strokes that are softly sounded to keep the rhythm going (on the jembe), or a tap by the fingers on the sound table (on the koni). Parentheses around a notehead indicate an optional additional note.

In the kora transcriptions the treble clef contains what the index fingers play and the bass clef contains what the thumbs play. In the jembe transcriptions only one staff line is used; noteheads in the upper space indicate slap strokes, noteheads on the line indicate tone strokes, and noteheads in the lower space indicate bass strokes. The guitar (and bass) transcriptions are notated as a guitarist would read them (an octave lower than they sound) and before a capo is put on. To sound at the same pitch as the recordings, a capo should be put on at the indicated fret. For example, in transcription 28 (*Muudo hormo*) the accompanying guitar plays in F but is capoed up two frets to sound in G, and the lead guitar plays in C but is capoed up seven frets to sound in G.

All the discussion surrounding the hand positions of the various instruments assumes the player is right-handed. For example, right-handed bala players play the bass end of the instrument with the left hand and the treble end with the right hand. Left-handed bala players turn the instrument around so that the bass end is on the right side of the body. Right-handed guitarists pluck the instrument with the right hand; left-handed guitarists pluck with the left hand. The same applies to koni players. Left-handed jembe drummers use the opposite hand from right-handed drummers. There is no difference on the kora.

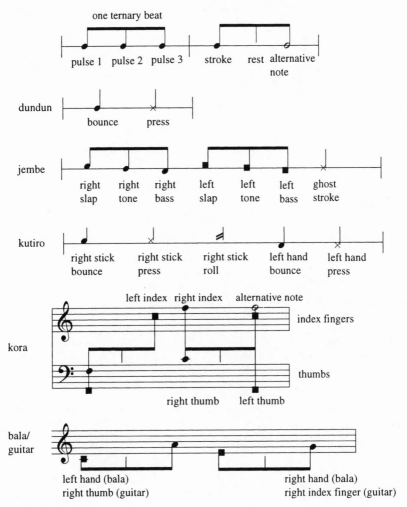

Key to the music notation

Early in the thirteenth century the West African Mande (or Mali) empire was established by the legendary warrior and hero Sunjata and his allies. The Mande homeland (also called Manden or Manding), situated along the Upper Niger River roughly between Bamako in southwestern Mali and Kouroussa in northeastern Guinea, gradually became the center of one of the largest and wealthiest empires in West Africa (see map 1). At its height in the fourteenth to the sixteenth century the Mande empire extended from Gao in the east and Timbuktu in the north all the way to the Atlantic coast in the west. As Mande peoples dispersed throughout the West African savanna they assimilated various local cultures and spread their own. Their descendants today make up significant parts of the population of many West African countries: in Mali and Guinea they are known as Maninka (or Malinke in French writing); in Senegal, The Gambia, and Guinea-Bissau they are known as Mandinka (or Mandingo in British writing).

Mande societies are marked by a class of hereditary professional artisans called *nyamakala* (Md: *nyamaalo*). Artisan classes are common throughout western Africa, perhaps owing in part to Mande expansion. The specific professions vary according to the ethnic group and geographic location, but within traditional Maninka and Mandinka society four are generally recognized: blacksmiths-sculptors (*numu*); leatherworkers and potters (*garanke* or *karanke*); musical-verbal artisans (Mn: *jeli,* pl. *jelilu;* Md: *jali* or *jalo,* pl. *jalolu*); and orators, expert in the Koran, specializing in genealogies (Bm: *fune;* Mn, Md: *fina* or *fino*). The musical-verbal artisans in various western savanna and sahel societies are sometimes collectively called griots, a word that first appeared in the written accounts of seventeenth-century French travelers to the Senegambia region. But jelis (griots) are not the only people who make music.

Maninka and Mandinka music culture, the focus of this book, encompasses four distinct spheres that call for professional musicians:

1. music related to hunters' societies and their legendary hunter heroes, sung to the accompaniment of the *simbi,* a seven-stringed calabash (gourd) harp
2. music of the jelis (called *jeliya*), played on the *bala* (xylophone), *koni* (lute), and *kora* (harp), which is associated with rulers, warriors, traders, and other patrons

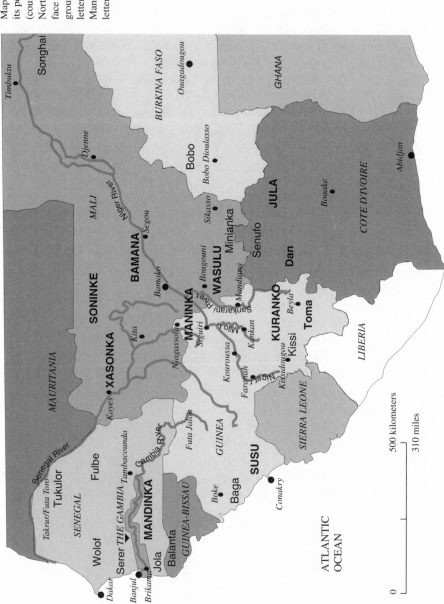

Map 1 Western Africa and some of its peoples. Place-names are in italics (countries are in capital letters). Northern Mande groups are in boldface capital letters. Southern Mande groups are in boldface lowercase letters after an initial capital. Non-Mande groups are in lowercase letters after an initial capital.

3. drumming related to various life-cycle, agricultural, and recreational events played on the *jembe* (struck with the bare hands) and *dundun* (struck with a stick) in Mali and Guinea or the *tangtango* (struck with one hand and one stick) in the Senegambia
4. modern urban electric groups (called orchestras), largely dominated by guitar-playing jelis, which draw from the other three spheres

The first three traditions are centuries, perhaps even millennia, old. Drumming, which has a close association with the blacksmith-sculptor artisanal group, and hunter's music are probably the oldest, predating the rise of the Mali empire, originating in a distant prehistoric past. *Jeliya* (the art of the jeli) goes back to the thirteenth-century origins of the Mali empire, although the institution of the griot in West Africa probably stems from the earlier Ghana empire (also known as Wagadu), which declined in the late eleventh century. The growth of hunter's music, drumming, and jeliya may track the shifting of political power in western Africa from hunters to blacksmiths to state builders, all having associations with sorcery. The fourth and latest tradition, guitar-based dance music, has its origins in Guinea about the 1920s. Rooted in European and Latin American popular dance music, it eventually drew heavily from the other indigenous traditions.

All the traditions above are distinguished from other kinds of Mande music making, such as certain activities designated as play, by the use of professionals—highly trained musicians who receive remuneration for their music making. Jelis, however, are the only ones who have guarded their profession through endogamy (restrictions on marrying outside certain groups). They are in effect the state-sanctioned guardians of certain Mande musical and oral traditions.

The distinction between jeli and nonjeli musical artists is fundamental in Mande society. As part of the *nyamakala* class—artisans who work with metal, wood, leather, clay, words, and music—it is the right, duty even, of jelis to devote their lives to music. Nonjelis making such a decision usually encounter resistance from their families, and with rare exceptions their avenues are limited to the nonjeli spheres of music.

Jelis have developed an exceptionally diverse and sophisticated musical system, stemming from the very origins of the Mali empire. Their music belongs to a variety of related peoples who populate a geographic area as great today as it was during the height of the Mali empire in the fourteenth and fifteenth centuries. The congeries of traditions represented by the three melodic instruments of the jeli (bala, koni, and kora), plus the guitar, along with the vocal aspects of jeliya and with hunter's harp music as its foundation, make up a "great tradition" of Mande music, an especially rich music culture. That great tradition is still vibrant today, and its latest practitioners are spreading its various manifestations throughout the world under the

Plate 1 Entrance to the compound of Lansana Diabate of the Lafiabougou Twins. Bamako, 1997. Photo by the author.

patronage of multinational recording companies, African expatriates living in Europe and North America, and people the world over who have an interest in African music.

Because of their primary roles in Maninka and Mandinka music culture, jelis deserve pride of place in any broad study of Mande music. Therefore a primary focus is the classical tradition of the jeli (jeliya) and its transformation into the modern musics of Mali and Guinea. The three melodic instruments that are exclusively reserved for jelis are covered in detail. They are the *bala,* a xylophone also known as *balafon,* indigenous to Maninka in the Mande heartland, the *kora,* a twenty-one-stringed calabash harp indigenous to Senegambian Mandinka, and the *koni* (also called *nkoni, ngoni,* or *kontingo*), a four- or five-stringed lute associated with Xasonka, Maninka, and Bamana in Mali. Special attention is given to the guitar, which has recently been integrated into the jeli tradition and is the foundation for one of the most fascinating musical syntheses in Africa. Jelis have welcomed the guitar, and it has in turn moved their music into the international arena of modern electric dance music.

Being public and cosmopolitan figures, jelis have been receptive to certain foreign influences that have not affected drummers and hunter's musicians. The primary influence can be heard in the singing, which bears marks of melodic ornamentation typical of musics of the core Muslim world. Mande instrumental music also reflects a mixture of indigenous and Muslim-tinged musical styles. The virtuosic, highly ornamented melodic flights that function as solos, especially on stringed instruments, exhibit Muslim aesthetics of ornamentation not often found among non-Muslim West African peoples.

Hunter's harp music and drumming are also focal points in this book. Maninka hunter's music is a historical source of jeliya and has also been an inspiration for some of the modern artists in Mali and Guinea. The two most influential hunter's harps are the seven-stringed Maninka *simbi* and the six-stringed *donso ngoni* played in the adjacent Wasulu region. Jembe drumming from Mali and Guinea has made major advances into the world commercial market over the past decade, with dozens of high-quality CDs released, overshadowing all other African drums. National ballet troupes and their former lead drummers are touring the world to enthusiastic audiences, and jembe teachers are proliferating outside Africa with legions of students. Two other drums with their own traditions are played with jembes: a large double-headed, cylindrical drum called *dundun* and a small double-headed, hourglass-shaped squeeze drum called *tama*. In Senegal and The Gambia the Mandinka three-drum *tangtango* (also called *seruba* or *kutiro*) ensemble predominates.

This book pulls together widely disparate sources. I have relied on early Arabic and European historical writings and travel accounts, Mande oral traditions, previous musicological research, personal and commercial recordings, private instrument lessons and interviews, and recent work from other relevant disciplines. My own involvement with Mande music began when I first met Djimo Kouyate in the United States in 1981 and began studying the kora with him several years later. From mid-1988 to mid-1990 I lived and studied in several western African regions where there is a strong Mandenka presence (Senegal, The Gambia, Mali, and Guinea). A shorter stay in Conakry in the summer of 1994 was spent researching modern Guinean music, and a trip to Bamako in March 1997 allowed me to renew friendships and further my understanding of music there. I also took several brief trips to Europe to speak with expatriate Malian and Guinean musicians and to carry out research in museums, libraries, and archives. And I have benefited greatly from my contact with Malian, Guinean, Senegalese, and Gambian musicians and scholars living in the United States.

Chapter 1 sets the scene for the rest of the book by summarizing current research on Mande history, culture, and society. Although it is out of the ordinary to begin a study of music by discussing human occupation of a region hundreds of thousands or even thousands of years ago, I have tried to fashion a deep historical lens to view the developments of various genres of Mande music and their relationships. Literature about African music history lags behind that of other areas of the world where writing has been used for a long time, fueling notions that African music is timeless and static. Drawing on the work of archaeologists, historians, linguists, literary theorists, and others, I have attempted to construct a multidimensional framework for the discussions in later chapters.

Chapters 2 through 5 each cover one of the major spheres of Mande music: hunter's music, jeliya, drumming, and modern urban electric groups. In each of these chapters I follow a similar line of investigation with variations dictated by the subject matter. First I place the performers in the historical context of the genre and discuss the occasions when they perform. Then I describe their instruments and repertories (the body of pieces played). Next I cover the tuning systems, and finally the playing techniques and styles, using musical transcriptions. Chapter 3 (on jeliya) is by far the longest in the book, primarily because of the extensive body of writing and research surrounding jelis, their instruments, and their pivotal role in Mande society. Despite its unwieldy length, I opted not to split it up, hoping that chapter subheadings will allow readers to negotiate it. In chapter 6 I examine Mande music theory, the terminology Mande musicians use when they talk about their music. Chapter 7 contains a personal view of what I did in Africa, how I did it, how my teachers may have perceived me (and I them), how they learn, and how their children learn.

A series of appendixes collects several kinds of resources: historical descriptions of Mande music making from the eleventh to the mid-nineteenth century (appendix A); a comprehensive list of musicians who have recorded (organized by instrument and country), keyed to the discography (appendix B); a select listing of recorded versions of some of the major pieces played by Maninka and Mandinka jelis, keyed to the discography (appendix C); and a complete listing of the albums released on Syliphone, the national record label of Guinea (appendix D). A glossary of African terms follows. The following overview summarizes some of the major points made in chapters 2 through 5, using the same progression found in each chapter: performers, performance, instruments, repertories, tuning, and playing techniques. The overview is followed by a brief survey of language and ethnicity in relation to Mande groups and their neighbors. The chapter concludes with brief discussions of Islam and Mande music and the terms traditional and modern in a Mande context. Having read the overview and survey, readers should be prepared to shift between various sections and chapters if they wish.

Performers

Lack of archaeological finds of musical instruments or music-related iconography makes it difficult to construct a deep history of music in West Africa, but much can be gleaned from other kinds of evidence. Before the age of great political entities such as ancient Mali and Ghana, the bravest, oldest, or most knowledgeable hunters may have held positions of high respect or leadership in small-scale nonpastoral societies. Hunter's musicians, such as the Maninka *sora* attached to hunters' societies, may represent vestiges of their ancient roles. Their musical and verbal art, including harp playing, narrating, praising, and singing, fulfilled a role in hunting societies similar to that of the jelis who were later attached to the leaders of the empire of Mali and possibly the earlier Ghana empire.

One indication that the jeli may have developed out of the hunter's musician can be seen in the specialization of the jeli. A single hunter's musician plays the simbi (harp), sings, and narrates. Among jelis, these are three distinct performance activities: speech (*kuma*), song (*dònkili*), and instrument playing (Mn: *fòli;* Md: *kosiri*). Male jelis usually specialize in one of these areas, although they are often trained and may also excel in the other two. Speech refers to oral history, storytelling, proverbs, negotiating, and various forms of praising. Song refers to sung melodies that are unique to named pieces of music, as well as the vocal elaborations of these melodies. Speech and song each require different training and call for different kinds of expertise. Speech entails a depth of historical and political knowledge that is usually the preserve of male jelis (*jelike*, pl. *jelikelu*). Singing requires a powerful delivery style and a voice to match, and in general the field is dominated by female jelis (*jelimuso*, pl. *jelimusolu*), though there are famous male singers.

During the first millennium C.E. a culture of jembe-based dance drumming may have originated with the rise to power of blacksmiths. Jembe drumming is associated with blacksmiths, in secret power societies (Kòmò) where they traditionally preside and also as the carvers of trees who make the drums and masks that are used in these societies. The strong tie of drumming events to the agricultural calendar (e.g., clearing fields and celebrating the harvest) also ties blacksmiths to drumming, because the iron hoe was crucial in transforming a hunter-gatherer society into an agricultural one. In contrast to jelis and hunter's musicians, drummers primarily engage in instrument playing; solo singing and speech are not major concerns.

In the early thirteenth century, the transfer of the magical bala (xylophone) of Sumanguru Kante, the sorcerer blacksmith who was defeated by

Sunjata, to Sunjata's jeli Bala Faseke Kouyate symbolizes a new era. The political power of blacksmiths was kept in check, and an epic age of mounted warriors began in earnest—what George Brooks (1993:97–119) has called "the era of Mandekalu horse warriors and state building." Jelis were essential to constructing and maintaining a balance of power. The bala not only is a symbol of the transfer of power but is also a bridge between the spheres of dance drumming and the jeli. As a percussion instrument, it can be played in ensembles with jembes; the grand epics of the jelis can also be played on it.

The preceding chronology, which is largely speculative, can be seen in the musical repertories of the hunter's musicians and jelis. Hunter's musicians sing songs inspiring bravery and praising past hunters, invoking animal spirits, presumably of pre-Islamic origin. Jelis do the same for their noble patrons, invoking Islamic wisdom or their noble ancestry that dates back to Sunjata's era. Drummers do not sing praise songs or recite epic stories. They play rhythms to move people: villagers clearing fields for planting or celebrating the harvest, youngsters dancing into adulthood, or masked dancers restoring stability in their villages and towns. Iron tools shaped by the blacksmith are present at these events in one form or another: the hoe, cutting knife, and sculpting ax. There is a significant difference between hunter's music and jembe drumming associated with secret societies, such as Kòmò led by blacksmiths. As Youssouf Cissé (1964:189) has pointed out, hunter's music (and I would add the jeli's music here too) is welcoming and public; Kòmò drumming and the like are threatening and private.

Performance

Sometimes events call for only one kind of musician, and sometimes different genres of music mix. Hunter's music is usually performed on occasions when jelis and drummers are not present, such as before or after a hunt or at the funeral of a great hunter. Similarly, many of the major occasions for drumming, such as the meetings of secret power societies, circumcisions and excisions, and agricultural labor, usually do not involve jelis. The most common meeting grounds for jelis and drummers are marriage celebrations and stage concerts. Traditionally they do not play together but perform at different times during a marriage celebration. Drumming is for dancing; the music of jelis is primarily for listening, although when augmented with drums it can also encourage dancing.

The verbal expressions of hunter's musicians and jelis often involve a second person whose role is to answer and encourage the vocalist with short interjections, such as *naamu* (a sign of affirmation with no literal translation), *walahi* (Ar: "I swear"), or *tinye* (Mn: "that's the truth"). The continuous responses of the *naamu-tigi* or *naamu-namina* (*naamu* answerer) may seem perfunctory in their constant placement in the short pauses after each phrase, but they are necessary just the same. This vocal aesthetic is typical throughout the African diaspora.

Mande musicians have responded to opportunities to perform abroad, just as their forebears have done in their widening zones of influence within Africa. They have accordingly shaped their music for foreign audiences, and it continues to, move in disparate directions. Drumming, for example, took to the stage when Fodeba Keita created Les Ballets Africains in the late 1940s. Jembe drummers have since recorded their rhythms in tight arrangements, a genre of recorded music that is so far absent in commercial markets within Africa, and since the 1980s drummers have developed a concert drumming tradition removed from its dance origins. Jelis have developed instrumental performances without the vocal praise singing that usually accompanies it in Africa. Modern electric groups have collaborated with European and American arrangers to open up their sound for an international market.

Instruments

West African music culture may be viewed as fertile ground on which instruments, ways of playing them, and tuning systems have sprung up from the cross-fertilization of the natural resources available with the cultural influences passing through them. The coastal forest regions, interior savanna lands, and dry sahel each have their own natural resources as well as natural barriers to human migration. The spread of cultural influences and the distribution of musical instruments in West Africa are often bounded within one of these three regions. Modern state boundaries have not significantly affected the distribution of musical instruments, but capital cities have acted as magnets attracting musicians to the national ensembles.

Mande musicians view their instruments according to the sphere of music in which they are used. For instance, the kora (a twenty-one-stringed harp) is a jeli's instrument and lives in a different world than the six- or seven-stringed hunter's harp. Even though they are all morphologically similar calabash (gourd) harps with similar playing techniques, it is uncommon to find a kora player who also plays a hunter's harp or vice versa. They live in two different musical realms. It is much more common to find one person playing both the guitar and the bala (xylophone) or a kora player whose father played the koni (lute), because they are all jeli instruments.

There are three principal families of melody instruments played by Mande peoples: harps, lutes, and xylophones. Members of these families are played by some neighboring groups, usually with different tuning systems and slightly different morphologies. Hunter's harps with calabash resonators are found in the savanna lands, particularly in the more southern parts. The Maninka play a seven-stringed hunter's harp called *simbi* (Md: *simbingo*). The kora is a more technologically developed calabash harp that is played uniquely by Mandinka jalis or other Mande jelis who would have picked it up from them.

Plucked lutes are primarily found in the sahel and northern parts of the savanna and stretch across West Africa to Cameroon. The name of the four- or five-stringed lute played by jelis varies according to who plays it: Maninka and Xasonka *koni,* Mandinka *kontingo,* and Bamana *ngoni.* All are essentially the same instrument with differences primarily in size. This kind of lute is widespread in the western African sahel and is also played by the Wolof (*xalam*), Moors (*tidinit*), Fulbe (*hoddu*), and Soninke (*gambare*).

Frame xylophones are found throughout Africa, but the particular type that Mandenka jelis play is limited to a compact area across the southern savanna of West Africa. The bala (or balafon) is the only Mande instrument whose history is so readily verbalized and agreed on by jelis. Indeed, a bala guarded by the direct descendants of Sunjata's jeli in a village in the old Mande region is believed to be the original thirteenth-century bala. The preservation of such a musical instrument is extraordinary in Africa, and it may be one of the oldest instruments preserved in Africa south of the Sahara, if not the very oldest.

The guitar was probably introduced into Mande music in Guinea in the 1920s and was soon well integrated into the traditional music culture. Nowadays it is considered a bona fide jeli's instrument, although it is of course recognized as a foreign import.

The three traditional jeli instruments (koni, bala, and kora) are associated with different eras and different geographical regions of the Mande diaspora: the northernmost Mande regions (or the sahel in general) for the koni; old Mande, particularly the southern reaches in Guinea, for the bala; and Kabu (the western Mande territories) for the kora. The meeting of these three distinct musical instrument cultures (harps, lutes, and xylophones) in the hands of jelis accounts for the unusual breadth of Mande music. The guitar, still primarily in the hands of jelis, has pulled this music system and its traditional instruments into the theater of international popular music.

The materials the instruments are made of and the ways they are played often reflect the close relation between the lifestyles of the musicians and their musical instruments. For instance, the original association of the bala with a blacksmith (Sumanguru Kante) is no coincidence. Blacksmiths work with both metal and wood, and heating the metal requires burning large amounts of wood. The construction of a bala is aided by the blacksmith's iron tools for carving, and it takes an ample supply of wood to smoke it dry. The physical motions of forging metal, downward strokes aimed toward the earth with a tool, are replicated in the action of playing a bala. And the mallets are made of wood wrapped in rubber tapped from trees. The hunter's lifestyle revolves around animals, and it is no coincidence that hunter's harps are sounded by plucking strings made of animal hide (or twine in some cases) and amplified by skin sound tables stretched over calabashes. Plucking their strings also replicates the action of shooting an arrow. Music traditionally associated with blacksmiths and hunters is created by drawing sounds from the raw materials of their daily life.

A musical instrument in the abstract is called *fòli fen* (saying thing) by Maninka or *kosiri fengo* (beating thing) by Mandinka (see the technical notes section for the sound changes between Maninka and Mandinka). Curiously, Maninka use the verb *fò* (to say) to refer to playing an instrument while Mandinka use *kosi* (to beat), regardless of whether the instrument is plucked with the fingers or struck with the hands or a stick. (The linguistic influence of their Wolof neighbors may be responsible: Wolof use the word *tegg* [to knock, beat] to refer to the way they play their lute.) Therefore "to play the bala" is *ka bala fò* in Maninka and *ka balo kosi* in Mandinka. This difference in dialect reflects a fundamental regional division between eastern Maninka and western Mandinka musical branches—what Senegambian Mandinka call *tilibo* (sunrise, east) and *tilijii* (sunset, west). This division is most clearly seen in the use of drums. Throughout the Senegambia region up to Tambacounda, Senegal, the Mandinka three-drum *tangtango* ensemble is used. From Tambacounda east to Mali the Maninka jembe is prevalent.

There are other instruments played by Mande peoples that are not covered here. Among them are a water drum (*ji dunun*) played by women, consisting of one or more half calabashes turned upside down in a basin of water (Chéron 1931; Rouget 1954a-disc, 1954b-disc, 1999-disc; Gibbal 1982; Modic 1993, 1994, 1996; Konate and Ott 1997:18–19; Konate 1997-disc), and trumpets (*buru*) made of ivory or wood (Joyeux 1910:51–52, 1924, fig. 2, 178–79; C. Monteil 1924:314–15; Toureille 1992-disc; Brandes, Male, and Thierno 1998-disc).

Repertories

Each of the three traditional spheres of Mande music (hunter's harp music, jeliya, and drumming) has its own body of music. Musicians are keenly aware not only of the boundaries that separate these bodies, but also of what is and is not supposed to be within their purview. Each is in turn made up of bodies of pieces that are tied together in various ways. Jeliya, for instance, is made up of pieces associated with each of the jeli's instruments, with particular geographic regions, empires, family lineages, and kinds of people (e.g., warriors, leaders, merchants, or generous patrons). These associations are linked in a thick web of relationships that lends itself well to a rich variety of analytical vantage points: simbi, kora, bala, or koni pieces; old or new pieces; pieces honoring ancient Malian heroes, eighteenth-century Segu kings, nineteenth-century Fulbe jihad leaders, or twentieth-century Mandinka chiefs; pieces from Guinea, Mali, Senegal, or The Gambia; and pieces musically derived from a parent piece.

The pieces jelis play are all named. Most often the name is that of the person to whom the piece is dedicated, such as Kelefa or Sunjata. The number of pieces a jeli knows might surpass one hundred, but the most important ones, those played most often, probably number in the dozens in any one jeli's repertory. A piece can last as long as the performer wishes—from a few minutes to an hour or longer, depending on the performance situation and the kind of piece.

Whereas jelis play pieces honoring specific persons, drummers play pieces honoring groups of people: strong men, children about to undergo the rituals of circumcision or excision, slaves, farmers, blacksmiths, neighboring ethnic groups, and so on. Other rhythms are associated with specific occasions, such as the cultivation of fields or meetings of secret power societies. Drum rhythms are more generic in this regard, though jeli pieces can also serve as generic prototypes and be reoriented to honor new patrons. For example, a common practice is for jelis to put new words to one of the classic pieces in the repertory. They often choose a piece by matching up some characteristic of the person being honored in the original piece with that of the new subject.

The introduction jelis often give to the stories behind pieces of music, that "every piece has its owner or meaning" (see chapter 3), can apply to a certain extent to all Mande music. Although drum rhythms are nowadays played outside their originally intended occasions and old pieces receive new words to honor new patrons, the original associations are still understood by many and are responsible for much of their power.

Lack of historical documentation precludes definitive statements about the age of most pieces. Stylistic analysis would prove untenable, given that musical change in Africa is poorly understood. With few alternatives, the person or persons to whom a piece is dedicated stands to symbolize its age for most Mande musicians. Whether a piece played nowadays was played in the same manner centuries ago is a moot question.

Tuning and Scales

The melodic instruments used by Mande musicians all have their own tuning systems—owing in no small part to their various geographic origins—which are often spoken of as differences in language or dialect. The simbi is tuned to a heptatonic scale that is close to a just intonation major scale. The bala is tuned to what seems to be an equiheptatonic scale, although it would be unusual to find an instrument that conforms closely to a theoretical model. The bala and simbi tunings do not have names, probably because there is no need for them with only one tuning. The koni can be tuned many different ways (I encountered eight), each named after an important piece played in that tuning. The kora has four distinct tunings, each of them named, but not after particular pieces (with one possible exception). The guitar also has a few alternative tunings, but they conform more or less to the European equal-tempered tuning system. Although these instruments have different tuning systems, they share parts of their repertories, and all the jeli's instruments may be played together in a single ensemble. Together they collectively define a northern Mande heptatonic tonal system.

The diversity of tuning systems and the willingness of Mande musicians to combine them in ensembles need not be interpreted as a lax attitude to a standard tuning. The unusually large number of languages in Africa comes into play here. It is not at all uncommon for Africans to be fluent in two, three, or more local languages plus French, English, and Arabic. Fluency in several local languages may be seen as showing respect for one's neighbors by learning to communicate with them in their own languages. Tuning systems and their regional and personal interpretations are like languages and dialects belonging to certain regions and peoples. Rather than tending toward monolingualism or a single tuning standard, Africans accept and appreciate other ways of speaking while taking pride in their own ways. Not only does the sound of an instrument itself evoke certain regions or peoples, but so does its tuning system. This approach is not confined to West Africa (e.g., see Berliner 1978:59–72 on Shona *mbira* tunings in Zimbabwe).

The simbi and bala have no allowance for altered degrees of their own single heptatonic tunings. Although the kora has four heptatonic tunings, most players specialize in only one or two, and pitches cannot be altered in the course of a single piece. Since the koni and guitar are lutes, they can easily accommodate degree alterations in performance, usually lowering the seventh or sharp fourth degrees in descending passages, or more rarely the second degree. The different tunings on the kora and koni, and the different uses of the kora tunings wherein the tonic is moved to a different string, thereby altering the scale structure, reveal a modal practice in which pieces associated with different regions are played in tunings and scales that reflect their diversity.

Playing Techniques and Styles

In addition to regional preferences for certain instruments, tuning systems, and repertories, there are also regional playing styles. This is probably most evident on the guitar. As the newest instrument and a foreign import without a long local tradition, the guitar was fertile terrain on which local styles could be transplanted and cultivated. The most significant contrast is between a Malian guitar style based on koni playing and a Guinean guitar style based on bala playing.

Most of the musical transcriptions in this book consist of a single cycle of a piece, usually lasting from two to eight seconds. That single cycle should be taken as a harmonic, melodic, or rhythmic model of a piece that may undergo various musical transformations. The model can be a short melody (on the koni or simbi), a short rhythmic pattern or melody of timbres (on the jembe or dundun), or a series of harmonic areas (on the bala) with idiomatic ways of working through those areas. Some of the transformations that may be exercised during a performance include using alternative tones, resulting in variations to the model, or alternative models (once again consisting of a single cycle of a piece), which are considered different ways to play the piece or different versions of it. Each of these ways of playing a piece may be thought of as an accompaniment pattern, a kind of playing that contrasts with another kind consisting of highly ornamented melodic solo lines. Kora players call accompaniment-type playing *kumbengo* and solo-type playing *birimintingo*. Jelis who are familiar with French often refer to these two kinds of playing as *accompaniment* and *solo*. Hunter's harp playing does not lay great emphasis on highly ornamented solos, with the possible exception of the Wasulu harp (*donso ngoni*).

Instrumental renditions of pieces by jelis combine steady accompaniment-type patterns with solo cascading lines. The accompaniment type of playing can embody African aesthetics of polyphony and polyrhythm where two or more interdependent parts combine into a whole. The solo lines integrate African aesthetics of melody—descending terracelike movement—with the highly ornamented melodic turns typical of the Muslim western sahel and savanna. Even when there is a vocalist, these two kinds of playing are involved. Vocal pauses can be punctuated with short solo melodic bursts or extended solo melodic instrumental playing.

Use of the term "accompaniment" should not be taken to imply that there is no instrumental music without voice. Although all the pieces jelis play have songs and stories attached to them, and though jeli performances in Africa typically center on a vocalist, recordings of instrumental music are growing (see chapter 3).

Much of the drama of Mande instrumental music comes from exploiting the possibilities of variation: within a single accompaniment pattern, within a single piece by creating new accompaniment patterns, and by juxtaposing accompaniment pattern playing and linear melodic-solo playing. An instrumental performance maintains the flow of the rhythmic and harmonic cycle while weaving in and out of these different kinds of playing. Although guitarists have absorbed this aesthetic of variation, few approach the depth and creativity of the masters of the traditional instruments.

A key part of Mande musical aesthetics is setting up two or more interdependent melodic parts that interact to create a polyrhythmic or offbeat texture (or both). This is evident no matter what the instrument, although it is less common on the koni. Bala accompaniments, for instance, often consist of the two hands (each holding one mallet) interacting to form a polyrhythmic or interlocking whole. This has transferred over to the guitar, with the thumb plucking the part of one mallet and the index finger that of the other. A typical bala ensemble of three players can achieve great polyrhythmic complexity with two players assuming accompaniment roles and the leader weaving in and out of each. Duos are the norm for guitar or koni players. A wide spectrum of musical expression is available to solo kora players, since their four fingers (two thumbs and two index fingers) can enter into a variety of relationships with each other.

Drums are usually played in ensembles, with each instrument maintaining a well-defined role. The drum ensemble of the Senegambian Mandinka is fixed at three: two accompanying drums that differ primarily in size (*kutirindingo* and *kutiriba*) and one lead drum (*sabaro*). Maninka jembe ensembles are not fixed but are typically made up of one to three dunduns (double-headed bass drums) of different sizes, one or two accompanying jembes, and one lead jembe. Typically the accompanying instruments—either the two Mandinka *kutiro* drums or Maninka jembes—set up short interlocking patterns over which the lead drummer plays phrases that interact closely with dancers.

Languages and Neighboring Peoples

In its most inclusive linguistic usage, "Mande" is a heading of one of the major branches of the large Niger-Congo language grouping that covers most of West Africa, the other branches being Kordofanian, Atlantic, and

Table 2 Mande and Other Niger-Congo Languages

Mande	Atlantic	Volta
Northern	*Northern*	*North*
Mandekan	Senegal languages	Kru
Mandinka (Senegambia)	Fulbe (Pulaar)	Gur
Xasonka (NW Mali)	Serer	Senufo
Bamana (central Mali)	Wolof	Mossi
Maninka (western Mali, NE Guinea)		Dagbani, Dagari,
Kuranko (SE Guinea)	Bak languages	Sisaala
Jula (SE Mali, Côte d'Ivoire)	Jola	Bwa/Bobo Wule
Soninke (northern Mali)	Balanta	
Susu/Jallonke/Yalunka		Dogon
(western Guinea, northern Sierra Leone)	Others	
Vai/Kono (eastern Sierra Leone, SW Liberia)		*Benue-Kwa*
	Southern	Benue
Southwestern	Mel languages	Yoruba
Kpelle/Guerze; Loma/Toma (SE Guinea, Liberia)	Baga	Bantu
Mendi (Sierra Leone)	Landuma	Kwa
	Temni	Ewe, Akan, Baoule
Southeastern	Kissi	
Bisa (Burkina Faso)		
Dan/Gio (Côte d'Ivoire)		
Mano (north-central Liberia)		

Source: Adapted from Brooks 1993:30–33 and Blench 1997:92–94.

Volta (table 2).[1] One of the four languages of the northern subgroup of the Mande branch is Mandekan, an artificial term (not found in local tongues) combining Mande with *kan* (language) introduced by Charles Bird, the primary language within the scope of this book. Mandekan has several major dialects stretching from the Senegambian coastline to the Mali–Burkina Faso border in a continuum blending into each other (table 1 [p. xxii]). At the distant borders these dialects are probably mutually unintelligible, and different speakers would have varying degrees of difficulty understanding speech as they move around. To nonnative speakers (especially foreign researchers) Gambian Mandinka, Guinean Maninka, and Malian Bamana, the three most prevalent dialects in those countries, are for all practical purposes different languages. My own usage of Mande in this book refers primarily to Maninka and Mandinka, but at times it may also include other speakers of Mandekan and of northern branch Mande languages. I will use

1. This section on Mande and other languages is based on Bird (1970, 1982), Blench (1997), Brooks (1993), and Vydrine (1995–96). For bibliographical and other information on the peoples discussed here see the various country volumes in the "Historical Dictionary" series from Scarecrow Press (e.g., O'Toole 1995). For musical surveys see the various country entries in Sadie (forthcoming).

the local terms, such as Maninka, Mandinka, and Xasonka, when referring to specific groups.[2]

A Mandekan linguistic core, perhaps encompassing a proto-Mande language area (though this is not clear), stretches from Segou (Mali) in the northeast to the headwaters of the Niger River near Faranah (Guinea) in the south, and west to the Faleme River at the Senegal-Mali border (Bird 1970:149). (See map 1.) Three exceptional features distinguish Mandekan from other West African languages (Bird 1970:148): its extensive geographic spread, covering vast amounts of Mali, Guinea, Senegal, Gambia, and Côte d'Ivoire; the large number of speakers, estimated (by Bird 1982:1) to be the native tongue of five to six million people and the second language of twice that many, combining to be more than half the population (in the early 1980s) of the five countries; and its relative cohesiveness as a language. These features are no doubt due to the expansion of the Mali empire and its trade networks.

Using language designations as ethnic labels can be especially problematic in Africa, for language is just one among many ways Africans define their group identities. Some markers of group identity that cut across boundaries of language can include family names indicating common origin (such as the widespread name Camara), family name equivalencies indicating common status or occupation within different ethnic groups, associations uniting members of the same age group, and nationality combining disparate ethnic groups in common cause.[3] The blanket ethnic designations used in late nineteenth- and early twentieth-century French colonial writing were matters of convenience that satisfied bureaucratic needs for classification into clear-cut categories and then took on a life of their own (Bazin 1985:92–94). Many of the language designations, which also served as ethnic designations, came from outsiders such as Fulbe or Moor interpreters who might not have been very discerning in their assessment of the group identity of others (Amselle 1998:49–50, 172).[4] Before gaining respect in

2. See Vydrine (1995–96) for a discussion of the confusing array of European and American uses of the term "Mande" and related variants and suggestions for standardization.

3. Maninka-speaking musicians on either side of the Guinea-Mali border can be shaped by very different cultural influences when they move to their capital cities, which are separated by eight hundred kilometers. Manfila Kante's (1995-disc) song *L'unité* is an example of the effort to unite the diverse peoples of a country in common cause: "Our country is not a Fula one . . . a Maninka one . . . a Sosso one . . . a Toma one . . . a Kissi one . . . a Guerze one, Our country belongs to everyone."

4. A notorious example is the designation "Bambara," which has taken on diverse references according to who is doing the speaking. They have been described variously as pagans and infidels by their Muslim neighbors, as warriors by Arab historians, as peasants by itinerant traders known as Jula, as farmers by pastoralists, as slaves by those in power, as slaves from the interior country by European slave traders, and as metaphysicians by French anthropologists (Bazin 1985:88, 106, 113, 117; Amselle 1998).

ethnographies, these terms may have had derogatory connotations, since they were used by members of one group to distinguish themselves from others, who may have been hostile neighbors or conquered peoples. French and British colonial writings have acted to reify these foreign designations: in French writing Bamana are known as Bambara, Maninka as Malinke, and Pulaar as Peulh; in British writing Gambian Mandinka are known as Mandingo and Pulaar as Fula or Fulani (in Nigeria). Even so, language and ethnicity are clearly means that Africans sometimes use to distinguish themselves from their neighbors. But they are not the only means, and they can be fluid according to the context.

Those who are considered part of the northern Mande language family include Bamana, Wasulu, Soninke, Xasonka and Susu.[5] Bamana, known as Bambara to outsiders such as Europeans, primarily inhabit the regions of Segou and Kaarta north of Bamako. Bamana is now the predominant language in Mali. Because they were persistent resisters of Islam, the term Bambara has often been applied to any non-Islamic people in the larger region, creating much confusion over their identity. Oral traditions attribute the origins of the Bamana in the Segou region to a migration led by Kala-jan Coulibaly in the mid-seventeenth century. In the early 1700s Mamari (also called Biton) Coulibaly established the Coulibaly dynasty and the Segu kingdom, which was expanded by Ngolo Jara (Diara) and the Jara dynasty in the mid- to late 1700s. Da Monson Jara (ruled 1808–27) is the subject of an important praise song, as is Bakari Jan (Dian) Kone, a great warrior chief under Da Monson. The other major Bamana kingdom, Kaarta, was founded in the mid-seventeenth century and ruled by the Massasi dynasty. Kaarta and Segu fell in the mid-1800s when they were taken over by al Hajj Umar Tal. Though Bamana and Maninka are mutually intelligible dialects, there are significant differences in their musics. Bamana music is pentatonic and Maninka music is heptatonic, which in effect means that the two live in different spheres. Bamana instruments include the pentatonic bala and ngoni (lute), both larger than the Maninka varieties.

Wasulu (Wassoulou) or Wasolon is the name of the region on the eastern border of old Mande, extending from the Sankarani River in the west to Bougouni in the east, with parts in northeastern Guinea and northern Côte d'Ivoire. A Wasulu identity formed as a centuries-long brew of waves of Fulbe migrants, initially from Massina in the second half of the fifteenth

5. For a survey of musical instruments in Mali see M. Diallo (1972) and Musée National du Mali (1996). For further references on Bamana, see Ba Konaré (1987), Bazin (1985), Conrad (1990), Imperato (1996), C. Monteil (1924), and Newton (1997); Wasulu, see Amselle (1998), Durán (1995a, 1996, forthcoming a, forthcoming b), and Imperato (1981); Soninke, see Boyer (1953), Mamadou Diawara (1990), Dieterlen and Sylla (1992), and Pollet and Winter (1971); Susu, see Bühnen (1994); and Xasonka, see C. Monteil (1915) and Cissoko (1986).

century and later Futa Jalon (Amselle 1998:47, 49, 74–78), settled into an area joining Maninka, Bamana, and Senufo farmers. The four Fulbe lineages Sidibe, Sangare, Diakite (Jakite), and Diallo (Jallo) are commonly found in the Wasulu region. Like that of the Bamana, their music is pentatonic. Their instruments include the hunter's harp called *donso ngoni,* a smaller version called *kamalen ngoni,* a one-stringed fiddle called *soku,* and a small jembe. The Wasulu Sogoninkun masked figure and its associated music have had an important impact on modern Malian music.

Soninke descend from ancient Ghana, which they refer to as Wagadu (see chapter 1). They are known as Maraka in the predominantly Bamana Segou and Kaarta regions and as Sarakhole or Sarahuli in the Senegambia region.[6] Soninke griots are known as *gesere* and *jaare,* but the distinction between the two is not so clear. They play a lute called *gambare* and are expert in the history of Wagadu. Sissoko (also spelled Cissokho; in the Senegambia region it is shortened to Suso) is a typical Soninke jeli name, and Tounkara and Sacko also have Soninke jeli branches.

The area between Kayes and Bafoulabé in northwestern Mali is the home of the Xaso kingdom (also spelled Khasso). Xasonka (Khassonka) are a mix of Maninka, Fulbe, and Soninke. Plucked lutes are associated with each of these three ethnic groups, and the Xasonka themselves are renowned koni (or *kontin*) players. Their language is readily identified by a predominance of velar fricative sounds (written as *x*), which are striking to the unaccustomed ear. Xasonka jelis may represent an old layer of griots, since the instruments they excel in—the koni, tama and dundun—are probably the oldest jeli instruments, perhaps dating back to the Ghana empire. Kanoute is a typically Xasonka jeli name.[7]

Susu (also called Sosso), with probable origins in Mali and historical relations to Soninke and Maninka, migrated southwest into Guinea as far as the coast after the defeat of their leader Sumanguru Kante at the hands of Sunjata in the thirteenth century. Having settled among coastal Guinean peoples and absorbed influences from them, they are in certain contexts considered distinct from the Maninka of Upper Guinea. Predominant in Conakry, they are known for their expertise on the bala. Doumbia (Dumbia, Doumbuya) is a typical Susu jeli name, though they may also consider themselves Maninka.[8]

The other major language family found in Mandekan regions is Atlantic

6. See Arnoldi (1995:137–48) for a discussion of the variety of peoples subsumed under the name Maraka, such as Maraka je, Maraka fin, and Maraka jalan, and a discussion of the ethnic identities of Boso (Bozo), Somono (Niger River fisherfolk), and Maraka in the Segou region.

7. The Senegambian jeli family name Konte may be a local version of Kanoute.

8. In a praise song, Oumou Dioubate (1995?-disc: *Amara Bangoura* [4'27"]) sings that Bangoura (a name occasionally found among Guinean musicians) is the Susu equivalent of the Maninka

(or West Atlantic), a Niger-Congo branch. Atlantic languages, unrelated to Mandekan except in grand linguistic classification systems, are divided into a northern branch from the Senegambia region, including Fulbe (Pulaar), Serer, Wolof, and Bak (Jola, Manjak, and Balanta) languages, and a southern branch from Guinea, including Baga and Landuma. Living near Mandekan speakers, Atlantic language speakers have both influenced and been influenced by the culture of their neighbors. A brief survey follows.

Fulbe are among the most widely dispersed peoples in West Africa and have had long and close contact with Mande peoples both as tenders of their cattle and, in the eighteenth and nineteenth centuries, as militant leaders of Muslim holy wars of conversion. Pieces dedicated to Fulbe leaders make up a significant component of the musical repertories of Mandinka and Maninka jalis (Knight 1983). The most widespread of such pieces is *Taara,* dedicated to al Hajj Umar Tal. Fulbe ancestors may have been nomads from the Sahara who migrated to the middle Senegal river valley during the first millennium C.E. This area was known as Takrur (Tekrur) when it was first described by al-Bakrī, who indicated that the ruler and his subjects had converted to Islam in the early eleventh century (Levtzion 1980:44, 183–85, 1985:143–46). By the early sixteenth century Futa Toro was established by Koly Tengela Ba in place of Takrur, stretching the length of the middle Senegal River (see map in Robinson 1985:61). In addition to Futa Toro there are several other major Fulbe centers: Futa Jalon, in the northern Guinean mountains; Massina, on the inland delta of the middle Niger River; and Fuladu, in eastern Gambia and the upper Casamance (southern Senegal). In terminology used in Senegal, the inhabitants of Takrur and their descendants are all considered to be Haalpulaaren (speakers of their Pulaar language), with two distinct groups identified: Tukulor (Fr: Toucouleur), sedentary agriculturists from Takrur; and Fulbe (Fr: Peulh, Md: Fula), nomadic pastoralist cattle herders whose migrations have brought them directly south to the Futa Jalon highlands of northern Guinea and east across the sahel into Mali, Niger, Nigeria (where they are known as Fulani), and Cameroon (Levtzion and Hopkins 1981:400 n. 9; Villalón 1995:51). Five major Fulbe holy wars (jihads) were responsible for the massive spread of Islam in West Africa over the past several centuries (Robinson 1985): the first began in Futa Jalon about 1700; the second was led by the Torodbe (Muslim clerics) of Futa Toro in the late 1700s (Willis 1978); the third and fourth took place in the early 1800s in Sokoto (northern Nigeria) and Massina (Mali); and the fifth began in 1852 led by al Hajj Umar Tal, who died

name Doumbuya: "Susu say Bangoura, Maninka say Doumbuya" (*Sosolu ko Bangura, Maninkalu ko Dumbuya*).

in 1864. The end result of these jihads is that Senegal, The Gambia, and Mali are over 90 percent Muslim and Guinea is approximately 85 percent Muslim. The most widely appreciated Fulbe instrument is the *serdu* (flute). Other instruments include the *hoddu* (lute) and *nyanyur* or *gnagnur* (spike fiddle).

The Wolof were the core people of the Jolof kingdom, founded in the distant past by the legendary figure Njanjan Njay (Ndiaye).[9] The Jolof state, just south of Futa Toro, probably developed sometime in the thirteenth or fourteenth century. In the mid-fifteenth century the Portuguese found a flourishing Jolof empire that included three other vassal states: Walo, just east of Futa Toro; Kajor (Kayor), south of Walo along the *grand côte* (from St. Louis to Dakar); and Baol, south of Kajor along the *petite côte* (from Dakar southward). The opening up of trade with Europeans along the coast shifted the economic flow of goods from north across the Sahara to west toward the Atlantic, and by the mid-sixteenth century the landlocked Jolof state lost power to the coastal states. Wolof society is organized similarly to Mande society, with two major classes of people besides slaves (*jam*): *geer,* the equivalent of the Mande *horon* (freeborn), and *nyeenyo,* equivalent to the Mande *nyamakala* (artisan-born). The equivalent to the Mandinka *jali* is the Wolof *gewel.* Sufism is particularly strong in Senegal, and there are several prominent orders: Qadiriyya, with twelfth-century origins in Baghdad; Murid, a predominantly Wolof offshoot of Qadiriyya founded in the early twentieth century by the highly influential Shaykh Amadu Bamba Mbacke; and Tijaniyya, an order with Moroccan origins that is particularly popular among the Haalpulaaren owing in part to al Hajj Umar Tal. Wolof gewels (griots) often have the family names Seck and Samb. Wolof instruments include the *sabar* (drum) and *xalam* (lute).

The term "Serer" encompasses several groups associated with the states of Sin and Salum, situated between the former Wolof states in the north and the Mandinka Kabu states in the south. Although some Serer may have originated in their present region, others probably migrated from Takrur in the north beginning in the eleventh century, being pushed south by Moors, Fulbe, and Jolof. By the fourteenth century the powerful state of Sin was established, led by a line of rulers of Mandinka origin known as Gelwar. The Salum kingdom was established in the late fifteenth or early sixteenth century by Mbegan Ndur (Ndour).

9. For further information on the Wolof, see Ames (1955-disc), Brooks (1993:167–257), A. Diop (1981), Gamble (1967), and Levtzion (1985:145); on the Serer, see Gamble (1967) and Gravrand (1983, 1990); on the Jola, see Irvine and Sapir (1976), Mark (1985, 1992), and Sapir (1965-disc); on the Senegambia, see Barry (1998), Clark and Phillips (1994), and Sonko-Godwin (1986); on the Baga, see Lamp (1996).

Jola (Fr: Diola), known in older European writing as Felupe, are predominant in the lower Casamance. Their stateless political structure is sometimes described as acephalous (headless). Although they are not linguistically related to the Mandinka, centuries of contact have led to mutual influence. Jola dancing, with torsos bent parallel to the ground and outstretched arms flapping like birds' wings, resembles Mandinka dancing. Jola instruments include a set of three or four large drums (called *bugarabu, bugarab,* or *bugareb*), played by a single person, and a hunter's harp. Balanta are related to the Jola and play a large xylophone called *kadj* (or *balo*), with two people on one instrument, that has influenced neighboring Mandinka kora playing styles (Knight 1997-vid).

In Guinea the musical influence on Mande groups by their neighbors appears to be limited to the sphere of drumming, primarily in the context of the national ballets. Baga, who live along the coast, have an extensive drumming and mask dancing tradition that is part of a larger West Atlantic tradition that reaches north to the *kankurang* fiber masked figure of Gambian Mandinka. Baga rhythms such as *Sorsorne* and *Kakilambe* (the Susu term for the highest Baga deity) have entered into the repertory of the national ballets, as have those of other small-scale groups from the southern forest region such as the Toma (Loma).

Islam and Mande Music

Various kinds of music in the Mande world have been influenced by the long association of Mande peoples with Islam. Only some basic features will be discussed here.[10] Islam has shaped and been shaped by local cultures wherever it has taken root. Certain Muslim holidays are cause for celebration or rest, certain local repertories have broadened to include pieces dedicated to Muslim leaders, and certain singing and playing styles bear marks of Arab Muslim musical sensibilities. During Ramadan (Mn: *sunkalo,* "fasting month"), the month of fasting from sunup to sundown, marriages are not held and drummers do not play. But the end of Ramadan (Ar: *'īd al-fitr;* Mn: *selifitini, selinin, selikalo, salikalo;* "lesser feast") is cause for celebration and music. The biggest Muslim festival, known as Tabaski (Ar: *'īd al-adhā;* Mn: *seliba, saliba;* "greater feast"), commemorates Abraham's sacrificing of a lamb and marks the end of the month-long pilgrimage to Mecca (*hajj*). It is a major time for music making, with drummers often making the rounds in their villages, going from compound to compound.

10. For more on Islam and music in Africa see Charry (forthcoming).

The spectacular music making at the fourteenth-century court of Mali described by Ibn Battūta took place on the two feast days *'īd al-fitr* and *'īd al-adhā,* as well as at the Friday Muslim prayers (Levtzion and Hopkins 1981:292–93, 416).

The vast majority of jelis are well educated in Islam, and many are devout Muslims. Quotations from the Koran are common in their narrations and singing, and pieces dedicated to religious leaders (such as *Taara,* dedicated to al Hajj Umar Tal) frequently attract such quotations. Sufi and other Muslim leaders are occasionally the subjects of popular songs, such as Baba Djan Kaba's (1992-disc) *Touba Famake* dedicated to the Senegalese Murid leader Shaykh Amadu Bamba (also see McLaughlin 1997).

One song from Upper Guinea sung by women in the course of circumcision celebrations demonstrates Mande recognition of the give-and-take between the religious demands of local interpretations of Islam and long-standing local traditions. The song honors Alpha Kabine, a Muslim leader who lifted earlier restrictions on music and dance in circumcision celebrations.

> Our dances and songs
> In honor of our children
> Will not at all kill
> Our faith in Islam.
> May you forever remain serene,
> Oh, Alpha Kabiné the great
> Our authentic ancestor!
> We devote the time
> For our cherished Islamic rites
> But without sacrificing our songs
> And dances for our cherished children.
> (Mamadi Kaba 1995:108)[11]

From a technical perspective, music of the jelis has been influenced by some of the musical aesthetics carried in the recitation of the Koran that is bound up in Islam wherever it travels. Two noteworthy features that sometimes distinguish the music of sahelian Muslim peoples from some of their non-Muslim neighbors include monophony, wherein vocal harmony is largely absent, and a high degree of melodic ornamentation. Although it is possible that these tendencies might predate the coming of Islam, they do conform to Arab musical practice and help to bind a large musical culture area.

11. My English translation of Kaba's French translation of the original Maninka. See M. Kaba (1995) for other songs related to Islam and local Maninka practices.

Traditional and Modern

After several decades of increasing interrogation, the concepts of traditional and modern have survived the late twentieth century bruised but intact.[12] Though these terms can conjure up outdated binary either/or ways of looking at the world, they can also provide valuable frames of reference for the very real possibility of nonexclusive dualities, with people drawing elements from here and there while forging multifarious ways of living in the world. The two terms continue to maintain their relevancy for certain aspects of life in Africa, and it is essential to address the issue of labeling and use. "Traditional" (Fr: *traditionnnel*) and "modern" (Fr: *moderne*) are embraced in their English, French, or local forms by many—certainly by Mande music makers—who effectively use them to make meaningful local distinctions.[13] It is perhaps best to understand these terms here intuitively, as shorthand ways to distinguish sensibilities associated with old local musical instruments, genres, and styles from more recent ones. Traditional and modern in a Mande context do not refer to opposing sides of battle with impenetrable lines, or to blind adherence to colonial lexical categories and mentalities, but rather reflect states of mind that can be fluidly combined and respected in innovative and often humorous ways.

That guitars, koras, konis, and balas can all be played in traditional and modern styles (see chapter 5) should give pause for thought. Acoustic guitars, koras, and konis are routinely used alongside each other to play the intimate repertory of the jeli plugged into huge sound systems at outdoor urban marriage celebrations that appropriate a whole city block, often alternating with drum ensembles that announce and dance arriving guests into, out of, and back into their seats (see plates 2 and 34, which are from the same event). Kora, koni, and bala players, in turn, have their ears tuned to musics from around the world. Dakar-based kora player Soriba Kouyate (shown in plate 2) has integrated African American musical sensibilities, as well as actual chord progressions and melodic lines, into an original musi-

12. See Geertz (1995:136–68) for a recent discussion of the two terms. Barber (1997:1–12) captures limitations of the two terms in some African cultural contexts but narrowly confines the references of each to advance an alternative interpretive vantage point ("popular culture"), which is ineffective, however, in confronting the deep-time creative cultural practices that continue to operate in the Mande world.

13. Local terms for "tradition" or "custom" include *fasaroo* (Gamble 1987b:39) and the Wolof word *coosaani* (Gamble 1987b:23), both used in Senegambian Mandinka, *laada,* from the Arabic *al-āda* or *l'ādat,* used in Bamana and Maninka (Bailleul 1996:242, Delafosse 1955:452–53, Kone 1995:115), and *naamè* (Kone 1995:137) or *naamu/namu* (Bailleul 1996:285) used in Bamana. "Modern" is conveyed by the term *bimògòw* or *bimòòlu* (today's people, nowadays people) in Bamana (Kone 1995:13) and Maninka/Mandinka (Séminaire-atelier 1994:47), respectively.

Plate 2 Stringed instruments at a marriage celebration in Dakar, 1989. Left to right: Mory Kouyate (guitar), Soriba Kouyate (kora), unidentified guitar and koni players. Photo by the author.

cal style that can be startling to those hearing him for the first time.[14] Koni player Basekou Kouyate (plate 3) shared the stage with American bluesman Taj Mahal at a Tennessee banjo institute in 1990, much to the enjoyment of all. Certainly many, mostly older, musicians do not venture far from their inherited traditions. But some of those who do have come up with stunning results.

The elderly Keletigui Diabate playing two balas that can emulate the European twelve-tone scale in an ensemble of musicians thirty to forty years his junior, including kora player Toumani Diabate, koni player Basekou Kouyate, a vocalist, and electric bass, electric guitar, tama, and drum set players, has been a familiar image for Bamako residents in the mid-1990s (plate 3). Diabate is grounded in the bala tradition, and he also occasionally pulls out a trombone to blow a jazz-oriented solo with this group. He has played electric guitar with state orchestras in Mali and Guinea at the dawn of independence (plate 44), violin with Mali's renowned Les Ambassadeurs in the 1970s (plate 45), and bala with Salif Keita in the 1990s. In a corner of the courtyard of his home, carved wooden bala slats are smoked dry in

14. "The fusion of African American and Mande music in Soriba's performance had blown me away. I had said to myself that, at last, African music was not afraid of becoming modern" (Manthia Diawara 1998:111).

Plate 3 Symphonie Mandingue. Top (left to right): Keletigui Diabate (bala), Mamadou "Santiago" Kouyate (guitar), Toumani Diabate (kora), Basekou Kouyate (koni). Bottom (left to right): same as above with Djibril Camara (bass), unidentified tama player and drummer. Club L'Hogon, Bamako, 1997. Photos by the author.

preparation for attachment to bamboo frames to be played with wooden mallets partially wrapped in rubber tapped from trees, a fabrication process used by his bala-playing ancestors for centuries. Keletigui Diabate may be unique in his own solutions to problems of old and new, tradition and modernity, but he is not alone.

There is something modern about Toumani Diabate's (1988b-disc) first solo recording—perhaps the European-inflected tuning of his kora, the laid-back tempos or other aspects of his musical sensibility, the lack of any vocalizing, or the warm acoustic ambiance of the studio. He plays *Kaira* and

Allah l'a ke, pieces that were staples of the repertory of his father, Sidiki Diabate, one of the great musical artists of his generation, whose death was cause for national mourning. In the home given to his father by the first president of Mali, Toumani Diabate lives in a world of fax machines, cell phones, recording sessions, local nightclubs, international tours, electrified jelimuso-led ensembles performing at traditional celebrations, extended family and the extended obligations therein, high infant mortality, young kora apprentices, respect for the jelis of his father's generation, and the proud legacy of the Diabate lineage of jelis. Like many of his contemporaries, he uses modern technological tools to honor traditional commitments. Traditional musics are likewise put in modern contexts in his ensembles, mixing diverse instruments with new arrangements. Traditional and modern worldviews complement each other, meld together, and also remain distinct in late twentieth-century western Africa. In the following pages I attempt to detail this process.

1

The Mande

This chapter summarizes the prehistoric and historic background of western Africa with particular attention to areas inhabited by peoples speaking Mande languages. I begin by discussing climate, then move on to the peopling of western Africa, subsistence strategies, artisanal occupations, political history, and finally Maninka notions of social organization and personality and the impulses that motivate the *ngara*—the master oral historian, singer, and musician.

The construction of a deep-time music history is hindered by very sparse writings on music sprinkled over a relatively short time span, barely one thousand years. Archaeological research in western Africa has yet to uncover prehistoric musical activity, but recent theories on the early appearance and spread of agriculture in Dhar Tichitt (in southern Mauritania), ironworking in the Middle Niger region (in Mali), and the growth of specialized artisanal communities several thousand years ago may have much to contribute to an understanding of early music making. Since certain instruments are closely associated with certain artisanal communities or subsistence activities, an understanding of the origins of these communities and practices is relevant.

Hunter's music, sung to the accompaniment of calabash harps played throughout the savanna, might be the oldest musical tradition with still-living vestiges. With the growth of an iron industry beginning about 2,500 years ago, political power may have shifted into the hands of blacksmiths, who have long been associated with the jembe (drum) and bala (xylophone), perhaps because they were the proprietors of the iron tools used to craft them. The introduction of Arabian horses in the late first millennium C.E. gave rise to a mounted warrior class that would eventually challenge and win rule over the savanna. They had their personal praise singer–musicians who would preserve their memories in a new epic age, perhaps drawn from the ranks of musician-priests associated with savanna hunters' societies. Their instrument was the koni or some other closely related variety of plucked lute. They also used the bala, and by the nineteenth century the relatively new kora (calabash harp) became the instrument of choice in the western territories. The koni, bala, and kora are emblems of the jeli, the most prestigious of the Maninka and Mandinka musical artists. In the twentieth cen-

tury the guitar has been absorbed into the tradition of the jeli, and it in turn
has extended that tradition into new terrain.[1]

West African Prehistory

West African life from prehistoric times to the present has been profoundly
shaped by climate.[2] Every year beginning about March, summer rains coming from the southwest sweep over western Africa in a northeasterly direction. The front, called the Inter-Tropical Convergence Zone (ITCZ), reaches
the northernmost latitudes of the Senegal and Niger Rivers by July and then
shifts back southward, leaving the continent by November or December.
The descending ITCZ leaves a dry winter in its wake, compounded by the
desiccating Harmattan winds coming from the northeastern Sahara, which
reach as far as southern Guinea by January and stop vegetative growth. The
environment-defining rainfall bands (called isohyets) are responsible for
varied east-west bands of vegetation that determine the lifestyles of the
people living within them. The bands expand and contract independently of
each other over the long term, and several thousand years ago a long dry
spell may have thrown together diverse peoples, funneling them toward the
Senegal and Niger river valleys and giving birth to civilization in western
Africa. Defined according to the amount of yearly rainfall received, West
African environmental regions are (from north to south): the Sahara Desert,
the transitional region called the sahel, the savanna (divided into a northern dry savanna and southern savanna woodland), and the coastal forest
(map 2).

Little is known about human populations in West Africa before
12,000 B.P. (before the present). There is little direct evidence from the western part of the continent of the earliest type of stone tools (Oldowan), consisting of flakelike knives and larger choppers, dating from 2.5 to 1.4 million years ago in East and South Africa. From about 1.5 million years ago

1. My thinking on the construction of a deep-time music history has been shaped by the writings of R. McIntosh (1993,1998) and S. McIntosh (1995) on Middle Niger archaeology, Y. Cissé
(1964, 1994) on Maninka hunters' societies, Bird (1972, forthcoming) on Wasulu hunters' epics and
jelis, and Brooks (1993) on Mande state building. For broad introductions to West African history
see Ajayi and Crowder (1985–87) and Vogel (1997); for early written sources see Hair (1967,
1997) and Fage (1994); for an introduction to Maninka social organization see Hopkins (1971); for
bibliographic guides to music in Africa see J. Gray (1991) and Lems-Dworkin (1991). The journal
History in Africa has been a major outlet for recent research in Mande studies.

2. Interpretations of archaeological material can vary widely within scientific communities,
and there is a vast literature debating the details of the prehistoric sequence that follows. I have
summarized in order to focus on the study at hand. The following information on West Africa up
to 12,000 years ago draws on J. D. Clark (1978:24–54; 1982), Church (1980), S. K. McIntosh and
R. McIntosh (1983:221–29; 1988:92–95), R. McIntosh (1993:195), and Muzzolini (1993).

Map 2 Climate zones and some foods of West Africa (after Brooks 1993; Church 1980). Sahara Desert: less than 150 mm rainfall; salt. Sahel: 150 to 400 mm rainfall; sorghum and millet. Savanna (northern): 400 to 1,000 mm rainfall; sorghum and millet. Savanna (southern): 1,000 to 1,400 mm rainfall; rice and kola. Coastal forest: 1,400 mm or more rainfall; tubers (yam, cassava), kola, malaguetta pepper.

a new stone tool technology (Acheulean) using hand axes appeared in East Africa for the first time. Two examples from the Malian Sahara have been dated to several hundred thousand years ago. The increasing aridity and depopulation of the Sahara Desert that peaked about 50,000 B.P. left layers of sterile windblown sands that covered up Acheulean tools. On top of these layers the later Mousterian and Aterian stone tool industries have been found, perhaps in use throughout the Sahara region during the increasingly humid period from 50,000 to 30,000 B.P. Another kind of stone industry was used about this time in the savanna woodlands and forest regions farther south, with heavier tools that may have been used as crude axes for working with wood.

The last major dry period in the Sahara, from 20,000 to 12,000 B.P., left the massive sand dunes that run the breadth of the continent and shifted the desert perhaps four hundred or more kilometers farther south. The hyper-arid Sahara was probably uninhabited north of Dakar or Mopti (15° N), and most of the population in West Africa lived south of the northernmost borders of Côte d'Ivoire and Ghana (11° N).

Approximately 12,000 years ago the Pleistocene epoch (Ice Age) gave way to the Holocene (sometimes called the Late Stone Age), coinciding with global warming and rising sea levels.[3] Over the next several thousand years a period of increased humidity ensued. The Niger River breached sand dunes and flowed three hundred kilometers northward, rainfall was ten to fifty times the amount of today, and lakes in a parkland environment dominated the landscape up to the northernmost deserts of present-day Mali and Niger (24° N). During this time the Central Saharan highlands were repopulated by groups, perhaps proto-Nilo Saharan speakers coming from the northeast and east, who engaged in a variety of fishing, hunting, and gathering.

Table 3 shows an overview of George Brooks's (1986) historical schema of western Africa based on climate periods over the past eleven thousand years. Correlating population movements with the major climatic fluctuations in the region, Brooks has provided a valuable framework for understanding certain forces motivating political, cultural, and social change.

A ceramic industry appeared throughout Central Sahara (in southern Algeria and Sudan) roughly between 9300 and 8000 B.P. The round-bottomed clay pots decorated with wavy and dotted wavy lines, as well as an apparent widespread use of microlithic tools and bone harpoons (which had a more limited distribution), have led some scholars to suggest culture contact over a broad band across the Sahara. Others have pointed out significant local differences, possibly indicating specialization in hunting, fishing, or grain processing. A renewed arid phase dried up southern Saharan lakes, eventually forcing many of the sites in the region to be abandoned by 7300 B.P.

Pastoralism appeared for the first time in the Sahara about 7000 B.P. This new economy spread throughout the central and southern Sahara between the Egyptian Nile valley and present-day Niger. Its origins and the ways it might have spread remain unclear. The growth of pastoralism signaled a new kind of social organization that contrasted with the small, highly mobile groups of hunter-gatherers with minimal personal possessions or surplus goods. Pastoralism entailed private ownership of animals and may have encouraged a social hierarchy, with those who owned much stock taking on leadership.

3. The following information on West Africa from 12,000 B.P. up to, but not including, the Dhar Tichitt tradition is based on S. McIntosh (1994:167–73), S. McIntosh and R. McIntosh (1983: 229–38, 1988:94–101), Smith (1992:32–77), Muzzolini (1993), and Brooks (1986).

Table 3 Historical Periods of Western Africa Based on Climate Periods

───

9,000 to 2,500 B.C.E.: Era of aquatic culture
Long wet phase interrupted by a dry period. Groups (perhaps proto-Nilo-Saharans) settled near
Saharan bodies of water. After the dry period (6,000 to 5,500 B.C.E.), new groups moved into the
Sahara, perhaps proto-Berbers from north who introduced shorthorn cattle, goats, and sheep, and
proto-Mande speakers from south.

2,500 to 300 B.C.E.: Era of progressive desiccation
Long dry period. Saharan peoples either stayed or moved out in all directions. Groups in southern Sahara began to cultivate grains. Pastoral groups migrated south and introduced cattle, goats,
and sheep to the Niger bend by 2,000 B.C.E. Saharan rock art from seventh to third century B.C.E.
shows horse-drawn chariots. Trans-Saharan trade in salt and copper.

300 B.C.E. to 300 C.E.: Era of advanced aridity
Trans-Saharan trade halted because of desiccation. Camel herding introduced from Nile valley
during first century C.E. and internal trade in West Africa elaborated. Jenne-jenno established by
third century B.C.E. Rice and yams probably domesticated in West Africa.

300 to 1100 C.E.: Era of plentiful rainfall
Trans-Saharan trade flourished. Arabs introduced horses in the seventh and eighth centuries in
the southern Sahara and sahel. During 700–1000 wet period the tsetse fly line advanced north
and Fulbe migrated east. Mande traders moved south seeking kola, malaguetta peppers, etc.,
contributing to the differentiation of three languages of the northern subgroup (Soninke, Susu-
Jallonke-Yalonka, and Vai-Kono). Western and eastern split of Susu with Vai-Kono may have
been due to different commercial networks on Senegal and Niger Rivers and tributaries.

1100 to 1500 C.E.: Era of progressive desiccation
Mande traders moved farther south, expanding trade networks. Mande smiths followed traders
and founded chapters of power associations. Smiths moved to exploit southern woodlands.
Mande horsemen conquered sahel and savanna zones. Mande golden age: smiths, leatherworkers,
and griots.

1500 to 1630 C.E.: Brief but eventful wet period

1630 to 1860 C.E.: Era of droughts, famines, warfare, and slaving

───

Source: Adapted from Brooks 1986.

The southern range of pastoralism in West Africa is largely determined
by the tsetse fly line, the latitude above which tsetse flies, carriers of try-
panosomiasis (sleeping sickness) cannot survive. The sickness is fatal to
camels, horses, donkeys, sheep, and zebu cattle. The tsetse fly line is directly related to the average annual rainfall bands, lying somewhere between 500 mm and 1,000 mm of annual rainfall. Over the past 12,000 years
the line has migrated between roughly 10° N and 15° N, triggering a related
migration of people and their animals. Since about the twelfth century C.E.,
the Gambia River has roughly marked off the 1,000 mm rainfall line, separating the tsetse-free dry savanna in the north from the wooded savanna to
the south (Brooks 1986:48; 1993:12, 22–23).

Cattle, sheep, and goat herding spread rapidly after 6500 B.P. over a wider range than the previous ceramic cultures, stretching farther west to the Tilemsi valley in the Malian Sahara and probably even to the Mauritanian Atlantic coast. Similar pottery styles and stone tools that could have been used for working wood have been found along this broad band, although regional variations in tool types may be identified. Material differences from earlier Saharan inhabitants include thinner-walled pottery, the decorative patterns on it, and personal adornment such as beads, ivory bracelets, and possibly leatherwork (A. Smith 1992:56–62).

Rock art in the Sahara consisting of drawings that are either painted on or cut into rocks (called petroglyphs) provides details of the lifestyles of early pastoralists and later Saharan populations. Beginning about seven or eight thousand years ago in southern Algeria and Libya, petroglyphs of large animals and of human figures with clubs, axes, or bows appear, and shortly thereafter there are found depictions of human figures with round featureless heads, sometimes masked. Later, throughout the Sahara multicolored paintings of domesticated herds of cattle with herders and milkers appear. About three thousand years ago horse-drawn carts or chariots with human figures armed with javelins were depicted along possible north-south routes across the Sahara terminating at the Niger River. Depictions of horses with riders become common about two thousand years ago. In the few centuries B.C.E. the camel was introduced into the Sahara, and its depiction was often accompanied by the Libyco-Berber script (also called Tifinagh or Tifinar). The populations illustrated appear to be from distinct cultural groups: proto-Berber, probably coming from the north, and black Africans coming from the south.[4]

About 4500 B.P. temperatures began to rise, and an erratic, indeed chaotic, decline in environmental conditions led to a new period of desertification. During this period humans and animals moved progressively southward, probably in well-defined north-south water channels connected to various parts of the Niger and Senegal Rivers. By this time the constant short- and long-term fluctuations of the ITCZ may have taken a serious toll on the Saharan environment. Formerly, populations that were forced farther south with the drying of the Sahara could move north again during wetter phases when the tsetse fly line would approach from the south. But with the long-term degradation of Saharan soils the northern migration swings may have become more and more restricted. During the dry spells after 4500 B.P. various populations may have come into contact along the northern tributaries and channels of the Niger and Senegal Rivers. Rather than continu-

4. For more on Saharan rock art see Muzzolini (1997), Smith (1992:154–63), and Willcox (1984:35–42). For the introduction of the horse in West Africa see Law (1980).

ally migrating, these populations may have found it more advantageous to settle near each other, specializing in certain activities such as hunting, fishing, herding, grain processing, or crafting with the intent of sharing resources. This is the "pulse theory" developed by Roderick McIntosh, who suggests that the shift from small-scale, simple societies to integrated networks of subgroups may have occurred in West Africa sometime in the last two millennia B.C.E. and the first millennium C.E. (R. McIntosh 1993:193; S. McIntosh 1994:169–70).

After 4500 B.P. evidence for agriculture, the deliberate cultivation of crops, appears in West Africa for the first time. The origin of agriculture in West Africa has received much scholarly attention with little consensus. One of the earliest examples comes from the Dhar Tichitt region, a line of sandstone cliffs standing over dry lake beds in south-central Mauritania.[5] The region may have been populated by 4000 B.P., and it appears that millet was cultivated there by 3000 B.P. if not earlier. Evidence of hunting, fishing, gathering, and cultivation is present, but it is so far unclear if the population as a whole was engaged in these tasks seasonally, if there were smaller communities specializing in certain occupations, or if they moved from hunting to fishing to herding to agriculture as primary means of subsistence during the course of the fourth millennium B.P. Dhar Tichitt provides clear evidence of a large gathering of people: in the three hundred kilometers between the modern-day towns of Tichitt in the northwest and Walata in the southeast there were hundreds of villages almost three thousand years ago. In one study area of forty-four kilometers by fourteen kilometers over forty sites have been identified, each comprising from a few to as many as two hundred compounds, supporting a total population of perhaps five to ten thousand people (although it is unclear if all the sites were occupied contemporaneously). By the last few centuries B.C.E. Dhar Tichitt was abandoned, perhaps owing to the combined pressures of increasing desertification and the arrival of mounted Libyco-Berber peoples from the north who were armed with weapons of metal. After this time occupation sites in the Sahara become rare. The political center of western Africa would soon become established farther south.

Dhar Tichitt is a laboratory for investigating early specialization that may have led to the emergence of large-scale societies. It has been suggested that its people might be considered proto-Soninke or proto-Mande (Munson 1980). They would be the ancestors of the founders of the ancient Ghana empire, which in turn encompassed ancient Mali. About the time of the de-

---

5. The following information on Dhar Tichitt is drawn from Munson (1976, 1980, 1989), Holl (1985a, 1985b), and Muzzolini (1989). See R. McIntosh (1997:414) for a recent synthesis linking Dhar Tichitt to "an emerging landscape of interacting specialists" in the southern Sahara.

cline of Dhar Tichitt in the last few centuries B.C.E., larger-scale communities began to appear around the Middle Niger region, the most stunning example of which is Jenne-jeno (old Jenne).

As the increasing aridity of the Sahara intensified in the last few centuries B.C.E. the Middle Niger region became a magnet for peoples in search of green pasture, farmlands, and water.[6] Iron-using peoples settled in the Inland Niger Delta (from Timbuktu in the north to Jenne-jeno 350 kilometers to the south), forming a patchwork of towns that probably had trade contact with each other. Jenne-jeno, just a few kilometers from present-day Jenne, was settled about 250 B.C.E. By 800 C.E. a wall two kilometers long surrounded Jenne-jeno, and within the next few centuries its population including nearby satellite settlements might have reached as high as 27,000. By 1400 these sites were abandoned. Archaeological remains indicate that there were occupationally specialized groups living separate from each other.

Among the archaeological finds at Jenne-jeno are domesticated rice, millet, and sorghum, mud-brick house foundations, concentrations of iron and slag, clay figurines, copper ornaments, hundreds of grinding stones, and hundreds of thousands of potsherds. Particularly enigmatic has been a glass bead dating from the last few centuries B.C.E. or the early centuries C.E. that was most likely manufactured in East or Southeast Asia, indicating some kind of long-distance trade well before Arab contact (S. McIntosh 1995:252–55, 390–91). A refined terra-cotta tradition flourished in the latter part of the first millennium C.E., and similar pottery traditions in the larger region indicate strong interaction in the early and mid-first millennium C.E. (R. McIntosh 1989). Other sites in the Middle Niger region, such as Dia, follow a pattern of settlement similar to that at Jenne-jeno. The region evidently developed in the early centuries C.E. as a major transport axis with exchanges of Saharan copper and salt for savanna gold, iron, and agricultural produce. Later Arab-controlled trans-Saharan trade would have been grafted onto this system.

The appearance of metalworking in West Africa in the mid-first millennium B.C.E. signaled the beginnings of an artisanal group, blacksmiths, who would eventually be an important force on the political, religious, and musical landscape. Metalworking was probably brought in by Libyco-Berber peoples, who themselves may have learned it from Phoenician and Greek colonists on the North African coast. By the end of the first millennium B.C.E. ironmaking technology spread rapidly in West Africa, but not uniformly.

6. The following information on Jenne-jeno is drawn from S. McIntosh and R. McIntosh (1983:246; 1993). For the spread of metalworking in West Africa see S. McIntosh (1994:173–77) and S. McIntosh and R. McIntosh (1983:240–45; 1988:102–10).

Part of the significance of Middle Niger civilization in the first millennium C.E. was the emergence of distinct artisanal groups and ethnic identities.[7] Perhaps it is during this period that a distinctly Mande music with professional music makers may have begun to take shape.

> The paradoxical pull of specialization versus the generalizing obligation has been resolved in the Middle Niger by the special relations that evolved between specialists, be they subsistence-defined ethnic groups or artisan associations. These relations allow each to pursue in ever more particularistic ways, their individual occupations while together sharing mutual obligations and accommodations. (R. McIntosh 1993:206)

This was the context in which the small chiefdom that came to be known as Manden (Mande, Mandeng, Manding, Mali, or Malal), some five hundred kilometers south on the Upper Niger River, arose to eventually become one of the greatest of all West African empires. Before that happened, though, the first great West African empire, Ghana (or Wagadu), would flourish and then decline.

Ancient Ghana (Wagadu)

The birth of Islam in the Arabian desert in the early seventh century C.E. would eventually have a profound impact on West African sahel and savanna society. Arabs conquered North Africa by the eighth century, and by the ninth century they were firmly established on the ancient trans-Saharan trade networks. Their Arabic names for the lands they encountered endure today: Maghrib (sunset, west) for North Africa; Sahel (shore, coastline) for the southern border of the Saharan desert sea; and Sudan, from Bilād al-Sūdān (land of the blacks), for Africa south of the Sahara. The historical era in West Africa begins with written Arabic accounts about the western Sudan dating from the early ninth century C.E. From the very beginning of Arab contact with western Africa the writers noted a land that they called Ghana, situated in southern Mauritania, just south of the Dhar Tichitt region.[8]

Ancient Ghana may have flourished for several centuries before it was first noted in early and middle ninth-century Arabic accounts (al-Khuwā-

---

7. For more on the idea of ethnic or artisanal identity in the Middle Niger region see R. McIntosh (1993:190–94, 1998) and R. McIntosh and S. McIntosh (1988:146–53); for the southern Sahara in the vicinity of ancient Ghana see McDougall (1985).

8. Levtzion's (1980) *Ancient Ghana and Mali* is the standard historical reference, and a forthcoming edition promises to set a new standard. See Conrad (1984) for a discussion about relating Ghana of the written Arabic sources to Wagadu of the Soninke oral traditions. Dieterlen and Sylla (1992) provide comprehensive coverage of Soninke oral traditions concerning Wagadu. Other versions of the legend of Wagadu include Courlander (1978), Frobenius and Fox (1937), and C. Monteil (1953). Mauny (1954:209) has summarized the importance of ancient Ghana and Mali in the world economy: "The Western Sudan was, from the eighth century until the discovery of America, the chief supplier of gold for the western world."

rizmī and al-Fazārī, in Levtzion and Hopkins 1981:6–7, 30–32). Its reputation as a wealthy country struck these early writers and continued for
several centuries. "Then there is the kingdom of Ghāna, whose king is also
very powerful. In his country are the gold mines, and under his authority
are a number of kings. . . . Gold is found in the whole of this country" (al-
Ya'qūbī 872–73, in Levtzion and Hopkins 1981:21).

The dominion of Ghana covered much of the area between the Senegal
and Niger Rivers. What may have been its capital, Koumbi Saleh, lay south
of Dhar Tichitt in Mauritania near the border with the modern nation of
Mali. The strength of Ghana, and perhaps its very existence, came in part
from its intermediary position in the trans-Saharan trade, which was firmly
established with the arrival of the camel many centuries before the coming
of the Arabs. Saharan nomads traded desert salt for savanna gold, each
commodity being out of reach of the other party. The Arab conquest of
North Africa by the eighth century greatly stimulated trans-Saharan trade,
since the Muslim monetary system depended on gold. By the ninth century
Muslim traders brought Islam to the Saharan nomads and into the sahel and
savanna.

The people of Ghana probably spoke Soninke, the northernmost branch
of the large Mande language family. Soninke oral traditions about their ancient kingdom Wagadu probably refer to the historical Ghana of the Arabs.
These traditions, as the historian Nehemia Levtzion (1980:18) has noted,
are not only stories of the origin of the Soninke but also accounts of the
beginning of the political history of the western Sudan. Nowadays Soninke
are reminded of their glorious past by oral historians and pop singers alike.
For example, in his well-known song *Mandjou,* honoring the former president of Guinea Sekou Toure (see table 18 for an extended translation), the
Malian singer Salif Keita declaims the names of the five renowned Soninke
mori (Ar: *murābit;* Fr: *marabout*) families of Wagadu, credited with the
early spread of Islam in West Africa. (*Mori* refers to Muslim savants versed
in religious science.) Simple declamation of their names is an important
form of praise, and a common practice among praise singers.

> Toure mande mori
> Kouma mande mori
> Jane mande mori
> Cisse mande mori
> Berete mande mori.
>
> (Les Ambassadeurs 1979c-disc/Salif Keita 1994a-disc: *Mandjou*)[9]

9. There is some irony in using the example of Salif Keita, from the founding Keita dynasty of
Mande, singing the praises of Soninke families. The practice of praise singing and oral history is
an exclusive right of other families, known as jelis. It is a common understanding that members of

In Mande oral traditions the oldest named family lineages go back to Wagadu. Before that time oral traditions of the jeli are linked with the East via Islam. Oral traditions of hunter's musicians may refer to an even deeper past, but family lineages are not named.

By the middle of the eleventh century the capital of Ghana was a major town in West Africa. "The city of Ghāna consists of two towns situated on a plain. One of these towns, which is inhabited by Muslims, is large and possesses twelve mosques, in one of which they assemble for the Friday prayer. There are salaried imams and muezzins, as well as jurists and scholars. . . . The king's interpreters, the official in charge of his treasury and the majority of his ministers are Muslims" (al-Bakrī 1068, in Levtzion and Hopkins 1981:79–80). In the late eleventh century Ghana came under the influence of a Muslim confederation of desert Sanhaja peoples known as Almoravids who converted the Soninke to Islam, and by the thirteenth century Ghana definitively declined.[10]

Soninke oral traditions attribute the end of the kingdom to a drought brought on by their not properly appeasing their guardian snake named Bida. Soninke dispersed, with some establishing long-distance networks as traders. These traders, called Wangara in Arabic sources or Jula by the Maninka, were also well versed in Islam owing to their contact with Muslims coming from across the Sahara, and they were instrumental in spreading Islam in West Africa. Along with them Soninke leatherworking artisans known as *garanke* may also have dispersed, providing leather goods for the Wangara and finding new local clients (Frank 1995, 1998).

By the early thirteenth century the Sosso, a related group also known as Susu, came to power in the region between the Senegal and Niger Rivers, shifting the political center of western Africa out of the sahel into the sa-

---

aristocratic lineages such as Keita should not engage in praise singing, and they are not regarded as authoritative sources of deep historical knowledge. Just the same, Salif Keita has done much to introduce wide audiences to Mande music and culture and has clearly absorbed much of the jeli tradition. The praises refer to these Soninke families as being great moris of the Mande diaspora and are common in jeli performances. For similar lists praising Soninke mori families in this same form see Lansine Diabate (in Jansen, Duintjer, and Tamboura 1995:156), Wa Kamissoko (in Cissé and Kamissoko 1977:413), Fa-Digi Sissoko (in Johnson 1986:108, 193), Nantenedie Kamissoko (in Ministry of Information of Mali 1971-disc: vol. 4: *Keme Birama*), Kerfala Kante (1994-disc: *Kaba Mory*), Fode Kouyate (1995?-disc: *D. C. Jane*), and Ebraima "Tata Dindin" Jobarteh (1994-disc: *Lala*). The name Kouma can be replaced by Fofana (by Lansine Diabate), Sanogo (by Wa Kamissoko) or left out (by Nantenedie Kamissoko). Rather than Kouma, Fa-Digi Sisoko gives the name Fodele the Tall. The list given by Dieterlen (1955:40) is Berete, Toure, Haydara, Fofana, and Saganogo. Salif Keita (1995-disc) leaves out Berete in his updated version of *Mandjou*.

10. Recent reevaluations of the nature of Almoravid presence in late eleventh-century Ghana have raised serious methodological questions about the historiographical tradition passed down in Arabic and French colonial writing. See Masonen and Fisher (1996) for a detailed discussion of the issues involved.

vanna. Oral traditions report the Sosso reign as one of oppression, finally broken by a Maninka hero who would establish a thriving empire ruled from the heart of the savanna.

Writing at the end of the fourteenth century, the North African historian Ibn Khaldūn succinctly summarized the political history of the Western Sudan from the eighth century to the thirteenth as seen from an Arab perspective.

> When Ifrīqiya and the Maghrib were conquered [by the Arabs] merchants penetrated the western part of the land of the *Sūdān* and found among them no king greater than the king of Ghāna. . . . Later the authority of the people of Ghāna waned and their prestige declined as that of the veiled people, their neighbours on the north next to the land of the Berbers, grew (as we have related). These . . . converted many of them to Islam. Then the authority of the rulers of Ghāna dwindled away and they were overcome by the Sūsū, a neighbouring people of the Sūdān, who subjugated and absorbed them.
>
> Later the people of Mālī outnumbered the peoples of the Sūdān in their neighbourhood and dominated the whole region. They vanquished the Sūsū and occupied all their possessions, both their ancient kingdom and that of Ghāna as far as the Ocean on the west. (Ibn Khaldūn 1406, in Levtzion and Hopkins 1981:332–33; brackets in the original; also see Levtzion 1980:52)

Mali

The earliest documentation of a place called Mali (Malal in Arabic sources) comes from the famous eleventh-century Cordova geographer al-Bakrī (appendix A). In the twelfth century al-Idrīsī provided details of its location. "[Malal] is a small town, like a large village without a surrounding wall, built on an unassailable hill of red earth. . . . From the town of Malal to the town of Great Ghāna is about twelve stages over dunes and deep sands where there is no water" (Al-Idrīsī 1154, in Levtzion and Hopkins 1981:108–9).

Stories of the rise of Mali from a small chiefdom ruled by a succession of great hunters to an expansive empire that ruled over western African sahel and savanna lands under the leadership of the legendary hero Sunjata (Fr: Soundiata) form a vast body of oral and written literature.[11] The range of accounts includes Ibn Khaldūn's late fourteenth-century encyclopedic royal history written in Arabic; French colonial collections elicited from local oral historians beginning in the early twentieth century; French novels written by Africans; lengthy Maninka versions recorded, transcribed, or translated into English or French and published by African, European, and

11. Bulman (1997) has identified sixty-four published versions of the Sunjata epic. Conrad's (1999, forthcoming) valuable translations of Sunjata and other stories from Upper Guinea will significantly broaden this body.

American researchers as well as African government institutions; radio broadcasts; performances at traditional ceremonies attended by Mande nobility; and recordings by modern dance bands. The epic recounting of the founding of the Mali empire is one of the primary sources of the musical repertory of Mandenka musicians, containing pieces dedicated to Sunjata, Sosso king Sumanguru Kante, and two of Sunjata's allies, Fakoli and Tiramakan Traore. The role of the Sunjata epic in forming modern Maninka identity and the national identities of Mali and Guinea cannot be overestimated. A summary of relevant portions of the Sunjata epic follows.[12]

> Two brothers of the Tarawele (Traore) clan, Danmansa Wulanin and Danmansa Wulantamba, killed a magic buffalo that was ravaging the countryside of a land called Do. The younger Traore brother proved the braver of the two, and the elder brother sang his praises, becoming the founder of the Diabate lineage of jelis. The brothers were rewarded with a local woman named Sogolon of the Konde lineage. They brought her to marry the chief of a land called Manden (Mali), named Magan Kon Fatta (or Farako Magan Cenyi) of the Konate lineage descending from Wagadu.
>
> Magan Kon Fatta's first wife was Sasuma (or Tasuma) Berete, who already had borne him a daughter, Nana Triban (or Tiriba). The first male children of first wife Sasuma Berete and second wife Sogolon Konde would become rivals for the chiefdom of Manden: Sasuma's son was Dankaran Touman; Sogolon's son was Sunjata. Sogolon later bore two more children: Manden Bukari (or Bori, a boy) and Kolonkan (a girl).
>
> King Magan Kon Fatta had his own jeli, named Gnankoman Duwa (or Jakuma Doka), whose son Bala Faseke (Fasalli or Facelli) Kouyate, was ap-

---

12. The countless episodes subsumed in the Sunjata epic have been conveniently summarized by Bird (1971:21) as falling into three major divisions: "the events leading to the birth of Sunjata, his youth and exile from the Mande, and lastly his return, victory over the invaders, and formation of the Mali empire." The two most popular accounts of the Sunjata epic are the novels of the Guineans Djibril Tamsir Niane (1965), based on his research with the jeli Mamadou Kouyate of Djeliba Koro (Siguiri, Guinea), and Laye Camara (1980), based on his research with the jeli Babou Conde of Fadama (Kouroussa, Guinea). One of the most entertaining accounts is that sung and narrated by Mory Kante with the Rail Band (1975/n.d.-disc). Also see *Soubale* by Las Maravillas de Mali/ Les Merveilles du Mali (1967/1998-disc; reissued on Musiques du Mali 1995a-disc) for a Cuban charanga-style piece with a chorus singing the praise line associated with Sunjata, *Subaa ni mansaya* (Sorcery and kingship). Differences among the wide variety of published accounts indicate regional and personal variations, so the following summary is just one among many possibilities. The salient features are generally agreed on, although some of the family relationships indicated in the summary may vary. Following Delafosse ([1912] 1972), Sunjata's reign has been commonly dated as beginning in 1230 or 1235 C.E. (e.g., Niane 1975a). This is based on Ibn Khaldūn's report that Sunjata ruled for twenty-five years and that his successor Mansa Wali (or Ulī) made the pilgrimage to Mecca sometime between 1260 and 1277. But there is no indication of when Mansa Wali made his pilgrimage or how long he ruled. Sunjata's reign therefore could have begun anytime between, say, 1225 (if Mansa Wali had ruled for ten years before he made the pilgrimage in 1260) and 1252 (if Mansa Wali made the pilgrimage during the first year of his reign in 1277). For further details see Levtzion (1963) and Levtzion and Hopkins (1981:333–34, 424–25).

pointed as the jeli of Magan Kon Fatta's son Sunjata. Bala Faseke Kouyate is the founder of the Kouyate lineage of jelis.

As a young child Sunjata was not able to walk. In a triumphant moment, Sunjata, upon seeing his mother Sogolon humiliated by her co-wife, sent for a great iron rod and finally pulled himself up to walk. He soon made up for lost time and became a great hunter.

When the king Magan Kon Fatta died, his son Dankaran Touman inherited the throne. Sunjata went into exile with his mother and family. They traveled throughout Maninka and Soninke lands making alliances with the local rulers: the blacksmith Camaras of nearby Tabon and Sibi, the Cisses of Wagadu, and the Tounkaras of Mema on the Middle Niger, where he settled in exile.

The young king Dankaran Touman sent Sunjata's jeli, Bala Faseke Kouyate, on a delegation to appease Sumanguru (Soumaouro) Kante, the blacksmith sorcerer-king who ruled Sosso territory and led an oppressive campaign against the Maninka. Mali soon fell under the domination of the Sosso king Sumanguru Kante, who refused to release Sunjata's jeli, Bala Faseke. One day Bala Faseke gained entry into Sumanguru's secret chamber and began playing his magical bala (xylophone). Sumanguru knew it was being played and returned to the chamber. Bala Faseke sang a praise song to him, and Sumanguru made him his jeli.

Sumanguru destroyed Mali's capital, Niani, and a party was sent to find Sunjata. They found him in Mema and convinced him to reclaim Mali. Sogolon died the next morning. Sunjata's return to his Manden homeland to claim the throne is celebrated by the famous song *I bara kala ta* (You took up the bow). Sunjata raised an army from the allies he visited during his exile, including Sumanguru Kante's nephew Fakoli, who was associated with the clan names Koroma, Dumbia, and Sissoko.

Sumanguru and Sunjata first battled with no victory. Bala Faseke Kouyate escaped and returned to Sunjata. Nana Triban (Sunjata's half-sister) discovered Sumanguru's *tana* (taboo), and in the grand battle of Kirina Sunjata grazed Sumanguru with a cockspur arrow. Sumanguru fled, never to be found. With the defeat of Sumanguru, Sunjata destroyed Sosso and was proclaimed *mansa* (king) of Mali. Sunjata gave all the social prohibitions that still exist among the Mande peoples.[13]

13. There is disagreement among sources on whether Gnankoman Duwa (Jakuma Doka) is the father of Bala Faseke Kouyate (e.g., L. Camara 1980:72, 120; Niane 1965:17; Cissé and Kamissoko 1991:81, 114) or whether they are the same person, with Sumanguru Kante renaming Gnankoman Duwa as Balla Faseke Kouyate (e.g., Kele Monson Diabate in Moser 1974:279–82; Jeli Kanku Madi Jabate in Ly-Tall, Camara, and Diouara 1987:49–51, 202–9; Sidiki Kouyate in Jansen 1991:92; Mory Kante in Rail Band 1975/n.d.-disc). See Wilks (forthcoming) for a wideranging discussion of this and other relevant issues. Many versions have the birth of Sunjata and his half-brother Dankaran Touman taking place on the same day but with their order of birth announcement reversed. Two versions from Kita, Mali, have Dankaran Touman being born first but Sunjata's birth announced first (Fa-Digi Sissoko, in Johnson 1986:129–31; Kele Monson Diabate, in Moser 1974:228–31). Two versions from Kela, Mali, have Sunjata being born first but Dankaran Touman's birth announced first (Jeli Kanku Madi Jabate, in Ly-Tall, Camara, and Diouara 1987:35, 156–59; Lansine Diabate, in Jansen, Duintjer, and Tamboura 1995:85–87). Two versions from Upper Guinea have Dankaran Touman as years older than Sunjata (Niane 1965:12–16; L. Camara 1980:114–16). See Bulman (1996) for a discussion of this birth-order dispute.

After the reign of Sunjata, Mali continued to expand. A golden era was marked by the reign of Mansa Musa (1312–37), whose lavish distribution of gold on a pilgrimage to Mecca in 1324 caused a devaluation of the precious metal in Cairo. The fame of Mali spread, and by the mid-fourteenth century drawings of the king of Mali holding a gold nugget began appearing on European maps (Levtzion 1980:209–14; 1985:141–42). Remembrances of Mansa Musa and Sunjata are particularly illustrative of different historiographical traditions. Muslim writers paid special attention to Mansa Musa, but he does not figure in the Mande grand epic tradition; his deeds were not on a par with those of Sunjata.

At its height in the fourteenth century the dominion of Mali stretched from the mouth of the Gambia River in the west to Gao in Songhai territory in the east. In 1352–53 Ibn Battūta visited the capital of Mali and left the most detailed description of royal court life, including performances of music and poetry.

By the middle of the fifteenth century Mali began losing its territories in the north. Tuareg had taken control of Timbuktu, and Soninke states between the Senegal and Niger Rivers were asserting their independence. Mali had lost control of its northern territories by the end of the fifteenth century to Sonni 'Ali, the founder of the great Songhai empire based in Gao, and through the sixteenth century Songhai expansion into Mali continued. At the end of the sixteenth century an invading force from Morocco defeated the Songhai and took over Gao, Timbuktu, and Jenne. Although Mali's territories in the sahel were lost to the Songhai and later Moroccans, its conquests in the west were still paying tribute. The loss of the Bambuk goldfields in the last decade of the sixteenth century marked the disintegration of the Mali empire.

A period of drought in the seventeenth century brought famine, warfare, and increased slavery to the Niger and Senegal river valleys. A series of smaller kingdoms filled the void left by the decline of Mali. In the middle of the seventeenth century the Bamana kingdom of Kaarta was established, and in the early eighteenth century the Bamana kingdom of Segu arose. They would endure until the advance of the Fulbe jihad leader al Hajj Umar Tal in the mid-nineteenth century.

Kabu

Mande oral traditions attribute a major westward Maninka migration to an expeditionary force against the king of the Jolof state (in present-day northwestern Senegal), led by one of Sunjata's generals, Tiramakan Traore. In Tiramakan's wake a wave of Maninka are believed to have left their Mande homeland to settle in the Senegambia region. They are called Mandinka or Mandinko in their western dialect. Senegambian Mandinka mixed with local peoples such as the Jola, assimilated local family names like Sane and Mane, and took up local customs. States that paid tribute to the king of Mali were established. With the decline of Mali in the mid-fifteenth century these states joined into a confederation that came to be known as Kabu (Gabu or Ngabu), which ruled from its base in Kansala (in present-day Guinea-Bissau). Senegambian Mandinka jalis maintain oral traditions about the Kabu empire, usually rendered in a piece of music called *Chedo* (Fr: *Tiedo*), primarily concerned with the dramatic downfall of the empire in the mid-nineteenth century. Oral traditions show little concern for the several centuries between the initial rise of Kabu and its demise. Senegambian Mandinka recognize their historical roots in ancient Mali, but over the course of centuries they have developed their own distinct culture that has much in common with their more recent neighbors.[14]

One story attributes the origin of Kabu to a woman from Manden in the east, who had three daughters by a *jinn* (genie). They married the chiefs of the provinces of Sama, Jimara, and Pacana, in the eastern regions of present-day Gambia, Senegal, and Guinea Bissau. Their sons, called *nyancho,* provided the kings (*mansaba*) of Kabu in strict rotation. *Nyanchoya* (*nyancho-hood,* eligibility to rule Kabu) is passed down matrilineally, and they had the family names Sane or Mane, now prominent in the Casamance (southern Senegal). Attached to the three nyancho provinces were other provinces ruled by princes called *koring.* Kabu social classes included freeborn (*foro*), equivalent to the Maninka *horon;* artisans (*nyamaalo*), equivalent to the Maninka *nyamakala,* consisting of *numu* (blacksmith), *karanke* (leather-worker), and *jali;* and slaves (*jon*).[15]

The demise of Kabu is attributed to an argument over succession to *mansaba* between the Sama and Pacana provinces. When Janke Wali Sane of Pacana finally rightfully became ruler about 1850 he made three predictions (*mansa daali*): a war would break out between Kabu and the Futanke

14. For an interpretation of Senegambian Mandinka history suggesting cultural transfer to western territories rather than waves of migration see D. Wright (1985). Also see D. Wright (1997) for a broad-based history of one region of the Senegambia. A large body of tapes, transcriptions, and translations concerned with the history of Kabu are kept in the Archives Culturelles in Dakar and in the Oral History and Antiquities Division of the National Council for Arts and Culture in Banjul, Gambia. Historical literature on Kabu includes works by Innes (1976, 1978), Mané (1978), Niane (1989), and Quinn (1972) and a collection of papers from a colloquium on Kabu (Fondation Léopold Sédar Senghor 1981). As with the Sunjata epic, stories about Kabu can reflect regional and personal variations. The following information on Kabu is primarily drawn from the research of Mané (1978).

15. Respected Gambian oral historian Bamba Suso (in Innes 1976:76–79, 117–18) reports that the first king of Kabu was Kelemankoto Baa Sane, a son or grandson of Tiramakan Traore, and that Kelemankoto's three sons by his wife Nyaaling were the founders of the three nyancho lineages.

(Fulbe from Futa Jalon); the fortress at Kansala would be called *turban* (hecatombe—the end of life in Kansala); and he would be the last king of Kabu. The defeated Sama province enlisted the aid of Fulbe from Futa Jalon to exact revenge. Their efforts were successful in part because of Fulbe resentment that the Mandinka were exploiting them and pillaging their animals and millet crops. In the piece *Chedo,* Mandinka jalis recount the exploitation of the Fulbe and tell of the ensuing siege of the fort of Janke Wali at Kansala, the capital of Kabu.

About 1865 the *turban kelo* (Kansala war) broke out (Mané 1978:142–45). The Futanke laid siege to the Kansala fortress. Sensing defeat, Janke Wali made plans for the escape of his jali, Jali Wali Kouyate, who refused to flee. Janke Wali ordered the gates open, and when the Fulbe entered he set fire to his ammunition cache, blowing up the fortress and killing everyone. The Mandinka women are said to have committed suicide in the wells of the town rather than submit to Fulbe slavery.

After the fall of Kansala, Alfa Molo Balde led a Fulbe revolt in 1867 and took over much of Fuladu (in eastern Gambia). Alfa Molo died about 1881 and was succeeded by his brother Bakari Demba and son Musa Molo, who ruled until 1919 when he was exiled by the British to Sierra Leone. Musa Molo is a major figure in the oral traditions of eastern Gambian jalis and was an important patron for them.

European Contact, the Colonial Encounter, and Independence

The rise of Kabu coincided approximately with the first arrival of Europeans in West Africa, although there was no immediate connection between the two occurrences.[16] The economy of the western savanna would soon shift from one that looked north across the Sahara to one that flowed westward toward the Atlantic Ocean. Documentation of Mande music would increase dramatically with European travel writing beginning in the mid-fifteenth century. Until the nineteenth century most of the references to music were limited to the Senegambia region and concerned either drumming and dancing events or the prominent presence of praise singers and court musicians.

In the 1440s the new Portuguese caravels, ships twenty to thirty-five meters long carrying crews of more than twenty men, first reached the Senegal and Gambia Rivers. They came to establish trade in commodities coming out of West Africa, such as gold and pepper, cutting out the middlemen of the Sahara and the Maghreb (North Africa). In the 1450s the Portuguese were trading with the Wolof of the Jolof kingdom, with the Fulbe of Futa

16. The following material on the European presence in West Africa is drawn from Brooks (1993:121–41, 167–83) and relevant chapters in Ajayi and Crowder (1985–87).

Toro, both in the vicinity of the Senegal River, and with Mandinka states along the middle and upper Gambia River. About 1530 French vessels began trading in the Senegambia, followed by the English about 1555. By the early seventeenth century European ships carried sloops with them to use for trading along the coasts and upriver. The French became the dominant trading force in the early eighteenth century and built fortified trading posts along the Senegal River. The British dominated trade along the Gambia River. With the abolition of the slave trade in the early nineteenth century, the French and British looked for alternative means of exploiting local commerce. Peanut (groundnut) farming emerged by the mid-nineteenth century, but West Africa never took on the plantation system that so marked the Americas.

European colonization of West Africa began in earnest in 1854 when a new French governor, Louis Faidherbe, began a period of military expansion along the Senegal River that would reach the Niger River by 1880. A string of French forts linked by telegraph lines were established in the 1880s, followed shortly by a railway link from Kayes to Bamako connecting the Senegal and Niger Rivers, completed in 1905. Commandant Gallieni's expedition in 1887–88 through Niagassola and Siguiri in Upper Guinea was responsible for what may be the earliest photographs of Mande musical instruments, including balas, konis, and jembes (plates 17 and 18).

The federation called French West Africa (Afrique Occidentale Française or AOF) was established by a series of decrees beginning in 1895, comprising what would become nine colonies and United Nations protectorates that would gain independence between 1958 and 1960: Senegal, Guinea, Mali, Mauritania, Niger, Burkina Faso (formerly Upper Volta), Côte d'Ivoire (Ivory Coast), Benin (formerly Dahomey), and Togo. By 1904 the colonies of Senegal and Guinea had the boundaries they have today, and Upper Senegal–Niger (Haut Senegal–Niger), formerly the French Sudan (Soudan Française), included Mali, Niger, and parts of Burkina Faso. The French pursued a policy of direct rule wherein French colonial officers exercised a great deal of administrative control over local African chiefs, who had few official powers. Villages were united into cantons headed by local chiefs, which combined into subdivisions and then into the largest administrative units of the colonies, *cercles,* headed by a French commandant. The British preferred a more indirect style of rule in their colonies such as The Gambia, and local African rulers were given much more autonomy.

In the early 1900s the French set up a European-style educational system including local primary schools taught by Africans, regional and urban schools with French teachers, and two schools of higher education in Senegal, serving all of French West Africa, one of which became known as

École William Ponty, an *école normale* specializing in teacher training. These schools were an important means of indoctrinating West Africans with French culture. Students at École William Ponty in the 1940s, such as Fodeba Keita (founder of Les Ballets Africains), were exposed to European music and culture and became important forces in modernizing African music in Senegal and Guinea. Another source for the importing of European culture and musical instruments were the hundreds of thousands of black African soldiers who fought in Europe during World War I and World War II.

The process by which Guinea gained its political independence made a hero of its first president, Sekou Toure, whose rule had a major impact on the growth of modern music in the former French West African colonies. With the return to power of Charles de Gaulle in June 1958, a draft constitution for the Fifth Republic was to be approved in a referendum throughout France's overseas territories, which were to vote on continued membership in the French Community. Guinea was the only French African territory to vote no, and on October 2, 1958, the Republic of Guinea became the first French West African nation to proclaim independence. France responded by withdrawing all administrative personnel and services, halting all aid and credit, taking Guinea off favored-nation status, and allegedly destroying files and tearing out telephones. Sekou Toure, head of the Parti Démocratique de Guinée (PDG), was elected president and remained in office until he died in a United States hospital in March 1984. The army seized power within weeks, and Colonel Lansana Conte became president. A failed coup attempt in July 1985 damaged the national radio and television station, destroying many valuables tapes.

The French West Africa Federation was dissolved in October 1958, and the other former territories chose political autonomy within the French Community. In June 1960 the Mali Federation, consisting of the Sudanese Republic (formerly French Sudan) and Senegal, proclaimed independence, but within months it broke up. The Republic of Mali became independent on September 22, 1960, with Modibo Keita as president. In November 1968 Keita was overthrown in a military coup, and Moussa Traore became president from 1969 until March 1991, when he was overthrown in a popular revolt. In June 1992 archaeologist Alpha Oumar Konaré became president after a democratic election. The Republic of Senegal chose April 4, 1960, as its independence day, the date the French accord of independence was signed. Leopold Senghor was the first president, serving until December 1980 when he resigned and his prime minister, Abdou Diouf, took over. The Gambia, a nation set inside the borders of Senegal, reaching approximately 15 kilometers on both sides of the Gambia River and 320 kilometers inland, gained independence from Great Britain on February 18, 1965, under the leadership of Prime Minister Dawda Jawara, who became president in 1970 when The Gambia became a republic. In July 1994 Yahya Jammeh became the head of state in a military coup.

In Guinea and Mali, music and dance festivals and competitions were organized according to the plan of administrative units in the country, with a series of local competitions eventually pitting regions against each other for national medals. Under President Sekou Toure the Republic of Guinea was divided into thirty administrative regions, each headed by a governor and each with its own federal orchestra. After 1984 Guinea was reorganized under President Lansana Conte into eight provinces, each headed by a governor, which in turn are divided into prefectures, subprefectures, and districts (*arrondissements*). The Republic of Mali consists of the autonomous district of the city of Bamako and seven regions: Kayes (northwest), Koulikoro (southwest), Mopti (north-central), Timbuktu (extreme north), Gao (northeast), Sikasso (southeast), and Segou (central).

Nyamakala and Notions of a Mande Class System

Mande societies are marked by a complex and shifting web of relationships that differentiate two major social groupings: *nyamakala* (pl. *nyamakalalu;* Md: *nyamaalo*) and *horon* (pl. *horonnu;* Md: *foro*). Nyamakalalu are artisans born into their profession who work with certain well-defined, spiritually charged materials, including metal, wood, clay, leather, words, and certain kinds of music. Horonnu do not, indeed cannot, work with those materials but instead farm, govern, defend, and conquer. The term *horon* is usually translated as freeborn or noble-born, possibly derived from the Arabic *hurr* (free) (Delafosse 1955:309–10). *Horonya* (horon-ness) translates as "freedom." The third part of the Mande tripartite social order, *jon* (slave), is now largely extinct.[17]

Horonnu (freeborn or nobles) depend on the nyamakala artisans for manufactured goods such as iron implements of agriculture and war, leather equipment and amulet cases, and services such as guarding and shaping the past and present through words and music. Nyamakalalu in turn depend on their horon patrons for nonmanufactured gifts such as food, livestock, or money and for services such as the administration of village and state affairs and physical protection. Nyamakala and horon guard their status

17. A landmark collection of writings on nyamakala (Conrad and Frank 1995a) offers a rich array of fresh perspectives on Mande society, pointing up the interpretive shortcomings of centuries of Eurocentric observations. An extended study of the late Massa Makan Diabate, a Malian writer from a jeli nyamakala family, written by Cheick Keita (1995a), a Malian from a horon family, brilliantly illustrates by implicit example modern redefinitions of traditional African identities.

by endogamy—marriage within certain well-defined communities—although the barriers are not so impermeable. In the best of times, services and goods are exchanged in a system marked by mutual respect, checks and balances, and occasional heroic generosity. In less opportune eras, especially when horonnu are not able to provide for the nyamakalalu who specialize in words, the system can break down into a crass play of begging, empty praising, public humiliation, and private disdain.

Among Maninka and Mandinka the term *nyamakala* encompasses four corporate entities of diverse origins: *numu* (blacksmiths/sculptors); *garanke* (leatherworkers); *jeli* or *jali* (verbal and musical artisans); and *fune* or *fina* (public speakers expert in genealogy and the Koran). Each group has its own oral traditions referring to prototypical ancestors, but their historical origins are not well understood. They may have originated as distinct communities sometime during the first millennium C.E. when groups living in the Niger and Senegal river valleys became increasingly specialized. The vast body of oral traditions surrounding Sunjata indicates that with the defeat of Sumanguru Kante, signaling the rise of the empire, the nyamakala groups were in place. The phrase *ngara naani* (four great artisans), or *nwara naani* in a dialect variant, is typically used by jelis to refer to these four nyamakala groups who were part of the core of the Mande empire.[18]

Nyamakalalu are all commonly believed to possess, through their birthright and rigorous apprenticeship in their extended families, special spiritual powers, called *dalilu,* which enable them to work with the dangerous forces, called *nyama,* of their raw materials. Dalilu and nyama are defining concepts in Mande society and culture and are relevant for understanding the place of various kinds of music and musicians in Mande society. Jelis, for example, have the exclusive right to play certain instruments that others do not take up. It is their birthright, honed by years of apprenticeship. This birthright, as well as the birthrights of the *numu* (blacksmith), *garanke* (leatherworker), and *fune* (public speaker), sets the nyamakala apart from the horon.

> One's birthright . . . provides an initial set of means to actions, the ability to perform particular acts and, more importantly, to be protected from the consequences of those acts. A blacksmith is born into a caste which enables him to smelt iron ore, to transform the shapes of iron, earth, and wood, and to survive the forces unleashed by his transformations. A freeman, *horon,* might, through madness or accident, perform a blacksmith's act, but his horon's birthright offers him no protection against its consequences.
>
> The means or powers required to perform an act are referred to as *dalilu.*

18. For examples of ngara or nwara naani, see Lansine Diabate (in Jansen, Duintjer, and Tamboura 1995:131, 155), Cissé and Kamissoko (1988:233; 1991:63–64, 214), and Dieterlen (1955: 40, 1959:125).

The dangerous forces released through the performance of *dalilu* are referred to as *nyama*. All acts and their associated instruments have *nyama*. A person's inherited *dalilu* may protect him from the *nyama* of his actions, or he may acquire protective *dalilu* in other ways—by acquiring fetishes and talismans, for example. Much of this protection comes from the *nyama-kala,* "nyama branch," who are casted smiths, bards, and leatherworkers. The inherent *dalilu* of the *nyama-kala* affords protection against the *nyama* they release, and they, in turn, protect their *nya* ["means"] by practicing endogamy. (Bird and Kendall 1980:16)[19]

As a consequence of the acts that nyamakalalu perform on behalf of horonnu, be it fashioning implements of war and agriculture for the horon to use, instilling pride and courage in warriors, leaders, or traders by recounting the deeds of their ancestors, or brokering marriages, the horon is obligated to provide for the nyamakala. The way this obligation often played out before European eyes was the impetus behind the view commonly held by early European travelers (and passed down to scholars) that at least one nyamakala group, jelis, are beggars, are despised, and depend on horonnu for their daily bread. Stories of *gewels,* Wolof counterparts of jelis, being buried in baobab trees for fear of polluting the earth fed this stereotype.[20]

Recently scholars have penetrated beyond these stereotypes to investigate the kinds of power that jelis possess. Measured against a social or political yardstick jelis may indeed be subordinate to their horon patrons. But as Barbara Hoffman has pointed out, this may be intentional on the part of the jeli. "The essence of griotness [jeliya, being a jeli] is in lowering oneself. To make yourself small to make others big" (El Hadji Yamuru Diabate, in Hoffman 1995:45).[21] Jeli power resides in other realms, such as the spiritual, and jelis may be willing to sacrifice their standing in one realm to increase their power in another.

> I have seen many a *horon*'s hand quake as it thrust forth a bill, sometimes accompanied by a verbal plea, "ka nyama bò" (Please take away the *nyama*). It is, perhaps, even understandable that some nobles resent the fact that the *jeliw,* "their" *jeliw,* as they say, have such power over them, power not only to stir them deeply and make them tremble, but to inspire them to part with hard-won cash or goods in the bargain. But it is incomprehensible that we, as scholars, should take note only of the nobles' anger and resentment and ignore the causes of the admiration and envy that underlie them. (Hoffman 1995:42–43)

19. Footnotes from the original have been omitted. A recent review of etymologies of the term *nyamakala* by Bird, Kendall, and Tera (1995) advocates caution in settling on any one interpretation.

20. For further references on baobab burials of Wolof gewels see Mauny (1955) and Conrad and Frank (1995b:4–7).

21. "Jeliya sindi nana yeremajigin le kan. K'i yere dogoya ka mogolu bonya."

The transfer of cash from patron to jeli during the course of a performance may in its ideal form be thought of as a necessary and willing sacrifice.

> When a praise song is sung for someone, his energy to act is augmented, thus forcing him to act, and these acts can lead to his destruction if not appropriately controlled. In order to maintain equilibrium, the most common means of controlling *nyama* is through a sacrifice, and such a sacrifice is often made to the bard or his instrument.
> The songs that the bards sing and the instruments that they play have a *nyama* which, if performed by the ordinary man, would destroy him. The bards are protected against the forces they release by their heritage. (Bird 1976:98)

Powerful in other ways are the numus, who are primarily blacksmiths but also have several important associations with music making. As sculptors, numus carve jembe drums and are also associated with jembe playing.[22] Although jembe playing is not a hereditary profession, the numu family names Camara, Kante, and Dumbia are common among professional jembe drummers (appendix B). Branches of those three numu families, along with a fourth, Sissoko, have moved into the profession of the jeli and are among the most prevalent names of jelis after Kouyate and Diabate, especially among bala players, no doubt owing to the origins of the instrument with Sumanguru Kante. The name Sissoko, or Suso in its Senegambian form, is particularly widespread among Senegambian kora players.

The history of *numuya* (the activities of the numu) may shed light on a general history of drumming in Africa because drumming is such an integral part of many of the numu's ritual activities. Numu hands perform circumcision and excision; all-night jembe drumming prepares the youth for the operation. Numu hands create agricultural tools; rhythms for agricultural work are played on the jembe. And numu hands sculpt the wooden masks of the secretive power societies that they also lead, whose ceremonies are marked by jembe drumming.

The numu represents another stage in the history of the savanna between hunter-based societies and the later mounted warriors who conquered the savanna, establishing the horon/nyamakala (nonartisan/artisan) division and relegating the numu to nyamakala status, void of political authority. Horonnu are accompanied by their string-playing jelis, validating their authority. Numus are also celebrated by jelis, who remind them of Sumanguru and Fakoli of the Sunjata era, evoking the transfer of power from numu to horon. The hunter's musician praises the hunter and the numu alike, but his

---

22. In parts of Senegal and The Gambia, drum making is sometimes done by Laobe, a Fulbe or Wolof artisan class associated with woodworking. Numu wives are the traditional potters of Mande society and the ones who perform excision on girls. For further information on numus see Brett-Smith (1994), Frank (1998), and McNaughton (1988, 1995).

praise of the numu refers not so much to the blacksmiths of Sunjata's era as to the more primordial aspects of numuya, as in the following excerpt from a performance by the renowned Wasulu hunter's musician Seydou Camara.

> The world's first child is the smith.[23]
> The forgers of hoes are smiths.
> The pen is from the smith.
> The ax handle is from the smith.
> The origin of the forge is from the smith.
> The source of the execution sword is the smith.
> The source of the bullet is the smith.
> The pestle is from the smith.
> The pounding mortar is from the smith.
> . . . .
> The skinning-knife is from the smith.
> The plow is from the smith.
> The beginning of killing the lion is from the smith.[24]
> The hoe is from the smith.
> (Seydou Camara in Bird, Koita, and Soumaoro 1974:21–22)

In contrast to the hunter's musician's praise of the numu referring to his artisanal creations and power, jelis praise their horon patrons with a call to bring in the horses (Md: *suolo kili;* Bm: *sow wele*), their source of military power. According to George Brooks, the association of horses with the horon gives a clear message in the history of the savanna:

> In the sahel and savanna zones Mandekalu horse warriors imposing the Mande tripartite social order prevailed over power associations, including the Great Python Society controlled by smiths. Essentially Sundiata and Sumanguru represent the two basic and conflicting principles of Mande society and of groups in western Africa generally. (Brooks 1993:100)

Some scholars see the Sunjata epic as representing a new order in which northern mounted warriors wrested power from blacksmith sorcerers who functioned like earth priests throughout the savanna.

> As Robert Launay has noted (Transcript, 1992), if we replaced Sumanguru's label, "blacksmith" with that of "earth priest," we would have in this story one more instance of the clash between the northern horsemen and the earth priest

23. "The blacksmith is considered to be the center of all activity. Without him, there would be no weapons for the hunters, no tools for the farmers and no utensils for cooking. According to at least one mythology, the blacksmith was the first human to descend from the heavens" (Bird, Koita, and Soumaoro 1974:113).

24. "According to tradition, man only had the power to attack the lion subsequent to the invention of iron" (Bird, Koita, and Soumaoro 1974:113).

rulers who preceded and opposed them throughout the western savannah. The rulers of Asante, the Mamprusi, the Gurunsi, the Dagomba, the Sonrai and the Zarma, to mention but a few, trace their history to these horse warriors. (Bird, forthcoming)[25]

The wresting of political authority from numus by Mande warriors did not eradicate any of the numu's functions. Horon and nyamakala could exist side by side as long as there was respect for the boundaries of each.

The dispersion of blacksmiths from northern Mande areas southward spread not only metalworking, but also their power societies. Based on the Kòmò society they led, numus established Simo and Poro societies among non-Mande groups along the upper Senegal and Niger River tributaries, respectively. A dry period from approximately 1100 to 1500 encouraged traders and blacksmiths to move southward into non-Mande areas and enabled mounted warriors from the north to follow in their path, penetrating southern lands made available by the receding tsetse fly line (Brooks 1993: 44–46, 73–77, 106).

Garankelu (leatherworkers) have little connection with music making, but there is a curious practice in certain regions where the term *jeli* refers to leatherworkers rather than musicians (Frank 1995).[26] It appears that on the eastern and southeastern extensions of the Mande diaspora (from northeastern Liberia through parts of Guinea, Côte d'Ivoire, southeastern Mali, and Burkina Faso) migrant jelis may have taken up leatherworking to fill a void. A map of the distribution of jeli leatherworkers drawn up by Barbara Frank (1988:192) shows that this occurrence effectively delineates the southeastern and eastern boundaries of the music culture in this book. Garankelu are probably of Soninke origin and may have been part of the long-distance migrations of Soninke traders (Jula) and clerics (Mori) in search of new clients, supplying leather goods such as amulet cases, beginning in the eleventh or twelfth century. They would also have accompanied later Mande state-building mounted warriors, supplying leather equipment (Frank 1995:142–43).

Very little research has been done on the *fina* or *fune* other than David Conrad's 1995 essay. Although they share the medium of speech with jelis, *finalu* differ in several respects: they have their own story of origin; they do

25. For further interpretation of the forces represented by Sunjata and Sumanguru see the discussion of *Janjon* (and the footnote) in chapter 3. Bird's reference to Launay's transcript is from the Sunjata Epic Conference (November 13–15, 1992), Northwestern University, Institute for the Advanced Study and Research in the African Humanities. See Austen (forthcoming) for papers from this conference.

26. The only notice of garanke in relation to music that I have come across is a jembe rhythm simply called *garanke,* presumably to be danced by, or in honor of them.

not sing or play musical instruments; and their realm of expertise usually complements rather than competes with that of jelis. The vast majority of finalu have the surname Camara.

The horon/nyamakala social distinctions of the Maninka are also well entrenched in several other western African societies, notably among the Soninke (*hoore/nyaxamala*), Wolof (*geer/nyeenyo*), and Fulbe (*dimo/ nyeenyo*).[27] The origins of these distinctions are unclear, but they do share geographic proximity to the early empires of the region, ancient Ghana and Mali. The specific artisan groups vary, but blacksmiths, woodworkers, leatherworkers, griots, and weavers are the most common. Societies with a high degree of social differentiation like the Mande contrast with other smaller-scale stateless societies, sometimes called acephalous in ethnographic literature, which do not recognize such strong social differentiation. Some of these groups include the Jola (Senegal), Baga (Guinea), and Senufo (Mali).

Mande Aesthetics and the Creative Artist: The Ngara

Jeliya (jeli-ness), the art of the jeli, finds its most profound and deeply appreciated embodiment in the *ngara,* a master of extraordinary integrity, knowledge, or skill. To be called a ngara by one's peers is one of the greatest signs of respect and an aspiration of all jelis. The ngara, whose field of play is speech and music, has a complement in the *ngana,* a hero whose field of play is action. The complementary relationship between speech and action—between the ngara and the ngana—and the similar social forces that motivate them are fundamental aspects of Maninka social and creative thought and practice. An examination of the motivations of *ngaralu* and their significance in Mande society is in effect a study of Mande aesthetics, innovation, and creative impulses.[28]

Among the intersecting sociopsychological forces that Maninka, and particularly performing artists such as jelis, must confront during their lifetime, three are especially defining: *fasiya* (the paternal lineage), *fadenya* (competition with that lineage to distinguish oneself), and *badenya* (obligations to the family and community). These forces find potent and richly multivalent symbols in the father (*fa*) and mother (*ba*). Both parents can in

27. See Tamari (1991, 1997) for comprehensive references to West African peoples marked by significant social differentiation, and for theories on their origins.

28. The writings of C. Keita (1995a, 1995b), Bird and Kendall (1980), and Brett-Smith (1994) are the basis for my understanding of the terminology of Mande aesthetics. I have tried to synthesize their findings, keeping them relevant to this book and paraphrasing frequently. Conversations with Cheick Keita have helped to clarify my understanding in this area.

their own ways act as inward-pulling communal forces encouraging conformity with tradition, and also as outward-pushing individualistic forces encouraging competition and innovation. The combination and interaction of the forces inspired by the mother and father make for a rich panorama of artistic possibilities and aesthetic viewpoints full of paradoxes that define the Maninka personality or *maninkaya* (Maninka-ness, what it is to be Maninka).

A person's name is a repository of the various forces surrounding the mother and father. The family name, or *jamu* (Md: *kontongo*), represents the paternal lineage, an axis of conservation of family traditions known as *fasiya*—from *fa* (father) *si* (lineage, race) *ya* (-ness). The family traditions are inherited at birth, and the formative years are spent learning how to live up to the fasiya. The given name, or *togo* (Md: *too*), which by extension also can mean reputation, represents personal achievements as measured against one's peers and ancestors. The earning of a togo, the identifying first name that distinguishes son or daughter from father or mother, is fueled by a competitive force called *fadenya*—from *fa* (father) *den* (child) *ya* (-ness)—which targets the father as the benchmark because it is his achievements that must be surpassed on the path to earning a reputation (Bird and Kendall 1980:14–15). The individual name (togo) and the family name (jamu) are sometimes balanced by placing the mother's first name (togo) in front of the son's name, distinguishing her child from those of the co-wives while honoring the mother.[29]

Fadenya, a motivating force for competitive behavior, has its complement in *badenya*—from *ba* (mother) *den* (child) *ya* (-ness)—an integrating force encouraging submission to authority and cooperation (Bird and Kendall 1980:15). The contrast of fadenya with badenya can be readily understood by their meaning without the suffix *-ya* that makes them abstract nouns. Both refer to sibling relationships in a polygamous family. *Baden* (pl. *badennu*) refers to children of the same mother, those who have suckled the same breast (as the genealogists say), the closest relationship children can have with each other. *Faden* (pl. *fadennu*) refers to children who have the same father but different mothers. The relationship between

---

29. The name Sunjata, a contraction of Sogolon (his mother's name) Jata (lion) in a popular etymology, is a well-known example of taking the mother's togo. There is little published material on the relationship between a female jeli and either of her parents, but Jackson's research with the Kuranko of Sierra Leone might be relevant. Jackson (1977:177) indicates that the elder daughter is never a rival to her mother's position in the way that the elder son competes with the father because the daughter's destiny is to marry out of the father's lineage into another home. Women retain their jamu (family name and lineage) after marriage; a daughter takes the jamu of the father and may therefore have a different jamu than her mother.

fadennu can be marked by extreme competition, reflecting the sometimes strained relations between co-wives. Mande epics are driven by the opposing forces of fadenya and badenya, typically marked by conflicting claims to inheritance between fadennu.[30]

Just as the father can represent two opposing forces—fasiya (paternal lineage) and fadenya (competition with that lineage)—so can the mother. In contrast to the stabilizing force of badenya, the mother can also be a strong source of inspiration for her children to succeed and surpass the accomplishments of the fadennu (children of the co-wives). The relationship between the child and mother

> is based on the undivided love that the mother gives to her child and the necessity for the child to honor his mother and to 'avenge' her sufferings [*ka monè bo ala*] by succeeding as much as if not better than the children of the other wives of the father. (C. Keita 1995a:135)[31]

The idea of avenging the suffering of the mother has its most celebrated illustration in Sunjata's finally lifting himself up to walk (and setting himself on the path to leadership) after a childhood of infirmity to avenge the insults heaped upon his mother by her co-wife. Even more than being an inspirational symbol, the mother can be an actual source of spiritual power.

> The father gives the name, but it is the mother who offers the barika, the mystical force that protects and conditions success in life. (Adam Ba Konaré 1993:13)[32]

In contrast to the widely recognized and well-documented motivations of fadenya and badenya with respect to the hero of social action (the ngana), the force of the paternal lineage (fasiya) and its central significance in the

30. See Bird and Kendall (1980), and Johnson (1986:8–29, 41–45) for more on the forces of fadenya and badenya on the ngana. The proverb "Your father is your first *faden* [competitor]" (Bird and Kendall 1980:14) indicates the significance of the father on the fadenya axis. The essential difference between faden and baden is captured in the common image of suckling the same breast (e.g., Fa-Digi Sissoko in Johnson 1986:112). A child inherits the father's blood but is nurtured with the mother's blood via the breast milk (see Arnoldi 1995:173 and Jackson 1977:84–87). The saying "It is said that a battle between milk brothers smokes but never flames" (Tayiru Banbera, in Conrad 1990:150–51) further illustrates the special relationship among badennu.

31. Brackets in the original.

32. Blessings from the mother is a recurring theme in Mande literature (e.g., see the song *Bele Bele* in M. Kaba 1995:94–95). A striking example is dramatically depicted in Souleymane Cisse's (1987-vid) film *Yeelen,* where the elderly mother passes on to her son her blessings (*barika*) and an amulet that would make him invincible and protect him from the sorcery of his vengeful father. Also see Manthia Diawara's (1992:157–64) discussion of womanhood in Mande literature and Zobel (1996a:639), "Comparable to divine grace (*baraka*), the gift of sorcery is transmitted to the children by the mother." Zobel (1996a:639–40) suggests that circumcision and agricultural rites as well as activities of the male Kòma society could be interpreted as male appropriation of reproductive powers detaching male children from the world of their mothers.

creative arts have only recently been the subject of analytical writing. The Malian Cheick M. Chérif Keita (1995a) has elucidated a rich Mande aesthetic of jeliya (what the jeli does), defining the motivating forces of fasiya and fadenya and their interaction. His focal point is the author Massa Makan Diabate, who was born into a jeli family and used the written rather than the spoken word to both continue and break away from the legacy of his family. Keita began his study by placing the artist in perspective with the forces of fasiya and fadenya.

> The first, *fasiya,* is responsible for the attachment of the artist to models in practice in society before his birth. It is the axis of apprenticeship and integration into a caste and a family, entities whose functions are defined in advance by society. It constitutes a kind of collective heritage from which the individual can draw according to his capacities and innate gifts. *Fasiya* is a centripetal force that mobilizes the artist to work toward the continuation of a tradition, generally following the canons personified by the father and the paternal lineage. The second force is *fadenya,* the axis of competition with past models as personified by the father. It is the strong desire of the individual to distinguish himself from his ancestors and to surpass their achievements. On the artistic plane *fadenya* promotes the opening up of new forms of expression and the individual discovery of new aesthetic limits. (C. Keita 1995a:9–10)

Mande creativity thrives in the social space where the inward pull of one's calling in life, one's fasiya, meets the outward push of individual initiative, innovation, and desire to surpass the achievements of the parents (fadenya) and make a name through extraordinary behavior. Control and creativity within this social space constitute a cherished trait.

> By his double image of preserver and innovator, Massa Makan Diabate manifests the most characteristic traits of the Mandingue personality, of *maninkaya.* . . . Nothing is more pleasing to the Malinke than this paradoxical image of one who unfailingly guards his attachment to the community in which he belongs while at the same time enlarging it, even bursting through its frontiers by the magnitude and importance of his personal action. (C. Keita 1995a: 36, 42)

The space within which social and artistic progress takes place is symbolized as the intersection of the village or home (*so*), representing conservation and security, and the bush (*wula*), representing innovation and adventure. Within this space the drama of the confrontation of the forces of fasiya, badenya, and fadenya takes place on either of two complementary planes: speech or action. Those who master these forces and distinguish themselves are known as ngara or ngana. The ngara, through his or her speech or music, inspires others and activates the dynamic energy of society. The ngana responds to this call and acts. The ngara in turn celebrates and conserves the memories of the significant acts of the ngana (C. Keita 1995a:84–85).[33]

The prototypical ngana is Sunjata, the horon who establishes a name through action, usually of a violent nature. A ngana can also be a nyama-kala (artisan), specifically a numu who acts on and shapes wood or metal, as Sarah Brett-Smith has found working with numu sculptors. Her observations about achieving ngana status also apply to ngara status, indicating their common motivations.

> Acquiring the status of *ngana* through the creation of important sculpture is not quite the same as acquiring a "name." . . . One may acquire fame and still remain a weak human being; but, if one is tough enough, one can be a *ngana* without having one's name on everyone's lips. In general, *nganaw* are those celebrated by the cognoscenti: the healers other healers consult, the black-smiths other ironworkers celebrate, and the sculptors other artists envy. (Brett-Smith 1994:163)[34]

Similarly, the ngara is the jeli's jeli.

The symbiotic relation between speech and action in Mande society is a significant part of Mande identity, if not a defining feature. Not only are the ngana and ngara motivated by similar forces, but one cannot exist without the other.

> Few people depend on their art for the affirmation and expression of their identity as much as the Mandingue. In their mythology as much as in their daily life, action appears to be made of the same substance as speech, so much so that the *ngana* is always accompanied by the *ngara,* the artist whose speech stimulates his courage and celebrates his exploits before the rest of the society. As guardian of the collective memory, the oral artist has a fundamental role in the manipulation of heroic symbols inherited from the past, for the act is condemned to disappear if its echo does not resonate in time and space. (C. Keita 1995a:49)

> From a sociological point of view, the Manden was since its origins until Sun Jata the *liaison of the n'gana and n'gara.* (Massa Makan Diabate, in C. Keita 1995a:82)

The contrasting pulls of the village and bush, symbolic in so many endeavors, and the liaison of speech and action may be a key to understand-

33. The term "speech" in the context of what the ngara does can also include song and musical instrument playing. For more on the bush as a source of artistic expression see Arnoldi (1995: 101–2).

34. L. Camara's (1954:31–41) description of a woman who brings along a kora-playing jeli while she commissions a piece of jewelry to be made by Camara's numu (blacksmith) father is an example of a numu's being inspired and celebrated by a jeli, a miniature ngara-ngana drama (see chapter 3). The phrase *ngara naani* or *nwara naani* (four *ngara*) used by jelis to refer to the four nyamakala groups (see the discussion in the nyamakala section above) implies that the term *ngara* is reserved for nyamakalalu.

ing the dynamism of Mande society and its grand spread throughout the savanna, taking in diverse peoples. Individual battles that were occurring within single families may have been replicated on larger and larger scales covering massive amounts of territory.

> From a spiritual point of view, the Mande [diaspora] was able to reconcile the space covered by waves of migrations—centrifugal movement—with the attachment to the spiritual principles of the original territory—centripetal movement. (C. Keita 1995a:47)

The role of the ngara in the expansion of Mande society may be much greater than one might accord to masters of speech and music, who are neither warriors nor political leaders. In Mande ideology the ngara is not just a master artist but also a guide and source of wisdom.

> Formerly the griot was . . . an extremely powerful man. So much so that Balla Fasseke Kouyate, the griot of Sunjata, said straight out to Sunjata: "We are two to lead the Mande; you do what I advise you to do." (Massa Makan Diabate, in C. Keita 1995a:119)

This implication that the jeli is the conscience and even the wisdom behind the horon may be startling to a modern sensibility colored by a profession sometimes marked by exchanges of "solid pudding for empty praise," as the Scottish traveler Mungo Park ([1799] 1983:213) noticed two centuries ago. But the power and respect ngaralu command in performance indicates that perhaps this view of power sharing is not so far-fetched, at least in its idealized form.[35]

Two recent examples will illustrate the driving forces of fasiya, fadenya, badenya, and loyalty to the mother, and a final example will illustrate the moral force of the ngara. The relationship between the renowned Malian author Massa Makan Diabate and his master and paternal uncle, the ngara Kele Monson Diabate, was marked by constant frustration over Kele Monson's unwillingness to share his knowledge, a common sign of fadenya in jeli families. "He [Kele Monson] never had any students; and everyone who tried to learn at his side had to leave, because Kele Monson never, never shared. '*Talali manyi* (sharing is not good),' he would say to anyone who would listen" (Massa Makan Diabate, in C. Keita 1995a:32). On the other hand, Massa Makan's relationship with his mother was quite different. He publicly declared that despite her illiteracy she "gave him pride in his

---

35. Another example of the power jelis may have wielded in earlier times comes from Segu: "If they [jelis] told the Bamana to eat beans, they [Bamana] would buy butter" (Tayiru Banbera, in Conrad 1990:83). Butter, used in the preparation of the beans, symbolizes the patron's readiness to follow the jeli's orders (Conrad 1990:83). For more on the power that Malian female jeli singers hold over their audiences, see Durán (1989a, 1995b, forthcoming a, forthcoming b), and the discussion in chapter 3.

finished work and the necessary encouragement to pursue his adventure through writing" (in C. Keita 1995a:135). The image of a nurturing mother and an unapproachable, even godlike, father is a classic one for Maninka.

> We say in the Mande that we are the children of our mothers; it is true that all of us have been brought up by our mothers, we have very distant relationships with our fathers. . . . in fact, in the popular imagination in Mali, the father is a little like God. . . . I am above all the child of my mother before being the child of my father. (Massa Makan Diabate, in C. Keita 1995a:138)

Cheick Keita has argued that by extending the fasiya and moving jeliya out of the realm of verbal performance into a previously uncharted literary form—and doing it in such a profound way—Massa Makan Diabate has achieved ngara status.

The fadenya (competitive) relationship between the great Malian kora player Toumani Diabate and his ngara father, the late Sidiki Diabate, one of West Africa's great kora players, is striking. Not only do they both specialize in the same field (kora), but Toumani has not shied away from performing and recording the same pieces on which his father built his reputation, accepting the challenge of his fasiya head on. When asked if he had learned from his father, Toumani replied,

> No. My father didn't teach me to play the kora, although generally speaking, the art of the griot is learned from the father. He passes his knowledge on to his sons, and his sons give it to their children. But I didn't learn the kora from my father. I already had the kora in my blood. I was born to it. My grandfather played the kora, and his father and grandfather before him. But my father didn't teach me because the kora was already there, waiting for me. Mostly, I would listen to cassettes, because I was a student and when I got home from school, my father was away playing somewhere. I listened to cassettes of my father, my grandfather, and other musicians as well. . . . (Toumani Diabate, in Prince 1989a:15)

His father confirmed this and added his own experience with fadenya.

EC: When you first studied the kora, was *Kelefa* the first piece that you studied?
SD: No, I did it the way Toumani did it. With me the kora is like a gift from Allah. Even up to now, I have not said to Toumani to do this or that. (S. Diabate 1990-per: 440–42)[36]

The concept of inheriting the kora, either through bloodlines or from Allah, is a fasiya-based conception: it is their heritage. Toumani Diabate's (1988a-disc, 1988b-disc) first recordings as a soloist are revealing. His solo recording, the first of its kind on the new CD technology, contains several pieces

36. EC: "Folo folo kabiring i ye kora karang, i la julo folo folo, wo mu Kelefa le ti i ye ming karan?" SD: "Hani nte. Tumani be nyameng nte be teng ne. Nte kan kora Ala le y'a sooneya n ye. Hani bi nte ma fo Tumani ma a ke teng a ke teng."

closely associated with his father but done in his own distinctive personal style. A second CD recorded soon after with a Spanish flamenco group was a groundbreaking session that placed the kora in a new context and contained novel pieces including a favorite of his, *Nene Koita,* named after his mother. The recent *New Ancient Strings* (Diabate and Sissoko 1999-disc) is an extraordinary example of the meeting of the fadenya and fasiya axes: Toumani is joined by kora player Djelimoussa "Ballake" Sissoko, whose father recorded kora duets with Toumani's father three decades earlier (Ministry of Information of Mali 1971-disc, *Cordes anciennes*).[37]

The aesthetic of ngaraya (the heroic art of the ngara) still serves as a viable source of inspiration despite widespread cynicism about the economics of the jeli's profession. By extending jeliya into the literary sphere, assimilating the guitar into the tradition, or forging new musical styles, jelis are continually pushing the frontiers while keeping one foot still in their villages. The moral and artistic integrity of the late Banzumana Sissoko, a legendary Malian ngoni (lute) player and vocalist, is a model of ngaraya: being true to the fasiya while distinguishing oneself through extraordinary accomplishments. His heroic stance harks back to the ideal role of the ngara in Mande society.

> From the late 1950s, when Banzumana Sissoko became known on the national scene, to his death in 1987, the entire Mandenka nation was witness to his categorical refusal to curry favor with any politician or rich patron. It is interesting that in his immensely rich repertoire of both traditional and original songs, not a single one contains praises for a living person. This fact seems extraordinary when considered in the context of the generalized political clientelism of our modern nations. In Mali today, society has lost its ability to effectively spell out and enforce the criteria of heroism; as a result, the immediate and short-term interests of the praise singers and the *jatigiw* (patrons) are placed above those of society as a whole. Today it takes a great deal of personal integrity and sacrifice to resist the temptation of the easy money and instant stardom which opportunistic praise singing guarantees. In integrity, Sissoko has few equals. (C. Keita 1995b:185)

Conclusion

In the late twentieth century increasing research on African soil in a variety of disciplines has begun to explore and reveal to the outside world the rich histories that inform the daily lives of those who live there. Although the era that binds Mandenka consciousness over a wide geographic region remains that of Sunjata, his allies, and his foes, there is much to be learned

---

37. The initiative of British journalist, producer, and scholar Lucy Durán in seeing these and other pioneering recordings to completion is responsible for some of the most creative African music recordings over the past decade and a half.

from the confluences of other forces that took place in western Africa over the past several millennia. The physical as well as psychological battles of hunters, blacksmiths, and mounted warriors not only have shaped social consciousness but have also left a deep musical legacy that continues to be played out in national musics and on international stages. Hunter's music, drumming, and the music of the jelis remain vital symbols of times past. Understanding the background to these symbols may bring us closer to appreciating the extraordinary continued relevance of these traditions as well as how these traditions have fared outside Africa.

2

Hunter's Music

Maninka hunter's music is largely unknown outside Africa. Consisting of praising, chanting, and singing accompanied by a calabash harp (often supplemented by a metal scraper as well as by someone providing vocal interjections), it probably represents the oldest surviving Maninka melodic instrumental tradition. There are many varieties of hunter's harp played across the western savanna region, but the two most influential ones are the Maninka *simbi,* made from a calabash resonator with a long neck holding seven strings tuned to a heptatonic scale, and the neighboring Wasulu *donso ngoni,* with a similar construction but having six strings tuned to a pentatonic scale (plates 4 to 8). The Maninka simbi is an important source of the music of the jeli, and it continues to nourish some of the modern music in Mali. The Wasulu donso ngoni has had little influence on Maninka music, but it is the source for the very popular music of a new generation of Wasulu singers in Mali. Although hunters' societies have taken on marginal roles in the modern nations of Mali and Guinea, they continue to provide musical inspiration for creative artists.[1]

Performers and Performance

Hunters have long held a special place in Mande society. Great warriors gained their prowess as hunters, whose powers came through their extensive knowledge and practice of sorcery associated with the bush. The very foundations of the Mali empire were laid by hunter-warriors with the aid of blacksmith-warriors, both being well versed in the arts of sorcery. Much of the training of a hunter consists of acquiring knowledge that will help not only in the act of killing an animal, but also in dealing with the potentially

1. My knowledge of Maninka simbi music is based on much more limited resources than musics discussed elsewhere in this book (see appendix C for recordings of the harps discussed in this chapter). Recordings of Bala Djimba Diakite, Coumoun Keita (Moussa Keita 1997?-disc), and Sidikiba Keita (Zobel, forthcoming-disc) form the basis of my understanding of the genre. Coulibaly (1985) and Y. Cissé (1964, 1994) both document Bala Djimba Diakite's sung texts, and Nakamura (1992) has carried out research with seven Maninka hunter's musicians (*soralu*) in the Kita region. (Diakite's middle name is sometimes spelled Guimba in French; his name is also spelled Bala Jinba Jakite.) An extraordinary video segment of Bala Djimba Diakite can be seen in a documentary about Salif Keita (Austin 1991-vid), and a simbi can be heard on Keita's (1993-disc) piece *Chérie.* Extended scenes of simbi players from Siguiri are in Dance of Guinea (1991-vid), and Knight (1992-vid) has a segment of a Gambian simbingo player.

dangerous life force or spirit (*nyama*) that is released when it is killed. The apprenticeship of the hunter prepares him to control these forces, as do the many spiritually charged objects that are put on the shirts hunters wear. Part of the protection against that potentially dangerous nyama is provided by the hunter's musician.

The Maninka hunter's musician is called *sora* (*sewa, sera, serewa,* or *sewra* in dialect variants).[2] The Wasulu hunter's musician is called *donso jeli* (hunter's jeli). *Kònò* (bird) is a common metaphor and title used for non-hereditary singers such as nonjelis who choose to take up singing, and it is a favorite designation for Maninka and Wasulu hunter's musicians (Y. Cissé 1994:139, 145, 185; Durán 1995a). In contrast to the jeli, there are no hereditary restrictions on becoming a hunter's musician; indeed, it is unusual for a jeli to be a hunter's musician. By his music, singing, and speech, the sora inspires bravery in the hunter and endows him with power as he goes off into the bush. When the hunter returns, the sora's praise of the hunter and his kill neutralizes the nyama (spiritual force) of the animal and ensures balance. The term "musician" does not adequately convey the spiritual side of what the sora does, since he functions more like a priest, an "intermediary between the hunter and the supernatural forces of the bush" (Bird 1972: 278–79). The relation between the hunter's musician and the hunter and also their respective roles are similar to that of the ngara (master of speech) and ngana (master of action) discussed in chapter 1. This might be taken as evidence that the hunter's musician was the historical antecedent of the ngara, who would have been a product of the nyamakala/horon social system associated with Sunjata's era in oral traditions.

The concept of nyama is a constant theme in traditional Mande society, and the sora is an important mediator in this regard: "Nyama is everything, and its destruction is a condition for the eternal rest of the soul" (Y. Cissé 1964:209). The sora's presence is required at the last rites of a hunter for the proper control of the nyama released from the body of the deceased.

> "When the final hour arrives for a *donsoba* (great hunter), his peers and the
> *sora* (chronicler of the hunters) go to his bedside and will be the only ones to
> witness his death. . . . And since the dying one is about to rejoin for eternity

2. The following material applies to both Maninka and Wasulu hunter's musicians unless otherwise noted. Differences between the two include slightly different instruments, different tuning systems, and different repertories. Sources concerning the Wasulu hunter's musician (donso jeli) are Bird (1972), Bird, Koita and Soumaoro (1974), Soumaoro et al. (1976), Cashion (1984), Thoyer (1995), Thoyer-Rozat (1978a, 1978b), and Thoyer-Rozat and Dukure (1978). Other relevant material includes discussions of sorcery (McNaughton 1988:11–21), hunter's shirts (McNaughton 1982), and the shirts of hunter's musicians, called *koli doloki* (Cashion 1984:148–51). See Durán (1995a, 1996, forth coming a, forthcoming b) for extended treatment of modern music in Mali based on Wasulu and Maninka hunter's traditions, and C. Keita (1996) for the hunter's influence in the music of Salif Keita.

the spirits of the great hunters of the Manding, it is essential that he make the passage to the somber sound of the *sūbi,* harp. That is why the *sora,* repository of traditions, historic chants and myths of the hunters, remains at the bedside and does not cease to extract from the cords of his instrument the whispers coming from the depths of the ages. As for the *donsoba,* their role is to gather the *nyama* of the deceased. . . ."

The preceding is the account of the death of one of their own that the hunters have given us. . . . After having finished collecting the *nyama,* the *donsoba* proceed to clean the body in his hut. The *sora* continues to play his harp. . . . When everything is ready the *sora,* the grand master of ceremonies, proclaims the praises of the great hunters of the Manding accompanied by his harp. Both eulogistic and humorous at the same time, the *fasa* [praise song] of the hunters that Moussa Traore has reported from Fuladugu, Kita, and Kaarta is common to all the peoples who speak the language of N'ko [Mandekan]. It exalts the virtues of the good hunter who is faithful to the tradition of Kontron as well as denigrates the unworthy hunter; . . . The aspiration of every hunter is to be honored one day by a hunter's *fasa* that will elevate him to the rank of a spirit in the pantheon of hunters. (Y. Cissé 1964:209–11)

The idea that the greatness of hunters is nothing if not chronicled by the sora finds a direct corollary in the function of the ngara in relation to the ngana.

The relationship between the hunter and his priest-musician is a close one, as can be seen from the following vivid lines praising the hunter, sung by the great Wasulu donso jeli (hunter's jeli) Seydou Camara.

> You who have offered me a skull
> As a face-washing bowl,
> And offered me a skin
> As a covering cloth.
> You have given me a great tongue
> So that I may speak to the world.
> The brave offered me fresh blood
> As face-washing water,
> And gave me a tail
> As a hut-sweeping broom,
> And offered me a thighbone
> To use as a toothpick.
> It is the hunter who has done this for me.
> (Seydou Camara 1968-disc; Bird, Koita, and Soumaoro
> 1974:9–10; also see Bird 1972:286–87)[3]

Although musical instruments or other direct physical evidence for the prehistoric origins of hunter's musician-priests is lacking, other kinds of evidence can be gleaned. For instance, the absence of social and hereditary

---

3. See chapter 1 for an example of Seydou Camara praising a blacksmith, Durán (forthcoming b) for a similar use of this hunter's musician's imagery by jelimuso singer Ami Koita (1993-disc) in her piece *Bambougoudji,* and B. Keita (1988:134–36) for more on the relation between a hunter and a hunter's musician.

restrictions on who may become a sora has been taken as an indication that the institution of the hunter's musician predates the rise of the Mali empire, when the endogamous artisanal professions (the nyamakala class) seem to have been reified.[4] The relative absence of social distinctions within the hunters' societies themselves also suggests that these societies may predate the more rigid social categories that came to the fore in Sunjata's era. Youssouf Cissé, a Malian scholar who has done important work both with hunters' societies and with jelis, has noted that the rules in the hunters' societies are different from those operating in Mande society at large.

> The hierarchizing of hunters into *koro* and *doko*—older and younger brothers—is a function solely of the length of time they have been hunting. No other considerations—notably that of age, *famaya* (strength), *horōya* (nobility), *dyō ya* (slavery), and especially *fasya* (the primacy of the generation of the fathers over that of the sons . . .)—which make up the rigid structure of Malinke society, are kept here in order to differentiate hunters among themselves. (Y. Cissé 1964:186)

Cissé believes that hunters' societies predate the formation of the "rigid structure of Malinke society" and the coming of Islam.

> Finally, the great interest that the *dōsotō* [hunters' society] presents for us is that it was able to guard almost intact the ancient foundations of Sudanese beliefs. By its songs, stories, and secular rites, it continues to vigorously perpetuate the most ancient myths of the Sudan, notably those relating to the vulture, snake, hyena, and *kulādyā* [eagle], despite the continually growing and destructive influence of Islam in the Manding. (Y. Cissé 1964:176)

Prompted by the following words of Mali's revered hunter's musician Bala Djimba Diakite, Cissé (1994:16) explains that "of all the institutions of the Manding, it is the hunters' brotherhood that remains the conservator of the true values of Malinke civilization."

> ". . . The primordial affair is hunting. The very foundations of Manding rest on hunting. Without hunting, what is known as Manding would have ended long ago." (Bala Djimba Diakite, in Y. Cissé 1994:16)[5]

The special status of hunters and their organization into brotherhoods may have been brought about by the decreased reliance on hunting as a major food source owing to the growth of agriculture several thousand years ago. In times of drought and famine, hunting may have been the critical

---

4. The relative absence of female hunter's musicians and singers compared with the strong presence of female jelis (who all sing) raises questions about the transition from hunter's musician to jeli that require further research.

5. Y. Cissé (1994:16) used the spelling "manden" in his Maninka transcription of Diakite and "Manding" in his French translation. In a scene featuring a performance by Bala Djimba Diakite, Salif Keita (in Austin 1991-vid) echoes Diakite's sentiment.

food source that enabled a society to survive, elevating hunters to heroes (Y. Cissé 1964:189, Bird 1972:276). One might speculate that the institution of calabash harp–playing hunter's musician-priests may have its origins in the first millennium B.C.E. when agriculture began to definitively take hold in the savanna, if not earlier. The iron tools of the blacksmith are not needed to construct the instrument.[6]

Explicit written accounts of hunter's musicians or their instruments do not appear before Jobson's ([1623] 1968:134) early seventeenth-century description of a six-stringed harp (appendix A). The lack of sources may mean that hunter's musicians were associated with activities that were secret and kept far from the view of foreign travelers. West Africans managed to keep the location of their gold mines secret from foreigners for centuries, so if they wanted to keep a source of their military strength secret they presumably were also able to do so. Jelis, on the other hand, were associated with the political leadership and maintained a high profile.

Arabic references to sorcery date back to al-Bakrī in the eleventh century. He described a country known as Malal and recounted a story about how the king of that country received the title El Moslemani when he was initiated into Islam by a Muslim visitor who told him that the drought afflicting his country would end if the king would accept Islam. Then the two men prayed, it rained, and so "the king ordered the idols to be broken and expelled the sorcerers from his country. He and his descendants after him as well as his nobles were sincerely attached to Islam, while the common people of his kingdom remained polytheists" (al-Bakrī 1068, in Levtzion and Hopkins 1981:82–83).

Although there is little early written documentation concerning hunters or their music, Mande oral traditions abound in references to hunters. Oral traditions about ancient Mande history refer to the immediate ancestors of Sunjata as hunters, and their names often have *simbon* (master hunter) attached to them (e.g., Johnson 1986:105–7; Jansen, Duintjer, and Tamboura 1995:44–52). Renditions of the Sunjata epic also usually include an episode telling how Sunjata's mother was brought to his father by two hunters who had killed a buffalo genie that had ravaged much of the countryside. Genealogical attribution of hunter ancestry to Mande nobility is standard practice among jelis. The hunter ancestry of Sunjata supports the common belief that hunters' societies and their musicians still preserve that preempire, pre-Islamic heritage. Epics recited by hunter's musicians have not been as extensively documented as those concerning Sunjata, but they are gener-

6. Y. Cissé's (1994:52) research in 1960 found that of thirty villages in Maninka country in the Upper Niger river valley, only one did not have a hunters' society (*donso ton*); he concluded that most Bamana and Maninka villages of four hundred or more inhabitants have one.

ally believed to refer to a mythic past that predates Islam and the socially differentiated society of the Sunjata era.[7]

The historical relation between the sora and the jeli may be very close, as Charles Bird (1972:291–92) has suggested in his comparisons of the epics of hunter's musicians and jelis. Similarities between the two genres may not be limited to stylistic and structural aspects. Seydou Camara (1996:773–74) has noted that the biographies of Sunjata and of Siriya Manbi, the last of the forty-five hunter heroes (*gwede*) in the repertory of Bala Djimba Diakite, are remarkably similar. The rise of the Ghana empire, which may have resulted from increased contact in the sahel between desert peoples from the north and savanna peoples from the south, might have caused a transformation in the hunters' societies that was accompanied by a related transformation of the hunter's musician into a court musician. As the master hunter became the ruler of the savanna, the sora may have been transformed into the jeli. This would help to explain why jelis and the like are prominent in those societies that came into close contact with the Ghana empire. The similarities in the verbal expression and the roles of the sora and the jeli lend further support.

The primary occasions for long epic singing by the hunter's musician are funeral ceremonies, which are also the most common times for the meetings of hunters' societies. Funeral ceremonies are usually concluded by the fortieth day after the death, but a few years later there may also be grander memorial ceremonies known as *simbon si* or *simbon na si* (evening for the master hunter). The actual seven-day celebration, which can involve epic recitations, singing, dancing, and beer drinking, is sometimes called *su sumun*.[8] Other than funeral ceremonies, the major ceremony for hearing hunter's music has to do with birth: the annual *dankun son* (crossroads sacrifice), which takes place after the harvest, signaling a rebirth of the hunting season, beginning at dawn at a crossroads. New initiates are accepted into the hunters' society during this ceremony, another symbol of birth (Cashion 1984:207–12; Y. Cissé 1994:110–14). Independence Day in Mali (September 22) is another occasion for hunter's music. Communal hunting is rare, especially since hunting was outlawed in Mali in 1978 to stem threats to the animal population posed by nontraditional hunters using modern guns. Hunting season commences after the harvest, since hunters are

7. Lengthy translations of hunter's songs and epics include Bird (1972), Bird, Koita, and Soumaoro (1974), Cashion (1984), Coulibaly (1985), Thoyer (1995), Thoyer-Rozat (1978a, 1978b), and Thoyer-Rozat and Dukure (1978).

8. Other names for *simbon na si* include *kon si* and *fugutege*. For information on hunter funeral celebrations see Cashion (1984:212–33), Y. Cissé (1964, 1994:115–58), B. Keita (1988:136–37), and M. Sidibe (1930).

occupied with their fields during the rainy season and in the few months after (Cashion 1984:107–20).

A fundamental feature of much music in Africa—a responding person— is usually present during performances of hunter's music. The most common interjection is *naamu,* a sign of affirmation akin to "yes," of probable Arabic origin (Delafosse 1955:535). Typically, a person called a *naamu namina* (naamu responder) or *naamu tigi* (person responsible for saying naamu) interjects vocal support between the phrases of the main vocalist, who is also usually the harp player. The naamu namina might also respond with *tinye* (truth) or say the name of the performer in support of what was just sung. Maninka simbi players prefer their naamu sayers to be numus or jelis; other traditions, such as those of Segou and Wasulu, do not have this preference (Coulibaly 1985:6, 19). Occasionally the singer may play off the naamu namina, calling for support by saying "numu" or "naamu namina," to which the response is "naamu!" The naamu namina must be sensitive to the phrasing of the singer so as not to interrupt the flow. The response can come after a single word, a phrase, or several phrases.

A hunter's whistle, called *fle* or *su fle* (sorcerer's whistle) may be played every so often with a hunter's harp (plate 6). The su fle is standard gear for a hunter (Y. Cissé 1994:64) and is used to communicate danger over long distances. About ten centimeters (four inches) long, the piercing whistle is blown across its top. A small hole near the bottom end is covered by a finger when the whistle is first blown, and it yields a pitch approximately a fourth higher when the finger is lifted.

Hunter's Harps

Throughout the southern savanna lands of western Africa there is a remarkable culture of calabash harps, including three used by Mande musicians: the three- or four-stringed *bolon* played for warriors (plate 4), the seven-stringed simbi played for hunters (plate 5), and the twenty-one-stringed kora played by jelis for their noble patrons (plate 9).[9] All of the dozen or more savanna harps share the feature of the neck's being spiked all the way through a calabash resonator, defining them as a unique West African branch of the larger world harp family. Despite their shared characteristics, each harp bears marks that identify it with one or another ethnic group. A less widespread related group of harps, with wooden box resonators, can be found farther south in the northern forest regions across Côte d'Ivoire and Ghana.

9. The soron, a close relative of the kora, is also played by Maninka, but with a much more limited distribution (see chapter 3).

Plate 4 Bolon player. Photo taken before 1922. Bibliothèque Nationale de France, Paris, Société de Géographie, We 222, no. 26 (Fierro 1986:76).

Plate 5 Bala Djimba Diakite playing the simbi. Apprentice Bakary Samake in background. Bala, Mali, 1990. Photo by the author.

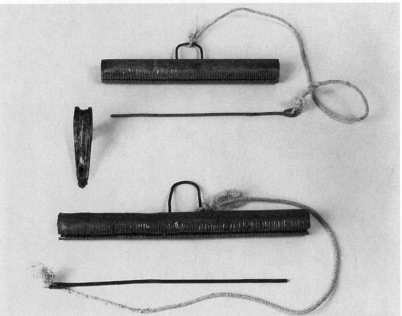

Plate 6 Top: Donso ngoni. Bottom: Nege (iron rasp), su fle (hunter's/sorceror's whistle). Donso ngoni made by Siaka Sidibe, Bamako, 1997. Photo by John Wareham.

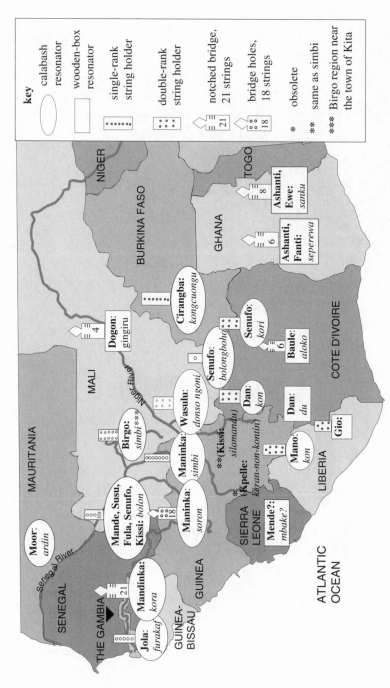

Map 3 Distribution of harps in West Africa.

Map 3 shows the distribution of harps in West Africa along with the name of the ethnic group to which they are indigenous, the name of the instrument, and various morphological features. Table 4 lists a variety of references for the instruments shown in map 3, and table 5 lists in chronological order early documentary references for these harps (reprinted in appendix A). Each illustration of a harp in map 3 is placed in the general area to which it is indigenous, but most of the instruments are found over a wider area than the space occupied on the map. Distribution maps of musical instruments in West Africa can be hazardous because of much population movement, reliance on published sources that may be inaccurate, and the inherent compromises involved in plotting fluid diachronic and synchronic processes onto a two-dimensional surface. Therefore the placement of the instruments on the map should be taken only as a general geographic guide. Harps with calabash resonators are found in the savanna belt that extends from the Atlantic Ocean to the western part of Burkina Faso. All these harps are closely related, although they may be tuned differently, and some may be seen as more technologically advanced versions of others. Harps with wooden resonators are less common and have a narrower distribution, primarily limited to the forest regions.

Table 4 Chronological Harp References for Map 3

Calabash Resonator

Ardin
Courbe 1685:172; Brue [1715] 1747:438–39; Duvelle 1966-disc; Norris 1968:63–65.

Bolon
Tellier 1898:178; Famechon 1900:204; Reeve [1912] 1969, facing 198; Joyeux 1924:182; Schaeffner [1936] 1980, pl. 21; Boulton 1957-disc; Schaeffner 1951:68–70; Béart 1955:680–83; Liberia 1971:24; Sory Camara 1976, figs. 14–16; Jenkins 1979-disc; Imperato 1983, pl. 15; Gourlay and Durán 1984b; Haydon and Marks 1984-vid; G. Meyer 1985:59; B. Keita 1988:67; Kubik 1989:184–89; Knight 1992-vid; Rouget 1999-disc; D. Traore 1999-disc.

Bolongboho (related to *bolon*)
Zemp, n.d.b.-disc; 1980:434; Glaze 1981:177–78, 240.

Donso ngoni
Metropolitan Museum of Art, n.d., 1889.2032 (bridge with notches); Frobenius 1921:40–41; Joyeux 1924:182, 194–99; Rouget 1954a-disc; Bird, Koita, and Soumaouro 1974; Peuls du Wassolon 1987-disc; Samake 1992-disc.

Furakaf (Jola *simbingo* or *esimbin*)
"African Curiosities" 1846:341; Irvine and Sapir 1976:70; Pevar 1978-disc.

Kon (belonging to Dan, Mano, or Vai peoples)
Ellis [1914] 1970, facing 138 (Vai); Donner 1940:75; Schwab 1947:153, fig. 80e (no name indicated); Zemp, n.d.a.-disc; 1971:54–57, 130–37, 219–22, 286–89, pl. 14.

Kongcuongu/konchuhun
Sadie 1984, 2:455; Soma 1988:478–80.

(*continued*)

Table 4 (*continued*)

Kora
Park [1799] 1983:213; Laing 1825, facing 148, 369; Gray and Dochard 1825, facing 301; Hecquard 1855:123; Moloney 1889:278; Mahillon 1893:420–21; Metropolitan Museum of Art, n.d., 1889.498; Ankermann 1901:15, 78–79; Reeve [1912] 1969, facing 198; Boulton 1957-disc; Ministry of Information of Mali 1971-disc, vols. 1, 4, and 5; King 1972; Knight 1973a, 1984a, 1991a, 1992, 1992-vid; Jali Nyama Suso 1992-vid; Pevar 1978; Durán 1981a; Aning 1982; Kubik 1989:184–88; Charry 1994b.

Kori
Zemp, n.d.b.-disc; R. F. Thompson 1974:154–55; Glaze 1981:42–45; Metropolitan Museum of Art, n.d., 1983.76.1; Wegner 1984:179; Brincard 1989:90.

Silamandu
Schaeffner 1951:70–72.

Simbi
Metropolitan Museum of Art, n.d., 1889.4.493 (bridge with holes) [6]; Tellier 1898:179 [6]; Frobenius 1921:40–41; Schaeffner 1946:25 [7]; 1951:68–72 [6]; Rouget 1954a-disc; Y.–Cissé 1964:209; Niane 1975b, facing 240; Jackson 1977, facing 182; Festival National 1979:10; Durán 1984; Coulibaly 1985; Austin 1991-vid; Dance of Guinea 1991-vid.

Soron
Tellier 1898:179 [12]; Mahillon 1909:117–18 [6]; Joyeux 1924:180–82, 210–11, pl. 2, fig. 4; Chauvet 1929:98–100; Rouget 1954a-disc, 1954b-disc.

Wooden Resonator

Aloko
Zemp 1967:81–86; 1972-disc; Fujii 1990-vid, tape 19 #1.

Du/luu
Schwab 1947:153, fig. 80a (Gio people); Liberia 1971:22 (*luu*); Zemp 1971:55–56, 286–89; 1971-disc.

Gingiru/koro
Griaule et Dieterlen 1950; Zahan 1950; Griaule 1954; Klobe 1977.

Ngoni (harp)
Binger 1892, 1:1, 184–85 (with calabash resonator) [5]; Dieterlen 1951:221–25 [8]; Dieterlen, in Paques 1954:106–7 [8].

Sanku
Bowdich [1819] 1966, facing 275, 361–69, 450–51, pl. 5; Bowdich 1821, pl. 14; Beecham 1841:168 (Ashanti people); Cruickshank [1853] 1966, 2:268; Ankermann 1901:14; Smend 1908:72–75 (*kasangu* of Ewe people); Schaeffner [1936] 1980:191; Hause 1948:54–55; Wachsmann 1973:48, 55; Wegner 1984:175–76, 269 (Tem people).

Seperewa
Nketia 1963:96; Hood 1969-disc; Nketia 1974:105.

Shiplike cork-in-a-bottle neck
Musée de l'Homme, n.d., 67.99.1.2; Staub [1936] 1958, pl. 18; Wachsmann 1973; Bebey 1975:118.

Unidentified
Barbot, [1746] 1992, 2:568, facing 570 #13; Kikius 1701; Bosman [1705] 1967:140; Metropolitan Museum of Art, n.d., Todes.Afr 13 (Minianka people? bridge with ten holes); Stone 1982:51, 132, xvi (obsolete Kpelle harp); Brincard 1989:189 (*sanku? seperewa?*).

Note: See references for complete citations. Brackets indicate number of strings on the instrument.

Table 5 Early Documentation of West African Harps

Date	Author	Page Numbers
1594	Almada	25
1623	Jobson	134
1685	Courbe	172
[1746] 1992	Barbot	2:568, and plate 47, no. 13 (facing 570)
1701	Kikius	
1705	Bosman	140
1715	Brue	439
1788	Matthews	105–6
1799	Park	213
1802	Golberry	2:417
1819	Bowdich	361–62, musical transcriptions between 364 and 365
1821	Bowdich	plate 14
1825	Gray and Dochard	facing 301
1825	Laing	369, facing 148
1841	Beecham	168
1846	"African Curiosities"	
1853	Cruickshank	2:268
1855	Hecquard	123
[1868] 1980	Mage	cover
1889	Moloney	278
1891	Gallieni	479
[1910?] 1989	Kubik	185
1912	Reeve	facing 198

Note: See appendix A and bibliography for complete citations.

The fundamental unity of West African harp culture may have its ancient roots in the bolon, which has the uncanny look of a calabash drum slipped onto a warrior's or hunter's bow. Hunter's harps (donso ngoni, *kori, kon,* simbi) look as if someone had straightened out the bow of the bolon and added a few more strings. The harp of the jeli (the kora) looks as though the neck has been completely straightened out, with many more strings added. The three harps used by the Mandenka (bolon, simbi, and kora) may indeed represent three stages of West African harp culture.[10]

Perhaps the earliest documentation of a harp in West Africa comes from the late sixteenth century, probably referring to the Senegambian Mandinka (Almada [1594] 1946:24–25, 1984:34). Not long after, the earliest known detailed description of a harp in Mande territories appeared, although the specific harp is unclear (Jobson [1623] 1968:134). The earliest documentation of a Mande harp by name appeared at the end of the eighteenth century: "I have now to add a list of their musical instruments, the principal of which are . . . the *korro,* a large harp with eighteen strings; the *simbing,* a small harp with seven strings" (Mungo Park [1799] 1983:213). As I noted

10. See Lamm (1968:32–33) for a brief discussion of the evolution of harps in the region.

earlier, hunters' activities may have been shielded from foreign travelers, leading to the relatively late documentation of their instruments.

Morphology

The morphology of the calabash harps has been covered in detail elsewhere (Charry 1994b), so here I will give only a summary. Early generations of musicologists considered the kora a cross between a harp and a lute (Hornbostel and Sachs 1961:22–23). In an article on African harps, Klaus Wachsmann (1964) omitted those from West Africa, apparently considering them "harp lutes" and not full harps. Knight (1973a, 1:19–26) pointed out several problems with the name "harp lute" and proposed the terms "bridge harp" and "quasi–bridge harp," effectively capturing the West African varieties. DeVale (1989) synthesized the findings of both Wachsmann and Knight, noting that Wachsmann's three types of African harps have "longitudinal string holders" that sit flat on or below the sound table, and that the West African variety has "vertical string holders or bridges." Furthermore, DeVale used the term "spike harp," in effect a fourth type of African harp, and for the first time brought West African harps into Wachsmann's African harp classification system based on how the neck and resonator fit together. The contrast of vertical (or upright) and longitudinal (or flat) string holders conveys an essential difference between West African and non–West African harps.

All four types of African harps share four basic structural components:

1. a neck fitted with tuning pegs or rings
2. a resonator
3. a sound table, usually animal skin stretched over the open side of the resonator
4. either a string holder or a bridge

West African harps have tuning rings and an upright string holder or bridge, features unique to the region. They differ from other harps in the way the neck is attached to the resonator: they are spike harps where the neck is spiked through the resonator and protrudes from the bottom end.[11] Spike harps have upright string holders or bridges. Since spike harps and upright

---

11. The two exceptions, the Moorish ardin and what Wachsmann (1973) has called "shiplike" harps, are discussed in Charry (1994b:36–40). Foreign (non–West African) features on the ardin are its longitudinal string holder, "spoon in a cup" (Wachsmann 1964) type of neck and resonator construction, tuning pegs, playing position, and its being played exclusively by women. The last two features point to Egypt. Foreign features on the "shiplike" harp, from the Mende people of Sierra Leone, include a "cork in a bottle" neck construction (prevalent in Central Africa) and the sculpture of a head protruding from the body (resembling the Fang *ngombi* harp of Gabon). It may have been made for the tourist trade.

string holders or bridges are found only in West Africa, one can conclude that these two features are indigenous there. Savanna spike harps have calabash resonators, and forest spike harps, which are not played by core Mande groups, have wooden box resonators. West African harps may be distinguished among themselves by their string holders, tuning systems, materials used for strings, playing techniques, and social functions.

Bolon

The bolon is played by several peoples in West Africa, including Maninka, Fulbe, Senufo, Susu, and Kissi (map 3, plate 4). Nowadays it is a rare instrument in its traditional setting, but it is often played in national ballets and in a variety of settings within jeli or Wasulu ensembles (see appendix B for recordings of the instrument). Most, if not all, of the published sources refer to the bolon as being associated with inciting warriors to battle (e.g., Tellier 1898:178; Humblot 1921:140; B. Keita 1988:67), distinguishing it from the other calabash harps, which are associated with hunters or jelis. Some other distinguishing features of the bolon are that it has the fewest strings (three or four) among the West African harps; its neck is the most curved, resembling a hunter's or warrior's bow more closely than do any of the other harps; the skin sound table is tied around the resonator as in a calabash drum rather than tacked onto it as in most other calabash harps; and it is played by the widest variety of peoples. There do not appear to be any hereditary restrictions on who may play the bolon. If one can posit an evolution of West African harps according to the number of strings, the curve of the bow, and method of attaching the skin sound table, the bolon would be the candidate for the oldest of the calabash harps. It conveys such a striking visual image of a calabash drum wedded to a hunter's or warrior's bow that there is no need to search outside West Africa for prototypes.

Maninka Simbi

The interchangeable use of the names simbi and donso ngoni has led to a confusing array of references. This confusion typically occurs when musicians apply the names of their own instruments to similar instruments of their neighbors or, conversely, when they use the names of their neighbors' instruments to refer to their own. The simbi (called *simbingo* by the Mandinka), traditionally played by the sora for hunters, is indigenous to Maninka in Mali and Guinea and is an important source of Mande instrumental music. It is the only one of the hunter's harps that is heptatonic, and it is also the only hunter's harp I know of with metal strings (see *dan,* below).

JELLIMAN OF SOOLIMANA.

Sambou, griot Malinké à Niantaneo.

Plate 7 Two nineteenth-century calabash harps. Left: from Laing (1825, facing 148); right: from Mage (1868:91; 1980, cover).

In the late eighteenth century Mungo Park noted that the simbi had seven strings, which it still has today in Mali and Guinea. The harp illustrated on the cover of Mage ([1868] 1980), perhaps the earliest drawing of what is probably a simbi, has eight strings (plate 7).[12]

The simbi is also distinguished from other hunter's harps in Mali in that the string holder has a single rank of strings and the two sticks that come up from the resonator do not curve into the neck as they do on the Wasulu donso ngoni. The sticks go straight out and act as handles just as they do on the kora, and the playing technique of the simbi, using the thumb and index

12. See chapter 3 for references to nineteenth-century instruments that show signs of a transition between a simbi and a kora. Tellier (1898:179) noted that the simbi had six strings (in the region of Kita, Mali), and Knight (1992-vid) has also recorded and photographed simbingos in The Gambia that have six strings. Schaeffner (1951:68–72) noted an instrument called *silamando* (or *silamandu*) among the Kissi in Guinea, but it is probably a local term for a simbi, because the accompanying drawing is of a six-stringed simbi (Charry 1994b:21–22). I have no information about the length of time that metal strings have been used on the simbi. The three simbis I saw in Bala (Mali) and Niagassola (Guinea) had metal strings, as did a fourth from Kita, Mali, that I have heard on a recording.

Plate 8 Calabash harp and unidentified instruments from 1825. (1) bala; (2) tabala (?); (3) tabala (?); (4) tama; (5) flute; (6) Mandinka sabaro or Wolof sabar; (7) kora; (8) lute (koni, molo?). From Gray and Dochard (1825), facing 301. Courtesy of Brown University Library.

fingers of both hands while holding on to the sticks with the rest of the fingers (or just one or two fingers), is much closer to that of the kora than are the playing techniques of any of the other harps.

Wasulu Donso Ngoni

The Wasulu donso ngoni (called *dunsu nguni* in a dialect variant) has six strings arranged in two ranks of three strings each, in a pentatonic tuning (plate 6). The donso ngoni is normally played with one hand on the neck so that only the thumb of that hand plucks the strings. The other hand holds the handle (which curves in and is attached to the neck), and both the thumb and index finger pluck. The historical relation between the names *jeli ngoni,* the lute played by jelis, and *donso ngoni* (hunter's ngoni) is unclear. I have seen only two references to a local name for the Wasulu donso ngoni: *burunuba* (Rouget, in Stone and Gillis 1976:103, and Langer, in Peuls du Wassolon 1987-disc:8–9).

The best-known donso ngoni player and singer is Toumani Kone (n.d.-disc), who has many commercial cassette recordings available in Mali. A derivative instrument called *kamalen ngoni* (young man's ngoni), tuned higher and typically smaller than the donso ngoni, is closely associated with the Malian music simply called Wassoulou (Wasulu), which has become very popular since the late 1980s, in part owing to the unprecedented success of a recording by Wasulu singer Oumou Sangare (1990-disc). According to research carried out by Lucy Durán (forthcoming b) in Bamako and the Wasulu region, the kamalen ngoni (*kamalengoni*) was created sometime in the 1950s by Allata Brulaye Sidibe, who was also the first to record on the instrument in 1977 with his niece Coumba Sidibe. The kamalen ngoni emerged as an instrument for youth to dance to, conveying the sounds of the donso ngoni, but without its forbidding sacred power.[13]

Other Harps

The Jola *furakaf,* sometimes called *simbingo* or *esimbin* after the Mandinka variety, differs only slightly from the Maninka simbi.[14] The instrument has a single rank of strings like the Maninka simbi but has only five strings, tuned pentatonically. The strings of the two instruments I saw were made from the roots of a palm tree. A description accompanying what may be the earliest drawing of the furakaf reports that it had five strings made of "common hemp" ("African Curiosities" 1846). The harp that Schaeffner (1951: 70–71) called *silamando* also had strings made of raffia (palm), but it had six strings. The playing technique of the Jola harp is closer to that of the donso ngoni than to that of the simbi: one hand holds the handle and uses the thumb and index fingers while the other hand holds the neck higher up and uses the thumb only. While the harp is being played it is common for a second person to beat a simple rhythm (often a straight three against two) with two sticks on the back of the calabash resonator. This may be the source for the tapping of patterns on the kora in Senegambian traditions that is absent in Malian and Guinean traditions.

A simbi of the Birgo region (southeast of Kita, Mali) is a curiosity that may not be very old or widespread. It has ten strings, divided into two ranks of five each, tuned pentatonically, and is played by the thumb and index fingers of both hands, which hold the two handles. The sound table skin is laced around the calabash resonator rather than tacked onto it. I have

13. For more on the kamalen ngoni and its music see Durán (1995a, forthcoming a, forthcoming b), whom I thank for giving me an advance copy of her forthcoming chapter. Research recently carried out in Mali by Cullen Strawn (personal communication, 1999) with Siaka Sidibe, Sekou Camara, and others is beginning to document Wasulu donso ngoni playing. *Ngoni sen* (leg) refers to the melodic pattern played on the donso ngoni. *Den* (child) and *ba* (mother) can qualify *ngoni senw* as accompanying (*ngoniden*) or solo (*ngoniba*) melodies, played by apprentices and master musicians, respectively, in performance. *Ngoni senw* may be named after certain ethnic groups or occupations, or great hunters. Similar naming practices in jembe traditions, as well as the use of den and ba (see chapter 4), point to a broad conceptual system at work. In addition to the tuning given below, Strawn has noted that some players sharpen the fourth degree and that some kamalen ngonis have eight strings, and consequently a wider tonal and modal palette.

14. Being bilingual in Jola and Mandinka, Jola harp players may refer to their instruments by the Mandinka name *simbingo.* My sources for the furakaf are two Jola musicians I recorded in Brikama, Gambia (Jiba and Koli 1990-per); see Charry (1994b:24–25) for photographs of them and of the Jola harp from "African Curiosities" (1846).

seen only one of these instruments and believe it may be a recent and local invention.[15]

The *dan* (*ndan* or *ndang*) is a pentatonic pluriarc (stringed instrument with multiple necks); each string is attached to a separate neck, which consists of a flexible stick. The resonator is a large calabash, but turned upside down so that the strings lie across the curved surface, each raised by a small cylinder bridge. The other side of the calabash is left open, with no skin covering. The dan probably originated in Wasulu, and it has associations with sorcery rather than with hunters or warriors.[16]

Simbi Repertory

Just as the simbi and donso ngoni are two distinct instruments with their own tuning systems, so are their musical repertories distinct; they do not play each other's music.[17] This is not surprising, given their different tuning systems and playing techniques. But it does impose limits on a conception of broad panethnic savanna hunters' societies in which the members lose their inherited social identities to become children of Sanin and Kontron (or Sanen and Kontoron), the mythical mother and archetype hunter son. While linguistic and ethnic affiliations may be fluid in the large region encompassing Kita, Segou, Wasulu, and old Mande, the musical identities of the Maninka simbi and Wasulu donso ngoni are less so. Although Maninka and Wasulu hunter's pieces may praise some of the same heroes, such as Fakoli (Coulibaly 1985:60) or Samori Toure, the musical vehicles that carry them, such as the harps and their tuning systems, are indicators of ethnic identity (*siya*).[18]

15. I thank Yusuke Nakamura, who was living and studying in Kita when I visited there, for introducing me to Sekou Diallo, who made and played this instrument (see Charry 1994b:27–28 for photographs of his harp).

16. See Knight (1992-vid) for photographs and a recording of a dan, Konate and Ott (1997:16–17), who refer to it as *koworo*, for a photograph, and Béart (1955:683–85), who also calls it *ko voro* (six backs), for a sketch and description. I thank Yusuke Nakamura, again, for introducing me in Kita to an elderly blind dan player named Coulibaly, the source of my information. Mr. Coulibaly learned the dan in the Wasulu region from Burema Coulibaly, whom he credits with replacing the unwieldy animal tendon strings with the more stable metal strings he uses. Lucy Durán (forthcoming b) notes that Allata Brulaye Sidibe played the dan before he created the kamalen ngoni (see above).

17. Nakamura (1992:364–65) noted that during hunters' festivals in Kita, Maninka and Wasulu hunter's musicians do not play together but alternate with one another. He also commented on a young simbi player who modified his style to accompany the donso ngoni players, indicating that this is more plausible for the heptatonic simbi than vice versa with the pentatonic donso ngoni.

18. Coulibaly (1985:3) notes three regional interpretations regarding Sanin and Kontron: they are a married couple (in Segou and Beledougou); mother and son (in the Manden); or a woman and a "*fétiche*" (also in the Manden), probably a translation of *boli* or *basi,* an object endowed with

Although Wasulu music has made a significant impact on a national Malian musical identity in the past decade owing to the donso ngoni player Toumani Kone, the singers Coumba Sidibe, Oumou Sangare, Sali Sidibe, Nahawa Doumbia, and others, Maninka simbi music has had a more far-reaching impact on western African music, most likely because of the spread of Maninka culture. Three pieces in particular, commonly believed to have originated on the simbi, have gained widespread currency: *Janjon, Kulanjan* (Long-crested eagle), and *Balakononifin* (or *Balakononinfin;* Little black bird of the river).[19] Appendix C lists recorded versions of these pieces, which range from performances in the classic tradition of the jeli to updated recompositions by pop singers outside the tradition. Simbi pieces have entered the repertory of jelis and others, but it is uncommon for simbi players to play pieces from the jeli's repertory.

Bala Djimba Diakite's repertory centers on the three best-known simbi pieces. *Balakononifin* is part of a group of three closely related pieces differing primarily in tempo: *Manden Mori* (slow tempo); *Mugutari* (medium tempo); and *Balakononifin* (fast tempo). According to Dosseh Joseph Coulibaly (1985:13), Diakite's core repertory of song texts concerns the odysseys of forty-five hunter heroes known as *gwede,* but it is unclear which musical accompaniments are used for these texts.[20]

The vocal melodies that jelis use for *Janjon* and *Kulanjan* are not the same as those used by Bala Djimba Diakite. The melody to *Balakononifin* as sung by Diakite has been incorporated wholesale by the Rail Band

---

spiritual or divine power. Y. Cissé (1964) reports on Maninka (Malinke) hunters' societies and does not explicitly address their relation to Wasulu hunters' societies, if indeed there are any differences. Two anonymous quotations that he cites imply this panethnic fraternity: "'The children of Sanin and Kontron' are neither Malinke nor Bambara, Senoufo, Bobo, Peuls, neither black nor white, although they may be a little of all that"; and "from the moment we consecrate ourselves to hunting, we are by rights the children of Sanin and Kontron, no matter what our religion, race, homeland, totem, customs, social condition" (Y. Cissé 1964:178, 186).

19. *Kulanjan* (or *kolanjan*), from *kulan* (anvil) *jan* (long), has been defined as an "eagle with a long occipital [back of the head] crest" (Delafosse 1955:422) and as "*Pelecanus rufescens, Pelecanus onocrotalus*" (gray or white pelican) (K. Kone 1995:228; Bailleul 1996:441). Y. Cissé (1994:134), who refers to the bird as a fisher eagle or royal eagle, provides an origin myth linking it to the primordial blacksmith's anvil. *Balakononifin* has been defined as "black ibis" (Cissé and Kamissoko 1988:25) or "little black bird of the river" (Y. Cissé 1994:129), and *balakononin* as *Pluvianus aegyptius* (K. Kone 1995:228; Bailleul 1996:439).

20. Out of five hours of Diakite's various recordings, only two pieces are not part of this core musical repertory: *Sori,* which he played when I requested something different during our recording session, and an unidentified song played between *Janjon* and *Balakononifin,* when a hunter is dancing solo in Austin (1991-vid). The film segment begins with *Mugutari* as the hunters enter. *Janjon* is played as Salif Keita describes the significance of the piece and of hunters' societies. Next comes the unidentified piece, and finally *Balakononifin* is played while Keita dances—the melody sung by the crowd can barely be heard in the background.

(1977-disc), by Mory Kante (1986-disc) in his piece *Teriya,* and by Salif Keita (1993-disc) in his piece *Donsolou* (Hunters). The melody to *Mugutari* as sung by Diakite has been recorded under the name *Simbon* (Master hunter) by jelis from Kela (Diabate Family of Kela 1994-disc).[21]

Charles Bird (1972:279–80) has grouped hunter's music into three interrelated categories, perhaps conflating the Maninka and Wasulu repertories. Songs for amusement are for dancing, and anyone may participate. They may be sped up to accommodate the athletic dancing of younger hunters. Ritual songs, such as *Janjon* and *Duga,* are related to the hunt and are restricted to those who have earned a reputation. Heroic works, such as the Wasulu piece *Kambili,* are for listening and are performed at the end of hunter's ceremonies. They are extended narratives about great hunters and warriors of the past. Using Bird's categories, I would classify *Balakononifin* as a song for amusement and the similar, but slower, *Manden Mori* as a heroic work.

The significance of ritual songs is still maintained in Mande society and widely respected.

> *Janjon,* for example, is exclusively reserved for hunters who by their coolness, their fearlessness, or their courage have triumphed over their "enemies" or escaped a danger. "Who can dance *Janjon* before having seen a calamity!" says the refrain of this hymn. As for *Kulanjan* (Hunter-eagle), it belongs to hunters renowned for their skill, while *Duga* (Vulture) is danced only by those who have been gravely injured in war and is sung only on the occasion of the funerals of great hunters. (Y. Cissé 1994:54)

In a rare film scene showing hunters dancing to *Janjon,* Salif Keita (Austin 1991-vid) calls it the most sacred of pieces and says he had to request permission to dance. He is shown dancing later, but to another piece, *Balakononifin,* not *Janjon. Janjon* is associated with the great warrior Fakoli, who left the side of his uncle Sumanguru Kante to join the ranks of Sunjata, and it is sometimes sung during renditions of the Sunjata epic when Sumanguru Kante makes an appearance. *Kulanjan,* also known simply as *Donso foli* (Hunter's music), has no associations outside hunting as *Janjon* does. *Janjon* and *Kulanjan* form the oldest layer of the jeli's repertory.[22]

21. At the 9'55" mark Lanfia Diabate sings *Mugutari.* For transcriptions of lyrics to *Balakononifin,* see Y. Cissé (1994:129), Durán (forthcoming b), and Mory Kante (1986-disc:5); for *Kulanjan,* see Y. Cissé (1994:133–34, 353–57) and M. Kaba (1995:62–63); for *Janjon,* see Y. Cissé (1994:148–52).

22. For an extended discussion of Fakoli see Conrad (1992). For more on *Janjon* see Bird (1972:280, 291), Bird and Kendall (1980:20–21), and M. Diabate (1970a:43–52). Bird and Diabate worked together in the middle to late 1960s (Bird 1972:441), so their publications in the early 1970s are probably based on a common pool of research. According to Soninke griot Diarra Sylla

Not only has the music of hunters been an important source for musicians in the modern sphere, but images of hunters have also served as a wellspring. Cheick Keita (1996), a childhood friend of Salif Keita, has pointed out that the latter's emergence as an international artist in the mid-1980s with his first solo recording coincides with a shift from the jeli-based persona of his earlier Bamako days to one that draws on the nobility of the hunter. In contrast to his earlier breaking of the traditions of his society by aligning himself with jelis, this shift moved Keita's artistic career more in line with his own fasiya, his paternal lineage. Cheick Keita identifies the piece *Sina,* a praise song dedicated to Salif's father, as a symbol of Salif's reconciling his broken relationship with his father, who was a hunter.

Simbi and Donso Ngoni Tuning

The simbi is the only heptatonic hunter's calabash harp I have encountered; all others are pentatonic or possibly hexatonic. Figure 1 is a diagram of the bridge of a simbi along with the layout and tuning of the strings drawn from the example of Bala Djimba Diakite. It appears that Diakite does not use other tunings, perhaps reflecting the provinciality of the simbi, although other regions might have their own tunings. In this respect the simbi contrasts with the kora and koni, which travel widely in West Africa and play pieces from a variety of repertories in different tunings.[23]

(Dieterlen and Sylla 1992:14, 96), *Janjon* was sung in honor of Dinga, the founding ancestor of the Soninke empire Wagadu. Sidiki Diabate (1990-per:15–18) attributed *Janjon* originally to Sumanguru's ancestor Sora Musa, and then to Sumanguru, finally taken over by Fakoli. A line from *Janjon* in praise of Sumanguru Kante, "First king of the Mande, And traditional King," has prompted Bird (forthcoming) to suggest the idea of a song's being captured. Bird and Kendall (1980:20–21) relate that *Janjon* was first sung in praise of Sumanguru Kante, and that on hearing it sung for Sunjata, Fakoli desired and ultimately won it because of his heroic sacrifices. "They [jelis] sing that Sumanguru is the first and traditional king; they say that Sunjata is. This sounds like good evidence for Sunjata's winning the song, and having its accompanying story adapted to fit the new circumstances, but the bards choose to preserve Sumanguru's original claim to the title, and they preserve the role of Fakoli as earning the right to the song" (Bird, forthcoming). The praises of Sumanguru were perhaps retained because "the hero's greatness is measured against that of his adversaries. . . . The more that is said of the terribleness of Sumanguru, the more terrible had to be the greatness of Sunjata who defeated him" (Bird, forthcoming). Bird uses this idea of transfer of song ownership to support his suggestion that Sunjata might have been a Soninke native son from Mema in the north who imposed himself militarily on the Mande to the south, defeating Sumanguru Kante. Bala Faseke Kouyate, who would have been Sumanguru's jeli, then helped legitimize the new ruler by singing *Janjon* for Sunjata. Furthermore, Bird sees this as symbolizing the victory of northern horsemen over blacksmith–earth priests farther south in the savanna.

23. Further research with other simbi players is needed to see if indeed there are regional differences in repertory, tuning, and playing styles. Although they cannot be heard clearly, it appears that the simbis shown in Dance of Guinea (1991-vid) are tuned differently. Also see Rouget (1999-disc:59–60).

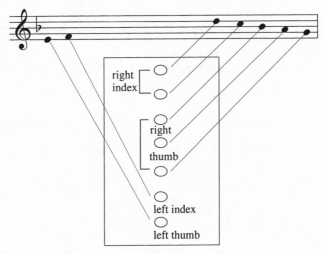

Figure 1 Simbi tuning, layout of strings, and fingering.

The circumstances of recording the simbi tuning shown in figure 1 illustrate some of the vagaries of African music research as well as the nature of the profession of a hunter's musician. I visited Mr. Diakite at his home in July shortly after the rainy season had started and learned that it was not a time for simbi playing because people were busy tending their land. During the dry season Mr. Diakite was in great demand and traveled extensively, as do other simbi players, as I had found in Kita several months earlier (during the dry season) when I was unable to reach two simbi players who were also traveling. Mr. Diakite explained that he had not touched his instrument for weeks, perhaps longer, and asked me to return in a week or two so he could have time to practice. Because I was about to leave Mali, he graciously agreed to tune up his instrument and be recorded that night.

The tuning rings on hunter's harps are not easy to manipulate, so it took some time to get his instrument in tune. His apprentice, Bakary Samake (who was probably in his early forties), evidently had been practicing because his simbi was already in tune and did not slip out during our recording. One of Mr. Diakite's strings slipped out of tune frequently during our recording session. Sometimes he stopped to tune it, but there were also stretches when he kept on playing. When he realized I could tell when his simbi was out of tune, he showed good humor and tried to correct it, against the wishes of a stubborn instrument. I did not have adequate time to build up a close relationship with Mr. Diakite, but he seemed to appreciate my initial approach, arriving by public transport with my family, giving him the traditional ten cola nuts and a few small gifts, and conversing with him in

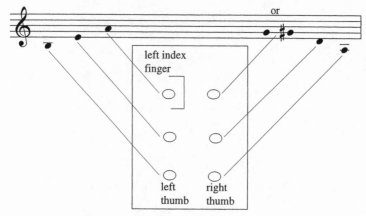

Figure 2 Donso ngoni tuning, layout of strings, and fingering.

Bamana rather than through an interpreter.[24] He accordingly made a sincere effort to accommodate my desire to record him. Negotiations involving money, expected when dealing with foreigners, took place only after lengthy conversation, when we felt comfortable with each other. My brief contact with Mr. Diakite contrasted with the longer and closer relationships I had with my kora, bala, koni, dundun, and jembe teachers.

The tuning given in figure 1 is that of Mr. Diakite's apprentice, Bakary Samake. When Diakite's simbi slipped out of tune he used Samake's instrument as a model, and at one point he even took Samake's instrument to record a piece on it by himself. Their simbis were tuned to a tonic around D-flat; the simbis in the *Salif Keita* film (Austin 1991-vid) were tuned closer to D, perhaps owing to the drier weather when they were filmed.[25]

A standard tuning for the donso ngoni is given in figure 2 (also see Rouget 1999-disc: 56–59). Kamalen ngoni tuning replicates that of the donso ngoni approximately a fourth higher (see Durán 1995a:118). Donso ngonis have their lowest string tuned in the vicinity of A-flat to B-flat, and kamalen ngonis typically have their lowest string tuned near D a fourth higher, perhaps the only structural difference between the two instruments. In practice, the kamalen ngoni is used for lighter dance music rather than the serious music of hunters.

24. He humorously referred to the dialect I was using as "Coulibaly kan," the language of the Bamana Coulibalys to the north.

25. The background scenery, including stacks of long branches, indicates the dry season. Diakite's apprentice in the film could be Bakary Samake, but identification is difficult because he wears a cap with hair extensions and sunglasses. The simbi on Diakite's (1995-disc) commercial cassettes has a tonic that ranges between D-flat and D; the Institut des Sciences Humaines recordings and market cassette (Diakite n.d.a-disc, n.d.b-disc) have a tonic a whole step or more higher, but variations in tape speeds in the many dubbing stages are notorious.

Simbi Playing Technique and Style

The simbi is plucked by both thumbs and both index fingers, each assigned to one or more strings (fig. 1). Like other Maninka music, simbi music consists of short melodies that are played over and over, sometimes with slight variations and occasional breaks for more extended variations. Typically, one person plays the simbi and also sings. He may be accompanied by a second simbi player, who also may inject vocal responses and join in chorus either with the lead vocalist or with a group of singers. Fast simbi music can also be accompanied by a *karignan* or *nege* (iron), a notched narrow metal tube held in one hand while the other hand rhythmically scrapes it with a thin metal rod (plate 6). Simbi music does not emphasize the kind of solo virtuosic playing that is typically found on the instruments of the jeli, although expert players can weave an array of variations around the basic compositions.

Vocal melodies, as in many other parts of Africa, consist of cascades of descending lines. Typically, single vocal phrases consist of a descent to the third or tonic degree. Longer phrases begin above the upper octave, often on the tenth or eleventh, descend to the octave or fifth, jump up, and then descend again to the third or tonic.

Transcriptions 1, 2, and 3 show basic simbi parts played by Bala Djimba Diakite for his most frequently played pieces: *Manden Mori* (1), also known as *Mugutari* or *Balakononifin; Janjon* (2); and *Kulanjan* (3). One feature typical of much hunter's music is a subtle shifting from a ternary to a binary division of the beats (or vice versa), illustrated in transcriptions 1 and 2. In the course of a performance the musician may move in and out of these two options, expanding or contracting the spaces between his strokes of the strings, creating and exploiting an ambiguity as to ternary or binary beat division. This type of tendency has already been noted on the kora (Knight 1973a, 1:270–74) and jembe (Beer, in Konate 1991-disc:12–13). Rainer Polak's (1996a, 1996b, 1998) research with Malian jembe drummers, suggesting that they systematically inflect their microtiming so as to move toward one or the other beat division, points to a broader Mande aesthetic of timing.

It is unclear how Diakite distinguishes the three musically related pieces known as *Manden Mori, Mugutari,* and *Balakononifin.* It may be that musically they are the same piece differing primarily in tempo: *Manden Mori* is played slow, *Mugutari* is played faster, and *Balakononifin* is played much faster. *Janjon,* like *Manden Mori,* can also be played with a ternary division (2.1) or with a binary division (2.2). *Janjon* is readily identified by the alternation between the first and fifth degrees followed by the alternation

Transcription 1 Simbi: *Manden Mori/Mugutari*. Typically, version 1 is played for *Manden Mori* and version 2 for *Mugatari*. Ternary and binary versions of each are given. From Bala Djimba Diakite (1990-per, 1995-disc).

Transcription 2 Simbi: *Janjon*. 1 and 1.var: ternary version and variation. 2: binary version. From Bala Djimba Diakite (1990-per).

Transcription 3 Simbi: *Kulanjan*. From Bala Djimba Diakite (1990-per).

between the first and fourth degrees.[26] *Kulanjan* (3) is marked by a steady beat on the tonic and a line descending from the fifth degree to the tonic. Each of these three pieces has been transcribed with eight beats to a complete cycle, and each cycle can be viewed as consisting of two halves, the second half differing from the first in some significant manner. The limited sample of pieces and musicians demands caution in making further generalizations on the structure of the music.

Conclusion

The music of hunters is of interest not just for its role as the foundation of the more widespread and public music of jelis, but also in itself. The explosion of secularized Wasulu donso ngoni–based traditions onto the national Malian and international music scenes in the past decade has provided a musical identity for Malians that is an alternative to the pervasive jeli's tradition. The Maninka simbi tradition has not yet enjoyed such a resurgence, although singers like Salif Keita are drawing on simbi music and the persona of the hunter in shaping their own musical identities. The precolonial and pre-Islamic past symbolized by hunters and their music is attractive to those struggling to define local identities in the face of increasing European and American influence. Although hunting has declined as a subsistence activity and the music consequently no longer thrives in its ancient contexts, images of a grand past of hunter heroes reflecting ancient local traditions nourish national identities. Hunter's music also contains keys to understanding the long-neglected musical past of a region rich in music and history.

26. A rare early musical transcription of a "Mandingo Air" (Moloney 1889:279, no. 2) has a melodic profile that looks very much like *Janjon* or its Senegambian musical descendant *Jula Jekere*.

3

Jeliya

Jeli (pl. *jelilu;* Md: *jali* or *jalo,* pl. *jalolu*) is the Maninka term for a special kind of musical and verbal artist. Jelis are highly trained professionals whose skills have been learned over a lifetime and passed down through generations within a limited number of families. *Jeliya,* the art of the jeli, is the field of music most closely associated with the ruling Mandenka elite, and it is appreciated by all. With the exclusive right to play the kora, bala, and koni (and in certain regions the dundun and tama) and to sing about certain aspects of Mande social and political life, jelis have shaped a unique musical world that is visible to all but accessible (in practical terms) to few. Although sometimes jeliya is intended to animate dancing, deep jeliya is for listening and is intended to inspire listeners to act. Jeliya can be chamber music, played in the open courtyard of a patron, or concert music, played in the halls or stadiums of large cities. Above all, jeliya is classic.[1]

Performers and Performance

Musician and oral historian are quick and convenient descriptions of a jeli, but important Mande concepts of sound may get lost in the translation. Jelis are artisans and shapers of sound (words and music) much as numus are artisans and shapers of metal, wood, and clay. Jelis shape and transform events and actions through their words and music. They are different from other kinds of Mande music makers and orators for several reasons: jelis are born into their profession and guard it through endogamy (restrictions on marrying outside their own group); they claim a common origin in just a few lineages; and they have the exclusive right to play the kora (a twenty-one-stringed harp), koni (a four- or five-stringed lute), and bala (also known as *balafon,* a xylophone). As performers, jelis specialize in any one of three fields: speech (*kuma*), the vehicle for historical narrative, stories, genealo-

---

1. The terms "classic" and "classical" as applied to African musics can be problematic owing in part to the absence of local written traditions canonizing them. Classical is also often narrowly interpreted as referring only to a style of European music. But from a social point of view, the similarities between jeliya and what are often called classical or traditional art musics of Europe and Asia need not be ignored. Bringing jeliya into this fold may help expand sensitivity to the varied status of music in Africa and beyond. For more on the concept of classical musics in Asia see Powers (1980a).

gies, and proverbs; song (dònkili), which refers to melodies and lyrics that are unique to named pieces as well as the art of singing and expanding them; and instrument playing (Mn: fòli; Md: kosiri). These three fields require different kinds of training, resulting in a high degree of specialization. Most male jelis (jelike; pl. jelikelu) are competent in at least two of these areas, but they usually gain professional expertise in just one. Female jelis (jelimuso; pl. jelimusolu) primarily sing, although they are also known for their powers of speech.

Since the founding of the Mande empire jelis have been attached to the leaders of their society. They retain political history and genealogies and convey this kind of knowledge through singing (Mn: dònkili dali; Md: donkili laali) or speaking (kuma), usually accompanied by music.[2] The high profile of jelis in Mande public life has attracted the attention of foreign visitors, and there is a significant body of writing describing them in Arabic sources beginning in the mid-fourteenth century, in Portuguese sources beginning a century later, and in French and English sources beginning in the seventeenth century. At present jelis are still active forces in the musical lives of Mali, Guinea, Senegal, The Gambia, and neighboring countries. Some of them have taken up the guitar and have extended their tradition into the realm of African popular music, receiving worldwide acclaim.

The institution of the jeli is not unique to Mande peoples. Jelis have their analogue in the Wolof gewel, Fulbe gaulo (gawlo), Moorish iggio (iggiw) and Soninke jaare, all of whom come from societies that have had close contact with the Ghana and Mali empires. The term guiriot was written down by early French travelers to West Africa, probably as a French transliteration of what they heard in the Senegambian coastal areas, referring to the praise singers and musicians they encountered. By the end of the eighteenth century the written form standardized to "griot," which has now gained widespread currency outside Africa. I will use that term when referring to jelis, gewels, gaulos, and such in general without reference to any specific ethnic group.

What Jelis Do

Jelis are musicians, singers, public speakers, oral historians, praisers, gobetweens, advisers, chroniclers, and shapers of the past and the present. Although most jelis have had a thorough Islamic education and routinely

---

2. Although the knowledge and duties of the jeli and the fune (Md: fina/fino) may overlap, the latter are distinguished in several ways: they do not sing; they usually speak without musical accompaniment; and they most often carry the jamu (family name) Camara (although there are also Camara jelis).

pepper their performances with quotations from the Koran, the knowledge they retain and transmit is essentially political and historical in nature rather than religious.[3] Jelis usually do not have a leading role in ceremonies where drummers are essential, such as circumcision ceremonies, agricultural festivities, or secret power societies. Jelis may indeed be present, praising the participants or playing their own drums (the tama and dundun), but they are usually still acting within their role of jeli as social or political motivator. Contrary to popular perception outside Africa, jelis do not hold a monopoly on the whole of the musical and verbal arts. But they do have a lock on a good portion and maintain the highest profile among Mande music makers. By virtue of their bloodlines, they also command the greatest respect in terms of their right and duty to perform.

It is uncommon for a jeli to be expert in all three fields of speech, song, and instrument playing. For example, I received a variety of reactions from my teachers, who were respected as instrumentalists, when I inquired about the history of their instruments, of jelis, of Mande subgroups, or even of certain songs. Some gave a candid "I don't know"; others may not have been so candid, wishing to guard certain secrets. Another said, "Did you come here to learn [such and such an instrument], or do you want to learn history? They are not the same." Still others gave lengthy responses reflecting their expertise in certain areas. My koni teacher Moussa Kouyate maintained that history (Fr: *histoire*), which for all intents and purposes was synonymous with speech (*kuma*), and instrument playing (*fòli*) are two different pursuits. Although he learned from his father, he was also sent to a separate teacher to learn history.

EC: But history . . . you . . .
MK: We learned it from our father. We also left home to learn it, yes.
EC: Song [*dònkili*] and history [*histoire*] . . .
MK: They are not the same. . . . The instrumentalist, the historian, and the singer are not the same. (Moussa Kouyate 1990-per:IIB)[4]

The practice of gaining a broad education by apprenticing with specialists is typical, especially given the extended family network that exists among jelis. For example,

> My father, who is deceased, entrusted me to Bintou Famo Diabate, the head of the griots of Kela, who, I suppose, knew the 74 Malinke family names and their history better than anyone. (Gawlo Madani, in Association SCOA 1980:12)

---

3. See Cutter (1968) and Schulz (1996) for discussions of the political nature of the jeli's activities.

4. EC: "Bari histoire fana . . . i . . . " MK: "An y'a kalan an fa fe. Anw wulila fana ka taag'a kalan, oui." EC: "Dònkili nin histoire . . . " MK: "E te kilin ye. . . . Fòli kela ani histoire benbaga ani dònkili kela te kilin ye."

The impetus for students to apprentice with specialists comes not only from a desire to gain a broad knowledge of a vast field, but also from the call of *fadenya* (competition with the father) to develop a distinct personal style.

It is to maintain such a spirit of competition and innovation in a family of artists that the young *mandingue* artist leaves the schooling of his father or uncle after a couple of years to learn from other masters. In this way he gathers the indispensable elements for the elaboration of a style that is distinct in some way from that of his father or patrilineage. (C. Keita 1995a:65)

Although jelikelu (male jelis) either receive training or gain competence by osmosis in all three fields, as they move into adulthood they specialize in their areas of keenest interest. Youssouf Cissé's assessment of his close friend and associate Wa Kamissoko is a case in point.

It should be mentioned that being a *nwara,* a master of the word, he no longer really played any musical instruments, even though he had played them until his adulthood. He was, according to everyone, an excellent player of the *jeli taman,* "griot drum" or "armpit talking drum," but a mediocre player of the ngoni, "guitar" or four-stringed harp. Neither did he sing anymore. (Cissé and Kamissoko 1988:24)

In short, jelikelu are usually minimally competent in speech, singing, and instrument playing but commonly specialize and excel in just one area.

The situation is different for jelimusolu (female jelis), who engage in speech and specialize in singing. The only instrument they play is a narrow tubular iron chime, about thirty centimeters (one foot) long, called *nege* (Md: *neo;* iron) or *karinyan (karignan)*, perhaps from the French *carillon* (chimes, bells). Jelimusolu twirl the karinyan in one hand while striking it with a metal rod held in the other hand, accompanying their song or dance.[5]

The specialized nature of jeliya (what jelis do) has drawn an equally specialized array of researchers, who have investigated the roles of the jeli in Mande society largely according to their own areas of expertise.[6]

The role of the griot which is usually stressed by Western scholars is that of historian, but those scholars who describe the griots as the historians of West Africa are perhaps reflecting their own interests rather than those of the griots; it seems that Western historians tend to regard the griots as historians, musicologists as musicians, and scholars with an interest in oral literature to regard them as expert narrators—and the griots are of course all of these. (Innes 1976:4–5)

5. See Kidel and Marks (1990-vid) for scenes of jelimusolu playing the karinyan.
6. Discussions of the jeli as verbal artist (or Mande verbal art in general) may be found in Austen (forthcoming), Bérenger-Féraud (1882), L. Camara (1954, 1980), Seydou Camara (1996), Sory Camara ([1976] 1992), Darbo (1972), Hale (1998), Hoffman (1990, 1998), Jatta (1985), K. Kone (1997), Leynaud and Cissé (1978), C. Monteil ([1924] 1977:24–26, 316–18), V. Monteil (1968), Niane (1965), Zahan (1963), and Zobel (1997).

Critical reading of descriptions of griots given by foreign travelers to West Africa from the fourteenth century onward yields fruitful information on the roles griots played in West African societies and how they were viewed both externally and internally. (Excerpts from many of these travelers' writings are reproduced in appendix A.)

Jelis refer to each other as singers (Md: *donkili laala;* Mn: *dònkili dala*), instrumentalists (Md: *kosirila;* Mn: *fòlila*), or speakers (*kumala*).[7] It is primarily in speech that jelis render the detailed political and social history of their people in the form of genealogies, storytelling, praising, and proverbs. All these kinds of speech may be integrated into song, and song may also be integrated into speech. But there is a distinction between jelis who primarily engage in kuma (speech) and jelis who primarily engage in dònkili (song). It is a distinction based on knowledge and gender (see Durán 1995b).

Verbal Sound Materials: Speech and Song

According to Sidiki Diabate, knowledge (Md: *londo*) is not an essential factor in the performance of song (donkili), but it is crucial in speech (kuma), to the point of being virtually synonymous with it. The important factor in song is the ability to move with the rhythm of the musical accompaniment.

> Someone may know how to sing—they may not have much knowledge [*londo*] in their head—but their voice is in with the music. That happens with people, with artists. You will find that the knowledge that is in their head, it is not great, but their voice, their voice moves well with the music. . . . You know X [a reference to a male singer], his voice is good . . . but knowledge is not there, knowledge is not in his head, but his voice is good, it goes with the music. . . . Yes, the voice is there, but speech [*kuma*] is not there. Anyone, for example, there may not be a lot of speech [*kuma*] in their head, but their voice can go well with the music. (S. Diabate 1990-per: 153–55)[8]

The contrasting images of a beautiful (and powerful) voice and a historically authoritative voice, captured by the categories dònkili and kuma, respectively, are typical in Mande aesthetic evaluations, and in many parts of the world for that matter. These two images in most cases might even be mutually exclusive, for it is expected that an authoritative voice is the prod-

---

7. See Durán (1995b: 202) for the use of the term *kumala* (speaker) to refer to jelimusolu who are competent rather than great.

8. "Kari, a ye donkilo noo, but a la donkilo, londo meng b'a kungo to, a man siya bari a kango be kumbengo la. Wo be moolu kono, artisolu kono. I s'a taara a la londo min b'a kungo to, a man wara bari a kango, a kango, a kara wuli kumbengo la a kara jii kumbengo. . . . I man [X] je, [X] a kango le diyata . . . bari londo ti jee, londo te kungo kono bari a kango diyata a be kumbengo la. . . . Bon, kan ne taara mais kuma te jee. I si moo doo je, kuma jama t'a kungo kono bari a kango a be kumbengo la."

uct of wisdom acquired by age and that a beautiful or pleasing voice comes with youth.[9]

Kuma is often delivered in a kind of a chant that Bird (1976:90) has observed might be an "intermediate form in the continuum between language and song." Although the content of what the jeli is rendering—be it genealogies, praising, narrative, or proverbs—seems to go hand in hand with the way it is rendered (as Bird has observed), I would consider anything short of song to be kuma. Dònkili (song) in this case could be defined as recognizable melody and words that are unique to the piece being rendered, as well as the vocal elaborations that accompany it, including those that are less specific to any one piece. Kuma covers most everything else. Kuma is word oriented; dònkili is melody oriented.

Those who specialize in kuma are believed to be the authoritative source of the knowledge of the jeli. They are the masters or guardians of the word, also known as *belentigi*, holders of the staff that gives the right to speak. For instance, my dundun teacher, a cofounder of the National Ballet of Mali and an elderly respected Xasonka jeli, did not wish to speak with me about the history of his own instrument, insisting that it was not his area of expertise. So when another elderly Xasonka jeli whose specialty was history rather than playing came to stay with him for a while, my teacher graciously arranged a session where all could hear him speak. The instrumentalist (*dundun fòla*) deferred to the speaker (*kumala*), both being jelis.

In contrast to speech, which is the forum for exegesis of fine, esoteric, and sometimes secretive detail, the song of the jeli is a matter of public record. Song is heard more often and is less detailed, although it takes a high degree of skill to deliver it, and it can be an extremely powerful force. The distinction between kuma and dònkili is heightened because it is primarily men who are considered to be the authoritative guardians of the esoteric knowledge of the jeli and primarily women who deliver major parts of it publicly in performance. I have often observed women praising the lineages of guests at marriages and naming ceremonies, sometimes in song, sometimes in a manner resembling scolding, as if they were enjoining the recipients to live up to the reputations of their ancestors. Their authority as guardians of esoteric knowledge, however, may reside in other kinds of cultural knowledge outside the borders of jeliya. I would posit a continuum in the delivery of kuma and dònkili moving through the calm, measured speech of the jeli speaking in public or narrating a story, the stylized metric public

9. See Jansen's (1991:29) discussion of a Malian family arguing the relative merits of the renowned elderly jelimuso Sira Mori Diabate, who knows more secrets, and her daughter-in-law in her early twenties, who has a pretty voice. The young apprentice would need to put in years learning some of Sira Mori's secrets before a comparison could be justified.

speech of the *fune* or *fino* (oral historian and praiser), the unaccompanied songlike praising of the jelimuso, and finally her flat-out, full-throated singing backed up by an array of male musicians.

The elite status of ngara, a master or authoritative artist, is a level that any jeli, male or female, can achieve, regardless of specialization. Ngaralu are recognized for the way they use their materials, whether it be speech, song, or instrumental music. Mastery does not necessarily entail a beautiful voice or even knowledge as conveyed by speech, but rather is based on what one does with the singing or speaking voice—the use of it. As the well-known Malian jelimuso Ami Koita has said about *ngaraya* (the art of the ngara), "It's not the beauty of the voice, it's the use of words" (Ami Koita in Durán 1995b:203).[10]

Some jelimusolu have earned a reputation for their authoritative and powerful singing that has no parallel among male performers. Their style of delivery, especially that of jelimusolu from Mali, is the stuff of fantastic stories about moving their patrons to bestow legendary gifts on them, such as cars, houses, airplane tickets, and even a small plane (Durán 1989a; also see her notes to Kandia Kouyate 1999-disc). Malian jelimusolu are indeed, as Durán (1995b) has called them, "superwomen of Malian music." The present generation of great Malian jelimuso singers, including Ami Koita, Tata Bambo Kouyate, and Kandia Kouyate, exude a powerful stage presence that controls their patrons in the audience. They are well versed in the history of their people and in Islamic as well as Mande proverbs, combining them in virtuosic performances.[11]

The Social Status of Jelis

Jelis often speak with pride of their crucial role in the proper functioning of society, yet members of the freeborn class (horon) sometimes speak of the

10. See Durán (1995b) and Knight (1984a:74) for further discussions on ngaraya and jelis, and Y. Cissé (1994:308–9), who in one context translates jeli as singer and *nwaara* (ngara) as narrator. Wa Kamissoko (Cissé and Kamissoko 1991:58) distinguishes a *nwara,* one who recites "real speech" (*kouma yèrè-yèrè*) to connoisseurs, from musicians (*fòlikèla djéliw*) and singers (*dònkilidala djéliw*), who are often incapable of explaining or commenting on what they play or sing.

11. See the video clips of a live performance (Ndao, n.d.-vid) showing a steady stream of audience members giving gifts of cash to the singer (Maimouna Dembele), and even one man filling out and giving to her what appears to be an airplane ticket. The performance of *Taara* sung by Tata Bambo Kouyate accompanied by her husband, guitarist Modibo Kouyate, in the BBC film *Bamako Beat* (Kidel 1991-vid) is a moving example of the raw vocal power of a jelimuso. For more on female singers in Mali see the pioneering works of Ba Konaré (1993) and Durán; for women's songs in general, see Luneau (1981) and Couloubaly (1990); for a certain class of Soninke women as oral historians and singers see Mamadou Diawara (1989). See Jansen (1991) for French translations of the song and speech of Sira Mori Diabate and other jelimuoslu from Kela, and Mamadou Diawara (1996, 1997) and Schulz (1996, 1998) for discussions of how electronic media may have boosted the star power and influence of jelimusolu. Amadu Bansang Jobarteh (1990-per:tape 11A) relates

public behavior of jelis as shameless. This paradoxical status of jelis within Mande society has recently received sustained critical attention (e.g., Conrad and Frank 1995a), with observers moving away from hierarchical assessments toward more multivalent interpretations of the nature of social roles determined at birth. The interdependent roles of speech and action (discussed in chapter 1) provide a key to understanding the power and standing of jelis (and their griot counterparts in neighboring societies). Laing's (1825:243) observation that "nothing is more dreaded by an African than a bad name from the Jelles" helps explain the history of resentment of jelis.

> Although people provide the raw materials for their own reputations, it is the bard who articulates, interprets, and perpetuates those reputations. . . . The *gewel*'s [Wolof griot] power is that of the presenter of social identity for *all* persons. It is not surprising, therefore, that bards are maligned, in a vain effort to call that power into question by attributing unsavory qualities to them. . . . Because the power of speech and the memory of action are granted to *gewel*, the *geer* [Wolof freeborn class] are deprived; and because the power of action is granted to *geer*, the *gewel* are deprived. But both groups, as human beings, retain both capacities, and it is only by an elegant cultural investiture that the speech/action dichotomy can be expressed in this particular way. (B. Wright 1989:52)

Early European reporting is permeated by derogatory remarks about the apparently unabashed soliciting of gifts by praise singers (called griots by the French). This perception of griots as beggars might be attributed to European alignment with the freeborn social classes, who were interested in currying favor and might have had a one-sided view of the role of griots. Or perhaps the status of griots in some parts of western Africa had degraded. The scene described by Ibn Battūta at the seat of the Mali empire in the mid-fourteenth century had no hint of degradation, while the account of Senegambian griots given by Fernandes in the early sixteenth century and thereafter by many French travelers (appendix A) could hardly have been more unsympathetic. How the changing economic and social order brought on by European encroachment affected the status of griots along the Senegambian coast and elsewhere is an open question.[12]

Perhaps the most glaring instance of undignified behavior (at least in the eyes of foreigners) is the way jelis are remunerated. Often in full performance jelis receive cash as they praise their patrons. Sometimes the cash might be laid on praise by praise. Jelis are professionals in that they get

---

a story of Bakari Jabate, who was so moved by a performance by the great jelike Wandifeng Jabate that he proposed to commit suicide because he did not have the proper wealth to offer Wandifeng.

12. See Mauny (1955) for a discussion of burying griots in baobab trees to avoid contamination, and Darbo (1972) and C. Keita (1995b) for sympathetic accounts of the plight of the modern griot.

something in return for what they do (some earn their whole livelihood from it), but not in the sense of selling their product. Whatever is provided to the jeli, be it cash, food, animals, land, or whatever, it is not traditionally considered to be payment, but rather is seen as cementing an ancient historical interdependence. Guinean Sory Camara contends that the gifts made to a jeli do not

> represent the price of the songs and music of the griot. They are an obliga-
> tion. . . . Therefore music and the songs of the griots escape the world of eco-
> nomic exchange, the law of supply and demand. It all takes place simply as if
> it were an occasion for demanding one's due, which one qualifies, however, as
> a gift: one says "to give to the griot," *kà jèlí só,* and not "to pay the griot," *kà*
> *jèlí sàrà,* a term one uses only to signify an act of remuneration for work or a
> service to which a value can be attached. In this case the relationship does not
> ordinarily indicate any kind of a personal tie between the parties at hand.
> (Sory Camara 1976:107; 1992:110–11)

The same point has been made by Gambian Sidia Jatta, whose family "is traditionally regarded as a source of patronage by Mandinka musicians" (Jatta 1985:187). "Contrary to what some Europeans believe, jalis are not paid for their performance. That is why in Mandinka we say: *Ka jaloo so* (to give to a jali), not *Ka jaloo joo* (to pay a jali)" (Jatta 1985:21).[13]

A relative social hierarchy among the constituent nyamakala (artisan) groups appears to exist, at least if one takes at face value what jelis say about the hierarchy, or who can solicit gifts from whom. Nyamakalalu tradition-ally solicit gifts from members of the freeborn class (horonnu), and they may also solicit gifts from each other. Even jelis may solicit gifts from each other. This hierarchy among nyamakalalu, and also among jelis, based on who has the right to solicit gifts from whom, varies by region. Three brief examples will help to clarify this practice, which might ultimately provide insight into the history of the various nyamakala groups.

As I was standing outside the music conservatory in Dakar talking with one of my teachers, an elderly bala virtuoso with the family name (Mn: *jamu;* Md: *kontongo*) Dounbouya (Doumbia), a student from the Kouyate lineage approached, greeted us, and asked my teacher for money to buy French bread at the corner stand.[14] Dounbouya symbolically searched his pockets and replied that he had nothing, at which point the student moved on. Mr. Dounbouya then explained to me that as a Kouyate, a pure jeli, the student had a right to solicit gifts from a Dounbouya. Though Dounbouya

13. One of the meanings of *son* (*so*) given by Delafosse (1955:674–76) is "to offer a sacrifice."
14. I am translating *jamu* (Md: *kontongo*) here as "family name" or "lineage." When meeting strangers, one asks for their jamu to situate them. By extension jamu also means to praise some-one. The simple act of saying someone's jamu (such as Kouyate or Diabate, for instance) is a typ-ical form of praise and is often heard as part of the greeting process.

himself was a practicing jeli—he taught the bala and frequently played at traditional events and on television—he was proud that his name had a nonjeli history. Indeed, one of his favorite pieces to play was *Fakoli,* a piece honoring Fakoli Doumbia, the nephew of Sumanguru Kante who joined ranks with Sunjata.

I also witnessed a hierarchy among nyamakalalu at the marriage ceremony of a son of my kora teacher in Bamako, when an endless array of people appeared soliciting money from my teacher, usually by praising and congratulating him. He took it all in stride, since he understood the pecking order very well. He was a jeli with the family name Diabate. When I later questioned him about this, he replied in part,

> A jali whose family name [*kontongo*] is Kouyate is a pure jali. For a Diabate, Suso, Kanoute, and Soumano, being a jali is not their heritage [*sii*]. It is just a profession [*métier*] for them. But a Kouyate jali, he can solicit gifts from all of us. Didn't you see the other day when jaliya was happening here, that I gave someone money? He is a Kouyate. . . . Kouyates can solicit gifts from jalis, from us, in the same way that we can solicit gifts from nobles [*foro*]. Yes, the *karanke* [leatherworker] and *fino* [public speaker] can also solicit us for gifts. The fino can solicit gifts from jalis, from Kouyates. The karanke also, they can solicit gifts from Kouyates and finos. (Question: A karanke can [ask] a fino?) Yes, they can solicit gifts from finos. Do you understand? The order goes like this. . . . A fino can solicit gifts from Kouyates and from all jalis, a karanke can solicit gifts from finos, a jali can solicit gifts from numus [blacksmiths]. (Sidiki Diabate 1990-per: 343–48)[15]

The idea of retaining one's hereditary status while practicing another profession is common, if confusing. After referring to members of his family who were illustrious musicians, ex-Ambassadeurs guitarist Manfila Kante wanted to make clear his own hereditary status.

> But something the journalists never get right is that we the Kantes are not "griots," we are blacksmiths; that's our hereditary profession. We're all descended from Sumanguru Kante. (Manfila Kante, in Durán 1991:21)

There is a widespread belief that the only pure Mande jeli jamu is Kouyate, originating with Sunjata's jeli Bala Faseke Kouyate. All other common jeli surnames, such as Diabate/Jobarteh, Sissoko/Suso, Kanoute/Konte,

15. "Jalo meng kontongo mu Kuyate ti, wo le mu jalo ti *pure*. Jebatewo Susowo Kanutewo Maraba Sumano, a sii te jali te. Metier le mu dorong. Bari jalo meng mu Kuyate ti, wo le ka ntolu bee daani. I m'a je wo lung meng ye jaliya ke jang fo nte y'a soo kodo la, Kuyate wo le mu. . . . Kuyate wo le ka jalol daani, ntol daani, n s'a fo ntol kara forol daani nyameng. Bon, karankewo fanang n kara, fino fanang ka ntolu daani. Fino wo ka jalol daani, a si Kuyatewo daani. Karankewo fanang, a si Kuyatewo, a si fino daani. [Question: Karanke si fino?] Haa, a si fino daani. I y'a moyi. A be nyo nooma teng ne. . . . Fino kara Kuyate daani, fino si jalo bee daani, karankewo si fino daani, jalo si numo daani." For a clip of Tata Bambo Kouyate praise singing for Sidiki Diabate and Serang Kanoute, see Kidel and Marks (1990-vid).

Doumbia, and Kante (the first three pairs reflect the French and English spellings, respectively, of the same name rendered in local Mandekan dialects), came about by their having entered the profession afterward. By indicating that he was just practicing a *métier* (profession), Sidiki Diabate may have been asserting his social rank in the same way that Mr. Dounbouya (above) had done. They still enjoyed all the rights and privileges of being a jeli, though perhaps not to the same degree as Kouyate jelis, while resting comfortably with the belief that their ancestors had a less tainted, noble social standing.[16]

Although the conventions of who may solicit gifts from whom may differ by region, there is general agreement that a fino (Mn: *fune;* public speaker) may solicit gifts from a jeli and that both of them may in turn solicit gifts from a numu (blacksmith) (S. Diabate 1990-per, Knight 1973a, 1:39; Hoffman 1990:152). In The Gambia, Knight (1973a, 1:39) places leatherworkers (Bm: *garanke;* Md: *karanke*) between jelis and blacksmiths; in Mali, Hoffman (1990:152) places leatherworkers below jelis, and Sidiki Diabate, a Gambian who spent most of his life in Mali, places leatherworkers below finos and jalis (see quotation above).

Perhaps the earliest documentation of a formal hierarchy among nyamakalalu comes from Sierra Leone in the early nineteenth century.

> There are four trades or professions, to which conjointly is given the appellation of Nyimahalah; they rank in the order in which they are enumerated, and consist of the fino, or orator; the jellee, or minstrel; the guarangee, or shoemaker; and the noomo, or blacksmith; all of whom are high in the scale of society, and are possessed of great privileges. (Laing 1825:132)

Other than the public act of soliciting gifts as members of different corporate social entities, the larger social significance of a relative hierarchy among nyamakalalu is unclear. This hierarchy may not be so important on the level of personal relationships.[17]

The relationship between a numu and a jeli was the subject of an extended narrative in *The Dark Child,* an autobiographical novel by Guinean writer Laye Camara (1954:31–41). A woman brought along a griot to Ca-

16. See Zobel (1996b) for a detailed discussion of the *jeli-horon* or "noble griot." Oumou Dioubate (1999-disc: *Mo ye banna*) has also eloquently sung of the jeli-horon.

17. See Frank (1995, 1998) for further information on the relative status of garankelu, and the related practice of jelis taking up the profession of leatherworking in outlying regions. Hoffman (in Frank 1995:146 n. 20) has cautioned against taking what nyamakala say about each other too literally, noting that they are framed in terms of general social categories, not with reference to particular families or individuals. B. Wright (1989:52) has made a similar point: "*Geer* [Wolof freeborn class] commonly describe *gewel* [Wolof griot class] in general as parasitic. . . . Such statements, however, are rarely if ever applied to specific individuals; furthermore, these statements are intended to describe *gewel* public behavior, not private."

mara's compound to help her persuade Camara's numu father to fashion a piece of gold jewelry for her on short notice. Camara (1954:32; 1953:25) writes that the griot would sell (Fr: *vendre*) his services to the woman, reflecting a cynical attitude toward the profession that is prevalent in modern urban areas.[18] But as the griot played his kora, praising the ancestors of Camara's father and touching his pride, he transcended his mercenary status.

> For the praise-singer [griot] took a curious part—I should say rather that it was direct and effective—in the work. He was drunk with the joy of creation. He shouted aloud in joy. He plucked his *cora* like a man inspired. He sweated as if he were the trinket-maker, as if he were my father, as if the trinket were his creation. He was no longer a hired censer-bearer [*thuriféraire:* "flatterer"], a man whose services anyone could rent. He was a man who created his song out of some deep inner necessity. (L. Camara 1954:38–39)

The griot played *Duga,* "the great chant which is sung only for celebrated men" (39), and Camara's father danced it. Profoundly affected, Camara's cynicism faded. The griot "found himself laden with gifts—almost his only means of support, for the praise-singer [griot] leads a wandering life after the fashion of the troubadours of old" (40).

It is not difficult to understand why jelis may be looked down on in modern Mande society. Although horonnu may enjoy a higher social status as the former warriors and present leaders of society, jelis may occasionally acquire substantial wealth through their work. This may cause resentment, particularly from horonnu who do not have wealth yet feel obliged by custom to give to a jeli at public events. Furthermore, jelis may be perceived as yes-men owing to their past and continued close association with the political leaders of their lands. For instance, the safety of a well-known Malian jelimuso and her home was threatened during the public uprising in January 1991 that led to the downfall of the dictatorial Traore regime and the subsequent democratic election of a new president. Her performance several weeks earlier at a march in which president Traore tried to garner support against the growing public resentment put her in the same league with other symbols of the state that were furiously attacked (Ba Konaré 1993:253).

Negative connotations wrapped up in the term "griot," reflecting local cynical views of the viability of the profession in modern times, have been part and parcel of public discourse, at least in Senegal. "What to do with them?" asked a journalist at the time of national independence (Ka 1959:32). "Do the griots themselves still want to remain griots according to the point of view of our century? That is to say, 'beggars,' 'parasites,' as

---

18. The English translation (L. Camara 1954:32) has the woman arranging a fee to pay the griot rather than the griot selling his services to her. It also replaces the word griot with "praise singer."

one is apt to call them at the present time?" (Ka 1959:32). Public perception had not changed after several decades of political independence. In a print scuffle in Senegal in 1989, editorial writers for the government newspaper defended themselves against charges from an opposition newspaper that they were not journalists, but rather media tools of the government. They had been accused of being "flunkeys," "mercenaries," and "griots" (Le Soleil 1989:5).[19]

European culture has had little effect on the traditional music performed by jelis on their indigenous instruments, but through the colonial encounter it has had a significant impact on the perception of jelis and the traditions they represent.

> The French set out to transform the structure of Mandenka society by blurring the traditional distinctions established between the *horonw* (nobles), the *jonw* (slaves or descendants of former slaves), and the *nyamakalaw*. [Footnote from the original: The French created the so-called freedom villages where the precolonial social distinctions were invalidated.] By dispossessing the *horonw* from the power they had exercised since the days of the empire and by placing the state apparatus beyond the reach of the masses, the colonialists planted the seed of disintegration and self-doubt, if not self-denial, in one of Africa's most elaborately structured and proudest societies. The radical changes which resulted from this encounter have forced the different components of Mandenka society to reassess the value of traditions several centuries old in the light of the new challenges of nation building and economic development. (C. Keita 1995b:182, 195)

This reassessment of the value and viability of certain traditions is a fundamental preoccupation of many modern African societies. In Mali in particular, the tradition of hereditary music makers has continued to maintain its relevance, albeit with adaptations to new challenges.

What Jelis Say about Their Origin

It is common for jelis and their counterparts among their neighbors to claim that they ultimately stem from Surakata, a companion of the prophet Mohammed. These claims have been well documented among Maninka jelis in Guinea and Mali, and to a lesser extent among Wolof gewels (griots) in

19. See Leymarie-Ortiz (1979) and Panzacchi (1994, 1996) for further discussion of Wolof griots in modern-day Senegal. C. Keita's (1995a:23) discussion of young Malian stars untrained in historical knowledge and unscrupulous in their praising of corrupt officials, and Mamadou Diawara's (1996, 1997) analysis of the transformation of the griot profession in Mali brought on by colonization and then electronic media may express feelings typical of many of their compatriots: "(1) Music takes precedence over the historical text; (2) the beauty of the voice takes precedence over sociological content; and (3) flattery and banal conversation take precedence over chronicle" (Mamadou Diawara (1997:44, 1996:604).

Senegal and Diawara (Soninke) griots in Mali.[20] I recorded a Surakata story from my bala teacher, Bala Dounbouya, but he also pointed out that the ancestor of jelis in particular, as opposed to the profession in general, is really Sunjata's father's jeli, Gnankoman Duwa (Jakuma Doka).[21] By that he was distinguishing the global (Islamic) tradition of praise singing from the local Mande one.

Renditions of the Sunjata epic often reach back to the time of Mohammed with the naming of the ancestors of Sunjata, but the first Mande jeli to be named (as opposed to an Islamic ancestor) is Gnankoman Duwa (Jakuma Doka in some other dialects). His son, Bala Faseke Kouyate, was Sunjata's jeli and is believed to be the founding ancestor of the Kouyate family. This is the source of the widespread belief that Kouyate is the only pure jeli family name, summed up in the well-known praise line *jeli ma kuyate bo* (no jeli can equal a Kouyate). The primacy of Kouyate jelis is played out in part in the rules of who may solicit gifts from whom: Kouyates have the right to solicit gifts from all other jelis.[22]

Kouyates are considered "pure" jelis in part because they did not split off from a horon or other nyamakala branch like the other jeli lineages. The best-known story of a jeli branch's splitting off from a horon lineage concerns Diabate jelis. For killing a great buffalo that was ravaging the countryside, two hunter brothers with the family name Traore (also called Tarawele) were rewarded with a woman whom they brought to Sunjata's father to be his bride. This woman, Sogolon Konde, would give birth to Sunjata. The older brother praised his younger brother's bravery in killing the buffalo, to which the younger replied, "Brother, if you were a jeli you could not be refused." The phrase "cannot be refused" in the Maninka language contracts into *diabate*. Diabate jelis trace their origins to the older brother and consequently to the Traore noble lineage.[23]

20. See Boyer (1953:117), Conrad (1985), Coolen (1979:48–50), and Zemp (1966). The earliest documentation of Surakata is in a biography of Mohammed written in the middle or late eighth century by Ibn Ishaq (1955; Zemp 1966:621–22), but this version does not contain references to Surakata's becoming a praise singer of Mohammed that are prominent in versions collected from griots.

21. Knight (1973a, 1:51) has made the same point.

22. As I noted in chapter 1, some sources have Gnankoman Duwa (Jakuma Doka) and Bala Faseke Kouyate as the same person. Bala Faseke Kouyate (or Gnankoman Duwa in versions where they are the same) is typically referred to as the Kouyate ancestor or patriarch (Kele Monson Diabate, in Moser 1974:279; Fa-Digi Sisoko, in Johnson 1986:150; Jeli Kanku Madi Jabate, in Ly-Tall, Camara, and Diouara 1987:203). The Kouyate matriarch is Tumu Maninyan (Fa-Digi Sisoko, in Johnson 1986:129; Kele Monson Diabate, in Moser 1974:266; Jeli Kanku Madi Jabate, in Ly-Tall, Camara, and Diouara 1987:52–55). Jeli Kanku Madi Jabate (in Ly-Tall, Camara, and Diouara 1987:26) also refers to a Jeli Dora, who was a jeli of the king of Do, the land of Sunjata's mother.

23. Many versions of this well-known story have been published. See, for example, Wa Kamissoko (in Cissé and Kamissoko 1988:62–67, 86–89), Fa-Digi Sisoko (in Johnson 1986:108–28)

There appears to be, then, a two-tiered ancestry among jelis: that of their profession in general, which is projected back to the time of Mohammed, and that of jelis in particular, which goes back to the time of Sunjata. The early tier establishes the prestigious link with Islam, and the later tier establishes the tie to the *jamana,* the homeland. In the syncretic societies of the western sahel and savanna, this presents no problem. One of Zemp's (1966:624) informants neatly telescoped these two tiers in saying that Gnankoman Duwa was Surakata's son, establishing the two links and making no attempt to fill in the gap of almost six centuries.[24] Tiers of ancestry can stack up further, with some jelis referring back many generations to the ancestor of their particular family branch, and there may also be recent ancestors who have distinguished themselves, such as the first ancestor to leave one region to establish himself in another. For instance, the Diabate lineage ultimately stems from Dan Mansa Wulanba (Wulantamba), the older of the Traore hunter brothers. Dan Mansa's descendant Kala Jula Sangoyi, believed by some to be a companion of Sunjata, is the next major ancestor of the Diabate lineage. The names of Kala Jula Sangoyi and his three sons Tuba Kate, Monson Kate, and Fatiya Kate are commonly used in praise songs for Diabates.[25]

Although further research among non-Maninka griots is needed, it appears that most griots endorse the idea of a common origin for the profession of praise singing. This might even be a diagnostic indicator of being a griot: if you claim descent from Surakata, then you are a griot. The details

---

and his son Magan Sisoko (in Johnson et al. 1979:39–65), L. Camara (1980:34–64), Lansine Diabate (in Jansen, Duintjer, and Tamboura 1995:62–82), and Niane (1965:4–9). For an early published version with a Wolof twist see Diagne and Télémaque (1916:276–78). See Conrad (1995:105, 125 n. 96) for references to other versions of the story. The National Ballet of Mali treated delegates to the Second International Conference of the Mande Studies Association held in Bamako in 1993 to an extended dramatic presentation of this episode. Les Ballets Africains, one of the national ballets of Guinea, has included this episode in its presentation of Sunjata, and a dramatic version can be seen in the film *Keita: The Heritage of the Griot* (D. Kouyate 1995-vid). The politics of older and younger brother relationships among the Mande are explored in Jansen and Zobel (1996).

24. For further discussion on the link between jelis and Surakata see Conrad (1985). Hunter's musicians, who have resisted the impact of Islam, make no comparable attempt to establish an Islamic ancestry. See Moraes Farias (1989) for a discussion of Mande history and Islam, particularly with regard to Kòmò society origin stories.

25. For written references to Kala Jula Sangoyi and his three sons see Kele Monson Diabate (in Moser 1974:205), M. Diabate (1970b), Fa Digi Sissoko (in Johnson 1986:121, 183, 203, 225), Lansine Diabate (in Jansen, Duintjer, and Tamboura 1995:150–55; Jansen 1996:672), Jeli Kanku Madi Jabate (in Ly-Tall, Camara, and Diouara 1987:63), Sine Diabate (in Jansen 1991:51), and Sanugwe Kouyate (in Jansen 1991:61). Sung references are widespread; for examples see Bajourou (1993-disc: *Hakilima, Jodoo*), Aboubacar Camara (199?-disc: *Baba Moussa*), Diaba Koita (199?-disc: *Seben djara seben*), and Mariam Kouyate, Diabate, and Diabate (1995a-disc: *Mamadou djon kounda*). Massa Makan Diabate (in Ministry of Information of Mali 1971-disc: vol. 1) writes that Kalajan Sangoyi Tubaka was the composer of the piece *Suba ni mansaya.*

of how the belief in a descent from Surakata spread in West Africa, or how his descendants got to West Africa (accepting the belief at face value), may be obscure and controversial, but it raises an intriguing possibility.[26] If a single figure is believed to be in some way the origin of West African griots, then a single term may be the root for the local variants of the terms for griot in West Africa. This is not to suggest that the professional activities of the griot are anything other than West African in nature. Muslim travelers, merchants, or scholars coming from the east, or West Africans who made the pilgrimage to Mecca and returned home, may have attached an Arabic name to a tradition that existed in West Africa, which then was picked up and diffused by the indigenous West African population.

Origin of the Word Griot

It was not until the fourteenth century when Ibn Baṭṭūta visited the seat of the Mali empire that someone resembling the modern-day jeli was first portrayed in print. For the next several centuries these musicians, singers, and orators were described in detail in Arabic, Portuguese, French, and English sources. They were known under a variety of names, and in the seventeenth century they were called *guiriot* by the French, who were, it seems evident now, writing down one or another of the local terms used by West Africans. By the late eighteenth century the spelling became standardized to "griot," which has since gained wide currency in francophone countries.[27]

Table 6 shows many of the written forms referring to griots from the fourteenth to the early nineteenth century (see appendix A for all references). They are terms used by several West African peoples that have been filtered through Arabic and European sound and writing systems. The language columns demonstrate that the French alone were responsible for the written introduction and acceptance of the term griot. Accounts in other languages used local African terms that in slightly different forms are still in use today: *jālī, gaul, guissiridonke, juddy,* and *jelli kea.*[28]

26. The controversial aspect of attributing a nonindigenous origin to a West African term or institution stems from outmoded theories that ascribed cultural advances in West Africa to supposedly civilizing forces from either North Africa or the Middle East. For a detailed refutation of the "Hamitic hypothesis" in relation to the origins of the ancient Ghana empire see Munson (1971: 149–54, 1980:458–59). See MacGaffey (1991), for a review of writings by Cheik Anta Diop and others that addresses this issue and related ones.

27. V. Monteil (1968) and Conrad (1981:8–19, 1990:4) have both provided concise surveys of many of the primary sources for early European writings on griots, and the following discussion of the term griot (but not of any of the other local variants) is in essential agreement with their conclusions with minor modifications and significant additions of sources. Also see Mauny (1952:40). For a recent broad-based study of griots see Hale (1998).

28. Gray and Dochard (1825:59, 112, 282, 284) used three different terms: *Jallikea* for the Mandinka; *Goulahs,* which probably refers to Fulbe *gaulos*; and *griot,* treated as a synonym of "bard." Winterbottom ([1803] 1969, 1:108) also makes a comparison to bards: "Among the Foolas

Table 6 Written Forms Referring to Griots from the Fourteenth to the Early Nineteenth Century

Date	Author	Arabic	Portuguese	English	French
1355	Ibn Battūta	julā, jālī			
1506–10	Fernandes		Gaul, gaul, judeus, judeo, judia		
1594	Almada		Judeu(s)		
1623	Jobson			Juddies, Juddy(es)	
1637	Saint-Lô				Guiriot(s)
1669	Coelho		Judeos		
1685	Courbe				guiriots, guiriote, guiriotte, griot
1695	Le Maire				*Guiriotz,* Guiriot(s), Guériotz
17th c.	Kati	guissiridunke			
1732	Barbot				*Guiriot(s)*
1740	Moore			Jelly kea, Jelly moosa	
1789	Lamiral				Griot(s), Griottes
1799	Park			*Jilly kea*	
1802	Golberry				griot(es)
1802	Durand				*guiriots, griottes*
1820	Mollien				griots
1825	Gray and Dochard			*Jallikea(s),* Goulahs, griot(s)	
1825	Laing			*jellē,* jellé, Jelle(s), *Jelle,* JELLEMAN, JELLEMEN, Jelle(-)men, griot	

Note: See appendix A and bibliography for complete citations. For the European sources, italics and capitals appear as in the source cited. Parentheses within a word indicate that it appeared both with and without the added letter or letters.

Seventeenth-century French voyagers most likely believed they were writing down a term from a local language that was subsequently assimilated into their own written language by adding French plural and feminine forms. The descriptions "instrumentalists called Guiriots, held in disgrace by this nation" (Saint-Lô 1637:87) or "they have people called *Guiriots* whose only occupation is to praise people" (Le Maire 1695:120) indicate that the term would not have been familiar to seventeenth-century French

---

there is a set of people called singing men, who, like the ancient bards . . . " He also noted similar people, called *kárramukko* (master, teacher), among the Bullom people in Sierra Leone.

readers. At least two French descriptions of *guiriots,* written within a century and a quarter of the first appearance of the word, are explicit about its being an indigenous African term. Barbot began a three-quarter-page description of the role and status of *guiriots* as follows. "The name of *Guiriot,* in their tongue, properly signifies a buffoon, and they are a sort of sycophants" (Barbot 1746:55). Adanson's footnote to his usage of the term *guiriots* clearly reflects an early French belief in an indigenous African origin of the term. "This is the name that the negroes give to the musicians and drummers of the country" (Adanson 1757:33). What may be the earliest documentation of European recognition of different African terms for the musical-verbal artisans under consideration here is from Astley, who edited a mid-eighteenth-century collection of reports by voyagers to Africa. It is also one of the most conclusive pieces of evidence for the origin of term griot.[29]

> Those who play on the Instruments are Persons of a very singular Character, and seem to be their Poets as well as Musicians, not unlike the Bards among the *Irish* and the ancient *Britons.* All the *French* Authors, who describe the Countries of the *Jalofs* and *Fûlis,* call them *Guiriots;* but *Jobson* gives them the Name of *Juddies,* which he interprets *Fidlers.* Perhaps the former is the *Jalof* and *Fûli* Name; the latter, the *Mandingo.* (Astley [1745–47] 1968, 2:278)

The French could have picked up a local term from any of the three languages spoken on either side of the Senegal River, since the terms for griot in this region are remarkably similar to each other: *iggio* (*iggiw*), *gewel,* and *gaulo* (*gawlo*) in the Hassaniya (Moor), Wolof, and Fulbe languages, respectively.[30] More significant than choosing which word was the source

29. Barbot initially wrote a French manuscript (dating from 1688 and still unpublished) and then an expanded English translation, which he worked on until his death in 1712 (it was published in 1732). The editors of the new Barbot edition (1992:128, 138 n. 19) omitted the quotation cited above and the section following it explaining that it was borrowed from Dapper and Le Maire. Astley's passage was reprinted in French a century later in C. A. Walckenaer's monumental collection (1842, 4:193).

30. Norris (1968:53) has suggested this connection: "*Iggīw* is a word borrowed from communities across the river. It is *gêwel* in Wolof and *gawlo* in Toucouleur [a Fulbe dialect]." Suggestions for the sources of the word griot include: "Our French griot then would come directly from iggio, with an r 'flap'—as the old form guiriot shows" (V. Monteil 1968:778); "The name Griot, which we have frenchified, belongs to the Wolof language; in the plural it becomes Guéroual or Guéwoual in the idioms of Cayor and Oualo [in northern Senegal]" (Bérenger-Féraud 1882:266); and the Portuguese word *criado* (Labouret 1959). Bird (1971:16–17) has suggested that *jeli* may have been pronounced "gerio" in the past, but the terms used by Ibn Battūta (1355), Jobson (1623), and Park (1799) do not support this; also see Conrad (1981:8–9) for further criticism of this theory. It appears that several centuries ago the French used *gui* or *gu* to convey *j,* as the following French (from Avezac 1845) and present-day Mandinka pairs show: *guion/jon* (slave); *guelou/jelu* (how many?); *guinné/jinn* (genie); *guoulou/julu* (rope); *guy/ji* (water); *guan/jan* (long). On the other hand, perhaps Mandinka pronunciation changed from *g* or *gy* to *j* over the centuries.

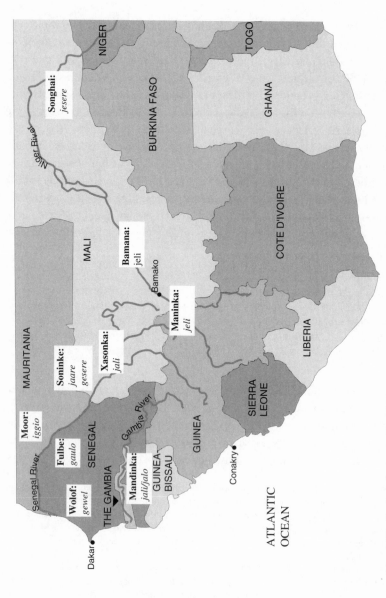

Map 4 Distribution of griots in West Africa.

for griot is recognizing that these local terms appear to be linguistically related even though some of the languages in which they are used are not.[31] If the various local terms used to refer to griots spring from a common source, then it would likely be the ancient Ghana empire (map 4). The scenario proposed here is that griots have roots in the Ghana empire, were diffused to other local kingdoms, whose fortunes in turn waxed and waned over the centuries, and flourished and developed in their own environments. This local development included the specialization on certain instruments and the local names by which they are known today. During this whole process they were in constant contact with their neighbors, sharing much of their musical repertory, which in turn was part of a larger western savanna-sahel musical universe extending from the Wolof at the Atlantic coast eastward to the Songhai of Mali and Niger. Not only would griots share the same name, but they all would also play a similar kind of lute (see below).[32]

I reserve the term griot exclusively for western African hereditary professional musical-verbal artisans whose calling in life is fundamental to the ethnic identity of their people. This definition limits their distribution to only a few societies, albeit highly influential ones, shown in map 4. Although music makers can be found in all West African societies, the peoples shown in map 4 are distinctive in that the institution of the griot is an old and integral, even defining, part of their culture.[33]

It is no coincidence that all the groups shown in map 4 inhabit a well-defined area of the western African sahel and savanna. All these societies had come into close contact with ancient Ghana, had early contact with Islam, and were nation (or at least confederation) builders. They also all distinguish between freeborn (noble), artisan born, and slave. Griots, by definition, come from the artisan-born group. Even though all of the core groups

31. Bird (1972:292) proposed that the "same word for the casted bard is reconstructible in all these areas" that were in contact with the ancient Ghana empire, but unfortunately he did not show how.

32. The Hausa, located farther east in northern Nigeria, probably have some cultural relationships with the groups under discussion here, owing in part to the long-distance traders known as Wangara, but their history is not closely tied in with that of ancient Ghana, and they will remain outside the scope of this book because of their geographic distance.

33. "Musical-verbal artisans" is an awkward phrase, but it encompasses succinctly the activities of griots. More than fifteen ethnic groups in West Africa have been identified by Tamari (1991, 1997) as having "castes" and griots, but many of these groups have borrowed the institution in recent times or absorbed griots from their neighbors. Tamari (1991:241–47) points out the foreign origins of griots in several societies, but my arguments here offer a somewhat different historical perspective. Tamari, along with many other historians, uses "bard" rather than griot. I prefer not to use "caste," even given Tamari's (1991:221–23) working definition of "endogamous ranked specialist group," because its connotations in English, perhaps broader than French usage, do not adequately convey the peculiarly African nature of social differentiation.

in map 4 have much in common and live close to each other, some of their languages are mutually unintelligible. For example, Fulbe and Wolof are Atlantic languages; Maninka and Soninke are Mande languages.[34]

Although the term griot can be useful as it points to a deep unity of Upper and Middle Niger and Senegal river valley savanna-sahel culture, its usage may also encourage glossing over cultural distinctions that strike to the very core of identity in Africa. These distinctions may not be important for many Western writers, who may be unaware of them—no doubt the indiscriminate use of griot by French voyagers was due to their lack of familiarity with local culture—and even for much of francophone West Africa, but in the lives of the artisans themselves they are crucial. Each ethnic group has its own language or dialect, history, heroes, and ways of singing and dancing, and these are all sources of identity and pride. Griots are cultural and historical curators as well as creative artists for their own people (though they may also be expert in neighboring traditions). For example, when one elderly Mandinka jali was discussing the piece *Taara*, a classic known in much of West Africa that is the vehicle for recounting the life of the Fulbe jihad leader al Hajj Umar Tal, his Mande pride was evident. "The first jali that Alhaji Umar had—I did not say *gaulo*, I did not say *maabo*, I did not say *sakewo*, but *jali*—he was Jali Musa Diabate" (Sidiki Diabate 1990-per: 79–80).[35] The word griot erases these significant local cultural distinctions.

There is no term in any of the local languages that can refer to hereditary professional musical-verbal artisans generically without specifying the ethnic group they belong to. In other words, jeli refers to the Maninka kind and gewel to the Wolof kind. The term griot has fulfilled that function and is commonly used as a cover term for any West African hereditary professional musical-verbal artisan regardless of ethnic origin, although Africans consider it a foreign term.[36] By extension, the term griot has also been used to refer to any kind of West African musician, regardless of hereditary social status, and the term griotism has been used to describe the soliciting of

34. See the introduction and Bendor-Samuel (1989) for a comprehensive overview of classification systems of West African languages. In the following discussion Bamana, Mandinka, Maninka, and Xasonka will be covered by the term "Mande," since they all refer to their griots as jelis or jalis.

35. "Alaji Umaru ye jali folo folo ming soto, n ma fo gawlo, n ma fo maabo, n ma fo sakewo, bari jalo, wo le mu Jali Musa Jebate ti." In this instance *maabo* and *sakewo* refer to certain kinds of Fulbe musicians. See below for more on Jali Musa Diabate.

36. I heard the word griot in West Africa only in the course of French or English conversation. When conversing in local languages I heard only the local terms. When conversing in English in The Gambia I sometimes heard "griot" pronounced phonetically (gree-aht) as if the speaker had read a foreign term and given it an English pronunciation.

money or favors through praise. Both terms can have derogatory connotations in modern usage. Griot is neither a French nor a West African term, yet at the same time it is both.

A New Etymology for the Local West African Terms for Griot

Sometime before Ibn Battūta's fourteenth-century visit to Mali, the Arabic term *qawal* (word, speak, sound) may have been attached to the musicians and orators attending the nobility of ancient Mali, or perhaps ancient Ghana. As new states rose and fell, the institution of the court musician spread, and the term would have been assimilated into local languages. The names now used in West Africa could all represent vestiges of *qawal:* Wolof *gewel,* Fulbe *gaulo,* Moorish *iggio,* Mandenka *jeli* or *jali,* and Soninke *jaare.* Ironically, the indiscriminate use of "griot" by the French, without regard to important local cultural distinctions, had the effect of unifying the institution under a single term after perhaps a millennium of multiple local linguistic forms, which in turn may have stemmed from a single form. Figure 3 summarizes this hypothetical historical process.[37]

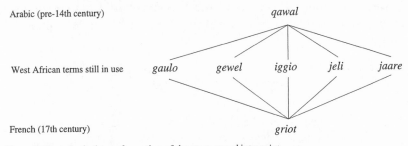

Figure 3 Hypothetical transformation of the term *qawal* into *griot.*

37. My hypothesis that the term *qawal* is the source of the local West African terms has not been embraced by editors and referees of two mainstream African history journals, and I have benefited from their comments. But I remain convinced that once the musicological evidence is understood, my conclusion is immediately apparent and opens up a significant and hitherto unexplored speculative path. Such musicological evidence includes the way *qawal* is used elsewhere in the Muslim world and the tight and controlled distribution of griot lutes only among those societies in which griots are significant presences (see below and Charry 1996b). Whether future arguments weaken or strengthen my hypothesis, African musicology and African historiography cannot afford to ignore each other, especially in a region where music and history are so intertwined that historians are also musicians.

The formulation in table 7 (p. 114) implies that the term *qawal* was assimilated directly by each of the groups listed, which is just one possibility among many. Untangling the various plausible paths of diffusion, lines of sound change, and reasons for adopting the term, and privileging one path over another, will take the joint efforts of specialists in several disciplines—notably early Islamic and African history and linguistics—to work through the details that as a nonspecialist in those areas I have had the luxury of neglecting.

The appearance of the word *jali* (*jālī*) in Ibn Battūta's account of his visit to the seat of the Mali empire in the mid-fourteenth century is the first time a West African term for a musician or poet has been documented. He used the term in reference to what he described as poets (*shu'arā'*; Ibn Battūta [1355] 1858:413), not the musicians he had seen. The words *jālī* and *julā* were used for the singular and plural, respectively. As was common practice for treating foreign terms in Arabic treatises of the time, Ibn Battūta specified the vowels to be used in pronouncing these words and so provided a clear idea of how he heard them. Within a few centuries other local terms appeared in writing: *gaul*, a reference to a Fulbe or Wolof griot, and *guissiridonké*, a probable reference to *gesere*, a griot of Soninke origins.[38]

Several etymologies of the words *jeli*, *gesere*, and *gewel* have been proposed and critiqued.[39] If the local variants (shown in map 4 and fig. 3) do indeed spring from a single source, however, the problem of reconciling the widely divergent etymologies given for each of the local terms is dramatically recast. The phonetic and semantic similarity between the words *gewel* (Wolof) and *gaulo* (Fulbe) on the one hand and *qawal* (Arabic) on the other suggests a striking etymology.[40]

The Arabic root *q-w-l* concerns speech. Some of the definitions of *q-w-l* given in dictionaries of medieval Arabic are virtual job descriptions of griots:

> He spoke in verse . . . poeticized . . . good in speech . . . loquacious . . . copious in speech . . . eloquent . . . the man who talks much. (Lane 1956, suppl., 2995)

> Man of the spoken word . . . singer . . . traveling poet . . . improviser . . . to recite verse that one has composed oneself. (Dozy 1967, 2:420–21)

---

38. The terms *gesere* and *jaare*, both referring to Soninke griots, are cause for confusion. *Gesere* may come from Gassire, the name of the local ancestor of Soninke griots who played a lute (see Conrad 1981:11). It may be that *jaare* is the Soninke equivalent of the Maninka *jeli*, a survival of a common source for the variant terms denoting musical-verbal artisans, and *gesere* is the name given to those griots who play the gambare, a lute similar to the Mande koni. The story "Gassire's Lute" can be found in Frobenius (1921:53–60) or Frobenius and Fox ([1937] 1966:97–110). For further references see Boyer (1953:72–73), Mamadou Diawara (1990:40, 108, 1995), Dieterlen and Sylla (1992:93–98), and Frobenius (1921:37).

39. See, for example, C. Monteil ([1924] 1977:24), Zahan (1963:125), Zemp (1966:630–32), V. Monteil (1968:783), and Bird (1971:17).

40. I thank my dissertation adviser Harold Powers for this fundamental observation. His extensive knowledge of music in the Muslim world undoubtedly allowed him to recognize the possible connection between the terms. Although I cannot take credit for spotting this initial connection, I take full responsibility for answering to criticisms of this hypothesis. I further thank Cheick Keita for pointing out to me that the Senegalese writer Birago Diop (1947:vii, 1966:xviii–xix) made this connection half a century earlier (see below).

Derivatives of the root *q-w-l* are frequently used in the Koran, mostly with the meaning "to say," but also "speech," "one who says, who speaks," and even "to invent, to fabricate [speech]." One usage has been cited as possibly supporting the use of music in Islam.

> In verses XXXIX, 17–18 the lines "So give good tidings to my servants who listen to *al-qawl* (the spoken word) and follow the fairest of it" are interpreted as referring to singing; incidentally, *al-qawl* is still used in folk music to designate singing of folk poetry. (Shiloah 1995:32)

The appearance of the root *q-w-l* in the Old Testament, with meanings related to speech and sound, particularly of the human voice and even of a ram's horn, indicates that it comes from Semitic rather than West African languages.[41]

Ibn Battūta's description of the people he called *julā* (sing. *jālī*) is relevant here (appendix A). The verbal aspect of the performance of the "poets called *julā*" conforms well with the usages of *qawal* given above. But several questions are raised. The bird-mask costume of the poets he referred to as *julā* is not a part of present-day jeli dress, although it may have been in the past. Dugha, whose performance on the bala and song of praise to the sultan fits contemporary jeli activity, was referred to as an interpreter (*turjuman*) and not a jeli. His role as interpreter may have been significant enough to Ibn Battūta to overshadow his role as jeli. Or jelis at that time may not have been associated with instrumental music. Perhaps the word *qawal* referred only to the verbal aspects of what griots did and it was local West African custom that expanded the term to include playing musical instruments. Indeed, "itinerant singer and musician" is one definition of *qawwāl* given in a dictionary of modern Arabic that is not present in dictionaries of medieval Arabic (Wehr 1976:797).[42]

Qawal therefore could have encompassed verbal-poetic performances that Arabic-speaking visitors to ancient Ghana (or Mali) may have seen at court ceremonies but that did not fit their conception of an interpreter. Alternatively, West African pilgrims to Mecca may have brought back the term. The local inhabitants might have taken up and Africanized the word, which then spread to neighboring areas.

The use of *qawal* to refer to musicians is by no means novel in the Mus-

41. See Kassis (1983:936–46) for occurrences of *q-w-l* in the Koran and Gesenius (1952:876–77) for appearances of the same root in the Old Testament. For other early references to the term *qawal* in a musical context see al-Faruqi (1981:261–63).

42. Genealogical research among the Kouyate family in Niagassola, Guinea, suggests that the bala player Ibn Battūta called Dūghā was a direct descendant of Bala Faseke Kouyate, Sunjata's jeli. This is taken up further in the section on the bala below.

Table 7 *Qawal:* hypothetical sound changes in West African languages

languages ⇒	Maninka	Soninke	Wolof	Fulbe	Hassaniya
transformations	*qawal*	*qawal*	*qawal*	*qawal*	*qawal*
⇓	*jawal*	*jawal*	*gawal*	*gawal*	*igawal*
⇓	*ja al*	*ja al*	***gewel***	*gaw l*	*igiw l*
	jaali	*jaale*		***gawlo***	***igiw***
	(*jali*)	***jaare***		(*gaulo*)	(*iggio*)

lim world. In Pakistan and northern India *qawwali* is a major musical genre associated with Sufism that is performed by professional musicians, known as *qawwals*, who are organized into endogamous patrilineal communities (Qureshi 1986:xiii, 96–98). Perhaps the first writer to link the Muslim *qawwal* to a local West African term (*gewel*) was Birago Diop, who defined griot as follows.

> *Griot:* Term from the colonial French-African vocabulary = *Diali* in the Soudan, *Guéwél* in Senegal (from the Arab Qawwal, a narrator of the Sufi sect). (B. Diop 1947:vii)

Islam, firmly entrenched in the western Sudan by the time of al-Bakrī's eleventh-century account (appendix A), introduced a variety of religious and nonreligious Arabic terms. Hiskett (1965:18–26) has discussed this process among the Hausa, and Hause (1948) and Blench (1984) have suggested possible Arab origins of some West African musical instruments or at least of their names. Evidence from an early vocabulary (Avezac 1845: 242) suggests that at least by the late seventeenth century Arabic words such as *duniya* (world) were common in Mandinka.[43]

Table 7 shows the sound changes *qawal* may have gone through to become the local variants in use today. The method shown assumes that all the local variants were derived from *qawal,* whereas some might have been derived from each other, but table 7 at least illustrates one possibility. The root may also have taken other forms, such as *qāli,* in which case slightly different transformational rules would apply in order to derive all the forms. Each of the particular sound changes that lead to the Maninka word *jeli* operate in Mande languages, but under slightly different conditions.[44]

43. Hair (1966:211) dates the vocabularies in Avezac (1845) to the late seventeenth century.

44. For example, there are Mandekan dialects where velars palatize (*k* > *c* or *g* > *j*) and medial consonants change or disappear (e.g., *sigi* > *sii*) (Bird 1982:22–23, 31). It is also common to add a vowel to foreign words that end in consonants. If the term *qawal* was originally recognized as an Arabic accretion onto a West African institution, then the term could have undergone the kind of local phonetic processes responsible for the forms known today much more readily than could Arabic religious terminology, which would retain its classical pronunciation, particularly since

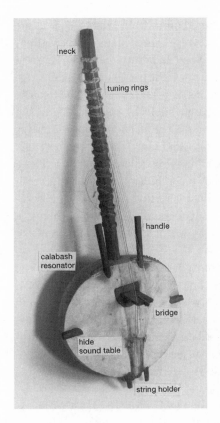

Plate 9 Kora. Instrument made by Alieu Suso, Bakau (The Gambia), 1989. Photo by Wendy Hood.

Jeli Instruments

Kora

The kora, a harp with a large calabash body and twenty-one strings, is played by Mandinka jalis and other Mande jelis who would have directly or indirectly picked it up from a Mandinka jali (plate 9). Although the kora is now found in many corners of West Africa, according to oral traditions it originated with the Senegambian Mandinka of the Kabu (Gabu) empire, which encompassed parts of present-day Guinea Bissau, southern Senegal, and The Gambia, with its seat in Kansala (in Guinea-Bissau). With a few exceptions, those who are not jalis do not play the kora.[45]

---

many West African Muslims are literate in classical Arabic. The linguistic path from *qawal* to *jali* or *jaare* is clearly the most speculative and demands further inquiry.

45. For a comprehensive listing of postal stamps issued by West African countries showing stringed instruments such as the harps discussed in chapter 2 and a variety of harps and lutes discussed in this chapter, see Eisenberg (1997). I thank Mark Schumacher for bringing this article to my attention.

The earliest known reference to a kora comes from Mungo Park at the end of the eighteenth century, but it is unclear where in his extensive travels up the Gambia River across land to Segu and down the Niger River he encountered the instrument (see appendix A). The earliest known drawings of calabash harps, perhaps early versions of a kora or the related soron, were published shortly afterward in separate books by Laing (1825, facing 148, 369), who referred to "Jelle-men" in the region known as Soolima (or Soolimana) in northeastern Sierra Leone, and Gray and Dochard (1825, facing 301), who traveled up the Gambia River (plates 7 and 8). These two harp illustrations show elements of modern-day koras (a bridge with what seem to be notches, a pad it sits on, many strings, and a metal buzzing leaf inserted into the top of the bridge) and also of hunter's harps (a slightly bowed neck and a metal buzzing leaf inserted into the top of the neck).[46]

In the middle to late nineteenth century koras began to be listed in the catalogs of museums outside Africa. The earliest listing might be of a thirteen-stringed instrument inexplicably labeled *kasso* in a catalog of the British South Kensington Museum (Engel 1874:308). The neck is bent like that of a simbi, and the strings are described as "the tough fibres of a creeping plant." A kora at the Metropolitan Museum of Art in New York (Metropolitan Museum of Art, n.d., 1889.498) acquired in 1889, has twenty-one strings made of finely twisted hide, and the one shown in the catalog of the Royal Conservatory of Music of Brussels (Mahillon 1893:420–21), labeled *kasso,* also has twenty-one strings. An early and extraordinarily clear photograph of a kora, possibly dating from the first decade of the twentieth century, shows the instrument with twenty-one strings and the metal buzzing leaf attached to the bridge (Kubik 1989:184–85).[47]

The kora does not seem to have traveled to any significant degree outside its indigenous area in Kabu before the twentieth century, but the closely related soron may have been used in Upper Guinea for at least a century. A postcard photograph of an "orchestra of a chief of Kissi country," at the southern range of Maninka influence, shows what appears to be a soron with sixteen strings (plate 10). Joyeux (1924) reported extensively on instruments in the Kankan and Kouroussa regions in northeastern Guinea but

46. See chapter 2 for structural distinctions among harps in West Africa and Charry (1994b) for further details and references. For documentation of the construction of a kora see King (1972), Pevar (1978), and Knight (1992-vid), which shows one being made, from the felling of a tree to the finished product.

47. Other early references include Tellier (1898:179), who described what he called a kora in Kita, Mali, as a guitar with two or three strings that is fretted with the finger, and a photograph in Reeve ([1912] 1969, facing 198) that does not have much detail.

COLONIES FRANÇAISES

HAUTE GUINÉE   17/2/06   Orchestre d'un chef du pays de Kissi

Plate 10 An early twentieth-century ensemble from Kissi (southeastern Guinea). "Orchestre d'un chef du pays de Kissi." Instruments include (left to right): tama, two jembes, a lute (Maninka koni or Fulbe hoddu), a soron or kora, a flute (Fulbe *serdu*), and a tama. Handwritten date indicates the postcard photo is from 1906 or earlier. From Guenneguez and Guenneguez (1998:39).

did not mention the kora, although he did photograph and describe the soron. Sidiki Diabate and Batrou Sekou Kouyate, two highly respected kora players living outside the indigenous kora region, may have been among the first or possibly second generation of kora players to flourish in Mali (plate 11). Sidiki Diabate's grandfather Jali Fili played the koni and migrated from Mali to The Gambia. Jali Fili's son Bala then took up the kora because he recognized its importance in The Gambia. Bala's son Sidiki was born in Tubanding and raised in Bansang (both in eastern Gambia), where he learned from his uncle Alhasan (Keeba). Sidi Diabate moved to Mali in his late teens during World War II, taking the kora with him, was based in Côte d'Ivoire from about 1948 to 1958, and lived the rest of his life in Bamako, where he was a founding member of the National Instrumental Ensemble of Mali about 1962 (S. Diabate 1990-per). Batrou Sekou Kouyate (1990-per: 171–216), from Kita in Mali, first saw the kora in the hands of Alieu Kouyate from The Gambia, who passed through Kita probably some-

Plate 11 The Malian old guard of kora players. Left to right: Nfa Diabate, Batrou Sekou Kouyate, Jalimady Sissoko, Sidiki Diabate. Photo courtesy of Batrou Sekou Kouyate.

time in the 1930s. The Dakar-Bamako railway, which ran through Tamba-counda, Senegal, close to the easternmost part of The Gambia, made it easier to travel between The Gambia and Mali. One of the earliest published recordings of the kora, if not the first, was made by Laura Boulton (1957-disc) in the early 1930s. The two kora pieces, *Kelefaba* and *Amadou Masina,* are still played the same way today.[48]

Nylon fishing line is universally used for kora strings because it is resistant to changes in the weather, does not break easily, and yields a good sound. Formerly the strings were made from thin strips of finely twisted hide of an antelope (Md: *minango*), a skin that Mandinka drummers prefer to use for the head of their *sabaro* (the long lead drum in an ensemble). The use of nylon strings may date from the early 1950s.[49]

Oral Traditions on the Origin of the Kora

Oral traditions agree on general points about the history of the kora but diverge according to the family and the geographic origin of the jali speak-

48. The titles are not specified, but they are readily recognized. Boulton was probably mistaken in stating that the unidentified kora player was Bambara—the pieces he played are staples of the Gambian repertory, and the kora has not often been associated with Bambara. Djimo Kouyate (personal communication 1997), from Tambacounda, Senegal, believes the kora playing is that of Dembo Sissokho from nearby Boraba, Senegal, who was a teacher of Kouyate's elder brother, the late Mamadou Kouyate. Although Kouyate had never met Sissokho, he recognizes the style of playing via his brother Mamadou.

49. Sidiki Diabate (1990-per:101–7) credits Burama Soumano with being among the first to use nylon fishing line on his kora in the early 1950s. Nylon line was evidently already being used on the koni at the time.

ing. Ultimately, my inquiries into the origin of the kora led to *jinns* (Arabic for "genies"), a common explanation in West Africa, and indeed my inquiries into all Mande instruments inevitably led to jinns.[50] With the available evidence it is reasonable to date the origin of the kora, the most modern calabash harp in West Africa, to the late eighteenth century, although there may have been transitional instruments of the kind shown in Gray and Dochard and in Laing.

Stories of the origin of the kora center on Jali Madi Wuleng, who is widely believed to have first discovered (Md: *bondi,* "caused it to come out") the kora with the aid of a jinn during the era of the Kabu empire.[51] The question of when Jali Madi Wuleng lived is linked with that of when a warrior named Kelefa Sane lived and is a subject of controversy among jalis. Kelefa's brave exploits have been canonized in *Kuruntu Kelefa* (Following Kelefa), associated with his lifetime, and *Kelefaba* (Great Kelefa), associated with his death. These two pieces are believed to be the earliest ones composed on the kora, associated with its very origins, and I have often heard them referred to as the ABC of the kora. Simplified versions of the pieces are the first items that beginning kora players from The Gambia and Casamance learn, and many pieces derived from them have entered the kora repertory. No other kora pieces are believed to predate them, nor is the kora associated with the repertories of thirteenth-century Mali or eighteenth-century Segu or Kaarta.

Some believe Jali Madi Wuleng was Kelefa Sane's jali and presumably the composer of *Kuruntu Kelefa* (e.g., Bamba Suso, Amadu Bansang Jobarteh, and Knight, in Jali Nyama Suso 1996-disc:19). The era they lived in can vary widely according to who is speaking. The late Sidiki Diabate, a Gambian who spent most of his life in Mali, relates that his own ancestor Tilimakan Diabate, from the Tomora region in Mali and a contemporary of Sunjata (thirteenth century), learned the kora from Jali Madi Wuleng and was the first to bring it from Kabu to Mali.[52] Mbady Kouyate, an elderly

50. Zemp (1971:93–168) has documented stories on the origin of musical instruments among the Dan in Côte d'Ivoire. I have found this subject to be elusive and beyond the interest of many of my teachers in Africa. On the other hand, they may have been unwilling to part with such information.

51. Sources used in this section are Bamba Suso (1969?-disc; in Innes 1974:40–41; 1978: 34–35, 62–67), Sidiki Diabate (1988-disc; 1990-per:171–73, 427–32), Amadu Bansang Jobarteh (1990-per:A3–23), and Mbady Kouyate (and Diaryatou Kouyate 1996-disc:8). Sanimentereng (Sanémèntin) is sometimes cited as the specific place of origin of the kora (Bamba Suso, Mbady Kouyate).

52. In his recorded concert performance in Conakry, Sidiki Diabate (1988-disc) named seven generations between Tilimakan and himself. My own interviews yielded one more generation (S. Diabate 1990-per:171–73, 216, 265–67). Sidiki Diabate's son Toumani also has noted that the

kora player from Boke (northwest Guinea) whose father came from Kabu (Ngabu), relates that the father of Jali Madi Wuleng came from Mali to visit the king of Kabu, who was the first descendant of Tirimakan Traore, one of Sunjata's generals. He also notes that Jali Madi Wuleng was of the Sissoko lineage (Suso in Gambian dialects). (*Wuleng* means red; it is not a family name.) There is an anachronism, characteristic in such matters, in a story from the late Bamba Suso, one of The Gambia's most respected jalis specializing in oral history. Although Suso says that Jali Madi Wuleng was Kelefa's jali and played the kora for him, he credits Koriyang Musa, a student of Jali Madi Wuleng, with not only witnessing Kelefa's death but also discovering the kora, which at the time, Suso says, was more like a *simbingo* (simbi). That Koriyang Musa, says Bamba Suso (in Innes 1978:67), "was my mother's father." That would place Jali Madi Wuleng sometime in the nineteenth century. Sidiki Diabate and his uncle Amadu Bansang Jobarteh both know Bamba Suso's story and contend that his maternal grandfather, Koriyang Musa, is recent history and that the kora is much older. Amadu Bansang Jobarteh, one of the oldest living kora players in The Gambia and a longtime colleague and accompanist for Bamba Suso, would not speculate any further about the age of the kora.

These stories could be interpreted as ways of legitimizing family associations with the kora, a common practice. The staggering number of kora players in the area once under the control of Kabu makes for a dense web of family connections, learning centers, personal styles, and rivalries. As an example of migration patterns of kora players, consider one of the most prestigious families associated with the instrument. Jali Fili Diabate played the koni when he migrated about a century ago to eastern Gambia from Gaalen, a Malian town in the division of Gadougou between Kita and Niagassola (Guinea). His first son, Bala, who made the trek as an infant, was the first in the family to take up the kora because he saw that it was the instrument of choice in The Gambia. He taught his younger brother Amadu Bansang Jobarteh, born about the time of the First World War, who in the 1990s is one of the most respected kora players in Africa. Bala Diabate's son (Amadu Bansang's nephew) was Sidiki Diabate, who migrated back to Mali as a youth and whose funeral was an occasion of national mourning in Mali in 1996. Sidiki Diabate's son, Toumani, was born and raised in Bamako and enjoys a reputation for being one of the most creative kora players of his generation, with five CDs to his credit. Jali Fili Diabate (Tou-

kora dates from the epoch of Sunjata (in personal conversations in 1990 in Bamako, and in Prince 1989a:15). In Prince, Toumani Diabate was probably misquoted in his reference to Sunjata's bala player.

mani's great-grandfather) and the father of Bamba Suso (see above) were cousins, and Bamba and Amadu Bansang lived as brothers. "Amadu Jebate's father's name was Griot [Jali] Fili Jebate. . . . My father, Griot [Jali] Musa, and Griot [Jali] Fili were the sons of two sisters. When my own father died it was Griot [Jali] Fili who took my mother; it was he whom I knew as my father" (Bamba Suso, in Innes 1974:41). Not only is the sheer number of active kora players and the network of family relationships that link them staggering, but so is the high level of expertise and the vibrancy of their tradition.

Soron

The soron (also spelled *seron*) is a curious instrument because it is so similar to the kora. It is localized in northeastern Guinea and has nowhere near the widespread popularity or documentation of the kora. Several defining features of the soron may be contrasted with the kora.[53] On the soron:

1. The bridge is pierced with holes through which the strings pass, not notches as on the kora.
2. The metal buzzing leaf is inserted into the end of the neck, not attached to the bridge.
3. The bridge usually sits on a long, thin wooden platform rather than a square platform wrapped in cloth.[54]
4. The way the hide sound table is wrapped around the resonator forms a kind of cross.

The harps sketched in Laing and Mage (plate 7) show the same kind of cross design attachment of the hide to the calabash as is used on the soron, a method not in general use on the donso ngoni or simbi hunter's harps today.

Documentation of the soron is very sparse. The earliest may be from Kita, in Tellier (1898:179); he simply noted that the "sorhon" had twelve strings and a calabash resonator. Joyeux (1924:180–82, 210–11) devoted one and a half pages plus a photograph to the soron, and Rouget (1954a-disc, 1954b-disc, 1955:153, 1999-disc) recorded Mamadi Dioubate [Diabate], known as Soronfo Mamadi, one of the most renowned players of

53. Soron sources are rare, and I have relied on three: the photographs in Joyeux (1924, fig. 4, facing 180) and Rouget (1954a-disc) and an instrument I photographed in Kankan, Guinea, in 1990 (see photo in Charry 1994b:30–31).

54. The eighteen-stringed "gora" from the Musée de l'Homme (pictured in Knight 1973a, 1:26) that has a soron-type bridge with holes and sits on a kora-type rectangular platform is an exception.

his generation and one of the grand notables of a thriving music scene in Kankan.[55]

The historical and geographical relationship between the soron and kora is puzzling. Joyeux (1924:210–11) reported that the soron players he had seen in the regions of Kankan and Kouroussa claimed they had come from Futa Jalon, the mountain range in north-central Guinea that was a Fulbe stronghold, and that the soron was not well known in Upper Guinea. An origin in Futa Jalon would bring the early history of the soron geographically closer to the region associated with the origin of the kora. Leopold Senghor's ([1964] 1973:250) definition of the soron (*sorong*) as a "word used by the Peuls [Fula] of Fouta Djalon to designate a kind of kôra" also points to the mountainous Fulbe region in northern Guinea.

Koni

The plucked lute is the instrument par excellence of the western African sahel, including parts of Senegal, Mali, and Niger. Mande varieties include the Maninka koni, Mandinka *kontingo,* Xasonka koni (or *kontin*), Bamana *ngoni,* and Soninke *gambare.* These instruments, and similar ones played throughout the sahel, resemble those used in ancient Egypt, but the nature of the historical relationship is not clear. The recent adoption of the guitar by Mande jelis may indeed have completed a circle out of northeastern Africa into Europe and back into West Africa, several thousands of years in the making.[56]

Plucked lutes are found among a wide variety of peoples clear across the breadth of the African continent throughout the sahel and northern savanna regions (map 5 and table 8). Some variety of lute is probably the oldest melody instrument used by griots (who did not play hunter's harps), dating back perhaps several centuries or more before it was first noted by al-'Umarī and Ibn Battūta in the fourteenth century. On West African lutes the neck, a round fretless stick, sits in an indentation in the body and is threaded

55. Knight (1968, 1:145–57; vol. 2, transcription 6) has transcribed and analyzed a soron piece from Rouget (1954a-disc). Schaeffner (1951:72) also noted a soron player he had seen in Kissidougou, Guinea, named Mamadi Yamate, probably the same Soronfo Mamadi with a local dialect pronunciation of Diabate. The soron shown in Charry (1994b:30–31) comes from the Kankan compound of Soronfo Mamadi's children. See Rouget (1954a-disc, 1972-disc, 1980:822, 1999-disc) for photographs of Soronfo Mamadi.

56. This section is based in part on Charry (1996b), which contains further technical details. Some variety (or varieties) of West African plucked lute was probably a model for the New World banjo. For documentation of the early banjo in the Americas see Epstein (1975, 1977) and Gourlay (1976).

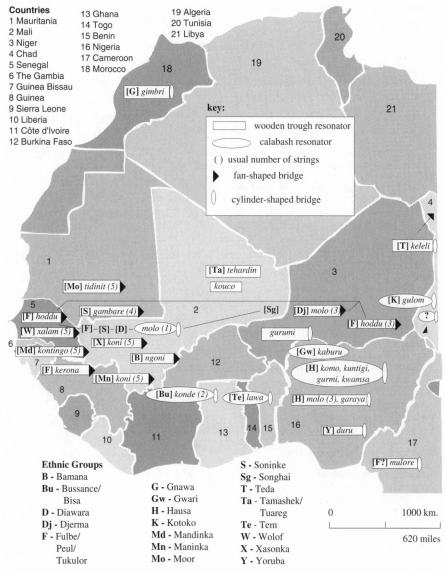

Map 5 Distribution of plucked lutes in West Africa and northwestern Africa.

through the hide sound table traversing most of the body, but not all. They are classed as spike, or more precisely semispike, lutes. The strings, attached at one end of the neck by the characteristically sub-Saharan African hide tuning laces, pass over a bridge and into a sound hole, where they are attached to the exposed end of the neck (plates 12, 13, 17, 18).

Table 8 Chronological Lute References for Map 5

Fan-Shaped Bridge

Gambare (Soninke)
Mahillon 1909:118–19; Frobenius 1921:53–60; Boyer 1953:117–18; Guignard 1975:171,
pl. 13; Coolen 1979:116–17; Mamadou Diawara 1990:108–9; Mangar 1993-disc.

Hoddu (Fulbe)
Nikiprowetzky 1965a-disc; Wane 1969:60–61, fig. 9; Ministry of Information of Mali 1971-disc:
vol. 2; Arom 1975-disc; Coolen 1979:118; Erlmann 1986:10; Maal 1991-disc.

Kerona (Fulbe from Futa Jallon)
Van Oven 1970:23; Jenkins 1979-disc; Coolen 1983:481; Jenkins 1983:22–23.

Koni/kontingo/nkoni/ngoni (Mandenka, Xasonka, Bamana)
Gallieni 1885:59; Moloney 1889:278; Frobenius 1921, facing 40; Humblot 1921:139; Joyeux
1924:180–82; Lamm 1968:18–21; Bazoumana Sissoko 1972a/b-disc; Fanta Damba 1971-disc;
Charters 1975a/b-disc; Dalby 1980; Ami Koita 1993-disc; Diabate Family of Kela 1994-disc,
1997-disc.

Molo (Djerma/Songhay)
Béart 1955:685; Nikiprowetzky 1966:72, 91, 1990-disc; Ministry of Information of Mali 1971-
disc: vol. 3.

Teharden (Tamashek/Tuareg)
Boulton 1957-disc, 1969, fig. 13 (repr. from 1957-disc); Bebey 1975:19.

Tidinit (Moor)
Béart 1955:684; Nikiprowetzky 1966:15, 22; Norris 1968:61–63; Guignard 1975:122, plates 5,
8, 11, 12; Coolen 1979:112–15; Collaer and Elsner 1983:176–79; Duvelle 1966-disc; Wegner
1984:139; Eide and Abba 1990-disc.

Xalam (Wolof)
Mahillon 1909:169; Nikiprowetzky 1965a-disc, 1966:38; Charters 1975a/b-disc; Ames 1955-
disc; Coolen 1979, 1982, 1983; Durán 1981b; Maal 1991-disc.

Not shown on map or unidentified

Diassare (eastern Senegal)
Nikiprowetzky 1966:45.

Goumbale (Diawara)
Boyer 1953:117–18.

Kook (Tukolor)
Coolen 1979:111.

Kouco/kubru (Tamashek?, Songhai?)
Jay 1976-disc; Sadie 1984, 2:477.

Xalam or *cambreh?*
Metropolitan Museum of Art 1907:19–20, "Lute types."

Hoddu or *xalam?*
Chauvet 1929:106, fig. 67.

Table 8 *(continued)*

Cylinder-Shaped Bridge

Duru (Yoruba)
Thieme 1969:384–92; Wegner 1984:142.

Garaya (Hausa)
Ames, n.d.b.-disc; Ames and King 1971:40–41; Erlmann 1986:11; Kubik 1989:80–81; Fujii 1990-vid: tape 17, no. 16; also see *komo*.

Gimbri (Gnawa)
Salvador-Daniel [1863] 1986, cover; Ankermann 1901:12–13; Metropolitan Museum of Art 1907:19–24, "Luke types"; Rouanet 1922:2929–31; Farmer 1928; Schuyler 1970-disc, 1972-disc, 1979, 1981; Collaer and Elsner 1983:128–29, 162–63, 166–71; Wegner 1984:123, 136–38, 255–57; Gnaoua d'Essaouira 1993-disc; Charry, forthcoming.

Gulom (Kotoko, Chad/Cameroun)
Brandily 1984.

Gurmi, aka *kumbo* (Hausa)
Ames and King 1971:43–44; Gourlay 1984a:111.

Gurumi (Dosso)
Jenkins 1983:23, 31; Gourlay 1984a.

Gurumi (Mawri/Maori)
Nikiprowetzky 1965b-disc, 1966:70, 86.

Kaburu (Gwari)
"The All-Nigeria Festival of the Arts—1970" 1971:18; Enem 1975:97.

Keleli (Teda)
Brandily 1974:31–64, 1980-disc; Wegner 1984:257.

Komo, aka *babbar* ("big") *garaya* (Hausa)
Nikiprowetzky 1965b-disc, 1966:77, 86–87; Krieger 1968:408–9; Ames, n.d.a.-disc; Ames and King 1971:40–41, fig. 8; Wegner 1984:258; also see *garaya.*

Konde (Bussance/Bisa)
Duvelle 1971-disc; Bebey 1975:45.

Kuntigi/kuntugi (Hausa, Songhai, Djerma)
Nikiprowetzky 1990-disc, 1966:91; Krieger 1968:409; Ames and King 1971:45–46; Jay 1976-disc; Surugue 1980:523; Gourley 1984b:487; Wegner 1984:140, 142.

Kwamsa (Hausa)
P. Harris 1932:124; Krieger 1968:407–8; Thieme 1969:385–86; Erlmann 1983:23–24, 34 (Fulani *garaya*).

Lawa (Tem)
Kubik 1989:167.

Molo/mola (Fulbe, Soninke/Diawara)
Boyer 1953:117–18; Nikiprowetzky 1966:36, 45–46, 1966:75 (Sonrai), 1965a-disc; Coolen 1979:116; Gourlay 1976; Gibbal 1994:68, between 70 and 71 (*djerkele*).

(continued)

Table 8 (*continued*)

Molo (Hausa)
Smend 1908:72–73; Krieger 1968:406–7; Thieme 1969:387–90; Ames and King 1971:46–47; Gourley 1976; Erlmann 1983:23–24, 35–36 (Fulani, Cameroun); Wegner 1984:137–40, 258.

Mulore (Cameroun)
Ankermann 1901:12–13 (abb. 11); Wegner 1984:257; Kubik 1989:86–87, 194.

Unnamed (from Kanem in Chad)
Brandily, n.d.-disc.

Not shown on map or unidentified

Genbra/gnaybra (Mauritania; calabash resonator)
Guignard 1975:171, pl. 13.

Gora (Hausa)
Nikiprowetzky 1966:86.

Gullum (Kilba)
Sadie 1984, 2:110.

Kola lemme/gesere (Diawara/Soninke)
Boyer 1953:117–18; Coolen 1979:75, 119, 235.

Kologo/kono/kpono (Ghana)
Kaye 1987.

Kuban/kubangu (Bassari, Togo)
Ankermann 1901:12–13 (abb. 12); Wegner 1984:258.

Yomshi (Birom, Nigeria)
Bouquiaux 1969:106; Wegner 1984:140.

Unnamed (Manjak, Jola, or Balanta, Senegal)
Djimo Kouyate 1991-vid; Huet and Keita 1996:112–14.

Unnamed (Togo)
Smend 1908:72–74.

Note: See references for complete citations.

West African plucked lutes may be broadly distinguished from each other by two basic features:

1. The bridge, which either is fan shaped and slips onto the end of the neck in the sound hole or is cylinder shaped and sits on top of the skin sound table.
2. The resonator, which is either a carved wooden trough or a calabash (or in some cases a sardine tin or some other kind of metal container).

Wooden trough lutes with fan-shaped bridges are played exclusively by griots, and their distribution conforms with the distribution of griots in West Africa. To distinguish them from other types of plucked lutes I refer to them as griot lutes. They are used in the western sahel and northern savanna from

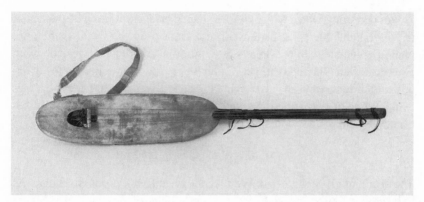

Plate 12 Koni. Instrument made by Kabine Cissoko, Bamako, 1990. Photo by John Wareham.

Plate 13 Lute (koni?) players at a jeweler-blacksmith's workshop, late nineteenth century. "Atelier de bijoutier forgeron—griots." Photo taken before 1885. Bibliothèque Nationale de France, Paris, Société de Géographie, We 44, no. 31 (Fierro 1986:70).

the Atlantic coast to Niger. Non-Mande griot lutes include the Wolof *xalam,* Moorish *tidinit,* and Fulbe *hoddu.* Griot lutes may sometimes be augmented with more strings (I have seen up to seven strings on a koni). Further research is needed to identify the distinguishing characteristics of each of the griot lutes, though size is one contributing factor (e.g., the Bamana *ngoni* is the largest).

Wooden trough lutes with cylinder-shaped bridges are used by the Hausa of Nigeria and others farther east. These kinds of lutes as well as the griot lutes are plucked with the fingers or with some kind of nail extension worn as a ring around the index finger. Calabash resonator lutes belong to yet another tradition; they all have cylinder-shaped bridges and fewer strings (usually one or two), and they are often plucked with a plectrum held between the thumb and index finger.

Origins of the Griot Lute

The origin of plucked lutes in West Africa is a difficult problem that has yet to be convincingly resolved. The eminent scholar of Arabian music Henry Farmer (1924:158, 1928:25–27, 1938:251, 1939:571–75) posited ancient Egyptian ancestry of both West African and North African lutes, which he grouped under the names *gunbrī* or *gunībrī* (references to a Moroccan lute), and he claimed they are all essentially the same instrument. Similar but less specific attributions of ancient Egyptian ancestry for West African lutes were made earlier by Sachs (1921:55) and Ankermann (1901:120–23). Little documentation of these instruments was available at that time, and prevailing views of West African culture, ultimately rooted in assumptions of racial and cultural superiority, saw Egypt as the wellspring. For example, "Up to the sixteenth century, the Western Soudan was a cultural offspring of Egypt. After the Moorish occupation . . . it is Morocco that determines the intellectual world of the Soudanese" (Farmer 1924:158). "The Egyptian lute, with the handle ending inside the body, has survived in the Northwest of Africa. It first degenerated to a clumsy Negro instrument, used in Morocco and Senegambia and called *gunbrī* in Sudanese" (Sachs 1940: 102). Scholarly work done in Africa in recent decades and the increasing number of recordings and world tours of musicians have illuminated the rich indigenous culture in West Africa to such an extent that the quotations above are of interest not so much for what they propose as for their place in African music historiography. Many of Farmer's observations have since been refined, questioned, or quietly repudiated.[57]

The earliest references to a lute in West Africa come from al-ʿUmarī and Ibn Battūta in the mid-fourteenth century (table 9): "When the king of this kingdom comes in from a journey . . . drums are beaten and guitars (tunbūr) and trumpets well made of horn are played in front of him" (al-ʿUmarī 1337, in Levtzion and Hopkins 1981:266–67). "The sultan comes out of a

57. For the renowned ngoni player Banzoumana Sissoko's version of how the instrument arrived in West Africa, attributing it to a black Arab named Djalita from Saudi Arabia during the time of Mohammed, see Baiko (1979).

Table 9 Early Documentation of West African Lutes

Date	Author	(Edition) Page Numbers
1337	al-ʿUmarī	(1981) 266–67
1355	Ibn Battūta	(1981) 291
1468	Ca da Mosto	(1937) 51
1493	al-Lamtūnī	(1933) 286; (1970) 14
1506–10	Fernandes	(1951) 8
1594	Almada	(1946) 24–25
1685	Courbe	(1913) 43, 73
1695	Le Maire	120–23
1781	Høst	in Collaer and Elsner 1983:168–70
1788	Matthews	(1966) 105–6; reprinted in French in Durand 1802:189
1799	Park	(1983) 213–14

Note: See appendix A and bibliography for complete citations.

door in the corner of the palace. . . . The singers come out in front of him with gold and silver stringed instruments (qunburī)" (Ibn Battūta 1355, in Levtzion and Hopkins 1981:291). Al-ʿUmarī referred to the lute by a term used for an ancient Egyptian or Persian lute, *tunbūr.* Ibn Battūta's term *qunburī,* however, is a mystery. It may have been a corruption of *tunbur,* for there is no evidence of the term *qunburī* (or any close variant) until the nineteenth century, and Ibn Battūta did not take special notice of the word as was his habit with other local West African terms. It may also be related to the name of the Soninke lute, *gambare,* which was probably the model for the *gimbri* played by Gnawa, black Moroccans of Soninke, Bamana, and Hausa origin.[58]

Compounding confusion about the diffusion of lutes in Africa is the variety of lutes in North Africa. Schuyler (1979:127–31) has identified three lute types used in Morocco (other than the *'ūd*), two of which have been called *gimbri* (*ginbri*).[59]

1. The Gnawa ginbri (also known as *l-hejhuj, sintir,* or *ginibri*) is a semispike lute with tuning rings and a rectangular box-shaped body (sometimes with a rounded back).
2. The Arab ginbri (large variety, also called *l-hejhuj*) or *ginibri* (smaller variety, also called *sinitra* or *suisin*) is a semispike lute with tuning pegs and a teardrop-shaped body. Berbers from the Middle Atlas region and some plains Arabs call this ginbri a *lotar.*

58. For references to the Gnawa of Morocco see Charry (forthcoming) and Schuyler (1981). See Farmer (1928) for many of the nineteenth-century sources for the term *gimbri,* Dozy (1967, 2:408) for other nineteenth-century sources, and al-Faruqi (1981:78, 84–87, 254, 267) for later sources. Ibn Battūta's *qunburī* is discussed in further detail in Charry (1996b).

59. Schuyler's recordings of the Gnawa ginbri (Schuyler 1972-disc), Arab ginbri (Schuyler 1971?-disc), and Rwais lotar (Schuyler 1978-disc) demonstrate the differences between these three instruments.

3. The Berber *lotar* used by professional musicians known as Rwais (singular Rais) is a semispike lute with tuning pegs and a bowl-shaped body.

The Arab ginbri is distinctly North African. It is not found farther south, nor does it bear much morphological resemblance to lutes found farther south, and it is played primarily by Arabs. The Gnawa ginbri was most likely brought to North Africa from the south by the Gnawa who played it or was fashioned by them once they arrived. There is no evidence that it traveled from Egypt directly across North Africa.

The question of the similarity of ancient Egyptian lutes and one or another variety of North African ginbri, Farmer's original point, is misplaced. It would be more relevant to examine the lutes of ancient Egypt and those found in a line farther south stretching across the Sahara and sahel to ancient Ghana. Furthermore, Fulbe migrations from their ancient homeland in Tekrur (northern Senegal) eastward to the nation of Cameroon should also be examined. And finally, the movements of Soninke and other peoples north into Morocco should be explored. Any link between ancient Egypt and the North African Gnawa ginbri would have come via the south, most likely the Soninke gambare.

The earliest evidence of lutes in the world comes from representations on two Mesopotamian seals from over four thousand years ago, and scholars have speculated on possible origins of the instrument among West Semitic nomads from Syria.[60] Eighteenth-century B.C.E. Hyksos invaders from the Near East are generally believed to be responsible for the first appearance of the lute in Egypt. Three basic kinds of lute are found in ancient Egypt, distinguished by their resonators: oval, pear shaped, and concave sided. The last two types do not resemble those in West Africa, nor have they had anywhere near the same number of representations as the oval type. In an exhaustive inventory, Manniche (1975:70–81) has listed seven surviving specimens and over ninety representations of ancient Egyptian oval-resonator lutes, primarily from the New Kingdom period (1580–1085 B.C.E.). With a few exceptions, representations of this kind of lute in Egypt stop at the end of the New Kingdom. These oval-resonator lutes can be divided into two types, once again according to their resonators: carved-out wooden trough and tortoise shell. Males and females are depicted playing both types.

60. For brief surveys of early lute history see Picken (1975:261–63) and Wachsmann (1984: 551–53). Turnbull (1972) and Rashid (1984) are authoritative sources for lutes in Mesopotamia, as is Hickmann for lutes in ancient Egypt. Rashid, Hickmann, and Sachs (1921) are excellent sources for photographs. All the lutes discussed here are considered long-necked lutes, in contrast to short-necked lutes such as those found in modern Egypt (e.g., *'ūd*), and various parts of Asia (see Picken 1955 and Wachsmann 1984).

The striking morphological similarities between ancient Egyptian and West African lutes are at least partially responsible for the ready acceptance of claims of direct ancestry, but there are a number of significant differences.[61] Such differences between a lute of ancient Egypt and one from modern-day Mali include the use of a plectrum versus the fingers; the placement of the striking fingers on top of or below the strings; the place on the instrument where the strings are plucked; the position of the instrument in relation to the body; the ratio of the length of the neck to the body (Egyptian lutes have longer necks and smaller resonators than West African lutes); the different bridges; the ways the neck is threaded through the body; and the use of frets on Egyptian lutes.[62] Despite these differences, there is a remarkable resemblance between West African and ancient Egyptian lutes, but the historical significance of this resemblance is still unclear. Calabash resonator lutes might be older than the wooden trough variety in West Africa, perhaps predating iron implements that could help in carving out a wooden body.

Whether the ancient Egyptian lute migrated to West Africa or vice versa or whether the two types arose independently is an open question. Transmission out of Egypt to the west or south would have to have taken place any time during the second millennium B.C.E. Transmission from the west into Egypt would have occurred before the beginning of this period. Could lutes have been used in West Africa before this time? At present there is no archaeological evidence for old lutes, but given the different climatological, cultural, and research contexts of western and northeastern Africa, absence of material evidence in West Africa proves little.[63]

The early attempts to posit directional flow of cultural traffic between western and northeastern Africa failed to address some significant questions. How might the diffusion of musical instruments compare with the dif-

61. See Charry (1996b: 18–19) for a photograph and table comparing a Malian lute and an ancient Egyptian lute. In evaluating these differences note that a comparison is being made between a tradition that may have disappeared three thousand years ago and one that lives today, represented by many distinct branches. Though there is little basis for projecting a living tradition thousands of years into the past, there are few alternatives.

62. Other less tangible differences include the tunings of the instruments (Hickmann [1948: 649–56] has speculated that the three strings on Egyptian lutes were probably tuned in unison, a rarity on West African lutes) and the playing of Egyptian lutes by both men and women (usually an either/or situation in West Africa). Women typically play stringed instruments among desert peoples, such as the Moorish harp *ardin* (see chapter 2) and the Tuareg one-string fiddle *inzad* (Huet and Keita 1996:30–31; Nikiprowetzky 1966?-disc), but that becomes rare farther south. Also see the fifteenth-century quotation from al-Lamtūnī about women playing the lute (appendix A).

63. Archaeological research into the settling of the Dhar Tichitt region in southern Mauritania during the third and second millennium B.C.E. may eventually turn up relevant information (see chapter 1).

fusion of other developments such as plant and animal domestication, pottery, pastoralism, or language? Why is there such a concentration of lutes in the sahel and northern savanna and not farther south? Why are lutes relatively sparse east of Nigeria up to Egypt and so numerous in Hausa land and in the Niger and Senegal river valleys? What is the significance of the two types of bridge? What is the significance of lutes' being used for hunters in Nigeria and for nobles and rulers farther west? How did it come to pass that lute playing is a hereditary profession in certain areas? Until these questions are addressed, a critical eye must be kept on simplified paths of musical instrument diffusion.

Etymologies: Gambare, Xalam, Hoddu, Koni

The marked similarity of griot lutes to each other suggests a common origin. Ancient Ghana would be a likely source; those cultures with griots and griot lutes were in close contact with it, and there are Soninke oral traditions about lute playing during the time of Wagadu, the Soninke name for ancient Ghana.[64] In contrast to the well-known story of origin of the Maninka bala (see below), Mandenka jelis do not claim they were the first in West Africa to have the lute. Nor do Wolof make any claims for having the lute first—quite the contrary, they may have taken up the instrument last, in part based on what they say and also because much of their repertory is of Mande or Fulbe origin (Coolen 1979:118; Durán 1981b:31–32). Fulbe may well have been responsible for much of the dispersion of the lute throughout West Africa, but further research is needed to properly assess their role in the history of the lute.[65]

A few possible shared etymologies of griot lutes might shed light on the historical dispersion of lutes in West Africa. The Soninke gambare could be the source for several lute names. The name *gambare* might even be a deformation of the Arabic term *tunbur,* retaining the *n-b-r* sound, as Farmer (1938:251) has suggested in relation to the North African ginbri.[66] But like the term *qawal* described above, this does not mean the Soninke got the in-

64. For the story of Gassire's lute see Frobenius (1921:53–60, translated into English in Frobenius and Fox [1937] 1966:97–110). For a story attributing the origin of the lute to Bida, the serpent guardian of Wagadu, via a jinn, see Dieterlen and Sylla (1992:96–97).

65. Not only does Arnott's (1980:23) map showing the main dialect areas of Fulbe peoples in West Africa conform well with the distribution of lutes, but the major split between Sokoto–West Niger dialects and Central Nigerian dialects also roughly conforms to the distribution of fan-shaped bridges versus cylinder-shaped bridges.

66. Nasals assimilate to following bilabials in Mande languages, so the consonant cluster written as *nb* is pronounced *mb.* As far as I am aware, the substitution of *g* for *t* does not occur in West African languages.

strument from the Arabs, simply that the instrument acquired the Arabic term. *Ginbri* probably comes from the name *gambare,* especially given the ancient associations that the gambare has and the probable Soninke origin of at least some of the North African Gnawa. Hause's (1948:58) linguistic derivation of the Wolof *xalam* from the Soninke *gambare* also seems plausible (*gambare/kambare/kambale/kalamb/kalam*). Long-distance Soninke merchants known as Wangara or Jula may have been responsible for the distribution of *gambare*-derived names farther east. Possible cognates between the terms *guimbri* and *gambare* and the lutes *gurmi* and *gullom* in Nigeria, *gurumi* in Niger and Chad, and *kubru* of Timbuktu have been noted by Gourlay (1984a).

The word for finger in Maninka, Mandinka, Wolof, and Fulbe might also be the source for the names of their lutes. Delafosse (1955:395) defined koni as "finger," and as "any string instrument that is played with the fingers, guitar, harp." The sound changes that occur for both terms in Mandinka are very similar: *koni* (for both finger and the lute) in Maninka and *konondingo/kontingo* (finger/lute) in Mandinka (Gamble 1987b:70–71). The terms for finger and lute in Wolof (*baram* and *xalam*) (Koelle [1854] 1963:45) and Fulbe (*hondu* and *hoddu*) (ibid.; Labouret 1955:89–90; Osborn, Dwyer, and Donohoe 1993:143) are similar enough to present plausible explanations.[67]

Bala

A culture of xylophone (from *xylo* [wood] *phone* [sound]) playing probably goes back several thousand years in West Africa. From slabs of wood placed over a pit in the ground or laid across the knees to finely tuned wooden slats tied onto a bamboo frame, there is a strong case for the indigenous development of the instrument on African, if not West African soil (plates 14 to 20).[68] Mande oral traditions are unusually explicit about the origin of the xylophone. It was played by Sumanguru (Soumaouro) Kante, the Sosso blacksmith sorcerer-king defeated by Sunjata. Little is said about

67. See Charry (1996b:15) for a discussion of Coolen's (1979:117–19) suggestion that the names for several lutes come from the characteristic knocking sound that the fingers make when tapping against the hide sound table. Erlmann's (1986:10) suggestion that the Fulbe term *hoddu* comes from the Arabic *'ūd* is quite plausible. It is possible that Ibn Battūta's *q-n-b-r* was a local West African term for lute and not a corruption of *t-n-b-r,* perhaps formed by a compound of *koni* (finger) with *mbara* (calabash) (see Delafosse 1955:395, 432). In that case the Soninke term *gambare* might have come from the Maninka *konimbara,* although it seems unlikely that the Soninke would have taken a Maninka term for their own lute.

68. See Blench (1982:84–85) for an extended criticism of older theories about the foreign (Indonesian) origin of African xylophones.

Plate 14 Bala construction. Top: bala slats drying out in a smokehouse; workshop of Salimu Kouyate, Brikama (The Gambia), 1989. Bottom: Bala Dounbouya tuning a bala slat, Dakar, 1989. Photos by the author.

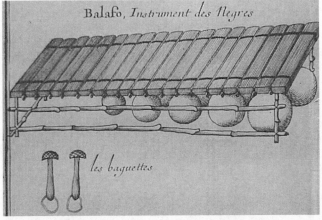

Plate 15 Bala drawings from the seventeenth century. From Froger (1698a:44–46); also published in Froger (1698b:33–35), Barbot (1732, pl. 3[2] after p. 55), and Astley ([1745–47] 1968, facing 278). Courtesy of Watkinson Library, Trinity College, Hartford, Conn.

the xylophone before Sumanguru, and like most other instruments, its ultimate origins are attributed to a jinn. The Maninka xylophone, called *bala* or *balafon,* is used wherever Maninka peoples have migrated, an area stretching along the Niger River from Segou to its source in southern Guinea, farther south into Sierra Leone and northern Liberia, west to the Senegambia, and east into northern Côte d'Ivoire, making it the best-known xylophone of West Africa. Frame xylophones in West Africa are very similar to each other, and it is not too difficult to imagine a more unified West African xylophone culture sometime in the distant past.

Plate 16 Drawing of unidentified musical instruments from Guinea in the 1880s. "Instruments de Musique du Fouta-Djallon et du Bambouk." Hanging on pegs on top row (left to right): dundun or sangba, lute (koni?), and horn. On ground (left to right): rattle, kora, three-legged drum, tama, flute, tabala, bala, and drum. From the voyages of Jean-Marie Bayol, Bibliothèque Nationale de France, Paris, Société de Géographie, We 13, no. 46 (Fierro 1986:68).

Plate 17 Musicians and dancers at Niagassola, Guinea, 1887–88. "Tam-tam à Niagassola." Left to right: drum (jembe?) on ground, French officers (standing), two dancers, koni player, bala player, women clapping. Photo from the Gallieni campaign of 1887–88. Bibliothèque Nationale de France, Paris, Société de Géographie, We 127, no. 27 (Fierro 1986:72).

Plate 18 Musicians at Siguiri, Guinea, 1887–88. Left to right: bala player, three koni players, two drummers (jembe on left; different drum on right?). Photo from the Gallieni campaign of 1887–88. Bibliothèque Nationale de France, Paris, Société de Géographie, We 127, no. 40 (Fierro 1986:72).

Plate 19 Four bala players with two dundun players. Photo taken before 1922. Bibliothèque Nationale de France, Paris, Société de Géographie, We 222, no. 96 (Fierro 1986:76).

Plate 20 Bala and tama players from Kita, Mali. Mid-twentieth century. From Collection Musée de l'Homme, D36-1461-41, Griaule N. 105.

The bala is a jeli instrument with close associations with numus (black-smiths), and it is a pivotal instrument linking not only the worlds of the jeli and numu, but also jelis and drummers. Many bala players come from Kante, Doumbia, and Camara families of numu origin, in addition to Kou-yate and Diabate families of jeli origin. Although stone tools in West Africa could have been used to carve crude xylophones long ago, several factors support speculation that the bala does not predate the introduction of metal-working in West Africa (ca. 500 B.C.E.) and that it was a blacksmith inven-tion. Mande blacksmiths work not only in metal, but also in wood. They also need ready access to wood for charcoal to heat their furnaces and as raw materials for their sculptures. Constructing a bala requires large amounts of wood, not just for the instrument itself, but also to keep a fire going for weeks to smoke its slats dry. The iron ax that the blacksmith uses to carve masks is also used to fashion balas. The bala is the only one of the jeli in-struments that is commonly played in drum ensembles, perhaps reflecting an earlier association with jembe drumming, which is also associated with blacksmiths. Finally, the very act of shaping metal, banging on it with a hammer, is replicated in the act of playing the bala, striking wooden slats with a mallet.

Maninka jelis prefer the term *bala* to *balafon,* which probably entered into European usage from *bala fo* (to play the bala). The name *balani* or *balanyi* (small bala) is occasionally used to distinguish the balas in use today from the larger ones that were used before the twentieth century (see below). The term *balafon* has been generally applied to all West African xylophones, but each group has its own name for its instruments. *Bala* is used here to refer explicitly to the Maninka/Susu instrument only.[69]

West African frame xylophones share at least one feature that distinguishes them from other African frame xylophones: the wooden slats are attached to the frame by cord wrapped around the ends of the slats rather than threaded through holes in the slats. In other parts of Africa they are held in place either by pegs inserted into holes in the slats or cord threaded through them, or by pegs inserted on either side of the slats. The consistency with which this morphological feature defines West African frame xylophones is remarkable.

Balas are constructed by cutting the wooden slats, made of an African rosewood (Md: *keno;* Mn: *genu*), to rough size and setting them in a hut where a fire is kept going day and night for weeks, if not months (plate 14). This dries the wood thoroughly, extracting any moisture. A bamboo frame is constructed, and when the slats are tuned (see below) they are tied onto the frame. Each slat has a small gourd attached below it to add resonance. The gourds have two small holes cut in their sides, covered with a thin membrane (formerly made from a spiderweb, nowadays usually cigarette paper or a piece of a plastic bag), so that a buzzing sound is made when a slat is struck and air passes through the gourd.[70] The heads of the wooden mallets are wrapped in very thin rubber strips cut from a flat sheet of the dried liquid tapped from a tree.

Map 6 shows the distribution of xylophones in West Africa, and table 10 lists references for each of the instruments. Frame xylophones are shown in the general geographic area where they are indigenous. Other kinds of xylophones—for example, those in which the slats are laid either across the player's legs or across banana stalks—are shown outside the land mass with lines pointing to the areas where they are indigenous.[71]

69. Early references (appendix A) use *balafo* (Barbot, Froger, Gray and Dochard), *balafeu* (Moore), or *balafou* (Park). Mandinka jalis call it *balo* (see technical notes for sound changes from Maninka to Mandinka). For documentation of variants of the term *balafo* in the Americas from the eighteenth century on, see Epstein (1977:55–58, 83).

70. Tellier (1898:181) and El Hadj Djeli Sory Kouyate (1992-disc) report the use of a spiderweb; Joyeux (1924:175) calls it the inner surface of a nest of spiders. Jessup (1983:36) translates the Mandinka term *talingjalo* as spider's egg case, rather than spiderweb as in Gamble (*taalingjaloo;* 1987b:120). Kersalé (1997-disc:3, 7), referring to xylophones in Burkina Faso, calls it "a very fine web obtained from the cocoon protecting the eggs of a type of spider."

71. Since local names for West African xylophones are poorly documented, the references in table 10 are organized according to ethnic groups. Dogon sculptures of two people playing a xylophone (Brincard 1989:182) may give the impression that the Dogon themselves play it, but they do not now do so (see Abspoel, n.d., 11–20 for descriptions of the instruments used in one Dogon village).

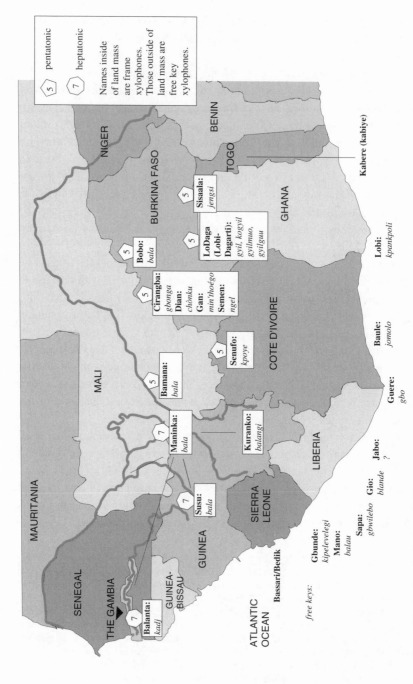

Map 6 Distribution of xylophones in West Africa.

Table 10 Chronological Xylophone References for Map 6

Frame Xylophones with Slats Tied onto Frame

Bala (Bamana)
C. Monteil 1924:177, 314–15; Zahan 1960:123, 234–35, 338, pls. 17 and 23; Metropolitan Museum of Art, n.d., 1986.467.73; Brandes, Male, and Thierno 1998-disc.

Bala? (Boba/Bwa)
Huet 1978:102–3, no. 165.

Bala (Maninka; twentieth century, small)
Moloney 1889:278; Tellier 1898:181–82; Famechon 1900:204–5; Arcin 1907:270, 547; Mahillon 1909:60–62; Joyeux 1924; C. Monteil 1924:177, Pl. 4, fig. 7; Schaeffner [1936] 1980, pl. 9; Staub 1936:137; Boulton 1957-disc; Schaeffner 1946:20; Alberts 1949-disc, 1954a-disc, 1998-disc; Lamm 1968:66–69; Rouget and Schwarz 1969; Rouget 1999-disc; Béart 1955:665–66; Van Oven 1970:24, 27; Sory Camara 1976, fig. 7 (22 slats); Jessup 1983; Gourlay and Durán 1984a; Panneton 1987; Ivorys 1987-disc; Sourakata Koite 1990-disc; L. Harris 1992; Djeli Sory Kouyate 1992-disc; Keletigui Diabate 1996-disc.

Bala (Maninka; pre-twentieth century, large)
Froger 1698a:44–46; 1698b:33–36 (19 slats); Moore 1740:84–85; Barbot 1732:55, pl. 3 (2) (repr. in Kubik 1989:182–83); Park [1799] 1983:213; Gray and Dochard 1825:54–55, facing 301; Metropolitan Museum of Art, n.d., 1889.492 (15 slats); Mahillon 1893:383–86 (19–slats); Jenkins 1970, pl. 1, no. 10 (19 slats); Niane 1975b, facing 217 (20 slats); Rouget 1999-disc.

Balangi (Karanko/Kuranko)
Jenkins 1979-disc.

Chònku (Dian)
Kersalé 1997-disc.

Gbonga (Cirangba/Cerma, Goin)
Soma 1988.

Gyil, kogyil, gyilmuo, gyilguu (LoDaga, Lobi, Dagarti, Birifor)
Chauvet 1929, fig. 52; Strumpf 1970; Foday Musa Suso 1977-disc; Jay 1979-disc; Godsey 1980, 1984; Mensah 1982; Aning 1989; Kubik 1989:170–71; Kersalé 1997-disc.

Jengsi (Sisaala)
Seavoy 1982.

Kadj (Balanta)
Kubik 1989:182; Mane 1996-disc; Knight 1997-vid.

Kpoye (Senufo)
Prouteaux 1929, facing 456; Huet and Keita 1954:33; Bebey 1975:86; Glaze 1981 (see xylophone in index); Jenkins 1983:71; Zemp, n.d.b.-disc; Förster 1987-disc.

Min'thorègo (Gan)
Kersalé 1997-disc.

Ngel (Semen/Siamu)
Kersalé 1997-disc.

Free Slats or Pegs on Side of Slats

Baule
Rouget 1954a-disc; Ménard 1963:65, 88; Kubik 1989:172–73.

(*continued*)

Table 10 (*continued*)

Bedik/Bassari
Ferry 1969.

Dan
Zemp 1971:288–89.

Guere
Zemp 1971:288–89, 1971-disc.

Liberia (with pegs on side of keys)
Schwab 1947:149; Herzog 1949 (Jabo).

Nigeria: Biron, Ekoi, Ibo, Ibibio, Igbo, Mbube
Jones 1964, pl. 3, no. 8; Ames, n.d.c.-disc; Nicklin 1975; Akpabot 1986:14; Quersin, n.d.-disc.

Togo: Kabere (Kabiye)
Verdier and Lavilleon, n.d.-disc.

Note: See references for complete citations.

There are four basic clusters of West African frame xylophones:

1. The heptatonic Maninka/Susu bala (all the same instrument), played in Guinea and Mali.
2. The heptatonic Balanta *kadj,* sometimes called *balo,* tuned differently from the Maninka bala and played by two people on one instrument in the Casamance region.
3. The pentatonic Bamana/Truka/Senufo/Bobo bala (different instruments with different local names), played in eastern Mali, Burkina Faso, and northern Côte d'Ivoire.
4. The pentatonic Lobi/Dagarti/Sisaala *gyil,* of northern Ghana and Burkina Faso.

The historical relationships and morphological distinctions among these instruments are unclear.

Mande oral traditions are unanimous that the Maninka received the bala from the Sosso (Susu) king Sumanguru Kante. The attributions of two respected Malian jelis are typical. "Sumanguru made a bala inside a cave. He played the bala for himself" (Kele Monson Diabate, in Moser 1974:279). "At that time, the bards did not have balaphones. . . . None but Susu Mountain Sumamuru [Sumanguru]. . . . The balaphone of seven keys" (Fa-Digi Sisoko, in Johnson 1986:148–49). The episode in which the bala is first noted in the Sunjata epic is a major one that figures in most renditions. When Sunjata's jeli, Bala Faseke (or Balla Fassali) Kouyate, gained entry into Sumanguru Kante's secret chamber, he began playing the bala. Sumanguru, who was out in the bush, was reputed to be able to hear his bala anywhere he was, and he magically appeared in his chamber ready to kill whoever was playing it. Bala Faseke Kouyate immediately began singing

Sumanguru's praises and won him over. Sumanguru is said to have cut Bala Faseke's Achilles tendons to ensure that he would remain his jeli.[72]

According to my teacher Bala Dounbouya (1989-per), the piece that Bala Faseke Kouyate played for Sumanguru was called *Boloba*. Wa Kamissoko was also of this opinion. "Having come back from the bush, Sumaworo found Faseke Kwate playing boloba, 'great arms,' which is the first hymn of the Mande. The Sunjata fasa [praise hymn], like boloba, was drawn from the music of the hunters" (Cissé and Kamissoko 1988:165). Djibril Tamsir Niane (1965:39) wrote that Bala Faseke played *Duga*, another of the oldest pieces in repertory.

Bala Faseke Kouyate had three sons: Missa, Massa Magan, and Batru Mori (S. J. Kouyate 1990-per; L. Camara 1980:207; Fa-Digi Sisoko, in Johnson 1986:151; Sidiki Diabate 1988-disc; Dembo Kanute, in Innes 1974:281). When Sumanguru was defeated by Sunjata his bala is believed to have been passed on to Bala Faseke Kouyate and then passed down to his son Missa (S. J. Kouyate 1990-per; L. Camara 1980:207). That bala, known as the Sosso bala, has remained in the hands of the descendants of Missa Kouyate and at present is guarded by the Kouyates in Niagassola, Guinea.

The preservation of an instrument such as the Sosso bala is extraordinary for Africa, and it represents one of the oldest instruments south of the Sahara. It is larger in all dimensions than the balas in use today, which may have attained their present smaller size in the late nineteenth or early twentieth century. A rare photograph of either the instrument or a more probably a replica of it was taken during the Gallieni expedition of 1887–88 (plate 17). The Sosso bala and *balatigi* (bala guardian) are pictured in Niane (1975b, facing 217) and Rouget (1999-disc). An equally rare recording of it (or perhaps of a replica) can be heard in Toureille (1992-disc). The Sosso bala is kept in a hut along with other relics from the time of Sunjata. The status of the Sosso bala in Niagassola is generally recognized (Cissé and Kamissoko 1988:388), but being a village with difficult vehicle access,

72. Examples of the Sumanguru bala episode include S. J. Kouyate (1990-per), Fa-Digi Sisoko (in Johnson 1986:148–50), Kele Monson Diabate (in Moser 1974:279–82), Cissé and Kamissoko (1988:165), Niane (1965:38–40), and L. Camara (1980:173–76). Caution should be taken with Gambian sources for bala history, such as Dembo Kanute (in Innes 1974:271–73) and his younger brother Banna Kanute (in Innes 1974:136, 173–213), since the instrument is not a major part of Gambian traditions. Banna Kanute was Jones's (1964) Mandinka informant for his problematic book on Indonesian influence on African xylophones. Dieterlen (1955:57) reported an episode in a Mande creation myth in which one of the ancestors of humanity created the first bala. She reports that a replica of this instrument, having seven keys, is guarded by the Keitas, presumably in Kangaba, and is supposed to be brought out only on the death of an important Keita or Kouyate. I have not come across any other information about this instrument either in written sources or in any other oral traditions.

Niagassola is visited less than towns such as Kela and Kita, which have reputations as jeli centers.[73]

I have personally seen four other balas similar to the one guarded in Niagassola: a replica with nineteen slats made perhaps a century ago by the Niagassola Kouyates; one with twenty slats that belongs to Bakari Diabate (who comes from Niagassola) in Kita, Mali, that is about seventy years old; one with fifteen slats in the musical instruments gallery of the Metropolitan Museum of Art in New York (Metropolitan Museum of Art, n.d., 1889.492); and one with nineteen slats in the instrument museum of the Royal Conservatory of Music in Brussels, dating from before the twentieth century (Mahillon 1893:383–86).[74] The earliest drawing of a bala, published in Froger (1698a:45–46, 1698b:33–35), Barbot (1746, pl. 3(2) after 55), and Astley (1745–47, vol. 2, pl. 7, facing 277), appears to have nineteen slats and looks as if it is the larger variety (plate 15).[75] The xylophone with eleven slats drawn in Smith (1744, frontispiece) and the one with eighteen slats drawn in Gray and Dochard (1825, facing 301) appear to be the large Maninka variety. Bala photographs from Guinea published in 1907 show the smaller variety that is prevalent today (Arcin 1907:270, 547).[76] The evidence above, supported by the opinions of some of my teachers, points to the relatively young age of the smaller balas—perhaps a century old.

The age of the bala guarded in Niagassola may never be determined according to Western scientific standards because there are strict rules regarding its care and the circumstances in which it may be taken out and played. But it is believed to have been passed down from Sumanguru Kante, and it remains a powerful symbol of Mande culture. I was repeatedly warned, even by a high government official, that dire consequences could befall one who does not properly observe the customs concerning the bala. When the *balatigi* passed away in the mid-1970s there was a question whether it should be moved to the next eldest in line, who was living in a village across the border in Mali. A major Kouyate family summit was

73. My information on the Sosso bala comes from Salikene Jemori Kouyate, who was my host in Niagassola in 1990, and Namankoumba Kouyate (1970, 1994-per), also from Niagassola. The preservation of material culture from the time of Sunjata may not be so rare: two spears believed to belong to Sunjata's general Tiramakan Traore are reported to be kept by the Diawara family of jelis in Kela (Leynaud and Cissé 1978:18–19; Cashion 1984:203).

74. Another large bala with nineteen slats, possibly acquired before the twentieth century, is pictured in Jenkins (1970:7, plate 1, no. 10).

75. The bala drawings in Froger, Barbot, and Astley are from the same source, most likely Froger. Astley summarizes the other two, and the editors of the new Barbot edition (1992:xlviii–xlix, 806) did not reprint the illustration, considering it to be borrowed from Froger.

76. There is little question about the smaller size of the bala shown on page 270, but the size of those on page 547 is less clear.

held, and for various reasons, one being the recognition of its status as a national treasure, the bala remained in Guinea. In 1999 Sekou Kouyate succeeded the late Fadjimba Kouyate as *balatigi* in a major festival supported by the Guinean government. A nongovernment organization has recently been created to promote the preservation of the instrument.

A genealogy of the Kouyate family in Niagassola may provide a rare example of oral and written history converging. My host in Niagassola, Jemori Kouyate (son of Salikene), who was in his middle thirties at the time, recited a genealogy starting from Sunjata's jeli, Bala Faseke Kouyate, who lived in the early thirteenth century, and going about twelve generations up to the present day, detailing the movement of the ancestral bala from village to village.[77] Out of all of the ancestors named, only the second, third, and fourth generation after Bala Faseke Kouyate had Doka (Duwa in another dialect) as part of their names. Any of these descendants named Doka could have been alive when Ibn Battūta visited the royal court of Mali in the midfourteenth century. The person who acted as Ibn Battūta's interpreter, and was also the intermediary between those who wanted to speak to the king and the king himself, was named Dūghā, a dialect variation of Doka. What is all the more compelling is that Dūghā is the one who played the bala for the king. Of interest for future inquiry is the relative lack of Muslim first names in the Niagassola Kouyate genealogy.

The Repertory of Jeliya

All the pieces played by jelis are named and have some kind of story behind them, some being of epic proportions and some just a few explanatory comments. In contrast to drumming, the pieces that jelis play, called *julo* (string, tune), *julu,* or *juru* in Mandinka, Maninka, and Bamana, respectively, are usually dedicated to a single person, such as a great leader, warrior, or patron. The person (or persons) the piece is dedicated to is called its *mari* or *tiyo* (Mn: *tii;* Bm: *tigi*), its "owner." Amadu Bansang Jobarteh often begins his recitation of the story behind a piece with the following formula. "All of our *kora julolu* [pieces], they each have an owner [*mari*], and each also

---

77. Since there are several people named Jemori Kouyate in the Kouyate Niagassola compound, they may be distinguished by prefixing each name with the mother's given name, in this case, Salikene. I am exercising discretion here by not publishing a full Kouyate genealogy. A genealogy collected a few years later by anthropologist Clemens Zobel (personal communication 1998) from the same Jemori Kouyate yielded only very minor differences. Niagassola Kouyates refer to their lineage as Dokala, as in Niagassola native Kaniba Oule Kouyate's (1994-disc) song *Adama Diarra,* in which she sings, "I, a jeli, come from Dokala, the guardians of the Sosso bala" ("Ne jeli bora Sosso bala tigilu ro Dokala").

has a meaning or story [*mana*] behind it" (Jobarteh 1990-per, A125, 203). "Every *kora julo* has an owner [*tiyo*]" (Jobarteh 1990-per, A231).[78]

Although many pieces are dedicated or belong to individuals, they are commonly used to praise and encourage those who are from the same lineage. This is an essential aspect of jeliya: instilling in the listeners pride and strength derived from the example of the deeds of their ancestors. The choice of a piece in performance is often dictated by the lineage of a person in the audience to whom the piece is directed.[79]

Julu, which can mean "string" (like a string on the koni) and by extension, "tune," usually refers to the musical accompaniment to a piece. Sometimes the French word *morceau* (piece) is used interchangeably with julu. *Dònkili* or *donkilo* (Bm: *dòngili*) refers to the melody sung in a julu. The deepest expressions of jeliya are bound up in the *fasa*—from *fa* (father) *siya* (lineage, race)—a praise song, or collection of songs, often of epic proportions, covering someone's lineage and deeds. The most widespread of all is *Sunjata fasa,* the epic recounting of the founding of the Mali empire, which can have any number of musical changes within it.

Each of the three traditional melody instruments of the jeli (bala, kora, and koni) has pieces closely associated with it, which most likely originated on that instrument. Each also borrows pieces from the other two instruments. In addition, some pieces from the hunter's repertory and from the repertories of neighboring ethnic groups are played by jelis. Therefore the bala, kora, and koni have idiomatic ways of being played and tuned connected with their own repertories, and they also have absorbed styles of playing (and even tunings in some cases) from the other instruments. The various streams that feed the repertory of the jeli are in turn part of a larger vast musical culture of the western African savanna and sahel. Piecing together the sources of the repertory of jelis is no easy task, although some well-traveled expert jelis can do just that.

Instrumental recordings of jelis without vocalists are not common, but the number is growing. The earliest complete instrumental albums celebrate Guinea's early years of independence (Guinea Compilations 1962a-

78. "Ntol la kora julu wo julu a bee ning a mari lemu, a dung a bee ye mana le fanang soto." "Kora julu wo julu a bee n'a tiyo lemu."

79. A concert I attended with Amadu Bansang Jobarteh in Brikama, Gambia, illustrates how singers make choices in performance. Just before the concert, the renowned Malian jelimuso Kandia Kouyate was introduced to Jobarteh, whose nephew Sidiki Diabate and grandnephew Toumani Diabate she knew well from Bamako. Kouyate opened her performance with a regal rendition of *Lamban,* a piece traditionally belonging to Kouyate jelis, and immediately went into the classic history of the Diabate lineage, citing the two Traore hunter brothers as well as Tiramakan Traore. Her choice of *Lamban* signaled a jeli orientation, and she specifically targeted Diabate (Jobarteh) jelis. Jobarteh and his son responded in traditional fashion by occasionally getting up and presenting her with offerings of cash.

disc, 1962b-disc) with kora duos, bala duos, and koni solos. *Ancient Strings* (Ministry of Information of Mali 1971-disc, vol. 5), features four of Mali's greatest kora players in duets and solos, a definitive statement of what is now the old guard of Malian kora players (plate 11). Eight of the eleven selections have been reissued on CD (Musiques du Mali 1995a-disc and 1995b-disc). That tradition had been brilliantly extended by kora players Toumani Diabate and Djelimoussa "Ballake" Sissoko (Diabate and Sissoko, 1999-disc), son of Jalimadi Sissoko, who accompanied Toumani's father Sidiki Diabate on *Ancient Strings*. Numerous other Senegambian kora players have recorded solo, including Jali Nyama Suso, Alhaji Bai Konte, and Amadu Bansang Jobarteh. Instrumental recordings of koni or bala playing are rare, except for sporadic field recordings. Increasing interest outside Africa, however, appears to be stimulating releases, including a comprehensive set of three CDs recorded by one of Guinea's finest bala players, El Hadj Djeli Sory Kouyate, and a trio called the Ivorys (1987-disc) consisting of two balas and one kora. Malian koni player Moriba Koita (1997-disc) has released what is probably the first complete recording of an ensemble of jeli instruments (ngoni, bala, kora, dundun) and jembe with no vocals, recorded not coincidentally in concert in France. Other well-known examples of instrumental music are the solo koni and duo kora renditions of *Sunjata* and *Tutu Jara,* respectively, that precede the news broadcasts on Radio Mali several times daily, and the solo kora rendition of *Jula faso* that is the signature tune for Radio Gambia.[80]

Sources That Feed the Repertories of the Jelis

Map 7 shows some of the most important pieces performed by jelis. It would be rare for a single jeli to be able to play all these pieces because they come from a wide variety of regional traditions, but most jelis are probably aware of most of them. The streams that feed the repertory of a jeli can be viewed according to several criteria; the first two are shown on the map:

1. The geographic and historical origin of pieces (old Mali, Bamana Segu, Mandinka Kabu, Fula Fuladu, modern Guinea, modern Mali, etc.).
2. The instrument on which it originated (kora, bala, or koni).
3. Musically related tune families.
4. The kind of person the piece is dedicated to (e.g., warrior, political leader, merchant).

Certain instruments hold pride of place in different geographic regions, and they are the principal media for singing, dancing, and storytelling in

80. See the discography for recordings by musicians named in this paragraph and chapter 5 for recordings of guitarists without vocalists. It is not uncommon for albums to include one or more instrumental tracks.

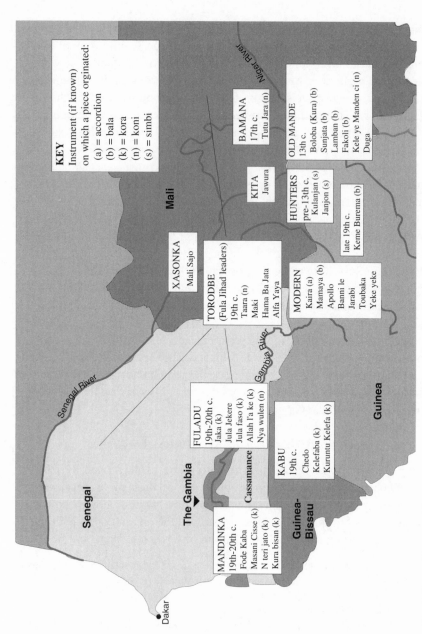

KEY

Instrument (if known)
on which a piece orginated:

(a) = accordion
(b) = bala
(k) = kora
(n) = koni
(s) = simbi

BAMANA
17th c.
Tutu Jara (n)

OLD MANDE
13th c.
Boloba (Kura) (b)
Sunjata (b)
Lamban (b)
Fakoli (b)
Kele ye Manden ci (n)
Duga

KITA
Jawura

HUNTERS
pre-13th c.
Kulanjan (s)
Janjon (s)

late 19th c.
Keme Burema (b)

XASONKA
Mali Sajo

TORODBE
(Fula Jihad leaders)
19th c.
Taara (n)
Maki
Hama Ba Jata
Alfa Yaya

MODERN
Kaira (a)
Mamaya (b)
Apollo
Banni le
Jarabi
Toubaka
Yeke yeke

FULADU
19th-20th c.
Jaka (k)
Jula Jekere
Jula faso (k)
Allah Ya ke (k)
Nya wulen (n)

KABU
19th c.
Chedo
Kelefaba (k)
Kuruntu Kelefa (k)

MANDINKA
19th-20th c.
Fode Kaba
Masani Cisse (k)
N teri jato (k)
Kura bisan (k)

Senegal River

Niger River

Gambia River

Senegal

The Gambia

Cassamance

Guinea-Bissau

Guinea

Mali

Dakar

Map 7 Some of the most important pieces jelis play.

those areas: the kora in The Gambia and Casamance, the bala in Guinea, and the koni in Mali. Consequently geographic region and instrument are often linked together, along with the heroes who had an impact on the rise and fall of local political power. But determining the instrument a piece originated on is not always clear-cut, since there are regions where several instruments coexist.

Although a significant body of pieces is intimately wrapped up in each instrument, some pieces transcend geographical borders and are known far and wide. A kora player from Mali, for example, may know Senegambian kora pieces even though they are of little interest to his Malian patrons. Such is the case with the kora player recorded by Laura Boulton (1957-disc) in Bamako in the early 1930s, who played the piece *Kelefaba,* celebrating a warrior (Kelefa) from the westernmost Mande region (Kabu) who had no influence on the Mali empire in general and was a Jola (neighbors of the western Mandinka). Politically, *Kelefaba* is not important outside the Senegambia region, but it is known to kora players all over because of its status as a prototypical kora piece; it is like an ocean that all can drink from, as Sidiki Diabate described it (see below). As with the kora, there are also prototypical pieces for the bala and koni.

The major direction of influence in the shared repertory of jelis is from old Mali (in the east) to more recent Mande territories in the west. For Gambian kora players, Mali is the ultimate source of their tradition, but they are more familiar with the traditions that spring from the Kabu empire and local cultures. Gambian jalis divide their repertory into *tilijii* (sunset, west)—pieces from The Gambia—and *tilibo* (sunrise, east)—pieces from Mali. A few pieces from The Gambia, such as *Masani Cisse* and *Allah l'a ke,* have also entered the repertory of Malians owing to their widespread popularity.

The simbi is sometimes cited as the ultimate source of the jeli's repertory, contributing pieces such as *Janjon* and *Kulanjan.* This flow of influence appears to be one-way; I do not know of any pieces the simbi has absorbed from any of the jeli instruments. Some modern pieces that probably developed on the guitar, such as *Apollo, Jarabi,* and *Tubaka,* have also entered the repertory of the jeli, and the guitar has absorbed virtually the whole of the jeli's repertory, being accepted since at least the 1950s as a bona fide jeli's instrument.[81]

Regional differences in Mande instrumental music are closely linked with the playing styles of instruments that are indigenous to those areas.

81. The recent work of Salif Keita as well as that of singer-composer Moussa "Segueledie" Keita points to a new trend of secularizing simbi music, opening it up to new instrumental combinations and new repertories.

Kora playing in Mali, for instance, has been influenced by the bala and koni in ways that it has not been affected in the Casamance region, where kora playing may show some influence from neighboring Balanta xylophone traditions (see Jali Mori Suso, in Knight 1992-vid). As another example, my principal bala teacher, Bala Dounbouya, who grew up in the region of Siguiri (Guinea), spent much of his life in Bamako (Mali), and then moved to Senegal, plays some of the more prominent pieces from The Gambia and Casamance, such as *Masani Cisse* and *Kelefaba* (as well as the Senegalese national anthem). He prefers pieces from his native Guinea, but many of them are virtually unknown in Dakar where he lives and teaches. Conversely, many of the Senegambian pieces he plays are insignificant in Guinea.

Roderic Knight (1973a, 1:100–109) classified the over one hundred pieces that he recorded in one year from Gambian kora players into three general epochs: early (thirteenth to fourteenth century); mid- (nineteenth and early twentieth centuries); and late (past forty years). These epochs effectively capture the distinctions significant to Gambian Mandinka. Jelis from Mali or Guinea might recognize other distinctions regarding the age of a piece. For example, the reign of the Bamana of Segu in the seventeenth and eighteenth centuries is an important source of pieces for Malian musicians. Several pieces associated with hunters, predating the Sunjata era, are also important.

Although the ngoni is the predominant instrument associated with the Bamana kingdoms of Segu and Kaarta and the simbi is the instrument of Maninka hunter's musicians, other kingdoms or peoples may have been associated with two instruments. Many of the pieces associated with old Mali are believed to come from the bala (such as *Boloba, Sunjata,* and *Lamban*), but one piece, *Kele ye Manding ci* (War has brought down the Mande), may come from the koni, according to Xasonka koni player Moussa Kouyate. Fulbe leaders from the nineteenth century might have had an entourage of griots that included jelis who played the koni, kora, and soron as well as Fulbe griots playing the *hoddu* (lute). Senegambian Mandinka chiefs from the nineteenth and twentieth centuries might also have had jelis attached to them who played the kora and *kontingo* (koni), owing in part to the influx of koni players from Xaso.

Two common techniques for generating new pieces in the Mande repertory are to lay new words on top of an older instrumental accompaniment and to alter the older instrumental accompaniment. The parent-child relationship of some pieces is common knowledge and is readily talked about as such among many musicians: *Saxo (Sacko) Dugu* comes from *Duga; Jula Jekere* from *Janjon;* and *Jaka* from *Hama Ba Jata.* The relationships between the parent and child pieces may be far removed in terms of region, instrument of origin, or tuning system, but once recognized they do give insight into Mande ways of musical transformation.

Similar kinds of transformations are now occurring in modern Mande dance music. Salif Keita (1991-disc) has taken one of the oldest pieces in the repertory, *Janjon,* and transformed it with new words, a new title (*Nyanafin*), and no reference to the original except the musical accompaniment. The same has been done by Baaba Maal (1991-disc), who took *Jula Jekere* (an important piece from eastern Gambia), which itself is a transformation of *Janjon,* changed the words, and retitled it *Joulowo.* They both took pieces that were important in their own countries: *Janjon* from old Mali for Salif Keita, and *Jula Jekere* from eastern Senegambia for Baaba Maal. (See appendix C for more examples.)

Another set of musical relationships among pieces is not articulated by Mande musicians as far as I can ascertain. Rather than a parent-child relationship, some pieces considered distinct and independent of each other appear to be cut from the same harmonic mold. I call one such set the Sunjata complex, not to be confused with the set of pieces that can be performed during a rendition of *Sunjata fasa* (the Sunjata epic). The pieces *Sunjata, Lamban,* and *Boloba* all have a similar harmonic progression (transcription 13), yet they differ enough in their realizations so that they are not spoken of as being musically related. A *Kelefa* complex, on the other hand, is recognized as a group of related pieces, most likely because of the idiomatic way of playing pieces that belong to it. The bala piece *Fakoli* and the more recent *Nanfulen* share the unique feature of having three harmonic areas rather than the usual two or four, but they are not spoken of as related.

Another way of viewing the repertory of the jeli is according to the people commemorated in the pieces. Knight (1983) categorized fifty pieces played by Gambian Mandinka kora players according to the ethnic origin of the people they are dedicated to and found that eleven were dedicated to Fula and seven more were dedicated to Wolof, Bambara, Jola, or Mauritanians. Knight (1973a, 1 : 100 – 109) has also categorized pieces according to the calling in life of the person the piece is dedicated to, such as kings, warriors, or traders. This categorizing based on the status of the patron lends itself to characterizations such as royal court music or light music. Pieces dedicated to kings and warriors are more serious and could be considered court or chamber music. Some pieces with more modern themes not dedicated to any leaders in particular, such as *Apollo* or *Jimbasengo,* are considered lighter, youth music. Amadu Bansang Jobarteh, whose repertory leans heavily toward older pieces from Mali, does not play *Jimbasengo* because he considers it light and for young people. By the same token, some younger kora players do not fare well with the older, serious pieces that Jo-barteh favors.

Descriptions of Important Pieces

Appendix C lists some of the more widespread pieces in the repertory of jelis and a variety of recordings on which they can be heard. The following brief descriptions survey those pieces.[82]

Simbi Pieces

Janjon and *Kulanjan* (also known as *Donso fòli*) belong to the oldest layer of the jeli's repertory. *Duga* is said to be of hunter origin, but I do not know of its being played on the simbi or donso ngoni. *Balakononifin* has curiously made the jump from hunter's music to modern dance bands without passing into the jeli's repertory. Descriptions of these pieces can be found in chapter 2.

Bala Pieces

The bala is one of the most potent symbols of Mande identity, as is the body of music associated with it surrounding the early formation of the empire. That music is exemplified in three musically related pieces that make up what I call the Sunjata complex: *Sunjata fasa,* a series of praise songs and narratives that recount the history of the Mali empire; *Boloba* (called *Kura* in The Gambia), dedicated to Sumanguru Kante; and *Lamban,* created by Kouyate jelis as a celebration of being a jeli. During a performance of *Sunjata fasa* a number of distinct songs praising Sunjata may be incorporated, including *Nyama nyama nyama, I bara kala ta,* and *Subaa ni mansaya.* Songs praising other figures in the epic might also be incorporated, such as *Janjon, Boloba,* and *Tiramakan. Boloba* and *Lamban* hold unique places in the jeli's repertory. *Boloba* is the only piece in any genre of Mande music in which the beats consist of five pulses each rather than the usual two, three, or four pulses (transcription 14). *Lamban* (Md: *Lambango*) is perhaps the only pre-twentieth-century piece played by jelis that has no story behind it. It is a celebratory piece dedicated not to any single person but to the whole Kouyate lineage of jelis, and it has become one of the most popular musical vehicles used by jelimusolu in Mali to create new praise songs for their patrons. *Lamban* is also one of the few pieces that has a specific dundun part to it, indicating that it is also a dance piece, and indeed there are distinctive movements associated with it danced by jelimusolu (see Knight 1992-vid). The bala-based piece *Mamaya,* created by Dioubate (Diabate)

82. For a brief discussion of the Soninke repertory see Dieterlen and Sylla (1992:97).

jelis in Kankan in the 1930s or 1940s, perhaps in collaboration with Kante jelis from the area, appears to be inspired by *Lamban,* not so much in its musical content but as a celebratory piece by and for jelis (and their nonjeli age-mates) with a distinctive dance associated with it. The same *Lamban* three-stroke dundun pattern can also be played for *Mamaya.*[83]

Jawura is a popular dance rhythm from Kita, Mali, that may have originated on the bala. It can be played with jembe and dundun accompaniment and is a favorite of Malian acoustic guitarists (two pieces on Bajourou 1993-disc come from *Jawura*). Sidiki Diabate (1990-per:37–40) considered it a wellspring for composers and cites it as the mother of the kora pieces *Allah l'a ke* and *Jula faso.* Djeli Mady Diabate (bala) and Kemogo Diabate (koni) from Kita also confirm its importance, citing *Hasiminka* and *Mamaya* as derivatives from *Jawura* (Diabate and Diabate 1990-per). *Fakoli* is a little-known bala piece that is probably the musical source for the unusual harmonic scheme of *Nanfulen,* a modern bala piece from Guinea that features three harmonic areas of equal duration.[84] *Keme Burema* is named after the brother of Almami Samory Toure, the late nineteenth-century general and political leader who conquered much of Upper Guinea, Wasulu in southern Mali, and Kong in northern Côte d'Ivoire. It is a praise vehicle for Toure that is very important in Guinea, in part because of his Guinean origins and also because Guinean president Sekou Toure has claimed a close family relationship with Samory Toure.[85] Like *Sunjata* in Mali, *Keme Burema* has been recorded by modern orchestras; the most ambitious effort is the album-length *Regard sur le passé* of Bembeya Jazz (1970-disc).

Koni Pieces

The koni is a wellspring for jelis of the sahel and northern savanna. The two most important and widespread koni pieces are *Tutu Jara* and *Taara. Tutu*

83. For Maninka transcriptions and English or French translations of some of the songs in *Sunjata fasa* see Kele Monson Diabate (in Moser 1974:257, 266, 289, 321) and Lansine Diabate (in Jansen, Duintjer, and Tamboura 1995:149, 157). See chapter 1 for further discussion of the significance of Sunjata in the Mande repertory and chapter 5 and Kaba and Charry (forthcoming) for more on *Mamaya.* Panneton (1987:231–32) has drawn up a list of fifty-eight pieces in the repertory of bala players from Tabato, Guinea-Bissau, in the order in which he learned them from his teacher Umaro Jebate; the first is *Lamban (Laa ban).*

84. The only performances of *Fakoli* I have heard were done by two of my bala teachers, both with the family name Doumbia, which is one of the lineages associated with Fakoli.

85. According to Sidiki Diabate (1990-per:83–85) Tasilimanga Konte was one of Samory Toure's jalis. His younger brother Harengale Konte was a jali of Muntaga Tal (son of Umar Tal). (Diabate's pronunciation occasionally alternated between Konte and Kone.) L. Kaba (1990:53) has recounted an occasion where Sekou Toure was publicly presented as a nephew of Samory Toure's nephew. Perhaps resulting from this, Samory Toure's lineage in Kankan and Sanankoro in Upper Guinea then adopted Sekou Toure, whose father came from Mali.

Jara, also called *Ba juru* (Mother's tune), dedicated to a Bamana king of the Jara (Diara) lineage, tells the story of a barren mother who sought help from a snake (Bm: *tutu*). With the aid of the snake she bore a child who would become a king of the Jara dynasty, and she named him Tutu Jara. The piece is one of the most popular musical accompaniments used in Mali by je-limusolu to create new praise songs for their patrons, and it is a major piece in the repertory of Malian guitarists, with countless variations.[86]

Taara is dedicated to the mid-nineteenth-century Fulbe jihad leader al Hajj Umar Tal, who from his base in Futa Toro conquered much of the Senegalese and Malian sahel including Segu. Given the expanse that Tal traveled and conquered, the piece is used to praise travelers. One of Umar Tal's jelis has been identified as Mustafa Jali Musa Diabate, who may have been the composer of *Taara.* Performances of *Taara* often move directly into *Maki,* a related piece apparently dedicated to Umar Tal's second son Maki, probably born in 1836 (Robinson 1985:105–6).[87]

Kora Pieces

Allah l'a ke (Allah has done It) has probably traveled the farthest of all kora pieces. The Cain and Abel–like story concerns the children of Falaye Kora, chief of Tumana district in eastern Gambia appointed by Fulbe leader Musa Molo at the dawn of the British colonial era in the late nineteenth century. The piece belongs to Mamady Kora, the eldest son who should have inherited the chieftancy when his father died. But his younger brother Kemonding convinced the town elders to give him the chieftancy instead, then banished his elder brother from Tambasansang, the seat of the district. When Mamady returned, Kemonding had him locked up. Mamady eventually had the chieftancy rightfully given to him, and rather than exacting revenge, he forgave his younger brother. Amadu Bansang Jobarteh, whose

86. My Xasonka koni teacher knew a large number of ways to play *Tutu Jara*—he often cited seventeen versions—and were it not for my impatience and a curiosity to see what other pieces existed, all our lessons would have been spent on *Tutu Jara.* Indeed, a koni class that I observed at the conservatory in Dakar, taught by respected koni player Numukumba Kouyate, played *Tutu Jara* exclusively for months. Moriba Koita's (1997-disc) recording of *Tutu Jara* (called *Badiourou*) goes through several of the variations.

87. According to Sidiki Diabate (1990-per:73–81), Mustafa Jali Musa's father, Amadu Jali Musa, was also Umar Tal's jali, and *Maki* was adapted from *Taara* by Jaliko Madi Diabate from Guinea, who played the soron. Based on information from Djigui Kouyate and Diely Baba Sissoko, M. Diabate (1970a:85–96) reports that *Taara* was composed by Moustapha Diabate, who was the jeli of Madani Tal, son of al Hajj Umar Tal. Ba Konaré (1993:239) notes that the jeli of al Hajj Umar Tal was Jeli Musa Diabate, whose son Karamoko Jeli Mamadi Diabate was the jeli of Muntaga Tal, son of al Hajj Umar. Karamoko Jeli's daughter Kiatou Jeli was a well-known singer in Mali in the 1940s and 1950s. One of the more idiosyncratic versions of *Taara* is Mory Kante's (1996-disc) *On yarama Foulbêh,* a tribute to Fulbe peoples done in the slow 6/8 style more typical of African American ballads of the past few decades.

father and in-laws were intimates of the parties involved in the story, believes the composers of *Allah l'a ke* were his father-in-law Kunkung Kanute and someone named Hamadi.

Masani Cisse, another very popular piece in Senegal and The Gambia, is the name of a wealthy merchant who lived in the early twentieth century. According to Amadu Bansang Jobarteh, Cisse wanted to marry a beautiful young girl of his village, but she was already engaged to another man who was very poor. Cisse offered the girl's family great bridewealth, and she was forced to marry him. On the first night of the honeymoon Masani Cisse died before the marriage could be consummated. The musical accompaniment is commonly believed to derive from an older piece named *Silati ngalen koyi.*[88]

As noted above, *Kuruntu Kelefa* and *Kelefaba* are widely believed to be the source of kora music.

> That is why any jali who is playing *Kuruntu Kelefa,* if it pleases them, with Allah's aid, they can create something from it and offer it to their patron. *Kuruntu Kelefa* is a great ocean. Everyone drinks from it. . . . It [*Kelefa*] is like the alphabet. Much has come from it. (Sidiki Diabate 1990-per, 3, 61)[89]

Other well-known kora pieces include *Tabara,* dedicated to a beautiful Fulbe woman from The Gambia, and *Jula faso,* dedicated to long-distance traders called Jula. Knight's (1973a, 1:98–99) selection of thirty-four pieces of diverse origins form a core Gambian kora repertory, "the songs most widely known and often heard," and could be taken as a general indication of the typical active size of any one player's repertory.

Unidentified Origins

The following pieces do not have close associations with any one instrument.

Duga (Vulture) is one of the oldest pieces in the Mande repertory, but it is not played on the simbi. Its basis in a minor mode indicates possible vocal or koni origins. It was originally played for warriors who had narrowly escaped death but has since been associated first with Duga Koro, king of Kore, and then with the Segu king Da Monson Jara who defeated him (Bird 1972:280, 468; Bird and Kendall 1980:21; M. Diabate 1970:69).[90] The piece *Sacko Dugu* is musically derived from *Duga.* According to Naman-

88. For an extended transcription and translation of the story of Masani Cisse (Maasaane Siise) by Yankuba Saaho, see Pfeiffer (1997:254–90).

89. "Wo le a tinna Kuruntu Kelefa, jali wo jali n'i be koriso la n'a diyat'i ye, ning Alla ye makoyi, i si feng bondi noo jee k'a dii jaatii ma la. Kurutu Kelefa baa jiiba lemu. Moo bee kara ming jee le. . . . Ate lemu komeng alfa bee. Jama le bota ate kono."

90. Wa Kamissoko (Cissé and Kamissoko 1988:354–55) adds that jelis sing *Duga* on the occasion of an execution when the body is thrown to the vultures. For a discussion of the significance of *Duga* in modern Mande literature, see Manthia Diawara (1992:164–66).

koumba Kouyate (1994-per) of Niagassola, *Sacko Dugu* was originally based on a piece commemorating the founder of Niagassola, Nasira Mady Keita, and his victorious battle against the Fulbe from nearby Birgo. The piece received its name later when Jemori Sacko, the chief of Kunjan, traveled to Niagassola to purchase it.

Chedo (Fr: *Tiedo*) or *Kedo,* the name given to a certain class of warrior during the time of the Kabu empire, is used as a vehicle for recounting the history of the empire. The Archives Culturelles in Dakar has commissioned many field recordings of it in the course of their research into oral traditions of the Casamance. *Chedo,* like *Sunjata,* has also been adapted by popular singers such as Ismael Lo (1985-disc) and Baaba Maal (1994-disc). *Chedo* most likely comes from the kora or koni.

Mali Sajo (Fr: *Sadio*) is associated more with the voice than with any particular instrument. The lyrics tell a story of a close friendship between a young girl and a hippopotamus (*mali*) from Bafoulabé in Xaso territory and its tragic end at the hands of a hunter. Classic versions have been recorded by Sory Kandia Kouyate (1956?-disc, 1970-disc), and Humblot (1921:139), reporting on life in Kankan (Guinea) in the early twentieth century, provided Maninka lyrics and a French translation.

Modern Pieces

Kaira, Arabic for "peace" and also a male first name, is very popular in Guinea and Mali and is often used as a standard musical accompaniment for creating new songs. Kora player Sidiki Diabate (Ministry of Information of Mali 1971-disc, vol. 5/Musiques du Mali 1995b-disc) has done much to develop the piece, and his son Toumani Diabate (1988b-disc) has continued that tradition. According to Sidiki Diabate (1990-per:455–72), *Kaira* was originally composed on the accordion by Gese Kemo Diabate in Guinea for a Fulbe interpreter named Kaira Barry in Kissidougou, at a time when there were few motor vehicles (perhaps in the 1940s or earlier). Gese Kemo's son Gese Mamady played it on the guitar, the instrument on which it may have disseminated. By 1949 it was widespread; Arthur Alberts (1949-disc) recorded versions of it by Sira Mory Diabate of Kela, the Kankan Diabates, and an unidentified guitar and kora group possibly from Siguiri (Alberts 1950-disc/1954a-disc).[91]

91. Notes to Ministry of Information of Mali (1971-disc: vol. 5; reprinted in Musiques du Mali 1995b-disc) state that the piece *Kaira* was born in Kela in 1946 and became a symbol of a Malian youth movement associated with the pan–West African political party RDA. Perhaps *Kaira* was composed earlier than 1946, but it gained popularity when the Kela jelis took it up. Djimo Kouyate (personal communication 1997) identified the composer of *Kaira* as Mecanicien Kemo, probably a reference to the same Gese Kemo, who may have been a bicycle mechanic.

Tubaka (*Toubaka*) stands apart from the bulk of the jeli's repertory not only because it is a love song, but also because of its extended harmonic scheme of four areas that unfold over a relatively long stretch of time. It probably originated in Upper Guinea, perhaps from Kankan, on the guitar or accordion in the 1930s if not earlier. It is a favorite of guitarists from Upper Guinea, who excel in playing it.[92]

Two songs attributed to Sira Mory Diabate of Kela have achieved widespread popularity: *Singya* (Mother's milk) and *Sara*. *Singya* has been recorded by Sira Mory's nephew Kasse Mady Diabate with National Badema (1983a-disc: *Kana bla n na*) and by singer-guitarist Ali Farka Toure (1988b-disc), whose guitar accompaniments bear a marked resemblance to Salif Keita's (Austin 1991-vid) solo guitar and vocal rendition of his own song *Primpin* (transcription 29). *Sara* has been taken up by modern Guinean orchestras, and two extended versions have been recorded by Balla et Ses Balladins (1993-disc).

Jaraby (Fr: *Diarabi*) is another popular love song that has two variants, one being distinguished as *Kankan Jarabi*, the other associated with Fanta Sacko (1972-disc).[93]

Jeli Tuning Systems

Kora

Four named kora tunings are in general use: *Tomoraba* (also known as *Silaba*), *Tomora mesengo, Hardino,* and *Sauta*. Each tuning is deemed more or less suitable for playing various pieces in the repertory, thereby reflecting local musical dialects. Many kora players recognize only three tunings, and still others play pieces in only two. Though some of the tunings may be historically related—for example, Sauta may have come about as a variant of Hardino—I do not see any one tuning as a standard reference. Rather, Tomoraba is predominant in the Casamance and western Gambia, Tomora mesengo and Hardino in eastern Gambia, and Sauta in Mali. The extensive work of King (1972) and Knight (1991a) collecting and analyzing kora tunings in The Gambia and Senegal provides a solid foundation for generalization, notwithstanding the absence of information from Mali, Guinea, and Guinea-Bissau. Figure 4, based on King (1972:136) and Knight (1991a: 22–23), shows the interval relationships for the four kora tunings. Figure 5

92. For lyrics to *Tubaka* see Fanta Sacko (1972-disc) and M. Kaba (1995:178).

93. For French translations of many songs in the jeli's repertory see M. Diabate (1970a) and M. Kaba (1995). For Maninka lyrics and French translations for a variety of songs see Perron (1930). See chapter 5 for more on repertories.

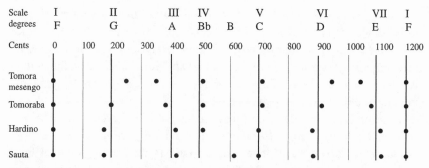

Figure 4 Kora: the four tunings (after King 1972:136 and Knight 1991).

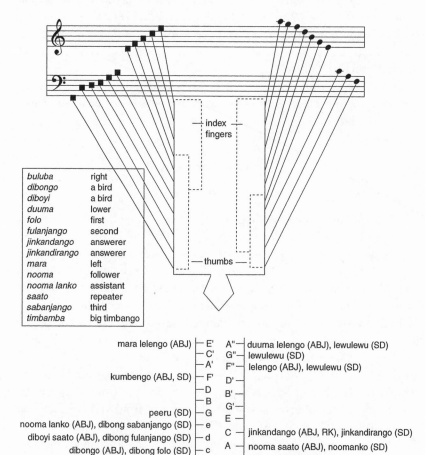

Figure 5 Kora: layout and names of strings. Distribution of strings, range of the thumbs and index fingers, and names of the strings, in Sauta tuning. ABJ = Amadu Bansang Jobarteh; SD = Sidiki Diabate; RK = Roderic Knight.

shows the layout and tuning of the strings on a kora, along with names of some of the strings.[94]

The origins of the various kora tunings are not clear, but the regional associations of pieces played in each tuning may provide clues. Mandinka kora players from the kora heartland (The Gambia, Casamance, and Guinea Bissau) generally agree that Tomoraba (big, great Tomora), also called Silaba (main way, main road), is the original kora tuning and that the oldest kora pieces (e.g., *Kuruntu Kelefa* and *Kelefaba*) are played in that tuning (Jobarteh 1990-per: A190, 534; King 1972: 126–33; Knight 1991a: 19).

Players who do not use or recognize Tomoraba as a distinct tuning may refer to Tomora mesengo simply as Tomora (Knight 1991a: 19). Sidiki Diabate, who spent relatively little time in western Gambia or the Casamance, referred to a recording of a piece in Tomoraba tuning I played for him as a Casamance tuning, a variation of Hardino, which he recognized as the original kora tuning. He considered Tomora as coming from the koni and Sauta, which he first heard from his uncle Amadu Bansang Jobarteh, as a later invention (S. Diabate 1990-per: 227–29). Jobarteh in turn recognized Sauta as a recent tuning; he first heard it from a jali named Keba Kouyate from Niumi and believes it originated on the koni (Jobarteh 1990-per: A49, B157, 233).

Tomora is the name of a region in Xaso in northwestern Mali renowned for its koni players, and according to Sidiki Diabate it is the source of the kora tuning of the same name.

> Tomora [either the name of a region in Mali or the tuning that takes its name from that region], it is the tuning of their kontingo players. Now, if you want to play with their kontingo players so that you are all in tune [*beng*], you should tune your kora to the Tomora tuning [*kumbengo*]. (S. Diabate 1990-per: 355–57)[95]

Here he was referring to Tomora mesengo tuning.[96] The qualifications *-ba* (big, great) and *mesengo, mesema,* or *-nding* (small, thin, little) could refer to the relative positions of the tonics in each of these tunings. Pieces in Tomora mesengo feature a tonic on the A string just above the *timbango* (F) string on the right hand side. Mesengo might refer to its thinness (its higher pitch in Western terminology), and *-ba* might then refer to the thickness (its lower pitch in Western terminology) of a tonic on the timbango string.

94. King (1972) took the tunings of the twenty kora players he sampled and arrived at an average tuning, which is reflected in figure 4. King's (1972: 133) proposal that Hardino and Tomora mesengo be considered derivatives of Tomoraba, rather than tunings arrived at independently, may be less appropriate for eastern Gambia, Guinea, and Mali.

95. "Wo Tomora, i la konting jalolu, i la konting jalolu la kumbengo. Ayiwa, n'i lafita i n'i la konting jalolu ye kosiro ke fò al ye beng i ka kora beng Tomora kumbengo le la."

96. Sidiki Diabate (1990-per: 228–32) also noted that in the Tomora region they refer to their tuning as Maranbandingo, but I do not know the significance of the term.

Tomora mesengo would then refer to the Tomora with the thinner or higher pitch or tonic and Tomoraba to the Tomora with the thicker or lower pitch or tonic.

Amadu Bansang Jobarteh believes that all three eastern tunings, Tomora mesengo, Hardino, and Sauta, come from the *kontingo* (the Mandinka term for koni). The kontingo was an important instrument in eastern Gambia for two reasons: as part of the Fulbe stronghold called Fuladu, its leaders were probably attended by *gaulo*s (Fulbe griots) who played the *hoddu* (the Fulbe version of the koni); and late nineteenth-century migrations of jelis from Mali into eastern Gambia brought the kontingo with them (including Amadu Bansang's father Jali Fili Jobarteh).

Hardino may be related to the word *ardin,* the name of the tuning that the lead koni player uses when two konis play together. Wolof *xalam* (lute) players also use the term *ardin* for a tuning. The word *ardin* may come from the Fulbe language with the meaning "to lead" (see the section on koni tuning below), conforming to the musical function of the tuning. When a kora and koni were played together, tuning adjustments would have to be made, and the kora-playing children of Malian koni-playing immigrants to eastern Gambia may have adapted a term and a tuning from the koni.

Kora players use Sauta tuning primarily to play pieces from Mali. Such pieces typically feature vocal melodies, usually sung by jalimusolu, that have a raised fourth degree, and Sauta is the only kora tuning that has a raised fourth degree. Knight (1991a:34) has noted that among kora players Sauta may also be called *jalimusolu la kumbengo* (female jali's tuning). The name Sauta may be related to the Arabic term *saut:* "sound . . . voice; tone; strain; melody; tune" (Wehr 1976:529).[97] Jalis who have had strong Koranic training, like the vast majority of my teachers, often use Arabic terms in the course of Mandinka conversation (I have heard Amadu Bansang Jobarteh use *saut* to refer to the sound of something). Kora players may have attached the Arabic term *saut* (or *sauta*) to a tuning typically used to play pieces from Mali with prominent vocal melodies sung by jalimusolu.

Amadu Bansang Jobarteh's tuning method is based on the timbango string as system tonic. First he tunes the answerer (*jinkandango*) string (C) to a fifth above the timbango string (F) (the first and third strings on the right hand side). He also checks the upper octave of the timbango (the string he calls *kumbengo*) against these two strings. He then fills in the lower tetrachord starting at the G immediately above the F (timbango) and then the A immediately above. The A is usually tuned in a 3-2-1 (A-G-F) pattern. In Sauta he tunes the sharp fourth degree (B-natural) against the C above it,

---

97. I thank Harold Powers for bringing the Arabic term to my attention. For more on the musical meaning of *saut* (*sawt*) in the Islamic world see al-Faruqi (1981:298–300) and Shiloah (1995:15).

immediately deadening the B-natural after it is struck, as if he were playing a piece. In the other tunings the natural fourth degree (B-flat) is tuned in a 4-3-2-1 (B-flat-A-G-F) pattern. Once the lower tetrachord is tuned he moves to the upper tetrachord, tuning the D string to the C below it and checking the upper F' in a 6-5-8 pattern. He then tunes the E in a downward pattern 7-6-5-8 (E-D-C-F').

Once the first octave spread is in tune, Jobarteh repeats the same process one octave higher; he does not tune each of the upper strings to their lower octaves one by one. It appears that the significant intervals for tuning are not octaves, but the intervals between adjacent strings and those between any string and the lower or upper tonic. Once the second octave is tuned, the two leftover treble strings on the right hand side (G″ and A″) are tuned, and then the bass strings below the timbango are tuned using the same process as was used for the upper tetrachord of the octave. At this point Jobarteh may begin to play a piece and then notice whether the various octave intervals are in tune. Often in the tuning process they may be out of tune, but they are not adjusted until after he has moved up and down the instrument tuning it and then begun to play a piece to check his tuning.[98]

There is no real sense of absolute pitch among kora players, so when two get together one must make an adjustment up or down to play with the other. Koras are usually tuned to match the range of the vocalist, who is often the player himself. Most are tuned with their system tonic, the timbango string (the first on the right hand side), within the range of E-flat to G above middle C (Knight 1971:29; King 1972:123–26), with younger players tending to have their instruments pitched higher than older players, at least in The Gambia.

By moving the tonal center to a string other than the timbango (F), kora players, especially those outside the Senegambia region, have expanded the scalar and modal vocabulary available on the instrument. Knight (1991a) has begun initial investigations of this practice, which is probably more prevalent outside the kora heartland, where jalis play repertories from other instruments and peoples. One common practice is to place the tonic on the sixth degree in either Hardino or Sauta tuning, which from a Western standpoint can be considered as playing in a minor mode, or more precisely, the Aeolian and Dorian modes, respectively.[99]

98. A brief excerpt of Alhaji Bai Konte (1989-disc) tuning reveals him at the tail end of the process checking octaves, other intervals, and descending scales. Also see Aning's (1982) description of Foday Musa Suso tuning his kora.

99. Knight (1991a:46–47) cites many examples of shifted tonal centers on the kora, which he correlates with various Western modes, including Sidiki Diabate's versions of *Duga* (Ministry of Information of Mali 1971-disc: vol. 5) and *Sacko Dugu* (Sidiki Diabate 1987-disc), both with tonics on the sixth degree of Hardino; and Toumani Diabate's (1988b-disc) version of *Jarabi*, with a tonic on the sixth degree of Sauta.

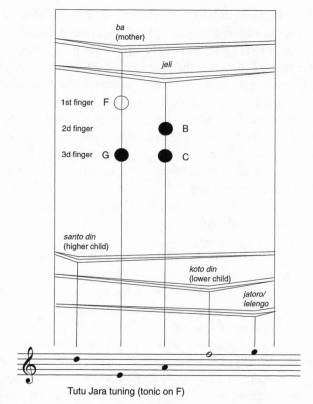

Tutu Jara tuning (tonic on F)

Figure 6 Koni: layout and names of strings and Tutu Jara tuning (according to Moussa Kouyate 1990-per).

Koni

Figure 6 shows the neck of a koni with the names of the strings and the tuning used for one of the most important pieces in its repertory, *Tutu Jara*. Figure 7 shows eight tunings along with the names of pieces played in each and the finger positions used in some of the tunings. All the information shown in these two figures is based on lessons with my koni teacher Moussa Kouyate, who comes from the Tomora region of Xaso in northwestern Mali. Tunings that appear in Michael Coolen's (1979) study of the Wolof xalam (lute) are also noted.[100]

Each tuning (called *kumben*) in figure 7 is named after an important piece played in that tuning. *Tutu Jara* kumben, then, refers to the tuning used to play the piece *Tutu Jara*. When two konis are played together the lead koni

100. Bamba's (Bamba and Prévost 1996:236) names for four ngoni strings (*ba juru, ko juru* [back string], *jeli juru,* and *den juru*) are similar to those of Moussa Kouyate, although their placement appears to be different.

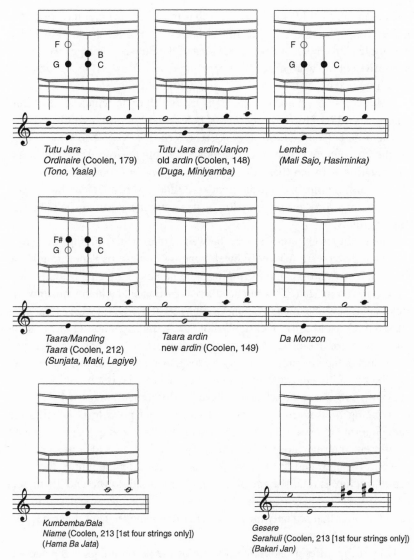

Figure 7 Koni: tunings and finger positions (according to Moussa Kouyate 1990-per). The tunings are named after important pieces that are played in them. Tunings that appear in Coolen (1979), transposed here, are also noted. Hollow noteheads indicate notes that serve as a tonic. Other pieces that are played in these tunings are listed in parentheses.

is tuned to a higher tuning generically called *ardin*. On the first line of music notation in figure 7 the first two tunings show the *Tutu Jara* accompanying and lead (ardin) tunings. *Tutu Jara* ardin tuning is also used to play the piece *Janjon*, in which case the tuning would be called *Janjon* kumben (tuning).

Coolen (1979:147) has suggested that the word *ardin* comes from the Fulbe word *ardo,* "to lead," or in another context, a certain kind of Fulbe warrior leader. Gaden's (1914:5) lexicon of the Pulaar language gives many derivatives of the word *arde,* all supporting Coolen's assertion: to come, arrival, to guide or lead, to go ahead, and a kind of chief.[101]

Ardin is also the name of a harp played by Moorish female griots (Guignard 1975:176; Norris 1968:63–65), described in print as early as 1695 by Sieur de la Courbe (appendix A). The term is also probably the source for the kora tuning called Hardino, most probably borrowed from the koni. The relation between these three uses of *ardin*—a Moorish harp, a koni (and xalam) tuning, and a Mandinka kora tuning—is not clear, but it does indicate some process of diffusion at work among griots of neighboring ethnic groups.

There is a strong concordance between xalam (lute) tunings and their names, collected from Wolof gewels (griots) in western Senegal and The Gambia (see figure 7), and the tunings and names I collected from my Xasonka teacher in Mali. This can be taken as evidence of a larger western African sahel-savanna music system. Coolen (1979:84–85; 1982:74) has discussed the Xasonka origin of the Wolof xalam tradition, noting that it is not uncommon for Wolof xalam players to learn from Xasonka koni players.

In each of the koni tunings many pieces may be played. Some pieces may also be played in several tunings, but they seem to be traditionally associated with only one. Pieces that are played in different tunings can be thought of as being transposed up or down to a different pitch level keeping the same internal interval relationships, as opposed to moving to a tuning with a different internal interval structure. This is the same idea as playing a piece in C major and in G major in open position on the guitar: the same scale structure is retained, the piece sounds higher or lower, and the fingering is different. There may also be cases where one piece is played in different tunings that not only move the general pitch level up or down but also change the scale structure.

One of the differences between some of the koni tunings is the accommodation of either a sharp fourth degree or natural seventh degree without having to use the fourth finger of the hand stopping the strings on the neck. In *Tutu Jara* tuning, for instance, the sharp fourth degree lies comfortably under the second finger. By contrast, *Manding* tuning is used for pieces that feature a prominent natural fourth degree; if the sharp fourth degree were used (and it is usually not), it would have to be played with the fourth finger.

---

101. Also see *'ardaade* (to lead, guide) and *ardinde* (to lead) in Osborn, Dwyer, and Donohoe (1993:10) and Labouret (1952:248).

Bala

Gilbert Rouget (1999-disc, Rouget and Schwarz 1969) did extensive work measuring Maninka (Malinke) balas, albeit on a limited sample, and concluded that they are tuned equiheptaphonically, seven equal intervals to the octave. Lynne Jessup (1983) did measurements on a larger but less select sample and came to the same basic conclusion, as did Panneton (1987:195–96), who used only one instrument measured with and without the gourd resonators. Knight (1991a) took up the work of Rouget and Jessup, reexamining the questions of interval size, octave tuning, and unison concordance, and coined the phrase "vibrato octaves" to describe a tolerance, or even possibly a desire, for intervals that deviate from a theoretical norm. My own observations of bala tuning follow.[102]

Most of the bala players I met were able to make their own instruments. The bala maker is also the one who tunes the instrument, which is done before the slats are tied onto the bala frame. If anything more than slight tuning adjustments are to be made to an assembled bala, all the slats must be untied, tuned, and then retied, taking the better part of a day. Tuning adjustments are made by shaving wood from the underside of a slat. Shaving from the ends raises the pitch; shaving from the center lowers it.[103]

I observed two methods for tuning a bala: either one bala is tuned directly to another or a bala is tuned to itself, the more taxing method. In both methods the tuner starts at the bass end and moves across the instrument one slat at a time toward the treble end. This is also true for the string instruments of the jeli. If he is tuning one bala to another, the lowest slat on one instrument is tuned to the lowest slat on the other (unless one has extra slats at the bass end), then the next slats are tuned to each other, and so on. If a bala is being tuned without reference to another, the tuner first decides on a pitch for the first slat (at the bass end), either referring to another bala or using an intuitive feel for an appropriate pitch and size of the slat. The second slat is then tuned to the first slat at an interval roughly equal to one-seventh of an octave (the seventh root of two, approximately 171 cents), which when replicated seven times will arrive at a perfect octave (1,200 cents). Throughout the process the most significant interval is that between any two adjacent slats. Once several slats are tuned, however, they are checked by playing a piece and also by playing arpeggio-like patterns, such as slats 1-3-5-8.

102. My understanding of bala construction and tuning comes from extended observation (and videotaping) of the process in the homes of Bala Dounbouya in Dakar and Salimu Kouyate in Brikama, The Gambia.

103. See Jessup (1983:34–37) for a description of the construction of balas and Strumpf (1970) and Seavoy (1982) for the construction and tuning process of xylophones in Ghana.

Octaves are also checked, and the octave is the only interval that is played simultaneously instead of sequentially. The tuning process itself is called *k'a kan ben* (literally, to-its-sound-meet, "to make its sound meet").

I have seen no evidence of intentional detuning of octaves, notwithstanding Knight's (1991a: 10–11) observation that bala octaves may be tuned wider as they move toward the treble end of the instrument. I attribute wide degrees of divergence from a theoretical norm of unisons, seconds, or octaves to factors other than an explicit desire to do so:

1. Some bala makers may be more expert in the construction (hand work) of the instrument than in its tuning (ear work).
2. There may be some leeway in the degree to which intervals are considered in tune.
3. The acoustics of the sound source—an unstable onset of the fundamental pitch—demand some subjective interpretation, which is why bala tuners sometimes take an inordinate length of time to decide whether an interval is wide, narrow, or just.
4. The hearing of elderly authoritative bala players may deteriorate more rapidly than their playing technique (at traditional dancing and drumming events balas are played at full strength to be heard and felt).
5. Balas intended for the tourist trade, or even for foreign collectors or researchers, may not be tuned with the same care as personal balas.

A vocabulary for expressing whether an interval (be it a unison, second, or octave) is wide, narrow, or right on, as well as my own observations, suggests that bala tuners strive for being right on rather than wide or narrow. Just the same, the general lack of conformity of balas to a theoretical seven equal-toned scale is puzzling. The set of instruments measured by Rouget was an ideal set to be measured, and Knight's (1991a: 5) comment that Rouget "happened upon the three best-tuned balos in all Mande!" is probably true. The Dioubate (Diabate) brothers recorded by Rouget (Sidi Mamady, Sidi Moussa, and Sidi Karamon) were the most renowned players of their time in Guinea.[104]

In his caption to a rare photograph of what is believed to be the original Sosso bala in Niagassola, Guinea, Niane (1975b, facing 217) indicated that

104. See the discussion of the bala-playing Diabate brothers in relation to *Mamaya* in chapter 5. Joyeux's (1924:175) description of the bala tuning process, tuning the slats of one to be in unison with another, concludes with praise for the tuner's accuracy: "During this process, he proves to have a trained ear and arrives at an accuracy equivalent to that which a European would obtain." Joyeux (1924:175) evidently never witnessed a bala being tuned to itself; he claimed that tuners only knew the unison and octave and could not tune other intervals against a single slat. Laura Arnston Harris (1992:225–27) describes a bala tuning process of tuning adjacent slats (i.e., the second to the first, the third to the second, etc.), and like Knight, she has found that "an amount of acoustic dissonance (a presence of 'beats' caused by a juxtaposition of close but dissimilar frequencies) appears to be desirable. The resultant musical or acoustic tension can be viewed as a quality that makes a sound fuller or stronger than that created by the sound of perfectly aligned frequencies."

the Sosso bala gives the "la" to all the balas of the old Mande. Perhaps this is so in the sense that some of the older, larger balas in the old Mande region may have been tuned directly to the Sosso bala. The smaller balas that are in widespread use today, however, are a much different affair. I do not know of any conscious effort to preserve any kind of absolute tuning with the Sosso bala other than the equiheptatonic interval found between any two adjacent slats. I suspect that on a practical level, other than balas in the Kouyate compound in Niagassola, the Sosso bala is not used to check the tuning of new balas in the old Mande region.

What is perplexing about bala tuning is that it is uncommon to find two instruments tuned by different people that are closely in tune with each other. Some of the slats might match between the two balas, but there are invariably slats that are out of tune with each other. If tuners were working with a strict interpretation of an equiheptaphonic tuning, there should be little variation. Balas, however, appear to reflect tuning preferences of the regions they come from, even though they also appear to roughly conform to a conception of an equal seven-tone scale. And the fact remains that any piece can be transposed up or down the instrument any number of slats without any acknowledgment of a change (e.g., of scale, key, or mode) other than pitch height.

Playing Techniques and Styles

This section is concerned with delineating the playing styles and techniques used on each of the three jeli instruments, with particular focus on the kora. The transcription guide (pp. xxvii–xxxi) explains the notation used here as well as some of the rhythmic concepts behind it, and the introduction (pp. 14–15) describes some of the basic features of a piece of music.

Most of the transcriptions in this section contain accompaniment patterns, or ways of playing pieces. Each line (containing one or two staves) in a transcription showing this kind of playing consists of one cycle of a piece that would be played over and over during a performance, usually with variations. Kora players refer to each of these accompaniment patterns as a *kumbengo* (pl. *kumbengolu*). Some koni players use the term *kumben*. Some bala players also may use a constituent term *ben* (see chapter 6). Accompaniment-type playing involves an ensemble relationship between the fingers or hands of one or more musicians in which African aesthetics of polyrhythm find full expression.

Accompaniment patterns are often interrupted with another type of playing consisting of fast descending melodic flourishes, often highly ornamented, which bear signs of Muslim musical influence.[105] Kora players call this kind of playing *birimintingo* (rolling). When questioned directly, my bala teacher Bala Dounbouya (1989-per) called it *bala wora;* other bala players may not have any terminology for this.[106] Mande instrumental music is driven by a mix of variations woven within a single accompaniment pattern, movement among different accompaniment patterns, and give and take between accompaniment-pattern playing and linear melodic-solo playing. An instrumental performance of a piece consists of maintaining the melodic or harmonic cycle while weaving in and out of these different kinds of playing. A piece may last as long as the performer wants.

Many pieces, particularly those originating on the bala, may be distinguished according to a unique harmonic pattern, a sequence of specific pitch combinations played in different parts of the cycle. Although the concept of a harmonic pattern is not explicitly verbalized, it can quite literally be seen, particularly on the bala, by watching which slats are sounded in different parts of the cycle.[107]

Kora

Using transcriptions of different versions of a single piece played by a variety of kora players and also by a single kora player, I will define some of the basic elements of kora playing. Many of these elements also apply to the bala, koni, and guitar and can serve as examples of a more general Mande aesthetic of music making.[108]

105. See al-Faruqi (1978, 1983–84, 1985) for concise descriptions of aesthetics of melody in the core Muslim world, and Charry (forthcoming) for more on the impact of Islam on music in Africa. See Moloney (1889:279–80) for transcriptions of various "Bambarra," "Mandingo," and "Volof" melodies.

106. *Wora* may be a dialect variant of *wara,* "to come down in torrents" (Bailleul 1996:417), or *woro(n),* "to flow or glide" (Delafosse 1955:818–19). Also see chapter 6.

107. Seavoy (1982) has devised a notation for Sisaala xylophone music from Ghana that shows a sketch of a xylophone with each harmony (i.e., the slats that may be struck) shaded with its own unique design so that at a glance one can see on a drawing of a single xylophone the movement of harmonies.

108. For further study see the comprehensive and richly detailed transcriptions and analyses of Gambian kora and vocal music done by Knight (1968, 1973a, 1984b). For tapping patterns on the kora, called *konkondiro,* see Knight (1973a, 1:192–205). King and Durán (1984:462) have proposed four predominant regional kora styles, one each coming from Guinea, Mali, The Gambia, and the Casamance. The imposition of colonial boundaries as well as government encouragement of national musical identities supports this view. So does the importance of the bala in Guinea, the koni in Mali, Fulbe influence in eastern Gambia, and Balanta and Jola influence in the Casamance. However, the tendency of jelis to travel weakens this classification in its practical application. Malian kora player Batrou Sekou Kouyate has spent much time in Guinea, as has Gambian-born Sidiki Diabate, who lived most of his life in Mali. Kora players from The Gambia and southern Senegal frequently travel across national borders, and there are relatively few native-born kora players from Guinea.

Kumbengo and Birimintingo in Allah L'a Ke

Transcriptions 4 through 9 show various ways the well-known Gambian kora piece *Allah l'a ke* is rendered by kora players over a wide geographic area. Transcription 4 shows *Allah l'a ke* as played by six different kora players. Each version (consisting of one system made up of one treble and

Transcription 4 Kora: *Allah l'a ke,* six versions of a standard kumbengo. In transcriptions 4 through 9 Sauta tuning is used.

one bass staff) is called a *kumbengo* in the terminology of Senegambian kora players. Any one kora player may have several ways of playing *Allah l'a ke,* so for the sake of comparison the kumbengos shown in transcription 4 are standard ones used by each of the six players. They are personalized versions of a traditional way of playing the piece. I have not attempted to posit any underlying model other than the skeletal harmonic scheme at the bottom of the transcription.

Even though there is a concept of an original version of *Allah l'a ke,* as there is with many pieces played by jelis, speculating on its exact form by comparing the versions in transcription 4 is hazardous. Transcription 5.4 shows what Amadu Bansang Jobarteh believes to be the original way of playing it (or at least the oldest he knows), from his father-in-law Kunkung Kanute, but this version would have been impossible to arrive at by comparing all the versions in transcription 4. According to Jobarteh, kora players have continually changed and developed this piece, as is the natural course for many kora pieces.[109]

Melodic and Harmonic Features of Allah L'a Ke

Certain common features of the kumbengolu in transcription 4 are unique and essential to *Allah l'a ke,* pointing toward a melodic-harmonic model for it, while others belong to the larger musical system. The right thumb part, shown as the round noteheads in the bass clef (F-C-F-A-F-C-F-A), is not usually heard outside *Allah l'a ke,* especially in the Sauta tuning in which it is played, although patterns very similar to it are common in other tunings. This type of alternating right thumb movement is characteristic of kora playing, and the simple substitution of a rest for the As in the right thumb part is enough to distinguish pieces like *N teri jato* and *Kelefaba* from *Allah l'a ke.* The left thumb part, shown as the square noteheads in the bass staff, combined with the right thumb part is enough to unequivocally identify *Allah l'a ke.* The bottom system in transcription 4 (harmonic scheme) is an abstraction of the harmony of *Allah l'a ke* taken from what is played by both thumbs. The basic tonal material of the first three beats is centered on F and C, beat 4 is centered on D and A, and this is repeated in the second half of the cycle. This reduction may be enough to identify the piece, since there are few if any other pieces with this same harmonic plan.

The harmonic scheme of *Allah l'a ke* represents a model of the basic musical structure of pieces in the Senegambian kora repertory: a binary form, eight beats divided into four plus four, apparently with no major differences

---

109. Amadu Bansang Jobarteh is an authoritative source on *Allah l'a ke* for several reasons. He comes from the region in eastern Gambia where the piece originated, he is one of the oldest living jalis from that region, and his father was the jali of the father of the two main characters in the story.

Transcription 5 Kora: *Allah l'a ke,* Amadu Bansang Jobarteh's kumbengos. From Amadu Bansang Jobarteh (1990-per). The tempo can vary from 144 to 208 beats (dotted quarter notes) per minute.

between the two halves. In actual realization, though, there is some change in the second half, no matter how subtle, that distinguishes it from the first half. Even disregarding the index fingers (treble clef), the change can be found in the bass part played by the thumbs. In *Allah l'a ke,* the second half of the cycle is distinguished from the first half on beat 6 by the thumbs striking together rather than staggered right-left on the analogous beat 2 in the first half.

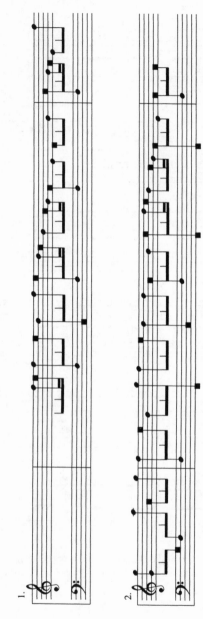

Transcription 6 Kora: *Allah l'a ke*, Amadu Bansang Jobarteh's birimintingo. From Amadu Bansang Jobarteh (1990-per). The tempo can vary from 144 to 208 beats (dotted quarter notes) per minute.

Transcription 7 Kora: *Allah l'a ke,* Amadu Bansang Jobarteh's index finger variations. From Amadu Bansang Jobarteh (1990-per). The top system (treble and bass staff) is reproduced from transcription 5.1. Each treble staff below it (numbered 1 through 6) represents a possible variation to the treble staff at the top, derived by substituting filled-in noteheads for the hollow noteheads.

Although the right thumb part usually maintains the rhythmic drive and does not vary greatly from player to player, the rhythmic and harmonic realization of the left thumb part is more subject to the player's personal style. For instance, c and f may be interchangeable in certain contexts (indicated by hollow noteheads in the transcriptions). Alhaji Bai Konte's placement of the ds on the third pulse of the fourth and eighth beats in transcription 4 creates a rhythmic shift that is characteristic of the way he personalizes kumbengolu. A d must be played on beats 4 and 8 to obtain the characteristic *Allah l'a ke* harmony; Bai Konte just delayed the attack point. A variation to a second kumbengo he uses (transcription 8.2 and 8.2.var 1), shows him using this same technique. In the index finger (treble) part in the second kumbengo (8.2) he places an E on beat 1 and a G' on beat 5. In the variation (8.2.var 1), he anticipates by one pulse the attack points of the E and G', placing them on the last pulse of beats 8 and 4, respectively.

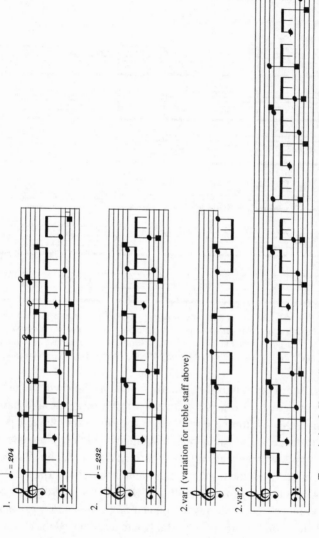

Transcription 8 Kora: *Allah l'a ke*, Bai Konte's kumbengos and variations. From Alhaji Bai Konte (1973-disc/1989-disc).

Another distinctive feature of *Allah l'a ke* is the melodic line, a descent from F' to D' to C' to G' (or back up to D"). The lower notes in the treble staff, usually F's played by the left index finger, serve a rhythmic function. This type of repetition of a pitch on the third pulse of every second beat is typical of kora music in general and can be heard in any number of pieces.

Kumbengo Variations and Birimintingo

Just as each kora player may have a personalized version of a widely known traditional kumbengo for *Allah l'a ke,* he may also have other kumbengolu for it, often his own creations that still retain the melodic-harmonic character of the piece. Amadu Bansang Jobarteh has at least two, and sometimes as many as five or more, kumbengolu for the pieces that are important in his repertory. Transcription 5 shows several kumbengolu and some variations that he uses in his performances of *Allah l'a ke*. Transcription 5.1 (reproduced from transcription 4 with a few added notes) is most readily identifiable as *Allah l'a ke,* and he starts his performances with it before moving on to the other kumbengolu. All of the kumbengolu in transcription 5 are unique to *Allah l'a ke,* and they would most likely be able to be identified as *Allah l'a ke* by a jali hearing them for a first time. I consider the systems labeled only with a number to be independent kumbengolu, and those with "var" tagged onto the numbers to be a variation to a kumbengo. For instance, transcription 5.1.var is a variation to 5.1 because it is a short melodic run inserted into 5.1 functioning as an embellishment.

Distinctions between a kumbengo and a variation to a kumbengo are not always clear-cut or verbalized. Transcription 5.2 is a borderline case that I consider to be a distinct kumbengo because each finger is altered just enough so that it sounds different from 5.1, and it was taught to me as a distinct unit. Transcription 5.3 is a clear case of a different kumbengo, distinguished by its emphasis on the upper register, a common technique for creating a new kumbengo. The bottom register has dropped out, and instead the left thumb plays in a register above the right thumb, which itself is slightly altered rhythmically (the A comes one pulse before its usual slot). The melodic profile of the piece remains intact, although it has become busier owing to octaves that are played as either harmonic (simultaneous) or melodic (sequential) intervals (from lower to higher or from higher to lower). Transcription 5.3.var is a subtle variation of 5.3.

Extended solo melody lines that contrast with kumbengo playing are known as *birimintingo* to Senegambian kora players. Short bursts of birimintingo may function as embellishment and ornament within a kumbengo (as in 5.1.var), and also as extended solo passages contrasting with a kumbengo. It is precisely this dual function that jalis exploit, integrating kumbengo and birimintingo in such a way that they feed off each other.

Transcription 6 shows two sample birimintingo passages that Amadu Bansang Jobarteh plays during the course of *Allah l'a ke.* Both passages descend stepwise, with the movement broken by occasional ascents, thereby creating a cascading motion. This kind of descending movement has been noticed in much sub-Saharan African music and has been linked with similar tonal movement in language, dance, and sculpture (see Thompson 1974:13).[110] Birimintingo passages as a rule descend in this way, although they may be continuously extended by brief melodic ascents (usually large leaps) in order to prolong the passage. The birimintingo passages are both relatively long, taking up a full cycle or more. They can often take the form of more extended excursions. Finally, they bear little relation to the kumbengo; they do not contain the kind of piece-specific information identifying a piece that a kumbengo does.

Most of the birimintingo passages that Amadu Bansang Jobarteh plays in *Allah l'a ke* are closely related to the two shown in transcription 6 in terms of where they start and end in the cycle, their length, and their kind of melodic descent. They also are unique to *Allah l'a ke* in that they do not show up in this exact form in other pieces. It appears the Jobarteh has particular kinds of birimintingo passages that, although they do not exhibit any of the features of the piece in the way the kumbengolu do, are nevertheless associated with specific pieces or groups of pieces.

The Relative Fixity of Kumbengo and Birimintingo

Mande instrumentalists are not usually confronted with the necessity of choosing a definitive version of a kumbengo, except perhaps by foreign students. Many of my teachers would initially simplify a kumbengo, suppressing variations, so that I could grasp it. But in performance it is common for kora players to vary a kumbengo so that it is rarely played the same way more than a few cycles in a row. Transcription 7 shows some of the options that Amadu Bansang Jobarteh's index fingers may exercise in one of his kumbengolu for *Allah l'a ke,* and it illustrates the open-endedness of a kumbengo. It is a working out of the options shown as hollow noteheads in the treble staff of transcription 5.1. This bundle of options should be considered part of Jobarteh's kumbengo rather than variations to a fixed sequence of notes. Some players might indeed arrive at definitive fixed kumbengolu for some pieces. *Allah l'a ke* in the hands of Amadu Bansang Jo-

---

110. Many Mandekan language dialects feature this kind of cascading movement (see Bird 1982:37–42).

barteh, on the other hand, is an outstanding example of an inventive musician playing a piece that allows room for his input.

This flexibility in the performance of a kumbengo, and the association of particular kinds of birimintingo with particular kumbengolu, has been noted by Lucy Durán in her study of Amadu Bansang Jobarteh's treatment of a Malian piece, *Tutu Jara*.

> There has also been a tendency to regard the kumbengo as the "fixed" part of a kora piece, and the birimintingo as the improvised element; however, this is not strictly true in the case of "Tutu Jara" and other pieces as played by Amadu Bansang. . . . [A]lthough a kumbengo may be repeated with some consistency for teaching purposes, it should not be regarded as a fixed composition, or indeed as anything other than a melodic idea whose realization into specific note patterns varies constantly from one player, and one performance, to another. While undoubtedly the kumbengo provides the musical framework, to describe a kora piece in terms of the kumbengo alone is insufficient; equally important are its associated variations and suitable places for inserting stock ornamental phrases. (Durán 1981a:187, 191)

I would further clarify the word "stock." Though all pieces may rely on a common grammar for creating ornamental phrases, individual pieces attract specific tokens created from this common grammar. Also, koni pieces from Mali such as *Tutu Jara* are often played slow and allow for more varied kinds of solo melodic playing. Kora pieces from the Senegambia region often feature fast accompaniment patterns that tend to attract more homogeneous kinds of solo melodic runs. This feature of tempo (fast versus slow pieces) is one major distinction between a western (*tilijii*) or Senegambian style and an eastern (*tilibo*) or Malian style.

The opposition of kumbengo with birimintingo is not necessarily characterized by fixed versus variable, composed versus improvised, or repeated pattern versus ornamentation-variation. Kumbengo and birimintingo both exhibit these features, though in varying degrees. Although kumbengolu are composed (i.e., they can have fixed sequences of finger movements), they also have built-in options that the experienced performer is expected to exercise. Some of these options are systemwide (the kinds of things that can be done to any piece), some are peculiar to the piece, and some are personal and may lead to the creation of a new kumbengo. Both Amadu Bansang Jobarteh and Sidiki Diabate have told me that new kumbengolu often come to them through their fingers' experimenting while playing a familiar kumbengo. Birimintingo, on the other hand, usually associated with expansion and hence improvisation, may also be composed, although once again the experienced performer probably would shy away from repeating passages too often without change. The performer's creative ability is taxed on several levels: in the continual play of kumbengo versus birimintingo, and also within the separate kumbengo and birimintingo areas themselves.

Roles of the Four Fingers

The four fingers used to pluck the kora often have well-defined roles, although this is probably more characteristic of kora styles from The Gambia and Casamance than of those from Mali and Guinea. Most pieces that originate on the kora feature regular right thumb alternation between pitches 1 (F) and 5 (C), often with pitches 2 (G) or 3 (A) used in place of pitch 5 at some point. The left thumb often has a standard rhythm (usually syncopated with the right thumb) that is played either on the low bass strings (involving pitches 1, 5, and 6) or on pitch 2 (G), in which case the string is deadened immediately after it is struck (the interval of a second with the recurring pitch 1 of the right thumb is considered dissonant, and it is not aesthetically pleasing to let it ring). This deadening of one of the pitches in a harmonic interval of a second is characteristic not only of kora playing but also of bala playing.[111] My bala teacher, Bala Dounbouya, would be visibly annoyed and would not hesitate to scold me if I failed to pick up his consistent dampening of one of the bala slats (see the discussion of the piece *Kulanjan,* transcription 12 below). The role of the left index finger is often to echo the right thumb on the offbeat. The right index finger probably has the least defined role, though it usually acts in melodic tandem with the left index finger. Two examples of the characteristic kinds of relationships that may exist among the four fingers in kora playing follow.

Transcription 9 Kora: *Allah l'a ke,* Toumani Diabate's kumbengo and variation. From Toumani Diabate (1988b-disc).

111. The tones deadened in the three most common harmonic intervals of a second are pitch 2 (G), if the pitches are 1 (F) and 2; the sharp fourth degree (b-natural) if the pitches are 4 and 5 (typical in Sauta tuning); or pitch 7 (E') if the pitches are 7 and 1 (F").

Kuruntu Kelefa, Mamadou Kouyate (1989-per)

Kuruntu Kelefa, Nyama Suso (from Knight 1973, 2:16)

Kuruntu Kelefa/N teri jato, Amadu Bansang Jobarteh (1990-per)

Jato, Dembo Konte (1989-per)

Hama Ba Jata, Amadu Bansang Jobarteh (1990-per)

Transcription 10 Kora: *Kuruntu Kelefa, N teri jato,* and related pieces. In Amadu Bansang Jobarteh's versions, the hollow and filled-in square noteheads indicate either *Kuruntu Kelefa* or *N teri jato*, respectively. In transcriptions 10 and 11 Tomoraba tuning is used.

Transcription 10 shows the kora piece *Kuruntu Kelefa* as taught by Mamadou Kouyate (at the National Conservatory in Dakar), Jali Nyama Suso (from Knight [1973a, 2:16], shifted left two beats to match the other transcriptions here), and Amadu Bansang Jobarteh. Also shown are several other pieces featuring similar playing techniques. In all these pieces (except Jali Nyama Suso's version, which may have been simplified for teaching) there is a steady right thumb alternation between the pitches F and C (round noteheads in the bass staff). Sometimes the pitch A is used (*Jato* and *Hama Ba Jata*), sometimes not (*Kuruntu Kelefa* by Jali Nyama Suso and Amadu Bansang Jobarteh). Against this steady right thumb, the left thumb (square noteheads in the bass staff) plays a standard pattern using the bass f and c strings or sometimes the G string (in which case it is dampened). The left index finger (square noteheads in the treble clef) typically alternates between F' and C' on the third pulse of every beat, echoing the right thumb. The right index finger's role (round noteheads in the treble clef) is the least defined.

In *Allah l'a ke* (transcription 4) both of the index fingers work together to play the descending melody. But the left index finger also plays constantly on the offbeat (pulse 3 of beats 1, 3, 5, and 7), in a characteristic conversation (usually on the note F' or A') with the constant onbeat of the right thumb (e.g., see the kumbengolu in transcriptions 4 and 10). In Toumani Diabate's kumbengo (in transcriptions 4 and 9) both index fingers join to play both the melody as two-note clusters (C'/F", A'/D', A'/D') and also the constant offbeat as two-note clusters (E/F'). In a variation to this kumbengo (transcription 9.1.var) he plays the two notes sequentially instead of simultaneously (i.e., he arpeggiates the cluster), thereby increasing the attack density by one-half. This creates twenty-four attacks in one kumbengo cycle as opposed to sixteen, an unusually high and sustained attack density at a fast tempo that stands out in a highly virtuosic performance. Three registral levels of activity are carried on simultaneously: low (the two thumbs in the bass staff); medium (the two index fingers in the lower treble staff); and high (the two index fingers in the upper treble staff). This kind of registral stratification is typical of kora music, Mande music, and indeed of much sub-Saharan African music. One might even discern four different activities going on in Toumani Diabate's variation, two rhythmic and two melodic: the right thumb playing the steady pattern; the left thumb playing a counterrhythm to the right thumb; and the two index fingers working together in two different melodic registers. These kinds of finger relationships are typical of kora music and may be one reason the kora is used more often as a solo instrument than the other jeli instruments, which are usually played in pairs.

Same Finger Movements, Different Pieces

The kinds of criteria significant in distinguishing pieces from each other are illustrated in transcription 11, which shows Amadu Bansang Jobarteh's kumbengolu for *N teri jato* and *Kuruntu Kelefa* (reproduced from transcription 10), and birimintingo passages that he plays in both the pieces.[112] The kumbengolu differ only in the strings that the left thumb plays: filled-in square noteheads in the bass clef belong to *N teri jato;* hollow square

112. Other transcriptions of *Kuruntu Kelefa* may be consulted for comparison in Durán (1978).

Transcription 11 Kora: *Kuruntu Kelefa* and *N teri jato* birimintingo. From Amadu Bansang Jobarteh (1990-per). In the kumbengo the hollow and filled-in square noteheads indicate either *Kuruntu Kelefa* or *N teri jato*, respectively. B1 and B2 = birimintingo; E = ending phrase, not played in *Kuruntu Kelefa*.

noteheads in the bass clef belong to *Kuruntu Kelefa.* The rhythm of the left thumb is the same for both kumbengolu, but the strings it plays are different. This is enough, for Amadu Bansang Jobarteh at least, to distinguish these two pieces. The birimintingo passages he plays—transcriptions 11.B1 and 11.B2 show two of his more common ones—are essentially the same for both pieces except that he invariably ends them in *N teri jato* with an ending phrase (transcription 11.E), which he does not play in *Kuruntu Kelefa.*[113]

Konkondiro

A tapping pattern played by a second person on the calabash of the kora is called *konkondiro,* the verbal noun form of the word *konkon* (an onomatopoeia for "knock"). Knight (1973a, 1:192–205) has identified four basic tapping patterns used in The Gambia, but Amadu Bansang Jobarteh uses only two; one of them for pieces from The Gambia and Casamance that originated on the kora, and the other for everything else. Tapping patterns are not routinely used by kora players from Guinea or Mali; perhaps the Jola practice of beating various patterns on the calabashes of their hunter's harps with two sticks is the source for this practice among their Mandinka neighbors.

Bala

Although balas may be played solo, they are more typically played in sets of two or three, with one person taking the lead and the others acting as accompanists. Tellier (1898:182) was impressed with the combination of bala playing and choral singing he heard in Kita and noted that as many as six balas might be played together at important events. Joyeux's extended description of performances in Kankan by eleven bala players associated with a large masked figure known as Konkoba is probably typical of Guinean bala-based traditions.

> The leaders place themselves in the middle. . . . The other balas are arranged in a line to the left and right of them. At both ends are placed the percussion instruments, and the singers are behind.
>
> The leader begins the concert by exercises of virtuosity on his instrument; he plays a "cadence," dare I say, characterized by rapidly descending lines. Then, calming down, he attacks the tune taken up by all the other players and

---

113. Another example is provided by the pieces *Hama Ba Jata* and *Jaka,* which, according to Amadu Bansang Jobarteh and Sidiki Diabate, are played the same way but are distinguished primarily by the tuning in which they are played. *Hama Ba Jata* is played in Hardino tuning and *Jaka* is played in Tomora mesengo tuning. This is the only case I know of two pieces being distinguished in this way.

sung by the singers, which the leader himself intones in case the memory of
the singers is at fault; in turn the drums come in and the piece is under way. It
continues in this way, the same theme repeating indefinitely; from time to
time the leader weaves variations, where he shows a real virtuosity, while the
other musicians continue the theme. I have seen them play nonstop for a whole
afternoon. . . . the moment a native approaches and appears ready to dance,
the musicians revive and beat on their balas with all their strength. . . .

The konkobas play music in all the normal circumstances, singing the
praises of leaders, of newlyweds, of the circumcised, eulogies for the deceased; in former times they encouraged the combatants and consoled the
wounded . . . their repertoire is made up of about thirty airs, whose words they
modify according to the needs of the moment. (Joyeux 1924:207–8)[114]

In general, one player solos at a time, while any number of others may
play accompaniment patterns, each usually sticking to a single one. Transcription 12 shows versions of *Kulanjan,* a signature piece of the hunter that
comes from the simbi, as played on the bala and simbi. Transcription 12.1
is the first version that Bala Dounbouya teaches (in my own private lessons

Transcription 12 Bala and Simbi: *Kulanjan.* The top four staves are bala versions from Bala
Dounbouya (1989-per). The fifth staff (marked simbi) is from Bala Djimba Diakite (1990-per).

114. For extensive discussion and photos of Konkoba performance in Siguiri see El Dabh and
Proschan (1979: 18–54); for additional photos see Joyeux (1924, fig. 8) and Huet and Keita (1954:
85); for a silent film and an audio recording of the event see Boulton (1934-vid; 1957-disc). Also
see the discussion of *Mamaya,* which probably is based in *Konkoba* performances, in chapter 5.

and in his classes at the national conservatory in Dakar), and it is the simplest. One hand articulates a ternary rhythm (three pulses per beat in the bass), and the other hand a binary rhythm (two pulses per beat in the treble). The steady repetition of a tone (F) in one hand is typical of bala playing, but the obvious polyrhythmic relation between the two hands is uncommon on the bala. Transcription 12.1.var is a variation created by adding a few strokes to the steady bass part, transforming it into a busier pattern, and grouping it into a clear framework of four beats plus four beats. This exemplifies a common technique for creating variations in much African music: adding strokes to a preexisting part, filling in gaps. This technique applies to percussion as well as stringed instruments. Teaching versions of pieces are usually stripped-down skeletal versions, which the teacher fleshes out as the student grasps them. Transcription 12.1.oct shows how a variation is created by reversing the roles of the hands. The bass hand now takes the binary rhythm and the treble hand the ternary one.

It is common to dampen one tone in a melodic or harmonic interval of a second, typically the note above or below the tonic. The notes marked with an x in transcription 12 show this dampening. Although the concept of a tonic may be inappropriate in some bala pieces, the steady repetition of a tone, such as the F in *Kulanjan,* can be taken as an indication of a tonic. Bala pieces that do not feature this steady repetition usually do not have much dampening of slats. Sometimes the repetition of a tone is shifted to the third or fifth scale degree in variations. The concept of a tonic receives support in the terminology of string players who, when preparing to play with a bala, ask to tune to its *kumben,* best translated here as tonic (see chapter 6). The bala player then chooses a slat that is closest to the tonic pitch of the string players.

Transcription 13 is a comparative view of three of the oldest pieces believed to come from the bala: *Boloba, Sunjata,* and *Lamban* (see their descriptions above). I refer to these three pieces as the Sunjata complex because they are all associated with the era of Sunjata, and they share a similar harmonic scheme. The transcriptions have been vertically aligned so that their common harmonic scheme (F/C to G/D and back to F/C) lines up. Boxes have been drawn around single cycles of each piece, but these reflect my interpretation of the simplest way to hear and play the pieces rather than a Maninka concept of a starting point in a musical accompaniment. At times I hear the starting points in each of the pieces in different places than those marked, typically halfway through the indicated cycles, so the boxes should be taken as one way (the simplest way for me) out of several ways to hear the pieces.

Transcription 13 Bala: the *Sunjata* complex (*Boloba, Sunjata, Lamban*). Pieces are arranged so that their harmonic schemes (F/C to G/D to F/C) line up. Rectangular boxes mark off single cycles.

Boloba is the only piece in the Mandenka repertory in which beats are made up of five pulses each rather than two or three (or their multiples). Although jelis recognize the piece as being different, I have been unable to elicit technical responses as to the nature of the difference, in part because I do not know of any technical vocabulary in Mandekan dialects that can communicate a concept of beats with pulses. *Sunjata* and *Lamban* are readily distinguished from each other by the placement of the harmonic change (G/D) within the cycle.

The versions in transcription 13 should not be taken as the only ways to play the three pieces, or even as standard ways, because every jeli would have his own way. But these are generic versions any jeli would recognize, and they could suffice as a second accompanying bala part. Just as I have given multiple versions of pieces played on the kora, transcriptions 14 through 16 show multiple versions of each of the three pieces shown in transcription 13 (also see King 1974 for several kora and bala transcriptions of *Sunjata*-related pieces).

Several typical kinds of bala accompaniments can be seen in transcriptions 15 and 16. Transcription 15.1 shows the constant offbeat F (which becomes G when the harmony changes) on the third pulse of every beat, characteristic of many bala accompaniments. This is the same kind of offbeat phrasing that the left index finger plays on the kora (see transcriptions 4 and 10). Transcription 16.1 shows a constant onbeat F (which becomes G when the harmony changes) on the first pulse of every beat, also characteristic of many bala accompaniments. Transcriptions 15.2, 15.3, and 15.5 show a constant repetition of C or F (which changes to D when the harmony

Transcription 14 Bala: *Boloba*. 1 and 2 are from Bala Dounbouya (1989-per). 3 and 4 are from Siriman Kouyate (1989-per).

Transcription 15 Bala: *Sunjata*. From Bala Dounbouya (1989-per).

Transcription 16 Bala: *Lamban*. From Siriman Kouyate (1989-per).

Figure 8 Bala: theoretical possibilities of offbeat and onbeat phrasing.

changes) on the first and third pulses of the odd-numbered beats. Transcription 16.5 shows similar phrasing, but on the even-numbered beats. Figure 8 shows these four theoretical possibilities in schematic form.[115]

115. Offbeat relationships are typical of bala playing, where one hand plays on the beat and the other hand plays on the offbeat. The independence and interdependence of parts were frequently

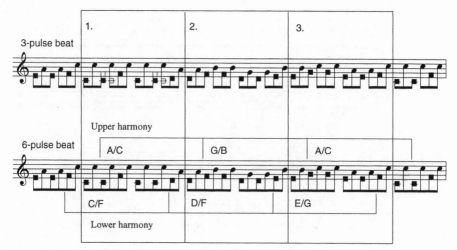

Transcription 17 Bala: *Fakoli*. From Doumbia and Doumbia (1990-per).

Transcription 17, a bala accompaniment part for *Fakoli,* illustrates rhythmic and harmonic tensions that are typical of bala music.[116] The piece can be analyzed as having three harmonic areas of twelve pulses each, labeled 1, 2, and 3 on the top staff. Three harmonic areas of equal duration are rare in the jeli's repertoire; the only other piece like this is *Nanfulen,* which I consider a musical child of *Fakoli.* The three-pulse beats on the top staff highlight the prominent beat that appears to be the frame of reference for the lead bala player. The alternating left-right two-pulse kinetic pattern of the player's arms is typical of many bala accompaniments, but the cross-rhythm between that and the three-pulse pattern of the main beats is less common. The second staff shows the same piece, but reorganized into six-pulse beats, highlighting the harmonic pattern. There are a number of ways to analyze this pattern, but I have highlighted how the groups of two notes (dyads) on the upper line and those of the lower line appear to be staggered to the right and left, respectively, of the main beats, giving an aural effect of tugging in opposite directions from the main beats. This kind of polyphonic laying out of a harmonic pattern is typical of bala music, as is the short variation

---

illustrated in my bala lessons. If I had trouble learning a new piece, my teacher Bala Dounbouya would play one hand (part) by itself and then the other hand (part) by itself. Sometimes the rhythm differed when he played the parts alone, as if he needed one part as a frame of reference for the other. They were rhythmically different—even independent—but each was necessary to define the other.

116. From Doumbia and Doumbia (1990-per); Mamadou Doumbia played the accompanying part while his older brother Fode Doumbia played solo parts. They are originally from Kindia, Guinea.

indicated as hollow square noteheads in the left hand part of the top staff, and it creates an aesthetically pleasing texture against which a lead player can work. It is ripe with the kinds of tugs and pulls in musical time associated with bala music.

Koni

The Maninka-Xasonka koni or larger Bamana ngoni is played in several contexts. The deep-sounding ngoni is often played solo to accompany the storytelling (Daouda Dembele, n.d.a/b/c/d-disc) or singing (Bazoumana Sissoko 1972a/b-disc) of the player himself, or to accompany a jelimuso singer (Fanta Damba 1971-disc). Among the Maninka and Xasonka the koni is usually played in pairs (Moriba Koita 1997-disc: *Badiourou*), in ensembles with other jeli instruments, and occasionally in electrified modern orchestras (Kasse Mady Diabate 1989-disc).

Sometimes a leather ring with an animal claw sticking out may be worn on the index finger to increase the volume of the plucking (Joyeux 1924: 181). The index finger plucks the two long main playing strings (most often with down rather than up strokes), the middle finger plucks the short bottom strings with up strokes, and the thumb plucks the short upper string (fig. 7). The third finger occasionally taps the skin sound table. Only the two long strings are fingered with the left hand; the short strings are played open.

Koni playing features a high degree of ornamentation involving hammering on and pulling off (indicated by grace notes and slurs, respectively, in the transcriptions). The melodic movement is usually downward. One characteristic of koni music is the limited melodic range, usually one octave with a few tones above or below the tonic. In the tuning for *Tutu Jara* (see above) the range of available pitches is one octave (F to F') with an occasional drop to the E below or the G' above (the open fifth string). Since solo koni music does not have the same melodic range as kora or bala music, a lead koni player extends the range by using a higher tuning when playing with an accompanist.

Koni music and kora music share some of the same principles. Music played on both instruments is based on a melodic or harmonic cycle that is repeated throughout a performance, usually with variations, with one part of the cycle (usually half) typically differing from the other by some harmonic or melodic change. Owing to the melodic orientation of the instrument, the distinction between accompaniment pattern playing and solo melodic flourishes is less clear in koni playing than in kora playing. Although Wolof xalam (lute) players use the term *fodet* for accompaniment playing and *tukull* for melodic flourishes much as *kumbengo* and *birimintingo* are

Transcription 18 Koni: *Tutu Jara*. 1a: Moussa Kouyate (1990-per) playing the koni. 1b: Modibo Kouyate playing the guitar (Kidel 1991-vid). 2a: Moussa Kouyate (1990-per) playing the koni. 2: A xalam version from Michael Coolen (1982:80, 1983:490).

used in kora playing, I have not encountered the term *birimintingo* in lessons with my koni teacher (see Coolen 1979:135–36; 1983:489; and chapter 6). Coolen (1982:80–81) has noted that in Wolof xalam music, which is largely drawn from Xasonka and Maninka traditions, the second half of a cycle is often distinguished from the first by a different tonal center, usually a whole tone above. The key characteristics distinguishing one piece from another are unclear, but they may involve a combination of the length of the cycle, the melodic movement and contour, the harmonic movement, and idiomatic ways of playing through these features.

Transcription 18 shows two renditions each of two ways of playing *Tutu Jara*, one of the most important pieces in the Xasonka and Maninka repertories. The two top staves (18.1a and 18.1b) show a version played by Moussa Kouyate (1990-per) on the koni that he refers to as *Kuluba*, and a similar version played on the guitar by Modibo Kouyate (Kidel 1991-vid). The two bottom staves (18.2a and 18.2b) show another way of playing *Tutu Jara* on the koni by Moussa Kouyate (1990-per) and a similar version played on the Wolof xalam taken from Coolen's research in the Senegambia region.[117]

There are a few other widely played versions of *Tutu Jara* and many more that Moussa Kouyate plays, but the two shown in transcription 18 are probably the most common. In contrast to bala and kora pieces, some of the versions of *Tutu Jara* are so different from each other that it may be futile to search for an underlying musical model. *Tutu Jara* might better be considered a collection of pieces, some closely related and others not. A few general features of koni playing technique and of the versions shown in the transcription can be identified, however.

The number of beats per cycle in *Tutu Jara* is greater than in most other pieces. Dividing the sixteen-beat cycle into four measures of four beats each, a contour emerges. In the first version (18.1a and 18.1b) there is a steady low F drone on each beat of the first two measures. Over this is the alternation between the high F′ and D after the first two beats. The last beat of the second measure invariably contains movement leading up to the fifth degree (C) on the first beat of the third measure. The third measure consists

117. In the several sources where Coolen's transcription of *Tutu Jara* appeared (1979:142, 195–98; 1982:80; 1983:490) a specific teacher is not cited. Abdulai Samba in Banjul was his principal teacher, and he also studied with Sait Camara in The Gambia and with Abdul Karim Ndiaye and Abdu Guisse in Dakar (Coolen 1979:6–8; 1982:83–84). Coolen's transcriptions are one sixteenth note short on beat 6, so I have rhythmically reinterpreted them here to fit. For more extensive and in-depth analyses of pieces from the related Wolof xalam tradition, Coolen (1979, 1982, 1983) is an excellent source. Also see Durán (1981a) for many other kora transcriptions of *Tutu Jara* played by Amadu Bansang Jobarteh.

of a descending line from C, sometimes ornamented. The fourth measure features another descending line, but starting from the high F', and contains the most ornamentation in the cycle.

Version 2 (specifically 18.2a) has a clearer harmonic differentiation within the cycle and can almost be read as a palindrome. Two beats of F/A/C, two beats of A/D, and two beats of G/C are followed by two beats of an ornamented F separating off the ensuing reverse movement of G/C, A/D, F/A/C ending again on an ornamented F. Another way of reading this harmonic movement is to divide the cycle in half, with the first half starting on F and the second half starting on G. Looking at both versions, a more basic contour can be discerned: F' to D to C to F' to low F. Whether this is enough to distinguish *Tutu Jara* from other pieces is unclear.

Conclusion

Among Mandenka music makers, jelis command the highest public respect for their authority. Although sometimes privately disdained or feared—the word griot carries these connotations much more so than jeli—they are seen, by themselves and others, as continuing long-standing traditions that still have relevance for many members of their societies. Naturally some are respected more than others for their musical or verbal artistry and integrity and are better able to move their audiences in deep ways that strike to the core of Mandenka social values. The virtuosity of the kora, bala, and koni players and the sheer power and beauty of the singers has attracted the attention of a world audience. Foreign interest in the musical traditions of jelis has contributed to a vital musical atmosphere, further stimulating the present young generation to continue the tradition, albeit in novel ways.

A century of colonial and postcolonial encounters has threatened, so far unsuccessfully, to eradicate the institution of the jeli. Despite French colonial efforts at breaking down the social system, and Sekou Toure's (1963: 254–55; n.d., 66–67) call to *dé-castiser* (decaste) Guinean society as well as the music profession, jeliya has not let up. How jelis will continue to adapt to the exigencies of modern Africa as well as new milieus in the cities of Europe and North America remains to be seen.

4

Drumming

Maninka and Mandinka drumming traditions belong to two major and distinct drum culture areas. Senegambian Mandinka dance to an ensemble of three drums, the kutirindingo, kutiriba, and sabaro, which bear similarities to drums used by their Wolof neighbors (plates 21 to 23). Malian and Guinean Maninka dancing is rooted in ensembles consisting of jembes and dunduns, and sometimes tamas (plates 24 to 35). This split between Senegambian Mandinka and Malian-Guinean Maninka, evinced in the drums they use, is remarkable for its consistency. Tambacounda, Senegal, long an important crossroads, may be the significant border area where both kinds of ensemble occur. To the west of Tambacounda the Mandinka ensemble is used; to the east the Maninka drums are used. This division also coincides with the use of the verb *kosi* (to beat) in the west as opposed to *fò* (to say) in the east to refer to playing musical instruments (see chapter 3).[1]

Outside the continent, the best known and most widespread African drum in the 1990s is the jembe, with dozens of CDs released since the late 1980s, far surpassing the number of recordings of any other African drum. The jembe was introduced outside Africa in the early 1950s in the tours of Les Ballets Africains led by the Guinean Fodeba Keita. Serious interest in the jembe in the United States began when Ladji Camara, a lead drummer with Les Ballets Africains, relocated there in the early 1960s to perform and teach. Since the late 1980s international interest in the jembe has taken an unprecedented upturn, owing in part to the death of Sekou Toure, which triggered a search for new sources of patronage by Guinean musicians. Former members of national ballet troupes of Guinea, Mali, and Senegal routinely settle abroad to teach and perform, jembe students flock to drum classes and camps, and major drum manufacturers have found a market for industrially produced synthetic jembe-like instruments. With this foreign interest a new genre of concert drumming has been created, an odd development from an African point of view, given the absence of jembe recordings within African markets.

1. A variety of other drums used by Mandenka in more limited and nonprofessional situations are not discussed here. These include the *tabala,* found outside mosques and used to announce various community events, the *ji dunun,* a calabash floating upside down in a tub of water, played by women (see introduction for references), and a variety of more localized drums.

Among Mande peoples, as in most parts of Africa, drumming is linked with singing and movement, be it dancing or agricultural labor. In public events a circle is formed with the drummers at the head. Dancers emerge singly or in twos and threes approaching the drummers, seriously engaging with them for short periods, then falling back into the circle. Those in the circle support the dancers by clapping, accentuating certain regulating beats in the drum parts. Song often breaks out as a respite from dancing. The circles can be very small, leaving barely enough room for the drummers and a dancer to move, or they can be as big as a city block where rented folding chairs are placed along the sides of the street for the guests. Stage presentations of jembe drumming and dancing probably date back to the late 1940s or early 1950s with the Paris-based efforts of Fodeba Keita that led to the formation of Les Ballets Africains. By necessity, the circle was broken and stretched out into a line so that a nonparticipating audience could view the events. Drumming and dancing were moved out of their ritual and sacred contexts into a more secular realm. Some rhythms have taken on a new status in the repertory of drummers, but whether they are popular because of their cultural associations or their musical properties or both is difficult to say.

The choreographing of traditional dances for the stage has led to two related, yet distinct, drum and dance genres among Maninka: a village tradition (which can be carried on in urban areas) and a ballet tradition. Although rooted in village traditions, regional and national ballets combine diverse local styles, which would rarely mix in a village context, with European ideas of group choreography and stage presentation. Concert drumming, featuring master drummers who left their village traditions to join regional and national ballets and eventually went on to forge solo recording, concert, and teaching careers in the United States and Europe, has recently emerged as a new drumming tradition. First Adama Drame and then Mamady Keita have become leading figures in this movement that is steadily growing in the 1990s.[2]

Surprisingly, out of the dozens, if not hundreds, of drums used in West Africa, the jembe is one of a relatively few that are played exclusively with

2. Comparative research between village and urban nonballet jembe traditions, such as that now being carried out by Rainer Polak in Bamako and points south in Mali, may provide evidence that the urban variety, while sharing elements of both village and ballet playing traditions, is distinct from them. Literature on the jembe has recently begun to proliferate. For overviews see Blanc (1993), Charry (1996a), Drame and Senn-Borloz (1992), Konate and Ott (1997), A. Meyer (1997: 27–36), and Zanetti (1996). For extended transcriptions of lead playing see Polak (1996a) and B. Michael Williams (1997). For a study of an African American transformation of a jembe-based tradition see Sunkett (1995); for a broad study of West and Central African drumming see A. Meyer (1997).

both bare hands, fewer still if one excludes those with bodies made of calabash rather than wood. Of those drums played with both bare hands, the
head of the jembe might be the tautest of them all, held onto the body by
extremely high tension, requiring iron rings (formerly animal hide) to bear
the pressure. This combination of bare-handed playing technique and a tight
drumhead contributes to a mystique that has surrounded the jembe outside
Africa.

Each of the Mandinka and Maninka drums is instantly recognizable by its
shape, method of attaching the skin head to the body, and playing technique.
They also are distinguished according to who may play them. It is unusual
for jelis to play drums, with the exception of the dundun and tama, which
are jeli instruments in certain regions. Among the Senegambian Mandinka
there are no hereditary restrictions on who may play drums. Neither does the
jembe have any hereditary restrictions on who may play it, but in the past
it may have been closely associated with numus (blacksmith-sculptors), the
ones who carve the instrument.

Although tamas, dunduns, and jembes are played together in the National Ballet of Mali (known as Troupe Folklorique Malienne [n.d.-disc: an-
nouncement] in the 1960s, and also as Les Ballets Maliens [198?-vid]), each
drum has its own traditions, repertories, and regions of predominance. Each
of these drums has a wider geographic and ethnic distribution than the
three-drum Senegambian Mandinka ensemble, even taking into account
similar Wolof drums that might make up a larger Senegambian drum complex. The broad sahel and northern savanna distribution of tama-like and
dundun-like instruments and the savanna distribution of the jembe contrast
with this more restricted Senegambian drum complex (map 8).

All of these drumming traditions are rooted in the practice of having at
least one drummer take the role of accompanist and one drummer act as
leader. In Mali dunduns can be played in pairs in this way, as can tamas. The
jembe requires one dundun for a minimal ensemble. In contrast to the fixed
size of the Mandinka three-drum ensemble, which has two accompanying
drums (kutirindingo and kutiriba) and one lead drum (sabaro), jembe ensembles can grow as large as one lead jembe, two or more accompanying
jembes, and from one to three dunduns. One or two contrasting jembe accompaniment patterns per rhythm is standard. Large groups of jembe players with many accompanying parts may be an invention of national ballets
or perhaps African teachers catering to the desires of their foreign students
in large jembe classes.

There is little historical documentation to support speculation on the age
of the various Mandenka drums. Table 11 shows some of the earliest written references to the drums in the western savanna and sahel, but it is often

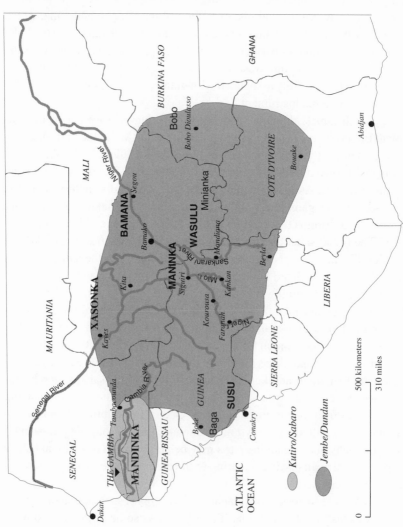

Map 8 Senegambian Mandinka and Malian/Guinean Maninka drum areas. Light shaded area shows the Senegambian Mandinka drum distribution. Darker shaded area shows the jembe and dundun ensemble cluster. Place-names are in italics (countries are in all capital letters). Northern Mande groups are in boldface capital letters. Non-Mande groups are in lowercase letters after an initial capital.

Table 11 Early Documentation of Mande Drums

1068	(al-Bakrī)
	"The royal meeting is announced by the sound of a kind of drum that they call *dubā* which is made from a long piece of hollowed-out wood." [*dundun?*]
1154	(al-Idrīsī)
	"Each one [of the king's officers on horseback] carrying a tabl which they strike." [*tama?*]
1355	(Ibn Battūta)
	"Each one of them has a drum tied to him and he beats it." [*tama?*]
1623	(Jobson)
	"Little drum which he holds under his left arm, and with a crooked stick in his right hand and his naked fingers on the left he strikes the drum."
1700?	(Avezac 1845)
	tantan (260)
1740	(Moore)
	"tantong"
1799	(Park)
	"*tangtang*" (Mandinka drum)
1825	(Gray and Dochard)
	Drawing of a tama, drawing of a sabaro
1885	(Gallieni)
	"tam-tam" (40)
1889	(Moloney)
	"Tang-tang" (278)
1898	(Tellier)
	"diembé" (159, 183)
1910	(Joyeux)
	"diembé" "doundou" (57)
1912	(Delafosse)
	photo of several jembe players with tama and flute (vol. 2, fig. 40)
1921	(Humblot)
	"'diémbé' et 'doun'doun'" (140)

Note: See appendix A and bibliography for complete citations.

unclear which drums are being described and who is playing them. With the exception of al-Bakrī's *dubā,* few are named. Because of the slow progress inland made by early European travelers, most of the references are to drums in the Senegambia region.

In contrast to the music of jelis or hunters, it is difficult to reconstruct with any detail drumming and dancing traditions of previous centuries. Whereas hunter's music may have remained insulated within esoteric hunters' societies and jeliya remained open to public scrutiny as part of a widespread conservative tradition guarded by and oriented toward an elite, drumming appears to have developed numerous local traditions. The combined wealth of these drumming traditions reflects a culture in which dancing is essential for everyone, although some are recognized as excelling in it. Accounts written by Europeans over the past several centuries describe dance events similar to those seen in villages nowadays, but European misunderstanding of the role of dancing in Africa may have hampered much keen detail. Some dance is viewed by Mande groups as play (*tulon*) or entertainment (*nyè-najè*); other occasions for drumming and dancing have more serious associations. With a few exceptions, such as hunters dancing to sounds of their harps and the dance pieces *Lamban* and *Mamaya* played on the bala, drums are the instruments of choice for dancing.

In the past, drum pieces and their dances may have been uniquely associated with specific occasions, each rhythm having a purpose, a time, and a place. Nowadays some rhythms and dances have less specific associations and may be performed at a variety of events. Drummers play rhythms that give people strength and courage before or during a trial and honor them when they have passed through it. Drumming is above all a communal event that demands participation from all present in the form of dancing, hand clapping, and singing. By participating, one honors those being celebrated, whether a bride and groom or children about to go into, or returning from, the bush.

Like the instruments of the jeli, the various Mandenka drums have rhythms and dances specifically associated with them, as well as rhythms that come from different drums of neighboring peoples. This can happen at the local level when, for example, the Mandinka three-drum ensemble is used to play neighboring Jola rhythms, or at the national level when a jembe-based ballet troupe plays rhythms from all over the country. But in general, drum rhythms and their associated dances are still closely associated with the region they come from. Despite differences between eastern (Maninka) and western (Mandinka) drumming traditions, there are features they both share, such as the occasions for drumming. After examining the kinds of drum and dance events that are common throughout eastern and western regions, I cover each of the drums in separate sections below.

Performers and Performance

Different drums are historically associated with different kinds of players. Among the Xasonka of northwestern Mali, the tama and dundun are played exclusively by jelis. Among the Soninke of northwestern and north-central Mali (where they are also known as Maraka), the tama is a jeli instrument. The Xasonka dundun, also called jeli dundun, is used to praise people by announcing their arrival at important events and invoking them to dance. Likewise, the tama is used to announce guests and to escort the bride and groom at marriage celebrations. In contrast, the jembe has no hereditary restrictions on who may play it, and it is uncommon (but by no means

Table 12 Occasions for Drum and Dance Events

Occasion	Name of Event	Name of Rhythm or Dance
Life-cycle events		
Infant naming	*Den kun li* (Mn.)	
	Ding kulio (Md.)	
Circumcision and excision	*Soli si, Fura si*	Mn: *Fura, Soli, Suku*
		Md: *Nyaka julo* (girls),
		Chingo (boys)
Marriages	*Konyo*	
Social and religious societies		
Secret power society (*jo*)	Kòmò	Kòmò
Masked figure	*Kankurango* (Md.)	Md: *Kankurang julo*
Other societies		
Older women	Md: *Kanyaleng kafo*	*Musuba julo*
Young girls	Md: *Asobi*	
Agricultural		
General	Konkoba	Konkoba
	Sansene ton*	
		Md: *Daba tantango*
Breaking up the field	Ciwara	
Clearing field	*Foro sonya***	Mn: *Kassa*
Rice transplanting		Md: *Nyaka julo****
Entertainment (*nyènajè*)		
Wrestling	*Nyoboring*	*Nyoboring julo*
Other	*Lenjengo, Seruba*	*Lenjengo, Seruba*
Stage performances		
Regional and national ballets		
Village theater	*Koteba*	

*D. Cissé 1970:230; **Leynaud and Cissé 1978:327–28; ***Knight 1995-vid.

unknown) for jelis to do so. The jembe is generally associated with numu communities, and a large proportion of jembe players bear the numu family names Camara, Kante, and Doumbia even though their families might not be practicing blacksmiths. Like playing other instruments (except perhaps hunter's harps), jembe playing carries a certain stigma among horon (freeborn, nonartisanal) families. Despite family resistance, however, many jembe players do have a horon background.

The kinds of occasions calling for drumming among the Mande are listed in table 12. The most common are celebrations surrounding two major life-cycle events that mark transitions: circumcision/excision ceremonies and marriages. Many of the other kinds of traditional occasions have become rare, if not extinct, but their dances are kept alive in the theatrical performances of professional government-sponsored regional and national ballet troupes. The continuity of old drumming traditions has been significantly affected in the twentieth century by several factors, including the impact of Islam and European colonialism, leading to the eradication of certain secret power societies; the mixing of diverse regional traditions in the hands of professional drummers in urban areas, especially the capital cities; and the vagaries of dance styles and drum rhythms.

Many dance occasions are tied to the seasonal calendar. The rainy season (Mn: *samiya;* Md: *saamo*), which begins in May or June in the savanna, is a time for agricultural labor and little else. Celebrations that occur during the rainy season most often take place in urban areas, where agriculture is not a major concern, and are often connected with infant naming ceremonies, which have no seasonal associations. Some communities, such as those around Segou, are renowned for their elaborate masquerade performances celebrating the coming of the rains signaling the new year, and also the onset of the dry season (Bm: *kawule*) signaling the fonio harvest (Arnoldi 1995). During the dry season (Mn: *tilema;* Md: *tili kandi*), which begins in late October or November, activities shift from agricultural to social. Marriages and initiation ceremonies are typically held during the dry season, and drumming is common. Drumming and dancing are generally absent during the holy month of Ramadan, when Muslims fast from sunup to sundown. The timing of Ramadan varies from year to year because it is based on the lunar calendar. The end of Ramadan (Mn: *selinin, salikalo*) and the biggest Muslim festival day Tabaski (Mn: *seliba, saliba*) are important occasions for drumming (Tellier 1898:159).[3]

Life-Cycle Events

Three major life-cycle events mark the lives of Mande peoples: a naming ceremony one week after birth; circumcision (boys) or excision (girls), which marks the passage into adulthood; and marriage. In observant West African Muslim societies, funerals are not a cause for celebration and drums are not played, although hunters' societies, which operate outside the confines of Islam, may have elaborate funeral celebrations that involve harp playing and dancing.[4]

3. The Segou Bamana youth association masquerades are known as *Samiyè da nyènajè* (beginning of the rainy season entertainment) or *Daba taa nyènajè* (taking up the hoe festival) and as *Fini tigè nyènajè* (fonio harvest festival) or *Daba bila nyènajè* (setting down the hoe festival). In addition to the tie to the agricultural calendar, the performances at the end of the rainy season are also related to the opening of the hunting season (Arnoldi 1995:109–10).

4. It is possible that drumming and dancing might be, or may have been in the past, part of a later memorial ceremony. Such was the case in the early twentieth century in Kita in a ceremony called *jonkalalate* that took place sometime after the requisite week of mourning (B. Keita 1988:

Plate 21 Mandinka three-drum ensemble. Set of instruments made by Mr. Juf, Kayaf (The Gambia), 1989. Left to right: sabaro (lead drum), kutiriba (big kutiro), and kutirindingo (little kutiro). Photo by John Wareham.

Infant Naming Ceremonies

One week after an infant is born it receives a name in a ceremony called *den kun li* (Md: *ding kulio*), "the shaving of the head," in which a tuft of hair is shaved off the infant's head. The ceremony usually begins in the morning. Typically a *mori* (Ar: *murābit;* Fr: *marabout*), a Muslim savant versed in religious science, pronounces the infant's name for the first time in its life, and at the same moment a goat is slaughtered nearby in accordance with Islamic law. The symbolism of a baby's coming into the world as an animal leaves it, to nourish the guests later, is vivid. Later in the day elaborate entertainment may be provided by the baby's family, most typically featuring jelis in varying kinds of ensembles. Brikama-based kora players Jaliba Kuyateh and Tata Dinding Jobarteh (son of kora player Ma Lamini Jobarteh) both lead very popular groups in demand for kulios throughout The Gambia and neighboring Senegal (plate 23). Both groups feature drummers who play a mixture of Mandinka and Wolof drums and draw enthusiastic crowds of

75–76). Modic (1996:73–74) lists four "life-cycle changes which involved the transition of individuals to different social statuses" that were occasions for musical entertainment by a Bamako women's association: the naming ceremony (*denkundi*), circumcision/excision (*bolokoli furasi*), the wedding engagement (*woro-tila*), and the wedding (*kònyò*).

Plate 22 Gambian Mandinka drumming and dancing. Top: Bakanding Camara (left) singing *Seruba* songs, Babanding Sanyang (right) playing sabaro, accompanied by kutirindingo and kutiriba (hidden). Bottom: Lenjengo dancing (Babanding Sanyang, sabaro). Brikama (The Gambia), 1989. Photos by the author.

Plate 23 Ebraima "Tata Dindin" Jobarteh and ensemble playing at a kulio (naming celebration). Left to right: jembe (partially out of photo), Wolof sabar ensemble drums, "Tata dindin" (kora) with Gambian dalasi (currency) bills pinned to his shirt, vocalist. Brikama (The Gambia), 1989. Photo by the author.

women eager to dance. Jelis and drummers may ply their craft together or in tandem at den kun li celebrations. There do not appear to be any pieces or dances specific to the occasion; it is a time for general celebration.[5]

Circumcision and Excision Ceremonies

According to Maninka thought, circumcision and excision (cutting off part or all of the clitoris) are necessary steps for the successful integration of children into society. Drums are an essential component of ceremonies leading up to the actual operations as well as the return of the children to their homes after healing. Local explanations of the significance of the operations are compelling.

> The child, who is at first considered a foreigner outside the rules of society, achieves the status of a person only from the moment he or she has undergone excision or circumcision, the first steps on the long path of social humanizing. The purpose of these operations, deemed necessary by the Mandingues, is to liberate from human beings *wanzo,* a cloud that renders the mind impermeable to the teaching that is necessary for proper socialization among the

5. See Dieterlen (1951:177–79) and Modic (1996:75–79) for brief descriptions of the naming ceremony among the Bamana, and Dieterlen and Sylla (1992:115–16) for the Soninke.

Mandingues. . . . once having passed under the knife of the *numu* [black-smith], thereby being shaped and fixed in their sexual identities, the new man or woman begins a long voyage through the maze of social relations (age groups, marriage, and others) and of mystical principals (initiation societies) that rule the visible and invisible universe. (C. Keita 1995a:40)

The force called *wanzo,* also known as *kono nyama* (spiritual force of the interior being), is believed to reside in the foreskin or clitoris of children and must be removed so they can marry and procreate (Dieterlen 1951:64–65; Y. Cissé 1973:161; 1994:68). Sarah Brett-Smith (1994:43–45) has likened the farmer's cutting and preparing of the earth with the blacksmith's iron hoe, thereby releasing *nyama* (potentially dangerous spiritual force) from the ground, to the cutting of unformed boys or girls with the black-smith's knife, thereby releasing their unchanneled nyama. Children are be-lieved to possess inordinate amounts of nyama, which permits them to com-mit acts such as eating anything and everything with impunity, which could be fatal in adults. But when children reach puberty there is a need to con-trol their unfettered power. Circumcision and excision not only control but also purify and cleanse. Women consistently told Brett-Smith that excision, "'releases the nyama' (*ka nyama bò*) of childhood, purifying the woman and guaranteeing her obedience to traditional rules of respect (*bonya*)" (Brett-Smith 1994:43–44).

The verb *ci* (to break or cut) can be used to refer to excision among the Bamana, as in *fura ci* (breaking or cutting of the leaf), and also to a numu's carving a sculpture. The concept of creation is present in both examples, whether creating a human being or a powerful wooden sculpture by carv-ing. *Teyi,* "to break" in Gambian Mandinka, is sometimes used as a verb to describe the creation or "cutting" of a new piece of music.

Maninka and Mandinka boys and girls undergo circumcision and exci-sion, respectively, sometime in the few years on either side of age ten. Both kinds of operation are called *bolokoli* (washing of the hands). The age at which it happens may have dropped over the course of the twentieth cen-tury, and modern city dwellers often have these operations performed in a hospital shortly after birth. In the villages, circumcisions and excisions may take place every few years, including all the eligible children as a group.[6]

6. For descriptions of circumcision and excision among Maninka see Tellier (1898:154–58), Chéron (1933), L. Camara (1954:111–35), D. Cissé (1970:215–25), and B. Keita (1988:44–50); for Mandinka see Innes (1972) and Schaffer and Cooper (1987); for Bamana see Henry (1910: 175–98) and Dieterlen (1951:179–88); for Soninke see Dieterlen and Sylla (1992:116–18); for Susu see Famechon (1900:206); for Kissi in Guinea see Schaeffner (1953); for Kuranko of Sierra Leone see Jackson (1977); and for Jola see Mark (1992). Circumcision- and excision-related song texts have been transcribed by Chéron (1933), D. Cissé (1970:216, 220), and Innes (1972) and translated into French by Luneau (1981) and M. Kaba (1995:25–41). A circumcision-related song called *Damadian* or *Siminka* has been transcribed by Joyeux (1924:189–90). Chéron (1933:297)

Before they are eligible for the operation, children are known as *bi-lakoro*. Once the date is set for the ceremony they are called *solima*. In the days and nights leading up to the operation there is drumming and dancing, culminating on the eve of the operation, when *soli si* takes place, an all-night event with singing and dancing. The exhausting dancing might have an anesthetic effect on the children and is intended to give them courage. When daybreak arrives they undergo the operation at the hands of an expert *numuke* (male numu) in the case of boys, or *numumuso* (female numu) in the case of girls. Afterward boys are called *solimake* and girls *solimamuso;* in Mandinka *ngànsing* is used for both sexes. After a few weeks or more of healing in seclusion they return to their families. The return from the bush is marked by a celebration involving drumming, dancing, and singing called *boloko dennu don bo* in Maninka or *ngansing jenjengo* in Mandinka (the dispersion of the newly circumcised/excised children). In the Senegam-bia region, sometimes the *kankurang* (*kankurao*), a feared figure dressed in long strips of tree bark, is brought out during the healing period to com-bat any problems (Knight 1995-vid; Mark 1992:121–24; and Schaffer and Cooper 1987:101–4). Once circumcised or excised, boys and girls move into the status of young men (Bm: *kamalen;* Md: *kambano*) and women (Bm: *npogotigi*), eligible for marriage.

The main Maninka drum rhythm and dance associated with circumcision and excision is called *Soli* (in Guinea) or *Suku* (in Mali). In an account of his own circumcision as a boy in Upper Guinea, Laye Camara (1954:113–25) writes of his dancing *Soli* during the whole week before the operation.[7] In the Senegambia boys dance *Chingo* and girls dance *Lenjengo* (which is more of a general recreational dance). Their mothers may dance *Nyaka julo* on this occasion.

Marriage Celebrations

Marriage (Mn: *kònyò* or *furu siri;* Md: *maanyoo bito* or *futuu sito*) is the most elaborate and costly event in Mande life, and weddings provide a major source of income for professional jembe drummers in large cities.[8]

---

noted that Bamana also use the term *nyagali* for female excision (also see *nyara* in Delafosse 1955:563). Perhaps this is related to the Gambian Mandinka dance *Nyaka julo.*

7. Camara also writes about a dance called *Koba* done only on the eve of the circumcision, and one called *Fady fady,* "the dance of manhood," done by his friends and neighbors when they heard the news of the successful operation.

8. Weddings can be so costly as to discourage early marriage for males. One Bamana-language newspaper story (in Bird and Kante 1976:122) reports on official community efforts in a neighbor-hood in Segou to regulate marriage expenses. See Zahan (1963:85–95) and Luneau (1981) for a discussion of songs related to marriage. For a description of marriages among the Maninka of Kita see Tellier (1898:113–24), D. Cissé (1970:76–104), and B. Keita (1988:53–59); for the Soninke

Negotiations and arrangements between the families of the bride and groom are usually done using a jeli as a go-between. There is one week of celebrating, beginning on the wedding night, during which the bride remains secluded in the husband's home. The entertainment that takes place during the week is called *kònyò nyènajè* (marriage entertainment). Music may be provided by a variety of jeli ensembles. In the capital cities one can often find jelimuso singers accompanied by the traditional jeli instruments and electric guitars. If these ensembles are present, they might alternate with a drumming group. If not, then drummers have complete reign over the event, often with a jelimuso acting as mistress of ceremonies leading group singing and dancing.

The broader the repertory of the drummers, the better they can accommodate guests who may come from diverse parts of the country and request their own regional dances. Drummers might be guaranteed a certain salary, with their earnings augmented by guests during and after the event. There may be rhythms specific to wedding festivities among the Maraka (played on the tama) in Mali, and among the Mandinka in The Gambia (e.g., *Maanyoo dondo*), but it is unclear if the term *koniofoli* (Tellier 1898:159) refers to jembe pieces specific to marriage celebrations or to drumming in general associated with the occasion.

Social and Religious Societies

Throughout much of West Africa traditional associations oversee or carry out certain community affairs, and they are also intimately linked with drumming. Often called initiation societies in French and English writing, they are of two fundamental types. In Bamana and Maninka the two types are called *jo* (*dyo*) and *ton*.[9] *Jow* and *tonw* are segregated by gender; there are male and female *jow* and *tonw*. A ton is based on age and it is oriented toward collective labor such as working in the fields or maintaining village property, entertainment, and dance. A jo is more like a power association. "They [power associations] focus on three types of activities: the containment and eradication of anti-social activities, the practice of divination, and the attainment of prosperity and happiness for their members and their cli-

---

see Dieterlen and Sylla (1992:119–21); for the Mandinka see Schaffer and Cooper (1987:80–85) and Van Hoven (1996).

9. This paragraph is based on McNaughton (1979:7–23), which contains a good summary of research over the past century on jow. For a discussion of the distinctions between jo and ton see Leynaud and Cissé (1978:307–37) and Brett-Smith (1994:285). Other relevant sources on jow include Dieterlen and Cissé (1972), Henry (1910), and Zahan (1960). I am using the Bamana plural marker -*w* for the terms jo and ton here because most of the research I am relying on has a Bamana rather than a Maninka slant.

ents" (McNaughton 1979:8). The names and specific activities of jow and tonw vary according to the region, but six have been widely recognized by researchers as being active in the Mande heartland through Segou. Ntomo and Kore are tonw; Kòmò, Nama, Nya, and Kono are jow. In essence, a ton is public, it deals with mundane matters, and its rules are human made. A jo is a secret association dealing with natural laws and supernatural powers.

Jow and tonw possess wooden masks, which are instantly recognizable emblems for their associations. The masks can take the form of elaborate vertical headdresses, face masks, or helmets that project horizontally. Horizontal helmet masks like those used in Kòmò societies are widespread in West Africa and are usually abstract depictions of bush animals (McNaughton 1991, 1992). These wooden masks are worn by dancers who are accompanied by drummers. Usually only the masks of tonw are taken out in public and danced in open performances. Well-known masks include those from the children's ton Ntomo (Zahan 1960), the agriculturally centered tonw Ciwara (Tyiwara) and Sogonikun (Sogoninkun) (Imperato 1981), and the most widespread of the jow, Kòmò (McNaughton 1979; Brett-Smith 1994).[10]

Jow and tonw use different drums associated with the regions where they operate. Although much important documentation has been written on tonw and jow, there is little information on the drumming that accompanies the masked dancers. In an otherwise highly informative musical account of the associations that were active in Upper Guinea in the early twentieth century, Joyeux (1924:206–7) devoted only half a page to Kòmò (Mn: Kòma), with a cursory reference to Kòmò flutes. Out of the more than one hundred named rhythms that have been recorded by jembe players, few are related to Maninka jow; the most readily identifiable one is simply called *Komo, Koma,* or *Komodenu* (Children of Komo).[11] Kòmò associations are traditionally led by numus, who also carve the masks and drums used in their rituals. The dispersion of numus from core Mande areas resulted in the dispersion of their jow, being redefined according to the milieus into which they were transplanted (Brooks 1993:44–46, 73–77).

Maninka and Mandinka acceptance and interpretations of Islam have had

10. For more on Bamana and Maninka masking traditions see Imperato (1980) and Arnoldi (1995); for a broad overview of the possible historical implications of West African masking traditions see McNaughton (1991, 1992). For a description of Kòmò mask performances among the Bamana see Travele (1929); among the Wasulu see McNaughton (1979:37–42); and among the Minianka see Diallo and Hall (1989:68–69). A photo in Delafosse ([1912] 1972, vol. 3, fig. 60) shows three musicians playing calabash drums and several females clapping for two Ciwara figures standing in front of field laborers.

11. For recordings see Ladji Camara (n.d.a-disc), Rouget (1972/1999-disc), Mamady Keita (1989-disc), and Yamadu Dumbia (in Polak 1994-disc).

varying effects on drumming and dancing. Muslims may object to drumming, especially that associated with masking traditions, for several reasons: the fashioning or creating of representational masks by human beings may be seen as an attempt to usurp the powers of Allah, the creator; the masks may represent spirits or deities in direct conflict with local Islamic doctrine; and drumming is often associated with dancing related to earthly pleasures. Although drumming thrives in most Muslim Maninka and Mandinka societies, different contexts may be more or less acceptable to devout Muslims. The least acceptable would be a jo such as Kòmò, which uses a wooden mask and draws on spiritual forces in direct conflict with Muslim teachings.[12] The Mandinka *kankurang* figure, wearing long strips of tree bark and accompanied by the Mandinka three-drum ensemble, would be more acceptable because it has no discernible face and does not represent a conflicting spiritual or power source.

Kòmò (or Kòma) societies, which use jembe drumming, may still be significant for some Bamana of Mali who have nominally accepted Islam, but Kòmò has declined among the Maninka, except in theatrical presentations by ballet troupes. In the early 1920s Joyeux (1924:206–7) noted that Kòma societies in Upper Guinea where he was stationed were formerly feared but were becoming more "inoffensive," perhaps owing to the French presence. He discussed several less feared figures accompanied by drummers or other musicians that are disappearing from village contexts, notably Mandiani and Konkoba (see below). In the early 1950s Rouget recorded Kòma singing and drumming in eastern Guinea, but not in its former context.

> Twenty-five years ago, traditional religion was still very much alive at Karala. In the Fifties, Islam zealots managed to get the "fetishes" burnt. The mysteries of the koma, the secret society of the masks, corner-stone of the religion, were exposed to the eyes of women and the non-initiated. Since then, koma rites have not been carried out in this village, now completely Moslem. (Rouget 1972-disc)

On the Mali side of old Mande, Leynaud and Cissé (1978:331, 338) have referred to rare outings of the Kòmò mask in the 1950s, noting that the tradition has died out, and Zobel (1996a:627, 638) has noted the recent decline of Kòma in Manding mountain villages southwest of Bamako. Arnoldi's (1995:99–100) research in the vicinity of Segou found that Kòmò was last performed in neighboring Kirango in the 1950s. Dieterlen and

---

12. Peter Mark (1992:143) has suggested that the presence of a face on a wooden mask, thereby conflicting with Muslim prohibitions on representation, might contribute to its demise at the hands of Muslim reformers. See Zobel (1996a) for a discussion of Kòma coexisting with certain interpretations of Islam in the Manding mountains.

Sylla (1992:114–15) also indicate that the outing of masks, including that of Kòma, had disappeared among the Soninke of Mali. Masks that were more in the realm of entertainment rather than religious rite, including secular outings of Kòmò masks in the performances of *kamalen tonw* (youth associations), were more apt to be tolerated by Muslims (Arnoldi 1995:19, 68). Consequently, drumming and dancing surrounding certain masks or figures, vital in village contexts in the early twentieth century, may exist only frozen in ballet troupes at the end of the century or used in a secular context in the masquerades of the youth associations.

Agricultural Events

Although it is not a major occupation, drummers are sometimes called on to encourage the work of clearing fields for planting or of weeding and to animate general fertility rituals. Jembe rhythms specific to this kind of work are *Kassa* (Mamady Keita 1989-disc:6, Chevalier 1991-vid) and *Sogonikun* (Meillassoux 1968b:96–100). Mandinka drummers also play for women working in the rice fields (Knight 1995-vid). Sometimes drumming is organized by a youth association (ton) charged with clearing someone's field (Mn: *foro sonya*), in which case the drumming accompanies work as well as dancing in honor of the owner of the field (Leynaud and Cissé 1978: 327–28).

Drumming can accompany the dancing of the famous Bamana antelope head Ciwara masks that celebrate the initial breaking up of the soil for planting (Brett-Smith 1994:34). *Wara* refers to a lion, but it can also refer to any animal with claws that scratch, hence the symbolism of scratching the earth. In Wasulu another mask, called Sogonikun (Sogoninkun), is used for similar purposes. Meillassoux (1968b:96–100) has described a dance association in Bamako named after the Sogonikun mask, made up of seasonal workers from Bougouni in Wasulu territory. Their dancing was accompanied by a jembe and a *gangan* (tama-like drum). *Sogonikun* is still danced in Bamako, and is an important component in the Wasulu sound, a recent genre in Malian popular music (Durán 1995a:113–15).[13]

Entertainment

The term *nyènajè* (entertainment), or the more general *tulon* (play), is used in several contexts to refer to drumming and dancing. The two terms can refer to nonprofessional drumming in general, such as that of the Bamako Ben

13. Joyeux (1910:56–58, 1924:209–10) described an association called Kourcikoroni whose purpose was to encourage agricultural labor with music. In a separate ceremony members would perform a special dance around a fire to the accompaniment of two jembes and one dundun.

Ka Di women's association (Modic 1996). The two terms can also refer to drumming and dancing that celebrates the completion of the life-cycle events of naming a child, circumcision/excision, and marriage. For example, the actual naming ceremony is a male-dominated event that takes place in the morning; celebrations, which can be considered nyènajè or tulon, are often female-dominated events (except for the professional instrumentalists, whether drummers or jelis) that take place in the afternoons. The all-night drumming that leads up to circumcision or excision is not considered tulon, but the celebrations that occur when the healed children return may be. Finally, the two terms can refer to public performance unrelated to life-cycle events.[14] The border between public entertainment and private ritual hinges on transformation, among other factors. The masquerade theater of youth associations in Segou is considered nyènajè.

> While the sentiments and flavor of the theatrical experience may extend into people's daily lives following the event, the theatre, unlike marriage and initiation rituals, does not permanently effect a transformation in the status and social identity of its participants. (Arnoldi 1995:22)[15]

This concept of life transformation distinguishes many of the activities of the ton, considered to be entertainment, from the jo, which has rites centered on power objects (called boli).

Based on her research with kamalen ton (youth association) masquerading traditions in Segou, Arnoldi has delineated a set of oppositions that distinguish Kòmò mask traditions from the nyènajè (entertainment) of the youth associations: "private/public, restricted/open attendance, bush/village, power object/plaything" (Arnoldi 1995:23). For instance, talk about Kòmò is private, attendance is restricted, and meetings take place in the bush and center on power objects (boli). The youth masquerades, on the other hand, are publicly discussed, may be attended by all, take place in a large village performance space, and use masks classified as playthings (tulon fen). In the late twentieth century there may be little drumming that is not considered entertainment. This is to say that various outside and internal forces have combined to secularize drumming traditions, bringing them to a broader public.

In the Senegambia a major source of entertainment is wrestling, which is accompanied by drummers. Among the Mandinka wrestling is known as nyoboring, and there is a specific rhythm, called Nyoboring julo, that is used to encourage wrestlers during their matches (Knight 1995-vid). Other forms of recreational drumming are usually organized by youth groups (ton). For

14. For more on distinctions between ritual and play in jembe drumming, see Polak (forthcoming); I thank him for allowing me to see his work in progress.

15. Arnoldi cites Handelman (1977) and Brink (1980) here.

instance, young Senegambian Mandinka girls sometimes form an association, called Asobi, and organize drumming, dancing, and singing events
where they all dress alike (see photo in Knight 1974:26–27).

Regional and National Ballets

One result of the creation of national ballets has been the reification of national canons or repertories of dances. Guinea led the way shortly after independence, with the nationalization of Les Ballets Africains, created by
Fodeba Keita in the late 1940s. Mali and Senegal also formed their own national ballets. These troupes have achieved world renown through their frequent tours, attracting the best dancers from all the ethnic groups living
in every part of the country, all bringing their own ways of dancing to the
troupe. The choreographer creates stage presentations of village dances,
combining different dance styles sequentially in long suites that take on a
life of their own, telling a story with a specific sequence of dances, rhythms,
and costumes. For example, the pieces called "The Sacred Forest" and
"Celebration" performed by Les Ballets Africains (1991-vid, 1991-disc)
present a sequence of fifteen dances from several regions of Guinea belonging to nearly half a dozen ethnic groups. Not only are dances from different regional traditions combined, but so are their associated musical instruments, an equally rare village event. This innovation of national dance
troupes is intended in part to promote a national identity based on the contributions of all members of society. New interpretations of traditional
rhythms are created and solidified, existing as perhaps the only living examples of abandoned traditional dance practices.

With the independence of Guinea, the national ballet became a showcase
directed to foreign audiences. In a curious charge from the new president,
a distinction was made between educating audiences (the role of domestic
troupes) and acquainting them with African culture (the role of the touring
ballet).

> While we insist, ever again, on the necessity for our artistic and cultural per-
> formances to be integrated into our popular revolution and to serve educa-
> tional purposes, this does not apply to the National Ballet, whose task does
> not consist in educating foreign spectators, but in acquainting them with our
> cultural values and artistic riches. The National Ballet should present Africa,
> make her known and esteemed. Its programmes are not chosen in view of their
> educational and mobilizing qualities, but rather of the artistic representative-
> ness of Africa and of the life of African peoples. (S. Toure 1963:261, n.d.:87)

The distinction here is between domestic presentations in support of local
political and social policy, deemed irrelevant for foreign audiences, and international presentations putting the country's best face forward.

The transformation that occurs when village traditions are adapted for stage presentation to foreign audiences was, and still is, a major concern of African ballet choreographers and their critics alike. Fodeba Keita understood the nature of this transformation and was a pioneer in presenting the culture of his country to international audiences. Even though there were historical connections with village traditions, ballet drumming and dancing constituted a new genre with different aspirations. Questions of authenticity were inevitably raised by foreign writers and were addressed by Keita.

> Nevertheless, the stage being different from life, it is necessary to resort to a certain amount of stage adaptation to make ourselves understood by a foreign public. In our African villages, the same dance may last a whole night without tiring anyone. The dances are, moreover, executed in the middle of a ring of spectators who also take part almost as much as the dancers and musicians. On the stage new conditions have to be created by means of different devices in order, on the one hand, to retain the freshness and reality of the dance and, on the other, to destroy the monotony which is quick to arise due to the non-active participation of the audience. That is the reason why we must take our dances only at their culminating point, shorten them and cut out a thousand details which are not important except in the public place of the village. (F. Keita 1958:176)

In the mid-1950s the Paris performances of Les Ballets Africains received a stunning endorsement from Rouget (1956), who knew the milieu in Upper Guinea that Keita stemmed from. But Rouget objected specifically to staging dances of possession.

> Possession is a complicated phenomenon that is produced only in very special circumstances and is totally incompatible with a stage presentation at a fixed hour without preparation and the inner necessity.
> Voluntarily sustained, deprived of its religious context, this conduct can only end up as a parody, a painful one in my opinion and without artistic value. (Rouget 1956:140)

There were enough dances that could be, and were, effectively extracted from their contexts for an audience, Rouget argued (1956:140), that Les Ballets Africains should not have to resort to the "exoticism, perhaps spectacular but surely facile and false," of dances of possession. And so was defined a classic conflict between Africans secularizing and popularizing some of their traditions for an uninitiated foreign audience and foreign critics sometimes objecting to it. But the discourse has rarely moved beyond these initial arguments to address deeper and subtler issues of local criticism.[16]

16. Reviews of various Ballets Africains tours can be found in Les Ballets Africains (1996). Photographs of key members of their February 1959 "triumph in New York" with attending celebrities such as Dag Hammarskjöld, Ralph Bunche, Geoffrey Holder, and Michael Olatunji, were pub-

Drummers migrate to capital cities not only for the prospect of employment in national ballet troupes, but also to find other lucrative work, such as playing for the sometimes lavish marriage celebrations. Some drummers, especially those like Adama Drame and Mamady Keita who are able to teach, perform, and even relocate abroad, prefer this kind of freelance work to the rigidity of a ballet. The capital cities function as a sort of melting pot for drummers from various regions. They come into contact with other rhythms and learn them in case people request these dances during a celebration. Rhythms that were not part of their formative regional repertory might receive generic names referring either to the ethnic group or to the instrument they come from (see below).

Jembe

The early history of the jembe is a mystery, but its association with numus may provide clues to its early dispersion. As providers of iron implements, numus were, and still are, guardians of certain kinds of power. Numu hands sculpt the power-laden wooden Kòmò masks that are emblems of the secret societies they also lead; they perform the circumcisions and excisions that lift the dangerous energies of boys and girls, marking their entrance into adulthood; and they forge the hoes used for agricultural labor. Jembes are directly tied to each of these enterprises. They are played for the Kòmò society, for circumcision and excision ceremonies, to accompany agricultural labor, and to celebrate the harvest. Numus are also the ones who carve the bodies of jembes, and they are often the ones who play them.[17]

The vast majority of jembe players have Maninka or Susu names, and many of them belong to numu lineages such as Camara, Doumbia, and Kante (appendix B). Most of the other family names (*jamu*) of jembe players, such as Keita and Konate, are of Maninka horon (nonartisan) heritage. Relatively few of the names are of jeli origin.[18] Although jelis in core Mande

---

lished in the African magazine *Bingo* ("Triomphe à New York" 1959). A review with special mention of Fodeba Keita, dancers Italo Zambo, Suzy Baye, and Issa Niang, vocalist Sory Kandia Kouyate, jembe player Ladji Camara, kora player Daouda Diabate, and musical director Facelli Kante appeared in the *New York Times* (Martin 1959).

17. Caillié's (1830:247–49) report of a blacksmith establishment in the hills near Kouroussa (in Upper Guinea), where iron is found in "great quantities," and of the surrounding chiefdom of Amana (Hamana) as being "idolaters" (i.e., non-Muslim), lends further support to a blacksmith connection with jembe drumming. Hamana is home to the most widespread jembe piece, *Dundunba* (see below). In neighboring Muslim communities, such as Kankan, traditionally violent *Dundunba* dancing has been suppressed.

18. Blanket generalizations based on a blind review of family names can be misleading, but the preponderance of evidence supports this particular example. The jeli side of jembe players such as Abdoul Doumbia of Segou (now living in the United States), who comes from a numu father and a jeli mother, is not reflected in an examination of family names only.

areas recognize that the jembe is not one of their instruments, in more distant areas this tradition may have been transformed, hence Adama Drame's assertion that the jembe is a jeli instrument in Burkina Faso (Drame and Senn-Borloz 1992). Despite the association of the jembe with numus, there do not appear to be any hereditary restrictions on who may play it.

The major axis of jembe playing runs along the Upper Niger River from Faranah (Guinea) to Segou (Mali), with extensions stretching east into Burkina Faso, south into Côte d'Ivoire, southwest to Conakry, and west toward Kita and Kayes (map 8). With increasing urbanization and the formation of national ensembles, the capital cities Conakry and Bamako are the two major centers of jembe playing. Abidjan and Bouake (Côte d'Ivoire), Ouagadougou (Burkina Faso), and Dakar (Senegal) also host important jembe-based groups. Farther south in Sierra Leone, Liberia, and Côte d'Ivoire, smaller jembe-like instruments are played. The wide dispersion of the jembe in West Africa may be due to numu migrations dating from the first millennium C.E.[19]

Although jembes vary somewhat in shape and size according to region, they all share certain characteristics. Jembes are carved from a single piece of wood, the most common kinds being *lenke* (*linge*), *dugura,* and *jala* among others (table 13). The preference for one wood over another might vary by region and availability; lenke is particularly prized in part because of the belief that it is spiritually charged. The upper part of the jembe body is shaped like a large bowl, with the diameter on top typically ranging from thirty to thirty-eight centimeters (twelve to fifteen inches). The lower part of the body is a cylinder about fifteen centimeters (six inches) in diameter (on those from Mali) or slightly flared at the bottom (on those from Guinea). A typical jembe from Mali or Guinea stands about sixty-one centimeters (twenty-four inches) tall. The drumhead is goatskin.[20]

A major distinguishing feature of the jembe is the way the head is attached, using three iron rings. A water-soaked goatskin is laid over the top

19. Some examples of jembe-like instruments in the southern Mande range are: from Liberia, the *samgba* (Liberia 1971:4), the triple *samgba* played by the Kissi (Liberia 1971:5), a Gbunde and Loma triple drum (Schwab 1947, fig. 79c), and one described in Donner (1940:76–77); from Sierra Leone, a *sangboi* played by Mendi (Alldridge 1901, facing 113; Lamm 1968:73–74, 100; Monts 1982:104–5); and from Côte d'Ivoire, a drum played by the Gouro (Vuylsteke n.d.-disc), the *baa* played by the Dan (Zemp 1971:40–44, plates 7 and 14), and a triple drum (Huet and Keita 1996:123).

20. Wa Kamissoko (Cissé and Kamissoko 1988:272–75; 1991:107) reported that a small jembe called *djemberenin,* from *djembe ren* (child) *nin* (small), was the first instrument played by blacksmiths during the smelting process, and that it is still played for blacksmiths in Sibi and Narena. The head, about twenty-five centimeters (ten inches) in diameter, is strung onto the clay or wood bowl with straps. It is played with the index fingers. Kamissoko also noted that blacksmiths would sing along with it.

Table 13 Woods Used for Making Drums

Jembe

Lenke, also known as *linge, danga, dagan, daganba* (*Afzelia africana*)
Pale straw sapwood (Lincoln 1986:22)

Dugura (*Cordylla pinata*)
Yellowish wood (*Cordyla africana*) (Delafosse 1955:142)

Jala (cailcedra, *Khaya senegalensis*)
African mahogany (Lincoln 1986:158; Mauny 1952:26)

Kasia (*Cassia*)

Balenbo (*Crossopterix febrifuga*)

Benbe (*Lannea acida*)

Kutiro and Sabaro

Dutoo (*Cordyla africana*)
Wild mango (Gamble 1987b:34)
Yellowish

Kembo
Deep red mahogany (Knight 1974:27)

Note: See Polak 1996a:8; Brett-Smith (1994:119–53, 291–306), and K. Kone (1995:230–31).

opening, and one ring is placed over it, around the outside of the bowl. The ends of the skin are pulled up over the ring (and eventually trimmed off), and another ring is placed on top of the first (which is now covered by skin). This second ring has small loops hanging down about every five centimeters (two inches). A third ring, with loops identical to those on the second, is slipped over the lower half of the body and slid up to the bottom of the bowl. A very long, strong cord is then threaded through the loops of the upper and lower rings in an up-and-down zigzag pattern. After an initial tightening, the skin may be left to dry for a few days. Then the cord is tightened again and again. To further tighten the skin, the excess cord can be woven horizontally through the vertical zigzag pattern, forming a diamond-like pattern starting with one row near the bottom ring and eventually requiring more rows as the rope and skin stretch. Just before playing, jembe players may place their drums close to a fire to further dry and tighten the skin (and hence raise its pitch) significantly. Formerly, leather cord was used and the pitch was lower (plates 24, 26, 29).[21]

21. Compared with recent recordings, the pitch on jembes recorded in the 1930s (Boulton 1957-disc) and 1950s (Rouget 1999-disc) is lower. Nowadays clear regional preferences for higher-pitched (Guinea) and lower-pitched (Mali and Burkina Faso) jembes can be discerned.

Plate 24 Assorted jembes from Mali, Guinea, and Senegal. The four jembes on the left are from Mali, the next two are from Guinea, and the one on the right is from Senegal. Photo by John Wareham.

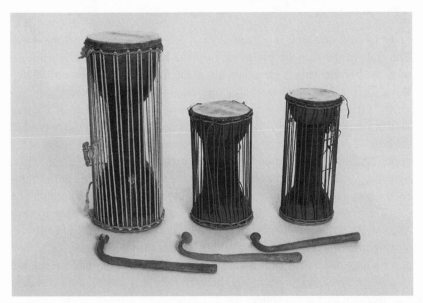

Plate 25 Tamas from Mali. Sizes (left to right): 42 × 17 centimeters (16.5 × 6.75 inches); 25.5 × 14.5 centimeters (10 × 5.75 inches); 28.5 × 13 centimeters (11.25 × 5 inches). The two on the left are Maraka style; the one on the right is Xasonka style. Photo by John Wareham.

Plate 26 Old jembe-like drums from the southern range. Top: "Beating the tom-tom or sang-boi, by Mendi boys," a jembe-like instrument from Liberia, from Alldridge (1901, facing 113, fig. 33). Bottom: mid-twentieth-century jembe (51 centimeters tall) from the region of Nzerekore, from Musée de l'Homme, M.H. 38.18.135; D-84-1026-493; photo by D. Ponsard.

Jembes are often played with three large flexible oval metal plaques attached to the drum. The plaques have small metal rings inserted so that when the drum is struck the vibration is transmitted to the plaque and the rings jingle. The plaques are called *sekeseke* (or *segesege*) in Mali or *sesse* in Guinea (by a common linguistic process, the hard *k* [or *g*] drops out). In parts of Guinea and Senegal they are called *kesekese* (through the linguistic process of metathesis).

Jembe repertories draw from many sources including widespread core Maninka rhythms and dances as well as more geographically limited dances. Many other rhythms played on the jembe are adaptations from other kinds of percussion instruments played by neighboring peoples, sometimes retaining those names: *Bougarabou* (Orchestre Africa Djembe 1993-disc); *Burun* (Polak 1996-disc); *Djabara* (Mamady Keita 1989-disc); and *Sabar* (Adama Drame 1987-disc; Polak 1996-disc). The influence of non-Maninka drumming is probably the greatest contributor to the emergence of national drumming styles and repertories, a recent development brought on by colonial boundaries. Such national styles can clearly be discerned among Maninka, whose Mande homeland was split into a Mali side and a Guinea side. Malian Maninka drummers head north to the capital city Bamako, where they encounter rhythms from the northern savanna and sahel regions. Since these rhythms are not from their home tradition, they label them simply by the ethnic affiliations of the people they come from: *Sarakole/ Maraka* (Abdoul Doumbia 1995-disc; Mamadou Kante 1993-disc; Polak 1996-disc); *Peuhls/Fula* (Mamadou Kante 1993-disc; Polak 1996-disc); *Dogons* (Mamadou Kante 1993-disc); *Bamanan* (Polak 1994-disc; 1997-disc); and *Wasulunka* (Polak 1994-disc). The same thing occurs in Guinea, where Maninka drummers head southwest to Conakry and play rhythms from the forest and coastal regions belonging to peoples such as the Baga, Toma, Mane, Temne, and Guerze.

Judging from the number of drummers who have recorded it, the most popular rhythm among jembe drummers by far is *Dundunba* (*Dununba, Dunumba*), a collection of related rhythms probably reflecting local variations played in Upper Guinea.[22] It is typically described as a dance of strong men bearing whips that they use to strike each other, originating in the Maninka chiefdom of Hamana in the region of Kouroussa in Upper Guinea. Its popularity as a dance spread north to Bamako and south to Conakry, where it entered the repertory of the national ballet troupes. In Conakry nowadays the term *dundunba* is popularly used for any kind of jembe-based dance celebration. Early documentation of the dance includes a photograph published by Chauvet (1929:152) captioned "un tam-tam à Kouroussa (Guinée)" (plate 27).[23] The attire of the dancers is very close to that of the

22. The bilabial consonant *b* in the suffix *-ba* (big) changes the nasal *n* to *m,* yielding the correct pronunciation *Dundumba* or *Dunumba.*

23. Another early piece of documentation of *Dundunba* comes from Joyeux (1924:210), who described what he called a "sect" called Bando (monkey), which consisted of dancers who wore goatskin (formerly monkey skin) collars. The head of the Bando dancers at the time was Diely Koro. Famoudou Konate (1991-disc:66–70) includes *Bandogialli* (probably named after *bando* and *dieli*) as a *Dundunba* variation. Konate's description of the dance (written by Johannes Beer) conforms with a scene in Les Ballets Africains (1991-vid).

Plate 27 *Dundunba* dancers at Kouroussa, Guinea. "Un tam-tam à Kouroussa (Guinée)." Photo by Lieutenant Bacot. From Chauvet (1929:152, fig. 12 bis).

dancers in modern Ballets Africains (1967-vid, 1991-vid, n.d.-vid) performances of the piece. In the early 1960s Claude Meillassoux (1968b:93–96) saw the dance performed in Bamako by migrants from Kouroussa and reported that it was danced regularly on Sundays. What he saw was relatively tame, but his description of how it is danced in Kouroussa vividly portrays its significance. Meillassoux indicates that, traditionally, circumcised males fifteen to twenty-eight years old prove their courage by dancing *Dundunba*. The dancers tie handkerchiefs around their heads.

> On both arms magic leather bangles sustain their strength; in one hand they carry a small war ax or a saber, in the other a *wene* (short whip) made of the plaited membrane of a donkey's penis. They walk in single file around the *bara* (dance ground), each whipping the man in front of him until the blood runs. Those who cannot bear the pain leave the file amidst the jeers of the crowd. . . . The *dunūba* formerly was danced only at great occasions, to celebrate a victory or a circumcision. Today, in the bush, the most usual occasion is at circumcision time. (Meillassoux 1968b:94)[24]

Other descriptions of the dance are given by Sory Camara ([1976] 1992:292) and in the notes to two extraordinary recordings by Famoudou Konate (1991-disc), who plays six *Dundunba* variations, and Mamady Keita

24. Notes by Beer (Famoudou Konate 1991-disc:68) and Flagel (Mamady Keita 1996-disc:13) indicate that the whips are made from hippopotamus skin, *manimfosson.*

(1996-disc), who, along with guest Famoudou Konate, plays twelve. Konate, lead jembe player with Les Ballets Africains in the early years of independence, comes from Kouroussa, the *Dundunba* heartland. In Keita's description, similar to Camara's, concentric circles of males are formed in the village dance space (*bara*) according to their age groups (*kare*). The *barati,* members of the oldest youth group, which owns the dance space, are in the center, and when someone from a younger group wants to join them he moves out of his circle and reciprocal whipping takes place with a member of the older group. The younger male is accepted into or rejected from the inner circle according to his courage. Konate's description indicates that an outside group collectively challenges the inner circle. In its village context, *Dundunba* had the status of a serious ritual. But Meillassoux (1968b: 96) suggests that, removed from the village, the dance had moved from ceremony to entertainment; the movements were done, but not the whipping—except on certain occasions. Meillassoux (1968b:96) had been told of an independence celebration in 1959 in which Kouroussa natives in Bamako held a *Dundunba* where "the whipping was very rough." Taking the examples of *Dundunba, Komo,* and *Manjani* (see below), it appears that jembe drumming in serious ritual contexts may have declined by the time of independence.

After *Dundunba,* the next most widespread jembe pieces are probably *Manjani* (*Menjani* or *Mandiani*), from Upper Guinea, and *Soli* (called *Suku* in Mali), the main dance done in all-night celebrations (called *soli si*) leading to the actual circumcision and excision surgery. *Manjani* is traditionally danced by young girls, but recent descriptions do not go into detail about its village significance, perhaps because the tradition no longer exists. A *manjani* is the best young female dancer in a village. Ladji Camara (1996-per) describes Fanta Kamissoko, the lead dancer with the original Ballets Africains in the 1950s and wife of guitarist Facelli Kante (see plate 36), as a manjani in Siguiri when she was younger. The earliest documentation of *Manjani* may be a photograph of a manjani dancer from Upper Guinea published by Joyeux (plate 28) and his extended description (1924, fig. 6 facing 182, 203–5). According to Joyeux (1924:203–5), a *mandiani* is a young girl chosen for her ability in a dance competition, a tradition local to Upper Guinea. Every village that can support one has a manjani, and if there is a rival political party, they too choose one. They were formerly sorceresses, but by the time of Joyeux's writing their powers had declined. They were fed and cared for by a principal family of the village. All their wants were taken care of, and they had several people constantly at their service. A daughter of a griot was attached to her and accompanied her during her

Plate 28 Early twentieth-century *Manjani* dancer from Upper Guinea. From Joyeux (1924, fig. 6).

dancing. She remained a manjani until puberty, at which time she returned to the ranks and another was elected in her place (Joyeux 1924:203).[25]

Jembe playing technique is particularly hard on the hands, since the drumhead is very tight and does not have much flexibility. The three basic strokes are known in English as tone (Fr: *tonique* or *médium*), slap (Fr: *claquement* or *claque*), and bass (Fr: *basse* or *grave*). Although African jembe players do not usually refer to these strokes by name except when teaching foreigners, they sometimes distinguish them from each other in Bamana using terms referring to relative height. In this way, high (*sanfè* or *sanma*), middle (*cèmancè*), and low (*duguma*), or high, low, and very low (*dugumaba*) may be used for slap, tone, and bass.[26] Though jembe players can vocalize their rhythms, the syllables used do not appear to be attached to the

25. Famoudou Konate (1991-disc:64) also indicates that the manjani dances by herself while another young girl dances in a circle around her, perhaps referring to what Joyeux calls the daughter of a griot.

26. Polak (1996a:13) uses the former set of Bamana terms; the latter set is from Abdoul Doumbia (1995-per). For examples of French and German terminology see Mamadou Kante (1993-disc), Mamady Keita (1995-disc), Famoudou Konate (1991-disc), and Konate and Ott (1997).

different strokes in any systematic fashion and can vary from player to player.

A basic theory can be discerned by observing the sequence of hand strokes used by jembe players, though it is not usually verbalized. The choice of the right or left hand is determined by the pulse on which the stroke lands in a steady fastest-pulse stream. Odd-numbered pulses belong to the right hand and even-numbered to the left (or vice versa if one plays left-handed). Therefore the same hand might strike several times in a row if there is one pulse or three pulses rest between strokes. There are naturally exceptions to such a generalized theory, and experienced drummers might even prefer to play with and exploit the predictability of hand placement.[27]

Jembe performances can range from a minimal ensemble of one jembe and one dundun, as is sometimes the case in Bamako marriage celebrations, to a full ensemble of one lead jembe, two or more accompanying jembes, and three dunduns, as is typical in Guinean ballet troupes. One or two dunduns is the norm in Mali; in Guinea three dunduns are more common. The actual parts played for any one piece can vary according to locality, but there are a few common traits shared from Conakry to Bamako and beyond.

Two fundamental accompaniment patterns are widely used in jembe playing, and one or the other can be played in almost any piece (transcription 19). Traditionally, most pieces may have only one or two accompaniment patterns, but pieces that have been adapted from other instruments for a jembe ensemble may have any number of additional ones. A second accompaniment pattern may be unique to a particular piece, or it might be a pattern that is used in a few other pieces. In Mali an accompaniment pattern on either a jembe or a dundun is called *den* (child), and a lead pattern on either drum is called *ba* (mother).

Although one of the dunduns typically plays a pattern that identifies the piece, most pieces also have unique identifiable lead jembe phrases. Accompanying (as opposed to lead) dundun parts are usually generic to any number of pieces. One complete cycle of a piece most often takes two repetitions of the generic accompanying jembe parts to complete, although four repetitions, as in *Dundunba* (see below), are not uncommon.

The lead jembe player controls the ensemble and engages in two fundamental kinds of playing. One kind is for singing or group dancing, and for this each named rhythm has at least one unique lead jembe part (*ba*) played at slower tempos. The other kind of playing is for solo dancing and consists

27. Polak (1996b:61) notes that at faster tempos younger drummers might vary their strokes to distribute the duties of both hands more equally, thereby conserving strength; but they risk being rebuked for laziness by older drummers. See Konate and Ott (1997:54) for a discussion of hand placement.

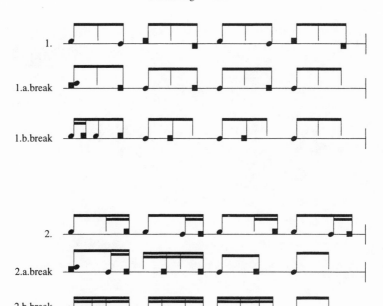

Transcription 19 Jembe: Two main accompaniments and associated breaks. 1: Generic ternary accompaniment pattern. 1.a.break and 1.b.break: two versions of breaks. 2: Generic binary accompaniment pattern. 2.a.break and 2.b.break: two versions of breaks. See transcription guide for explanation of strokes.

of fast rolling patterns in which every pulse within every beat in the cycle is usually struck. The tempo of the whole ensemble speeds up during this kind of dancing. There are generic rolling patterns that can be played in any number of pieces, and there are also patterns that are based on the lead parts, filling in the spaces. The dance is considered to "heat up" or "speed up," and sometimes drummers describe this kind of playing with the French term *échauffment* (heating) or the Bamana term *golobali* (running, speeding up). The roll used for the vigorous solo dancing is finished off with one of several cadence patterns, called *tigeli* (cutting, breaking) in Bamana, "break" in English, or *bloquage* in French. The break is a signal for the dancer to end, and another dancer may then approach. In ballet performances and in drum classes for foreigners, the breaks that end the rolls are also used to begin a piece. A few generic breaks are widespread (transcription 19).[28]

Although over one hundred named jembe pieces have been recorded, an

28. For further information see Polak's (1996a: 76–87) discussion and examples of solo jembe playing. Polak discusses three aspects of jembe playing separately: lead patterns, rolls, and breaks. Konate and Ott's (1997; and Konate 1997-disc) pioneering collaboration is an excellent source for technical information on jembe playing.

Plate 29 Early twentieth-century jembe players. Top: "Scène de danse guerrière chez les Malinké" [Malinke war dance scene]. Jembe players with tama and flute players, dancer holding sword, and onlookers holding muskets in Mali, from Delafosse (1912, vol. 2, fig. 40). Bottom: jembe players with buru/budu (horn) players in Upper Guinea, from Joyeux (1924, fig. 2, facing 176).

urban jembe player may use only perhaps one or two dozen in the course of his professional practice. Famoudou Konate's case is probably typical of most master jembe players. "I once wrote down the names of all the rhythms I knew, and came up with more than eighty" (Famoudou Konate, in Konate and Ott 1997:24). Based on his research in Bamako among professional jembe players Polak (1996a:59–89) has analyzed approximately one dozen important pieces. In addition to a generic jembe accompaniment pattern (*den*), he has also given one unique jembe accompaniment pattern and at least one lead pattern (*ba*) for each rhythm. Also given are dundun accompaniment parts that can be played in any number of pieces and at least one lead dundun part for each rhythm. Polak has also shown that some rolling patterns can be played in several pieces, whereas others are unique to certain rhythms, being based on the lead part. He has also given three breaks (*tigeli*) that can be used to end any number of rolls.

The description above is based on village-style playing, albeit in an urban context, which can be contrasted with ballet style. Village playing can take place in urban areas, but it follows the village practice where solo singing, group singing, and group dancing alternate with frenetic, fast-paced solo dancing, all within an unbroken circle of participants. Relatively few rhythms are played for long stretches during the course of the event. Ballet drumming is more choreographed, with many more rhythms played in rapid succession for short periods.

Transcription 20 shows a Malian version of *Dundunba,* one of the most difficult pieces for non-Africans to perceive rhythmically. *Dundunba* is immediately identifiable by the accompanying dundun (*kenkeni* or *konkoni*) part, three strokes that surround the main beats. Heard in isolation, the first and last of the three stokes can easily be misapprehended as falling on the main beats. But compared with the second jembe accompaniment, it can be

Transcription 20 Jembe: A Malian version of *Dundunba.* From Drissa Kone (1990-per). The dundun part can be played without any of the hollow noteheads (Yamadu Doumbia in Polak 1994-disc), or adding either the hollow oval noteheads or the hollow diamond notehead.

Transcription 21 Jembe: *Dundunba* played solo by Adama Drame. From Adama Drame (1987-disc), beginning at 2′52″.

seen that the kenkeni part is replicated by the bass and two tone strokes on the offbeats.[29]

Transcription 21 shows how Adama Drame incorporated the lead dundun part to *Dundunba* in his solo jembe performance of the piece, and tran-

---

29. When I first learned *Dundunba* in Bamako, I was having trouble understanding the jembe parts against an accompanying konkoni part that would start first. I asked my teacher how people in a dance circle would clap to this part, and he replied by telling a nearby youngster to clap. Without any further prompting, she immediately did so, placing the claps where they should be, match-

Transcription 22 Jembe: *Dundunba* arrangement in Oumou Dioubate's *Lancey*. From Oumou Dioubate (1993-disc), beginning at 3'54".

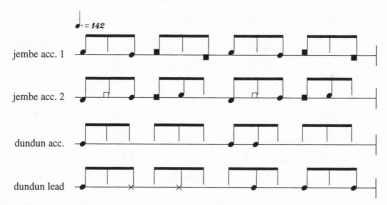

Transcription 23 Jembe: *Maraka*. From Abdoul Doumbia (1995-disc, 1995-per).

scription 22 shows how the dundun part has been used as a bass line in Oumou Dioubate's *Lancey*. Transcription 23 shows *Maraka*, one of the most popular pieces played at Bamako marriage celebrations. The second jembe part (with the optional stroke played) is the same as the second jembe

---

ing the slaps on the jembe parts. The claps also match the dancer's footsteps, called *don sen* (dance step). *Dundunba* versions from Guinea often feature a different lead dundun (or sangba) part.

part for *Dundunba,* but shifted left two pulses so that the bass stroke on pulse 3 in *Dundunba* falls on pulse 1 in *Maraka.*

Transcription 24 shows versions of *Soli,* known as *Suku* in Mali, as played by my teacher Drissa Kone in Bamako, by Mamady Keita (1989-disc), and by Famoudou Konate (1991-disc). Note that even though they come from three different (although neighboring) regions, the lead jembe part is very similar in all three versions.

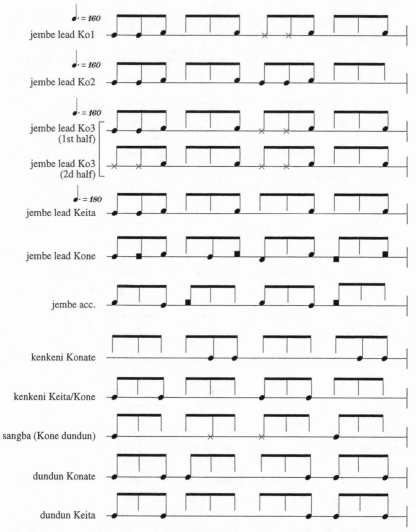

Transcription 24 Jembe: *Suku/Soli,* three versions. Ko1: Famoudou Konate (1991-disc: no. 3, 1′05″). Ko2: Famoudou Konate (1991-disc: no. 4, 0′13″). Ko3: Famoudou Konate (1991-disc: no. 6, 0′36″). Keita: Mamady Keita (1989-disc: no. 7, 5′26″, 6′40″). Kone: Drissa Kone (1990-per).

Plate 30 National Ballet of Mali (Troupe Folklorique du Mali) drummers at the First Panafrican Cultural Festival, Algiers, 1969. Seated (left to right): Balani Samake, Burema "Tindo" Diakite, Madou Faraba, Mare Sanogo. From Collection Musée de l'Homme, BF 83-804-842, pl. 38, no. 16. Photo by D. Nidzgorski.

Dundun, Sangba, and Kenkeni

The dundun (also called *dunun* in parts of Mali and Guinea and *junjun* or *junjungo* in the Senegambia) is a double-headed cylinder-shaped drum that is used to accompany jembe playing and also as a solo instrument in Mali. Dundun sizes vary, as do the materials they are made from, the shape of the stick used for striking them, and the shape of the bell played with the other hand. In general, in Mali dunduns are played in pairs and in Guinea they are played in sets of three. In Guinea the three sizes are the small *kenkeni,* medium-sized *sangba* (or *sangban*), and large *dundunba.* In Mali the three are known as *dununin* (small dundun) or *konkoni, dununba* (large dundun) or simply dundun, and *dundunbelebeleba* (very large dundun). Dundun-like instruments are widespread in the sahel and savanna, played as far west as the Senegambian coast by the Serer (Nikiprowetzky 1965-disc) and as far east as northern Ghana (Locke 1990), Niger, and Nigeria (Ames and King 1971).

Among the Xasonka in the region of Kayes in western Mali the dundun is a solo instrument that is played by jelis, usually accompanied by a second dundun. Carved from a single piece of wood, the lead dundun is approximately thirty-three centimeters (thirteen inches) in diameter and sixty-nine centimeters (twenty-seven inches) long; the accompanying dundun is approximately thirty-three centimeters (thirteen inches) in diameter and fifty-six centimeters (twenty-two inches) long. Both have goatskin heads. The dundun is slung low over the left shoulder and played with a curved stick held in the right hand. The left hand holds a cone-shaped bell, called *nganga* or *nege,* "metal," hung around two fingers by a short string and struck with a ring worn on the thumb of the same hand. Typically, Xasonka dunduns are played in pairs, and they may also be played with one or more tamas. The curved stick may be an identifying feature of drums played in the sahel; dunduns played farther south in the savanna region use straight sticks or sticks with short right-angle extensions.

The most developed repertory specifically for dunduns comes from Xasonka jelis. Elsewhere it appears that the dundun is an accompanying instrument, albeit an essential one, in jembe ensembles. The drumming group in the national ballet of Mali utilizes Xasonka dunduns; one of the founding members was Serang Kanoute, a Xasonka dundun player from Bafoulabé in northwestern Mali. Kanoute's repertory consists of pieces that could be played on dundun only (along with a smaller accompanying dundun), and also pieces that can be played with jembes. Some of the most important pieces in his repertory include *Jeli don* (also called *Lamban* or *Sandiya*), *Woloso don* (Dance of the house slaves), *Jon don* (Dance of the slaves), and *Dansa* (a dance from Xaso celebrating the harvest). Other rhythms include *Sidiyasa* (played at Maraka marriages), *Sanda Gundo* (from Xaso), and *Take* (from Xaso, referring to Soninke blacksmiths).[30]

Writing about the region of Kita, Tellier (1898:183) referred to what must have been a Xasonka dundun as a "*jali dunu* (griot's drum), also called wulusu-dunu (slave's drum)."[31] *Woloso* (*wulusu*), literally *wolo* (born) *so* (house), is a special status of slave, the offspring of two people of *jon* (slave) status born and raised in the home of his or her master, and *wolosolu* are associated with both drumming and dancing (Meillassoux 1968b:44–45, 101–4). Tellier (1898:164) briefly described *danses des captifs de case* (dances of captives of the house), what was probably *Woloso don,* in Kita as mimicking a kind of combat with sexual overtones: "It is executed by a male and female with a naturalism that leaves nothing to be desired." Such an explicitly sexual dance, described in detail in Meillassoux's (1968b: 103–4) account of woloso dancing as part of a Segou dance association in Bamako in the 1960s, may have been unique to wolosolu.[32]

30. Serang Kanoute's dundun playing can be heard with the Ensemble Instrumental du Mali (Ministry of Information of Mali 1971-disc: vols. 1 and 4). The only recording devoted to the Xasonka tradition so far is by Mamadou "Kunkun" Camara (1997-disc). See Tellier (1898:158–59) for brief references to *dansa* and dances of "captives," "griots," and "blacksmiths."

31. "Le *dialli-dounou* (tambour de griot), appelé aussi ouloussou-dounou (tambour de captif)."

32. Tellier (1898:152–66) provides much descriptive material on dancing, commenting, "The most surprising is that all these movements are executed perfectly in time, as difficult as they may

The tradition of the ancient aristocratic society is that people of slave condition must perform grotesque and obscene dances for the enjoyment of their masters. Many *wolo-so* still accept their condition and volunteer for such performances. Unlike the *horō*, *wolo-so* of both sexes can dance together. (Meillassoux 1968b: 103)

In southern Mali the small dundun (dununin, konkoni, or kenkeni) is usually played without a bell. Used exclusively to accompany the jembe, rather than as a solo instrument, the dununin in Mali is not a jeli's instrument. Nowadays it is made from a small metal barrel (called *barigon,* perhaps from the French *barrique,* "large barrel"). Rather than being curved, the stick is straight with another much shorter stick attached at a right angle.

In Guinea, none of the trio of dunduns (kenkeni, sangba, and dundunba) is exclusively associated with jelis. All three can be fashioned from oil drums ranging from ten to fifty-five gallons, but they also can be carved from a single block of wood. Each has a bell tied onto it, and they are usually played by one person on each drum holding a single straight stick in one hand and a metal rod or ring in the other hand to strike the bell. The largest can be played horizontally or vertically, in which case two sticks can be used. Sometimes one or two kenkenis are attached to a dundunba, either in vertical or horizontal position, and one person can play two parts. Typically, the sangba plays the identifiable lead pattern (as in *Soli;* see transcription 24), the kenkeni plays a part generic to several rhythms, and the large dundun plays another lead part (see Beer, in Konate 1991-disc: 57).[33]

Dundun patterns consist of a combination of bounces and presses where the stick is pressed into the skin, momentarily deadening it. An accompanying dundun part generally consists of a short pattern with little allowance for variation. A lead dundun part for a piece may consist of one or more patterns identified with that piece, leaving room for improvising within the patterns.[34]

---

be, and quite often over furious rhythms" (161). See Gallieni (1885:40–44) for descriptions of warriors dancing to drums, horns, and flutes (accompanied by a drawing) and of the "graceful poses of Khassonka ballerinas" in the vicinity of Kayes. Humblot (1921:137–38) noted that in 1910 Mori Kaba, a religious and political leader from Kankan, liberated wolosolu from their servitude. Also see Y. Cissé (1994:28) on the status and liberties enjoyed by wolosolu.

33. See the front and back cover photos from Mamady Keita (1996-disc) for the set of three Guinean dunduns.

34. It is not uncommon for jeli vocalists who use the full complement of jeli melody instruments in their ensemble (kora, koni, bala, and guitar) to have a solo dundun as the only percussion instrument. Such was the case with the 1990 Senegambian tour of Kandia Kouyate. Other examples are Diaba Koita (199?-disc) and Aboubacar Camara (1994-disc), who also includes a jembe. In Burkina Faso a bell similar to that used by Xasonka dundun players is used, but it is longer, is played without drums, and is played in groups (Huet and Keita 1996:56–57).

Plate 31 Les Ballets Africains rehearsal, Conakry, 1994. Top (left to right): Diely Kanni Diawara (female dancer), Abou Sylla (bala), Naitu Camara (female dancer), Gbanworo Keita (first jembe soloist), Laurent Camara (second jembe soloist), Seny Toure (jembe), Mohamed Diaby (jembe), Lancine Keita (jembe), Mohamed Lamine Sylla (jembe), Younoussa Camara (sangba and kenkeni), Ali Diabate (dundunba). Bottom (seated on bench facing the troupe, left to right): Mohamed Kemoko Sano (choreographer), Hamidou Bangoura (technical director). Photos by the author.

Tama

The tama is a small double-headed squeeze drum in the shape of an hour-glass (plate 25). It is held under the left arm and struck with a curved stick held in the right hand and also with the fingers of the left hand. The heads on each end of the drum are connected by a long, thin cord laced back and forth along the length of the drum through approximately twenty loops attached to each of the heads. Because the middle of the instrument tapers into a narrow cylinder, hence the hourglass shape, there is space for the cord to be squeezed inward toward the drum body. This pressure tightens the heads on both ends and raises the pitch. Releasing the pressure lowers the pitch again. The instrument is usually played by Soninke and Xasonka while kneeling, in which case the upper left side of the chest pushes down on the drum, which rests on the left knee. When played standing, the drum is strapped tightly under the left arm, which can be squeezed toward the side of the chest to apply pressure.

The tama, like the dundun, is widespread throughout the sahel and savanna regions, from the Wolof tama in the Senegambia region to the Dagbamba *lunge* (or *donno*) family in northern Ghana (Locke 1990) and similar, though larger, dundun drums of the Yoruba in Nigeria (Euba 1990). Among the Dagbamba and Yoruba, tama-like drums have been called talking drums because they can communicate with those who know the language. Outside the western sahel and savanna, the fingers of the free hand are used less to strike the drum. The Xasonka tama is perhaps the smallest of all. The Wolof tama is very similar.[35]

The two tama stick strokes, a bounce and a press, are similar to the dundun strokes. The fingers of the left hand are also used to strike the drum, being held together and striking all at once. Tamas are typically played in pairs, where one takes the lead and the other accompanies. The accompanying tama usually plays a short pattern, very similar to that played on accompanying dunduns, and repeated without variation. The lead player has one pattern, or possibly a few, unique to each piece and may also improvise within those patterns. The squeezing pattern on the tama is typically timed so that one full cycle of rest, squeeze, rest occurs during a single repetition of a lead pattern. The drummer's body is constantly in motion, so there is a constant rise and fall of pitch on the instrument.

A single lead tama is a staple of popular music groups from Senegal, such as those led by Youssou Ndour and Baaba Maal. It is occasionally used

35. Tellier (1898:183) referred to the tama as *douncan*. A tama used by Maninka in the Mande heartland has a very large diameter, about twenty centimeters (eight inches), and is played with a straight stick that has another very short stick attached to its end at a right angle. One is kept in the same hut with the Sosso bala in Niagassola, Guinea.

Plate 32 Conakry jembe-based celebration, 1994. Ensemble consists of one dundunba, one kenkeni, and two jembe players. Lead jembe: Ansuman "Yeye" Kante. Photos by the author.

in some of the traditional groups that accompany Malian jelimusolu, but it is relatively rare in the modern orchestras of Guinea and Mali. The few recordings featuring solo tama music to date include Nikiprowetzky (1965-disc), Assane Thiam's (n.d.-disc) extraordinary group with tamas, sabars, and jembes, and the group Tama Walo (1998-disc).

Plate 33 Bamako jembe-based celebration, 1997. Ensemble consists of two konkoni players and two jembe players. Top: Drissa Kone (lead jembe, seated), Madou Diakite (konkoni, standing). Bottom: unidentified (konkoni), Drissa Kone (lead jembe), Madou Diakite (jembe), unidentified (konkoni). Photos by the author.

Mandinka Kutiro/Tangtango Ensemble

Senegambian Mandinka use a three-drum ensemble consisting of a lead drum, called *sabaro,* and two accompanying drums, called *kutiriba* (big *kutiro*) and *kutirindingo* (little or small *kutiro*). The term *tangtango* (or *tantango*) is often used to refer to any of these drums, and sometimes the

Plate 34 Dakar marriage celebration, 1989. Unidentified Xasonka dundun, tama, and jembe players. Photos by the author.

ensemble is called a *Seruba* (or *Saoruba*) ensemble after the name of an important dance event in which they are played. The ensemble is used throughout The Gambia and Casamance as far east as Tambacounda.[36]

Evidence from neighboring drumming traditions suggests that the Mandinka may have fashioned their drums after models used in their new Senegambian homeland or even acquired them there. Both the name and the shape of the Mandinka sabaro and Wolof sabar drums are very similar, and the method of attaching the head to the body is the same for these two as well as for the other Mandinka and Wolof drums. But in contrast to the Mandinka ensemble, fixed at three drums and rarely augmented, Wolof sabar-based ensembles consist of more drums and can accommodate large numbers of players. In the case of celebrations with many participants, the Mandinka ensemble is still not augmented; rather, many ensembles play for smaller groups within the larger crowd.[37] In addition to Wolof influence, there is also an exchange of rhythms between Jola and Mandinka, even though the Jola play the very different *bugarabu* (*bugarebu, bugarab*), a group of three or four large drums played by a single person with bare hands. The practice of wearing iron jingles (*jawungo*) around the wrist is widespread among Mandinka and Jola drummers as well as bala players.[38]

36. Knight's article (1974) and video (1995-vid) on Mandinka drumming are excellent introductions to the subject. Other important sources include Baldeh (1996-disc), Ly (1992-disc), and Zanetti (1997-disc). Knight (1995-vid:7) suggests that *tantango* is an onomatopoeic Mandinka word that may be the source for the word "tomtom," a drum in a jazz drum set. Tellier (1898:159) suggests that the name "tam-tam" was imported into Africa by the French: "The name tam-tam does not at all come from local [African] languages. We imported it [the name], and the locals take it for a French word." References to Mandinka drums as "tantan" (Avezac 1845:260), "tantong" (Moore 1740:77), and "tangtang" (Park [1799] 1983:213) date back to the late seventeenth century. Gallieni (1885:40) used "tam-tam" to refer to a drum as well as to Bambara, Wolof, Tukulor, and Sarahole (Soninke) dance events. Other names include *junkrandingo* for the kutirindingo (R. L. Thompson 1993, 1994) or *jonkurango* for either of the small drums (Knight 1995-vid:7) and *jilamba* for the sabaro (Zanetti 1997-disc). Amadu Bamba Baldeh (1996-disc) gives Fula names for the two smaller drums.

37. Such was the case when I attended a large celebration for the return of newly circumcised boys from the bush. Different families hired their own drummers, who escorted them through the village, meeting up in the large town square, where separate circles formed. For a four-drum ensemble using two kutiriba players see Knight (1995-vid).

38. For Wolof sabar recordings see Ames (1955-disc), Diop (1992-disc), Thiam (n.d.-disc), Rose (1994-disc), and Soule and Millot (1993-vid); for Jola drumming see Badjie (1996-disc) and Sapir (1965-disc). Mandinka drummer Mamadou Ly (in Baldeh 1996-disc), a founding member of the National Ballet of Senegal, has claimed that the Mandinka drums come from the Fula of the Firdu region around Kolda in central Senegal; see Baldeh (1996-disc) for a recording of this tradition. Two drums shown in an early twentieth-century photograph titled "Jola youths at an initiation" (Mark 1992:45) resemble Wolof sabars or Mandinka sabaros beaten with a stick.

Plate 35 Jembe atelier of Issou Koumare, Bamako, 1997. Top: tools for carving. Bottom: three stages of preparation; hollowing out the log (background), chipping away at the inside of the bowl (middle ground), and carving the outside (foreground, Koumare). Photos by the author.

The method of attaching the heads on the three Mandinka drums is not related to that of the jembe. The skin of a goat (*baa*) or small bush antelope (*minango*) is used for the heads on all three. Laces threaded through holes in the perimeter of the head and tied around five thick pegs set into the upper body are used to tighten the head. Although they are roughly the same shape, the different size of the two kutiro drums ensures that the larger ku-tiriba is pitched lower and that the dialogue between the two drums is sufficiently emphasized. The sabaro, with a much smaller circumference, is the highest pitched. Compared with those of the jembe, the two kutiro heads are more resilient, looser, and deeper pitched. The lead sabaro is shorter than the Wolof sabar, though older sabaros were bigger than those in use now. Preferred woods are *dutoo* and *kembo,* a deep red mahogany (Knight 1974:27).

Each drum is played with one hand and a short stick (approximately twenty centimeters or eight inches long); the two kutiro drums are some-times played with both bare hands. The minimal vocabulary necessary to play the drums consists of two different hand strokes and two different stick strokes. Vocables with no apparent literal meaning are sometimes used to refer to the strokes, although a widespread uniform system does not appear to be in place. The hand strokes are an open bounce (*kun*) where a clear tone is produced, and a closed damped stroke (*ba*) where the fingers press on the head and remain there. The stick strokes are a bounce (*din*) and a press (*da*).[39] With two hand sounds and two stick sounds on each drum, a strik-ingly full orchestral sound can be created by just the two kutiro drums (see transcriptions below).

The signature Mandinka dance is the recreational *Lenjengo* (or *Lin-jingo*), danced primarily by girls and young women. A *Lenjengo* event typ-ically includes a collection of rhythms, songs, and dances leading up to *Lenjengo* proper. The preliminary dances could last twenty or thirty min-utes, and *Lenjengo,* which could also include respites of singing going back to the earlier pieces, could go on indefinitely. Once *Lenjengo* is finished, *Seruba* is usually performed, featuring a lead singer and a different set of rhythms. During *Lenjengo,* singing is usually done by the participants; someone in the crowd leads a song, and everyone else responds. In *Seruba* the lead singer, who is often the leader of the drum group, is in charge. Dur-ing his initial singing, the participants come up and pin local currency onto his shirt. The kutirindingo and kutiriba are played with both bare hands in *Seruba.*[40]

As a village rather than urban event, *Lenjengo* can be contrasted in or-ganization with analogous urban jembe drumming events in Mali and Guinea. In *Lenjengo* a long-term compositional process is at work with a specific sequence of pieces. These pieces were systematically taught to me,

39. My own teachers did not use any vocables, so I am relying on Knight's (1974:28) research here.

40. This description of *Lenjengo* is based on my observations in and around Brikama (The Gambia) in 1989 and 1990.

first on the kutirindingo, then on the kutiriba, finally on the sabaro, and my teachers usually went through them in performances in the same order they were taught to me. Jembe events, on the other hand, appear to be more loosely organized with a more open-ended flow of dances.

Besides *Lenjengo* and *Seruba,* several other rhythms are important. *Chingo* is associated with the return of boys from the bush after undergoing circumcision. *Nyaka julo,* also called *Musuba julo* (Elderly woman's tune), is danced by older women, often members of an association of older women (called Kanyaleng kafo), to impart fertility to barren younger women.[41] *Daba tangtango* (Hoe drum) is done to encourage agricultural labor. *Nyoboring julo* is done to accompany wrestlers, a specialty of the Senegambia. *Kankurang julo* accompanies the *kankurang (kangkurang),* the feared figure covered in strips of bark who helps to maintain order in times of crisis, especially in the context of circumcision.

While the sabaro drummer plays the phrases linked with the entrances, exits, and other movements of the dancers, the two kutiro drummers play the identifying parts that are unique to each dance. Transcription 25, kutirindingo and kutiriba parts for *Nyaka julo,* illustrates the role of the different strokes in constructing a composite rhythm. The same rhythm is played on both drums (long, long, short, short), but different strokes are used to create a dialogue between the two drums. A variation (kb.var) on the kutiriba changes the character of the rhythm, creating a two-against-three polyrhythm.

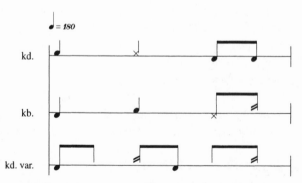

Transcription 25 Kutiro ensemble: *Nyaka julo.* kd = kutirindingo. kb = kutiriba. From Camara and Sanyang (1989-per). See transcription guide for explanation of strokes.

41. Knight (1974:30, 34) makes a distinction between *Nyaka julo,* which he associates with girls' initiation dancing, and *Musuba julo,* which he associates with the Kanyaleng kafo (Older women's association).

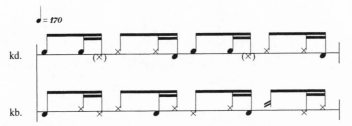

Transcription 26 Kutiro ensemble: *Chingo.* kd = kutirindingo. kb = kutiriba. From Camara and Sanyang (1989-per).

Transcription 26, kutirindingo and kutiriba parts for *Chingo,* illustrates in a similar way the concept of a play of different sounds conversing with one another. Both drummers play essentially the same rhythm, but the different strokes create a composite sound that belies the regularity of the hand patterns. The open left-hand strokes on each drum are the loudest in the ensemble and define the character of the piece.

Conclusion

In the last decade of the twentieth century, jembe drumming has had world exposure that is unprecedented for any African drumming tradition. Although it is difficult to gauge the impact of this international interest on local traditions, it is clear that drumming has not lost any of its power and relevance at home. Local economies have been stimulated by burgeoning study tours to Africa, by world tours of local drummers and troupes, and by an explosive jembe export trade. The ecological impact of the last on an extremely fragile sahel and savanna should be a major concern of government agencies in the future.

The stage presentation of Mandenka drumming and dancing has a history that is now over half a century old. New traditions have developed, moving drumming in a variety of directions. Although some of these traditions flourish abroad, the general recognition of Africa as a wellspring of a deeply entrenched culture of drumming and dancing still operates. The number, diversity, depth, and uniqueness of drumming traditions in Africa are astounding. So is the musical sophistication and power that can be routinely achieved by a small ensemble of instruments with a limited palette of sounds.

5

The Guitar and the Modern Era

Modern music in Guinea and Mali is rooted in two parallel worlds that had little contact with each other before independence: small urban orchestras playing European and Latin American popular music, primarily made up of a French-educated African elite, and jeliya, the music of jelis. At the time of independence in Guinea these two worlds merged into a national orchestra, giving birth to a new era. The guitar proved to be the bridge. An especially rich two decades of musical experimentation in dance orchestras followed, marked by increasingly inward-looking sensibilities. By the late 1970s the exhilarating promise of government patronage played itself out, and many musicians began a slow exodus first to Abidjan, then to Paris. The European successes of artists like Guinean Mory Kante and Malian Salif Keita by the late 1980s may have provided a stimulus for new thinking back home. By the early 1990s Guinean and Malian musicians were digging deeper into their past and coming up with novel combinations of instruments, definitively shedding the earlier Latin American and European influences. Nearing the end of the century, several streams coexist and feed off each other: hi-tech Euro-American-based dance music fronted by vocal stars; electrified ensembles of local instruments and guitars led by jelimusolu; acoustic guitar summits; virtuoso jeli instrumental combinations; hunter's harps mixing with jeli and European instruments; and all of the above animated by jembes and dunduns rather than a Western drum set.

The term "modern" has been widely embraced by African musicians, and they consistently use it to talk about the music discussed in this chapter. Although the term may sometimes invite awkward formulations, as when the introduction to a concert of the Guinean orchestra Bembeya Jazz referred to their music as "the neoclassicism of modern African song" ("le neoclassicism de la chanson moderne africaine") (Bembeya Jazz 1970-disc: introduction), there is a clear and consistent concept of the difference between traditional, modern, and European music. Malian musician Sorry Bamba's usage is typical.

> At the debut of our career, we interpreted the melodies that were in fashion in France, Cuba, or elsewhere. After having been the interpreters of European

music, we became, after the independence of our countries, the pioneers of modern African music [*la musique moderne africaine*].

Our modern music, born in the sixties, is not structured like European music.

[Referring to the genre called Apollo] It is the griots who have modernized [*modernisé*] their Mandingue music by adding to it a bass guitar, a drum set, amplifiers. (Sorry Bamba, in Bamba and Prévost 1996:6, 8, 176)

Novel styles and combinations using local instruments can also be referred to as modern.

We had kora, djembe, ngoni, and bolon [four-string bass harp] for the bass. But it was modern music we were playing on those traditional instruments. (Mory Kante, in Durán 1998:47; brackets in the original)

African usage of the French terms *orchestre* for modern musical groups using European instruments and *ensemble* for traditional music groups is also consistent and widely accepted by those involved. Although many musicians are active in both worlds, many other musicians draw sharp boundaries. Older jelis in particular often express the view that modern electric dance music does not have the historical depth of their own tradition, and they distance themselves from modern dance bands because they do not uphold the ancient hereditary sanctions on who may play certain kinds of music. Younger jelis may be less concerned with such social distinctions, yet they remain keenly aware of the different kinds of training and sensibilities involved in the two worlds.

Performers and Recordings

Preindependence History

The way the guitar first spread through Guinea and Mali is unclear, but it probably was brought to Guinea in the 1910s or 1920s, perhaps by soldiers returning from fighting in Europe in World War I. No mention was made of the guitar in the earliest detailed account of Maninka music from Upper Guinea (Joyeux 1924), so it may not have had much impact by then. One of the earliest Guinean guitar players was also one of the most influential: El Hadj Sidikiba Diabate (1906–76), charged with organizing government-sponsored ensembles at the time of independence, and the father of two of Guinea's great guitarists, Kerfala "Papa" and Sekou "Docteur" Diabate. In the 1920s Sidikiba Diabate worked at Kindia, 135 kilometers outside Conakry. There he formed Philharmonie Jazz, probably the first group of its kind in Guinea, playing tangos, waltzes, and polkas. Sidikiba could read music and played the banjo, mandolin, and guitar. His knowledge of both the jeli

Table 14 The First Orchestras in Guinea (1920s to 1950s)

Instrument	Philharmonie Jazz	La Joviale Symphonie*	La Douce Parisette (1945)	École William Ponty**
Banjo	Sidikiba Diabate Gomez	Mamadou Ndow (alto) Sekou "Dra" Camara (tenor) Momo "Wandel" (1952–55)	Mory Camara (alto) N'Fa Toure (tenor) N'Famara Keita (tenor)	Fodeba Keita Mory Camara (alto) Mamadou Sow (tenor)
Guitar	Sidikiba Diabate		Kanfory Bangoura	
Piano		Wilfred Kairu Samuel		
Accordion		Wilfred Kairu Kanfory Sanoussi	Jean Camara (founder ca. 1936–37) Damantan Camara	
Violin			Kanfory Bangoura	Kanfory Bangoura
Voice				Fodeba Keita Guro Soumano (Niger)
Trumpet			Sada Musa Toure	
Clarinet		Momo "Wandel" (1952–55)	Momo "Wandel" (1955–58)	
Tumba			Bangaly Camara (1950s)	
Drum set		Paul Quinn		
Unknown	Dianfode Kaba	Georges Demaison (founder) Ibou Diallo (leader, 1950s)		

Sources: *Kanfory Sanoussi, in J. Williams 1990; **Mory Camara, in J. Williams 1993; Diabate family 1994-per; and Momo "Wandel" Soumah 1994-per. La Douce Parisette was created by Jean Camara about 1936–37 and included Ndiaye, Bicaise, and Boubacar Sow.

tradition, inherited by virtue of being a Diabate, and European music was unusual for his time and would place him in an important and influential role at the time of independence.[1]

In the 1930s two other groups were founded in Conakry: La Joviale Symphonie and La Douce Parisette (table 14). They were the two major dance

---

1. Information on Guinean music from the 1930s through the 1960s is drawn from radio interviews conducted by Jean Baptiste Williams (1990, 1993) with Kanfory Sanoussi and Mory Camara and from my own interviews with Balla Onivogui, Pivi Moriba, "Soba" Manfila Kante, Manfila "Dabadou" Kante, Manfila Kante "ex-Ambassadeurs," Momo "Wandel" Soumah, Kerfala "Papa" and Sekou "Docteur" Diabate, and Sekou "Bembeya" Diabate. I have included many of the recollections of the sources above (primarily in footnotes) because so little has been published about this period in Guinean music. Sidikiba Diabate's children report that Philharmonie Jazz was created in the early 1920s. Kanfory Sanoussi, who was musically active in the 1930s, believes the group was created in 1932. Sanoussi also named Dianfode Kaba and Gomez as members of the group.

bands in Guinea through the 1950s, playing rhythms they called beguine, bolero, waltz, tango, fox trot, slow fox, conga, spirot, march, and swing. Playing from sheet music ordered from France, they would also occasionally adapt what they called folkloric tunes of their native Guinea, most often to a beguine or bolero rhythm.

After the Second World War, foreign trends entered at a quicker pace, owing in part to the returning soldiers. The saxophone became more prominent, and the banjo was eventually dropped in favor of the guitar. École William Ponty, a teachers' college in Senegal, had a major impact in disseminating European-based dance music in the 1940s and 1950s. Each French West African colony had one *école primaire supérieure* (secondary school), and the most promising students were sent to École Ponty, where they received a thorough French-style education, including training in the arts.[2]

Members of a dance orchestra at École Ponty in the early 1940s, located at the time at Sebikotane outside Dakar, would play major roles in shaping Guinean music of the next few decades. Consisting in part of graduates from the *école primaire supérieure* in Conakry, where they also had a small orchestra, the École Ponty orchestra gained notice from students and faculty alike (see table 14 for personnel and instruments). The leader, Fodeba Keita (1921–71), who played banjo and sang, would profoundly change the perception of African music outside the continent with a group he established in the late 1940s call Les Ballets Africains. Other Ponty graduates, such as Mory Camara and Kanfory Bangoura, would inject fresh musical styles into the older Conakry orchestras on their return to Guinea. Kanfory Bangoura (violin and guitar) joined La Douce Parisette and later became artistic director of the first Guinean national orchestra when it was created in 1959.[3]

The leader of the national orchestra (called the *chef d'orchestre*) was Kanfory Sanoussi, who played accordion and vibraphone in La Joviale Symphonie. Sanoussi, like Bangoura, did not come from a jeli background, but he learned some bala from his childhood friend Djeli Sory Kouyate, one of Guinea's great bala players, an experience that whetted his appetite

2. École Ponty originated as an *école des otages* (school for hostages) established in Saint-Louis, Senegal, in 1857 by Louis Faidherbe, the French governor of Saint-Louis. Intended to indoctrinate the sons of local rulers into French culture, it trained interpreters, teachers, and later, civil servants when it became the École Normale William Ponty in 1918, named after the governor-general of French West Africa (1908–15). The first institution of higher learning in French West Africa, it changed locations to Gorée Island, then Sebikotane (in 1930), and finally Dakar, where after independence it was called École Normale Supérieure.

3. According to Mory Camara (J. Williams 1993), members of the Guinea École Primaire Supérieure orchestra included Fodeba Keita, Mory Camara, Michel Collet, Philip Collet, and Mamadou Sow. They played French music as well as adaptations of local music, such as *Mariama Debori,* on instruments including a banjo, mandolin, guitar, saxophone, and trumpet. Philip Collet would later play guitar on a recording with Facelli Kante (1954?-disc).

for keyboard instruments. Sanoussi started with tenor banjo in 1934, studied theory for a few years, and inspired by Mamadou Ndow of La Jovial Symphonie, began playing alto banjo in 1937. After the war he moved to Kankan, where he formed a group and was joined about 1950 by Momo "Wandel" Soumah playing drums.[4]

Other groups active in Conakry in the early 1950s include Abele Jazz, consisting of Benin nationals, Vingt-cinq, and Harlem Jazz, which included saxophonist Keletigui Traore and was one of the few Conakry orchestras integrating African and European musicians. According to Mory Camara, who fondly remembered his French teachers at École Ponty in Senegal appreciating their orchestra, La Douce Parisette played for African and European patrons in Conakry. After independence, École Ponty graduates in these Guinean orchestras would leave to take up posts in their new government, and a new generation of musicians would take over.[5]

One of the earliest and most influential guitarists to bridge the divide between the urban orchestras and the music of jelis was Facelli Kante (1922–61) from Siguiri. The prominent use of the guitar by Fodeba Keita, also from Siguiri, in his theatrical presentations probably sprang from his meeting Facelli Kante in Senegal about 1947, a partnership that would be the nucleus of Les Ballets Africains. Kante was responsible for the musical arrangements of Les Ballets Africains, transferring what he knew on the bala to the guitar. After several years of informal rehearsals and performances in Paris, Les Ballets Africains debuted at the Théâtre de l'Étoile in Paris in November 1952, with Kante as assistant director. About 1954 Kante made a series of recordings under his own name and that of Les Ballets Africains on the French Chant du Monde and Vogue labels, among the very first commercial recordings of Mande guitar playing.[6]

Facelli Kante came from a distinguished family of musicians, connected by a web of relationships to a staggering array of influential musicians (fig. 9). He is the product of a union between the Kankan (maternal side) and Kissidougou (paternal side) branches of the Kante lineage. On the

4. The accordion was well known in French West Africa at the time. Sorry Bamba (Bamba and Prévost 1996:29–30) noted several players active in Mopti, Mali, before independence.

5. This account of African orchestras in Guinea contrasts with that reported in Harrev (1992: 217–18), which indicates that Africans were not playing in the Conakry orchestras of the 1950s. Also see Collins (1985:53–54, 1996:28–30).

6. Legend has it that one summer night in 1947 Facelli Kante was playing his guitar on the Saint-Louis (Senegal) bridge when Fodeba Keita met him for the first time (Les Ballets Africains de Keita Fodeba 1981a-disc; Ladji Camara 1996-per). See Les Ballets Africains (1959, 1996) for early documentation of their history. Facelli Kante studied European guitar styles either in Dakar or in Conakry with Mory Camara, who in turn studied guitar at the Conakry École Primaire Supérieure with a teacher named Ibrahima Jula Naby about 1939 (J. Williams 1993).

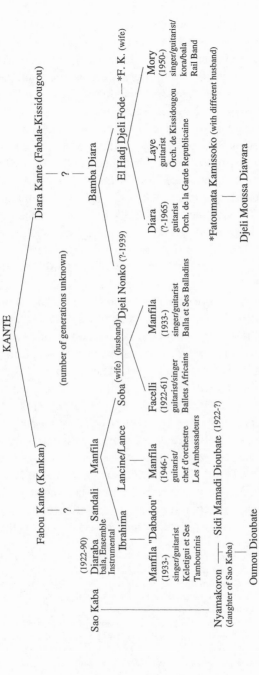

Figure 9 Lineage of Kante family of Kankan and Kissidougou.

mother's side, his granduncle Diaraba Kante was the lead bala player with the National Instrumental Ensemble of Guinea, and an aunt was Nyamako-ron Kante, one of Guinea's great jelimuso singers, who married Sidi Ma-madi Dioubate (Diabate), one of Guinea's most respected bala players of the 1940s and 1950s and cofounder with his brothers of the musical move-ment known as Mamaya. Nyamakoron and Sidi Mamadi's daughter Oumou Dioubate is at present one of the most important singers in Guinea. Facelli Kante's younger cousins and brother, the three Manfila Kantes, were major players in postindependence music in Guinea and in Mali.[7] On the father's side, Facelli's cousin Diara Kante was an influential electric guitarist, whose younger brother Mory Kante is Guinea's most internationally successful musical artist. Through the 1950s Facelli Kante toured the world with Les Ballets Africains (plate 36). As he was returning from Prague after one such tour in March 1961, his airplane ran out of gas while waiting to land in Casablanca, and he died in the crash ("Soba" Manfila Kante 1994-per).[8]

By the 1940s the acoustic guitar was evidently already in use in Upper Guinea, according to Laye Camara's autobiographical account of his child-hood. "I would take down my guitar which Kouyaté had taught me to play. In the evening, instead of staying in my hut, we would stroll through the town [Kouroussa] strumming our guitars while Check played the banjo; all three of us would sing in harmony" (L. Camara 1954:173).[9] The earliest written source specifically indicating that Mande music was being played on the guitar may be Fodeba Keita's (1948) *Chansons du Dioliba,* a twenty-to twenty-five-minute play consisting of one actor rendering Keita's poetry accompanied by a guitarist. Keita, most likely inspired by his relationship with Facelli Kante, named a dozen pieces of music (such as *Kaira* and *Nan-fulen*) to be played throughout the performance. In a collection of works published in 1950 as *Poèmes africaines,* Keita continued this idea, naming pieces from a wide variety of regions and historical eras, including *Duga,* one of the oldest pieces played by jelis, *Lamban,* one of the oldest bala

7. The three Manfila Kante cousins, all with the same grandfather, Manfila Kante, are identified here as "Soba" Manfila Kante (singer with Balla et Ses Balladins), Manfila "Dabadou" Kante (singer with Keletigui et Ses Tambourinis), and Manfila Kante "ex-Ambassadeurs" (guitarist with Les Ambassadeurs). Identifying someone by the mother's first name (Soba) or the place of birth or youth (Dabadou) is a common practice.

8. The influential Senegalese record producer Ibrahima Sylla has credited Facelli Kante as "the first Guinean to play modern Guinean music. He replaced the kora with the guitar, percussion by timbales as in Afro-Cuban music, and above all, he introduced the notion of an arrangement. Un-til then, it was the griot who took his microphone and sang until he was tired and then he stopped. But for Les Ballets [Africains] an arrangement was necessary. It was Faceli Kante who invented the modern arrangements of Mande music" (Ibrahima Sylla in Lee 1988:86).

9. The guitar was probably in use in Mali by the 1940s. Boura Sako, father of the Malian singer Monkontafe Sako, has been cited as playing the guitar; he passed away in the late 1930s or early 1940s (notes to Monkontafe Sako 1976a-disc).

Plate 36 Facelli Kante and dancers, mid-1950s. Left to right: Hawa Diawara (dancer), Fanta Kamissoko (lead dancer), Mansaba Camara (dancer), Facelli Kante (in center). Photo courtesy of "Soba" Manfila Kante.

pieces, *Kelefaba,* one of the oldest pieces that is believed to have originated on the kora, and *Taara,* dedicated to al Hajj Umar Tal.[10]

The earliest nonstudio recordings of Mande music played on a guitar may be those made by Arthur S. Alberts in Kissidougou, Guinea, in 1949 (perhaps further research will uncover earlier recordings). One piece, *Kahira* (*Kaira*), with two guitars and a kora, has been released on an LP (Alberts 1954a-disc), but he recorded fourteen more pieces by this group (Alberts 1949-disc). These recordings demonstrate that a Mande guitar style had developed by then and was well integrated into the jeli tradition. They show a broad knowledge of the repertory of the jeli, including *Lamban, Sakodugu, Sunjata,* and *Nanfulen.* One of the guitarists often sang along with his guitar lines and appears to have been the leader of the group, which also included a female singer.[11]

10. Fodeba Keita (1950:26) noted that as early as 1947 the piece *Sini-Mory* was played with guitar accompaniment on Radio Dakar.

11. Several older musicians from Kissidougou, Kankan, and Siguiri whom I interviewed could not identify the guitarist or vocalist recorded by Alberts in Kissidougou, but they noted that the

The first commercial studio recordings of Mande musicians date from the 1950s, and the guitar was an essential part of them. The Malian singer Koni Coumare (1918?-93) from Segou may have been the first Mande singer to record commercially, probably in 1953, accompanied by her husband Fotiqui Diabate on the guitar (Coumare, n.d.-disc). The Chant du Monde label issued the first recordings of Fodeba Keita's ensemble about 1954, which featured the guitar playing of Facelli Kante. In the late 1950s and early 1960s the Vogue label issued a series of recordings that featured various members of Fodeba Keita's Ballets Africains, including guitarist Facelli Kante, Guinean singer Sory Kandia Kouyate accompanying himself on guitar, and singer-guitarist "Soba" Manfila Kante, younger brother of Facelli. Included on the Vogue series is the Malian jelimuso singer Monkontafe Sacko (1937–) from Segou accompanied by Dialy Madi Sissoko (kora) and Mamadou Diabati (bala). In 1960 the Phillips label released a series of 45 rpm recordings of Malian music, two of them solo performances by singer-guitarist Nouhoum Djallo (Djallo Nouhoum). Other recordings in the Phillips series featured Senufo xylophones, a one-stringed fiddle, a Maninka bala, and other guitar recordings. The electric guitar had not yet made its recorded appearance in this preindependence era.[12]

Older pieces from the jeli's repertory were rare on commercial recordings before the 1960s.[13] Among the several twentieth-century jeli pieces recorded were *Kaira, Yarabi (Diarabi)*, and *Mamaya* (also known as *Bandian Sidime*), all three recorded by both "Soba" Manfila Kante (1961?-disc) and Nouhoum Djallo (Nourrit and Pruitt 1978, 1:49–50). Other well-known recent pieces included *Nanfulen* ("Soba" Manfila Kante 1961?-disc) and *Tubaka* (Sory Kandia Kouyate 1956?-disc).

In addition to those musicians recorded in the decade before independence, there must surely have been itinerant musical ensembles that used

singer was young and inexperienced. They also recognized the vocal dialect as probably coming from Siguiri.

12. For Koni Coumare's Fiesta recordings see Nourrit and Pruitt (1978, 1:32–34, 74–75); for the Phillips recordings of Djallo Nouhoum and others see Nourrit and Pruitt (1978, 1:46–50). Ba Konaré (1993:236, 248) indicates that Koni Coumare and the duo of Fanta Damba (no. 2) and Dionkouta Kouyate were the first Malian female singers to release a disc (on Fiesta in 1953). Coumare (n.d.-disc) appears to be an LP reissue of her early recordings. Alan Merriam's (1970) discography provides information on the recordings of Facelli Kante (items 27, 28, 345, 347, 349–51, 380–81), Sory Kandia Kouyate (items 347, 380), "Soba" Manfila Kante (items 354–56, 365–67), and Monkontafe Sacko (item 353). The Chant du Monde recordings appear to have been released in 1954; Rouget (1955:157–58) refers to them in general, and an advertisement for them appears in a Ballets Africains program from the mid-1950s (Les Ballets Africains 1996). The Vogue recordings probably date from 1956–61.

13. The few traditional jeli pieces with guitar accompaniment recorded before independence include *Malisadio* (Sory Kandia Kouyate 1956?-disc), and *Sakodugu* and *Samory,* on a Phillips 45 rpm from about 1959 featuring Kabine Kouyate, Kelema Doman, and Odia Conde (Nourrit and Pruitt 1978, 1:48–49).

Plate 37 Diabate Family of Kela, Mali, about 1949. Photo courtesy of Jan Jansen and Diabate
Family of Kela.

the guitar with other jeli instruments. A remarkable 1949 photo of the Diabate family from Kela gives some indication of what these groups were like
(plate 37). The Kela Diabates are among the most renowned in Mande lore,
since they preside over the sacred septennial reroofing ceremony at nearby
Kangaba (Ganay 1995). Their use of a guitar alongside a bala confirms the
guitar's acceptance within the tradition of the jeli, as does its use during the
actual ceremonies at Kangaba at least as early as 1968 (Meillassoux 1968a:
177–78, photo facing 179) and its use in the rendition of the Sunjata epic
by the venerable Malian jeli Kele Monson Diabate (n.d.-disc).

While the guitar was making significant inroads into traditional Mande
music during the 1950s, the vestiges of the old Conakry orchestras had lost
the energy that drove them in the previous decades. Guinea's resounding No!
to France's offer of membership in the French Community and the rise of
Sekou Toure to the presidency would cause a revolution in the music of francophone West Africa. Guitarists from jeli families would be in the vanguard.

The Modern Era in Guinea from Independence to the Mid-1980s

Shortly after gaining independence on October 2, 1958, the new government of the Republic of Guinea under the leadership of President Sekou

Toure initiated a revolutionary cultural policy establishing a network of regional and national performing groups that set the standard for francophone West Africa. The groups took on the French titles *orchestre, ensemble,* and *ballet* with very specific and mutually exclusive references. *Ensemble* was used for groups that brought together musicians schooled in the local traditions of their country using indigenous African instruments exclusively, often with female vocal soloists and choruses. Their repertory was primarily based on that of the jeli but also drew from nonjeli traditions. *Orchestre* was used for groups that played modern renditions of traditional pieces as well as newly composed pieces using primarily European instruments. *Ballet* was used for dance troupes accompanied by drum ensembles, usually jembe based.[14]

The Paris-based Ballets Africains, established almost a decade earlier by Fodeba Keita with Facelli Kante, became the national ballet of Guinea, and Fodeba Keita was appointed minister of the interior. European musical instruments, including electric guitars, were handed out, musicians were made civil servants, and their creations, recorded in the state-run Studio de la Voix de la Révolution (Studio of the Voice of the Revolution) and distributed on the state Syliphone label beginning in the mid-1960s, belonged to the people—that is, the republic.[15]

The immediate formation of the Syli National Orchestra, charged with creating a Guinean music that drew on local rather than foreign traditions, is a convenient marker for the beginning of the modern era in Guinean music (plate 38). According to a government report,

> The first typically African national orchestra was founded on 15 January 1959 in Conakry under the name Syli National Orchestra. Imbued with a new spirit, the orchestra was composed of our best instrumentalists and led by dedicated musicologists who were prepared to research and advance our musical cul-

14. For accounts of modern music in Guinea and Mali see Bamba and Prévost (1996), Barlow, Eyre, and Vartoogian (1995), Bender (1991), Durán (1989a, 1994, 1995a, 1995b, forthcoming a), Ewens (1991), Graham (1988, 1992), Harrev (1992), Lee (1988), Seck and Clerfeuille (1986, 1993), and Stapleton and May (1990). For a description of the bureaucratic arrangement of the arts festivals and competitions see Sekou Toure (1963:257). For an account of the political climate in independent Guinea in relation to the arts see L. Kaba (1976).

15. Ladji Camara (1996-per) indicates that Les Ballets Africains was in the United States from early 1959 to early 1960 and became the national ballet about May 1960 after returning to Guinea. One example of the new government policy came in 1965 when Les Amazones "proceeded in the modernization of their orchestra" with new kinds of instruments: electric guitars, tenor and alto saxophones, a trumpet, and a drum set (Justin Morel Jr. in notes to Les Amazones de Guinée 1983-disc). A fleeting clip of Les Amazones playing mandolins, probably before they modernized in 1965, can be seen in Achkar (1991-vid). See Toure (1963:259–60) for the Guinean government's position on artistic property rights belonging to the state. This question with regard to Mali has been taken up in Bamba and Prévost (1996:133–35).

Plate 38 Syli National Orchestra, about 1962. Top (left to right): Sayon Camara (clarinet, out
of photo), Pivi Moriba (trombone), Balla Onivogui (trumpet), unidentified, Keletigui Traore
(tenor saxophone), Sekou Kouyate (accompanying guitar, second row), Blaise (tumba, second
row), Clement Dorego (tenor saxophone), Alex (drum set, second row), Mamadi Kourouma (alto
saxophone), Kanfory Sanoussi (orchestra leader, standing), unidentified bass player [Kerfala
"Tambourini" Camara?] (second row), Sekou "Docteur" Diabate (lead guitar), Momo "Wandel"
Soumah (alto saxophone), Honoré Copé (alto saxophone). Bottom left (left to right): Onivogui,
Soumah (hidden), Camara (bass), Dorego, Copé, Traore, Moriba, Kouyate, Sanoussi (maracas).
Bottom right (left to right): Dorego, Traore, Onivogui, Soumah. Photos courtesy of Balla Onivogui.

tural heritage. This was in accordance with the approach adopted by the PDG
[the ruling national party], which imposed on them a sacred obligation to draw
their inspiration solely from the wealth of epic and popular folk traditions,
which was henceforth to be rid of alien contrivances. (Ministry of Education
and Culture of Guinea 1979:80)[16]

16. The leader of the national orchestra, Kanfory Sanoussi, recalled in similar language in 1990
that the orchestra was formed "with the order that we must valorize our own national music based
on our folklore" ["avec le consigne qu'il faut que nous mettions en valeur notre propre musique

National orchestra leader Kanfory Sanoussi (from La Joviale Symphonie) and artistic director Kanfory Bangoura (from La Douce Parisette) presided over auditions that took the form of a *stage* (workshop) lasting several months. Some musicians from the older Conakry orchestras were invited, such as saxophonists Keletigui Traore and Momo "Wandel" Soumah (1926–), but those who had attended École Ponty were needed for their administrative expertise in the new government. A new generation of musicians, most of them in their twenties, would give birth to the new Guinean music. Those who were in Dakar studying at the conservatory, including trumpeter Balla Onivogui (1938–), trombonist Pivi Moriba (1939–), and guitarist Kerfala "Papa" Diabate (1936–), returned to Guinea to serve their country in the orchestra.

Because horn players were primarily influenced by American and French styles of playing and also tended not to come from jeli families, the guitar turned out to be the major link between the old and the new. Having been integrated into traditional Maninka music for decades, the guitar cut a path into orchestras throughout the country that enabled traditional musics to flood in. But now the guitar was electrified. The most influential guitarist in Guinea at the time of independence was Kerfala "Papa" Diabate, son of Sidikiba Diabate of Philharmonie Jazz fame. Born in Faranah at the southern fringe of Maninka influence, Papa Diabate attended the conservatory in Dakar from 1954 to 1958, playing in the group Guinea Jazz along with singer Laba Soce, and also with his conservatory teachers in nightclubs. Papa returned to Conakry to play in the national orchestra, and in the early 1960s the minister of the interior, Fodeba Keita, appointed him leader of the Orchestre de la Garde Républicaine, where he trained Diara Kante, another pioneering electric guitarist of the era, and older brother of Mory Kante (plate 39). In the 1960s Papa moved between Abidjan, where he played in clubs, and Conakry, in part owing to his strong individualistic personality and objections to the overt politicization of music by the ruling PDG party in Guinea. He was in Mali in the early 1970s with the group Tiawara Jazz from Kati, which won a prize in the biennial competition in 1972. Returning to Abidjan about 1974, Papa was joined a few years later by younger brother Sekou "Docteur" Diabate, who had left Balla et Ses Balladins. In 1986 they returned to Conakry, where they now live.[17]

nationale à partir de notre folklore"] (J. Williams 1990). For a photograph of the Syli Orchestra brass section (other than plate 38) see Toure (1963, facing 80).

17. The group Guinea Jazz was formed in Dakar by several Guineans in Senegal, including Mory Camara (from École Ponty), Naby Conte, and Konate. At the time of Senegalese independence some Guinea Jazz members helped to form Star Band de Dakar. Multi-instrumentalist Keletigui Diabate was the first guitarist in Orchestre de la Garde Républicaine and was replaced by Diara Kante in 1961 when he returned to his native Mali.

Plate 39 Three early Guinean orchestras. Top left: Orchestre de la Garde Républicaine, early 1960s. Left to right: unidentified (maracas), Nyessa (trumpet, orchestra leader), Fanton (saxophone), unidentified (sunglasses), Kemori (saxophone, hidden), Diara Kante (lead guitar). Top right: Orchestre du Jardin de Guinée (Balla et Ses Balladins), about 1964. Left to right: Bamba Kourouma, Pivi Moriba (hidden by microphone), "Soba" Manfila Kante (vocalist), Balla Onivogui (trumpet), Sankumba Diawara (guitar). Photos courtesy of Balla Onivogui. Bottom: Keletigui et Ses Tambourinis, about 1972. Left to right: Sana Kouyate (bala), Kaba Sylla (drum set), Sekou Conde (accompanying guitar), Labile (tumba), unidentified (bass guitar), Linke Conde (lead guitar), Manfila "Dabadou " Kante (vocalist), Momo "Wandel" Soumah (alto saxophone), Keletigui Traore (tenor saxophone, orchestra leader), Bigne Doumbia (alto saxophone), Kerfala Camara (trumpet). Photo courtesy of Momo "Wandel" Soumah.

Guitarists who cite Papa Diabate as their teacher or inspiration are a Who's Who of Mande guitar playing in the 1960s and 1970s. Guinea's renowned guitarist Sekou "Bembeya" Diabate considers himself a student of Papa. Manfila Kante, guitarist with Les Ambassadeurs, cites Papa Diabate as the source for modern Mande guitar playing and remembers him when they were both living in Abidjan in the 1960s. Papa also trained his younger brother Sekou "Docteur" Diabate. Papa's playing with a guitar plectrum rather than the fingers, and his breaking away from open-position playing by the use of scales learned at the conservatory, enabled the electric guitar

Table 15 The Syli National Orchestra of Guinea and Its Offshoots in the 1960s

Instrument	Balla (Jardin)	Keletigui (Paillote)	Demenageurs	Miscellaneous
Guitar solo	Sekou "Docteur" Diabate	Sekou Kouyate*	Sekou Kouyate*	Kerfala "Papa" Diabate
Guitar acc.				Leonard
Voice		Kerfala Camara*		Hamet Ndiaye (bongos) Fatou Sylla Makali Camara Angeline Dafe
Trumpet	Balla Onivogui			Christophe Bossard Raymond Malo
Trombone	Pivi Moriba			
Alto sax	Souleymane Sylla*	Momo "Wandel" Soumah Bigne Doumbouya	Momo "Wandel" Soumah Souleymane Sylla* Honore Cope	Mamady Kourouma
Tenor sax		Keletigui Traore Clement Dorego		
Clarinet	Souleymane Sylla*	Momo "Wandel" Soumah	Momo "Wandel" Soumah Honore Cope Souleymane Sylla* Sayon Camara	
Bass		Kerfala Camara*	Kerfala Camara*	Remetteur
Tumba	Sory Camara	Blaise*	Blaise*	Englebert
Drum set		Alex*	Alex*	Jean Fanga
Unknown				Soriba Nabi Konte

Note: All the musicians listed were members of the Syli National Orchestra at some point. The Syli Orchestra artistic director was Kanfory Bangoura; the *chef d'orchestre* was Kanfory Sanoussi (who also played accordion and vibraphone). An asterisk indicates musicians who joined the Syli Orchestra in a second wave about 1961. Those in the "miscellaneous" column did not join Balla or Keletigui. Les Demenageurs became Camara et Ses Tambourinis when they were nationalized, and later Keletigui et Ses Tambourinis. Clement Dorego later joined Bembeya Jazz; Souleymane Sylla joined Balla et Ses Balladins later. Full orchestra names: Balla et Ses Balladins; Keletigui et Ses Tambourinis; and Les Demenageurs Africains.
Sources: Balla Onivogui (1994-per) and Manfila "Dabadou" Kante (1994-per).

to cut through an orchestra like a horn while still evoking the polyrhythm of the bala.[18]

Sometime around late 1963 the Syli National Orchestra was split into two national orchestras because it had grown too large (table 15). At first the

18. Testimonies of Papa Diabate's influence include the following. "In 1959, Papa Diabate, from Syli Orchestre, taught me the electric guitar. He was the best guitarist in Guinea" (Sekou "Bembeya" Diabate, in Stapleton and May 1990:110). "The Diabate brothers, Papa the older and Sekou 'Doc-

groups were known by the nightclubs where they were in residence, Orchestre de la Paillote and Orchestre du Jardin de Guinée, which was the way they were billed on the first three albums released on the Syliphone label in the mid-1960s (plates 39 and 40). Orchestre de la Paillote was initially led by bassist and vocalist Kerfala Camara but eventually was taken over by tenor saxophonist Keletigui Traore and came to be known as Keletigui et Ses Tambourinis. Featured members included Momo "Wandel" Soumah on reeds and vocalist Manfila "Dabadou" Kante, an electric bass player and accomplished acoustic guitarist who in the late 1980s had a solo success with the song *Momangi*. Orchestre du Jardin de Guinée was led by trumpeter Balla Onivogui and came to be known as Balla et Ses Balladins. "Soba" Manfila Kante, a fine acoustic guitarist, was the main vocalist, and Sekou "Docteur" Diabate was the guitar soloist. In the late 1960s multi-instrumentalist Kemo Kouyate joined the group on guitar.[19]

In 1961 the regional Orchestre de Beyla, soon to become Guinea's most famous band, was formed under the patronage of Émile Konde, governor of the region. After winning medals in the national music festivals of 1964 and 1965, it attained national orchestra status and became known as Bembeya Jazz National, named after a river that flows through Beyla. In 1966 the group toured Cuba for a month and a half along with the newly created Djoliba National, the second national ballet. Bembeya Jazz had two stars: vocalist Aboubacar Demba Camara, whose death in a car accident outside Dakar in 1973 was an occasion for national mourning and a commemorative album (Bembeya Jazz 1974-disc), and guitarist Sekou "Bembeya" Diabate (plate 41).

Sekou "Bembeya" Diabate (1944–) got his first guitar about 1954 as a gift from his father for going to Koranic school in Sierra Leone. His father,

teur' the younger, come from a great family of traditional artists in which everyone plays the guitar from infancy. 'La Famille Diabate' was the first to introduce the Spanish guitar into Guinean dance music. They have also contributed to the creation of an original style of accompaniment, support, and improvisation, and to integrate this important participation of the guitar section into every orchestra of note" (Ibrahim Khalil Diaré, in Guinea Compilations 1972a-disc). Papa Diabate rarely recorded, but he can be heard on Guinea Compilations (1972a-disc), which has recently been reissued on CD, Djessou Mory Kante (1998-disc), and Papa Diabate (1999-disc).

19. The time of the national orchestra split was remembered as being somewhere between 1962 and 1964 by those I interviewed in 1994. I am using Balla Onivogui's recollections here, since he appears to have retained a clear picture of the era. He also prepared a detailed list of the musicians in the national orchestra that is the basis for table 15. See Balla et Ses Balladins (1993-disc) for a CD reissue of some of their classics. A group active in the early and mid-1960s called Les Demenageurs Africains was the nucleus of Keletigui et Ses Tambourinis. The exact relation between the national orchestra, Les Demenageurs, and Keletigui is unclear. In the early 1970s a small group known as the Guinean Quintet, including Keletigui members Kemo Kouyate and percussionist Papa Kouyate, recorded and toured with South African vocalist Miriyam Makeba (see appendix D, Syliphone SLP 22).

Plate 40 Early Syliphone album covers. Orchestre Paillote, SLP 1 (Keletigui et Ses Tambourinis 1967a-disc), Jardin de Guinée, SLP 2 (Balla et Ses Balladins 1967-disc), Bembeya Jazz, SLP 4 (1967-disc). Courtesy of Günter Gretz.

Plate 41 Bembeya Jazz (about 1964) and Sekou "Bembeya" Diabate. Top (left to right): sitting on hood of car, Salif Kaba (vocalist), Askene Mohamed Kaba (trumpet), Mamadi "Vieux" Camara (accompanying guitar); second row, Aboubacar Demba Camara (vocalist), Sekou "Bembeya" Diabate (guitar), Hamidou Diaoune (bass), Lamin Kaba (chauffeur), Siaka Diabate (tumba); next row, Bangaly "Gros Bois" Traore (tenor saxophone); top row, Sekou "LeGros" Camara (trumpet), Mori Mangala Konde (drum set). Bottom: Sekou "Bembeya" Diabate about 1970 (left), and with his first guitar, about 1956, Sierra Leone (right). Photos courtesy of Sekou "Bembeya" Diabate.

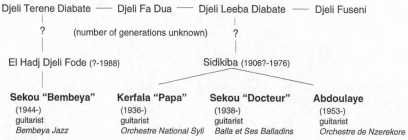

Figure 10 Lineage of Diabate family of Duako.

El Hadj Djeli Fode Diabate (d. 1988), played the koni and bala, as well as the guitar in the 1930s. Djeli Fode Diabate and Sidikiba Diabate, father of Papa Diabate, were very close, having family connections that went back to four brothers from Duako; El Hajj Djeli Fode descended from Djeli Terene, and El Hajj Sidikiba descended from Djeli Leeba (Layeba) (fig. 10). Sekou studied the guitar with Papa Diabate in 1959, learning scales and how to play with a plectrum and without a capo (a bar tied across the neck to make transposing easier). He got his first electric guitar about 1964.

Through the 1960s and early 1970s, the three leading bands in Guinea were Balla et Ses Balladins, Keletigui et Ses Tambourinis, and Bembeya Jazz National, all celebrated in the Syliphone LP *Guinée an XI* (Guinea Compilations 1971-disc) (table 16).[20] How completely just a few lineages of jelis dominated modern Guinean guitar playing and singing can be seen in the abbreviated family trees shown in figures 9 and 10. Most of the great guitarists of Guinea and Mali through the 1970s either belong to these Diabate or Kante families or learned from them.

The first recordings of postindependence Guinean music were made by Leo Sarkisian and issued on ten LPs from 1961 to 1963 on Tempo, an American label. Sekou Toure himself had given Sarkisian free rein to record throughout the country, and he appointed as his guide Philharmonie Jazz founder Sidikiba Diabate, who had organized the new national instrumental ensemble. The recordings included l'Ensemble Instrumental Africains de la Radiodiffusion Nationale ("Africains" was eventually dropped from their name), which recorded staple pieces from the jeli repertory on traditional instruments; the Groupe Folklorique de Kankan; a variety of other traditional music from across the country; and three modern regional groups: Orchestre Danse de Gueckedou, Orchestre de Beyla (later known as Bembeya Jazz), and Orchestre de Kissidougou. The three orchestras featured

20. According to Sekou "Bembeya" Diabate, Syli Orchestra brought in "the true Guinean folklore," and Bembeya Jazz took it to "new levels," opening the door for other countries to abandon "other music in favour of their own folklore" (Stapleton and May 1990:110).

Table 16 Guinean and Malian Orchestras of the 1960s and 1970s

Instrument	Orch. Beyla (1963)	Bembeya (1970)	Balla (1970)	Keletigui (1970)	Les Amb. (1979)	Rail Band (1977)
Guitar solo	Sekou Diabate	Sekou Diabate	Sekou Diabate	Linké Conde	Manfila Kante	Djeli Mady Tounkara
Guitar acc.		Mamadi Camara	Kemo Kouyate	Sekou Conde	Ousmane Kouyate	Djeli Moussa Koite
						Mamadou Diakite
Voice	Jenne Camara	Demba Camara	Manfila Kante	Keletigui Traore	Salif Keita	Mory Kante
		Salif Kaba (2d)	B. Nestor Wallas	Kerfalla Camara	Ousmane Dia	Makan Ganessy
					Sambou Diakite	Djeli Mady Sissiko
Trumpet	Mohamed Kaba?	Mohamed Kaba	Balla Onivogui	*Kerfalla Camara*	Kabine Traore	Moussa Kone
	Sekou Camara	Sekou Camara				Tidiane Kone
Trombone			Pivi Moriba			
Alto sax			*Souley*	Momo Wandel	Moussa Cissoko	Tidiane Kone (a/t?)
				Bigné Doumbouya		
Tenor sax	Hamidou Diaoune	Clément Dorego	Fodé NDiaye	*Keletigui*	*Moussa Cissoko*	
		Bangaly Traore				
Soprano sax			Souley			Ledy Youla
Clarinet			*Fodé NDiaye*			
Flute				*Momo Wandel*		
Bass	Abou Camara	Hamidou Diaoune	Famoro Kouyate	*Keletigui*	Sekou Diabate	Cheick Traore
				Man. Dabadou Kante		
				Mbemba		
Bala				Samah Diabate	Kaba Kante	
Percussion						*Moussa Kone*
Tumba	Siaka Diabate	Siaka Diabate	Thiam	Papa Kouyate	Nouhoun Keita	Dramane Koumare
Drum set	Mori Conde	Mori Conde	Abdou	Kaba Sylla		Mamadou Bagayoko
Maracas	Sekou Konate	*Salif Kaba*				
Claves	Sekou Kande					
Organ					Smith	Alfred Coulibaly

Sources: Bembeya Jazz (1967-disc), Guinea Compilations (1971-disc), Keletigui et Ses Tambourinis (1975-disc), Les Ambassadeurs (1979c/1984b-disc), and Rail Band (1977-disc). Full orchestra names: Orchestre de Beyla, which became Bembeya jazz; Balla et Ses Balladins; Keletigui et Ses Tambourinis; Les Ambassadeurs; and Rail Band.

Note: Orchestra members whose names are in italics appear twice, doubling on certain instruments.

Plate 42 Tempo LP labels of Orchestre Danse de Gueckedou and Orchestre de Beyla, 1963.
From Orchestre Danse de Gueckedou (1963b-disc), and Bembeya Jazz (1963-disc). Courtesy of
Leo Sarkisian.

the guitar, did not record any of the older pieces from the jeli's repertory, and were strongly influenced by Caribbean popular music. On the disc labels many of the song titles had parenthetical descriptions of the rhythms, such as beguine, bolero, calypso, or cha-cha-cha (plate 42).[21]

The importance of Latin American music may be attributed to its preindependence popularity in Africa and the strong postindependence political ties between Guinea and Cuba. Fashions in France, including a taste for Latin American popular music, quickly reached the francophone colonies. Recordings of South American and Cuban music edited for African consumption were released as the GV series, from Grabado en Venezuela (pressed in Venezuela), on the HMV label beginning in the early 1930s. By the end of World War II these recordings were well known in francophone African countries and influential in the popular music of the time. Cruise ships carrying rumba bands went ashore, furthering the appreciation of Latin music, and Guinean bands such as Horoya Band (1971-disc) recorded new versions of GV successes (Ewens 1991:56, 69; Harrev 1992:235–36). Malians and Guineans traveled to Cuba to study and perform in the mid-1960s, and the great Cuban Orquesta Aragon performed in Guinea at the ninth National Arts Festival in 1968 (notes to Guinea Compilations 1974b-disc). The Cuban-influenced lineup of Orchestre de Beyla was typical of orchestras in the 1960s (table 16).

From the mid-1960s to the early 1980s the national recording company Syliphone documented a classic era of Guinean music with about eighty LP albums and dozens of seven-inch singles. Comparing the earlier Tempo recordings, one can hear the Latin-based sound of the early 1960s giving way to a distinctly Mande-based sound by the end of the decade. The claves and maracas players in Orchestre de Beyla in the early 1960s were dropped in favor of a second guitarist about 1964. The 1968 Bembeya Jazz album-length epic *Regard sur le passé,* based on the jeli piece *Keme Burema,* featured Djeli Sory Kouyate on bala, a sure sign of a shedding of Cuban influences in favor of local music. But other than a single bala, traditional instruments did not enter into the orchestras. Rather, bala playing styles entered via the guitar, played primarily by those coming from jeli families. In the modernizing process of the 1960s, jeli guitarists and vocalists provided the link with local culture.[22]

Throughout the 1960s and 1970s there sprouted many excellent bands prominently featuring Maninka electric guitar playing, with eight eventu-

21. See Merriam (1970) items 327–35 (Tempo 7008 to 7016). For more on Sarkisian's work in Guinea and later with the Voice of America see Gwamna (1992).

22. Keletigui Traore has been credited with introducing the bala into an orchestra (Ibrahim Khalil Diaré in Guinea Compilations 1971-disc).

Table 17 Guinean Orchestras on the Syliphone Label

National orchestras as of 1971
Keletigui et Ses Tambourinis
Balla et Ses Balladins
Bembeya Jazz (formed 1961, nationalized 1966)
Orchestre de la Garde Républicaine (formed 1959), later became Super Boiro Band
L'Orchestre Féminine de la Gendarmerie (formed 1960), later known as Les Amazones
Horoya Band (from Kankan, formed 1965, nationalized 1971)

National orchestras added by the late 1970s
Kaloum Star (from Conakry)
22 Novembre Band (from Kankan)

Regional orchestras
Beyla: Simandou
Boke: Sorsornet Rythme
Conakry: Camayenne Sofa
Conakry: Sylli Authentique
Farannah: Tropical Djoli Band
Fria: Sombory Jazz
Gueckedou: Kebendo Jazz
Kissidougou: Niandan Jazz
Macenta: Palm Jazz
Mamou: Bafing Jazz
N'Zerekore: Nimba Jazz
Siguiri: Manden Kono
Telemele: Tele jazz
Dirou Band
Kebali Jazz
Kakande Jazz
Kolima

---

ally rising to the status of national orchestra by winning regional and national competitions (table 17). Horoya Band and 22 Band (22 Novembre Band), both from the Maninka cultural metropolis Kankan, extended the guitar-based tradition through the 1970s. Government patronage of the regional orchestras had begun to decline in the late 1970s, and the death of Sekou Toure in 1984 signaled the end of an era for Guinean orchestras. Syliphone had folded, and while the country endured years of economic disaster, many musicians emigrated.[23]

23. The thirty regions each had what were called federal orchestras (Guinea Compilations 1974b-disc). Twenty-four Syliphone selections have recently been reissued in celebration of Guinea's fortieth year of independence (Guinea Compilations 1998-disc), and much of the Syliphone catalog is being reissued on CD (see appendix D). An excellent, almost textbook survey of this classic era of modern Guinean music by the group Kouyate et Kouyate (1990-disc) covers some of the great Syliphone recordings of Bembeya Jazz, Horoya Band, Keletigui et Ses Tambourinis, Balla et Ses Balladins, Camayenne Sofa, and Sory Kandia Kouyate (1970-disc, 1971-disc). Although the sound is updated, the singing and arrangements are faithful to the originals. Kemo Kouyate's guitar solo on *Sara* (Kouyate et Kouyate 1990-disc) is remarkably similar to his solo on *Sara 70* recorded with Balla et Ses Balladins (1993-disc/Guinea Compilations 1971-disc).

The Modern Era in Mali from Independence to the Mid-1980s

The history of dance orchestras in Mali before independence is ill documented, and perhaps for good reason. Unlike Guinea and Senegal, whose cosmopolitan port cities Conakry and Dakar attracted cultural influences and communities from Europe, the Caribbean, and other parts of coastal West Africa, landlocked Mali had remained resistant to cultural influences arriving via the Atlantic—if not by will, then by geography. Bamako, a town of fewer than 1,000 people when the French first built a fort there in the 1880s, did not really begin growing until the railway from Kayes was completed in 1905; by 1920 it had about 15,000 inhabitants. Besides being an administrative center, Bamako was a major transit station for trade such as kola nuts moving from Côte d'Ivoire north and westward to Senegal and other goods moving from Senegal eastward and to the south. Although there was a significant European population of several thousand by the 1950s (the population of Bamako in 1960 was 130,000), the kind of dance orchestras playing foreign music in Conakry and Dakar do not appear to have been present in Bamako before independence. Jelimuso singers backed by ensembles of jeli instruments including the guitar were, and continue to be, one of Mali's most powerful musical forces.[24]

Mali lagged behind Guinea in the African-style modernizing process of drawing on local traditions to nourish Cuban-inspired dance orchestras, but by the early 1970s it had caught up. A Malian musical identity was firmly established with the launching of the three top Malian bands of the 1970s,

---

almost two decades earlier. (Early printings of the notes to Balla et Ses Balladins 1993-disc were mistaken about Famoro Kouyate's playing the solo on *Sara 70.*) Equally remarkable is the way guitarist Zoumana Diara pays homage to Kemo's solo (all but reproducing it) on *Wentere*, a piece sung by Adama Diabate (1995-disc) in praise of Mali's great artists, including Sira Mori Diabate, composer of *Sara.*

24. Recordings from Radio Mali (1977-disc) made in the early 1960s, including an homage to Facelli Kante by jelimuso Mokotafe (Mokontafe) Sako accompanied by a guitar, conga, and a fine trumpet player, provide an important window into the early modernization process in Mali. Bamba and Prévost (1996) contains a wealth of information on music in Mali just before independence, including descriptions of l'Orchestre de Kati (52), Bani Jazz, which became l'Orchestre Régional de Mopti and then Orchestre Kanaga (59, 70–72, 91–96), the impact of trumpeter Louis Armstrong's concert in Bamako (probably during his 1960 tour of Africa) (62), and the First Youth Festival in Bamako (perhaps about 1958), of which he wrote, "For the first time, I discovered a modern orchestra made up of black musicians, Senegalese. They wore elegant dark European style suits, which was new in the Soudan" (50). According to Djeli Mady Tounkara (in Durán 1992a: 35), Kita was "the first place in Mali to have a dance orchestra under French colonial rule. In the early '50s not even Bamako had an orchestra. The French expatriates used to take the train to Kita every weekend to hear the band, which was led by 'BK'—Bourahima Keita, Mali's first saxophonist." See B. Keita (1988: 12) for an early twentieth-century postcard photograph showing a small brass band from Kita. For a history of Bamako see Meillassoux (1968b) and Perinbam (1997); for a view of one corner of the city in the early 1990s, see Modic (1996); for political and social histories of Kita, an important center of Maninka music, see D. Cissé (1970) and Hopkins (1972).

The Rail Band, Les Ambassadeurs, and National Badema. Leaders of these bands would move on to solo careers in the mid-1980s, via Abidjan and then Paris, to become some of the most creative and successful artists on the international music scene: singer Salif Keita and guitarist Manfila Kante of Les Ambassadeurs; singer and kora player Mory Kante and guitarist Djeli Mady Tounkara of the Rail Band; and singer Kasse Mady Diabate and arranger Boncana Maiga of National Badema.[25]

From 1962 to 1968 annual regional and national arts festivals, called Semaines de la Jeunesses (Youth Weeks), were organized by the Ministry of Culture. They were suspended because of the coup in late 1968 and were replaced in 1970 by the Biennale Artistique et Culturelle de la Jeunesse (Biennial Youth Arts and Cultural Festival) held every two years until 1988. The first Biennale in 1970 was the occasion for a collaboration between the Ministry of Information of Mali, under the direction of novelist Massa Makan Diabate, and Barenreiter Musicaphon that over the next two years produced an extraordinary series of recordings of regional and national orchestras, the national instrumental ensemble, the jelimusolu Fanta Damba and Fanta Sacko, and revered ngoni player and vocalist Bazoumana Sissoko. These recordings were the first systematic survey of Malian music, similar to that of the Tempo label recordings made in Guinea a decade earlier.[26]

The relative lack of Malian recordings from the 1960s makes it difficult to reconstruct the growth of orchestras during this time, but the Ministry of Information recordings of the Rail Band, Orchestre National "A," and regional orchestras of Kayes, Segou, Mopti, and Sikasso shed light on the previous decade. The orchestras were modeled on those of Guinea, with brass sections, drum sets, congas, and prominent electric guitars. The orchestras of Segou, Mopti, and Sikasso, however, differed from those in Guinea in their use of the pentatonic melodic systems of their regions.

Perhaps the most crucial (and undocumented) grassroots development in Malian music during the 1960s was the growth of Apollos, popular dance events featuring groups having congas, Western drum sets, bass guitars, and

25. The following survey of the Rail Band, Les Ambassadeurs, and National Badema is drawn from Mandel (1983), Lee (1988), Durán (1991, 1995c), Austin (1991-vid), Manfila Kante ex-Ambassadeurs (1994-per), Les Ambassadeurs (1994-disc), Kabine "Tagus" Traore (1995-per), Musiques du Mali (1995a/b-disc), and Bamba and Prévost (1996). I have tried to reconcile conflicting histories by selectively choosing from each of these sources.

26. The Biennale was not held in 1990 owing to the political unrest that ultimately led to the democratic election of Alpha Konaré as president in 1992. Although intended to reflect the diversity of the nation, the national arts festivals had the effect of glossing over local differences in favor of bringing out a regional identity emphasizing shared characteristics (e.g., see Arnoldi 1995:138 on puppet masquerading traditions). A similar process is at work in the national ballet troupes that perform abroad. The Malian recordings from the early 1970s include Ministry of Information of Mali (1971-disc, 1972-disc), Rail Band (1972-disc), Orchestre National "A" (1972-disc), and a variety of regional orchestras.

Plate 43 Lafiabougou Filani/Les Jumeux de Lafiabougou/The Lafiabougou Twins. Fousseni and Lansana Diabate in the 1950s. Seated person in bottom middle photo is Sekou Kouyate, son of Ntenin Sory Kouyate. Photos courtesy of Lansana Diabate.

electric guitars, all amplified by a sound system. The movement centered on a famous family of jelis in the Lafiabougou section of Bamako, featuring the twins Fousseni and Lansana Diabate, known as Lafiabougou Filani or Jumeaux de Lafiabougou (Lafiabougou Twins). Born in Niagassola, Guinea, home of the ancestral Sosso bala (see chapter 3), the Lafiabougou Twins embodied both the old and the new; they grew up playing the bala and also embraced the guitar (plates 1 and 43). Their use of electric instruments brought the jeli tradition in line with modern urban Bamako life. As they played for traditional events such as naming ceremonies and mar-

268 · CHAPTER FIVE

riages, the new electrified sound ultimately made its way into the more ur-
bane hotel orchestras that featured brass sections. The Apollo space mis-
sions symbolized the modern world, and the Bamako events named after
them were equally viewed as "modern" (Bamba and Prévost 1996:175–76)
and "progressive" (Mory Kante, in Durán 1998:45).

Apollos may have grown out of elaborate Bamako marriage celebrations
popular in the early 1960s called Ambiance. Meillassoux (1968b:107–12)
described an association of over eighty-one people registered under the
name of *jeli ton* (jeli association) in 1956, which in 1963 changed its name
to Association des Artistes du Mali, l'Ambiance, with more than three hundred members. Performances at Ambiance events included an orchestra including a kora, bala, jeli dundun, tama, and electric guitars. These Ambiance
events may themselves have grown out of an event from Kankan, Guinea,
called Mamaya that was popular there from the 1930s to 1950s (Kaba and
Charry, forthcoming). Although the term Apollo might not have been applied to the new Bamako genre until at least 1967, it was brewing throughout the 1960s.[27] Notes to a Horoya Band (1971-disc) 45 rpm recording of
the tune Apollo released about 1971 refer to it as "at present all the rage to
dance in Guinea" ("Apollo est en ce moment la grande fureur à danser en
Guinée"). The tune *Apollo* is now a standard in the repertory of many jelis.

One of the most influential orchestral musicians during the 1960s was
multi-instrumentalist Keletigui Diabate (1931–).

> Immediately after Mali had become independent [1960], her young genera-
> tion, through the . . . Board of Youth and Sports, decided to form a national
> orchestra. . . . [It] is dominated by that great figure, Kélétigui [Diabate], the
> orchestra-man, the leader of this formation. . . . At the age of seven this artist
> born at Kita (the cradle of the greatest musical traditions of the country) al-
> ready was a virtuose on the *balafon*. . . . As his closest admirers suggested to
> him to try his hand at the modern instruments (the guitar, for example) in or-
> der to prepare a career for himself, Kélétigui began to travel across Western
> Africa in search of instructors and, above all, of a style appropriate to his de-
> velopment. Thus he stayed several times in Senegal, Guinea, and Ivory Coast
> before definitely returning to this country in 1960.
> For virtuoso Kélétigui Diabate these journeys have been very productive
> of learning: he has become master in the arts of playing the guitar, the trum-
> pet, the flute, the saxophone, the counter-bass. But he is fondest of his guitar,

27. The Apollo program to land on the moon was announced in 1961, but the first significant
notice in Africa of an Apollo spacecraft may have been a January 1967 ground test that killed the
three astronauts inside *Apollo 1,* delaying the program until October 1968 when the first manned
Apollo flight was launched, circling the earth. In December 1968 *Apollo 8* circled the moon, and
in July 1969 the famous *Apollo 11* landed on the moon. Sekouba "Bambino" Diabate (in Durán
1997:43), from Siguiri, Guinea, believes that the piece *Apollo* was composed by his mother, Jeli
Marayam Samoura, who settled in Bamako after remarrying, to a Malian guitarist, Wusu Diabate.

Plate 44 Orchestre National "A" de la République du Mali, about 1970. Keletigui Diabate playing the guitar. From Orchestre National "A" de la République du Mali (1972-disc).

which he plays as soloist in the "A" formation of the National Orchestra, in a style reminiscent of the late Guinean guitar-player Facély Kante. (English notes to Orchestre National "A" de la République du Mali 1972-disc)[28]

Diabate apprenticed as a guitarist in the Guinean Orchestre de la Garde Républicaine when it was first created, and he returned to Mali just after independence to help form Mali's own national orchestra (plate 44). His younger brother Daouda Diabate played and recorded with Les Ballets Africains, and Keletigui appears to have been influenced by guitarist Facelli Kante. Just as the order was given in Guinea to create a dance orchestra rooted in local traditions, so it was in Mali. Modernization as defined in Guinea and Mali was based on this process of assimilating local traditions into Latin American–based dance orchestras. Keletigui's role in Mali may

28. Keletigui Diabate (in Prince 1989b:19) has reported that he was in Guinea from 1957 to 1961.

have been similar to that of Papa Diabate in Guinea, who initiated a generation of electric guitarists.

> I was put in charge of the Premier Formation du Mali (Orchestre national,
> Number One); it was me who introduced Manding and Bambara songs played
> on modern instruments. The idea was to make traditional music, but in a mod-
> ern way. At the time (the early '60s), we received delegations from Europe, or
> other African countries, and at such occasions we'd perform our traditional
> ceremonies. Each time we received a European delegation, an official recep-
> tion would be arranged, and those delegates, they couldn't dance our tradi-
> tional dances. So we had to find international rhythms and put our traditional
> sound within that, using a (kit) drum and so on. (Keletigui Diabate, in Prince
> 1989b:17)

While the regional and national orchestras supported by the Ministry of
Youth and Culture were exploring their own folklore in the 1960s trying to
forge regional and national identities in their synthesis of local and foreign
musics, bands outside the system had no such charge. A major venue for
one such band was the restaurant attached to the hotel at the railway station
in Bamako. The band that played there in the middle and late 1960s was the
Star Band de Bamako, consisting of former members of the Star Band de
Dakar, which itself was formed in August 1960 to help in the Senegalese
independence celebrations from remnants of Guinea Jazz, a group active in
Dakar in the 1950s. The repertory of Star Band de Bamako catered to foreigners, whether Africans from other countries or Europeans, and by 1970
the manager of the rail station, Aly Diallo, wanted something new.[29]

Saxophonist, trumpeter, and ngoni player Tidiani Kone was charged by
Aly Diallo with forming a band that would bring Malian music away from
French and Latin American influences and back to its roots—to "revalorize
the cultural patrimony," as the saying goes (Musiques du Mali 1995a/b-
disc; Seck and Clerfeuille 1993:200). The Rail Band was formed with the
aim of "transposing" traditional music onto modern instruments.

> At the moment when the independent countries of Black Africa incessantly
> co-ordinate their activities in search of appropriate ways and means to coun-
> tenance the restoration of their own civilization, an essential attribute of their
> national sovereignty, it is important to reserve a choice position for traditional
> music, which, in its transposition for modern instruments, will significantly
> answer to the legitimate aspirations of the peoples of Africa.
>
> For this end, the Station Hotel And Refreshment-Room of Bamako (Hotel
> Unit of the Railway Administration of Mali), anxious to contribute its mod-
> est share to the revalorization and diffusion of the rich Malian folk-lore,

---

29. The Star Band de Dakar was a training ground in the 1960s and 1970s for Senegalese
musicians such as Youssou Ndour, and several bands had spun out of it (see Durán 1989b; Graham
1988:149, 1992:52; and Ewens 1991:69).

was to put on its legs, in July 1970, a young group of musicians called "Le Rail-Band." . . .

Because of its permanent search for the due interpretation of Negro art, this orchestra of the rail has quickly developed toward being able to leave the simple stage of adaptation and to set out for new horizons of creativity. (English notes to Rail Band 1972-disc)

Ironically, the singer specifically chosen to bring this folklore into the band was Salif Keita (1949–), initially disowned by his horon (freeborn nonartisan class) father when he moved to Bamako about 1967 to play guitar and sing on the streets and in bars after being refused admission to a teachers' college because of poor eyesight. Although not a jeli, Keita had absorbed their singing and playing style, and his voice proved irresistible. In his native Djoliba he heard hunter's music, jelis, and schoolteachers who played pop songs of the day on the guitar. These schoolteachers who were willing to entertain village children with their guitar playing were a significant inspiration for Keita, as his former schoolmate Cheick Keita has suggested.

Their example as modern Malians, who had freed themselves from the social taboos surrounding music and musical instruments, may have made Salif Keita less hesitant to embrace music as a means of earning his living. . . . Through the model of teachers who played music, although not professionally, and under the pressure of dire necessity, Salif was determined to stand up to the opposition of his family and assert his new identity as a professional musician in a society where caste affiliation remains the decisive criterion. (C. Keita 1996:101)

Although not directly sponsored by the Ministries of Culture or Information, Rail Band members were considered civil servants of the Railway Board under the Ministry of Public Works. Led by Tidiani Kone and driven by the vocals of Salif Keita, the Rail Band quickly established a reputation as doing something new in Mali. "[The] Rail Band [is] considered by the Malian public as an orchestra in the avant-garde of the flowering of Negro African Culture" (my translation of the French notes to Rail Band 1972-disc). Salif Keita had become so popular that when he decided to leave about 1973 to join Les Ambassadeurs, which was under the direction of the Ministry of the Interior, a near crisis occurred. But Mory Kante, who would achieve unprecedented commercial success in Europe a decade and a half later, filled the void.

Mory Kante (1950–) is from a distinguished family of jelis in Kissidougou, Guinea, and is a cousin of Facelli Kante (fig. 9). He moved to Bamako in the mid-1960s and stayed with an aunt, Manamba Kamissoko, who sang with the national ensemble. Kamissoko was married to one of the famous

Lafiabougou Twins, who were major organizers of Apollos. Kante initially earned his reputation playing guitar at the Apollos and was known as Le Petit de Lafiabougou (Durán 1998:45; Lee 1988:43–44). About 1971 or 1972 he joined the Rail Band as a bala player, and a year later he switched to the guitar when Baba Nabe left. Mory Kante took over as lead singer in the Rail Band when Salif Keita left.

When Kante switched from guitar to lead vocals, Djeli Mady Tounkara was the guitar soloist in the Rail Band.[30] Tounkara, from a jeli family from Kita, played guitar accompaniment in the National Orchestra under Keletigui Diabate's direction in the late 1960s, and he also played at Apollos about this time with Mory Kante. Tounkara's lead guitar playing has become a signature of the Rail Band since the mid-1970s. The twenty-seven-minute album-length version of *Sunjata* recorded in Nigeria in 1975 featuring the singing and speaking of Mory Kante and guitar playing of Djeli Mady Tounkara is a classic (Rail Band 1975/n.d.-disc). In 1978 Kante left the Rail Band to pursue a solo career in Abidjan, where he played in hotels with his own group until he moved to Paris five years later. The rest of the Rail Band followed Kante to Abidjan about 1979, and Tounkara recorded several albums as leader of the band (Tounkara, n.d.-disc) and also with the "Manding Trio" (Sadio Kouyate, n.d.-disc). The band and Tounkara soon returned to Bamako, where he still lives.

Les Ambassadeurs was formed about 1969 to play at the government Motel du Bamako, which was managed by the chief of police, Tiekoro Bakayoko. Some of the musicians, notably saxophonist Moussa Sissoko and Guinean trumpeter Kabine "Tagus" Traore, came from Elephant Noir, a group working in Bouake, Côte d'Ivoire. In 1972 they were joined by Guinean guitarist Manfila Kante (1946–), who would become one of the most influential electric guitarists in francophone West Africa. Initially from Kankan, as a teenager Kante moved to Abidjan,where he recorded several 45 rpm discs. In 1969 Kante went to Mali, where he played with Sorry Bamba, leader of the regional orchestra of Mopti. Kante become orchestra leader of Les Ambassadeurs in 1972, and Salif Keita joined the orchestra the next year. The guitar playing and arrangements of Manfila Kante and the singing and songwriting of Salif Keita combined to form one of the great partnerships of modern music in West Africa and would make Les Ambassadeurs one of the most important West African bands of the 1970s (plate 45).

Les Ambassadeurs had released three 45 rpm recordings and three LPs

---

30. It is not clear exactly when Djeli Mady Tounkara became lead guitarist in the Rail Band. Durán (1992a:35, 1995c:45) and Lee (1988:45) report that he joined about 1971; notes attributed to Rail Band manager Modibo Nianzon Traore (Musiques du Mali 1995a/b-disc) imply that he became the guitar soloist in 1973. For more on Tounkara see Eyre (forthcoming).

Plate 45 Manfila Kante, Salif Keita, and Les Ambassadeurs. Top left: early 45 rpm record of Manfila Kante (1969?-disc). Courtesy of Günter Gretz. Top right: Salif Keita (left) and Manfila Kante (right), from Les Ambassadeurs (1981a-disc). Bottom: Les Ambassadeurs (1977a/b-disc). Bottom row (seated left to right): Moussa Cissoko, Amadou Bakayoko, Salif Keita, Dama; top row (standing left to right): Keletigui Diabate, Modibo Cone, Ousmane Dia, Kabine "Tagus" Traore, Issa Niare, Idrissa Soumaoro (with glasses), Manfila Kante.

by August 1978, when half of the group relocated to Abidjan because of civil unrest and the arrest of their corrupt manager Bakayoko. In Abidjan, Les Ambassadeurs Internationaux (as they were now called) recorded their most famous hit, *Mandjou,* a praise song for Guinean president Sekou Toure written by Salif Keita. The lyrics to *Mandjou,* the first part of which

Table 18 Excerpt of Lyrics to *Mandjou* by Salif Keita

Maninka	English
Manju woi, kana kasi	Manju woi, do not cry
Alifa Toure la den, kana kasi	Alifa Toure's son, do not cry
Manju woi, kana kasi	Manju woi, do not cry
Na Aminata Fadiga den, kana kasi	Ma Aminata Fadiga's son, do not cry
Manju woi, kana kasi	Manju, woi, do not cry
Andrée Toure ke, kana kasi	Andrée Toure's husband, do not cry
Manju woi, kana kasi	Manju, woi, do not cry
Andrée Madu fa, kana kasi	Andrée Madu's father, do not cry
Ne na n'i jigiya le ma,	My hope is with you
kasi tuma ma se, Manju	The time to cry has not yet come, Maju
Ala Manju jo sanu jo ye	May Allah reward Manju with gold
Manju woi, kana kasi	Manju woi, do not cry
Alifa Toure la den, kana kasi	Alifa Toure's son, do not cry
Manju woi, kana kasi	Manju woi, do not cry
Minata cinin fa, kana kasi	Little Minata's father, do not cry
Duniya dalen i jigi le ma,	Everyone believes in you
kasi tuma ma se, Manju	The time to cry has not yet come, Maju
Ala Manju jo sanu jo ye	May Allah reward Manju with gold
Manju fa tigi be fa ko waa so la,	Manju, fatherhood is a source of pride
Fama Ala y'o k'i ye	Allah the Great has done it for you
Manju den tigi ye den ko waa so la dinye lo wolon,	Manju, having children is a source of pride
Fama ala y'o k'i ye	Allah the Great has done it for you
Manju tinye tigi ye tinye ko waa so la tulon kuma te,	Manju, the truth is a source of pride
Fama Ala y'o k'i ye	Allah the Great has done it for you
Manju woi, kana kasi	Manju, woi, do not cry
Alifa Toure la den, kana kasi	Alifa Toure's son, do not cry
Maju woi, kana kasi	Manju, woi, do not cry
Andrée Madu fa, kana kasi	Andrée Madu's father, do not cry
Si fin na saya ma nyi n fa,	The death of a young person is not good my father
kasi tuma ma se, Manju	The time to cry has not yet come, Maju
Ala Manju jo sano jo ye	May Allah reward Manju with gold
	Instrumental solos

Sources: From Les Ambassadeurs 1979c-disc/1984b-disc/1994-disc, and Salif Keita 1994a-disc. Transcribed and translated by Amadou Wat and Eric Charry.

are excerpted in table 18, illustrate aesthetics of praise that Keita absorbed from the jelis who surrounded him. In addition to naming Toure's family members, a common form of praise, Keita sings about Toure directly, and finally (after the instrumental solos) uses phrases and images commonly found in *jelikan* (language of the jeli), the sometimes archaic speech of the jeli (not shown in table 18). About this time Manfila Kante and Salif Keita recorded an unusual two-album set featuring traditional jeli pieces accompanied on the acoustic guitar (Les Ambassadeurs 1979a-disc, 1979b-disc). In December 1980 Kante, Keita, guitarist Ousmane Kouyate, and saxophonist Moussa Sissoko went to the United States for several months and recorded two LPs of material (Les Ambassadeurs 1981a-disc, 1981b-disc). These LPs yielded two of Manfila Kante's finest guitar solos, *Toubaka 81* and *Djata* (both on Les Ambassadeurs 1984a-disc; see transcription 36 below), and another Keita classic, *Primpin.* After their return in early 1981, Kante and Keita began to drift apart, each taking part of the band with him. By 1983 Keita was giving concerts in France with Super Ambassadeurs without Manfila Kante, bringing to a close a classic era of modern electric Malian music that lasted from the early 1970s to the early 1980s. The Kante-Keita partnership established about 1973 was very much reminiscent of another Kante-Keita partnership begun twenty-five years earlier, that of guitar player Facelli Kante and writer Fodeba Keita that gave birth to Les Ballets Africains.[31]

The success of Les Ambassadeurs was due in large part to the way they reconciled their ties to Mande culture with the modern sensibilities of urban Africa. Like his cousin Facelli, Manfila Kante came from a celebrated family of musicians grounded in the traditions of the jeli.[32] He had thoroughly integrated the bala style of playing on the electric guitar and also understood the application of that style in an orchestra with a bass, drum set, keyboard, and brass instruments. Salif Keita, the horon (nonartisan), was the one injecting the local Muslim-tinged praise singing tradition for which jelis are known, the very reason he was recruited into the Rail Band. Les Ambassadeurs were joined by Keletigui Diabate in the mid-1970s for some of their recordings, but he remained in Mali when they left for Abidjan.

With the ascent of the Rail Band and Les Ambassadeurs, the Orchestre National "A" fell out of favor and disbanded. In the 1970s a new national orchestra arose to become the third major band active in Mali: National

31. Salif Keita and Manfila Kante remain close friends in Paris. They were reunited for Keita's 1991 release *Amen.* For more on Kante's early career in Côte d'Ivoire and Mali, see Bamba and Prévost (1996: 103–7, 126–27), according to which Manfila Kante, Mory Kante, and Djeli Moussa Diawara all rehearsed with the regional orchestra of Mopti in preparation for the Second Biennial of 1972. After several months, the three of them tried to return to Guinea because of the death of Manfila's father. When they learned in Bamako that Sekou Toure had closed the border because of political troubles in Guinea, Manfila Kante joined Les Ambassadeurs and Mory Kante joined the Rail Band.

32. Despite the preponderance of bala and guitar players in his extended family, Manfila Kante claims numu (blacksmith) rather than jeli status (Durán 1991:21; also see chapter 3), a common claim among some nyamakala (artisan class) musicians whose names are not Diabate or Kouyate. One explanation could be that they find the aspect of jelis' praising others for remuneration to be contrary to the sensibilities they were raised with.

Badema. The history of the orchestra goes back to 1964 when a group of Malian students were sent to study at the conservatory in Havana, Cuba. In 1965 they formed an orchestra, Las Maravillas de Mali (Les Merveilles du Mali), with Boncana Maiga as leader and arranger, and were soon giving concerts and appearing on Cuban television. They released an album on the Cuban state record label EGREM in 1967 (Las Maravillas de Mali 1967-disc/1998-disc), which was a remarkable mix of Cuban charanga style with Malian inflections. Maiga spent eight years in Cuba, and on his return to Mali Las Maravillas became a national orchestra. The members were joined by Kasse Mady Diabate, a singer and koni player from the distin-guished Diabate family in Kela, who stayed with them for about twelve years. In the mid-1970s the orchestra was renamed National Badema, and it too recorded an album-length forty-three-minute version of *Sunjata* with Diabate singing and Mama Sissokho playing guitar.[33]

Les Vedettes du Mali

Another major musical genre related to, but distinct from, the orchestral tradition of Mali and Guinea is that of jelimusolu, primarily from Mali, who are accompanied by jelis playing their instruments, including the guitar, without the brass arrangements and drum sets of the urban orchestras. Lucy Durán's (1995b) description of them as superwomen is right on target; they are the *vedettes* (stars) of Malian music. They come from a proud tradition of jelimusolu active before independence, many of whom are documented in Malian first lady Adam Ba Konaré's (1993) pioneering *Dictionnaire des femmes célèbres du Mali.* The first generation to be recorded were Mokon-tafe (Monkontafe) Sako, Fanta Damba, Sira Mory Diabate, and several oth-ers with the Ensemble Instrumental du Mali. The next generation, active in the 1980s and 1990s, is led by Ami Koita, Tata Bambo Kouyate, and Kan-dia Kouyate (plate 46), generally considered three of the greatest vocalists of their time.

Jelimusolu with their ensembles are staples of marriage festivities in Ba-mako (usually taking place on a Sunday), which are major sources of in-come for them and their musicians. In a direct line from the Apollos of the 1960s, these ensembles in the mid-1990s typically blend some or all of the traditional melody instruments of the jeli (koni, bala, and kora) plus an electric guitar and one or more local drums or sometimes an electronic drum machine. The instrumentalists take second billing to the jelimuso, who by

---

33. Written sources on National Badema and Las Maravillas are often contradictory. This para-graph was drawn from Kasse Mady Diabate (1989-disc), National Badema (1983b-disc), Seck and Clerfeuille (1993:95), Prince (1990), and Musiques du Mali (1995a/b-disc).

Plate 46 Kandia Kouyate in performance in Brikama, The Gambia, 1990. Middle: Receiving a gift of cash from a patron. Bottom: Bouba Sacko (electric guitar, in middle), Djelimoussa "Ballake" Sissoko (kora), Burema Kouyate (bala). Photos by the author.

Plate 47 Bouba Sacko and Djesira Kone ensemble. A Sunday Bamako celebration, 1997.
Top: Sambiri Kouyate (dundun), Issa Kone (koni), Bouba Sacko (electric guitar), Dembele
(animateur, standing). Bottom: Djesira Kone (vocalist). Photos by the author.

virtue of her praise singing commands the highest profile, a fact of Malian
urban musical life not lost on the instrumentalists (plates 46 and 47).[34]

34. See guitarist Bouba Sacko's comments in Eyre (1994:98, 100). Mamadou Diawara (1996:
599, 1997:43) considers the radio an important factor in the *"féminisation"* of the profession,
where jelimusolu take top billing. For studies of some of the great Malian jelimusolu, see Durán
(1989a, forthcoming a). The ensemble that accompanied several Malian jelimusolu on a 1990

A related and more intimate genre features a jeli vocalist accompanied by just one or two stringed instruments. Examples include Fanta Damba's (1971-disc, 1975b-disc, 1976-disc) recordings with Mady Tounkara (koni) or Batrou Sekou Kouyate (kora), Fanta Sacko's (1972-disc) recording accompanied by two acoustic guitarists, and Tata Bambo Kouyate's (Kidel 1991-vid) performance accompanied on the guitar by her husband, Modibo Kouyate. Fanta Sacko, from Kankan, Guinea, knew the music of Facelli Kante and Fodeba Keita well (Durán 1989a:35), and her recording has a particularly Malian signature, where the guitarists play the kind of hammering on and pulling off typical of sahelian lute music that distinguishes it from Guinean recordings. The brilliant acoustic guitar playing of Djeli Mady Tounkara and Bouba Sacko (Bajourou 1993-disc) moved this genre to a new level where the guitar playing dominates the singing, owing in part perhaps to the presence of a male, rather than female, vocalist. A unique recording of guitar trios and quartets (without any vocals) led by Djessou Mory Kante (1998-disc) with a rare appearance by Papa Diabate has further moved this genre in new directions.

Modern Mande Music from the Mid-1980s to the Late 1990s

In contrast to the jelimusolu and the jelikelu (male jelis) accompanying them, all of whom kept their base in Mali, where they performed at marriages and naming ceremonies, most orchestra musicians earned their living in nightclubs and hotels and began to search abroad for patronage in the late 1970s. Civil unrest in Mali and increasing economic and political problems in Guinea, capped by Sekou Toure's death in 1984, contributed to a climate where Mande musicians relocated to Abidjan and then Paris. By 1979 Abidjan was home to Salif Keita and Manfila Kante of Les Ambassadeurs, Mory Kante and Djeli Mady Tounkara of the Rail Band, Boncana Maiga of National Badema, Guinean guitarists Sekou "Docteur" and Papa Diabate, and Mory Kante's younger half-brother Djeli Moussa Diawara. Supporting a full-size band proved to be difficult without government support, so with cosmopolitan Abidjan as a stepping stone, a modest exodus to Paris began within a few years. There artists forged solo careers, gained record contracts with multinational labels, and recorded in state-of-the-art studios directed by African producers and European arrangers. The two most prominent artists were Mory Kante, who set the standard for record sales with his dance-floor beat, and Salif Keita, who set the standard for innovation, drama, and wit with his mix of African and European sensibilities. Others arrived as backup musicians and to cater in various ways to the

---

Senegambian tour consisted of two small konis, one large ngoni, one acoustic and one electric guitar, a kora, a bala, and a dundun (plate 46).

mushrooming African community, which included tens of thousands of Malians living together in Montreuil, a suburb of Paris. The 1987 advertising campaign of London-based record producers promoting the slogan "World Music" to help market their releases from Africa and elsewhere (Broughton et al. 1994: introduction; Graham 1992: 13; Sweeney 1992: ix) gave African music an important boost. By the late 1980s, several years after the definitive arrival of Mande musicians, Paris was a thriving place for Mande music, which was undergoing significant international exposure (Durán 1998; Knight 1989, 1991b). The atmosphere would change dramatically by the late 1990s, however. With a still-growing African community in and around Paris, a combination of new laws and xenophobic public sentiment has created an inhospitable atmosphere for many Mande musicians (Durán 1998; see Salif Keita's [1989-disc] *Nous pas bouger* [Don't move us] for warning signs). Some have migrated to New York and other parts of the United States, the next frontier; others talk about returning to Africa.

Mory Kante was the first to go solo, with *Courougnegne/N'Diarabi* in 1982, and *À Paris* in 1984. Installed in Paris by then, he began working with his new manager Otis Mbaye on a series of recordings for the Barclay label. In 1986 Kante released *Ten Cola Nuts,* coproduced by David Sancious (former keyboardist with Bruce Springsteen), and then in 1987 Mory Kante demonstrated the commercial viability of modern Mande music and opened the doors for his compatriots. The album *Akwaba Beach,* selling close to half a million copies, and its 45 rpm single *Yeke Yeke,* selling well over that amount, constituted an unprecedented commercial success for an African artist. Since then he has maintained a high-profile performing career, releasing a CD every few years featuring French, British, and American guest musicians and arrangers.[35]

The year 1987 was also when Salif Keita made his international mark with *Soro,* the first in a series of critically acclaimed recordings on the Mango label. Keita had moved to France about 1984 and pioneered a new mix that included former Ambassadeurs Souleymane "Solo" Doumbia (percussion) and Ousmane Kouyate (guitar), Malian keyboardist and arranger Cheick Tidiane Seck, and French arrangers François Bréant and Jean-Philippe Rykiel. Keita's 1991 release *Amen,* produced by Joe Zawinul (formerly with Weather Report and Miles Davis) and with cameo appearances by Wayne Shorter (saxophone), Carlos Santana (guitar), and former partner Manfila Kante (guitar), was nominated for a Grammy award in the World Music

---

35. For detailed information on Mory Kante see Lee (1988: 35–48) and Durán (1998); for an overview of the commercial success Kante achieved with *Akwaba Beach* (1987-disc) see Afrique Élite (1989). According to Graham's (1992: 10) figures, the *Akwaba Beach* 45 rpm outsold any African release through 1989.

category. Keita, too, continues to maintain a high-profile performing and recording career through the late 1990s.[36]

After the success of the former stars of the Rail Band and Les Ambassadeurs, National Badema vocalist Kasse Mady Diabate and arranger Boncana Maiga teamed up to release *Fode* in 1989. Influential Senegalese executive producer Ibrahima Sylla had them record at Studio Harryson in Paris, which would become established as a major center for the new African-Parisian mix produced by other Syllart artists such as Salif Keita, Djeli Moussa Diawara, Sekouba "Bambino" Diabate, Oumou Dioubate, Baaba Maal, and Ismael Lo.[37] Kasse Mady's work is distinguished by the use of a Malian arranger (Maiga) and the prominent guitar and koni playing of National Badema's Mama Sissokho. Kasse Mady released *Kela* shortly thereafter, reflecting a parallel trend of using traditional instruments combined with a guitar.

This parallel track of jelis moving their tradition intact into the World Music market is one of the major stories of modern African music. Ensembles of jeli instruments with guitar were playing for traditional events in the decades leading up to independence, but it was not until *Fote Mogoban/Yasimika,* by Djeli Moussa Diawara (Jali Musa Jawara), released in 1983 (and reissued in 1990), that these ensembles received significant international attention.[38] Stemming from the 1950s Ballets Africains recordings featuring Diawara's cousin, guitarist Facelli Kante, *Yasimika* bridged a gap between music of the jelis and the larger orchestras. This genre would blossom in Guinea in the 1990s with a plethora of (mostly male) singers, many of whom came up through the ranks of the network of orchestras. Drawing deeply from Mande traditions, these singers were equally at home with ensembles of jeli instruments or with brass-based orchestras. Many of them play guitar, kora, or koni and arrange their own music. Typically, they release cassettes in Guinea, which a year or two later appear on CD for Guinean communities in France and elsewhere. The number of outstanding creative, individualistic artists active in the middle and late 1990s is astounding, including Aboubacar Camara, Ibro Diabate, Sekouba "Bambino" Diabate, Oumou Dioubate, Kerfala Kante, and Baba Djan Kaba among others. It is no coincidence that they have roots in Maninka Upper Guinea, specifically Siguiri and Kankan.

Aboubacar Camara's work, especially *Telephone* (1994-disc), is distinguished by his use of a jeli dundun and jembe along with a kora, bala, and electric guitars. It is dance music, orchestral even, but without brass in-

---

36. A book in progress by Cheick Keita on Salif Keita and his music, certain to break new ground in African artistic criticism, is eagerly awaited.

37. For more on Ibrahima Sylla see Darlington (1994) and Kidel and Marks (1990-vid).

38. For information on Djeli Moussa Diawara see Stapleton (1988).

struments or a drum set; it is modern Mande music firmly in the jeli's tradition. Baba Djan Kaba does not come from a jeli background, but he has clearly absorbed the tradition like Salif Keita. Unlike Keita, Kaba's orchestral mixes include all the jeli instruments on equal footing with guitars, brass, and a drum set. Sekouba "Bambino" Diabate, from a jeli family, apprenticed in Bembeya Jazz in the 1980s and has also achieved a thoroughly integrated mix of tradition and modernity in his music, well appreciated within Guinea and also abroad.[39]

Oumou Dioubate's work presents a new direction for jelimusolu. The daughter of one of Guinea's most celebrated jelimuso singers (Nyamakoron Kante) and bala players (Sidi Mamadi Dioubate), her lyrics occasionally break with tradition, leaving behind the sometimes unabashed praising of living patrons (often businessmen) for more topical matters. Her piece *Lancey* is a case in point, expressing a direct and public critique, unusual for a female in the jeli tradition (table 19). Based on an old custom called Moribajassa, Dioubate tells her personal story of making a pact with Allah in the hopes of bearing a child who could survive infancy.[40]

The impact of arrangers Boncana Maiga and Ibrahima Soumano demands special notice. Having worked with Mande musicians in Mali and Côte d'Ivoire for decades, Maiga is the most prolific of the African arrangers. He retains much of the Malian flavor in his arrangements and is the driving force behind Africando, an ensemble of New York salsa musicians that collaborates with African vocalists. Guinean Ibrahima Soumano is a bala player and first-class guitarist who is behind many of the arrangements of Guinean singers in the 1990s. His strongly guitar-oriented arrangements retain much of the Guinean flavor and continue the direction of shedding foreign (Cuban and European) influences for local ones. Arrangements by both Soumano and Maiga can be heard on Sekouba "Bambino" Diabate (1997-disc).

While vocal music still reigns supreme among Maninka listeners, allinstrumental recordings (with no vocals) of guitar ensembles have begun to proliferate. Guineans Manfila Kante (ex-Ambassadeurs) (1994-disc), Sekou "Bembeya" Diabate (1995-disc), Djessou Mory Kante (1998-disc),

39. Sekouba "Bambino" Diabate's (1997-disc) *Kassa* was ranked fourteenth in a poll of one hundred critics for the "finest folk, roots and world music releases" of 1997 in the British magazine *Folk Roots* (Folk Roots 1998:37).

40. An earlier version of *Lancey* was recorded by Oumou Dioubate (1992?-disc) as *Moribadjassa*. A traditional version of *Moribajassa* from Guinea can be heard on Rouget (1972/1999-disc). Y. Cissé (1994:68), M. Kaba (1995:74), B. Keita (1988:107–8), and Traore (1942) give descriptions of the custom (called *maribayasa*, *moribayasa*, or *maraba yaasa* in local dialects), which involves dancing in public in tattered clothes, along with lyrics. A similar custom, called *dembajasa*, exists among the Senegambian Mandinka (Knight 1995-vid:13–15, Schaffer and Cooper 1987:60–61).

and the legendary Papa Diabate (1999-disc), have all released recordings that brilliantly continue the acoustic guitar tradition pioneered by Facelli Kante. Other all-instrumental recordings including a variety of nonjeli instruments are also beginning to appear. Malian guitarist and ngoni player Zoumana Diarra (1997-disc) performs classics and new pieces with overdubbed acoustic and electric guitars along with a piano, bala, and other instruments. Guinean saxophonist Momo "Wandel" Soumah (1991-disc) leads an ensemble of Maninka and Fulbe instruments playing Guinean pieces as well as John Coltrane's *Afro-Blue.* Cheick M. Smith (1992-disc), pianist with Les Ambassadeurs, has released a solo piano recording combining European classical, jazz, and Guinean bala styles. Like drumming, instrumental music (without vocalists) has not had a significant presence in local cassette markets. And also as with drumming, Western tastes for instrumental music may be the major catalyst for recordings and concert performances in this area.[41]

Repertories of Modern Music

The single most important wellspring in the repertories of Mande acoustic guitarists and the postindependence dance orchestras alike is jeliya, the music of the jelis. Words and titles are usually changed, but the musical accompaniments remain the same, albeit sometimes transformed so much that only the musicians themselves can identify the original. A significant body of pieces not originally related to jeliya is acknowledged to have been composed in the twentieth century, with some of them coming from youth movements. Originating on diverse instruments such as the guitar and accordion, they have entered the standard repertory of jelis and orchestras alike. They are distinguished from the jeli repertory in that they are not praise songs dedicated to a single hero or lineage.[42]

The orchestras of Mali and Guinea have clear preferences, determined by their respective histories, for the kinds of pieces they draw from the traditional jeli repertory. In Mali the epic *Sunjata,* a part of which is the national anthem, has been recorded by the three major male vocal stars of the Bamako bands in major extended renditions: Salif Keita (Rail Band 1972/n.d.-disc); Mory Kante (Rail Band 1975/n.d.-disc); and Kasse Mady Diabate (National Badema 1977-disc). That the first president of Mali was a Keita and the second president a Traore has no doubt contributed to the importance of the piece. Three other jeli pieces are standard in the repertory of Malian acoustic guitarists, once again because of their traditional

41. See chapter 3 for a listing of instrumental recordings of jeli instruments.
42. See chapter 3 for further descriptions of many of the following pieces and appendix C for listings of multiple versions by jelis and orchestras.

Table 19 Lyrics to *Lancey* by Oumou Dioubate

Maninka	English
I ko kenyolu kan ile le ma	Your friends talk about you behind your back
k'i bara bono i la wodiro	saying you were throwing away your money
ka don duniya kani musoro	giving it to a prostitute
ko n te den soro na	because I could not bear a child.
I laliba dolu yere kilali	Some of your closest friends said
k'i bara bono i la wodiro	that you were throwing away your money
ko don duniye kani musoro	giving it to a prostitute
ko ne tena den soro na	because I could not bear a child.
I siginyogon ma dolu yere ko ile nye	Even your neighbors said right in front of you
k'i bara bono i la wodido	that you were throwing away your money
ka don duniya kani musoro	giving it to a prostitute
ko n te den soro na	because I could not bear a child.
Fama Alla ye to mansaya ro bee nya na	Allah (God) is lord of the whole universe
ka nde so filani kono la Alla	who granted me a pregnancy with twins
k'o ke denke fila di	they turned out to be boys
Alla ma ke ti wulu ye mogoya ke n bolo	but Allah did not allow them to survive.

chorus (2x):

Fama Alla, Alla ye mansa le di	Master Allah, Allah is the ruler
Mansa Alla, Alla ye mansa le di	Lord Allah, Allah is the ruler

Maninka	English
Ka n to konodo fili sigi do n nalu	My mothers, I was ashamed
ka n to konoro ban do Alla	Allah, I had lost hope
ka n to konoro kasila	I was devastated
fo nye n dakan de ta	If only I could make a pact
ka n to kelena miri sigido	I remained alone thinking
ka ne to konodo fili do Alla	Allah, I was ashamed
ka n to konoro kasila	I was devastated
fo nye n dakan de ta	If only I could make a pact.

2x:

n ye n dakan ta Alla nye	I made a pact with Allah.
Ahh n ye n dakan ne ta Allaba ye	Ahh, I made a pact with the great Allah.
n koni den do sera ka fo nde ma lu mina n na	If I can give birth to a child who lives to say "Mommy,"
nde be jassa le don Alla ye	on that very day I will do the jassa dance for Allah.

chorus:

Moribajassa Alla tala kusan	Moribajassa, Allah merciful master of the universe,
Lance kan nde le ma ko n na	Lancy called me Mommy.
Moribajassa alu y'a lamina	Moribajassa, all of you answer me,
Lance kan nde le ma ko n na	Lancey called me Mommy.

Break, jembe enters, *Dundunba* bass drum and bass begins.
Between each of the following lines the chorus sings *joso jassa*.

Maninka	English
Musolu le bee ye n deme jassala	Women of the world help me with the jassa dance.
Bee ye n deme moribajassa la	Everyone help me with the Moribajassa dance.
N'an dakan de ta Alaba ye	We made a pact with the great Allah.

Table 19 (*continued*)

Maninka	English
M baden soron ko ndi moribajassa don	My brothers and sisters, dance the Moribajassa.
N tun bara bee nyafo berelalalu nye	I explained everything to the traditional healers,
Berelalalu fo ko n ye saa ke saraka di	They said that I should sacrifice a sheep.
Den be muso min koninu fe	To the women who have children,
Alla ma bee ta balo la	may Allah grant them long lives.
Ani don fana nte muso min koninu fe	And to the women who are childless,
Ala ma bee sora	may Allah grant children to you.
Kebon na si tono ye den de di	The meaning of marriage is in having children.
Ahh, jamana ke tono ye den ye di.	Ahh, the meaning of life is in having children.
Asta Penda le be ye n deme jassa la	Asta Penda help me with the jassa dance
Bee ye n deme moribajassa la	Everyone help me with the Moribajassa
Nyamakoron Saran ne	Nyamakoron Saran
n k'i ye n deme n den namoola	help me bring up my child
Ah, moo te wa don i baden bere ko	People cannot move forward without good parents
Sididu Mahawa le be ye n deme eh Alla	Mahawa of Sididu help me, Allah
Bee ye n deme moribajassa la	Everyone help me with the Moribajassa
Jassa, moribajassa	Jassa, Moribajassa
N Namama le be ye n deme jassa la	N Nanama help me with the jassa dance
Sao le be ye deme jassa la	Sao help me with the jassa dance
Jefadima le be ye n deme jassa la	Jefadima help me with the jassa dance
Bee ye n deme moribajassa la	Everyone help me with the Moribajassa
jassa, moribajassa,	Jassa, Moribajassa
moriba ye la le kamma ko n na	
Jekaba le be ye n deme jassa la	Jekaba help me with the jassa dance
Sonosa le be ye n deme jassa la	Sonosale help me with the jassa dance
Mama Kande le be ye n deme eh Alla	Mama Kande help me, eh Allah
Bee ye n deme moribajassa la	Everyone help me with the Moribajassa
Kabes Fanta le be ye n deme eh Alla	Kabes Fanta help me, eh Allah
Bee ye n dembe moribajassa la	Everyone help me with the Moribajassa

Source: From Oumou Dioubate 1993-disc. Transcribed and translated by Alpha Camara, Kabine Kante, and Eric Charry.

associations: *Tutu Jara,* associated with the Bamana Segu kingdom; *Taara,* dedicated to al Hajj Umar Tal; and *Lamban,* a piece associated with Kouyate jelis. Pieces based on *Jawura,* a dance rhythm from Kita, are widespread throughout Mali.

In Guinea, *Sunjata, Tutu Jara,* and *Lamban* hardly figure in the modern orchestra repertories. One of the most important pieces is *Keme Burema,* which is used to tell the story of Almami Samory Toure, a central figure in late nineteenth-century Guinea. The album-length version by Bembeya Jazz, titled *Regard sur le passé* (1970-disc), is a classic. Like *Jawura* in Mali, the jembe and dundun rhythm known as *Dundunba* can often be heard in arrangements of modern Guinean music.

Most of the twentieth-century pieces that have entered the repertories of jelis and orchestras come from Upper Guinea. *Nanfulen* (*Nanfoulé*), a piece protesting French colonial rule, was probably drawn from the bala.[43] Both *Kaira* (see chapter 3) and *Tubaka* are among the most popular musical accompaniments used in both Mali and Guinea and continue to inspire Mande musicians. Probably originating in Upper Guinea, *Tubaka*, with its extended harmonic scheme, has challenged guitarists for decades, and Manfila Kante's electric guitar solo on the version recorded by Les Ambassadeurs (1981b/1984a-disc) ranks among the finest.

Mamaya, a social event that arose among youth in Kankan sometime in the 1930s, deserves special notice (Kaba and Charry, forthcoming). Although the actual event, which includes slow group dancing in a circle, fell out of favor by the 1960s, it continues to provide musical inspiration for Guinean musicians. The music of Mamaya comes from the bala, and it originated among the bala-playing family of Sidi Dioubate and the virtuoso bala ensemble of his sons Sidi Mamadi, Sidi Karamon, and Sidi Moussa (plate 48). The reverence in which these musicians were, and still are, held and the continued interest in this piece make *Mamaya* an extraordinary phenomenon in the history of Mande music.

The documentation of Mamaya may begin as early as the early 1930s with silent film shot by American anthropologist Laura Boulton (1934-vid). Part of the film shows a Konkoba celebration, named for a large masked figure local to Upper Guinea, with musical accompaniment by an elderly man with three young men all playing balas, probably a father and his sons. Boulton recorded a tape concurrently, and the music is reminiscent of *Mamaya*. Although unidentified, the musicians might be from either a famous jeli family from Siguiri known as the Konkoba Kouyates or the Dioubate creators of *Mamaya* from Kankan.[44] Alberts (1949-disc, 1998-disc) made recordings in Kankan in 1949, and the bala players and singers, identified by Alberts as being recorded at Sidi Djelli (the name of the family patriarch), are certainly the Kankan Dioubate family performing *Mamaya*. Rouget (1954a-disc, 1954b-disc) recorded the Dioubate brothers in Kankan in

43. M. Kaba (1995:221) translates *Nanfulen* as "Come, release me" (*na n fule*), and dates it to World War II when the French imposed draconian rations on their colonies and prohibited trade with neighboring British colonies such as Sierra Leone. Kaba attributes the piece to a "griot merchant" caught in the contraband traffic who was tortured by colonial customs officers.

44. A few musicians have identified the Boulton (1957-disc) bala recording for me as *Mamaya*, but they may be referring to the music in general rather than the specific piece being played. The piece follows the harmonic scheme of *Nanfulen* (and also *Fakoli*), a rare form having three harmonic areas of equal duration rather than the usual two or four. This same form, but with a subtle difference in one of the harmonies, is transcribed as a Konkoba bala piece by Joyeux (1924:208), who would have witnessed it in Kankan, the very heartland of both Konkoba and Mamaya. Perhaps Konkoba was one of the main sources of inspiration for the young generation of the 1930s that created Mamaya. See M. Kaba (1995:187) for a song dedicated to Bandian Sidime, a noted Mamaya personality.

Plate 48 Dioubate Brothers of Kankan, 1952. From Rouget and Schwarz (1969, facing 48).

1952 and published an article on bala tuning based on measurements he made of their three balas (Rouget and Schwarz 1969).[45] Recent recordings associated with *Mamaya* are revealing of change and renewal in Maninka music. Oumou Dioubate (1992?-disc), daughter of Mamaya cocreator Sidi Mamadi Dioubate, pays homage to her grandfather Sidi Dioubate in *Sididou* (Sidi's place) by systematically naming the children and grandchildren, thereby praising Sidi for his progeny. An extended sung genealogy like this in a modern music setting is uncommon (especially when one's own family is concerned), but Sidi Dioubate's heroic status as Mamaya creator merits this special treatment. Oumou's older sister Nakande Diabate (daughter of Sidi Mamadi and Namama) has recently re-

45. Although Boulton's film is cataloged as being shot in Bamako and Bankumana, Mali, several African viewers believe that parts of it may have been shot in Guinea. The Kankan musicians playing on the Alberts (1949-disc) recordings were easily identified during my 1994 trip to Conakry. Ntenen Janka Saran, younger sister of the bala-playing Dioubate brothers and aunt of my host Kabine Kante, made the most moving identification, recalling that she was one of the young girls singing on the tape (see Alberts 1998-disc for a photo of the female chorus; Rouget 1999-disc has a photo of the bala players and their wives). Hearing old recordings is not a common experience for many Africans, and she broke down in tears on hearing her long departed family members, just as her nephew had predicted.

corded a version of *Mamaya* with jembe player Mamady Keita (1995-disc), with lyrics all but identical to the version recorded by Alberts forty-five years earlier. Another version of *Mamaya* by Baba Djan Kaba (1992-disc), titled *Kankan* after the town that gave birth to Mamaya, is extraordinary on several accounts. Baba Djan belongs to the aristocratic ruling Kaba lineage, also known as Maninka Mori, known for its Islamic scholarship and theocratic rule; the family had no previous association with music making. Kaba's singing therefore is not bound by the jeli's aesthetic of praise, much as the female Wasulu singers are free to comment on contemporary matters in Mali. Kaba's musical sensibility is a fascinating mix of the Kankan jeli tradition freed of the Cuban-influenced, brass-dominated orchestras of the immediate postindependence period of the 1960s and 1970s. In Kaba's hands the bala-based Mamaya is transformed into a powerful orchestra of 1990s Guinea featuring one bala, one kora, three electric guitars, a jembe, electric bass, synthesizer, drum machine, and female chorus.

Guitar Tuning

The equal-tempered tuning system of the guitar is accepted as yet one more dialect in the Mandenka heptatonic system. Perhaps the plethora of spoken languages and dialects in West Africa, and the concomitant widespread fluency in several languages, has contributed to a cosmopolitan ear that is willing to accept what elsewhere might be considered a clash of tuning systems.

Electric guitarists in orchestras typically use the standard widespread Western tuning (E-A-D-G-B-E) and do not use a capo. Acoustic guitarists accompanying jeli singers, and some electric guitarists in this context, may play in a few alternative tunings and use a capo.[46]

Alternative tunings (Fr: *accords*) on the acoustic guitar (Fr: *guitare sèche*) do not deviate significantly from the Western equal-tempered system (other than perhaps having perfect fifths), but rather involve tuning one or more of the open strings to pitches other than those in the standard tuning. Although not often verbalized as such, acoustic guitar tunings are each based on one principal chord, which is the tonic chord of the mode in which a piece is played. The most common tunings and chords are F and C, although G, A minor, and B-flat are sometimes used (transcription 27).[47]

46. Limited lessons with Siriman Kouyate, Jemori Kouyate, and Namankoumba Kouyate, study of videos of Modibo Kouyate (Kidel 1991-vid) and Solo and Fadiala Tounkara (Tounkara and Tounkara 1990-per), and brief visits with Djelimady Tounkara, Bouba Sacko, and Manfila "Dabadou" Kante have greatly helped my understanding of acoustic guitar technique and tunings. The tunings and transcriptions that follow supersede those in Charry (1994a); see note 60 below regarding Djeli Mady Tounkara's *Fanta barana*.

47. In his brief demonstration of kora style on the guitar, Modibo Kouyate (in Kidel 1991-vid) plays in B-flat. He tunes his A string to B-flat, and it appears that his B string was already tuned to C. It is unclear if his high E string was tuned to F, but if it was, it would have the effect of

Transcription 27 Guitar: Some common acoustic guitar tunings and sample pieces. *Taara* 1 (in C tuning) is from Jemori Kouyate (1990-per). *Taara* 2 (in F tuning) is from Modibo Kouyate (Kidel 1991-vid). *Jarabi* (in F tuning) and *Cinquante-six* (in G tuning) are from Namankoumba Kouyate (1994-per). Hollow oval and diamond noteheads are alternative choices. In *Taara* 2 they alternate every repeat; in *Cinquante-six* they indicate two versions. The parentheses in *Jarabi* indicate an optional additional note.

In C tuning (transcription 27, *Taara 1*) either no strings are retuned or the bass is tuned down to a low C (e.g., Kasse Mady Diabate in Kidel and Marks 1990-vid). In F tuning (transcription 27, *Taara 2*) the bass E string is tuned up to F and the B string up to C. This may be the most popular tuning among present-day Malian guitarists. F major mode pieces that exploit the natural fourth degree (B-flat), such as *Lamban* and *Taara,* as well as F Lydian mode pieces exploiting the sharp fourth degree (B), such as *Tutu Jara,* may be played in F tuning.[48] In addition to altering the E and B strings, Guinean guitarists playing *Jarabi* (or any of its variants) may tune the A string to C to maintain a strong F-C to G-C (1-5 to 2-5) bass alternation (transcription 27, *Jarabi*). G tuning (transcription 27, *Cinquante-six*) may have been popularized in Guinea in a piece known as *Cinquante-six* (referring to the year 1956) or *Makale,* a variant of *Jarabi* (N. Kouyate 1994-per). Like *Jarabi* F tuning, in *Cinquante-six* a strong G-D to A-D (1-5 to 2-5) bass alternation is made easier by the two altered bass strings.[49]

Acoustic guitarists, who usually accompany singers solo or with a second guitar, prefer open-string tunings, in which just the first three or four frets are used, for several reasons. Because several of the open strings can be tuned to the first, third, or fifth degrees of the tonic chord and mode, they constantly ring out when plucked, yielding a fuller sound without the player's having to keep the fingers pressed on the frets. Bass strings can be tuned down to expand the range of the instrument. Certain solo melodic flourishes can conveniently fall under the first three fingers without having to use the fourth finger. And most important, pieces learned in open position can be easily transposed to suit the voice (or to match other instruments) with the use of a capo without the player's having to adjust the fingering. Usually the range of the vocalist and the particular tuning used determine the exact placement of the capo, which can be the commercial variety or contraptions consisting of a pencil or stick tied onto the neck with string. Open-position playing on the guitar is similar to koni playing, which primarily makes use of the first few finger positions and open strings.

When two acoustic guitarists play together, the accompanying guitar

transposing F tuning up a fourth. The lowest five strings in F tuning (F-A-D-G-C) and the highest five strings in B-flat tuning (B-flat-D-G-C-F) have the same interval structure (1-3-6-2-5). F tuning pieces can then be played by using the next higher strings.

48. For "Malinke and Bambara repertoires," Malian Bassi Kouyate (Zanetti 1993:208) uses F tuning (as described above); for the "Wassolon repertoire or to develop the Bambara repertoire" he additionally tunes his low F up to G. Eyre (1997a:37) reports that Songhai guitarists favor the key of G, sometimes tuning the low E string up to G.

49. It appears that "Soba" Manfila Kante (1961?-disc: vol. 6) is using G tuning on the piece *Makale 2.* Namankoumba Kouyate (1994-per) indicates that the *Jarabi* tuning (F-C-D-G-C-E) was also known as *Soixante* (referring to 1960) or *Jarabi Soixante.* Perhaps G tuning fell out of fashion after independence, to be replaced by *Jarabi* F tuning.

might tune to F capoing low on the neck (e.g., second fret, sounding G), and the lead guitar might then tune to C capoing high on the neck (e.g., seventh fret, sounding G). The opposite might also occur, where the accompanying guitar plays in C capoing low or not using a capo at all and the lead guitar plays in F capoing high (e.g., seventh fret sounding C).[50] These arrangements duplicate the relative tuning of a koni duo where the lead koni is in the higher ardin tuning (see chapter 3).

Mande electric guitarists in orchestras typically do not use capos or alternative tunings, for several reasons. The combination of an independent bass guitar and an accompanying guitar (also called rhythm or second guitar), as well as other brass or keyboard instruments, precludes the necessity for electric guitarists to exploit the bass range of their instruments or to maintain a constant ringing sound. They play polyphonic patterns, but the melodic lines usually lie within a single octave and are played much higher up on the neck, which, owing to the cutaway body design, allows easy access to the higher frets (transcriptions 34, 35, and 36). This style of playing is characteristic of Guinea, perhaps because of the influence of Papa Diabate, who played with a plectrum and used his theory studies to break away from open-position playing and use the whole neck of the instrument. Electric guitarists in jeli ensembles, who generally come out of an acoustic guitar tradition closely associated with jeli instruments, typically use a capo.

Guitar Playing Styles

The style of acoustic guitar playing pioneered by Mande jelis shares characteristics with guitar styles found throughout Africa, chief among them is the technique of plucking with only the thumb and index finger. Electric guitar playing typically, but by no means exclusively, makes use of a plectrum. Guitar styles of neighboring peoples are similar to Mande styles and point to a larger western savanna and sahel style. A brief survey will introduce a more detailed study of Mande guitar playing.

The Larger Sahel-Savanna Culture

In and around the vast regions where Mandekan dialects are spoken, a diverse array of guitarists who are not part of the core Mande style share in a grand sahel-savanna music culture. They are located within an arc that stretches from the Casamance (southern Senegal) up to Dakar, east to Kayes and Timbuktu, and south through Segou and the Wasulu region. This whole area was once part of the Mande empire.[51]

50. Such is the case with *Hakilima* (Bajourou 1993-disc), in which Djelimady Tounkara plays in C with no capo and Bouba Sacko plays in F capoed at the seventh fret.

51. See appendix B and the discography for recording information on the following guitarists.

Senegalese bands featuring Dakar-based Wolof or Serer guitarists rival those of Mali and Guinea with their following in and outside Africa. The Faye brothers—Vieux, Lamin, Habib, and Adama—are to a large extent responsible for the sound of many of Senegal's greatest bands. Although there is a strong Wolof xalam (lute) tradition in Dakar, Senegalese electric guitarists do not bear much of an African melodic imprint. They are primarily influenced by American and European styles of guitar playing, and also by a Wolof rhythm called *Mbalax* that injects a unique spark into their rhythm guitar playing. Dakar, the sub-Saharan capital closest to Europe by sea, has undergone more European influence than most other African cities, and it shows in the playing of Senegal's most active electric guitarists.[52]

Most of the other nonjeli guitarists reflect diverse local traditions, and their guitar technique only occasionally approaches the virtuosity of the great jeli guitar soloists. They most often sing and accompany themselves on the acoustic guitar. Pascal Diatta, for example, is a Balanta acoustic guitarist from Ziguinchor, Senegal, whose playing has been influenced by Balanta xylophone music with its stops and starts and strong use of parallel thirds. Boubacar Traore is a nonjeli Xasonka acoustic guitarist and singer whose music captures local traditions from his native Kayes, in northwestern Mali. Amadou Bagayoko is a blind electric guitarist from Mali who plays solo guitar while singing with his wife Mariam Doumbia. His style and tuning are based on pentatonic Bamana music. The guitar playing of Madou Bah Traore and Boubacar Diallo is based on the six-stringed pentatonic *kamalen ngoni* (youth harp; see chapter 2) from the Wasulu region in southern Mali.[53]

Singer-songwriter-guitarists Baaba Maal and Ali Farka Toure stand apart in their unique reflections of sahelian music culture.[54] Although Baaba Maal has Tukulor origins from Podor in northern Senegal and Ali Farka Toure has Songhai origins from Niafunke, near Timbuktu, their guitar playing shares some basic characteristics with Mande playing and can serve as an introduction to Mande guitar styles. Baaba Maal is primarily known as a

---

52. For a good demonstration of Mbalax-influenced rhythm guitar playing, see the examples played on the acoustic guitar by singer-songwriter-guitarist Ismael Lo (Brice 1990-vid). For more on Mbalax and the modern music scene in Senegal see Panzacchi (1996). Two Senegambian bands in particular have drawn on local Mandinka traditions: Ifang Bondi (formerly Super Eagles) from The Gambia, who were highly influential in their shedding of foreign influences in favor of local culture in the 1970s (Graham 1992:58; Ifang Bondi 1994-disc), and Toure Kounda from the Casamance (see Tenaille 1987).

53. For an overview and musical transcriptions of Malian nonjeli guitarists playing in various pentatonic traditions see Eyre (1997a, 1997b).

54. For background information on Baaba Maal see Cathcart (1988); for Ali Farka Toure see Anderson (1988), Durán (1992b), and Ali Farka Toure (1996-disc).

capo on 2nd fret to G major; bass E string tuned up to F (B string may be tuned up to C)

capo on 7th fret to G major; standard tuning

Transcription 28 Guitar: *Muudo hormo* (Baaba Maal). The main accompanying and lead acoustic guitar parts played by Baaba Maal and Mansour Seck, respectively, and a short lead guitar solo excerpt (beginning at 0′45″). From Baaba Maal (1989-disc).

singer, but he is also a tasteful acoustic guitarist. Though he is not a hereditary musician (griot), he has drawn on several pieces from the jeli's repertory, including *Massani Cisse* (1989-disc: *Lamtooro*) and *Jula Jekere* (1991-disc: *Joulouwo*). He is equally at home fronting all-electric bands supplemented by European studio musicians, as well as singing and playing guitar in all-acoustic contexts, where he is joined by other musicians playing the kora, hoddu (Fulbe lute), and xalam (Wolof lute).

Some fundamental characteristics of western savanna-sahel acoustic guitar playing are illustrated in transcription 28 (*Muudo hormo*) from one of Baaba Maal's (1989-disc) earliest and finest recordings, featuring two guitars and one bala.

1. Both guitars use capos so they can use one of a limited number of open position tunings, which may be transposed up to suit the voice by moving the capo.
2. The lead guitar is played in open-position C tuning/mode and capoed higher on the neck than the accompanying guitar to put it in a higher register.
3. The bass string of the accompanying guitar is tuned to the tonic pitch for added resonance (up a half step from E to F).
4. In both guitar parts the index finger continuously strikes a repeated tone (in this case on the even-numbered beats), and the thumb works independently playing a bass line (in this case descending) with occasional octave doubling or anticipation by the index finger.
5. The lead guitar solo excerpt consists of a koni-like descending melodic flourish, based on a common pattern that makes use of open strings and pulloffs, where one finger pulls off to an open string (A-G, marked by a slur), followed by another finger that lands on the next string (F-sharp); the pattern is then repeated on a lower pitch level (E-D-C).

Transcription 29 Guitar: *Singya* (Ali Farka Toure) and *Primpin* (Salif Keita). 1, 2, 3, and 4 are acoustic guitar accompaniments played by Ali Farka Toure (1988b-disc). *Primpin* is an acoustic guitar accompaniment played by Salif Keita (Austin 1991-vid).

Ali Farka Toure's guitar playing, sometimes reminiscent of the blues guitar recordings he listened to in his youth, is rooted in the pentatonic sound characteristic of the Songhai and Tamashek (Tuareg) music from his native region. Transcription 29 shows several of Toure's (1988b-disc) acoustic guitar accompaniments for *Singya,* a Maninka piece that he attributes to the great jelimuso Sira Mori Diabate from Kela, Mali. Toure's versions bear a marked resemblance to the way Salif Keita, who grew up near Kela, plays his own piece *Primpin* on the acoustic guitar in a revealing video clip (Austin 1991-vid).[55] The similarity of *Primpin* to *Singya* indicates common musical material, if not a common source. Setting up a continuous repeated upper tone (or tones) played by the index finger against a moving bass line played by the thumb is characteristic of much sahel-savanna acoustic gui-

55. Keita's guitar playing is a revelation not only because of his fine technique, which is unusual for someone of noble, nonjeli birth (horon), but also because it provides a window into the process of arranging guitar music for an electric ensemble (compare his electric band version on Les Ambassadeurs 1981b/1983b-disc and on Salif Keita 1989-disc). According to Durán (1995c:45), Salif Keita has credited Rail Band guitarist Djeli Mady Tounkara with teaching him to play the guitar. No doubt Keita also learned during his long association with Manfila Kante.

tar playing. One way of creating rhythmic variation is by shifting the repeated upper tone (G) from the first to the second pulse within each beat (version 3) or by changing the index finger pattern to repeat every two beats (version 4).

Maninka Guitar Styles

The partition of the Mande homeland into a Malian side and a Guinean side has had important ramifications for guitar playing styles in those countries. For government and other patronage, those on the Malian side move north to Bamako, where they encounter lute traditions of the sahel. Those on the Guinean side move southwest to Conakry, where a savanna bala tradition dominates. This has led to distinct Malian and Guinean Maninka guitar styles because guitar versions of pieces from the jeli's repertory tend to bear the playing style of the instrument from which the piece originates. (The guitar is not widespread in The Gambia, where the kora predominates.)

In Guinea there is a special relation between the bala and the guitar. Many guitar players started out on the bala, and many bala players also play the guitar. Some musicians, such as Ibrahima Soumano, Kemo Kouyate, and Keletigui Diabate, have even recorded on both instruments. Such a pervasive and direct relation between an indigenous instrument and the guitar may be unique in Africa.[56]

Transcription 30 (*Keme Burema*) illustrates how Guinean guitarists have literally grafted bala pieces and styles of playing onto the guitar. The thumb takes the part of the bala player's left hand (indicated by square noteheads), and the index finger takes the part of the right hand (oval noteheads). Each staff in transcription 30 shows a basic accompaniment pattern that could be repeated indefinitely or combined with other versions during the course of a performance. These accompaniments provide the backdrop for a singer, or for a lead bala or guitar player. Though the actual notes may differ when

---

56. Among the guitarists who studied the bala are Keletigui Diabate (Prince 1989b:17), Sekou "Bembeya" Diabate (Stapleton and May 1990:110), Sona Diabate (Anderson 1990:27), and Manfila Kante "ex-Ambassadeurs" (Durán 1991:21). Keletigui Diabate reproduces the European equal-tempered tuning system by using two balas, one placed behind the other, so that he can get all twelve tones of the scale (see his performances with Salif Keita's group in Finch 1989-vid, Austin 1991-vid, and Perry 1991-vid and his solo demonstration in Kidel and Marks 1990-vid). The Guinean Demba Camara has recorded on both the guitar and the marimba (Sona Diabate 1983-disc, 1990a/b-disc; M'Mah Sylla 1983-disc). Several members of the Kouyate family of Niagassola, guardians of the old Sosso bala (see chapter 3), including "Salikene" Jemori Kouyate and his uncle Namankoumba Kouyate, are accomplished on both the bala and the guitar. Jemori Kouyate can be seen playing guitar on Sayon Kane Diabate (n.d.-vid). Female vocalists Sona Diabate (noted above) and Mama Diabate are reported to have been the bala section of the Instrumental Ensemble of Faranah (Günter Gretz in Mama Diabate 1995-disc).

Transcription 30 Guitar and bala: *Keme Burema.* Gtr. 1 is the second electric guitar part on *Regard sur le passé, deuxième partie* (Bembeya Jazz 1970/1990-disc). Gtr. 2 is the second electric guitar part from Horoya Band (n.d.-disc). Gtr. 3 is an acoustic guitar version from Jemori Kouyate (1990-per), who comes from Niagassola, Guinea. Bala 1 is an accompanying part from Bala Dounbouya (1989-per). Bala 2 is from Fode Doumbia (1990-per) who comes from Kindia, Guinea. Bala 3 is the second bala part from El Hadj Djeli Sory Kouyate (1992-disc: vol. 2).

comparing versions, they all conform to the harmonic scheme of the piece. Some of the guitar versions are very similar to the bala versions (especially gtr. 1 and bala 1). The continuous eighth-note pulse throughout is characteristic of bala playing and is standard practice for second, or accompanying, guitarists in Guinean orchestras.

Transcription 31 shows how jelis have transferred music from the simbi (Maninka hunter's harp) to the guitar. The simbi version (from transcription 1) would typically be repeated indefinitely in performance, serving as musical accompaniment for narrating and singing. The guitar versions preserve the simbi's melodic line but add ornamentation (sixteenth notes) that is typical of koni playing and atypical of simbi playing (see especially gtr. 2). The absence in simbi music of the kind of melodic flourishes that char-

Transcription 31 Guitar and simbi: *Balakononifin.* Simbi 1 is from Bala Djimba Diakite (1990-per/n.d.-disc; also see transcription 1). Gtr. 1 and 2 are acoustic guitar parts from *Mankan* (based on *Balakononifin*) played by Djeli Mady Tounkara (Bajourou 1993-disc). The gtr. 2 excerpt comes at the 4'03" mark. Gtr. 3 is the accompanying electric guitar part from *Balakononifin* played by the Rail Band (1977-disc). The simbi and guitar parts have been transposed to the key of C to make comparison easier.

acterize Muslim musics (and koni playing) might be taken as one piece of evidence that hunter's harp music reflects a pre-Islamic music culture.

Malian guitarists, particularly those from north of Bamako, are primarily influenced by the koni or other closely related lutes that are played by griots throughout the sahel (see chapter 3). Many Malian guitarists play one or another variety of griot lute, and some, like Mama Sissokho and Sayan Sissokho, have even recorded on both the guitar and a griot lute. Because sahelian peoples came into early and extended contact with Islam, there is a strong Muslim component in griot lute playing that has greatly influenced guitar playing in the sahel and northern savanna. This is apparent in the high degree of melodic ornamentation and the concomitant frequent flurries of activity of the fingers on the neck. The technique of hammering on and pulling off the fingers doing the fretting on the neck is responsible for the very fast melodic lines that one often hears on the griot lutes and the guitar. The practice of playing griot lutes in pairs, with the lead one played in a higher range than the accompanying one, is standard for Mande acoustic guitar duos.[57]

57. Malian guitarists reported to play the koni or ngoni include Djeli Mady Tounkara and Bouba Sacko (Eyre 1994:98; Durán in notes to Bajourou 1993-disc:4), and Bassi Kouyate (Zanetti 1993:206). The influence of griot lute playing technique on the guitar can be heard on the various

In the film *Bamako Beat* (Kidel 1991-vid) guitarist Modibo Kouyate was asked to demonstrate the relation between the guitar and local instruments. Speaking from a Malian jeli's perspective, Kouyate noted the three traditional instruments (ngoni, kora, and bala) and pointed out that the guitar can give the sound of the ngoni and kora. Kouyate's brief virtuosic demonstration of the guitar played in ngoni style (transcription 32), marked by quick grace notes and trills that explode out of the more leisurely unfolding of the piece *Tutu Jara,* brilliantly illustrates his point.[58]

The bala orientation of Guinean music and koni orientation of Malian music may have had at least one notable effect on the modern musics of these two countries. Balas are both melody and percussion instruments in one. They are used for epic narration as well as for dancing. Konis are much more quiet and intimate instruments, and they are not usually used for dancing. Perhaps because of its dance orientation, bala playing features a more regular and consistent attack density than does koni playing (compare the steady eighth-note streams in transcription 30 with the longer note durations in transcriptions 31 and 32). The slow, spacious, and regal quality of Maninka music from Mali, and the faster, busier quality of Maninka music from Guinea may be due in part to these instrumental influences.[59]

---

guitar, koni, hoddu, or xalam introductions on recordings by Baaba Maal (1991-disc), Kasse Mady Diabate (1989-disc, 1990-disc), Bajourou (1993-disc), Ami Koita (1993-disc), and Tata Bambo Kouyate (1985-disc, 1988-disc). To date, the clearest and best-recorded example of an ngoni (koni) duo is Moriba Koita's (1997-disc) extraordinary *Badiourou* (*Tutu Jara*). An example of two guitars taking the roles of two konis is the Malian recording by the singer Fanta Sacko (1972-disc). For examples of a higher lead instrument in xalam or hoddu pairs see Nikiprowetzky (1965-disc: side 1, no. 9, and side 2, nos. 7 and 8), and Baaba Maal (1991-disc), especially the piece *Joulouwo;* for examples in a guitar duo see Bajourou (1993-disc), especially *I Ka Di Nye.* The piece titled *The Five-Year Plan* (Radio Mali 1977-disc) recorded in the early 1960s features a singer accompanied by a guitar and ngoni duo.

58. The movement in transcription 32 from a four-pulse division of the beat in the first cycle to a three-pulse division in the second cycle is another example of the kind of rhythmic inflections often used in Maninka music (see transcription guide, chapter 2, and chapter 4). See transcription 18 for koni versions of *Tutu Jara.*

59. The contrasting acoustic guitar styles between Mali and Guinea can readily be heard by comparing recordings of Djeli Mady Tounkara and Bouba Sacko (Bajourou 1993-disc) from Mali with those of Sekou "Bembeya" Diabate (1995-disc), Sona Diabate (1990a/b-disc, 1996-disc), Manfila Kante (1991-disc, 1994-disc, 1998-disc), or Djessou Mory Kante (1998-disc) from Guinea. As noted in chapter 3, it is common to reinterpret on the guitar (or in a modern orchestra) pieces drawn from local instruments. A non-Mande example is Baaba Maal's (1991-disc) *Mariama* and *Yero Mama,* which strongly resemble two unidentified hoddu (Fulbe lute) pieces recorded by Thiam Sy of Dagana, not far from Podor, where Maal was born (Nikiprowetzky 1965-disc: side 2, nos. 7 and 8, respectively). The simbi piece *Balakononifin* has likewise generated many modern versions (see appendix C). An example of another type of transformation is when an artist reinterprets (and renames) one of his own pieces, such as *Mali Denou* (Les Ambassadeurs 1977a-disc) turning into *Waraya* (Salif Keita 1991-disc).

Transcription 32 Guitar: *Tutu Jara* played by Modibo Kouyate. From Kidel (1991-vid).

Transcription 33 Guitar: *Fanta barana* played by Djeli Mady Tounkara. From Bajourou (1993-disc).

Djeli Mady Tounkara's (Bajourou 1993-disc) accompaniment to *Fanta barana* (transcription 33) is a particularly fine example of one kind of interaction between the thumb and index finger favored by Maninka guitarists. Although just a single exemplar of his accompaniment is shown, he adds subtle variations in performance. The index finger (the upper part) plays a bala-like melodic accompaniment consisting of Cs struck every beat dropping down to pick up other tones (G, A, or B), chosen according to the harmonic scheme. The thumb (lower part) interacts with the index finger by weaving a line around it to create a typically Maninka musical texture.[60]

Cross-rhythm in the context of a modern electric orchestra can be heard in Sekou "Bembeya" Diabate's (Bembeya Jazz 1976/1990-disc) electric guitar solo in the piece *Akukuwe* (transcription 34). Where the transcription starts (about halfway through his solo), Diabate takes up a rhythm that divides twelve-pulse units into three beats of four pulses each. This puts him in a cross-rhythmic relation with the rest of the band, which has been delineating a rhythm of four beats of three pulses each. The electric bass moves into a rhythm that could be interpreted in either of these two ways, or perhaps six beats of two pulses each or two beats of six pulses each. In addition to cross-rhythm, Diabate consistently strikes the high A to create offbeat phrasing. At the end of each cycle (or staff line) he interrupts that rhythm with a descending line that leads back to the first part of the cycle. This mix of cross-rhythm, offbeat phrasing, and accompaniment-pattern playing interrupted by a descending line that fills out the cycle is typical of bala playing and is a signature of Maninka electric guitar playing.

60. Djeli Mady Tounkara may have tuned his B string up to C for *Fanta Barana,* making transcription 33 easier to play. In an earlier transcription (Charry 1994a:39–40) I had not considered the possibility that his whole guitar could be tuned a minor third below concert pitch, but it now appears that this was the case. I had mistakenly transcribed *Fanta barana* in G major, indicating it should be played with a capo on the second fret (sounding A major) with an alternative tuning that could account for bass notes below E. That transcription (as well as the others) should be transposed up a fourth to C, played with no capo and with no alternative tunings other than tuning the whole instrument down a minor third (i.e., C-sharp-F-sharp-B-E-G-sharp-C-sharp), which is the tuning that should be used for transcription 33 if a reader wishes to play along with the recording.

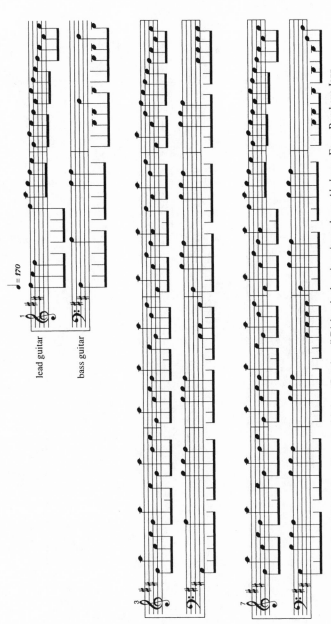

Transcription 34 Guitar: Excerpt of Sekou "Bembeya" Diabate's electric guitar solo on *Akukuwe*. From Bembeya Jazz (1970/1990-disc), beginning at 6'28".

(*continued*)

Transcription 34 (*continued*)

Transcription 35 Guitar: various accompaniments for *Djata*. From Les Ambassadeurs (1981b/ 1984a-disc). Accompanying guitar parts (1.tri, 1.tri.oct, 2, 3, 4) played by Ousmane Kouyate; lead guitar parts (1.dup, 1.tri.oct in duple time, 1.var, 2, 2.var) played by Manfila Kante.

Manfila Kante's (Les Ambassadeurs 1981b/1984a-disc) electric guitar solo on *Djata* is another outstanding example of the Mandenization of the guitar. Transcription 35 shows some of the accompanying guitar parts played by Ousmane Kouyate and lead guitar parts played by Kante. Transcription 36 shows Manfila Kante's complete lead guitar solo. My reduction of the harmonic scheme that guides the accompanying and lead guitar parts is shown as the top staff in transcriptions 35 and 36.[61] Throughout his

61. Although in transcription 35 the accompanying guitar (1.tri) and lead guitar (1.dup) parts differ only on pulses 10, 11, 20, and 21, it is clearer for me to hear a ternary accompanying and binary lead guitar. On the recording the jembe (or perhaps conga) accompaniment pattern joins the accompanying guitar in a ternary pattern (see chapter 4, transcription 19.1), supporting this interpretation. In the lead guitar solo (transcription 36) I hear a ternary beat in the first cycle and binary

harmonic scheme

Transcription 36 Guitar: Manfila Kante's complete electric guitar solo on *Djata*. From Les Ambassadeurs (1981b/1984a-disc). Lettered brackets group together repetitions or variations of the same accompaniment pattern. Accidentals are valid up to the bar line.

solo Kante alternates between static repeated accompaniment-like patterns, usually played for several cycles (marked off by bracketed sections) and more dynamic descending melodic lines. This kind of juxtaposition of two types of playing, as well as the balance and pacing between them, is also

---

beat in the second cycle on the basis of pulses 7 through 12 in each cycle. The rest of the solo has been notated as binary with exceptional spots at the end notated otherwise.

Transcription 36 (*continued*)

typical of bala playing. The pattern he plays in the bracketed section d is particularly interesting. The melodic line groups into four beats of six pulses
each, but the constant upper B-flats accent the offbeats of groups of six
beats of four pulses each. This is a brilliant, subtle combination of cross-
rhythm (four beats in the space of six beats) with constant offbeats, again a

Transcription 36 (*continued*)

typically Maninka texture featuring a kind of polyrhythm that can be created between two instruments, between two fingers or two hands playing the same instrument, or even with a single plectrum.

Conclusion

The merging of Guinean dance orchestras and the jeli's tradition into the Guinean national orchestra created at the dawn of independence inaugurated a new era in Mande music. The electric guitar, primarily played by musicians coming from a jeli background, was the bridge between these two traditions. National guitar styles emerged, owing to the strong influence of the bala in Guinea and the koni in Mali.

The power of Mande guitar playing, and the orchestral music it drives, is due in part to the continued vitality of the koni, bala, and kora. These three instruments, long in a symbiotic relationship with each other, have welcomed the guitar into their vibrant tradition, Africanizing it in the process. But the acceptance of the guitar as a bona fide jeli instrument should be taken with certain reservations. The koni, bala, and kora all have very definite ethnic, regional, and social associations that are a source of pride and identity for the jelis who play them. The guitar lacks these associations. The guitar also represents the modern and the non-African world; and it embodies the Africanizing of that world, a concept suggested by Salif Keita's former manager, Mamadou Konte. "The Europeans colonised us. . . . Now we've come to Europe. Not to colonise but to civilise" (Mamadou Konte in Chris Stapleton 1989:10).

Mande guitarists have arrived at a synthesis in their music that is unique. Throughout Africa the guitar has been the instrument of choice for taking local traditions and moving them into the international arena of popular dance music. In this arena musics based on local traditions vie for international attention in ensembles in which indigenous melody instruments are for the most part absent. It has been the responsibility of guitarists to maintain the local melodic instrumental traditions in these more global and less African contexts of keyboards, horns, bass guitars, and drum sets. Perhaps nowhere else in Africa do guitarists accept and honor that responsibility with as much depth as they do in the Mande world.

6

Music Terminology

This chapter is concerned with the words that Mandinka, Maninka, and Xa-sonka musicians use when they talk about music. The vocabulary used by the kora players Amadu Bansang Jobarteh and his nephew Sidiki Diabate, the two jalis with whom I have had the most extensive discussions about music, will illustrate some general principles of their music as well as ways of talking about specifics in the music. Certain principles of Mande musical organization apply to music played on all the jeli instruments (koni, bala, kora, and guitar), and indeed even to music of griots belonging to neighboring ethnic groups, pointing to a larger musical system common to griots throughout the western African sahel and savanna. However, some modes of musical thought are idiomatic to each of the jeli instruments, and I discuss them separately.

The examination of terminology related to a tonal system is focused on the kora and koni because a specialized vocabulary has grown up around these two instruments. The terms *ben* (Md: *bengo*) and its compound *kumben* (Md: *kumbengo*) receive particularly extensive analysis. Finally, after discussing the bala and pointing out which terms are not used and why, I take up terminology for tonal movement and rhythm.

The following is a summary of the terminology used in this chapter, based on chapters 2 through 5. There are four realms of Mandenka professional music: *donso fòli* or *donso jeliya* (hunter's music); *jeliya* (what the jeli does); *jembe fòli* (*jembe* drumming) or *tangtang kosiro* (*tangtang* drumming); and *musique moderne,* the music of the modern urban electric *orchestres.* In the performance of jelis there are three major components: *kuma* (speech), *dònkili* (song), and *fòli* or *kosiro* (instrument playing in Maninka and Mandinka, respectively). Jeli instrumentalists play pieces (Md: *julo,* pl. *julolu;* string, tune) named after the person they are dedicated to (the piece's *mari,* "owner, patron"), usually a leader (Md: *tiyo;* Mn: *tii;* Bm: *tigi*), warrior (*kelela*), or merchant (*jula*). Kora players divide a *julo* (piece) into two kinds of playing: *kumbengo* (pl. *kumbengolu*), which refers to one or more accompaniment patterns unique to the piece, and *birimintingo,* solo melodic excursions, certain aspects of which may be piece specific while other aspects may be more generically associated with one of four standard named tunings (Md: *bengo, kumbengo*) used on the kora. Different accompaniment patterns for the same piece may be thought of as versions or ways of playing a particular piece (Md: *kosiri nya, siifa, sila,* or *taarango*). The creation or composition of *julolu* (pieces) and *kumbengolu* (accompaniment patterns) is often attributed to a specific jeli, the one who "discovered it" or "caused it to come out" (Md: *bondi, funtindi*), or who "cut it" (Md: *kuntu, teyi*).[1]

Because the kora and koni both have tunable strings that can change for different pieces of music, they have acquired a tonal vocabulary that is more technical than that of the bala, in which the tuning is part of the fabrication process and is fixed. (Beginning a piece on the bala on a higher or lower slat will not effect a theoretical change in tuning system because the instrument is tuned equiheptatonically.) The layout and naming of the strings on the kora, as well as the tuning process, indicate that there is in effect a system tonic. On the koni, however, the idea of a system tonic is less appropriate because there are far fewer strings and the intervalic relationships between them can change from piece to piece, as can the finger under which the tonic for any given piece may lie. Therefore some of the terminology appropriate to one instrument may not be appropriate to another.

Senegambian Mandinka drummers play pieces (*julolu*); Malian and Guinean Maninka drummers play dance rhythms (*dòn,* pl. *dònnu/dònw*). When dancers approach, the tempo increases and gets hot (*kalan*). Jembe drummers play rolls that speed up (*goloba*). The drummer plays a short cadence pattern or break (*tigeli*) to signal the end of one person's dancing. When singing takes over, the tempo slows down and gets cold (*sumaya*).

Designations of pitch height on all the jeli instruments are the opposite of Western terminology: *sanfe* (Md: *santo;* up, high) designates the bass (larger or longer) strings or slats; *duguma* (Md: *duuma;* down, low) designates the treble (smaller or shorter) strings or slats. *Yèlè* (to ascend) designates moving toward the bass end of the instrument, and *jigi* (Md: *jii;* to descend) designates moving toward the treble end.

Julu, Dònkili, Fasa

Although there is a term that connotes a collection or conglomerate of pieces (*fasa*), the largest abstract musical unit of reference commonly used is that of a piece of music (Md: *julo;* Mn: *julu;* Bm: *juru*). Literally meaning "string," referring to a string on an instrument, *julu* can also refer by ex-

1. See technical notes for the sound changes that occur between Bamana, Maninka, and Mandinka. Some dialect alternations in Bamana and Mandinka, respectively, include *dòngili/donkilo, jeli/jalo, juru/julo, kumben/kumbengo,* and *ngoni/kontingo*. When referring to language usage by Mandinka jalis I use Gambian Mandinka spellings, usually signaled by the *-o* suffix.

tension to a tune or a piece of music in the abstract.[2] *Julu* is often used interchangeably with the French word *morceau* (piece), even by those who do not speak French. Similar terminology is used in Soninke, where *nyiime* can refer to a string on a lute and to a piece of music (Mamadou Diawara 1990:87). The person the piece is dedicated to is called its *mari* or *tiyo* (Mn: *tii;* Bm: *tigi;* "owner"), not to be confused with the person who created, composed, or discovered it. If the composer of a piece of music is known, he is often a jeli of the person to whom the piece is dedicated.

I have encountered four Mandinka terms routinely used by both Amadu Bansang Jobarteh and Sidiki Diabate that correspond to the notion of composing or creating a piece (see Gamble 1987b:17, 44, 77, 123):

> *bondi,* to take out or discover
> *funtindi,* to take out
> *kuntu,* to cut
> *teyi,* to break, or to cross, as in crossing a river

Bondi and *funtindi* are formed by adding the causative suffix *-ndi* to *bo* (to come from, to leave) and *funti* (to go out). The Bamana verb *ci,* equivalent to the Mandinka *teyi* (to break), is used by blacksmith-sculptors to describe their creation of a sculpture (Brett-Smith 1994:44–45). All four of these words are used in conjunction with the word *julu: julu bondi, julu funtindi, julu kuntu,* and *julu teyi.* When used with the Mandinka agentive suffix *-laa* (one who does), equivalent to -er in English (e.g., worker), the words roughly correspond to the notion of a composer: *julu bondilaa, julu funtindilaa, julu kuntulaa,* and *julu teyilaa.*[3]

In addition to creating a piece of music from scratch, there is also a concept of deriving one piece from another in a musical parent-child relationship. Usually the term *bo* is used, as in *bot'a kono* (came from it, came from inside of it), but the term *wulu* (to give birth to) is also used. The parent tune is referred to as the mother (Md: *baa;* Bm: *ba*), of the derived tune.[4]

Two verbs are used to refer to the physical act of playing, regardless of what instruments are being used. *Fò* (to say) is used in Bamana/Maninka, and *kosi* (to beat) is used in Senegambian Mandinka. Versions of a piece or ways of playing them can be described in several ways. *Kosiri nya* or *kosi nya* (a way of playing) is perhaps the most literal way of referring to a version of a piece. It comes from *kosi* (to beat, to play music) plus the verbal

2. A late seventeenth-century manuscript (Avezac 1845:220) defined *julu* as *corde,* French for rope or string.

3. Also see Yankuba Saaho in Pfeiffer (1997:255) for a subtle distinction between *bondi* and *teyi:* "The old Jali Keemoo, he had brought this tune about [*bondi*], but he composed [*teyi*] it for Sulatii Ngaling" [Jali Keemo keeba, wo le ye nying juloo bondi, bari a ye a teyi Sulatii Ngaling ne ye].

4. *Ba* is a homonym meaning "mother," "river," or "big" (when used as a suffix).

noun suffix -ri (kosiri, "beating, playing"), and nya (way, means). Sila (road, path, way) also can refer to a version of a piece. Taarango is formed from the verb taa (to go) and the suffix -rango, which is used to "derive the instrument that performs the action described by the verb" (Bird, Hutchison, and Kante 1977:241).[5] A few examples from Gambian Mandinka will help to illustrate the use of this suffix in a musical context (Gamble 1987a:8).

sii (to sit); siirango (seat)
muta (to hold); mutarango (peg, handle)
fita (to sweep); fitarango (broom)
taa (to go); taarango (way of going)

Taarango in a musical context, then, is a way of going or a version.

Sometimes the verb yelema (to change) or its causative form yelemandi (to make something change) is used to describe the process by which one version of an accompaniment changes or develops into another version. Sidiki Diabate, who spent much of his life in francophone West Africa but did not speak French to any appreciable degree, also used the French terms modifier (to modify) and changer (to change) to describe this process.

Whereas julu refers to the instrumental aspect of a piece of music, a vocal melody or song is called dònkili (or dòngili in some Bamana dialects; Md: donkilo), perhaps from dòn (dance) and kili (call). To say "to sing," dònkili must have a verb attached to it, either laa (to lay, to lie down) in Maninka/Mandinka, or da (to create) in Bamana. A singer is called a dònkili laalaa in Maninka/Mandinka or dònkili dala in Bamana.[6]

The song (dònkili) aspect of jeliya, like the speech (kuma) aspect, is a world of its own.[7] Jeliya shines in all its glory in the meeting of the three worlds of instrumental music, song, and speech. Extensive transcriptions and descriptions of singing by Gambian Mandinka jalis have been done by Knight (1973a, 1:246–341, also see vol. 2, 1984b), who divides the vocal aspect of jaliya in The Gambia into donkilo (song) and sataro (recitation or narration). The content of sataro is broken down further into four basic areas: "(1) jamundiro, or surname praise, (2) jali kumolu, or words of the jali, (3) mansalingo, or proverbs, and (4) extemporized jamundiro, related to jamundiro but personalized for a specific audience" (Knight 1984b:30).

Knight (1973a, 1:288–89) has noted that when Gambian jalis sing pieces of Malian origin their vocalizing consists primarily of sataro (reciting)—the kind that would be appropriate in any piece of music. They sing

5. This quotation is in reference to the equivalent Bamana suffix -lan. Gamble (1987a:8) describes the Mandinka -rango simply as "instrument."

6. See Couloubaly (1990:11–14) for an extended discussion of the etymology of dònkili.

7. Zahan (1963:132–41) has detailed terms that describe the use of speech by Bamana jelis; also see Seydou Camara (1996), Hoffman (1990:139–43), and K. Kone (1997).

very little donkilo—melodies that are unique to the pieces. When they sing pieces of local Gambian origin, however, donkilo is heard much more frequently. This difference in emphasis might be attributed to regional differences in the makeup of the songs, or possibly to the Gambian jali's lack of training in songs of Malian origin. Malian female jelis are renowned for their vocal skills, and their singing often includes strong doses of donkilo in addition to the kinds of speech that Gambian jalis call sataro. It is often a mark of prestige for a Gambian jalike (male jali) to have a Malian jalimuso (female jali) for a wife.

A term used in Mali to describe vocal improvisation is *teremeli* (Durán in notes to Bajourou 1993-disc), which could have several relevant meanings including bargaining, carefully examining, calculating or accounting, and cutting (Delafosse 1955:742; Bailleul 1996:398). In Segou, *teremeli* or *tige* (to cut) is used "to describe how they revise and creatively play with the basic structure of a song, drum rhythm, or dance" (Arnoldi 1995:103).

The verb *kasi* (to cry, chirp), usually used to describe the singing of a bird (*kònò*), is sometimes used to describe human singing. In these cases the singers are called *kònò,* and they are typically nonjelis, those who sing by choice rather than hereditary calling, such as hunter's musicians and Wasulu singers (Delafosse 1955:347, Durán 1995a:108–12, 125). Similar terminology exists with reference to Wolof gewels (griots), where the verb *sab,* used to describe the sounds birds make, is applied to the singing of gewels (Panzacchi 1994:192).[8]

Mande professional musicians, no matter what sphere of music they are involved in, have reasonably well defined repertories for which they are responsible. These various repertories, and also significant parts of them, are referred to by their most salient features: *jeliya, donso jeliya* (hunter's music), *tangtang julolu* (Mandinka drum pieces), and so forth. The closest term that could correspond to the idea of a collection of pieces related in some way to each other is probably the word *fasa.* The Malian writer Massa M. Diabate explains *fasa* as follows: "The fasa is dedicated to an ancestor, but is also addressed to all of his descendants. From a linguistic point of view, fasa is the contraction of Fasya (the race of the father)" (Diabate 1970a:43). Delafosse (1955:188) defines *fasa* as "genealogy" or "to recite the genealogy of" (as a verb). Its usage in Gambian Mandinka may have been superseded by the more common Wolof term *cosaan* (custom, tradition) (Gamble 1987b:23). *Fasa* appears in Gamble's (1987b:39) Mandinka dictionary as *fasari* (to explain) and *fasaroo* (tradition, account). The sig-

8. See Arnoldi (1995:92–97) for a discussion of the singing that accompanies the masquerade theater in Segou, done by nonjelis.

nificance of the word *fasa,* still vivid in Mali, may have been lost among Gambian Mandinka.

Fasa is most commonly used in a musical context to refer to the rendition of a collection of stories and praise songs associated with Sunjata. *Sunjata fasa,* therefore, could refer to a lengthy rendition of the Sunjata epic that could include many related pieces of music, such as praise songs for Sunjata himself and for any number of other important figures who are part of the epic.

Narratives or epics of Mande hunters are sometimes called *maana* (Coulibaly 1985:5; Seydou Camara 1996:766–67). Of the several definitions for various spellings of the term given by Delafosse (1955:486–88), the most relevant are *maana,* which may have Arabic roots, with a single definition, the French *signification;* and *mana,* "flame, glimmer, light, clarity (literally and figuratively), clear sense (of a discourse)." Y. Cissé (1994:81) prefers the second set of definitions. Coulibaly (1985:5) referred to a popular etymology relating it to rubber (*manã* in Delafosse 1955:487), which would have to do with the narrative's extending in time in the way that rubber stretches.

The Many Uses of *Ben*

Ben (Md: *bengo;* to meet, agree, harmonize) is one of the most important words used by musicians. An African worldview of agreement, personal contact, and working out differences might be gleaned from the significance and multiple meanings of this word. *Ben,* or compound words using *ben,* can refer to the tuning of an instrument, a tonic, a coming together of combinations of strings in an instrumental accompaniment pattern, and finally, the rhythm of a piece. Close scrutiny of what musicians are referring to when they use the term *ben* and its compound *kumben* (Md: *kumbengo*) is important for understanding the way they theorize about their music making.

Ben essentially means "to meet." Bafoulabé (Bafoulaben), a town in Mali, is an example of its usage as part of a compound word: *ba* (river) *fula* (two) *ben* (meet). The town is at the confluence of two rivers. Delafosse (1955:44–45) has given *ben* an extended treatment so as to include its many compound and derivative uses. One compound used by kora and koni players is formed with the word *kun* (head), which has one of the longest entries in Delafosse's dictionary (1955:417–20) owing to its extensive usage in other compound words. The compound *kumben* also concerns meeting or coming together. Specific usages of *ben* and *kumben* are tied in with specific instruments, so I will examine first the terminology of kora and koni players and then that of bala players. The tonal terminology of kora and koni players is more extensive than that of bala players, perhaps an indication that a concept of a hierarchy of pitches in the single equiheptatonic system of the bala is less relevant than in the various tunings used on the kora and koni.

Kumbengo/Birimintingo: Accompaniment Pattern/Solo

A basic principle of instrumental music played by jelis is that it is divided, in terms of terminology and teaching, into two parts: cyclic melodic or harmonic patterns identifiable as versions of named pieces that may take ornamentation and variation, and relatively long, fast-moving virtuosic melodic lines that may be considered as extended ornamentation or as expansion and variation of some element of the cyclic pattern. Kora and koni players use the Mandinka words *kumbengo* and *birimintingo,* respectively, to refer to these two parts. Some bala players from Guinea and Mali may use *ben* and *bala wora* (or *woron*) to distinguish between these two parts, but it is unclear whether this terminology is widespread.[9]

The various meanings of *kumbengo* have to do with a sense of meeting, agreement, and consonance, as in a tuning, certain kinds of intervals, or combinations of tones that go together. *Birimintingo* literally refers to curving or rolling (Delafosse 1955:59–60; Gamble 1987b:16). Some jelis use the French terms *accompaniment* for kumbengo and *solo* for birimintingo to describe these two main parts of instrumental performance, reflecting the musical function of the two parts rather than the literal meaning of kumbengo or birimintingo.

Kumbengo translates into accompaniment because whenever someone is singing or reciting, the instrumentalist plays a cyclic pattern, a kumbengo, over and over again, usually varying or ornamenting it, so as to support the vocal aspect but not draw attention away from it. The kumbengo accompanies the voice. Birimintingo translates into solo because it consists of relatively long melodic runs that are played when the voice is resting or is a featured part of instrumental performance without voice. Jelis sometimes use a third word, the French *variation,* to signify either additions to an accompaniment or an alternative, often elaborate, accompaniment.

Evidence for a larger western sahel-savanna music system is found when searching for equivalents to the kumbengo-birimintingo opposition among

---

9. My teacher Bala Dounbouya gave me the term *wora* (or perhaps a dialect variant of *wara* or *woron*) as a response to my questioning him on a bala equivalent in his language (Guinean Maninka) to the Senegambian Mandinka kora term *birimintingo.* Definitions of *wara,* "to come down in torrents" (Bailleul 1996:417) or *woron,* "tube, ring, to flow or glide" (Delafosse 1955:818–19) are close, but not identical, to the meaning of *birimintingo.*

neighboring peoples. Although Wolof griots, northern neighbors of the Mandinka, use a pair of terms that are different, *fodet* and *tukull,* the contrasted pair of musical meanings is remarkably similar to that of the Mandinka pair.

> The Wolof divide a piece of xalam [lute] music into two parts, the *fodet* and *tukull.* The former term carries the implication both of a tune and a tuning. It is apparently a Fulbé term, carrying the meaning of "pulling." Tukull is an onomatopoeic word, used to describe the bleating of a camel.
>
> The fodet is a basic melodic and rhythmic pattern, of a given length, played repeatedly in accompaniment to a specific song and to the story associated with that song. Normally the melody of the fodet is closely related to the main melody of the song. The tukull is an instrumental improvisatory interlude interspersed between several statements of the fodet. (Coolen 1983:489)

This similarity in terminology is not surprising. "Most Wolof *xalamkats* [lute players] credit the Khassonke of Mali and Eastern Senegal with being the source of their expertise on the *xalam.* . . . the majority of tunes played by the Wolof are borrowed from other groups, including the Fula and Mandinka" (Coolen 1982:74).

The word *fodet* may shed light on the meaning of *kumbengo.* In addition to "pulling," as Coolen has noted above, it has an extended meaning in Fulbe.

> *foododirde:* to pull together things from different directions towards the same object. To mutually hold together. (Gaden 1914:70)
>
> *foodude:* to pull; . . . to attract to oneself. (Osborn, Dwyer, and Donohoe 1993:96)

This sense of pulling or holding together conforms well with the sense of meeting associated with the Mandinka word *kumbengo.*

Kumbengo on the Kora and Koni

Kumbengo as used by kora players has acquired several related musical meanings: [10]

1. a tonic, the name of a string that functions as a tonic, the octaves of a tonic and possibly its fifths, and by extension the interval of an octave or fifth
2. a tuning in general (usually qualified by the name of a specific tuning)
3. rhythm, or the particular rhythmic characteristics of any accompaniment pattern
4. any accompaniment pattern in general

10. For a discussion of *kumbengo* as a tuning and as an accompaniment pattern see Knight (1973a, 1:69; 1984b:14) and Durán (1981a:186–87).

Kumbengo: Tonic, a Tonic String, and Its Octaves and Fifths

Both Amadu Bansang Jobarteh and Sidiki Diabate refer to the string that is one octave above the first right-hand string (called *timbango*) as *kumbengo*. When Jobarteh refers to that string (F′) as *kumbengo,* however, he also plays the other F strings on the kora and then the C strings.[11]

> This [1], this is the kumbengo [2]. If I say to you, strike the kumbengo [3] . . . that is the kumbengo [4]. Don't you see, all of the strings are the same [5]. (Jobarteh 1990-per: A389–91)[12]

Jobarteh is apparently using *kumbengo* to refer to several closely related items in this context: a particular string; octaves of this string and fifths of the string and its octaves; and, in a more abstract sense, a tonic. Because the other F strings have names (see *timbamba, timbango,* and *lelengo* in fig. 5), the term *kumbengo* seems to have become attached to the F without a name, although I have heard him on other occasions referring to the other F strings as kumbengo. Jobarteh's statement that "all of the strings are the same" must mean that they have the same role, that of a tonic.

Jobarteh's explanation of the string (F″) he calls *lelengo* (one octave above the string labeled *kumbengo* in figure 5) clearly articulates that he is thinking about the function of the strings that are notated here as F; they function as tonics.

ABJ: Here is the *lelengo* [6]. . . .

EC: Does it have a meaning?

ABJ: Lelengo . . . it is the lower kumbengo.[13] This and this [7],[14] this one's sound is little, but it and all of these others have the same role [*loo dulaa*] [8]. Do you understand? (Jobarteh 1990-per: A397–99)[15]

Lelengo (or *lewulewu* as Sidiki Diabate pronounced it) may refer to the highest several strings on the kora (as Knight 1973a, 1:171 has observed),

11. Bracketed numbers (e.g., [1]) in the following quotations refer to the appropriate music examples in figure 11, which indicate the strings that were struck at that particular moment. See figure 5 for the layout and names of the kora strings.

12. "Nying [1] wo lemu kumbengo ti [2]. Ni n ko i ye kumbengo maa bang [3] . . . wo lemu kumbengo ti [4]. I m'a ye julu bee mu kiling ti [5]."

13. The African practice of referring to pitch height opposite from the way it is referred to in Western music is taken up below.

14. Hollow diamond-shaped noteheads in figure 11 indicate that he accidentally struck that string in reaching for another one, a common occurrence when demonstrating something on the kora out of the context of a piece. It is clear, by looking at the diagram of the string layout on the kora as well as the rest of the transcription, that he was reaching for the F′.

15. ABJ: "Lelengo fele [6]. . . . " EC: "A koto mu mune ti?" ABJ: "Lelengo . . . nying kumbengo duumalanko mu nying ne ti. Nying nin nying [7] nying kango be dooyaring bari a nin nying bee be loo dulaa kiling ne [8]. I y'a *understand*?"

Figure 11 Kora: Examples of kumbengo as a tonic string.

but Jobarteh qualifies the other lelengo strings by position, *mara* (left) or *duuma* (lower). In the two previous examples Jobarteh first strikes the string he is referring to (labeled [1] and [6] in the music notation) and then strikes the other strings in the category kumbengo.

Jobarteh's key phrase is *loo* (to stand) *dulaa* (place), a place to stand, meaning role or function. The role of the kumbengo is that of a tonic, or most important pitch.[16] "Yes, this is the kumbengo. No playing can be done without it" (Jobarteh 1990-per: A393).[17] Durán has also noted that accord-

16. Use of the Wolof word *danné* (resting point) to signify a fundamental pitch in Wolof xalam music (see reference to Coolen 1979:152 below) may suggest that *loo dulaa* (standing place) could be translated as tonic rather than role, but Jobarteh's usage as well as its more general usage points to the latter translation.

17. "Haa, nying ne mu kumbengo ti. Kosiro wo kosiro, a te ke noo la n'i m'a bendi."

ing to Amadu Bansang Jobarteh, the string marked kumbengo in figure 5 "is specifically called kumbengo since it must be present in every statement of the theme" (Durán 1981a:187).

Two further usages of the term *kumbengo* by Amadu Bansang Jobarteh support its translation as "tonic." First of all, in the tuning known as Tomora mesengo Jobarteh calls the A strings and their fifths (E) kumbengo.

EC: I think that in Tomora mesengo this string [9], it is very important.
ABJ: Yes, its kumbengo is here. This is its kumbengo. Tomora mesengo, this is its kumbengo [10]. (Jobarteh 1990-per:A197)[18]

Many pieces played in Tomora mesengo tuning revolve around the A and E strings just as pieces in Tomoraba tuning revolve around the F and C strings.

Finally, when adjusting his kora so that he could play with a bala, Jobarteh listened to the tones of various bala slats to see which one was the "kora's kumbengo," the slat that matched his string called *timbango*. When the slat that was closest to his timbango string was found, he said "That is the kora's kumbengo," retuned his timbango string to match it exactly, and then retuned the rest of the kora to the timbango string (Jobarteh 1992-per).

The relation of the term *kumbengo* to the fifth degree above the tonic is puzzling because when Jobarteh refers to kumbengo as a string or tonic he invariably plays the fifths along with the octaves. When he says "all of the strings are the same" I interpret that to mean that all the F strings are tonics and that C strings have some kind of close relation to the F strings. This relation might be considered as the most consonant interval with the tonic or perhaps a subsidiary tonic, but the best label is provided by kora players themselves. The name of the C string above the F that gets the most use (the one that is called *timbango*), is *timbango jinkandango,* "the one that answers the timbango." And it does. Most of the pieces that are believed to have originated on the kora feature a prominent F-C alternation played by the right thumb. Furthermore, the timbango (F) is played more often than the timbango jinkandango (C), thereby establishing some kind of tonal hierarchy of F over C.[19]

Jobarteh also articulated the relation between the everyday literal meaning of *kumbengo* and its musical meanings, but I find translating what he said into English to be especially problematic.

18. EC: "Nga miira ko nying Tomora mesengo to nying julo [9], a nafa warata baake." ABJ: "Haa. A kumbengo be jan ne. Nying ne mu ate kumbengo ti. Tomora mesengo, a kumbengo mu nying ne ti [10]."

19. See the kora transcriptions in chapter 3 for several pieces that show the predominance of the F over the C in the right thumb part.

ABJ: If I say to you strike the kumbengo you should do this [11].[20]
EC: But *kumbengo,* its meaning is . . .
ABJ: The leader of all of the strings comes together there. Yes, kumbengo, that is kumbengo. The leader of all of the strings is met there. No matter what song you are playing (*kosi*), it cannot be played (*fo*) without it. (Jobarteh 1990-per: A401)[21]

A literal translation of the key phrase "julolu bee kungo benta (or nata beng) jee le" would yield: "strings all head is met (or happened to meet) there emphatic marker" = "the head of all of the strings is met there."[22] Applying terminology that developed around one music system to another system can be a dangerous road to travel, but tonic seems to match well with *kumbengo* in this particular context.

One other point about Jobarteh's terminology above is the usage of both *kosi* (to beat, play) and *fo* (to say, play) to mean the same thing in the same sentence. As noted above, *kosi* and *fo* are used by Mandinka and Maninka, respectively, as verbs for playing an instrument. The word *fo* is unusual in Jobarteh's speech in this context, but perhaps Mandinka may be more apt to use it in the passive sense used here rather than the active sense in which *kosi* is used.

As far as my inquiries have led, koni players do not use the term *kumbengo* either to refer to a tonic or to name a string. The reason seems to be tied in with the nature of their instrument, a lute on which each individual string can sound any number of pitches according to the placement of the fingers stopping it. The particular pitch that can be called a tonic may be found on different strings and under different fingers according to the particular tuning the player is using. Though I did not come across any term used by koni players that would justify defining *kumbengo* as tonic, Coolen, who studied primarily with Wolof xalam (lute) players, did find one.

> Ardiné tuning, like all the other tunings, recognizes one pitch as its *danné* (what the Manding call the *jindi*), which translates from the Wolof as 'resting point,' or the 'sitting down point.' This pitch serves as a kind of fundamental for ardiné tuning (although there are a few exceptions), and it plays an important harmonic and melodic function in the music. (Coolen 1979: 152)

Kumbengo as tonic, and the concept of a system tonic, provide fruitful points of comparison in the tonal systems of the kora, koni, and bala. On the

20. In this case the hollow diamond-shaped noteheads indicate that he reached for the C and accidentally struck the E.
21. ABJ: "Ni n ko i ye kumbengo maa bang, i s'a ke teng [11]." EC: "Bari kumbengo fanang wo koto mu. . . . " ABJ: "Wo le mu julolu bee kungo benta jee le. Haa, kumbengo, wo le mu kumbengo le ti. Julolu bee kungo nata beng jee le. Julo wo julo n'i b'a kosi la a te fo noo la nying kooma."
22. *Benta* comes from *beng* (meet, agree) plus *ta* (past tense marker). *Nata* comes from *na* (come) plus *ta* (past tense marker).

kora the pitches of the strings are not changed during a piece. The layout of the instrument, with a gapped fifth in the bass, the bottom pitch of which and its octaves are called kumbengo, implies that the F strings are system-wide tonics. Some pieces can have tonics other than F (see Knight 1991a), but they are most often from Mali or Guinea, not part of the core Senegambian kora repertory. The lack of a system tonic on the koni may be due to its having fewer strings and more ways of tuning them than on the kora, so that they have different functions in different pieces. Different strings may act as tonics in different pieces, similar to the guitar, and unlike the north Indian sitar, for instance, which has drone strings that always reinforce the system tonic. Each piece or group of pieces on the koni has its own tonic (or strong tonal center) that is not viewed in relation to some kind of system tonic. Because any piece can be transposed anywhere on the bala, the concept of a system tonic is inappropriate, and there are even some pieces where the concept of a tonic within a single piece may also be inappropriate. In *Teninke Madi,* for example, who is to say if an alternation between the harmonic areas defined by the first, third, and fifth slats and the second, fourth, and sixth slats should be considered as 1-3-5 to 2-4-6 or as 7-2-4 to 1-3-5? There is no verbal evidence to guide the analyst. The best kind of evidence comes when bala pieces are played on one of the other jeli instruments, thereby causing them to fit into a system where the concept of a tonic is more appropriate.

Kumbengo: A Tuning

Perhaps the most common usage of *kumbengo* among kora and koni players is as an abstract reference to any tuning used on the instrument. In this sense *kumbengo* translates directly as the noun "tuning," and it is often preceded by a specific name of a tuning.

Koni tunings are named after important pieces that are traditionally played in that tuning, so *Tutu Jara kumben* refers to the tuning of the koni strings that is used to play the piece *Tutu Jara.*[23] The names of the four tunings used on the kora do not come from pieces, except perhaps Sauta. It is unclear whether the piece *Sauta* was named after the tuning Sauta or vice versa. The distinction between *Sauta* the piece (julo) and Sauta the tuning (kumbengo), though, is clear with kora players who know both the tuning and the piece. Although *kumbengo* may also refer to an accompaniment pattern in the abstract, there is little question that Amadu Bansang Jobarteh is using it as "tuning" in the following example.

23. I am using the dialect of my Xasonka koni teacher, Moussa Kouyate, who used *kumben* rather than *kumbengo.*

This is the Sauta tuning [*kumbengo*]. I just played the piece [*julo*] *Sauta*. This here is its tuning [*kumbengo*]. You can play *Tutu* [*Jara*] in it, you can play *Allah l'a ke* in it. No matter what the piece, if it pleases you, you can play it there [in the Sauta tuning]. (Jobarteh 1990-per: A51)[24]

There is also little question as to how Sidiki Diabate used *kumbengo* in the context of discussing the piece and tuning called *Sauta*. Sauta is the only kora tuning I know where two varieties of a single pitch class, the natural and sharp fourth degree, may be present (but in different octaves). Sidiki Diabate indicates that the sharp fourth degree is the norm for Sauta, but the piece *Kaira* sounds better if one of the strings is lowered to become a natural fourth degree.

EC: You said that Sauta is also a song [*donkilo*], a piece [*julo*]. Is it the name of a piece [*julo*]?

SD: Sauta is a tuning [*kumbengo*].

EC: A tuning [*kumbengo*]?

SD: Yes, it is a tuning [*kumbengo*], many pieces [*julu*] can be played in it. *Allah l'a ke* is good in it. *Kaira* also, *Kaira* is good in it, but there is a place that is not played in it. If you want to play *Kaira* in Sauta you have to lower this string. (S. Diabate 1990-per: 41)[25]

When Diabate explained the tuning he calls Tomora (called Tomora mesengo, "little Tomora," by many jalis) there is little question once again about the usage of *kumbengo* as a tuning.

Tomora [either the name of a region in Mali or the tuning that takes its name from that region], it is the tuning [*kumbengo*] of their kontingo players. Now, if you want to play with their kontingo players so that you are all in tune [*beng*], you should tune [*beng*] your kora to the Tomora tuning [*kumbengo*]. (S. Diabate 1990-per: 355–57)[26]

Kumbengo: Rhythm

According to Sidiki Diabate one definition of *kumbengo* is "rhythm": "*Kumbengo* . . . yes, you all say *rythme,* the French say, white people say *rythme,* we say *kumbengo*" (S. Diabate 1990-per: 145).[27] He is not alone in linking

24. "Sauta kumbengo, wo lemu nying ti teng. Sauta julo nga wo le kosi teng. A kumbengo wo lemu nying ti teng. Bitung i si Tutu kosi jee, i si Allah l'a ke kosi jee. Julo wo julo ning a diyat'i ye i s'a kosi jee."

25. EC: "I y'a fo ko sauta fanang mu donkilo le ti julo le ti. Julo le too mu. . . . " SD: "Sauta kumbengo lem." EC: "Kumbengo?" SD: "Haa, kumbengo lemu, julu jamaa si kos'a la. Tutu Jara nyol bee ka diya ate le la, Allah l'a ke bee ka diya ate le la. Kaira fanang, Kaira ka diy'a la bari bari a dula dool be jee wol buka fo noo Sauta la. N'i lafita Kaira fo la Sauta to fo nying i jigi."

26. "Wo Tomora, i la konting jalolu, i la konting jalolu la kumbengo. Ayiwa, n'i lafita i n'i la konting jalolu ye kosiro ke fo al ye beng i ka kora beng Tomora kumbengo le la."

27. "Kumbengo. . . . Haa, altolu ko *rythme,* faransi ko, tubabol ko *rythme,* ntolu ko kumbengo."

rhythm with *kumbengo*. As will be seen below, my bala teacher Fode Doumbia translated the French word *cadence* (beat) into Maninka with the word *ben*. When pressed further he used the French word *rythme* to further clarify the meaning of *ben*. Doumbia speaks French well and understands the usages of both *cadence* and *rythme* in the French language.

Sidiki Diabate made a distinction between words that jalis use and the rhythm they use to convey those words, likening rhythm to the sound of the jali's voice. Regardless of dialect, the jali's voice should fit with the kumbengo, which I interpret to mean the rhythm of the musical accompaniment. The key terms that he used were *nengo* (tongue, dialect), *kango* (neck, voice, sound), and *kuma* (speech, words). His point was that even though the dialect and words (or what is said) may differ from jali to jali, their vocal performance, be it speech or song, should fit with the rhythm of the musical accompaniment. Once again, he used the term "rhythm."

> [Regarding different Mandekan dialects in which jalis speak and sing] Whoever says *n ko*,[28] they may speak [*kuma*] in the dialect of their own people, but when they are speaking they should speak in the rhythm [*rythme*] of the jali, yes. That is, whatever their tongue [*nengo*] says [i.e., whatever their dialect may be], it may be different, their dialects may be different, but the sound [*kango*], the *rythme,* they are all the same. . . . So, the speech [*kuma*] may not be the same, but the sound [*kango*], the *rythme,* it should all fit with the *kumbengo* [the rhythm of the musical accompaniment]. (S. Diabate 1990-per: 139–41)[29]

Diabate also used the terms *kango* (sound, language) and *diyamu* (speak) to describe how the different tuning systems reflect the language of their lands of origin.

> An instrument plays the language [*kango*] of the land to which it belongs. The way the people from that land speak [*diyamu*], the instruments also play [*fo*] like that. (S. Diabate 1990-per: 39)[30]

Although Knight did not explicitly link kumbengo directly with rhythm, his elaboration of kumbengo as accompaniment pattern applies just as well to kumbengo as rhythm. "When a singer is performing, there is only one thing for an instrumentalist to do, and that is to hold the kumbengo (*kum-*

---

28. *N ko* literally means "I say," an opening phrase often used by Mandekan speakers, regardless of their particular dialect, that is considered to be an important symbol of peoples claiming origins in the Mande heartland.

29. "Moo moo n'a kara fo n ko, moo bee kara kuma i la moo le ma, bari n'i be kuma l'a ma i si kum'a ma jaliya kango rythme la, haa. Ça fait, i nengo be mun fo la, wo koni kilingu te, nengo ka min fo kilingu te, mais kango, *rythme* wo bee kiling. . . . Bitung kuma kiling te bari bitung kango, *rythme,* a bee si beng kumbengo ma."

30. "Fo kosiri fengo banko meng fengo mu wol le, a ka wo kango le fo. Banko mool la diyamu nya kosiri fengo fanang kara wo le fo."

bengo muta)" (Knight 1973a, 1:69). One need only substitute "rhythm" for *kumbengo* in the quotation above to see how effective it is as a translation.

Kumbengo: Accompaniment Pattern

Kumbengo as accompaniment pattern is probably the most widespread meaning that has been used by Western scholars. It is often contrasted, by both scholars and jalis, with birimintingo, a word that describes a highly ornamented single line melodic kind of playing. A few quotations from Sidiki Diabate and Amadu Bansang Jobarteh will illustrate kumbengo as accompaniment pattern in the abstract. There may be many accompaniment patterns for any one piece, and although they are usually not named, they are sometimes referred to by the names of those who created them.

> You know, there are many kumbengos in *Allah l'a ke.* This is its first one. Yes, Amadu Bansang [created] that one. This is another kumbengo, they are all *Allah l'a ke.* I play it like this. This also is mine. (S. Diabate 1990-per:33)[31]

> Yes, it is the alphabet [of the kora]. If someone wants to learn the kora, if you want to learn the kora, if someone wants to teach you the kora, he should play *Kelefaba* for you. It is the alphabet because it has the kumbengo of every piece in it. (S. Diabate 1990-per:445)[32]

The piece called *Lamban* (Md: *Lambango*) is the one of the few I encountered in which Jobarteh had names for some of the different accompaniments.

ABJ: This is *balanding* [little bala] kumbengo. It came from the bala, all of this came from the bala. . . . Balanding kumbengo, yes, you know if you want to play with a bala this is very good. . . .

EC: First, first you started with . . .

ABJ: *Lambang silaba* [main way]. I left that one and I went to *Nganga kumbengo.* I left that and I came to this balanding kumbengo. (Jobarteh 1990-per:A353–56)[33]

The qualification *silaba* (main road, main way) refers to a standard accompaniment pattern. For example, Jobarteh has his own ways of playing the piece *Jula faso* and also a standard way, which he calls *silaba.* Once again,

31. "I y'a lon *Allah l'a ke* ate kumbeng jama le b'a la. Folo folo nying nemu a folo ti. Bon, Amadu Bansang ate le ye wo [dadaa?]. Nying nemu kumbengo doo ti, a bee mu *Allah l'a ke* la ti. Nte le y'a fo teng. Nying fanang mu nte ta le ti."

32. "Oui, *alphabet* don. Ni moo min lafita niking na, n'ite lafita kora niking na, ni kari lafita i karandi la kora la, a si *Kelefaba* fo i ye. *Alphabet* bawo julo bee la kumbengo b'a kono."

33. ABJ: "Balanding kumbengo, wo lem nying ti. . . . A bota balo le bala, nying bee bota balo le bala. . . . Balanding kumbengo, yoo, bitung i y'a lon, n'i lafita bitung i ning balo ye taa kataba[?] a ye diya beteke. . . . " EC: "Folo, i y'a folo. . . . " ABJ: "*Lambang* silaba la. M bota wo to n taata nganga kumbengo to. M bota wo to n nata nying balanding kumbengo to."

the context precluded any ambiguity as to which meaning of *kumbengo* was intended.

ABJ: The person who taught me this version [*siifa*] of *Jula faso,* he is no longer living . . . there are not many people who can play it this way.

EC: The way that *Jula faso* is usually played . . .

ABJ: Yes. [He then played a standard version.]

EC: All jalis know this one?

ABJ: Yes, yes.

EC: Is there another kumbengo?

ABJ: No, not now . . . *Jula faso?* . . . except for this one . . . [He then played his own version where the treble strings were emphasized and the bass strings dropped out.]

EC: This one is yours.

ABJ: Yes, it is mine. I put it there. But the main way [*silaba*] of playing it is this. [He plays the standard version that he had played before.] (Jobarteh 1990-per: A517)[34]

The last quotation above illustrates the usage of *siifa* (kind, type) to refer to a version of a piece. Three other ways that I have heard Amadu Bansang Jobarteh or Sidiki Diabate refer to accompaniment patterns were discussed above: *kosiri nya* (way of playing), *sila* (road, path, way), and *taarango* (means or way of going).

Ben on the Bala

I have not heard bala players using the term *kumbengo* (or *kumben*), but some recognize it as a term that kora and koni players use. Gambian bala players may use the term *kumbengo,* but I suspect that they have acquired it from kora players. Bala players use the term *ben,* however, with reference to tuning their instrument, and also with reference to rhythm.[35]

Ben: To Tune

Ben is used by bala players primarily as a verb for tuning their instrument: *k'a kan ben* (to make its sound meet). Because there is only one tuning used on the Maninka bala, there is no need for a term referring to a tuning in the

34. ABJ: "Nying *Jula faso* siifa ming ye nte karandi a la, a faata . . . ning Jamba[?] si sii i nahi[?] *Jula faso* kosi, bari ming be taa nying taarango la, a man siya." EC: "*Jula faso* be kosi jamaa jamaa, a kosiri nya, wo mu. . . . " ABJ: "Yoo, haa. [He plays the standard version.] EC: "Jalol bee ye nying lon?" ABJ: "Haa, haa." EC: "Kumbengo doo bi jee?" ABJ: "Hani silang, *Jula Faso,* fo nying de." [He plays his own high version.] EC: "Wo mu i ta le ti." ABJ: "Haa, n ta lem. Nte le ye wo bula jee, haa. Bar'a silaba wo lemu." [He plays the standard version.] Malian donso ngoni players use the term *siraba* (main way) to refer to a very important melodic pattern that can be used in many pieces (Cullen Strawn, personal communication 1999; see chapter 2).

35. According to Laura Arntson Harris (1992:140), Sankaran Maninka bala players in Sierra Leone use the term *balabolo* to designate a bala pattern and also "the collection of musical, verbal, and metaphoric elements that go into the creation and perception of a praise-song." *Bolo* (hand) in Sierra Leone and *julu* in the Senegambia region would be roughly comparable.

abstract. The tuning is done as part of the fabrication process, not every time the instrument is picked up, as it is on the kora and koni. Also, because any piece can be played at any pitch level on the bala—perhaps the strongest confirmation of its equidistant tuning—there is no question of a system tonic as there is on the kora, of a tonic for different tunings as there is on the koni, or even of a tonic in some pieces. One of the problems with notating bala music in cipher (number) notation arises because many pieces are ambiguous regarding which slat can be considered pitch number one. This is a familiar kind of built-in ambiguity that is often found in African musics: sometimes rhythms can, even should, be felt in both a binary and ternary rhythm at the same moment.

Ben: Rhythm

As I noted above, my bala teacher Fode Doumbia, who spoke French well, used the word *ben,* and its causative form *laben,* as a Maninka translation of the French word *cadence* (beat). Once he arrived at the word *ben* he retranslated it, or rather agreed with my retranslation of it, into French using the word *rythme.*

FD: Solos are not difficult. It is just necessary to know the beat [*cadence*]. To know the beat [*cadence*]. If I depart from this slat I must arrive at this slat at a specific beat [*cadence*]. If a musician understands that, you can play solos as you please.

EC: Is there a word in Malinke for *cadence?*

FD: *Cadence?* . . . There is a word in Malinke for *cadence,* yes . . . *ka ben a ma* . . . *ka laben a ma.* That means to meet with [*rencontre avec*].

EC: To agree with [*être d'accord*]? But regarding rhythm [*rythme*]?

FD: Yes, *rythme, rythme.* (Fode Doumbia 1990-per)[36]

Doumbia's explanation for playing solo lines on the bala indicates that he has a keen awareness of the duration in beats of a rhythmic cycle, and that melodic excursions are made with reference to these beats.

Terminology for Pitch Height

Mande terminology for pitch height is directly opposite from Western designations. Indeed, this may be the case for much of sub-Saharan Africa. The treble end of an instrument, whether the shorter strings on a kora or the shorter slats on a bala, is called low (Bm: *duguma,* Md: *duuma*), and the bass

---

36. FD: "Les solos ne sont pas difficiles. Seulement il faut connaître les cadences. Connaître les cadences. Si je quit ici, je dois arriver ici à tel cadence. Une fois que le musicien connaît ça tu pourra faire les solos comme tu veux." EC: "Il y a un mot en Malinke pour cadence?" FD: "Cadence? . . . Il y a le mot de cadence en Malinke pour cadence, oui . . . *ka ben a ma* . . . *ka laben a ma* . . . c'est à dire rencontre avec." EC: "Être d'accord? mais sur le rythme?" FD: "Oui, rythme, rythme." The phrase *ka laben a ma* might be alternatively transcribed as *k'a la ben a ma.*

end is called high (Bm: *sanfe, sanma;* Md: *santo*). Balas can be played with the bass end on the left- or right-hand side, depending on how the musician first learned, so terminology relating the hand to the pitch (i.e., left hand — bass end), as observed by Hugh Tracey (1970:120–21, 150) among Chopi xylophonists, is not common among bala players. Neither are the terms "small" and "large" (treble and bass, respectively) that have been noted as widespread in Africa by Kubik (1985:32). Melodic runs moving from the treble end of a kora or bala to the bass end were consistently referred to as ascending (Mn: *yèlè*), and melodic movement from the bass to the treble end as descending (Bm: *jigi;* Md: *jii*) (Jobarteh 1990-per; S. J. Kouyate 1990-per). I found this terminology very consistent regardless of instrument or geographic region.[37]

A related area is the significance of the downward movement in Mande languages, Mande melodic music, and African dance and sculpture.[38] Most Mandekan dialects are tonal and feature a sawtooth kind of descending tonal movement (Bird 1982:37–42). The descending character of melodic motion in Mandinka vocal and kora music, and its connection with language, has been discussed by Knight (1973a, 1:249–69; 1984b:10–11). The earth-directed motion of much African dance and sculpture displays what Robert Farris Thompson (1974:13) refers to in his title "'The Get-Down Quality': Descending Direction in Melody, Sculpture, Dance."

The terminology used for tuning the strings of a kora conforms more closely with Western usage, probably because of the physical action involved: the verb *sabaa* (to pull) is used for tightening a string to sharpen its pitch, and the causative verb *jiindi* (to make lower) is used for loosening a string to flatten its pitch. Knight has also observed a parallel usage in the evaluation of a tuning. "One kora player observing another tuning an instrument might offer verbal commentary: *A mang futa* ('It hasn't reached yet,' i.e. it is flat), or *A tambita* ('It has gone past,' i.e. it is sharp)" (Knight 1991a:3). I would add a further technical specification that *futa* (to reach or arrive) and *tambi* (to pass) not only signify flat and sharp but also function as relative directives for the person to continue tuning the string in the same direction in the case of the term *futa,* and to tune the string in the opposite direction in the case of *tambita.* For example, a string judged flat (*a mang futa*) would then be sharpened, but if it passed the mark (*a tambita*)

---

37. Joyeux (1910:52) reported the use of "mother" and "daughter" to distinguish high from low: "The right hand strikes the high notes, called daughter [*fille*] notes in the Malinke language; the left hand strikes the mother [*mères*] or bass notes." L. Harris (1992:225–28) reports similarly from Sierra Leone: the lowest slat on a bala is called mother (*ba*); the middle register slats are called children (*dennu*); and the upper register is called the "song place" (*dònkili yòrò*).

38. Here I am using downward in the Western sense.

it would be flattened, in which case the evaluation *a mang futa* could indicate that the string should be further flattened until it reached its mark.

Rhythm

I have not encountered a Mande vocabulary that corresponds to Western technical concepts of measuring musical time, such as beats grouping into a meter. But there are terms to describe other features of the meshing together of sounds over time. Two words used for tempo conform well with general African and African American usage: *sumaya* (cool) for slow; and *kalan* or *kandi* (hot) for fast. Although "cool" and "hot" may designate similar meanings in musical contexts throughout the world, they are not universally linked with slow and fast. In the United States, for example, summer heat can be equated with a slow, laid-back lifestyle whereas fall or winter cold is often associated with briskness, particularly when walking outside. The usages of the terms "cool" and "hot" do seem to exhibit some conformity, however, in the African diaspora, as Robert Farris Thompson (1973) has argued for the former term and Richard Waterman (1948) for the latter. The word *sabari* (patience) can be used to describe slowing down or adjusting the tempo (S. Diabate 1990-per: 159–61), and *goloba* (to speed up, to rush; Bailleul 1996: 143), or its verbal noun *golobali,* is sometimes used to refer to fast rolling jembe patterns (Polak 1996a: 86).

Senegambian kora players sometimes have a second person tap one of several tapping patterns (*konkondiro*) on the calabash of the kora; other instrumentalists do not use them, nor do kora players from Mali. *Konkondiro* (knocking) is the verbal noun of *konkon,* an onomatopoeia for "knock" (Knight 1973a, 1: 192–205).

In Mali and Guinea many drum pieces have the term *dòn* (dance) attached to their titles, as in *Jeli dòn* (Jeli's dance). The term functions like *julu* (piece) in that drum pieces may be called *dòn* in the abstract. Curiously, in the Mandinka tangtango drum ensemble, pieces are usually referred to as *julo* (piece). The verb *ke* (to do) is used to form the verb "to dance" (as in *dòn ke*). *Dòn sen* (dance foot, dance step) refers to a dance step, and *dònsen cogo* (dance step way of doing) refers to the pattern of steps in a dance in the Bamana language (Arnoldi 1995: 103).

In jembe drumming the hand strokes on the drum are not commonly named, but on close questioning drummers might respond with names corresponding to Western notions of high and low. High (*sanfè* or *sanma*), middle (*cèmancè*), and low (*duguma*), or high, low, and very low (*dugumaba*) may be used for slap, tone, and bass, respectively. The break to end dance solos is called *tigeli* (breaking).

Conclusion

From musical items to tuning systems to the basic structure of the music, Mandenka terminology reflects to a certain extent how the music is conceptualized. Perhaps because of the variety of melody instruments, jelis have the most extensive musical terminology, which sometimes allows them to talk about pieces in the abstract, removed from any particular performance context. While drummers might freely voice aesthetic evaluations of performances, discourse about technicalities in their music is less common. But then there are whole fields of Mandenka musical practice in which guiding yet unvoiced theories have yet to be explored. The explication of these worlds of musical thought, still barely begun, promises to reveal rich ways of thinking about music.

7

Perspectives

Here I begin to demystify how I went about gaining access to music in Africa, how I felt I was perceived, the activities I engaged in, the contexts where I worked, and the ways in which music is learned.

Shortly after arriving in Senegal on my first trip in 1988, I took part in an incident that illustrates some of the ironies and clashes that marked my work in Africa. It occurred in a kora class I was taking at the Conservatoire National de Musique in Dakar. There were about fifteen students in the class, all of them about high-school age except me. Most of us took the class seriously, but we also enjoyed the sometimes adolescent humor that went on in class. The professor was an elderly, respected kora player whose surname indicated that he was a member of a long lineage stemming from the premier family of thirteenth-century Malian court musicians.

In the classroom our chairs formed a square backed against the four bare walls, and three or four of us at a time would get instruction, since there were only four instruments at the school. One day a student walked in late, a few minutes after class had started. Respecting traditional protocol, he went around the room and greeted everyone personally by shaking hands one by one. He had gotten halfway around the room, and the professor, busy tuning one of the koras, was next in line. Everyone was watching, trying to restrain laughter, for the late student had been scolded before for bringing this custom, essential in much everyday African life, into the classroom. The student offered his hand, but the professor did not acknowledge it. The student (who was something of a class comedian), seeing that we all were waiting for his next move, snapped his fingers to call the professor's attention to his outstretched hand so he could move around the rest of the room and finally take a seat. Snapping one's fingers in this case is evidently not rude—there is an amusing scene in the film *Keita* (Dani Kouyate 1995-vid) in which eager young classroom students all thrust their hands into the air snapping their fingers, hoping the teacher will call on them. But there did seem to be a bit of mockery involved in the kora class, given the professor's aversion to shaking hands in the classroom.

I have been in this professor's home and have experienced the genuine warmth of being acknowledged personally by people going around and shaking everyone's hand, a practice strictly observed there. But after the student had snapped his fingers a few more times waiting for a response, it became evident that the professor was ignoring him. When the student started to walk away, the professor launched into a monologue, with appropriate breaks to accommodate the sporadic outbursts of laughter from the class, asking the student what he thought he was doing, hadn't he been told several times before not to do that in the classroom, and so on. I could not gauge the seriousness of the occasion, since the professor did not seem to mind the laughter from the rest of the class, but he went on at length before finally turning to me for a closing argument. So much for the naive concept of anonymous observer. He asked me if students where I come from go around shaking everyone's hand when they enter a classroom. Being new to the country and to the three languages that were operating in the classroom (Wolof, one or another Mandekan dialect, and French), I could not think quickly enough, nor did I want to appear insubordinate, so I briefly imagined how that might play in the United States and simply said no. At which the professor looked at the class and said *Voilà* (There you have it), and the case was closed.

The problem was whether the student should drop a traditional African practice in a modern African context. Or it could have been seen as whether the teacher should insist that it be dropped. But what if I had come late to the next class and gone around the room shaking hands with everyone? Better still, what if had I done that wearing the traditional African clothing that most of the teachers, and few of the students, wore to school? We all enjoyed the humor of the situation, and it was not the last time similar incidents played themselves out in that same classroom. I found this incident especially ripe with varying perspectives, particularly that of a non-African moving in the cultural depths of an African society that many Africans take for granted and few write about.

The way French *solfège* syllables (*do, re, mi . . .*) were used in that same classroom to teach kora pieces is another illustration of the clash of values in modern Africa, perhaps with more resounding implications for the study at hand than disagreements over classroom etiquette. These *solfège* syllables, used to name the strings of the kora, were written down, but they lacked any rhythmic precision. The advantage of this system was not clear to me other than the prestige involved in linking kora music with the European music that was taught under the same roof at the conservatory. The kind of syllabic notation used was very limited compared with staff notation, which, when modified to reflect the particularities of the music, has been used by Westerners to preserve, analyze, and teach kora music. There is little question among all involved, though, that the most effective way to teach the kora (at least in terms of turning out competent players) is the traditional oral-aural-tactile method used by kora players, passed down from father, uncle, or some close relative.

The irony—and audacity—of a non-African (myself) criticizing a traditionally grounded African musician for using dated European pedagogical methods (inherited from a French colonial past) instead of traditional African ones should not be lost. It is easy to bemoan the loss or trading in of certain African practices, and the line of non-Africans of varying motivations and agendas who have criticized African artists for not being African enough is long. The line of non-Africans questioning the motivations of these non-African critics is not so short nowadays either. Africans have also eloquently responded (see chapter 4; Fodeba Keita 1958; Fleming 1993; and Manthia Diawara 1998), although the voices of those who might object to the packaging and export of their traditions have been underrepresented. It is crucial to view each case on its own merits in order to go beyond stereotypes and facile dismissals. The aims of traditional African teaching and those of African conservatory teaching should not be confused. Doing so is similar to confusing the aims of village dancing with those of African national ballet dancing. They are different entities (although closely related). In Europe and North America, a conservatory education is part of the path to a performance career, though perhaps not a requirement; not so in Africa. Of the dozens and dozens of kora players I know personally or through their reputations or recordings, I do not know one who has gone through a complete conservatory or music institute education, though I do know a few who have taught in such places. The psychological boost in prestige attained by using French methods such as *solfège* to teach African music may have had great value for a generation brought up in a colonial era. A younger generation may have benefited in a more practical way. Naming the strings on the kora according to Western scale degrees makes it easier to integrate the instrument into guitar- and brass-based dance orchestras.

Later on during my stay in Africa I gained a better appreciation of the complexity of sticking one's nose into other people's business. Some simple lessons were constantly reinforced: it is essential to keep track of who is doing the talking, including questioning the sources of their knowledge and their motives, and also to question one's own motives and critical reactions. Of course this is not always easy to do, particularly when the medium is writing. But one can and should at least strive.

The study of music, and the communication of that study, has its own special problems, and sticking one's ears into other people's music calls for stances and skills that are in some ways significantly peculiar to that undertaking. This book does not explicitly advocate any one methodological model for going about this, other than an ad hoc approach informed by a familiarity with both the music and its local contexts. There must be some kind of play between theoretical knowledge and empirical knowledge to guide research in the music of any culture, and the script for the play between these different kinds of knowledge has to be given room to develop while the game is in session.

This book is, of course, a documentation of how I went about putting my ears, hands, and mind into Maninka and Mandinka music. It is more than my own reflections on music in Mandenka society. I have made a point, surely painful to the casual reader, of meticulously acknowledging throughout the text the debt I owe to the thought of others. Surely this study is skewed by my own experience, for better or worse. It is expected that other people might go about this in other ways, and that I might go about studying other music in other ways.

I have tried to make readers aware of the perspectives of my African teachers and how they have informed my own perspective. As far as possible, this book is about what Mande musicians do, and about what they say about what they do. It includes what I say as well: about what they do, and about what they say about what they do. At times I have tried to separate out these perspectives; at other times they are indissolubly intertwined.

Identity

While in Africa, I found resonance in a classic Mande proverb, well known among foreigners:

> No matter how long a canoe remains in water, it will never become a crocodile. (Versions of this can be found in Malian Bamana [Bird and Kante 1976:8], Gambian Mandinka [Gamble 1987a:71], and Songhai [Stoller and Olkes 1987:v])

Becoming a crocodile was not part of my plan in Africa. Learning to do some of the things that certain crocodiles—musicians—do, was. (And it still is.) There were times when people would comment on the state of my "crocodileness"—with the instruments I was learning, with the Mandinka language or other dialects, or in drawn out bargaining sessions with merchants—but there is a big difference between learning to do some of the things others do and actually being, or believing oneself to be, one of them. I was not after, nor could I hope to get, the type of insights on African life that African writers have, such as Laye Camara, Sory Camara, Diango Cissé, Youssouf Cissé, Massa Makan Diabate, Lansiné Kaba, Mamadi Kaba, Cheick Keita, Fodeba Keita, or Djibril Tamsir Niane in the case of the Maninka. I was after making music like a Mandenka musician—

something few African musicians write about—and understanding how they understand music.

Making music can sometimes lead to delusions about how well we do it. The time one spends learning the music of a foreign culture (both abroad and at home) rarely approaches the time spent by those who are recognized as being good at it in those foreign societies, almost never for those considered masters. A few conclusions might be drawn from this. Perhaps the music does not demand specialized skills, and so anyone can become competent, including foreigners who put forth the effort. Or maybe our ways of learning can be effective in making up for lost time. Or more commonly, we may delude ourselves into thinking that our ways of learning are effective, reinforced by local approval of our musical competence, the possible motives for which are usually not critically assessed.

There is a great gulf between musical competence and musical creativity, and also between local approval of the musical competence of a foreigner and local acceptance of the authoritative expertise of a foreigner. It is a difference like the one between participating and mastering, between following rules and creatively formulating, stretching, manipulating, or breaking them. Research skills appropriate for investigating musical competence may be inadequate for investigating musical creativity. Conclusions about, and theories of, music making based on one quality may not be relevant to the other. On the other hand, the notion of creativity in the performance of music just may not be as important in some cultures as in others. Where it is important, one must draw on appropriate research skills. I do not know of many serious musicologists or theorists of the classical traditions of European musics, for example, who have not gained at least minimal competence on a musical instrument, and I suspect that many have been highly skilled at some point in their lives. Should the case be any different for serious musicologists or theorists of music outside Europe?

Between the impossible extremes of going native and being an anonymous observer there exists quite a lot of ground that has been occupied by music researchers. I suppose I have tried to occupy different parts of that ground at different times and in different ways, but there was never any question about my own identity. It was clear that I am not African, and it became clear that my interests were centered in music. Holding on to my own identity was a kind of emotional insurance policy that enabled me to solicit and compare information from a wider variety of sources than is the norm within Africa. It also put me in a better position to evaluate the information I was receiving by making it easier to keep open several points of view at once.

Actually, I had no choice. In jeliya (the music of Mande hereditary professional musicians) one does not become initiated, as Mande hunter's musicians do, for example. One has to be born into the profession. Nevertheless, my teachers were able to accept me as an American musician who was interested enough in their music to live in their country to learn it. A case could be made that they were willing to open up their knowledge to me precisely because I was a foreigner. I was not perceived as a threat, I would not compete with them professionally, and the more I could appreciate and understand what they did, the more I could transfer that understanding to non-Africans and open up opportunities for them to travel abroad and find alternative sources of income.

The knowledge I sought, moreover, was essentially hand knowledge, and the secrets to be guarded in this realm are not politically charged. The musical technique of jelis takes years to develop, and it cannot be absorbed, and hence abused, by a novice in the same way as potentially dangerous information (such as scandalous personal history). Sounds coming from instruments do not have the political power of words, so musicians are more concerned with guarding their political-historical knowledge than their hand knowledge. The other kind of knowledge I sought out, however—the stories behind the pieces and the histories of their instruments and profession—is another matter. Here there are some secrets and jealousies, and in that respect there is a sharp distinction between playing music and talking about it.

Methods

My initial inquiries in Africa were primarily oriented toward learning a highly specialized skill that was not so far removed from other skills I was practicing before going to Africa (playing stringed and percussion instruments). This skill would stay with me after I returned to the United States. In Africa I took private lessons (and sometimes classes) several times a week, sometimes on several instruments with different teachers. As I moved from country to country (Senegal, The Gambia, and then Mali; I made much shorter trips to Guinea), I repeated the same schedule but with different teachers and sometimes different instruments. Although I spent much of the time with my teachers with an instrument in my hands, I also spent much time with a microphone recording their music and their words. Probably the best preparation for my work in Africa was my training as a musician.

My interests in Africa primarily revolved around who plays music professionally, what their instruments are like, what their pieces of music are about, how they play their instruments, how they have modernized their traditions, and how they talk about their music. The progression of topics within chapters 2 through 4 moves through the first four questions, and chapters 5 and 6 address the last two. Although anthropology and ethnography have informed my work, I do not consider myself to be primarily engaged in either. That is, I like to think that the scope of musicology and music theory is not limited by geography but rather is informed by it. At least it should be.

When a Context Modernizes

Anonymity and privacy are just two facets of Western urban life usually surrendered by Western students in Africa. Showing up at a musical event or approaching a teacher for information in Africa is not the same for a non-African as it is for an African. (Actually, it is not even the same for an African who belongs to the freeborn social class [horon] as for one who belongs to the artisan class [nyamakala].) It is precisely this point that must be understood when evaluating claims of music in its context. Often when I showed up at an event, typically a marriage or naming ceremony, African hospitality would take over and I would be treated as a guest and pulled through the crowd to a front-row seat. It took some time to get used to this. I do not think that my presence altered the events in any significant way, except for occasional attempts by praise singers to practice their craft on me and solicit gifts.

As for the music I recorded, it was largely taken out of its traditional context, except for videotaping of drumming and dancing. The concept of authenticity has many points of view, as the example of Les Ballets Africains has shown (see chapter 4), but I consider much of what I recorded to have been in an ideal context in that the musicians were in the unusual situation of having their every sound preserved for posterity with few distractions. Some of my teachers who were going abroad and had earned enough money so they could make the choice no longer played often for traditional events in Africa. They had no problem lifting the music out of its social context and moving around pieces as if they had a life of their own. Requests from the sons of my teachers for copies of the music I had recorded was evidence enough for me that the music was valid in its own right.

The question of the context (or contexts) in which music lives has been a great concern of much ethnomusicological writing. Carl Dahlhaus's observation on the relation of social history to music history in Europe has ramifications that go beyond the historical study of European music.

> The decision as to whether social history is part of music history or *vice versa* is not necessarily a choice between mutually exclusive principles. . . . For

[written] music is at once a work of art and a document. Either it forms the object which the historian wishes to comprehend and around which he marshals his explanations, or it can be simply the material he uses to illustrate structures and processes from social history. . . . In any event, the thesis that a collection of music-historical facts does not make a *history* of music until put in the context of social history is faced with the antithesis that in such a context it ceases to be a history of *music*. (Dahlhaus 1983:124)

For some contemporary Euro-American music theory the term "context" has just the opposite sense.

> Those middle-period works of Schoenberg, the middle-period works of Berg, the middle-period works of Webern have this particular property in common. They are to as large an extent as possible self-referential, self-contained, and what I'm given to call "contextual." Contextuality merely has to do with the extent to which a piece defines its materials within itself. (Milton Babbitt, in Dembski and Strauss 1987:167)

Which sense of the word "contextuality" predominates—an ethnomusicological sense, that music does not live in a vacuum, or a music-theoretical sense, that it sometimes may effectively be examined (or created) in one— is a question of balance, appropriateness, and the interests of the person doing the looking.

> Some musics can be managed apart from cultural context more readily than others, Western and Indian art musics being two notorious examples, while other musics are so intimately tied in with a cultural or even a material context as to be incomprehensible except in that context. (Powers 1980b:8)

Some Mande music, particularly the instrumental music of the jeli, can be managed, in my opinion, outside its own social context—for instance, in a concert hall, on a recording, or even perhaps transcribed on paper. Other Mande music—dance drumming and singing, for example—may be much more comprehensible (and interesting) when it is examined in its natural habitat. There, dancers heat up the drummers, or singers heat up their patrons, whose pride has been lit when they hear their ancestors being praised; they in turn heat up the singers with gifts, and one can feel the ebb and flow of these ancient symbiotic relationships at work.

Much of my work was done in a nontraditional context, in one-on-one situations with two instruments and a cassette recorder. Drum lessons, however, usually included at least two other players (and at times dancing schoolchildren and grandmothers), evidence that the importance of hearing how the different parts fit together to make the whole cannot be overstated in African drumming. There is a distinction that needs to be emphasized between some of the melodic musical traditions and some of the drumming traditions in Africa. Whereas drumming is intimately linked with dance, some melodic instrumental music may stand on its own—certainly to my ear, and perhaps even to an African ear. A thriving local cassette industry in which drumming traditions are effectively absent seems to bear this out. Live drumming can be heard throughout the cities, towns, and villages as an integral part of most marriage ceremonies, but people do not seem to want to hear drumming on cassette tapes out of its traditional context as a dance event. Cassettes of singing with melodic instrumental accompaniment and even extended instrumental solos, however, are ubiquitous.

One reason instruction on some of the melodic instruments differs from that of drums is that some of the solo melodic instruments have a built-in representation of an ensemble in the ways the fingers or the two hands relate to one another, providing reciprocal frames of reference. This has been remarked on by Ruth Stone with reference to solo instrument playing among the Liberian Kpelle, distant relatives of the Maninka.

> An instrument played alone simply incorporates the various roles assumed by different performers in an ensemble into a single instrument played by a single performer. Therefore, one person playing the konîn [Kpelle triangular-frame zither] symbolically manipulates many voices as opposed to several performers each manipulating one or more voices. (Stone 1982:90, 93)

The kora does not require a second instrument to create cross-rhythms in the way that a drum does, and kora instruction usually takes place in a more intimate setting.

Mande Ways of Learning Music, Ways of Learning Mande Music

Most of the musicians I learned with normally pass on their knowledge only to their children and the children of those considered to be their brothers and sisters (which can be a pretty large community). Those born into nonartisan families have little hope or desire to learn music because they are the traditional patrons. In one sense I was at an obvious disadvantage, falling into a class of people even further removed from music performance than the freeborn patrons: *tubab*—"white person" or, as it is sometimes applied to African Americans or Europeanized Africans, one who is perceived to have adopted the white people's ways. But in another sense I enjoyed certain advantages that enabled me to monopolize my teachers' time to an extent that even their own children would find difficult (over a period of months, though, not years). I had money to pay my teachers, I came from a country that they had either visited as artists or heard about and wanted to go to, and I had recording equipment that could capture their sounds and enable me to go home, learn their pieces, and return in a few days playing what they had recorded. The first advantage (money) enabled me to give them a kind of respect that is difficult to come by in a continent that has a fatal cash flow problem. The second advantage (coming from America) earned me respect (among musicians at least) for leaving a wealthy and powerful nation to learn the music of an economically poor and politically powerless one. The third advantage (a good cassette recorder) enabled me to challenge their musicianship in ways that were new to them.

Foreign researchers are often able to break into the traditional heredi-tary system because of their money, their potential for helping with travel abroad, and also because they pose no competitive threat. The problems that local researchers encounter, however, demonstrate the kind of knowl-edge that is held sacred and the difficulty of gaining access to it. Mamadou Mané has noted one of the problems he had in researching the history of the Kabu empire for his master's thesis at the university in Dakar. His family name Mane indicates that he is a descendant of one of the ruling families of Kabu. He therefore ought to be in a patron-client relationship with any of his informants who are hereditary professional oral historians (jali or griot). That is to say, the ancestors of his jali informants would have been the royal chroniclers and historians for the ancestors of Mane, who in turn would have been responsible for the well-being of their jalis.

> Although some of them have given us information, others, more numerous, have kept silent, believing that their knowledge is esoteric and cannot be di-vulged to simply anyone, especially to "those who go to the school of the whites," as they say. This expression refers to any African who has received instruction in a European language. We therefore have come to understand the reason behind the refusal of these informants. In fact, this mainly concerns griots (who are professional), whose knowledge of the history of our coun-tries serves as their bread and butter when during the course of a grand Afri-can soirée they would recite that knowledge before a wealthy patron. There-fore many griot traditionalists today sell their knowledge. And this is an important obstacle that researchers lacking money go up against.
>
> In effect, research into oral traditions requires great financial means to "loosen tongues," if one may permit the expression. (Mané 1978:91)

In some respects foreign researchers may have more access to certain kinds of knowledge than their African counterparts, owing in part to their greater financial means. But a patron—researchers eliciting information usually fall into this category—who does not recognize the value of a jali's knowledge, as demonstrated by a seeming unwillingness to part with money, may not be deemed worthy of such knowledge. A more sympathetic view of the value of a jali's knowledge would be that if they gave their knowledge away freely they would have no livelihood. It is the patron's re-sponsibility to see to the well-being of the jali, which is in effect like sup-porting one's local library, museum, concert hall, and university.

To be sure, foreign researchers cannot work effectively simply by loading up on cash. Those receiving the cash must answer to their families and friends as to what they are giving away. They will be ostracized if it is believed that they are selling knowledge that should not be sold. Most jalis understand the relative value of knowledge and cash in their own society and are able to guide foreigners in local customs of civility. Breakdowns occur when there is a breach of confidence on either side.

Some knowledge is sacred and should not be given out, least of all to those who might write about it. Djibril Tamsir Niane, a Guinean who published a version of the Sunjata epic in the form of a novel that has become a classic, has given the words of his jali informant on this matter.

> Other peoples use writing to record the past, but this invention has killed the faculty of memory among them. They do not feel the past any more, for writing lacks the warmth of the human voice. With them everybody thinks he knows, whereas learning should be a secret. (Mamadou Kouyate, in Niane 1965:41)

Niane himself then comments on those words.

> Here is one of the dicta that often recurs in the mouths of the traditional griots. This explains the parsimony with which these vessels of historical traditions give their knowledge away. According to them, the Whites have vulgarized knowledge. When a White knows something everybody knows it. One would have to be able to change this state of mind if one wanted to know some day all that the griots decline to give away. (Niane 1965:92)

Even so, African government institutions have managed to record a remarkable amount of material, most of it related to oral history. Unfortunately they lack the funds to publish transcriptions and translations.

It is not just the vulgarization of knowledge that jelis object to. There is a fundamental difference between written words and spoken (or sung) words that is not always appreciated in Western societies. Throughout much of Africa there is a privileging of the human voice over writing. The renowned jeli Kele Monson Diabate expressed this sentiment eloquently during the course of a Maninka conversation with linguist and pioneering scholar Charles Bird.

BIRD: If you help us, if you help us, we will write down your words and they will live forever.

DIABATE: You and your dried words. What are they to me? The meaning of my words is in the moisture of the breath that carries them. (Bird, forthcoming)

In general my teachers were agreeable, encouraging even, to my taping our lessons. They were familiar with the lifestyle of urban centers such as

Dakar, Bamako, Paris, or London and understood perfectly well the time constraints that a tape recorder helped to overcome, and they knew I was not going to spend the rest of my life in Africa. In some lessons my teacher would keep playing the same thing over and over again with me until I could play it up to speed. At other times we found it more effective for me to start in this way but then move on to another item and put off the hand work until I got home and could work it out at my own speed with a tape recorder— a distinctly non-African way of learning music, but one that at times produced results that could engage my teachers on a more challenging level. African students usually did not have this luxury, which enabled me to cover a larger repertory, but with less hand knowledge. I was aware of the dangers of not getting something into my hands before moving on to more sophisticated items, and my teachers were able to effectively evaluate my potential and either veto or encourage rapid progress. At any rate I would not, and could not, move on until I could play my previous lesson satisfactorily.

In contrast to the way I learned the kora in Africa, the son of one of my African teachers once described himself to me as being self-taught. I took that to mean that his father did not give him formal lessons. The designation "self-taught" in general is problematic, often entailing an apology for not being able to explain technically what one is doing, along with a sense of pride for having achieved so much despite a lack of formal education. Among the Mande, the significance of being self-taught may have more to do with a kind of competition with one's own ancestors, called *fadenya* (see chapter 1).

The hereditary nature of musicianship in Mande society is responsible for the relative absence there of the kind of formal training I know in the United States. As far as music is concerned, ancient Mande learning institutions —the family and the small community of blood-related musicians—still work. This is in contrast to the system of conservatories and schools of music that have been operating in Europe and elsewhere for several centuries, which among other things are theoretically open to anyone regardless of birth and operate on a basis of monetary exchange. The endogamous nature of the jeli's profession is also a reason behind the postindependence creation of schools of music to teach traditional African music to nonhereditary musicians. Among the Mande, as among some of their neighbors, certain aspects of music making, though by no means all, are traditionally relegated to a few patronymic groups. Growing up in an extended family of musicians, one cannot help but be educated in music; one is destined to be a musician.

The Mandenka notion of being self-taught, therefore, does not have the connotation of bucking the system that it has in the United States. It is instead an expression of family tradition in which music is inherited rather than learned. Music is the birthright of the jeli rather than something to be acquired through formal means. When I asked Sidiki Diabate, one of my teachers, how he learned the kora, he expressed this belief in inheriting music rather than acquiring it through formal training: "We are the kora, with us it just comes" (S. Diabate 1990-per:445–46). His son Toumani echoed his father's sentiments (with the added ingredient of fadenya) when asked if he had learned from his father. "But I didn't learn the kora from my father. I already had the kora in my blood. I was born to it" (Toumani Diabate, in Prince 1989a:15).

There were two contexts of musical instrument teaching that I observed in Africa: classes at the national conservatory in Dakar and private instruction at the homes of my teachers. The difference between what I learned at the conservatory and what I learned at the homes of my teachers was more a matter of degree than of kind. Outside the conservatory I saw a good bit of practicing, including that of a six-year-old son of one of my teachers, but I was not around to see much of how the things being practiced were actually picked up. The practice of young boys with miniature instruments sitting next to their fathers and, if not striking the exact pitches, then at least trying to imitate the finger or hand movements, is probably typical. The practicing I saw was not the type one would find in India, for example, where melodic or rhythmic patterns can be abstracted out of their performance context and practiced as exercises (Bhattacharya 1979:133–222; Shankar 1968:97–152). In other words, I did not see scales being practiced, or patterns that were not actually pieces. Knight's experience in The Gambia was similar: "Structured lessons, exercises, and practice are largely foreign to the tradition" (Knight 1984a:76).

There is a distinction here that is very important for understanding much African music. What Africans, Mande melody instrumentalists in particular, practice are exemplars of pieces. The very nature of the music makes this possible. Instrumental renditions of pieces consist of harmonic-melodic patterns, usually lasting from a few seconds to less than fifteen seconds, that are played cyclically, with various kinds of input expected from the performer. One cycle of a piece, then, can be repeated over and over without variation as practice. I refer to one cycle of a piece as an exemplar of that piece. These exemplars would usually not be less than one cycle long, so that contact with the musical whole is retained. The density of hand or finger movement can be pared down for beginners, and they can also be elaborated internally—that is, the length always remains the same, but more movements can be added to increase the density, or new movements can be substituted for old ones. No matter how simplified an exemplar may be made, it is still considered to be the piece, albeit a beginner's version.

When Teaching Westernizes

In 1948 the Conservatoire de Dakar opened offering training in European music (Ministère de la Culture, Senegal 1986). In 1960 a division of Musique Traditionnelle was added, which in the late 1980s (when I was there—the following section refers to this time period) offered classes (group lessons) in bala, kora, xalam (Wolof lute), sabar (Wolof drum), jembe, and riti (Fulbe fiddle). After several name changes the conservatory became the Conservatoire Nationale de Musique, de Danse, et d'Art Dramatique. It is the only institution of its kind in Senegal. A similar institution exists in Bamako, Mali (L'Institut National des Arts), but there is none yet in Guinea or The Gambia.

The melodic instruments that are taught at the conservatory are the exclusive preserve of the professional hereditary musician. The philosophy behind having a conservatory open up these traditionally closed hereditary pursuits to anyone is one particularly visible example of a postindependence policy of democratizing culture. There are problems, though, in the clash between African and European learning institutions that are quite evident in the conservatory's traditional music division.

The teachers in the traditional music division are all recognized artists of the highest quality. The politics of selection or their qualifications are not in question here. The environment in which they operate, however, from the name of the institution itself to the monthly salaries and the giving of final exams, was largely brought over from France and then inherited by the Senegalese from colonial times. In its purpose of teaching anyone to play some of the traditional instruments of the region (albeit at an elementary level), regardless of gender, inherited social status, or ethnic origin, the conservatory succeeds. Whether its goals are more ambitious than that is unclear.

One cultural clash can be found in the way the teachers are paid—by a regular salary. The earliest reference to the professional aspect of music among the Mande was given by Ibn Battūta in the fourteenth century (appendix A). Dūghā, whom Ibn Battūta referred to as an interpreter, received a purse of gold from the king of Mali after playing the bala and singing his praises. The next day each of the king's commanders gave to Dūghā "according to his rank." The concept of giving according to one's standing or rank is fundamental, just as giving a fixed amount for a performance seems to be alien, notwithstanding al-Bakrī's eleventh-century report that imams, muezzins, jurists, and scholars in ancient Ghana were salaried (appendix A).

The norm for performances that I saw in a wide variety of contexts in West Africa was that money was given to the praise singers as they were singing, especially while they were praising the families of their patrons. As the praises deepen, so do their patrons' pockets empty. Giving beyond one's means can be considered an act of heroism, at least from the jeli's point of view. The lack of a ceiling on what can be given, and consequently on what can be expected or hoped for by praise singers, is illustrated in *Jula faso,* a piece dedicated to itinerant traders known as Jula. Amadu Bansang Jobarteh's (1990-per) renditions of *Jula faso* contain detailed descriptions of a battle among wealthy patrons gathered at the end of the wedding of Musa Molo, an important Senegambian leader, to see who can give the most to the singers and musicians. In concert performances in Dakar, where tickets are sold and the performers are under contract, patrons routinely get up from the audience and give money to the singers on stage. This practice had to be banned in the main concert hall in Bamako because it had gotten out of hand. Even when the performers are under contract, they know that at least the possibility of augmenting their income exists (or used to exist in that concert hall in Bamako), according to their ability to awaken their patrons' pride and move them.

The economic aspect of traditional teaching contrasts directly with that of performance; money does not usually change hands from student to teacher. This is probably because teachers are working within an extended network of family ties, and the social and economic dichotomy between the patron (freeborn) and the performer (artisan) does not come into play. Although there may be some exceptions, it seems that some family tie, the kind that normally would not exist between endogamous freeborn and endogamous artisan born, along with the giving of ten kola nuts, would suffice to gain admittance and possible acceptance into an artisan family compound. But once teachers are paid to teach by salary there is a rupture with traditions of the past. That is compounded when the students are not only not members of the extended family network, but also not hereditary musicians, or even from the same ethnic group. There is no reason to expect that teachers would pass on anything more than a cursory knowledge of their tradition in such a context, particularly if they think they are underpaid. And there is not even the added incentive of a bonus, always present in a live performance. The use of *solfège* to teach kora music (described in the beginning of this chapter) is tailor-made for this situation.

Jelis make a clear tripartite distinction between the verbal rendition of history (*kuma*), song (*dònkili*), and instrument playing (Mn: *foli*, Md: *kosiri*), even though they all are part of their profession. In the setting of the national conservatory in Dakar little historical knowledge is formally taught. Teachers may generalize about the subject of a piece, but they usually offer nothing more than what most schoolchildren know. This is further evidence that the speech-related aspects of the jeli's profession are more politically powerful, and to be more judiciously guarded, than the instrument-playing aspects. I encountered little objection to my recording the music of jelis (after preliminary negotiations involving money, of course), but their recitations and historical knowledge were quite another matter. One elderly and respected kora-playing jali from the Casamance region graciously recorded any number of kora pieces for me, but his memory uncannily failed him when he was questioned on even some of the most widely known historical traditions. Although it may be advantageous for some jelis to guard their knowledge closely, other jelis just may not have been trained in historical knowledge beyond a basic competence, owing to the highly specialized nature of their profession.

Conclusion

How one goes about gathering information, acquiring knowledge and skills, and reporting on the experience is a sensitive topic that in the past few decades has increasingly occupied the thoughts and writings of professional observers and researchers. (In the academic cottage industry that has grown up around these concerns, the work of Clifford Geertz has been particularly seminal and enduring.) Artists sometimes shroud their early training in secrecy. Researchers sometimes neglect or dismiss the day-to-day details of text gathering. But the soap operas of daily life may just as easily contain necessary keys to understanding as may the more rehearsed and less frequent public displays. In this chapter I have tried to address the imbalance in the other chapters by revealing a bit about my own approach. I have kept the personal relations I entered into with my teachers and friends at bay in this book, partly out of respect for those I have and have not met, and partly to maintain the academic veneer of objectivity that is necessary in such an undertaking. We should not forget, however, that my own reporting, and the things I report on, are products of a wonderful infinity of accidents of the moment.

Manden Te Banna

Any story of Mande music, and perhaps any music for that matter, would be too long and dynamic to be told in a single book by a single person. Rather, this is *a* story of Mande music. I have tried to convey some of the breadth and depth of the musical expression of some of the peoples who claim origins in Old Mande and provide readers with an extensive body of references, including recordings, videos, and written materials, to explore the music further. At times my story may be filled with generalizations, lacking in appropriate detail, excessive in unnecessary particulars, and negligent or indulgent in many other ways. Even so, I hope I have supplied a preliminary foundation for understanding the music and the people who make and listen to it, and more ambitiously that I have made a move in the direction of a history of music in West Africa, and ultimately the whole of Africa. To conclude, I will first address the areas I have omitted and then discuss some current issues.

During the several years that elapsed between the time I first sent this manuscript (in an incomplete state) to a publisher and the completion of a final version, I worked on it feverishly. I constantly fought two opposing forces, familiar to many writers. On the one hand, I wanted to cover as much territory as possible as comprehensively as I could. On the other hand, I was eager to present my material, have it read and critiqued, and stimulate others to revisit, refine, refute, and go beyond my work. Although it is time for me to let go of this book, I am also aware that much is lacking. I briefly lay out some of the major areas I have missed, not only as a warning that this study is incomplete in many ways, but also as a call for others to move into these neglected areas and to reassess my writing and also the music.

One major area I have barely broached is differences in musical training, performance, and reception between males and females. This is partially a result of my primary interest in instrumental music, a male pursuit in Mande music. In retrospect, I did not question my teachers about their views on gender and music, nor did I spend much time asking women about their involvement with music, although I did observe a good bit. Consequently I do not specifically address these issues to any appreciable extent (other than in chapter 3 and parts of chapter 5). Of course, this is negligence on my part. Adam Ba Konaré, Sarah Brett-Smith, Mamadou Diawara, Barbara Frank,

Barbara Hoffman, and Kate Modic have done important work with gender in Mande society, and Lucy Durán's work with women and music sets a high standard showing the significance of this area.

One result of my neglect of women and music is the noticeable lack of discussion of vocal music, which is largely a female pursuit in Mande music. Once again my interest in instrumental music shaped my studies in Africa, and I missed out on a major—some might say, the major—aspect of Mande music making. Roderic Knight has done important work in this area, which still awaits extended study.

Another side effect of my instrumental music focus has been my neglect of song texts, another major area of Mande music making. The content and deeper cultural meanings of musical lyrics are often difficult to penetrate for one who is not a native speaker. Furthermore, foreigners typically do not have a lifetime of hearing the songs that go in and out of public consciousness, contributing to the shared memory of a community. Historians or linguists like Djibril Tamsir Niane, Charles Bird, and David Conrad have done important work in presenting and interpreting canonic historical texts. But the subtleties of everyday life and the histories of peoples and their nation that go into contemporary song texts can sometimes be too much for all but the most astute lifetime observers to fully grasp and to interpret for others. One only has to imagine the lyrics of one's own favorite songwriters to appreciate such subtleties. I wait with great anticipation more writing from critics like Cheick M. Cherif Keita to illuminate this so-far hidden dimension of modern-day African music.

Although I have collected and reprinted together for the first time a number of early European travel accounts on music made by Mande peoples, I have by no means exhausted the sources. In particular, I have not explored to any significant degree early colonial reports from the late nineteenth and early twentieth centuries, nor have I searched European or African archives for unpublished material from this era. Any comprehensive history of music and dance from West Africa will have to come to terms with this vast material that only occasionally takes note of local customs.

I regret not being able to spend time in Guinea-Bissau, Burkina Faso, or Côte d'Ivoire to deepen my understanding of core and more peripheral Mande musical traditions. Abidjan has been an important capital of modern music in West Africa, and many Mande musicians have recorded there as well as taken up residence there at one time or another. The cities of Bobo Dioulasso and Ouagadougou in Burkina Faso have fostered important jembe traditions that merit further exploration. Documentation of music in Guinea-Bissau, the ancestral home of the kora, has suffered because of the political strife that has decimated the country in the past several decades.

The ways music moves with the times can be unnerving for those trying to make some sense of it. This applies to the four countries covered here (The Gambia, Guinea, Mali, and Senegal) as much as anywhere else in the world. Some of the major historical events that have acted as catalysts for musical change can be readily identified. These include the early spread of metal-working, the rise of a mounted warrior class that would rule the savanna, the decisive rise of the Mali empire, the growth of tributary states in the western territories, the advent of European colonization, the return of African troops from the two world wars, political independence, declining political and economic conditions in the late 1970s, an exodus to Paris and a thriving West African community there in the mid-1980s, new compact disc technology and the growth of a commercial world music market, world tours of Mande musicians, and increased migration establishing core communities outside France in other European countries and in North America.

Along with these major historical processes there are countless individual initiatives that have moved musical exploration in new directions. Like the Mande hero of action (ngana), Mande musical artists have moved out into the unexplored space symbolized as the bush while still keeping one foot in the village, the symbolic space of tradition. They have created new traditions by reconciling old ones with modern ways of life and thinking in especially fascinating ways. Their ability to retain the essence of old traditions while integrating them into an international musical language sets them apart in a world of music long marked by dilution of local dialects or, more recently, by unabashed, uninformed one-time musical encounters. The continuity and integrity of their musical language—whether formulated in forty-eight-track Parisian recording studios, in jembe workshops packed with students during Northern Hemisphere winters, in life-cycle celebrations in rented New York halls, or in Bamako clubs playing for a mix of foreigners and locals—is truly remarkable.

Mande innovators bringing their traditions to new frontiers are an extraordinarily diverse and numerous lot. In living memory one can begin with the first Guinean orchestras in the 1920s (Sidikiba Diabate's Philharmonie Jazz) and 1930s (La Joviale Symphonie and La Douce Parisette). In the 1930s and 1940s there was the creation of the bala-based music and dance event Mamaya by Sidi Djeli Dioubate (Diabate) and his children Sidi Karamon, Sidi Mamadi, and Sidi Moussa of Kankan. Sidi Mamadi's daughter Oumou Dioubate is at present a leading light coming from deep in the tradition (her mother Nyamakoron Kante was one of Guinea's great jelimuso vocalists), propelled by an international ensemble including jeli instruments, electric guitars, and a brass section. Mamaya continues to inspire artists like Baba Djan Kaba (1992-disc), whose piece *Kankan* brilliantly revisits the glory days of the 1940s, but with electric guitars played in bala styles dominating and modernizing the texture (Kaba and Charry, forthcoming).

Beginning in the late 1940s Fodeba Keita, Facelli Kante, and Les Ballets Africains exposed much of the world to previously unknown Mande performance traditions. Their staging of these traditions opened up new genres, confronting difficult issues of authenticity and modernization, and ultimately served as a frame of reference for double standards that will not go away.

> How often do we hear the word authentic used here, there, and everywhere to describe folkloric performances! Come to the point! Authentic compared to what? To a more or less false idea which one has conceived about the sensational primitiveness of Africa? (Fodeba Keita 1958:172)

> When European artists borrow from Africa, this does not detract from the originality of their work, whereas African artists cannot borrow from Europe without being considered inauthentic. (Manthia Diawara 1998:194–95)

Some questions of borrowing were raised regarding beloved Ballets Africains vocalist Sory Kandia Kouyate's "Spanish-flamenco" style, a journalist's reference really to a shared Muslim heritage (Fodeba Keita 1958:175). Although there may have been little explicit Spanish influence on Sory Kandia's singing, the exquisite flamenco summits of kora players Toumani Diabate (1988a-disc, 1994-disc) and Djeli Moussa Diawara (1997?-disc) bask in the mutually sympathetic radiance of two distant musics meeting like long-lost cousins.

As I briefly alluded to in the introduction and chapters 4 and 7, discussions of tradition and authenticity occasionally lack subtlety and can especially suffer from the absence of those artistic voices that are not engaged in presenting their culture for foreign audiences. Outside Africa one can read about African musicians selling out and diluting their tradition, and one can also read defenses from the artists and their non-African supporters alike pointing out the hypocrisy of such a position. What gets swept aside is the range of local opinion on packaging local music for foreign consumption. Rather than subscribing to knee-jerk reactions, sensitive observers evaluate each case and express preferences for specific songs, arrangements, and artists. The range of aesthetic views is as broad as anywhere else in the world. Blind defense of authenticity or of attempts to borrow, integrate, and experiment may serve the political agendas of critics and artists, but they do not necessarily further the understanding of local debates. The drum machines accompanying jelimusolu so prevalent in Abidjan recording sessions may sound tacky to ears trained on high-fidelity hi-tech acoustic and electric musics of more industrialized nations. One might criticize the use of drum machines as inauthentic. One might in turn criticize the hypocrisy of such a conception of authenticity, not allowing Africans rights of experimentation. But let us recognize that the Africans who both utilize and criticize drum machines—including, no doubt, the arrangers looking for convenient solutions and the drummers seeing their traditions diluted—can think for themselves and are not just reverberant echoes of Euro-American images of Africa. Let us also recognize artistic diversity and competence, as well as the grounding of critics. Some efforts may be interesting, subtle, sophisticated, innovative, and far reaching; others may be derivative, simpleminded, pandering, overly formulaic, and excessively market driven. Many of us may not be well enough informed to pronounce which is which.

Moving out and embracing is a hallmark of Mande style. The Lafiabougou Twins' Bamako Apollos of the 1960s embraced sound-amplification technology—under a space-age heading—leading to novel combinations of instruments. The embracing of Cuban music by francophone Africans cannot be overemphasized, and it took several decades to loosen that embrace in favor of forging national styles based on local traditions. Still the love for Cuban music endures, in occasional arrangements (e.g., Oumou Dioubate's *Kalil* [1999-disc]), in reissues (Las Maravillas de Mali 1967-disc/1998-disc), and in the stunning Africando (1996-disc) project of Malian Boncana Maiga uniting Guinean singer Sekouba Bambino Diabate with a New York–based salsa orchestra.

Moving out and proselytizing has also been a hallmark of Mande style. Since the 1960s Ladji Camara, Famoudou Konate, Adama Drame, and Mamady Keita, all former lead jembe players with national ballets, along with many of their compatriots, have established new and enduring jembe traditions abroad, expanding frontiers and bringing questions of authenticity face to face with literally tens of thousands of new players. Mamady Keita's Tam Tam Mandingue school in Brussels has hundreds of jembe students; there are half a dozen branches in as many countries throughout the world, and it is still growing. Many expatriate drummers bring groups of foreign students to Africa on study tours, resituating foreign perceptions of Africa and charging the energy and commitment of students and teachers alike. These individual initiatives bode well for international relations.

Mande musical continuity rests on the relevance and vibrancy of old instrumental and vocal traditions as well as on Mande conceptions and practices of expansion, assimilation, integration, and respect. Old patronage systems have been upset by the colonial experience, as some Malian writers have noted (e.g., C. Keita 1995a, 1995b; Mamadou Diawara 1996, 1997), and by postcolonial national policy, such as Sekou Toure tried to effect in Guinea. But they were not wiped out. Local passions and exigencies are as compelling reasons for youth to take up the professions handed down from their elders as is the economic stimulus of recent international interest. Because of this combination of local and global demand for expertise in their musical traditions, young Mandenka still apply themselves to the expressive culture of their parents. Just as their parents and grandparents have made use of new musical material and stimuli—the case of Mamaya in Kankan and Apollo in Bamako are perhaps the two most striking examples—so do new generations. In the late twentieth century, however, the economic stakes are higher with the promise of foreign capital. The commercial successes of Salif Keita and Mory Kante have shown the viability of Mande musics in the crowded industry known as world music. The empowering of Mande musical artists, although certainly limited, is surely stimulating musical activity back home.

The praise singing associated with jelimusolu is going to have a tough time surviving, as the surge of popularity that Wasulu female singers have been enjoying in the 1990s has demonstrated. The sometimes drastic reshaping of history, such as the invention of noble bloodlines for powerful patrons who have not inherited them, is but one aspect of jeliya in the modern world that grates on the sensibilities of many. Being "opposed to handing out money to griots, period" yet occasionally succumbing to the "flattery of the griot" (Manthia Diawara 1998:110) is probably a common experience for some seeking to modernize their countries (for other examples see Schulz 1996:310–12). Stories of how great a patron is because he or she is so generous to griots are of little interest to non-Mande audiences and to growing numbers of those at home, no matter how beautifully and powerfully sung. Some of Oumou Dioubate's (1993-disc, 1999-disc) songs taking on social issues represent what might appear to be a new direction for jelimusolu, but they actually hark back to a perceived glorious age when jelis were the conscience and wisdom of Mande society, as in the examples of the revered Banzumana Sissoko (see chapter 1 and C. Keita 1995b) and Siramory Diabate (Y. Kone 1990; Durán 1995b). In other words, modernizing or reforming the tradition is effected by digging deeper into it. Witness the utter freshness of an ensemble of jeli instruments driven by a jembe and dundun (Moriba Koita 1997-disc), with added guitars (Aboubacar Camara 1994-disc) or just a trio of kora, bala, and koni complemented by an upright bass (Toumani Diabate 1995-disc). Mande codes of respect and graciousness may ensure that praise singing continues to maintain its relevance, much to the dismay of many. How to honor these codes of behavior and reform others, such as public praise based on political or economic power rather than morality or heroism, has no facile answer.

Just as there are people able to buy reputations and those willing to accommodate them, there are also key actors working to break out of long-standing social systems that some perceive to have lost their relevancy. National and regional ensembles, ballets, orchestras, and schools of music with salaried artists are one route established in force since independence to revamp patronage systems and democratize music. But one need only look at the family names of those who have made recordings (appendix B) to see where the expertise still lies. These government-patronized groups can be major revenue-producing agencies for their countries. Like other civil servants, though, the artists suffer from the same low salaries typical of economically distressed countries. Some of the more successful artists have forsaken this system and forged solo careers moving between continents the way their forebears would move between villages, towns, and chiefdoms. Some remain abroad on tours establishing careers as performers and teachers in foreign lands, once again like their forebears, who migrated with Mande expansion to new regions. And like the new traditions that developed in the Senegambian territories, new traditions are developing in Europe, North America, and elsewhere.

The story of the guitar in Mande music culture dramatically illustrates Mandenka values of change, marked by a tenacious respect for meaningful old traditions. Initially imported from abroad and used to play foreign music, the guitar has been integrated into the jeli's tradition, typifying continentwide processes but with a difference. Perhaps nowhere else in Africa has the guitar been so completely integrated into an old tradition and at the same time been the major force for expanding the language of that tradition and moving it into an international arena. It has also attracted female players like Sona Diabate. The guitar represented the modern and the non-African world, but as it came to be integrated into local traditions and ultimately move them into an international spotlight, it also came to symbolize the Africanizing of that world. With the definitive presence in Europe by the mid-1980s of Malian and Guinean musical artists, a new concept began to take shape, that the francophone West Africans flooding Parisian suburbs might have something to offer their hosts other than manual labor. In the documentary about his career, Salif Keita (Austin 1991-vid) talks about the enormous steps Africans have made toward integration into French society, suggesting that the French (and others) may have something to learn from their new neighbors if they would just take a few steps in that direction. For many decades the civilizing forces of African writers have been recognized by non-Africans, no doubt owing to the respect accorded to written literature. Music is apparently more subtle in this regard.

Discussions of Africa's moving into the modern world and into the twenty-first century (as the saying goes nowadays) will have to take account of the creative work of a diverse spectrum of African musical artists or risk irrelevancy. This risk is as real to Africanists as it is to the growing number of writers selectively scanning the continent in support of theories of musical globalization. But we are still unprepared. Relatively few Africans write about music. Of those who do, few have direct practical experience in their indigenous musics. On the other hand, most traditional musicians (as defined in the preceding pages) have had little access to or interest in a thorough Western-style education. Therefore those who write about the music do it from a distance, and those who play the music do not write about it. Although this situation may be less extreme in anglophone Ghana and Nigeria, it is the case in francophone western Africa, particularly among the Mande, where there are strong social expectations about who may play music, who should go through a university education, and what fields are respectable scholarly pursuits.

Because musicological writing about and from Africa lags behind other kinds of writing, key dimensions of African life that cut across disciplinary boundaries are missing in studies of Africa's past, present, and future. Questions of identity are so keenly played out in music that to neglect them impoverishes analyses. The staggering plethora of musical instruments uniquely associated with any one region and group of people should signal that these instruments and the traditions they represent are strong markers of group identity and history. For example, the nonmusical lives of Wasulu and Maninka hunters are probably not very different, but their musics are. Drums, styles of playing, and ways of dancing to them are instantly recognized, identified with, and appreciated by those who know their languages. Even the guitar has taken on regional styles and allegiances. If, as the wisdom passed down has taught us, music is such an integral aspect of African life, then the study of music should provide an essential key for understanding African life.

This book, then, is about identities, musical and otherwise, and some of the raw materials of what it is to be Maninka or Mandinka. Some of these materials are also shared by Soninke, Susu, Xasonka, Bamana, and peoples farther afield in southern Guinea, Sierra Leone, Côte d'Ivoire, Burkina Faso, and beyond. These materials—such as instruments and ways of playing them, melodic and rhythmic sensibilities, stories, songs, and social, moral, and psychological stances—are being used, performed, and shaped not only within Africa but also outside it. Those who do not know the language can, and have, responded to Mandenka performance on a variety of levels. I hope I have opened a door to a wondrous area of musical expression wide enough that those with the desire may enter and explore. As the expertise of those who make and grew up with the music we study can be challenged on deeper and deeper levels, they will respond in kind and bring us deeper and deeper into their traditions. The journey will be long, for the wisdom of those who understood the nature of history, geography, and society appears more and more evident: *Manden te banna* (Manden has no end).

References Related to Mande Music in Historical Sources from the Eleventh to the Mid-Nineteenth Century

When possible, I use published English translations; otherwise I have translated the source myself. African or French-African terms appear in my English translations as they do in the source (e.g., italicized, capitalized). I have tried to be selective in what I consider relevant and have left out much material, so readers may wish to refer directly to the sources for further information. After some of the quotations I have added commentary, either my own or from other sources (in which case quotation marks are used and the source is cited). The references appear in chronological order, with the initial date of the manuscript or publication followed by the date (in parentheses) of the edition quoted. See the bibliography for complete citations.

1068 (1981)   al-Bakrī
The city of Ghāna consists of two towns situated on a plain. One of these towns, which is inhabited by Muslims, is large and possesses twelve mosques, in one of which they assemble for the Friday prayer. There are salaried imams and muezzins, as well as jurists and scholars. (79)

Around the king's town are domed buildings and groves and thickets where the sorcerers of these people, men in charge of the religious cult, live. In them too are their idols and the tombs of their kings. . . . The king's interpreters, the official in charge of his treasury and the majority of his ministers are Muslims. . . . The audience is announced by the beating of a drum which they call *dubā*, made from a long hollow log. (80)

On the opposite bank of the Nīl is another great kingdom, stretching a distance of more than eight days' marching, the king of which has the title of Daw. The inhabitants of this region use arrows when fighting. Beyond this country lies another called Malal, the king of which is known as *al-musulmānī*. . . . [al-Bakrī then relates a story of how a visiting Muslim persuaded the king to accept Islam in order to bring rain to his drought-stricken land. When they prayed together for the first time rain came.] So the king ordered the idols to be broken and expelled the sorcerers from his country. He and his descendants after him as well as his nobles were sincerely attached to Islam, while the common people of his kingdom remained polytheists. (82–83)

Between Tādamakka and the town of Kawkaw is a distance of nine stages. . . . When their king sits down [to partake of a meal] a drum is beaten, the Sudanese women dance with their thick hair flowing, and nobody in the town goes about his business until he has finished his repast. . . . They maintain that they are called Kawkaw because this word can be heard in the noise of their drums. In the same way the names of Āzwar, Hīr, and Zawīla are heard in the drumbeats of these peoples, saying: "Zawīla, Zawīla." The people of the region of Kawkaw trade with salt which serves as their currency. [Brackets in the original.] (87)

COMMENTARY: See Farmer (1939:570) for a discussion of the term *dubā*.

"They announce the session by means of a great drum called *dubā* made from a long hollow log covered with a skin and having an awesome sound at which the people assemble" (*Kitāb al-Istibsār,* written in 1191, in Levtzion and Hopkins 1981:147). Much of this text was adapted from al-Bakrī, so it is unclear where the added description of a skin to the drum came from.

"The earliest detailed account of the Western Sudan, that of Abū 'Ubaydallāh al-Bakrī, written in 1067–8. Al-Bakrī, a resident of Cordova in Spain, never left his country. He based his writings on various written sources . . . al-Bakrī also collected oral information from traders who visited the Sudan" (Levtzion 1980:22).

1154 (1981)   al-Idrīsī

The people of Barīsā, Silā, and Ghāna make forays into the land of Lamlam, and capture its inhabitants. They bring them to their own countries, and sell them to the visiting merchants. The latter export them to all the countries. In the whole land of Lamlam there are only two small village-like towns, one called Malal and the other Daw. (108)

The people of this land [the Sudan in general] build their houses of mud, because wide and long pieces of wood are scarce there. . . . The townsmen in that country cultivate onions, gourds and watermelons, which grow very large there. (108–9)

It [Malal] is a small town, like a large village without a surrounding wall, built on an unassailable hill of red earth. . . . From the town of Malal to the town of Great Ghāna is about twelve stages over dunes and deep sands where there is no water. (109)

[The king of Ghana] has a corps of army commanders who come on horseback to his palace every morning. Each commander has a drum, which is beaten before him. When he reaches the gate it is silenced. When all the commanders have assembled, the king mounts his horse and rides at their head through the lanes of the town and around it. (110)

1337–38 (1981)   al-'Umarī

Chapter Ten: The kingdom of Mālī and what appertains to it (261)

Their king at present is named Sulaymān, brother of the Sultan Mūsā Mansā. He controls, of the land of the Sūdān, that which his brother brought together by conquest and added to the domains of Islam. There he built ordinary and cathedral mosques and minarets, and established the Friday observances, and prayers in congregation, and the muezzin's call. He brought jurists of the Malikite school to his country and there continued as sultan of the Muslims and became a student of religious sciences. . . . This king is the greatest of the Muslim kings of the Sūdān. He rules the most extensive territory, has the most numerous army, is the bravest, the richest, the most fortunate, the most victorious over his enemies, and the best able to distribute benefits. (261)

In all the countries, especially Ghāna, sorcery (*sihr*) is much employed. (265)

The king of this realm [Mali] sits in his palace on a big dais. . . . In front of him there stands a man to attend him, who is his executioner [or swordbearer: *sayyāf*], and another, called *shā'ir* "poet" who is his intermediary (*safīr*) between him and the people. Around all these are people with drums in their hands, which they beat. Before the kings are people dancing and he is pleased with them and laughs at them. [Second brackets in the original.] (265)

Whenever one of the emirs or another comes into the presence of this king he keeps him standing before him for a time. Then the newcomer makes a gesture with his right hand like one who beats the drum of honour (*jūk*) in the lands of Tūrān and Īrān. . . .

As for this gesture likened to beating the *jūk,* it is like this. The man raises his right hand to near his ear. There he places it, it being held up straight, and places it in contact with his left hand upon his thigh. The left hand has the palm extended so as to receive the right elbow. The right hand too has the palm extended with the fingers held close beside each other like a comb and touching the lobe of the ear. (266)

When the king of this kingdom comes in from a journey a parasol (*jitr*) and a standard are held over his head as he rides, and drums are beaten and guitars (*tunbūr*) and trumpets well made of horn are played in front of him. (266–67)

Ibn Amīr Hājib said also that . . . [t]he ceremonial for him who presents himself to the king or who receives a favour is that he bares the front of his head and makes the *jūk*-beating gesture towards the ground with his right hand as the Tatars do. (267–68)

COMMENTARY: "Al-ʻUmarī (d. 1348) speaks of the royal entourage of the ruler of Mālli being preceded by drums (*tabl*), pandores (*gunībrī*), and horns (*būq*)" (Farmer 1939:571)

1355 (1981)   Ibn Battūta

I arrived at the town of Mālī, the seat of the king of the Sūdān. . . . I met the interpreter Dūghā [spelled out], one of the respected and important Sūdān. . . . [Brackets in the original.] (288)

I spoke with Dūghā the interpreter, who said: "Speak with him, and I will express what you want to say in the proper fashion." (289)

When he [the king] is sitting they hang out from the window of one of the arches a silken cord to which is attached a patterned Egyptian kerchief. When the people see the kerchief drums are beaten and trumpets are sounded and there come forth from the gate of the palace about 300 slaves. . . . Dūghā the interpreter stands at the gate of the council-place wearing fine garments of silk brocade (*zardakhāna*) and other materials, and on his head a turban with fringes which they have a novel way of winding. Round his waist he has a sword with a golden sheath and on his feet boots and spurs. No-one but him wears boots on that day. . . . Each *farārī* has his followers before him with lances and bows, drums and trumpets. Their trumpets (*būq*) are made out of elephant-tusks and their [other] musical instruments are made out of reeds and gourds and played with a striker (*sattāʻa*) and have a wonderful sound. . . . Anyone who wishes to address the sultan addresses Dūghā and Dūghā addresses that man standing and that man standing addresses the sultan. [Brackets in the original.] (290–91)

The sultan comes out of a door in the corner of the palace with his bow in his hand and his quiver between his shoulders. . . . The singers come out in front of him with gold and silver stringed instruments (*qunburī*) in their hands and behind him about 300 armed slaves. . . . As he sits the drums are beaten and the trumpets are sounded. (291)

At Mālī I was present at the two festivals of the Sacrifice and the Breaking of the Fast. . . . Dūghā the interpreter comes with his four wives and his slave girls (*jawārī*). There are about a hundred of these, with fine clothes and on their heads bands of gold and silver adorned with gold and silver balls. A seat is set up for Dūghā and he sits on it and plays the instrument which is made of reed with little gourds under it, and sings poetry in which he praises the sultan and commemorates his expeditions and exploits and the women and slave girls sing with him and perform with bows.

With them are about thirty of his slave boys (*ghulām*) wearing red *jubbas* of cloth and with white *shāshiyyas* on their heads. Each one of them is girt with a drum which he beats. Then come his young followers who play and turn somersaults in the air as the Sindī does. In this they show unusual elegance and skill. They play with swords in the most beautiful way and Dūghā [also] plays remarkably with the sword. At this the sultan orders him to be given a bounty and a purse is brought in which there are 200 mithqals of gold dust. He is told what is in it publicly. The *farāriyya* stand and twang their bows in thanks to the sultan. On the next day each one of them gives to Dūghā a gift according to his rank. Every Friday, in the afternoon, Dūghā goes through the same performance as we have mentioned. [Brackets in the original.] (292–93)

An Amusing story about the poets' reciting to the sultan
On the feast day, when Dūghā has finished his performance, the poets come. They are called *julā* [spelled out], of which the singular is *jālī*. Each of them has enclosed himself within an effigy made of feathers, resembling a [bird called] *shaqshāq*, on which is fixed a head made of wood with a red beak as though it were the head of a *shaqshāq*. They stand in front of the sultan in this comical shape and recite their poems. I was told that their poetry was a kind of exhortation in which they say to the sultan: "This *banbī* on which you are sitting was sat upon by such-and-such a king and of his good deeds were so-and-so; so you do good deeds which will be remembered after you." Then the chief of the poets mounts the steps of the *banbī* and places his head in the lap of the sultan. Then he mounts to the top of the *banbī* and places his head on the sultan's right shoulder, then upon his left shoulder, talking in their language. Then he descends. I was informed that this act was already old before Islam, and they had continued with it. [Brackets in the original.] (293)

COMMENTARY: See chapter 3 for a discussion of Ibn Battūta's term *qunburī* (also see Farmer 1928). See Farmer (1939:573–75) for a discussion of Ibn Battūta's description of the instrument made of "reeds with tiny calabashes below it." It most likely was a bala and is the earliest description of one.

1468 (1937)   Alvise Ca da Mosto
[Regarding Cayor in northern Senegal] In this country they have no musical instruments of any kind, save two: the one is a large Moorish "tanbuchi," which we style a big drum; the other is after the fashion of a viol; but it has, however, two strings only, and is played with the fingers, so that it is a simple rough affair and of no account. (51)

1493 (1970)   al-Lamtūnī
[possibly describing the south-central Sahara and its southern peripheries, inhabited by Tuareg and Fulbe] Most of the women play the flute and the lute and the tambourine and wail the *zaghārīt* [ululation] and play all manner of musical instruments. (14)

COMMENTARY: An Arabic facsimile (1933, 286) shows *'ūd* to be the word translated as lute.

Fifteenth century (1937) Diogo Gomes

COMMENTARY: Does not contain anything directly related to music but has historical information on the extent of the Mandinka Kabu empire.

1506–8 (1937) Duarte Pacheco Pereira

COMMENTARY: Does not contain anything directly related to music but has much on Mandinka in The Gambia and the Casamance.

1506–10 (1951) Valentim Fernandes
In this country and in *Mādinga* there are *judeus* and they are called *Gaul* and they are black like their countrymen; however they do not have synagogues and do not practice the ceremonies of other Jews. They do not live with the other blacks, but in separate villages.

These *Gaul* are often buffoons and play the viol and *cavacos* and are singers. And because they do not dare enter into the villages they hide behind the compound of the village nobleman and sing his praises until dawn, until they are given a ration of millet, and then they leave.

And when the nobleman leaves his home the *judeus* go ahead of him singing and crying their buffooneries. (9)

The blacks treat them [*judeus*] like dogs, and they do not dare enter into any home except that of the nobleman, and if they are found in the village they are beaten with sticks. (11)

COMMENTARY: "They [*Gaul*] evidently do not have any Jewish ancestry, and the connection made by V. Fernandes must be solely because in the 15th century Jews and griots were despised and were kept apart from the rest of society.

Still today in Portuguese Guinea [Guinea Bissau] griots are universally known as *Judeus* (in Portuguese) and *Jideus* (in creole)." (152)

"Cavaco (Port.). A plucked string instrument midway between a guitar and a mandolin, used in Portugal. It usually has four strings" (Sadie 1980, 3:18).

1594 (1984) André Álvares d'Almada
Throughout this land of the Jalofos, Barbacins, and Mandingas can be found a nation of blacks who are considered and treated by them as Jews (are among us). I do not know where they come from. They are a handsome people, especially the women. The men have noses of generous size. Most of them will not eat pork.

They are importunate beggars, going from kingdom to kingdom with their women, like gypsies with us. They take up the same manual trades as the gypsies do, that is, (they work as) weavers, shoemakers, and blacksmiths. They are employed as drummers in the blacks' wars, and they sing to spur on those who fight, reminding them of the deeds of their ancestors; and in this way they persuade them to conquer or die. In war they beat three kinds of drums. One kind is like ours; another is smaller, and they carry it under the arm and beat it while on horseback; another kind is made of a single skin, seven hand-spans long. With these instruments they announce anything they want known, for instance, they make signals in battle or give warnings of fire. When the blacks hear drums, they can tell instantly which king or captain the particular drums belong to. The Jews also play (stringed instruments,) violins and another sort which is like a harp. . . . When these Jews die, they do not bury them in the ground like other blacks, but (leave their bodies) in holes in trees. If there are none, they hang their bodies in the trees, because the other blacks hold the erroneous belief that if Jews are buried with other persons, the rains will not come and there will be no new crops on the land that year. (Chap. 4, pp. 34–35)

[Regarding a log slit drum played with two sticks] All the Guinea blacks use the instrument, called by them *banbalo,* except the Mandingas, Barbacins, Jalofos, Fulos and all the other blacks who live North of the Gambia River, either on the coast or in the interior, for these people use hand-drums and side-drums. (chap. 11, pp. 107–8)

COMMENTARY: Brief discussion of dancing to drums, ivory trumpets, and conch shells at funeral ceremonies (chapter 8, pp. 69–70, chap. 11, p. 105), and of female initiates in the vicinity of present-day Conakry dancing to an ensemble of slit drums called *bambalos* (chap. 15, p. 16).

1623 (1968)   Richard Jobson

The Kings house is in the middle of the Towne, inclosed by it selfe, onely his wives severall houses about him, to which you cannot come, but as it were through a Court of Guard, passing through an open house, where stands his chaire empty, unlawfull for any but himselfe to sit in, by which hangs his drummes, the onely instruments of warre which we see amongst them, neither are the drummes without dayly imployment, for this is their continuall custome every night after it seemes they have filled their bellies, they repaire to this Court of Guard, making fires both in the middle of the house, and in the open yard, about which they doe continue drumming, hooping, singing, and makeing a hethenish noyse, most commonly untill the day beginnes to breake, when as we conceive dead-sleepes take them, by which meanes sleeping one part of the day . . . ; for this manner of course is held amongst them, not only in their fortified Townes, but also in every particular village, and habitation, whereof few of them is without such poore drums they use, and if they be, yet they continue the custome, through hooping, singing, and using their voyces, but when it happens musicke is amongst them, then is the horrible din, as I shall signifie when I overtake their fidlers. (58)

They also assembled themselves, in the most convenient place, to receive the multitude, and nearest unto the grave, and sitting downe in a round ring, in the middle came foorth a Mary-bucke, who betwixt saying and singing, did rehearse as it were certaine verses, in the praise and remembrance of him departed, which it should seeme was done *extempore;* or provided for that assembly, because upon divers words or sentences hee spake, the people would make such sodaine exultations, by clapping their hands, and every one running in, to give and present unto him, some one or other manner of thing, might be thought acceptable, that one after another, every severall Mary-bucke would have his speech, wherein they onely went away with the gratifications, who had the pleasingest stile, or as we terme it, the most eloquente phrase, in setting forth the praises of him departed, in which the people were so much delighted. (90–91)

[More on jelis, praising, singing extempore]

They have little varietie of instruments, that which is most common in use, is made of a great gourd, and a necke thereunto fastned, resembling, in some sort, our Bandora; but they have no manner of fret, and the strings they are either such as the place yeeldes, or their invention can attaine to make, being very unapt to yeeld a sweete a musicall sound, notwithstanding with pinnes they winde and bring to agree in tunable notes, having not above six strings upon their greatest instrument: In consortship with this they have many times another who playes upon a little drumme which he holds under his left arme, and with a crooked sticke in his right hand, and his naked fingers on the left he strikes the drumme . . . their most principall instrument, which is called Ballards made to stand a foot above the ground, hollow under, and hath uppon the top some seventeene woodden keyes standing like the Organ, upon which hee that playes sitting upon the ground, just against the middle of the instrument, strikes with a sticke in either hand, about a foote long, at the end whereof is made fast a round ball, covered with some soft stuffe, to avoyd the clattering noyse the bare stickes would make: and upon either arme hee hath great rings of Iron: out of which are wrought pretty hansomly smaller Irons to stand out, who hold upon them smaller rings and juggling toyes, which as hee stirreth his armes, makes a kinde of musicall sound agreeing to their barbarous content: the sound that proceeds from this instrument is worth the observing, for we can heare it a good English mile, the making of this instrument being one of the most ingenious things amongst them: for to every one of these keyes there belongs a small Iron the bignesse of a quill, and is a foote long, the breadth of the instrument, upon which hangs two gourdes under the hollow, like bottles, who receives the sound, and returnes it againe with that extraordinary loudnesse; there are not many of these, as we can perceive, because they are not common . . . the most desirous of dancing are the women, who dance without men, and but one alone, with crooked knees and bended bodies they foot it nimbly, while the standers by seeme to grace the dancer, by clapping their hands together after the manner of keeping time; (134–36) . . . and this one especiall note, howsoever the people affect musicke, yet so basely doe they esteeme of the player, that when any of them die, they doe not vouchsafe them buriall, as other people have; but set his dead corps upright in a hollow tree, where hee is left to consume: when they have beene demanded a reason for so doing, they will answer, they are a people, who have alwayes a familiar conversation with their divell *Ho-re:* and therefore they doe so dispose of them: which opinion of theirs caused us to neglect and especially in their hearing to play upon any Lute or Instrument which some of us for our private exercise did carry with us, in regard if they had hapned to see us, they would in a manner of scorne say, hee that played was a Juddy: The greatest resort of people, with the most aboundance of these Juddies, is at their times of Circumcision, wherein they observe one due season. (137)

1625 (1977)   André Donelha

COMMENTARY: Contains much description of groups in the southern Mandinka diaspora (Guinea and Sierra Leone), including a description of a long wooden idiophone called *bombalo* that can communicate messages.

1637   Alexis de Saint-Lô

At the end of the feast everyone gathered in a large area to dance, having no other instruments but drums that their Guiriots played rather harshly, although keeping the time. They scream at the top of their voices, singing and often repeating the same things over again. They have small iron plaques with rings around it that they call Casquabelles wrapped around their arms and knees and it makes a noise like cymbals.

The dancers make grimaces that inspire fear more than amusement: for they roll their eyes, grit their teeth, open their mouths, stick out their tongues, twist their necks, threaten the sky, and hold the rest of their body so straight and stiff that one could say that they were made of a single piece, doing nothing but stamping their feet, and in a half hour advancing only three or four feet, and feeling exhausted, they turn back along the same path they have traced. Surely, I thought at first when I saw this kind of dance that the dancer was possessed; one sees a girl or woman opposite the man who is dancing making the same postures and silly antics.

[Heading in the margin] *Musicians called Guiriots, held in disgrace by this nation.*

The Guiriots who play for the dancers are looked down upon by the community and when the French want to anger a black they call them a Guiriot. These Guiriots are a great nuisance because on seeing someone after some absence they accost them and sing all of the praises that they can come up with and do not leave them alone until they have been given something. Seeing that the person does not want to give them anything they scream and shout until at last one is forced to give them something. They are not deemed worthy of burial for when they die they are placed upright inside the hollow of a tree. I have seen the body of one in this kind of burial. (85–88)

COMMENTARY: First appearance of the word griot (guiriot).

1670   Olfert Dapper
[Heading:] *The Kingdom of Zenega, or Country of Jalofs* (339)
When a Drummer dies, they will not permit him to be buried in the Earth, or thrown into the Sea or River, but he must be cast into some hollow Tree: for they imagine that his being entomb'd in the one, or engulph'd in the other, would make them fruitless and empty: yet these sorts of People, though so abominated when dead, yet in their life time are in great esteem with the Kings, and other great Lords, who being minded to recreate themselves, send for them to beat on their Drums, as we in these civilized Parts have Musitians. In the Wars also they go before, yet never permitted to come into the place where the King reposes or sleeps: and if any of his Courtiers be known to have been familiar with a Drummers Wife, or Daughter, he dares no more appear in the King's House: In short, they are neither better nor worse than Beggers, or to speak more properly, then itinerant, or vagabond Fidlers, and not unlike them in conditions; for where they are liberally rewarded, they will extol their Master with the highest Eulogies, and descend even to the basest insinuations of colloguing flattery; on the other, not sparing the most contumelious reproaches to such as answer not their immerited expectation: for their Musick it self, or Drum, is nothing but a piece of a hollow Tree, three, four, or five Foot long, at one end covered over with a Buck-skin. (349)

COMMENTARY: French translation ([1686] 1970:235) contains a drawing of a griot being buried in a large tree.

1684 (1985)   Francisco de Lemos Coelho
[Regarding the kingdom of the "Jalofos" south of present-day Dakar] In these kingdoms there is also a race (*casta*) of blacks called *Judeos* (Jews). They are a despised people, and only make a living by the men playing musical instruments and the women dancing, which the latter are very skilled in doing after their own fashion, and so agile that it seems as if they were born without bones; also they are skilled jugglers and very good-looking. Although they make their living this way only, they earn plenty, because the blacks of the land give them all they ask for. Yet the blacks treat these *Judeos* with so little regard that none of them may enter their houses and they have to perform in the street, where they display their contortions. Nor will any local black touch any of the *Judeo* women, though they are very immodest. The local blacks consider all those of this nation contemptible, and when the *Judeos* die they do not

permit them to be buried in the ground, but instead the corpses are placed in the hollows of certain large trees called *cabaceiras*. . . . True, these *Judeos* have nothing of the Jew other than the name. (Chap. 1, pp. 7–8)

1685 (1913)   Sieur de la Courbe
[Regarding the Jalof or Wolof] The day after the wedding night the husband had a white skirt cloth that was slightly bloodied put on a lance and paraded around the village as a sign of the virginity of his wife, which was accompanied by guiriots singing the praises of the couple. (31)

The prince, an important person and relative of the king of Houal . . . came to visit me. . . . Having arrived at my place, he stayed by the door sitting on his backside like a monkey with all of his people around him armed with sabers, knives, lances, and shields of antelope [oryx] skin while the interpreter or master of language entered and inquired if I was disposed to receive him. Then he introduced the prince with only four of his people, two of whom were his principal officers and the two others were griots who never left their master. . . . he sat on a stool facing me, or rather he crouched on it, for they can never put their feet down like us. His two principal officers sat at his sides in the same posture, and the griots sat on the ground close to him. (40–41)

The guiriots were marvelous singing praises to me and to their master, and they accompany their voice with a small lute with three horsehair strings that is not unpleasant to hear; their songs are martial, saying that you are of a great race, which they call *grands gens* in corrupt French, that you will overcome your enemies, that you are generous and other things of this nature. Finally they conclude so that you may give them something. (43)

I gave them some small things, especially to the guiriots, who otherwise would have cursed me as much as they had praised me. (44–45)

[Regarding men working in the fields] All of this done to the sound and beat of a furious music made by six guiriots with their voices and drums; it was a delight to see them work as if they were possessed, and they would augment or diminish their work according to how the drums were beaten. . . . afterward it was necessary to give something to the guiriots, who, to impress me, used every effort of their symphony and howling to incite the others to work more feverishly. (51–52)

All the women of the village took us back to the riverbank while singing. Their manner of singing is extraordinary: a soloist sings all that comes to her in thinking of the praises of the person for whom she is singing, while the others keep the beat by clapping their hands. At the end of each couplet or reprise they all sing a chorus together and strike up a refrain that is still on the same tone, but is not disagreable. (54)

The guiriots who were by the door of the room shouted at the top of their lungs by way of singing my praises, accompanying their voices with their three-stringed instrument that had bells attached to the end of it: they said that it could be seen I was a great person because of the presents I gave to their king, that no other commandant before me had been so generous, and that they hoped I would also be generous with them; the other guiriots who remained by the riverbank made a frightful noise with a dozen drums, shouting at the top of their voices calling me Samba Bourguaye, which means master of the sea. (73)

The guiriots of the village did not fail to come and give us a symphony with their drums, all of which were made from a carved-out tree trunk, some long, others much shorter, which they play with a hand and a stick with much precision. It is to the sound of these instruments that the young girls and boys, after having dinner, relax from their work and dance with all kinds of diabolical postures and contortions well into the night. (77–78)

[Description of a circumcision] All the griots, numbering more than twenty, who had been occupied with the feast throughout the night, came with their drums to serenade us at dawn and went around our hut causing a row and racket like the devil; I thought that giving them something would quiet them down, but instead they redoubled their efforts in gratitude; this went on for about the whole eight hours that they had requested us to come and see the ceremony. (116)

[Regarding the Moors] The Moorish women are as modestly dressed as the black women are not; their followers were dressed the same, except for a guiriotte or female musician who was heavily adorned with all kinds of trinkets. (171)

Then they had their guiriote sing; she held a kind of harp, which had a calabash covered with hide that had ten or twelve strings, which she played well enough; she began to sing an Arab song that was melodious but quite languishing, somewhat in the manner of the Spanish or Portuguese, accompanying herself with her harp with much care; but what was even more delightful were her passionate movements and the way that she moved her head, causing all of her gris gris and pendants to shake in time and showing the most beautiful teeth in the world; I took exception, however, to her words, which seemed extremely rude and coarsely uttered. (172)

[Near Albreda on the Gambia River] Some time after, a musician came and began to play an instrument that is not unpleasant, but could be improved; it is made of many pieces of strong, hard and flat wood, the thickness of a thumb and the length of two fingers, arranged one after the other like on a spinet keyboard, and resting on two tightly stretched leather cords; underneath there are many calabashes of different sizes suspended; when he wants to play it, he strikes it with two small batons on the slats of wood in the manner of a tympani, which resonates in the calabashes and makes a very pleasant sound; they call this instrument *bala,* or Barbarie organ, because the batons are normally like organ pipes, and the person who plays it is called a *balafon.* (195–96)

[More on 91–92, 142, 144, 161, 169]

COMMENTARY: contains the earliest description of the Moorish harp called *ardin.*

1695   Sieur Le Maire

Even though they have no mind nor aptitude, they love praise so much that the have people called *Guiriotz* whose only occupation is to praise people. The Guiriotz carry around a kind of drum that is four or five feet long and made from a hollowed-out tree trunk that is played either with the hands or with sticks. They also have Moorish drums that resemble a Corbillon d'Oublieur, with thin cords going across it, which they play with one hand while the other strikes it with a stick.

I have noted before that they use a very harmonious instrument that they play quite well which sounds like a psalterion. It is made of many calabashes of different sizes suspended under keys that are arranged like that of a spinet.

I have seen another of their instruments that is more suited to a sick person's room. It is a kind of lute, made from a piece of carved wood covered with leather, with two or three horsehair strings. The neck is covered with small iron plaques and fitted with small bells like a Basque drum.

The Guiriotz tune their instruments to the sound of their unmelodious voices and sing the praises of eminent people. The kinds of praises they usually give are that they are great noblemen, rich, as powerful as the whites, who are the great slaves of the king, and an infinity of other such foolishness.

The nobles are delighted with these praises and generously reward the Guiriot who praises them. They even go so far in this regard that I have seen them take off their own clothing to pay for these insincere and false praises. When they fail to pay these rogues, they are discredited in the villages by their praisers, who say as much bad of them as they had said good, which is the greatest insult that they could get.

For them it is the greatest honor when the king's Guiriot sings their praises, and he is well rewarded: for they give him up to two or three bulls and even most of what they own.

These Guiriotz even thought to sing our own praises, shouting that we are great, rich, and masters of the sea. But they do not get their due from us, who do not appreciate them as much as the blacks. (120–23)

The Guiriotz incite them into combat with the sound of their instruments. (177)

[Also more on how they earn their living]

1698b   François Froger

The King appear'd a little while after, without any regular Train, in the midst of a great number of Negroes, and attended with some Drummers. (27)

The most part of the Negroes divert themselves therein, with discoursing about the *Alcoran,* or with playing on a certain Musical Instrument, which they call *Balafo,* whilst their Wives are employ'd in tilling the Ground. The *Balafo* is nothing else but several Pipes of very hard Wood set in order, which diminish by little and little in length, and are ty'd together with Thongs of very thin leather. These Thongs are twisted about small round Wands, which are put between every one of those Pipes, to leave a small Space: This instrument very much resembles one of ours in that particular; but that of the Negroes is compos'd of many more parts, in regard that they fasten underneath ten or twelve Gourds, the different Sizes of which perform the same effect as our Organ-Pipes: They usually play upon it with Sticks, the Ends of which are cover'd with Leather, to render the Sound less harsh. (35–36)

COMMENTARY: Contains two drawings of a bala: the first is of someone playing it inside a hut titled "A Negro Playing on a Balafo" (between 33 and 34); the second is of a bala and two sticks titled "The Balafo an Instrument of the Negroes" and "The Sticks" (between 34 and 35).

Seventeenth century (1964) Mahmūd Kâti

In a royal audience no one can call the prince by his name, except for the *guissiridonké.* (14, also see 177)

I report these details from the *guissiridonké* Boukâri who told me about these events. (276)

COMMENTARY: *Guissiridonke* may come from *gesere,* a Sonike word for griot. Songhai griots (called *jesere*) are believed to be of Soninke origin.

1705 (1967)   William Bosman

Their second sort of Instruments are their Drums; of which there are about ten several sorts, but most of them are excavated Trees covered at one end with a Sheepsskin, and left open at the other; which they set on the Ground like a Kettle-Drum, and when they remove it they hang it by a String about their Necks: They beat on these Drums with two long Sticks made Hammer-Fashion, and sometimes with a streight Stick or their bare Hands; all which ways they produce a dismal and horrid Noise: The Drums being generally in consort with the blowing of the Horns; which afford the most charming Asses Musick that can be imagined: to help out this they always set a little Boy to strike upon a hollow piece of Iron with a piece of Wood: which alone makes a Noise more detestable than the Drums and Horns together.

Of late they have invented a sort of small Drums, covered on both sides with a Skin, and extended to the shape of an Hour-Glass: The Noise they afford is very like that our Boys make with their Pots they play with on Holidays, with this difference only, that these have Iron-rings, which makes some alteration in the Sound. 'Twould be ridiculous to tire you with all the Instruments of the Negroes: I shall therefore take leave of this Subject, by describing the best they have; which is a hollow piece of Wood of two hands breadth long, and one broad; from the hinder part of this a Stick comes cross to the fore-part, and upon the Instrument are five or six extended Strings: So that it bears some sort of Similitude to a small Harp, or if you will, is not very unlike the Modern Greek Musical Instruments, and affords by much the most agreeable Sound of any they have here. (139–40)

1715 (1747)   André Brue

Moorish ardin: She had her play an instrument made of a calabash that was covered with a red parchment and with twelve strings, some silver and some brass. The sound resembled that of a harp. (439)

1738 (1740)   Francis Moore

One of the Emperors of *Fonia* came to the fort. . . . He and his retinue came in a large Canoa, holding about sixteen People, all armed with Guns and Cutlasses; with him came two or three Women, and the same Number of *Mundingo* Drums, which are about a Yard long, and a Foot, or twenty Inches diameter at the Top, but less at the Bottom, made out of a solid Piece of Wood, and covered, only at the widest End, with the skin of a Kid. They beat upon them with only one Stick, and their left Hand, to which the Women will dance very briskly. (44–45)

In every Town, almost, they have a large Thing like a Drum, called a *Tantong,* which they beat only on the Approach of an Enemy, or some very extraordinary Occasion, to call the neighbouring Towns to their Assistance. This same *Tantong* can, in the Night-Time, be heard six or seven Miles.

They are naturally very jocose and merry, and will dance to a Drum or a Balafeu sometimes four and twenty Hours together, dancing now and then very regular, and at other Times in very odd Gestures, striving always to outdo one another in Nimbleness and Activity. (77–78)

On my Arrivrl at *Nackway* they welcomed me with some Musick called a *Balafeu,* which at about an hundred Yards distance sounds something like a small Organ. It is composed of about twenty Pipes of very hard Wood, finely rubbed and polished; which Pipes diminish by little and little both in Length and Breadth, and are tied together with Thongs made of very thin fine Leather. These Thongs are twisted about small round Wands, which are put between every one of these Pipes, in order to leave a small Space. Underneath the Pipes are fastened twelve or fourteen Calabashes of different Sizes, which have the same Effect as Organ Pipes. This they play upon with two Sticks, which are cover'd with a thin Skin out of a Ciboa-Tree Trunk, or with fine Leather, to make the Sound less harsh. Both Men and Women dance to this Musick, and very much like it, and they are highly delighted to have a White Man dance with them, or drink with them. (84–85)

On the 5th, in the Morning, we left *Joar,* having taken in a Linguister for *Barracunda,* viz. *Tagrood Sanea;* we also hir'd a Balafeu (which is a Country Musician) to chear up the Men, and recreate them in an Evening. (189)

I shall now describe the *Pau de Sangue,* or Bloodwood, so call'd from a Red Gum which issues from it; it grows plentifully all up the River, but here at *Fatatenda* it is larger than ordinary, and by the *Mundingoes* call'd *Cano,* of which they make the *Balafeu,* a Musical Instrument. It is a very hard Wood, of a beautiful Grain, and polishes finely, very proper for Escrutores, or Inlaying, and they say that the *Buggabuggs* never touch it. . . . it grows generally in a dry rocky Soil, and against and on the Tops of Hills. (200–201)

[Included at the end of the book (X2)] A List of Words, *English* and *Mundingo* [with about two hundred entries, including]

A Man, *Kea*
A Woman, *Moosa* . . .
A Singing-Man, *Jelly kea* . . .
A Whore, *Jelly moosa*

COMMENTARY: The drum that Moore calls *tantong* is nowadays called *tabala.* The Mandinka at present use the word *tantong* for the other drums that Moore describes but does not name. Moore may have confused the two names. Mungo Park's description (see below) is in accordance with present usage. The wood Moore calls *cano* (called *keno* nowadays) is still used today for balas.

1732   John Barbot

The name of *Guiriot,* in their tongue, properly signifies a buffoon, and they are a sort of sycophants. (55)

COMMENTARY: See notes 29 and 75 in chapter 3 above. Plate 3(2) (after p. 55) contains drawings of a bala that were most likely reproduced from Froger.

1744   William Smith

We all went ashore, at the opposite Side, to pay our Respects to the King of *Barra* [on the north bank at the mouth of the Gambia River]. . . . The King came about a Quarter of a Mile out of the Town to meet us, attended with three or four Hundred of his Subjects, several of them beating on large loud Drums, while others sounded Trumpets made of Elephants Teeth; all which together made a loud and warlike Noise. . . .

When we were all seated, the King sent for his Musician, who play'd on a strange Kind of *African* Instrument call'd, a BALLAFOE. The Instrument was well tun'd, and made a very agreeable Sound. It is made of short Pieces of very hard Wood tied together, with Callabashes under them, being all of different Sizes, and is play'd upon, as describ'd in the Draught [the drawing on the frontispiece].

His Majesty, for our farther Diversion, caus'd several of the Natives to dance before us, the Men having drawn Swords in their Hands, which they brandish'd about with wonderous Dexterity. (20–22)

The Day, I din'd with the King of *Barra,* I observ'd, that his Musician, who play'd on the Ballafoe, had fix'd to the Top of his Cap, the Tuft or Crown of a Bird, as in the Draught, of which more hereafter; it being the largest and finest I ever saw. I went to take off the Fellow's Cap to look at it, but he, in a Surprize got up, and ran away: Some of the Gentlemen of the Castle who saw the Action smil'd, and told me, that was his *Fittish,* which ought to be handled by no Man, but himself. (27–28)

COMMENTARY: There is a drawing on the frontispiece captioned "A Negro playing on the Ballafoe." The instrument has eleven keys. Although he describes large calabashes used as bowls (29–31), he makes no mention of kora-like instruments.

1745–47 (1968)   Thomas Astley
Those who play on the Instruments are Persons of a very singular Character, and seem to be their Poets as well as Musicians, not unlike the Bards among the *Irish* and the ancient *Britons.* All the *French* Authors, who describe the Countries of the *Jalofs* and *Fûlis,* call them *Guiriots;* but *Jobson* gives them the Name of *Juddies,* which he interprets *Fidlers.* Perhaps the former is the *Jalof* and *Fûli* Name; the latter, the *Mandingo.* (2:278)

COMMENTARY: Contains a section titled "Of the Negro Music, Dancing, Fishing, and Hunting" that summarizes writing by Le Maire, Barbot, Jobson, Brue, and Labat (2:277–81).

1757   Michel Adanson
[In a footnote explaining the term "guirots"] This is the name that the negroes give to the musicians and drummers of the country. (33)

1781 (1983)   Georg Høst (Hoest)
Gnawa guitar, which is used only by the blacks. . . . It is played with the fingers. At the upper extremity a thin metal plate with rings is inserted which gives off a strong noise. (170)

COMMENTARY: Includes drawings of a Gnawa gimbri with a metal rattle stuck in the end of the neck (168). The shape resembles the large Bambara ngoni, rather than the modern-day rectangular box.

1788 (1966)   John Matthews
Their favorite amusement of singing and dancing, which they term a *cullunjee.* When a *cullenjee* is performed on any great occasion, they introduce dancers dressed in a grotesque style; on their heads they wear a high cap made of rushes, stuck round with feathers, and their faces are painted about the eyes, nose, and mouth, with chalk, or white clay, and they wear a pettycoat of rushes round their waist, which in dancing spreads in every direction. In their hands they have pieces of flat wood, which they clap together, and with which they keep time during the dance. (100)

[Regarding Bullam and Timmaneys(?)] They begin singing the praises of the deceased, and dancing to the music of a drum. In the dance they frequently vary the figure; sometimes forming one great circle round the music, and clapping hands at every period or repetition of their song. Sometimes one person performs the dance, the rest sitting or standing round in a circle, joining chorus and clapping hands as before: at other times two, three, or four, will dance together till they are weary, and then relieved by others; the rest singing and clapping hands. (101)

They have various kinds of national music; but the drum seems to be the principal instrument, of which they have three sorts, but they are of different sizes, according to the use for which they are intended. (104)

They beat upon them with two sticks. . . . They have also two kinds of string instruments; one is a sort of guitar, and is the same as the bangou in the West Indies; the other is in the form of a Welsh harp, but not above two feet long: the strings are made of the fibres of a plant and the hair of an elephant's tail. (105–6)

COMMENTARY: The information above is reported almost word for word (in French) by Durand (1802:186–87, 189).

1789   Dominique Harcourt Lamiral

[Among the Moors] On his right the king has the master of language, or interpreter, who is in charge of cutting and preparing morsels of meat for him. His Griot is behind and amuses him with songs or stories during the meal; the king also has much regard for him; from time to time he passes him some morsels of meat or commends him to the whites. (99–100)

[Regarding the blacks of Senegal and Gambia] The boys and girls gather together in the middle of the village; they sit in a circle, and in the middle are the musicians who entertain the party with dances and lascivious gestures. They pantomime all of the caresses and raptures of love, the griottes approach the onlookers and seem to provoke them into an amorous combat, the young girls accompany them with their voices and say things appropriate to the matter at hand: they all clap their hands in time and encourage the dancers by their clapping. At first the music starts slow, the dancers approach one another and back off, the rhythm doubles, the gestures become quicker; the musicians thunder and the movements of the dancers gets faster and faster, their bodies take all sorts of shapes; they hold each other and push each other away: finally out of breath, they fall into the arms of each other and the onlookers cover them with their pagnes [skirt cloths]; during this time the drums make such a racket that it is impossible to understand anything that is said.

Sometimes young girls take the place of the Griottes to show off their abilities and arouse the young men who watch them. They display more grace and finesse than the Griottes; when they have danced for a while they throw themselves into the arms of their friends, hiding their faces as if they were embarrassed at what they have done.

Often men dressed in the costume of war simulate the actions of combat, of a battle; the spectators and the music incites them by their war songs. (266–67)

Griots are the entertainers and musicians of the country; they are also seasoned storytellers; they also know psalmistry and divination: they know the art of making grisgris like Marabouts. It is a practice that is passed down from father to son: they are regarded as despised, and no families intermarry with them; however, everyone seeks them out, and everyone gives to them; the wealthy always have one of them with them; kings never go anywhere without having several of them in their entourage singing their praises. (269)

COMMENTARY: First appearance of the modern spelling griot.

1799 (1983)   Mungo Park

The wrestling was suceeded by a dance, in which many performers assisted, all of whom were provided with little bells, which were fastened to their legs and arms; and here, too, the drum regulated their motions. It was beaten with a crooked stick, which the drummer held in his right hand, occasionally using his left to deaden the sound, and thus vary the music. The drum is likewise applied on these occasions to keep order among the spectators, by imitating the sound of certain Mandingo sentences. (31)

On entering the town, the singing man began an extempore song in praise of the blacksmith, extolling his courage in having overcome so many difficulties; and concluding with a strict injunction to his friends to dress him plenty of victuals (61)

[I] was informed that a *Jilli Kea* (singing man) was about to depart for Sibidooloo . . . throwing his drum upon his back [Park was near Bamako at the time]. (182–83)

Of their music and dances, some account has incidentally been given in different parts of my journal. On the first of these heads, I have now to add a list of their musical instruments, the principal of which are the *koonting,* a sort of guitar with three strings; the *korro,* a large harp with eighteen strings; the *simbing,* a small harp with seven strings; the *balafou,* an instrument composed of twenty pieces of hard wood of different lengths, with the shells of gourds hung underneath, to increase the sound; the *tangtang,* a drum, open at the lower end; and lastly, the *tabala,* a large drum, commonly used to spread an alarm through the country. Besides these they make use of small flutes, bow-strings, elephants' teeth, and bells; and at all their dances and concerts, *clapping* of hands appears to constitute a necessary part for the chorus.

With the love of music is naturally connected a taste for poetry: and fortunately for the poets of Africa, they are in a great measure exempted from that neglect and indigence which, in more polished countries, commonly attend the votaries of the Muses. They consist of two classes; the most numerous are the *singing men,* called *Jilli kea,* mentioned in a former part of my narrative. One or more of these may be found in every town. They sing extempore songs, in honour of their chief men, or any other persons who are willing to give "solid pudding for empty praise." But a nobler part of their office is to recite the historical events of their country; hence, in war, they accompany the soldiers to the field, in order, by reciting the great actions of their ancestors, to awaken in them a spirit of glorious emulation. The other class are devotees of the Mahomedan faith, who travel about the country, singing devout hymns and performing religious ceremonies, to conciliate the favour of the Almighty, either in averting calamity, or insuring success to any enterprise. Both descriptions of these itinerant bards are much employed and respected by the people, and very liberal contributions are made for them. (213–14)

COMMENTARY: Park notes that there are only two sorts of artisans: *garanke* (leatherworker) and *numu* (blacksmith) (216).

1802 (1979)   Richard Bright

The only professed artists among the Mandingoes and Soosoos [Susus] are Blacksmiths who work in gold and silver as well as in iron; and a Class of men called Garangies, or Yellies [Yelies], whose functions are very complex and diverse. As artists, they work in leather with skill and even elegance. Besides this, they are professionally and exclusively the Musicians, Poets, Historian, Orators, and Heralds of the country. Thus, the superintendance of religion and law, and the practice of medicine excepted, they exercise throughout the interior of Nigritia, as well as on this coast, the functions of our ancient Druids and Bards. Satire and Panegyric are equally within their province; but they are to consider truth in the use of these powerful applications to human pride, as a sacred obligation. In some instances I am told they practice it, which if done from pure motives, must be in them a virtue of no vulgar stamp; for, being the most important beggars in the world, they are under constant temptations to be influenced by self interest both in the use of praise and dispraise. These men always attend the army, exciting the youth to acts of valour by rehearsing the deeds of their ancestors, or reproving their degeneracy if they perceive in them a disposition averse from war and military enterprize. [Brackets in the original.] (76–77)

This evening I was present at a grand concert of vocal and instrumental music with dancing performed in honour of Dalla Moodoo [Modu]. The instruments consisted of a Balanghiee, three large drums, and a small one. The Balanghiee is composed of a row of sticks of unequal length placed horizontally on the tops of empty calabashes of sizes gradually diminishing, and making a tenor, treble, and Bass. In the choice of these sticks the instrument maker is very particular with respect to grain, texture, and hardness upon which qualities the harmony very much depends. They [drums?] are struck with the palms of the hands. The drummers play and dance at the same time, whirling round with great rapidity and shifting their drums alternately from the waist to the neck. Small bells are fastened to the loins and ankles of the Drummer which emit a tinkling sound like the cymbal. Numerous voices singing in unison swell the concert, the effect of which is almost deafening and to an unaccustomed hearer cannot fail of producing a head-ach. These Musicians are called Yellies [Yelies] or Jellies, a class of people whose functions I have already described. [First and third brackets in the original.] (82)

COMMENTARY: Garankes (Bright's garangies) are leatherworkers and are distinct from jelis (Bright's yellies) in the geographic area under consideration in this book but in other parts of the Mande diaspora, in Sierra Leone where Bright was, for example, there are leatherworkers who call themselves jelis. Barbara Frank (1988, 1995) has documented the distribution of this phenomenon.

1802   Silv. Meinrad Xavier Golberry
The [circumcision] ceremony starts with the boys, and then come the girls. The songs of the griots and griotes and the din of the musicians cover the moans and cries that often come from the young victims. (1:596)

[Regarding the king of Barra (in The Gambia) named Sonko] He spent all his days surrounded with a group of young people his own age [he was twenty-six], with all of his entertainers, griots and griotes of the country. (2:161)

1822 (1967)   Gaspard Théodore Mollien

COMMENTARY: See 40, 94–96 on griots.

1825   Major William Gray and Staff Surgeon Dochard
The instrument which accompanies this dance is called a ballafo, and affords better music than might be expected from such rude materials; it is composed of cane and wood, in the following manner. A frame, three feet long, eighteen inches wide at one end, and nine at the other, is made of cane, split very thin, and supported at the corners, about nine inches from the ground, by four upright sticks of nearly an inch diameter; across this frame are laid twenty pieces of hard wood, diminishing in size in the same proportion progressively, from one end to the other, as the frame to which they are slightly attached with thin twine. Under each of these cross pieces, is suspended an empty gourd, of a size adapted to the tone of note required, having a hole

in the part where it comes in contact with the stick, and another at the bottom; the latter is covered with a thin piece of dried sheep's gut. It is played on with two small sticks, by a man who sits cross legged on the ground, and is accompanied by one or more small drums. (54–55)

The king . . . was attended by a troop of drums and singing people (*Jallikeas*), making a most hideous attempt at instrumental and vocal music, intended to inspire their royal master with a high idea of his own dignity. (59)

Goodeerie is a small straggling village, inhabited by Surrawoollies and Foulahs. . . . Since our arrival here, we were beset by a multitude of beggars of all descriptions. . . . Goulahs, or singing people, who in Africa always flock around those who have any thing to give, no doubt thought this a good opportunity to turn to good account their abilities in music, and we were continually annoyed by their horrid noise. Dozens of them would, at the same moment, set up a sort of roaring extempore song in our praise, accompanied by drums and a sort of guitar, and we found it impossible to get rid of them by any other means than giving something. (110–112)

The proceedings commenced by a griot or bard proclaiming in a loud voice the object of their meeting, and desiring that all those who had any thing to say on the subject, should do so. . . . One person only presumed to speak at a time, and that in a low voice, and the person speaking never received any interruption before he announced his having finished, which, as well as all that each had said, was repeated in a loud and distinct voice by the respective bards, or griots of the chiefs. (282–84)

COMMENTARY: Has a plate (facing 301) with drawings of many musical instruments including a tama, flute, tabala, bala, sabaro, kora, and lute. "Goulah" is probably the Fula *gawlo*.

1825   Major Alexander Gordon Laing

There are four trades or professions, to which conjointly is given the apellation of Nyimahalah; they rank in the order in which they are enumerated, and consist of the *fino,* or orator; the *jellē,* or minstrel; the *guarangē,* or shoemaker; and the *noomo,* or blacksmith; all of whom are high in the scale of society, and are possessed of great privileges. They travel throughout the country unmolested, even in war; and strangers, if of the sable hue, are always safe under their protection. The guarangé and noomo earn their livelihood by the exercise of their respective trades; the fino by his oratory and subtlety as a lawyer; and the jellé by singing the mighty deeds and qualifications of rich men, who, in his opinion, have no faults. Like the minstrels of old, they are always at hand to laud with hyperbolical praise the landlord of a feast, and headman of a town.

The distinctions of rank, although kept up among the Mandingoes more than among the generality of African tribes, are nevertheless few. The priests and teachers of the Koran are held in estimation next to the king or ruler of a country; the respect which they shew to learning is a trait in their character much to be admired: the next in order to the priests and teachers, are the subordinate chiefs and head-men; then follow the Nyimahalahs, (no matter from what country); after them, dependant freemen; and, lastly, slaves divided into domestic, or those born in the country, who are not liable to be sold contrary to their inclinations, and those taken in war, or enslaved on account of debt, or by way of punishment. (132–33)

The news of my appearance was soon spread abroad, and the yard was forthwith crowded with dancers, musicians, and singers; among the latter of whom I was not a little annoyed to behold the females whose stentorian lungs had so stunned me in the morning, and I was obliged not only to submit to a repetition of Yarradee's war-song, with their diabolical chorus, (which is a favourite air among the Soolima musicians,) but to pay them for their trouble; otherwise, according to Musah, I should have had a bad name amongst them, and nothing is more dreaded by an African than a bad name from the Jelles. (242–43)

They are passionately fond of music, and fonder still of flattery, which is lavishly bestowed upon them by the Jelle-men, when they have liberality and means enough to pay for it. The Jelle-men appear to answer the description of the Gallas of Abyssinia, who amuse the rich people in the morning and evening, and exaggerate their merits. The principal instruments used are the kora, in sound and shape resembling a guitar; the ballafoo, which I have already described; different-sized drums; and a flute with three notes, which is only used as an accompaniment to other instruments, and is sometimes introduced with tolerable effect. (368–69)

COMMENTARY: Includes drawings of musicians playing a calabash harp (facing 148), one-stringed viol (facing 148), xylophone (facing 369), and tama (facing 369).

1830 (1968)   Réné Caillié
[Reporting from Kankan] Music and dancing are forbidden among the Musulmans, and consequently their amusements are far from equalling in frolic and gaiety those which prevail among the pagans. (1:269)

[Reporting from Time, Mali] On the very day of her death, I had been attracted to the neighbourhood by the sound of the music. I saw in the court-yard, two large drums, made like ours, and some persons were beating them, and clashing cymbals. These cymbals consist of two pieces of iron, about five inches long, and two and a half wide. The two negroes who were beating the drums, held these cymbals in their left hands. Each of the pieces of iron has a ring, one is passed over the thumb, and the other over the fore-finger, and by a movement of the hand they are struck together in regular time. (1:341)

[Reporting from Bangoro, Mali] I saw several men parading about, beating large drums, and women with tambourines, suspended from their necks; to these tambourines were affixed small boards covered with bells and little bits of iron, which being shaken struck against the instrument, and produced a very pleasing sound. I concluded that all these musicians were what are called at the Senegal *griotes,* or wandering minstrels, who make it their business to sing songs in praise of any who will pay them; those whom I saw at Bangoro were very modest, and did not, like their fraternity at the Senegal, teaze passengers for presents. (1:391)

1855   Hyacinte Hecquard
[Regarding Mandinkas in Pakao in the Casamance] Their way of life is the same as the Peulhs [Fulas]; however, they are greater lovers of music and dance. Griots hold a special place of honor among them. Their principal musical instruments are the *balafon,* a kind of harmonica where the glass is replaced by pieces of soft wood to which calabashes of different sizes are attached. These new kinds of keys, which are struck with two pieces of wood with an elastic gum around the ends, make a beautiful sound; there are some that have three octaves. Griots from Kasso, reputed to be the most skilled in this part of Africa, put this *balafon* to a truly remarkable use. The other instrument is a guitar with twenty-one strings that is played with great taste and

renders a very striking sound; it is made with a large calabash that is covered very carefully with a tanned deerskin; into the calabash they fit a neck to which the strings are attached, and the strings are raised up by a hard wooden bridge. The strings are made from thin strips of deerskin cut more or less fine according to the desired thickness. They twist the strips and take out the roughness by rubbing them with sand. (123; also see 172–73, 187)

Be that as it may, these walls enclose about a hundred huts that lodge those who are called the king's people, that is to say, those who are particularly important in the service of the king. Among them the griot and the blacksmith have a very high rank and enjoy special privileges. For example, every time a bull is killed in the village, even for the king, the head goes to the griot, the sirloin and tenderloin to the blacksmith, and the skin to the leatherworker who for that must provide His Majesty with shoes and also supply him whatever his needs may be.

The king's hut is distinguished from the others' by the bull horns that are set on a baton in front of his door, it is also larger, but the furnishings inside are no different. The wives occupy a separate residence where only the griot has right of entry. (205)

Appendix B

Keys to Vocalists, Musicians, and Their Instruments

If known, the town of birth and the birthdate are given in parentheses after the name. The line below each name lists the recordings on which they play. Those who have recorded as leaders and are listed in the discography under their own names are marked with asterisks. I have been selective in listing vocalists on jembe recordings.

Bala

Côte d'Ivoire

Diabate, Mamadou
  Adama Drame 1994
Jobarteh, Mori
  The Ivorys 1987

Kamara, Kalifa
  The Ivorys 1987
Kouyate, Kaba
  Adama Drame 1994

The Gambia

Cissoko, Mohammed
  Ifang Bondi 1994
Jassy, Haruna
  Pa Bobo Jobarteh 1997
Jobate, Jali Kabele
  Pevar 1978
Kanuteh, Alhaji Fabala
  Charters 1975b
Kuyateh, Salun
  Pevar 1978, Suso and Laswell 1990

Suso, Foday Musa
  Foday Musa Suso 1984a
Suso, Mahamadou
  Suso and Laswell 1990
Suso, Mawudo
  Charters 1975b, Suso and Laswell
  1990, Konte, Kuyateh and Suso 1995

Guinea

Bangoura, Abdoulaye Epizo
  Djeli Moussa Diawara 1992, Ladji
  Camara, n.d.b.
Camara, Alikhali [Khali]
  Soumah 1991, Ibro Diabate 1995?,
  Mamady Keita 1995
Camara, Kalifa
  Djeli Moussa Diawara 1988
Camara, M'Mabou
  Mory Djeli Dienne Kouyate
  1993
Camara, Naby
  Morikeba Kouyate 1997
Camara, Seny
  Macire Sylla 1996

Camara, Soriba
  Mamady Keita 1995
Camara, Yacouba "Bruno"
  Fatala 1993
Conde, Adama
  Mama Diabate, n.d., 1995, Sekouba
  "Bambino" Diabate 1997, Oumou
  Dioubate 1999, Kandia Kouyate 1999,
  Amadou Sodia 1999?
Dambakate, Karamba
  Mandeng Tunya 1997
Diabate, Famoro
  Sekouba Kandia Kouyate 1990?
Diabate, Mory
  Manfila Kante 1998

Diabate, Sourakata
  Kerfala Kante 1994
Diawara, Ibrahima
  Horoya Band 1971, 1974, 1997
Dioubate Brothers of Kankan [Sidi Ma-
madi, Sidi Karamon, and Sidi Moussa]
  Alberts 1949, 1950, 1998, Rouget
  1954a, 1954b, 1972, 1999
Dioubate, Koca Sale
  Les Ballets Africains 1991, 1995
Kante, "Djessou" Mory
  Manfila Kante 1991
Konde, Adama
  Mory Kante 1996
Kouyate, Bakary
  Wofa-Tambou Bo Kannal 1997?
Kouyate, Djeli Mady
  Baba Djan Kaba 1993, Kaniba Oule
  Kouyate 1994, Sona Diabate 1996,
  Nimba 199?
Kouyate, Djeli Moridjan
  Djeli Moussa Diawara 1983
Kouyate, [El Hadj] Djeli Sory*
  Percussions de Guinée 1994
Kouyate, Isiaga
  Famoro Kouyate 1992
Kouyate, Kemo
  Aboubacar Camara 199?, Fode Kou-
  yate 1995?, Sacko and Kouyate 1991,
  Ami Koita 1992

Kouyate, Lansana*
Kouyate, Mamadou
  Famoro Kouyate 1992
Kouyate, Mohamed
  Sekouba "Bambino" Diabate 1992
Kouyate, Sandali "Bala Kala"
  Manfila Kante 1991
Kouyate, Sory
  Sekouba "Bambino" Diabate 1992
Kouyates of Niagassola
  Toureille 1992
Sissoko, Mohamed
  Ousmane Kouyate 1990
Soumano, Ibrahima
  Kasse Mady Diabate 1990, Manfila
  Kante 1994
Sylla, Abou
  Les Ballets Africains 1993, 1995,
  Lansana Kouyate 1996, Mohamed
  Diaby 1997
Sylla, Ibrahima
  Les Ballets Africains 1995
Sylla, Mohamed
  Les Ballets Africains 1993, 1995
Unidentified from Conakry, Kissidougou,
and Niagassola
  Toureille 1992
Wadje, Aliou
  Missia Saran Dioubate 1995?

Mali

Diabate, Djely Mady
  Walde Damba 1989b, Hadja Soumano
  1988
Diabate, Keletigui*
  Les Ambassadeurs 1975–77, Tata
  Bambo Kouyate 1985, Ami Koita
  1986, Adama Diabate 1995, Toumani
  Diabate 1994, 1995, Salif Keita 1991
Diabate, Lassana
  Nainy Diabate 1997
Diabate, Loutigui
  Ministry of Information of Mali 1971,
  vols. 1 and 4, Kandia Kouyate 198?
Diabate, Makan
  Ami Koita 1995
Kante, Kaba
  Les Ambassadeurs 1979c, 1984b, 1994

Kouyate, Bourema
  Ministry of Information of Mali 1971,
  vols. 1 and 4, Mokontafe Sako 1976a,
  1976b, 1977a, 1977b, Tata Bambo
  Kouyate 1985, Sidiki Diabate 1987,
  Ousmane Sacko 1987, Divas from
  Mali 1997
Kouyate, Lassina [Lansine "Boua," Las-
sana, Lansana]
  Kasse Mady Diabate 1990, Sacko and
  Kouyate 1991, Baba Djan Kaba 1992,
  Dogomani Dagnon 1993, Mangala
  1993, Kaniba Ouele Kouyate, n.d.,
  Aboubacar Camara 1994, Diaba Koita
  199?, Salif Keita 1995, Seck and
  Jones 1995, Sekouba "Bambino" Dia-
  bate 1996, 1997, Zoumana Diarra

1997, Moriba Koita 1997, Divas from
Mali 1997
Kouyate, Nancoman
Ministry of Information of Mali 1971,
vol. 1

Kouyate, Diombo*

Sissoko, Baba (#2)
Habib Koite and Bamada 1999
Unidentified
Laura Boulton [1939] 1957

Senegal

Dundun, Sangban, and Kenkeni
Burkina Faso

Coulibaly, Kassoum
Fà Kiyen Yiriwa 1997
Coulibaly, Lassina
Les Frères Coulibaly 1992
Coulibaly, Mamady
Kassama Percussions 1996, Lassina
Coulibaly and Yan Kadi Faso
1998?
Dambele, Dedougou
Farafina 1997?
Dao, Seydou
Kassama Percussions 1996

Dembele, Souleymane
La Famille Dembele 1996
Diara, Baba
Farafina 1992a
Diarra, Kassoum*
Kassama Percussions 1996
Keita, Tiawara
Farafina 1992a
Naba, François
Koko du Burkina Faso 1993
Sanou, Souleymane
Farafina 1992a, 1993, 1997?

Côte d'Ivoire

Bamoro, Siaka
Adama Drame 1992
Diabate, Mamadou
Adama Drame 1996
Drame, Amadou
Adama Drame 1994

Traore, Adama
Adama Drame 1994
Traore, Yacoumba
Adama Drame 1994

The Gambia

Kanuteh, Dembo
Suso and Laswell 1990
Suso, Foday Musa
Foday Musa Suso 1984a

Suso, Mahamadou
Suso and Laswell 1990

Guinea

Badilifu, Mahiri
Mamady Keita 1995
Bangoura, Hamidou
Les Ballets Africains 1991
Bangoura, Moustapha
Les Ballets Africains 1991, 1993, 1995
Bangoura, Sekouba Gbemgbedi
Wofa-Tambou Bo Kannal 1997?
Camara, Fanyuma Mamadi
Ladji Camara, n.d.
Camara, Mbemba
Nimba 199?

Camara, Seny
Macire Sylla 1996
Camara, Younoussa
Les Ballets Africains 1991, 1993, 1995
Cissoko, Keba
Les Ballets Africains 1995, Lansana
Kouyate 1996
Conde, Koumgbanan
Percussions de Guinée 1989, 1994
Dama[n], Karamoko
Famoudou Konate 1991, 1997, 1998,
Mamady Keita 1996

Dama, Mfamori
  Famoudou Konate 1991
Diaby, Mohamed*
Diakite, Amadou
  Famoudou Konate 1997, 1998
Diallo, Ahmadou Sadio
  Soumah 1991
Dioubate [Diabate], Aly [Ali]
  Lansana Kouyate 1996, Mohamed
  Diaby 1997
Dioubate, Koce Sale
  Les Ballets Africains 1991, 1993, 1995
Djabi, Moustapha
  Mamady Keita 1995
Kante, Lancei
  Percussions de Guinée
Keita, Mamady*
Keita, Nansedy
  Famoudou Konate 1998
Keita, Ntoman
  Mamady Keita 1992
Konate, Fode
  Famoudou Konate 1998
Konate, Ibro
  Mamady Keita 1995
Konate, Nankouma
  Famoudou Konate 1991, 1997, 1998

Konate, Sekou
  Mamady Keita 1995, 1996
Kourouma, Daouda
  Famoudou Konate 1991, Mamady
  Keita 1995, 1996
Kouyate, Lansana
  Ladji Camara, n.d.
Kouyate, Lansana*
Oulare, Bandou
  Mamady Keita 1995
Soumah, Amara
  Fatala 1993
Soumah, Bekaye
  Famoudou Konate 1998
Soumah, Yamoussa
  Mohamed Kemoko Sano 1992,
  1994-vid
Sylla, Abou
  Lansana Kouyate 1996, Mohamed
  Diaby 1997
Sylla, Aly [Aliseny]
  Soumah 1991, Famoudou Konate 1997
Traore, Kaloga
  Africa Djole with Fode Youla, n.d.a
Unidentified from Mandiana and
Koumana
  Toureille 1992

Mali

Camara, Mamadou "Kunkun"*
Camara [Kamara], Vieux
  Polak 1997
Camara, Sidi Mohammed "Joh"
  Mandeng Tunya 1997
Dembele, Mamady
  Mamadou "Kunkun" Camara 1997
Diabate, Brehima
  Kasse Mady Diabate 1997
Diabate, Modibo
  Divas from Mali 1997
Diabate, Sambou
  Moriba Koita 1997
Diakite, Modibo
  Rhythms of Mali 1995
Jakite [Diakite], Madu
  Polak 1994, 1996, 1997
Kanoute, Serang
  Ministry of Information of Mali 1971,
  vols. 1 and 4

Keita, Draman
  Polak 1994
Keita, Fasiriman
  Polak 1994, 1997
Keita, Moussa
  Moussa Keita 1997?
Kone, Toumani Papa
  Nahawa Doumbia 1997
Kouyate, Modibo
  Rhythms of Mali 1995
Mangala*
Samake, Solo
  Polak 1997
Sanogo, Mare
  Seck and Jones 1995
Sanou, Lassine
  Soungalo Coulibaly
Traore, Moussa*

Senegal

Ndiaye, Ken
  Mamady Keita 1989
Ndiaye, Moonha
  Mamady Keita 1989

Sy, Latyr
  Drums of Gorée

Guitar
Côte d'Ivoire

Diabate, Lassana
  Papa Cissoko 1986

Diabate, Sory
  Papa Cissoko 1986, Les Go de Koteba
  1997

The Gambia

Beyai, Ousmane
  Abdel Kabirr 1991, Ifang Bondi 1994
Camara, Alagie
  Pa Bobo Jobarteh 1997

Jobe, Badou
  Super Eagles 1969
Suso, Foday Musa
  Foday Musa Suso 1984a

Guinea

Camara, Aboubacar
  Djely Mousa Diawara 1988
Camara, Ansoumane "Petit Conde"
  Sekouba "Bambino" Diabate 1994,
  Kerfala Kante 1994, 1995?, Sekouba
  Kandia Kouyate 1990?
Camara, Demba
  Sona Diabate 1983, 1990a, 1990b,
  M'Mah Sylla 1983
Camara, Mamadou
  Kaloum Star 1996
Claver, Honomou Jerome
  African Virtuoses 1983
Conde, Adama
  Mory Kante 1996, Manfila Kante
  1998, Oumou Dioubate 1999, Kandia
  Kouyate 1999
Conde, Linke
  Keletigui et Ses Tambourinis 1967a,
  1967b, 1972, 1975
Diabate, Abdoulaye
  Virtuoses Diabate, African Virtuoses
  1983
Diabate, Kaba
  Sona Diabate 1990b
Diabate, Kerfala "Papa"* (Faranah,
  1936–)
  Guinea Compilations 1972a, Djessou
  Mory Kante 1998
Diabate, Kissima[n]
  Sekouba "Bambino" Diabate 1992,
  Mory Djeli Dienne Kouyate 1993

Diabate, Lancine
  Sekouba "Bambino" Diabate 1992
Diabate, Maltho Mory
  Mama Diabate, n.d.
Diabate, Sarati "Vieux"
  Mama Diabate 1995, Oumou Diou-
  bate 1995?
Diabate, Sekou "Bembeya"* (1944–)
  Bembeya Jazz National 1963–,
  Sona Diabaté 1990a, 1990b,
  1996, Sambala Kanoute 1995,
  Sekouba "Bambino" Diabate 1996,
  1997
Diabate, Sekou "Docteur" (1938–)
  Balla et Ses Balladins 1967, 1993,
  Virtuoses Diabate, African Vir-
  tuoses 1983, Guinea Compilations
  1972a
Diabate, Sire
  Horoya Band 1971, 19174, 1997
Diabate, Solo
  Oumou Dioubate 1995?
Diabate, Sona*
Diabate, Sorel
  Baba Djan Kaba 1995?, 1996?, Mama
  Keita 1995
Diawara, Djeli Moussa* [Jali Musa
  Jawara]
Diawara, Fadiala
  Kandia Kouyate 1999
Diawara, Ibrahima
  Horoya Band 1974, 1997

Diawara, Karan-Mady
    Super Boiro Band 1972, Ibro Diabate
    1995?
Doukoure, Amadou
    Mory Kante [1982b] 1993
Habas, Nyepou
    Les Amazones 1983
Kaba, Baba Djan*
    Sekouba "Bambino" Diabate 1992,
    Mama Keita 1995
Kamissoko, Ansoumane
    Mama Diabate, n.d., 1995
Kante, Bakary
    Djessou Mory Kante 1998, Manfila
    Kante 1991, 1998, Kerfala "Papa"
    Diabate 1999
Kante, Diara (?–1965)
    Orchestre de la Garde Republicaine
    1967 (1ère formation)
Kante, "Djekoria" Mory
    Mory Djeli Dienne Kouyate 1993,
    Djessou Mory Kante 1998
Kante, "Djessou" Mory* (1963–)
    Manfila Kante 1991, 1994, 1995,
    1998, Aboubacar Camara (1994.
    1996?), Djeli Sory Diabate and Djes-
    sou Mory Kante, n.d., Sekouba "Bam-
    bino" Diabate 1996, 1997, Sona Dia-
    bate 1996, Missia Saran Dioubate
    1995?, Kerfala "Papa" Diabate 1999,
    Amadou Sodia 1999?
Kante, Facelli* (1922–61)
    Les Ballets Africains de Keita Fodeba
Kante, Kaba
    Manfila Kante 1990, Ousmane Kou-
    yate (1990), Sabre Soumano 199?,
    Ibro Diabate 1995?, Missia Saran
    Dioubate 1995?, Fode Kouyate 1994?,
    Aboubacar Camara, n.d., Diabate and
    Diabate 1997
Kante, Manfila* [ex-Ambassadeurs]
    (Farbannah/Kankan, 1946–)
    Les Ambassadeurs [Internationaux]
    1973–, Salif Keita 1991, Oumou
    Dioubate 1992?, Sona Diabate 1996,
    Aboubacar Camara, n.d., Djessou
    Mory Kante 1998, Kerfala "Papa"
    Diabate 1999, Amadou Sodia 1999?

Kante, Manfila [Jr.]
    Manfila Kante 1998
Kante, Manfila "Dabadou"* (1933–)
Kante, Mory* (kora player and singer
    from Kissidougou)
Kante, "Soba" Manfila*
Konde, Lansana
    Horoya Band 1974, 1997
Kouyate, Djeli Moussa
    Rail Band, Nahawa Doumbia 1988,
    1990, Djanka Diabate 1991, Kasse
    Mady Diabate 1990, Baba Djan Kaba
    1992, 1993, 1995?, 1996?, Mangala
    1993, Sona Djely Kouyate 1993,
    Sanougue Kouyate 1990, Aboubacar
    Camara 1994, 199?, 1996?, Kaniba
    Oule Kouyate 1994, Fode Kouyate
    1995?, Sekou "Bembeya" Diabate
    1995, Salif Keita 1995, Mama Keita
    1995, Abdoulaye Diabate 1995, Se-
    kouba "Bambino" Diabate 1996, 1997,
    Diabate and Diabate 1997, Mama
    Sissoko 1997, Oumou Dioubate 1999,
    Amadou Sodia 1999?
Kouyate, Fatiya
    Kaloum Star 1996
Kouyate, Gramo
    Manfila Kante 1991
Kouyate, Ibrahima
    Balla et Ses Balladins 1980, 1993
Kouyate, Kemo [Tiemoko] (1946 or
    1947–)
    Oumou Dioubate 1993, Djanka Dia-
    bate 1991, Sanougue Kouyate 1990,
    Kouyate and Kouyate 1990, Balla et
    Ses Balladins 1993, Aboubacar Ca-
    mara 199?, Sacko and Kouyate 1991,
    Diaba Koita 199?, Fode Kouyate
    1995?
Kouyate, Lamine
    Djeli Moussa Diawara 1983
Kouyate, Moriken
    Djessou Mory Kante 1998, Kerfala
    "Papa" Diababe 1999
Kouyate, Moutou [Mamoutou, Routou]
    Mory Djeli Dienne Kouyate 1993,
    Kerfala Kante 1994, 1995?, Sona
    Djely Kouyate 1993, Sekouba

"Bambino" Diabate 1992, 1994, Fode
Kouyate 1994?
Kouyate, Ousmane
Les Ambassadeurs Internationaux
1976–, Salif Keita 1987, 1989, 1994,
1995, Seck and Jones 1995, Oumou
Dioubate 1999, Kandia Kouyate 1999,
Amadou Sodia 1999?
Kouyate, Sandali "Bala Kala"
Horoya Band 1971, 1997
Kouyate, Sekou
African Virtuoses 1983
Kouyate, Setouman
Guinea Compilations 1961a
Kouyate, Sory
Sekouba "Bambino" Diabate 1992
Kouyate, Sory Kandia *
Les Ballets Africains de Keita Fodeba
1956?
Seck, Mamadou
Seck and Diabate 1977

Soumano, Ibrahima
Aboubacar Camara 1994, 199?, Ibro
Diabate 1993, Djeli Moussa Diawara
1992, Oumou Dioubate 1993, Baba
Djan Kaba 1992, 1993, 1995?, 1996?,
Manfila Kante 1994, Kouyate and
Kouyate 1990, Sabre Soumano 199?,
Mama Keita 1995, Sekouba "Bam-
bino" Diabate 1996, 1997, Missia
Saran Dioubate 1995?, Diabate and
Diabate 1997, Kandia Kouyate 1999
Toure, Rakesh
Mama Diabate 1995
Williams, Jean Baptiste "Jeannot"
Camayenne Sofa 1975, 1976, 1977
Unidentified from Kissidougou
Toureille 1992
Unidentified
Guinea Compilations 1961b,
Arthur Alberts 1949, 1954a

Guinea Bissau

Kanoute, Sambala *

Mali: The Jeli Tradition

Bah-Sadio
Cissoko, Moussa
Tata Bambo Kouyate 1995
Coulibaly, Saffre
Abdoulaye Diabate 1995
Dembele, Ali
Rail Band 1995
Diabate, Cheick Oumar
Nainy Diabate 1987, 1990, 1992,
1997, Ami Koita 1993, Babani Kone
1998
Diabate, Fodekaba
Diabate Family of Kela 1994
Diabate, Fotiqui
Koni Coumare, n.d.
Diabate, Foussenou
Fanta Sacko 1972
Diabate, Keletigi (1931–)
L'Orchestre National "A" de la
République du Mali 1972
Diabate, Modibo
Nainy Diabate 1992, 1997, Assa
Drame, n.d., Babani Kone 1998

Diabate, Moussa
Hadja Soumano 1988
Diabate, Sambou
Diaba Koita 199?
Diabate, Solo
Ministry of Information of Mali 1971,
vol. 4, Mokontafe Sako 1976a
Diakite, Don Modia
Ami Koita 1989
Diarra, Zoumana *
Adama Diabate 1995, Aminata Ka-
missoko 1997, Benkadi International
1997
Doumbia, Mamadou
Salif Keita 1991
Guindo, Mamadou
Super Biton de Segou 1986
Kamisoko, Chaka
Diabate Family of Kela 1994
Kanoute, Abdrahame Gatta
Kanoute, Santoutou *
Mariam Kouyate, Mamadou Diabate,
and Sidiki Diabate 1995a, 1995b

Keita, Bako
Kandia Kouyate 1999
Koita, Harouna
Macire Sylla 1996
Koite, Habib*
Toumani Diabate 1993
Kouyate, Bassi*
Kouyate, Demba
Kasse Mady Diabate 1997
Kouyate, Fanta Mady
Rail Band 1992
Kouyate, Modibo [Modibo Koita]
Mokontafe Sacko 1976–77, Tata
Bambo Kouyate 1985, 1988, 1995,
n.d., Ami Koita 1988, Kasse Mady
Diabate 1990, Assa Drame, n.d.
Kouyate, Saki
Kaniba Ouele Kouyate n.d., 1995,
Sanougue Kouyate 1990, Tata Bambo
Kouyate 1985
Kouyate, Sidiki
Diabate Family of Kela 1997
Kouyate, Tiemoko (see Kemo Kouyate
under Guinea)
Mangala*
Sacko, Bouba
Santoutou Kanoute 1988, Kandia
Kouyate 198?, Ami Koita, n.d., 1986,
1987?, Bajourou 1993

Sacko, Ousmane* (Kayes, 1940–)
Sissokho, Baba
Sekouba "Bambino" Diabate 1996,
1997
Sissokho, Kambou
Diaba Koita 199?
Sissokho, Mama
Kasse Mady Diabate 1989, 1990, Na-
tional Badema 1977, 1983a, 1983b
Sissokho, Mamadou [Mama]*
Super Biton de Segou 1986
Sissokho, Moussa
Kasse Mady Diabate 1997
Sissokho, Sayan
Baaba Maal 1991
Sissoko (see Sissokho)
Soumano, Lamine
Ami Koita 1995, Aminata Kamissoko
1997
Thera, Amadou
Mama Sissoko, n.d.
Tounkara, Djeli Mady
Rail Band 1973– Hadja Soumano
1988, Bajourou 1993
Tounkara, Mamadou
Fanta Sacko 1972
Unidentified
Radio Mali 197?

Mali: Bambara, Wasulu, and Other

Bagayoko, Amadou
Bagayoko and Doumbia 198?, 1999?
Bagayoko, Ngou
Nahawa Doumbia 1988, 1990, 1997
Diabate, Zani*
Diakite, Bemba
Nahawa Doumbia 1997
Diallo, Boubacar
Oumou Sangare 1990, 1993, 1996
Doumbia, Moussa
Daouda Bakayoko 199?, Ousmane
Doumbia 1997

Koita, Bayini
Yorro Diallo, n.d.
Ngueye, Kader
Ousmane Doumbia 1997
Salah, Baba
Oumou Sangare 1996
Sidibe, Boubacar
Habib Koite and Bamada 1999
Traore, Boubacar*
Traore, Ma(ma)dou Bah
Djeneba Diakite 1992
Toure, Ali Farka*

Senegal

Cisse, Assane Ndoye
Baaba Maal 1988, 1990, 1994,
1998, Mansour Seck 1994,
1995

Cissokho, Youssouph
Sedhiou Band 1998
Dia, Ibrahima "Sylla"
Sedhiou Band 1998

Diatta, Pascal *
Diop, Ousmane Hamady
  Mansour Seck 1994
Faye, Adama
  Ismael Lo 1985
Faye, Habib
  Youssou Ndour 1989–
Faye, Lamine
  Super Diamono Youssou Ndour 1992
Faye, Vieux
  Ismael Lo 1987, 1989

Konte, Lamine *
Kouyate, Alioune
  Sedhiou Band 1998
Maal, Baaba *
  Mansour Seck 1994
Mbaye, Mamadou "Jimi"
  Youssou Ndour 1989–
Ndoye, Assane (*see* Assane Cisse)
Seck, Mansour *
  Baaba Maal 1989, 1991

Hunter's or Warrior's Harps
Bolon

Bangoura, Bangaly (Guinea)
  Les Ballets Africains 1995
Camara, Aly (Guinea)
  Fatala 1993
Camara, Amadou (Guinea)
  Les Ballets Africains 1995, Mamady
  Keita 1995
Coulibaly, Mamadou
  Sali Sidibe 1993a
Diallo, Ahmadou Sadio (Guinea)
  Soumah 1991
Diallo, Massambou Wele (Mali)
  Oumou Sangare 1996
Dioubate, Koca Sale (Guinea)
  Les Ballets Africains 1993
Kamara, Bajao (The Gambia)
  Knight 1992-vid

Keita, Bilali (Guinea)
  Rouget 1954b, 1972, 1999
Keita, Nansedy (Guinea)
  Famoudou Konate 1998
Kouyate, Djeli Sara (Guinea)
  Manfila Kante 1998
Kouyate, Saky
  Moussa Keita 1997?
Kuyateh, Jali Lamin (The Gambia)
  Ifang Bondi 1994
Sano, Mohamed Kemoko (Guinea)
  Les Ballets Africains 1993
Sodia, Amadou * (Guinea)
  Sona Diabate 1996
Traore, Djigui * (Mali)
  Unidentified from Kissidougou
  Toureille 1992

Donso Ngoni

Balo, Sedu (Mali)
  Polak 1994
Camara, Seydou * (Mali)
Coulibaly, Duguye (Mali)
  Zobel, forthcoming
Coulibaly, Lassina (Burkina Faso)
  Les Frères Coulibaly 1992
Coulibaly, Ousseni (Burkina Faso)
  Les Frères Coulibaly 1992
Coulibaly, Siaka
  Daouda Bakayoko 199?
Coulibaly, Souleymane (Burkina Faso)
  Les Frères Coulibaly 1992
Konate, Famoudou (simbi? Guinea)
  Famoudou Konate 1998
Kone, Toumani * (Mali)

Mazonkoro (Guinea)
  Rouget 1954a, 1999
Samake, Adama (Mali)
  Sibiri Samake 1991
Samake, Sibiri * (Mali)
Sidibe, Siaka (Mali)
  Zobel, forthcoming
Sinayogo, Alou
  Daouda Bakayoko 199?
Suso, Foday Musa (The Gambia)
  Foday Musa Suso 1984a
Traore, Boubacar (Mali)
  Djeneba Diakite 1992
Traore, Burlaye (Mali)
  Zobel, forthcoming
Traore, Zoumana *

Furakaf (Jola Simbingo)
Unidentified player (The Gambia)
  Pevar 1978

Kamalen Ngoni

Berthe, Abdoul Wahab
  Habib Koite and Bamada 1999
Diakite, Brehima (Mali)
  Oumou Sangare 1993
Diallo, Yorro*
Diarra, Dian (Mali)
  Toumani Diabate 1995

Doumbia, Ousmane*
Samake, Harouna (Mali)
  Sali Sidibe 1993a
Sangare, Amadou*
Sidibe, Kassim (Mali)
  Oumou Sangare 1996

Simbi (Maninka)

Diakite [Jakite], Bala Djimba*
  (Mali)
Drahme, Adame (Mali)
  Salif Keita 1993
Dyoubate, Alifa (Guinea)
  Rouget 1954a, 1999

Keita, Coumoun Balla (Mali)
  Moussa Keita 1997?
Keita, Sidikiba (Mali)
  Zobel, forthcoming
Samake, Bakary (Mali)
  Bala Djimba Diakite 1995

Simbingo (Mandinka)

Fatti, Malang (The Gambia)
  Knight 1992-vid

Jembe
Burkina Faso

Adama, Paco Ye
  Farafina 1992a, 1992b
Coulibaly, Lassina*
  Sacko and Kouyate 1991, Dogomani
  Dagnon 1993?, Les Frères Coulibaly
  1992, Lassina Coulibaly and Yan Kadi
  Faso 1998?
Coulibaly, Ousseni
  Les Frères Coulibaly 1992
Coulibaly, Souleymane
  Les Frères Coulibaly 1992
Diarra, Kassoum*
  Kassama Percussions 1996
Diarra, Samana
  Kassama Percussions 1996
Keita, Chaka
  Fà Kiyen Yiriwa 1997

Keita, Daouda
  Fà Kiyen Yiriwa 1997
Konate, Amadou
  Kassama Percussions 1996
Kone, Jacouba
  Koko du Burkina Faso 1993
Kone, Mama
  Fà Kiyen Yiriwa 1997
Kone, Salif
  Farafina 1997?
Poumayeli, Brahima
  La Famille Dembele 1996
Ouattara, Yaya
  Farafina 1993, 1997?
Unidentified from Bobo Dioulasso
  Danses du Burkina Faso

Côte d'Ivoire

Bakayoko, Karim
  Adama Drame 1994

Bakayoko, Mamady
  Adama Drame 1994

Drame, Adama*
  Huraux and Migeat 1988-vid
Drame, Yacouba
  Adama Drame 1996

Keita, Issa
  Adama Drame 1994
Keita, Moussa
  Adama Drame 1992

The Gambia

Gueye, Serigne
  Ifang Bondi 1994

Unidentified
  Pevar 1978

Guinea

Bangoura, (M)Bemba
  Djimo Kouyate 1992b, Lansana
  Kouyate 1996
Camara, Aboubacar "Fatouabou"
  Soumah 1991, Percussions de Guinée
  1994
Camara, Alpha
  Baba Djan Kaba 1993, Aboubacar
  Camara 199?, Kerfala Kante 1995?,
  Sekouba "Bambino" Diabate 1996,
  1997, Sona Diabate 1996
Camara, Aly
  Fatala 1993
Camara, Dumais
  Famoudou Konate 1991
Camara, Fode
  Africa Djole with Fode Youla, n.d.a
Camara, "Papa" Ladji* (Norasoba,
  1923–)
  Art Blakey 1976
Camara, Lamine Dibo
  Nimba 199?
Camara, Laurent
  Percussions de Guinée 1989, Les
  Ballets Africains 1991, 1993, 1995,
  Mamady Keita 1995
Camara, Mamadouba "Mohamed"
  Percussions de Guinée 1994
Camara, Moussa
  Mamady Keita 1995
Camara, Segou
  Africa Djole with Fode Youla, n.d.a
Camara, Yamoussa
  Mohamed Kemoko Sano 1992,
  1994-vid
Cherif, Alseny Solo
  Wofa-Tambou Bo Kannal 1997?
Conde, Lamine
  Famoro Kouyate 1992

Conde, Mamady
  Mamady Keita 1995, 1996
Conte, Ibrahima
  Les Ballets Africains 1991
Diabate [Dambagate], Karamba
  Karamba Diabate 1996-vid
Diaby, Mohamed*
  Lansana Kouyate 1996
Diop, Idrissa
  Mory Kante 1993
Kante, Amara
  Sekouba "Bambino" Diabate 1996,
  1997, Mory Kante 1996
Kante, Lancei
  Percussions de Guinée 1994
Kante, [Ansuman] Yeye
  Oumou Dioubate 1999, Kandia Kou-
  yate 1999, Amadou Sodia 1999?
Keita, Gbanworo
  Percussions de Guinée 1989, Les
  Ballets Africains 1991, 1993, 1995
Keita, Lancine
  Les Ballets Africains 1995
Keita, Mamady* (Balandugu, 1950–)
Keita, Nansedy
  Famoudou Konate 1998
Keita, Noumody
  Percussions de Guinée 1989, 1994
Keita, Ntoman
  Mamady Keita 1992
Konate, Diarra
  Famoudou Konate 1997
Konate, Famoudou* (Sangbarala,
  Kouroussa 1940–)
  Mamady Keita 1995, 1996
Konate, Fode
  Famoudou Konate 1997, 1998
Konate, Ibro[u]
  Famoudou Konate 1991, 1998

Kourouma, Mamady
    Mamady Keita 1995, 1996, Famoudou
    Konate 1997, 1998
Kouyate, Lansana*
Kouyate, Papa
    Ousmane Kouyate 1990, Nahawa
    Doumbia 1990, Kouyate and Kouyate
    1990, Kasse Mady Diabate 1989,
    1990, Baba Djan Kaba 1992, Mangala
    1993, Oumou Dioubate 1993, Ab-
    doulaye Diabate 1995
Oulare, Fadouba
    Mamady Keita 1995
Sano, Mohamed Kemoko*
    Les Ballets Africains 1991, 1993,
    1995
Soumah, Lamine
    Percussions de Guinée 1989, 1994
Sylla, Abdoulaye
    Mohamed Kemoko Sano 1992,
    1994-vid

Sylla, Aly "Kanya"
    Soumah 1991, Percussions de Guinée
    1994
Sylla, Mohamed Lamine
    Les Ballets Africains 1991, 1993,
    1995
Traore, Kaloga
    Africa Djole with Fode Youla, n.d.a
Toure, Arafan
    Fatala 1993
Toure, Seny
    Les Ballets Africains 1991, 1993,
    1995
Undidentified from Karala
    Rouget 1954a, 1972, 1999
Unidentified from Mandiana and
Koumana
    Toureille 1992
Youla, Fode*

Mali

Camara, Sidiki
    Habib Koite and Bamada 1999
Cissokho (*see* Sissokho)
Coulibaly, Soungalo*
Dembele, Sekouba
    Ami Koita 1995
Diabate, Fodekaba
    Diabate Family of Kela 1997
Diabate, Mamadou
    Kasse Mady Diabate 1997
Diabate, Siaka
    Soungalo Coulibaly
Diakite, Amidou
    Rhythms of Mali 1995
Diakite, Toumani
    Mama Sissoko 1997
Diarra, Adama
    Nainy Diabate 1997, Babani Kone 1998
Diarra, Dramane
    Benkadi International 1997
Diarra, Zoumana
    Super Biton de Segou 1986
Diawara, Issa
    Diabate Family of Kela 1994

Doumbia, Adboul*
    Mandeng Tunya 1997
Doumbia, Souleymane "Solo"
    Salif Keita 1989, 1991, 1993, 1994a,
    1995
Dumbia, Yamadu
    Polak 1994, 1996, 1997
Fall, Abdramane
    Adama Diabate
Jakite [Diakite], Jaraba
    Polak 1994, 1996, 1997
Kane, Boubacar
    Sali Sidibe 1993a
Kante, Mamadou*
Keita, Basidi
    Oumou Sangare 1996
Keita, Seydou
    Moussa Keita 1997?
Kone, Drissa (Kourouba, Mali)
    Zobel, forthcoming
Kouyate, Burama
    Rhythms of Mali 1995
Kouyate, Jeli Madi [Djeli Mady]
    Polak 1994, 1996, 1997

Sarr, Ibrahima
Oumou Sangare 1993
Sissokho [Cissokho], Moussa
Manfila Kante 1990, Sacko and Kou-
yate 1991, Seck and Jones 1995,
Kaloum Star 1996, Moriba Koita 1997

Sissoko, Alassane
Nahawa Doumbia 1997
Traore, Ibrahima
Djeneba Diakite 1992
Traore, Moussa *

Senegal

Balde, Ibrahime
Orchestre Africa Djembe 1993
Batakan, Joseph Gomez
Orchestre Africa Djembe 1993
Camara, Mamadou
Orchestre Africa Djembe 1993
Kabo, Yaya
Morikeba Kouyate 1997
Kande, Abdoulaye
Orchestre Africa Djembe 1993
Kouyate, Amadou
Djimo Kouyate 1996
Kouyate, Djimo *

Mbaye, Thio
Salif Keita 1987, Baaba Maal 1998
Ndiaye, Ken
Mamady Keita 1989
Niass, Alassane
Orchestre Africa Djembe 1993
Seck, Bakane
Baaba Maal 1998
Sidebe, Mamadou
Sunkett 1994
Sow, Lamine
Nimba 199?

Unknown Country

Diabate, Boubacar
Les Go de Koteba 1997

Keyboards
The Gambia

Baldeh, Amadou
Ifang Bondi 1994

Guinea

Camara, Mamadou
Kaloum Star 1996
Smith, Cheick M. *
Les Ambassadeurs 1979c, 1980,
Sekouba Kandia Kouyate 1990?,

Mory Djeli Dienne Kouyate 1993,
Sekouba "Bambino" Diabate 1994,
Kerfala Kante 1994, Oumou Dioubate
1995?

Mali

Coulibaly, Soro
Mariam Kouyate, Mamadou Diabate,
and Sidiki Diabate 1995a, 1995b
Diabate, Abdoulaye
Baba Djan Kaba 1992, 1995?, 1996?,
Dogomani Dagnon 1993, Mama
Keita 1995, Sekouba "Bambino"
Diabate 1996, 1997, Les Go de
Koteba 1997

Diara, Modibo
Mama Sissoko, n.d.
Maha
Assa Drame, n.d.
Seck, Cheik Tidiane *
Manfila Kante 1990, Salif Keita 1987,
1991, 1995, Adama Diabate 1995, Ou-
mou Dioubate 1992?, Aboubacar Ca-
mara, n.d., Diabate and Diabate 1997

Koni (Ngoni)
The Gambia

Mangara, Abdou Rahman* (Soninke
gambare)

Sahone, Alhaji Amara
Charters 1975b

Guinea

Diabate, Sekouba "Bambino"
Sekouba "Bambino" Diabate 1992
Kante, Kerfala
Kerfala Kante 1994
Kante, Mory
Mory Kante 1982b, 1993
Koroma, Sekou
Rouget 1972, 1999

Kouyate, Sory
Sekouba "Bambino" Diabate 1992
Maga
Sekouba "Bambino" Diabate 1992
Sissoko, Sadio
Sabre Soumano

Mali

Cissoko, Sayon (see Sissokho, Sayon)
Cone (see Kone)
Dante, Tiedjo
Tata Bambo Kouyate 1985
Diabate, Balla
Ministry of Information of Mali 1971,
vol. 1
Diabate, Komanwulen
Diabate Family of Kela 1994
Diabate, Lanfia
Diabate Family of Kela 1994, 1997
Diabate, Lassana
Babani Kone 1998
Diabate, Mamadu
Diabate Family of Kela 1994
Diabate, Solo
Mokontafe Sako 1976a, 1976b,
1977a, 1977b
Diarra, Zoumana*
Drame, Mama
Ami Koita, n.d.
Fimani
Assa Drame, n.d.
Kamisoko, Kasemadi
Diabate Family of Kela 1994, 1997
Koita, Moriba*
Ami Koita 1986, Hadja Soumano
1988, Tata Bambo Kouyate 1988,
Santoutou Kanoute 1988, Kaniba
Ouele Kouyate, n.d., Kasse Mady
Diabate 1990, Baba Djan Kaba 1992,
1993, 1995?, 1996?, Diaba Koita
199?, Salif Keita 1995, Seck and

Jones 1995, Sekouba "Bambino"
Diabate 1996, 1997, Missia Saran
Dioubate 1995?, Mory Kante 1996,
Oumou Dioubate 1999, Kandia
Kouyate 1999
Kone, Amadi
Walde Damba 1989
Kone, Mouctar [Mocktar]
Fanta Damba 1983?, 1986?
Kone, Tidiane
Mory Kante 1996
Kouyate, Ba Foussayur
Tata Bambo Kouyate 1995
Kouyate, Baba
Ami Koita 1995
Kouyate, Basekou
Nainy Diabate 1992, 1997, Toumani
Diabate 1994, 1995, Keletigui Diabate
1996
Kouyate, Bassi*
Kouyate, Mamaye
Abdoulaye Diabate 1995
Kouyate, Noumoudjon
Kandia Kouyate 1999
Kouyate, Souleymane
Salif Keita 1993
Sare, Nassourou
Ali Farka Toure 1996
Sissokho, Bazoumana* (ca. 1890–1987)
Radio Mali 197?
Sissokho, Djeli Baba
Ministry of Information of Mali 1971,
vol. 1, Musiques du Mali 1995a

Sissokho, Mama
  Kasse Mady Diabate 1989, 1990
Sissokho, Mamadou
  Kandia Kouyate 198?
Sissokho [Cissoko], Sayon [Sayan]
  Baaba Maal 1991, Sacko and Kouyate
  1991, Baba Djan Kaba 1992, Dogo-
  mani Dagnon 1993, Salif Keita 1993,
  Moussa Keita 1997?, Kasse Mady
  Diabate 1997

Sissoko, Baba (#2)
  Habib Koite and Bamada 1999
Tounkara, Garba
  Mory Djeli Dienne Kouyate 1993
Tounkara, Mady
  Fanta Damba 1971
Tounkara, Makan
  Ami Koita 1993, Adama Diabate 1995
Traore, Samba
  Ami Koita 1995

Senegal

Kouyate, Dindy
  Oro and Loudes 1976

Kora
Burkina Faso

Dembele, Piohanou
  La Famille Dembele 1996
Diabate, Mamadou
  Farafina 1997?

Keita, Tiawara
  Farafina 1993
Traore, Bakari
  Farafina 1993

Côte d'Ivoire

Jajo, Sidiqui
  The Ivorys 1987

Kamissoko, Mamadi
  Oumou Dioubate 1995?

The Gambia

Jobarteh, Amadu Bansang*
  Knight 1972, Knight 1992-vid
Jobarteh, Demba
  Knight 1992-vid
Jobarteh, Ebraima "Tata Dindin"*
Jobarteh, Malamini*
  Pevar 1978, Jobarteh and Konte,
  n.d., Konte, Konte, and Jobarteh
  1979
Jobarteh, Pa Bobo*
Jobe, Badou
  Ifang Bondi 1994
Kamaso, Keba
  Knight 1972
Kanuteh, Amadu
  Knight 1972
Kanuteh, Jewuru
  Suso and Laswell 1990
Konte, Alhaji Bai* (ca. 1921–83)
  Pevar 1978, 1979, Knight 1992-vid

Konte, Dembo*
  Alhaji Bai Konte 1973/1989, Pevar
  1978, Konte and Kuyateh 1987a,
  1987b, 1992, 1998, Knight 1992-vid,
  Konte, Kuyateh, and Suso 1995
Kuyateh, Falie
  Charters 1975b
Kuyateh, Jali Lamin
  Ifang Bondi 1994
Kuyateh, Jaliba*
Sacko, Sekou*
  Baba Djan Kaba 1992, Dogomani
  Dagnon 1993, Diaba Koita 199?,
  Diabate and Diabate 1997
Saho, Kunye
  Knight 1972
Saho, Yan Kuba*
Suso, Bolong
  Suso and Laswell 1990
Suso, Foday Musa*

Suso, Karanka
  Charters 1975b, Suso and Laswell 1990
Suso, Jali Mori
  Knight 1992-vid
Suso, Jali Nyama*
  Charters 1975b, 1977, Knight 1972,
  Knight 1992-vid, Suso 1992-vid
Suso, Manjako
  Suso and Laswell 1990

Suso, Musa Makan
  Knight 1972
Suso, Papa*
Suso, Salieu*
  Ladji Camara, n.d.b.
Suso, Suntu
  Knight 1972, Knight 1992-vid
Suso, Surakata
  Suso and Laswell 1990

Guinea

Camara, Aboubacar*
  Djeli Moussa Diawara 1988
Cissoko, Keba
  Les Ballets Africains 1995, Lansana
  Kouyate 1996
Cissoko, Mohammed Kelontan
  Mamady Keita 1995
Conde, Djely Moussa
  Baba Djan Kaba 1993, 1995?, 1996?,
  Kerfala Kante 1994, Mama Keita
  1995, Seck and Jones 1995, Sekouba
  "Bambino" Diabate 1992, 1996, 1997,
  Les Go de Koteba 1997, Oumou
  Dioubate 1999
Diabate, [Djeli Sory] "Papa"* (1962 or
1963–)
  Manfila Kante 1991, 1994, Djeli Sory
  Diabate and Djessou Mory Kante,
  n.d., Sona Diabate 1996

Diabate, Mama
  Mama Diabate, n.d.
Diawara, Djely Moussa* [Jali Musa
Jawara]
  Divas from Mali 1997
Kalissa, Fode
  Les Ballets Africains 1991, 1993, 1995
Kante, Mory*
Kouyate, Djelimakan
  Nimba 199?
Kouyate, Kemo [Tiemoko]
  Djanka Diabate 1991, Oumou
  Dioubate 1993
Kouyate, Sekou
  African Virtuoses 1983, Soumah 1991
Sodia, Amadou Doumbouya*
  Baba Djan Kaba 1992, Missia Saran
  Dioubate 1995?, Sekouba "Bambino"
  Diabate 1997

Mali

Anonymous
  Laura Boulton [1939] 1957
Diabate, Bakari
  Ami Koita 1992
Diabate, Mamadou
  Mariam Kouyate, Mamadou Diabate,
  and Sidiki Diabate 1995a, 1995b
Diabate, Nfa
  Ministry of Information of Mali 1971,
  vol. 5
Diabate, Sidiki* (?–1996)
  Ministry of Information of Mali 1971,
  vols. 1, 4, and 5, Mokontafe Sako
  1976a, Mariam Kouyate, Mamadou
  Diabate, and Sidiki Diabate 1995a,
  1996b

Diabate, Toumani* (1965–)
  Adama Diabate 1995, Sidiki Diabate
  1987, Keletigui Diabate 1996, Kasse
  Mady Diabate 1997, Diabate with Sis-
  soko 1999
Kouyate, Batrou Sekou*
  Ministry of Information of Mali 1971,
  vols.1, 4, and 5, Fanta Damba 1975a,
  1975b, 1976, 1986?
Kouyate, Fode*
Sissoko, Amara
  Kandia Kouyate 198?
Sissoko, Djelimadi
  Ministry of Information of Mali 1971,
  vols. 1, 4, and 5, Mokontafe Sako
  1976a

Sissoko, Djelimoussa [Jeli Moussa]
"Ballake"*
    Santoutou Kouyate 1988, Lassina
    Coulibaly and Yan Kadi Faso 1998?,
    Diabate with Sissoko 1999, Kandia
    Kouyate 1999

Sissokho, Yakhouba
    Moriba Koita 1997
Soumano, Lamine
    Aminata Kamissoko 1997

Senegal

Cissokho, Kauwding
    Baaba Maal 1994, 1998, Mansour
    Seck 1994, 1995
Cissoko, Sunjul* [Soundioulou] (1924–)
    Maa Hawa Kouyate, n.d.a, n.d.b
Diabate, Boubacar
    Seck and Diabate 1997, Tata Bambo
    Kouyate 1985
Drame, Lalo Keba*
Koite, Sourakata*
Konte, Lamine (Kolda)
Kouyate, Diombo*
    Sourakata Koite 1990

Kouyate, Djimo
Kouyate, Morikeba*
    Mandeng Tunya 1997
Kouyate, Soriba
    Youssou Ndour 1994
Kuyateh [Kouyate], Kausu
    Konte and Kuyateh 1987a, 1987b,
    1992, 1998, Konte, Kuyateh, and Suso
    1995
Sissoko, Bana
    Oro and Loudes 1976
Suso, Jali Mori
    Knight 1992-vid

Soron

Dioubate, Mamadi (Guinea)
    Rouget 1954a, 1954b, 1999

Tama
Burkina Faso

Dambele, Dedougou
    Farafina 1997?
Keita, Tiawara
    Farafina 1992a, 1992b, 1993

Poumayeli, Brahima
    La Famille Dembele 1996
Sanou, Keresse
    Koko du Bukina Faso 1993

The Gambia

Sen, Usmane
    Pevar 1978

Suso, Foday Musa
    Foday Musa Suso 1984a

Guinea

Percussions de Guinée 1994

Mali

Baba, Walde
    Fode Kouyate 1995?
Dia [Ja], Ndulay
    Polak 1997
Kanoute, N'Dia
    Mamadou "Kunkun" Camara 1997
Kouyate, Bassi*

Sissokho, Moussa
    Seck and Jones 1995
Sissoko, Baba (#1)
    Walde Damba 1989, Ami Koita 1992
Sissoko, Baba (#2)
    Habib Koite and Bamada 1999

Senegal

Dieye, Diebril
  Tama Walo 1998
Diop, Massamba
  Baaba Maal 1994, 1998
Gueye, Abdoul Rakhmanne
  Tama Walo 1998
Mbaye, Essa
  Zoumana Diarra 1997
Mboup, Ibrahima
  Tama Walo 1998

Samba, Abdou Boy
  Tama Walo 1998
Thiam[e], Assane*
  Youssou Ndour 1989–
Thiam, Mamadou
  Tama Walo 1998
Thiam, Ousseynou "Papa"
  Tama Walo 1998

Vocalists
Côte d'Ivoire

Cissoko, Papa*
Kante, Niama
  Les Go de Koteba 1997
Keita, Maate
  Les Go de Koteba 1997

Sangho, Awa
  Les Go de Koteba 1997

The Gambia
Fina

Camara, Mahame
  Suso and Laswell 1990

Suso, Bobo
  Suso and Laswell 1990

Jeli

Jebateh, Fatumata
  Knight 1972
Jebateh, Nyulo
  Knight 1972
Jobarteh, Ebraima "Tata Dindin"*
Jobarteh, Malamini*
  Jobarteh and Konte, n.d., Konte,
  Konte, and Jobarteh 1979
Jobarteh, Pa Bobo*
Jobarteh, Siffai
  Pa Bobo Jobarteh 1997
Konte, Alhaji Bai*
  Konte, Konte, and Jobarteh 1979
Konte, Dembo
  Jobarteh and Konte, n.d., Konte,
  Konte, and Jobarteh 1979, Konte and
  Kuyateh 1987a, 1987b, 1992, 1998,
  Konte, Kuyateh, and Suso 1995

Kuyateh, Jali Lamin
  Ifang Bondi 1994
Kuyateh, Jaliba*
Kuyateh, Kausu
  Konte and Kuyateh 1987a, 1987b,
  1992, 1998, Konte, Kuyateh, and
  Suso 1995
Sakho, Mabinty
  Ifang Bondi 1994
Samba, Sheikh
  Ifang Bondi 1994
Suso, Bintou
  Yan Kuba Saho 1998
Suso, Foday Musa*
Suso, Jali Nyama*
Suso, Salieu*

Guinea

Bangoura, Fatoumata "Ngadi"
Sona Diabate 1990a, 1990b
Bangoura, M'Mah
Famoro Kouyate 1992, Lansana
Kouyate 1996
Barry, Maimouna
Sekouba Kandia Kouyate 1990?,
Sekouba "Bambino" Diabate 1994,
Kerfala Kante 1994, 1995?, Ibro Dia-
bate 1995?, Oumou Dioubate 1995?,
Fode Kouyate 1994?
Camara, Aboubacar* (Brikakoma,
Siguiri, 1964–)
Camara, Fatou
Lansana Kouyate 1996, Mohamed
Diaby 1997
Camara, Malik
Kaloum Star 1996
Camara, Mama Adama
Mamady Keita 1992
Camara, Mamadou
Balla et Ses Balladins 1980, 1993
Camara, Mamasata
Mohamed Diaby 1997
Cissoko, Keba
Lansana Kouyate 1996, Mohamed Di-
aby 1997
Conde, Naba
Manfila Kante 1991
Conde, Nagnouma
Mamady Keita 1995
Conde, Nansouba
Famoudou Konate 1998
Dembele, Assitan
Djanka Diabate 1991, Oumou
Dioubate 1993
Diabate, Batourou
Famoudou Konate 1998
Diabate, Cadet
Famoudou Konate 1998
Diabate, Djanka*
Djeli Moussa Diawara 1983, 1992,
Papa Cissoko 1986, Toumani Diabate
1988a, 1994, Kandia Kouyate 198?,
Kouyate and Kouyate 1990, Ousmane
Kouyate 1990, Sabre Soumano 199?,

Aboubacar Camara 199?, n.d., Sacko
and Kouyate 1991, Diaba Koita 199?,
Baba Djan Kaba 1992, 1995?, 1996?,
Oumou Dioubate 1993, Salif Keita
1989, 1991, 1993, 1995, Kaniba
Ouele Kouyate, n.d., 1994, Sambala
Kanoute 1995, Sekouba "Bambino"
Diabate 1996, 1997, Sona Diabate
1996, Mory Kante 1996, Kandia
Kouyate 1999, Amadou Sodia 1999?
Diabate, Djeli Kani
Mamady Keita 1995
Diabate, Djelinouma
Manfila Kante 1991, 1998
Diabate, Domani
Manfila Kante 1991
Diabate, Doussouba
Missia Saran Dioubate 1995?
Diabate, Fanta
Manfila Kante 1994, Mama Diabate,
n.d., 1995, Missia Saran Dioubate
1995?
Diabate, Fode
Horoya Band 1971, 1974, 1997
Diabate, Ibro*
Diabate, Mama*
Diabate, Mariama
Djeli Moussa Diawara 1988, Famoro
Kouyate 1992
Diabate, Nahawa
Famoudou Konate 1998
Diabate, Nakande
Mamady Keita 1995
Diabate, Namassa
Manfila Kante 1998
Diabate, Sadjo
Sambala Kanoute 1995
Diabate, Sambou
Papa Cissoko 1986
Diabate, Sayon
Sabre Soumano 199?, Kaniba Ouele
Kouyate, n.d., Sona Diabate 1990a,
1990b, 1996, Diabate and Diabate
1997
Diabate, Sekouba Bambino*
Bembeya Jazz 1985?, Kouyate and

Kouyate 1990, Africando 1996, 1998,
Kandia Kouyate 1999
Diabate, Sona*
Sabre Soumano 199?, Manfila Kante
1994, Kerfala "Papa" Diabate 1999
Diaby, Fode
Djanka Diabate 1991
Diaby, Mohamed*
Lansana Kouyate 1996
Diawara, Djeli Moussa* [Jali Musa
Jawara]
Diawara, Kade*
Dioubate, Kandet
Baba Djan Kaba 1993, 1995?, 1996?,
Mama Keita 1995, Rail Band 1995,
Mory Kante 1996
Dioubate, Missia Saran*
Dioubate, Oumou*
Djanka Diabate 1991, Aboubacar
Camara, n.d., 199?, Manfila Kante
1994
Habass, Fassou
African Virtuoses 1983
Kaba, Baba Djan*
Missia Saran Dioubate 1995?
Kamissoko, Sayon
Oumou Dioubate 1995?
Kante, Kerfala*
Kante, Lansine
Horoya Band 1971, 1974, 1997
Kante, Mahawa [Mawa, Nawa]
Mory Djeli Dienne Kouyate 1993, Se-
kouba "Bambino" Diabate 1992, 1994,
Kerfala Kante 1994, 1995?, Oumou
Dioubate 1995?, Fode Kouyate 1994?
Kante, Makone
Manfila Kante 1998
Kante, Manfila* (ex-Ambassadeurs)
Kante, Manfila "Dabadou"*
Kante, Massaranke
Manfila Kante 1998
Kante, Mory*
Kante, Nyalenfi
Manfila Kante 1991
Kante, "Soba" Manfila* (1933–)
Balla et Ses Balladins
Keita, Fanta
Macire Sylla 1996

Keita, Mariamagbe
Djeli Moussa Diawara 1988, Baba
Djan Kaba 1993
Konde (see Conde)
Koroma, Sekou
Rouget 1972, 1999
Kouyate, Djefarma
Famoro Kouyate 1992
Kouyate, Djeli Sara
Manfila Kante 1998
Kouyate, Domani Damba
Mamady Keita 1995
Kouyate, Fadima
Mory Djeli Dienne Kouyate 1993
Kouyate, Fanta
Djeli Moussa Diawara 1983
Kouyate, Hadja [Adja] Manimgbe
Oumou Dioubate 1993, 1999, Mama
Keita 1995, Sambala Kanoute 1995,
Sekouba "Bambino" Diabate 1996,
1997, Sona Diabate 1996, Missia
Saran Dioubate 1995?, Mory Kante
1996, Kandia Kouyate 1999, Amadou
Sodia 1999?
Kouyate, Kabine "Kabus"
Kouyate and Kouyate 1990
Kouyate, Kande
Manfila Kante 1991
Kouyate, Konde
Rouget 1954a, 1972, 1999
Kouyate, Maryam
Kouyate and Kouyate 1990
Kouyate, Mory Djeli Dienne*
Kouyate, Ramata
Famoro Kouyate 1992
Kouyate, Sekouba Kandia*
Kouyate, Sona Djely*
Kouyate, Sory Kandia* (1933?–77)
Les Ballets Africains de Keita Fodeba
1956?
Kouyate, Wande
Sekouba "Bambino" Diabate 1992
Mara, Fanta
Oumou Dioubate 1999
Seck, Mamadou
Seck and Diabate 1977
Sodia, Amadou Doumbouya*
Missia Saran Dioubate 1995?

Sylla, Abou
  Lansana Kouyate 1996
Sylla, Macire*
Sylla, Sekou
  Kaloum Star 1996

Wallas, B. Nestor
  Balla et Ses Balladins 1993

Guinea Bissau

Kanoute, Sambala*

Mali
Jeli

Dagnon, Dogomani*
Damba, Assa
  Abdoulaye Diabate 1995
Damba, Dialou*
Damba, Fanta*
  Ministry of Information of Mali 1971,
  vol. 1
Damba, Hawa
  Polak 1997
Damba, Kadiatouni
  Moussa Keita 1997?
Damba, Mah*
  Abdoulaye Diabate 1995, Divas from
  Mali 1997
Damba, Manian
  Baba Djan Kaba 1993, Seck and Jones
  1995
Damba, Umu
  Polak 1997
Damba, Walde*
Dembele, Assitan
  Salif Keita 1991
Diabate, Abdoulaye*
Diabate, Adama*
Diabate, [El Hadji] Bala
  Diabate Family of Kela 1994
Diabate, Djelimadi
  Ministry of Information of Mali 1971,
  vol. 4
Diabate, Djenebou
  Ami Koita 1995
Diabate, Fanta
  Diabate Family of Kela 1994
Diabate, Jetenne
  Diabate Family of Kela 1994
Diabate, Kasse Mady*
  National Badema 1977, 1983a, 1983b,

Toumani Diabate 1994, Seck and
  Jones 1995
Diabate, Lanfia
  Rail Band 1982, 1985, 1992, Bajourou
  1993, Diabate Family of Kela 1994,
  1997
Diabate, Lansine
  Diabate Family of Kela 1994
Diabate, Modibo
  Rail Band 1992
Diabate, Nainy*
Diabate, Sira Mori
  Diabate Family of Kela 1949, 1997,
  Ministry of Information of Mali 1971,
  vol. 1, Musiques du Mali 1995b
Diabate [Jabate], Sita Ye
  Polak 1997
Diabate, Vieux
  Kasse Mady Diabate 1997
Diabate, Yakare
  Ousmane Sacko 1987
Diabate, [El Hadji] Yamourou [Yamadu]
  Ministry of Information of Mali
  1971, vol. 1, Diabate Family of Kela
  1994
Doumbia, Djenne (see Doumbouya)
Doumbouya, Djenne
  Djeli Moussa Diawara 1983, Oumou
  Dioubate 1992?, Baba Djan Kaba
  1992, 1993, Salif Keita 1987, 1989,
  1991, 1993, 1995, Sekouba "Bam-
  bino" Diabate 1996, 1997, Missia
  Saran Dioubate 1995?
Drame, Assa*
Drame, Mamou
  Tata Bambo Kouyate 1995, Assa
  Drame, n.d.

Fomba, Adama
   Rail Band 1995
Kamisoko, Kassemadi
   Diabate Family of Kela 1997
Kamissoko, Aminata*
   Ami Koita 1995
Kamissoko, Nantenedie
   Ministry of Information of Mali 1971,
   vols. 1 and 4
Kanoute, Abdrahamane*
Kanoute, Yayi*
Keita, Assitan "Mama"*
   Fode Kouyate 1995?, Sacko and
   Kouyate 1991, Salif Keita 1989, 1991,
   Mangala 1993, Kaniba Oule Kouyate
   1994, Seck and Jones 1995, Rail Band
   1995, Abdoulaye Diabate 1995, Baba
   Djan Kaba 1995?, 1996?, Sekouba
   "Bambino" Diabate 1996, 1997, Sona
   Diabate 1996, Mory Kante 1996
Koiate, Orakya
   Ministry of Information of Mali 1971,
   vol. 4
Koita, Ami*
Koita, Diaba*
Koite, Habib*
Kone, Babani*
Kouyate, Bassi*
Kouyate, Bintan
   Diabate Family of Kela 1994, 1997
Kouyate, Damory
   Rail Band 1992, 1995
Kouyate, Diaw
   Toumani Diabate 1988a, 1994
Kouyate, Dipa
   Kasse Mady Diabate 1990
Kouyate, Fatoumata "Mama"
   Seck and Jones 1995
Kouyate, [Djely] Fode*
   Sacko and Kouyate 1991
Kouyate, Kandia* (Kita, 1959?)
   Sidiki Diabate 1987, Sekouba "Bam-
   bino" Diabate 1997, Divas from Mali
   1997
Kouyate, Mah
   Nainy Diabate 1997, Babani Kone
   1998
Kouyate, Mama
   Abdoulaye Diabate 1995

Kouyate, Mariam*
   Sidiki Diabate 1987
Kouyate, Oumou
   Fode Kouyate 1995?
Kouyate, Ramata
   Fode Kouyate 1994?, Sacko and
   Kouyate 1991, Diabate and Diabate
   1997
Kouyate, Sadio*
Kouyate, Sanougue*
   Kasse Mady Diabate 1990, 1997
Kouyate, Saranfing
   Ministry of Information of Mali 1971,
   vol. 4
Kouyate, Sekou
   Abdoulaye Diabate 1995
Kouyate, Tata Bambo*
Kouyate, Tenin
   Nainy Diabate 1992, Babani Kone
   1998
Kouyate, Wande
   Ministry of Information of Mali 1971,
   vol. 4
Magassa, Idrissa
   Benkadi International 1997
Mangala*
Niang, Dja
   Nainy Diabate 1997, Babani Kone
   1998
Sacko, Fanta*
Sacko, Ousmane*
Sako, Mokontafe* (1937–)
   Ministry of Information of Mali 1971,
   vol. 4, Radio Mali 1977
Seck, Djeneba
   Assa Drame, n.d., Nahawa Doumbia
   1997
Sissoko, Djeli Mady
   Sidiki Diabate 1987
Sissoko, Hama
   Nainy Diabate 1992, Babani Kone
   1998
Sissoko, Mama*
Sissoko, Samba
   Rail Band 1995
Soumano, Hadja*
Toure, Assetou
   Moussa Keita 1997?

Wasulu

Diakite, Djeneba*
Diakite, Ramatou
  Nahawa Doumbia 1997
Diakite, Tom
  Seck and Jones 1995
Doumbia, Nahawa*
Keita, Fatou
  Moussa Traore 1999

Sangare, Assitan "Tata"
  Moussa Traore 1999
Sangare, Oumou*
  Divas from Mali 1997
Sidibe, Sali*
  Divas from Mali 1997

Other

Bagayoko, Amadou
  Bagayoko and Doumbia 198?, 1999?
Coulibaly [Kulibali], Fatumata
  Polak 1997
Coulibaly [Kulibali], Na
  Polak 1997
Coulibaly, Soungalo
  Farafina 1993, 1997?
Dia, Ousmane
  Les Ambassadeurs 1975–

Diakite, Sambou
  Les Ambassadeurs 1979c, 1980, 1983a
Doumbia, Mariam
  Bagayoko and Doumbia 198?, 1999?
Keita, Karamoko*
Keita, Moussa
Keita, Salif* (Djoliba, 1949–)
  Les Ambassadeurs
Toure, Ali Farka*
Traore, Boubacar*

Senegal

Diate, Djime
  Sedhiou Band 1998
Diabate, Boubacar
  Mamadou Seck and Boubacar Diabate
  1977
Kouyate, Djali Sekou
  Sedhiou Band 1998
Kouyate, Djimo*
Kouyate, Maa Hawa* (originally from
Guinea)
  Sunjul Cissoko 1992
Kouyate, Morikeba*
  Mandeng Tunya 1997

Lo, Ismael*
Maal, Baaba*
Ndao, Seydou
  Sedhiou Band 1998
Ndiaye, Aminata Dieng
  Sedhiou Band 1998
Ndour, Youssou*
Sakho, Fanta
  Oro and Loudes 1976
Sarr, Amadou Laye
  Sedhiou Band 1998
Seck, Mansour*
  Baaba Maal 1989, 1998

Unidentified

Bamba, Amy
  Missia Saran Dioubate 1995?, Kandia
  Kouyate 1999
Diabate, Awa
  Sekouba "Bambino" Diabate 1992,
  Tata Bambo Kouyate 1995
Kouyate, Diaou
  Sacko and Kouyate 1991

Maiga, Hawa
  Sekouba "Bambino" Diabate 1996,
  1997, Missia Saran Dioubate 1995?,
  Amadou Sodia 1999?
Soumbounou, Oumou
  Kandia Kouyate 198?

Recordings of Traditional and Modern Pieces in Mande Repertories

When titles are within parentheses, the performer (or performers) has composed a new piece based on the musical accompaniment under which it is categorized.

Simbi
Balakononifin/Mugutari/Manden Mori
Rail Band (1977); Mory Kante (*Teriya*, 1986); Bajourou (*Mankan*, 1993); Diabate Family of Kela (*Simbon*, 1994); Salif Keita (*Donsolou*, 1993); Kandia Kouyate (*Sa kunu sa*, 199?), Moussa Keita (*Sabamanigna, Sankin, Dossomosso, Dossolou, Kede fassa, Mambi fassa*, 1997?).

Janjon
Nantenedie Kamissoko (Ministry of Information of Mali, 1971, vol. 1); Sory Kandia Kouyate ([1973] 1990); Les Ambassadeurs (1976b, 1979a); Bembeya Jazz (n.d.); Ami Koita (*Idjodo*, 1986); Kandia Kouyate (*Dalla*, 199?); Baaba Maal (*Joulowo*, 1991); Salif Keita (*Nyanafin*, 1991); Lamine Konte (1990); Diabate Family of Kela (1994); Keletigui Diabate (1996); Moussa Keita (1997?).

Kulanjan
Ensemble Instrumental [Africain] de la Radiodiffusion Nationale (1970, Guinea Compilations 1998, vol. 1); Batrou Sekou Kouyate and N'Fa Diabate (Ministry of Information of Mali, 1971, vol. 5); Kandia Kouyate (*Balassama*, 198?); Kasse Mady Diabate (1990); Diaba Koita (mislabeled as *Lelile-Mireille Gassama*, 199?); Moussa Keita (*Mambi fassa*, 1997?).

Bala
Fakoli/Nanfoulen
Alberts (1949); "Soba" Manfila Kante (1961?, EPL-7836); Jardin de Guinée/Guinea Compilations (1967); Les Ambassadeurs (*Ntoman*, 198?); Mory Kante (1988); Maa Hawa Kouyate (n.d.b.); Mory Djeli Dienne Kouyate (*Kalilou Camara, Karifala Doumbouya*, 1990); Salif Keita (*N B'i Fe*, 1991); Djimo Kouyate (1992a); Sona Diabate/M'Mah Sylla (*Kinikiniko*, 1983); Aboubacar Camara (*Nadiyaba*, 1994); Ladji Camara (n.d.a).

Keme Burema
Unidentified (*Sily*, Guinea Compilations 1962a; Guinea Compilations 1962b); Orchestre de la Garde Républicaine; Bembeya Jazz (*Regard sur le passé*, 1970); Nantenedie Kamissoko (Ministry of Information of Mali, 1971, vols. 1 and 4); Sory Kandia Kouyate ([1973] 1990); The Ivorys (*Yanburi Pa Koura* [1984] 1987); Baaba Maal (*Dogota*, 1991); Dogomani Dagnon (1993); Djimo Kouyate (1992a); Baba Djan Kaba (*Djanfa* 1992); Mansour Seck (*Quinze Ans*, 1994).

Lamban

Sory Kandia Kouyate ([1973] 1990); Amadu Bansang Jobarteh (1978, 1993); Ousmane Sacko (*I yee i y'ata*, 1987); Ami Koita (*Banny Kebe*, 1986; 1992); Tata Bambo Kouyate (*Mah Drame*, 1988; 1995); Hadja Soumano (*Sosso*, 1988); Walde Damba (*Balabolo*, 1989a; *Lamba*, 1989b); Suso and Laswell (1990); Wassa (*Sikiri*, 1991); Konte and Kuyateh (1992); Amadu Bansang Jobarteh (Knight 1992-vid); Soungalo Coulibaly (*Ya Marouwo*, 1992); Diabate Family of Kela (*Jeliya*, 1994); Konte, Kuyateh, and Suso (1995); Toumani Diabate (*Cheick Oumar Bah*, 1995); Diaba Koita (*Seben Djara Seben and Waye*, mislabeled as *Ndiaye Makhanse*, 199?); Ladji Camara (n.d.a); Mariam Kouyate (*Dendiougou, Silama Kamba*, n.d.); Mariam Kouyate, Mamadou Diabate, and Sidiki Diabate (*Assa Cissé*, 1995a); Morikeba Kouyate (1997), Kerfala "Papa" Diabate (1999); Toumani Diabate with Ballake Sissoko (1999).

Sunjata

Ensemble Instrumental [Africain] de la Radiodiffusion Nationale (1970); Keletigui et Ses Tambourinis (Guinea Compilations 1970); Sira Mori Diabate (*Tirimagan*, Ministry of Information of Mali 1971, vol. 1); Yamourou Diabate (Ministry of Information of Mali 1971, vol. 1); Sidiki Diabate and Batrou Sekou Kouyate ([Ministry of Information of Mali 1971, vol. 5] Musiques du Mali 1995a); Bazoumana Sissoko (1971a); Kele Monson Diabate (n.d.); Rail Band with Salif Keita ([1970] n.d., 1976a, 1976c); Rail Band with Mory Kante ([1977] n.d.); Foday Musa Suso (1972); National Badema (*Tiramakan*, 1983a); Cheikh M. Smith (1992); Kouyate Family of Niagassola (Toureille 1992); Diabate Family of Kela (*Tiramakan*, 1994); Keletigui Diabate 1996; Kandia Kouyate (*Mandenkalou*, 1999).

Koni

Taara

Orchestre de la Garde Républicaine (1967); Ensemble Instrumental de la Radiodiffusion Nationale (1970); Orchestre Régional de Mopti (1972); Fanta Sacko (1972); Fanta Damba (1971); Bazoumana Sissoko (1971b); Batrou Sekou Kouyate and N'Fa Diabate ([Ministry of Information of Mali 1971, vol. 5] Musiques du Mali 1995a); Sory Kandia Kouyate (1971); Orchestre National "A" de la République du Mali (1972); Mamadou Seck and Boubacar Diabate (1977); Camayenne Sofa (1975, 1977); Les Ambassadeurs (1980a); Diabate Family of Kela (1994); Oumou Dioubate (*Super Bobo*, 1995?); Mariam Kouyate (n.d.); Mariam Kouyate, Mamadou Diabate, and Sidiki Diabate (1995a); Mory Kante (*On Yarama Foulbêh*, 1996); Moriba Koita (1997).

Tutu Jara

Unidentified (Guinea Compilations 1962a); Fanta Damba (1971); Sidiki Diabate and Batrou Sekou Kouyate (Ministry of Information of Mali 1971, vol. 5); Sory Kandia Kouyate ([1973] 1990); Bah-Sadio; Ami Koita (*Bambougoudji*, 199?; *Den Te Sanna*, n.d.); Tata Bambo Kouyate (*Mama Batchily, Goundo Tandja, Amadou Traore*, 1985; *Nene Sow*, 1988); Walde Damba (*Djeli Diourou, Toto*, 1989a); Maa Hawa Kouyate (n.d.b.); Sunjul Cissoko (1992); Diaba Koita (mislabeled as *Kulanjan*, 199?); Mariam Kouyate, Mamadou Diabate, and Sidiki Diabate (*Moussa Diakite, Aladji Sata*, 1995b); M'Bady Kouyate (1996, vol. 1); Moriba Koita (*Badiourou*, 1997).

Kora
Kuruntu Kelefa/Kelefaba
Jali Nyama Suso ([1972] 1996); M'Bady Kouyate (1996, vol. 1); Seck and Diabate (1977).

Allah L'a Ke
Unidentified (Guinea Compilations 1962b); Bembeya Jazz (Guinea Compilations 1971); Note: *Allah l'a ke* attributed to Sidiki Diabate and Djelimady Sissoko on Ministry of Information of Mali, 1971, vol. 5/Musiques du Mali 1995a is actually *Hama Ba Jata*; Batrou Sekou Kouyate (Ministry of Information of Mali 1971, vol. 5/Musiques du Mali 1995a); Santoutou Kanoute (*Tapa Sora*, 1988); Konte and Kuyateh (1992); Sunjul Cissoko (1992); Jali Nyama Suso (1992-vid); Jali Nyama Suso and Alhaji Suntu Suso (Knight 1992-vid); Mory Kante (*Mali-ba*, 1996); M'Bady Kouyate (1996, vol. 1).

Masani Cisse
Sory Kandia Kouyate ([1973] 1990); Sekou Conde (n.d.a); Quintette Guinéenne (Guinea Compilations 1976); Jali Nyama Suso (1992-vid); Habib Koite and Bamada (1999).

Tabara
Unidentified (Guinea Compilations 1962b); Jali Nyama Suso ([1972] 1996); Djeli Mady Tounakra and Bouba Sacko; Amadu Bansang Jobarteh (1993); Moriba Koita (*Niani Mankan*, 1997).

Unidentified Instrumental Origin
Chedo/Kedo
Unidentified (Guinea Compilations 1962a); Jali Nyama Suso ([1972] 1996); Sory Kandia Kouyate ([1973] 1990); Ismael Lo (1985); Sunjul Cissoko (1992); Ifang Bondi (1994); Baaba Maal (1994); Morikeba Kouyate (1997); Farafina (1997?).

Duga/Saxo Dugu
Unidentified (Guinea Compilations 1962a); Keletigui et Ses Tambourinis (1967b); Fanta Damba (1971); Sidiki Diabate and Djelimady Sissoko ([Ministry of Information of Mali 1971, vol. 5] Musiques du Mali 1995b); Sory Kandia Kouyate ([1973] 1990); Orchestre National "A" du Mali (1970); Orchestre Régional de Kayes (1970); Bah-Sadio; Balla et Ses Balladins (1967); Quintette Guinéenne (Guinea Compilations 1976); Tata Bambo Kouyate (*Ainanah Bah*, 1985; *Diadie Diawara*, 1988); Maa Hawa Kouyate (n.d.b.); Sunjul Cissoko (1992); Moussa Keita (*Ntani gnini*, 1993?); Ami Koita (*N'-Darila*, 1995); Moriba Koita (1997); Mama Sissoko (1997).

Maki
Bazoumana Sissoko (1971b); Amadu Kanuteh (Knight 1972); Mory Kante (*On yarama foulbeh*, 1996); M'Bady Kouyate (1996, vol. 1).

Malisadio
Sory Kandia Kouyate (1970); Setouman Kouyate (Guinea Compilations 1961a); Orchestre Régional de Kayes (1970); Cheikh M. Smith (1992).

Jawura

Sidiki Diabate (*Kounady La Beno,* 1987); Kandia Kouyate (*Niamadyla,* 198?; *Kitakou-rou, Lagare,* 199?; Divas from Mali: *Djaoura,* 1997; Doninke, 1999); Walde Damba (*Sabougnouma,* 1989b); Kerfala Kante (*Moriba Conde,* 1992); Soungalo Coulibaly (*Ya Kegne Nya Fuye,* 1992); Bajourou (*Sora,* 1993); Ami Koita (*Lolan,* 1993; *Tounya Tigui,* 1995 [also on Divas of Mali, 1996]); Diabate Family of Kela (*Tiramagan fasa,* 1994); Kerfala Kante (*Moriba Conde,* 1994); Djeli Sory Diabate and Djessou Mory Kante (*Mory Kone,* n.d.); Mariam Kouyate (*Ben Baliya,* 199?a-disc); Rail Band (*Niamatoutou Kono,* 1995); Macire Sylla (*Guiné Faré,* 1996).

Modern
Banankoro–Fanta Barana

Fanta Sacko (1972); Bajourou (1993).

Jarabi

Fanta Sacko (1972); Ami Koita (1988); Lamine Konte (1989); Mah Damba (Divas from Mali, 1987); Cheikh M. Smith (1992).

Kaira

Arthur Alberts (1954a); Diabate Brothers of Kankan (Rouget [1954a] 1999); "Soba" Manfila Kante (1961?, vol. 3); Balla et Ses Balladins (1967); Orchestre de la Garde Républicaine (1967); Sidiki Diabate and Batrou Sekou Kouyate ([Ministry of Information of Mali 1971, vol. 1] Musiques du Mali 1995b); Rail Band (1975, HNLX 5148); Kandia Kouyate (*Tono,* 1988); Ami Koita (*Ami Kaira,* 199?); Kasse Mady Diabate (1990); Mansour Seck (*Kairaba, Elimane Boubacar Kane,* 1994); Aboubacar Camara (*Deri,* 199?); Rail Band (*Dounia,* 1995); Moriba Koita (1997); Toumani Diabate with Ballake Sissoko (1999).

Mamaya

Arthur Alberts (1949); Keletigui et Ses Tambourinis (1967b); "Soba" Manfila Kante (1961?, vol. 8); The Ivorys (1987); Jali Musa Jawara (1988); Ami Koita (1992); El Hadj Djeli Sory Kouyate (1992, vols. 2 and 3); Djimo Kouyate (1992a); Nahini Diabate (1998); Mamady Keita (1995); Keletigui Diabate (1996).

Tubaka

Arthur Alberts (1949); Sory Kandia Kouyate/Les Ballets Africaines de Keita Fodeba (1956?); Fanta Sacko (1972); Keletigui et Ses Tambourinis (Guinea Compilations 1971); Bah-Sadio; Les Ambassadeurs (1980a, 1981b, 1984a); Ladji Camara (n.d.b); Kouyate and Kouyate (1990); Mory Djeli Dienne Kouyate (*Assetou Kouyate, Rokiya Kaba,* 1990); Aboubacar Camara (*Derimagni,* 1994); Manfila Kante (*Samadi,* 1994); Mama Keita (*Attention Coco,* 1995); Sekou "Bembeya" Diabate (*Balake,* 1995); Missia Saran Dioubate (*Yereko,* 1996?); Macire Sylla (*Ia,* 1996).

Singya

Ali Farka Toure (1988b); National Badema (*Kana bla n na,* 1983a).

Syliphone Recordings

Most albums do not contain copyright dates; those that do are listed. The dates of some albums can be estimated as a year or two after the year they commemorate; for example, *Guinée an X* commemorates the tenth anniversary of independence (1968).

GUI 1   *Kan Ni Mankan: Sons et echos.* Kindia, Paillota, Jardin de Guinée, Palm-Jazz, Tele-Jazz, Kissidougou.

GUI 3   *1967: Quinzaine artistique nationale, selections des choeurs.* Farana, Konakri 2, Labe, Mamu, Kindia.

SLP 1   *Orchestre Paillote sous la direction de Traore Keletigui, vol. 1.*

SLP 2   *Orchestre du Jardin de Guinée sous la direction de Onivogui Balla.*

SLP 3   *Orchestre Paillote sous la direction de Traore Keletigui, vol. 2.*

SLP 4   *Bembeya Jazz sous la direction de Diaoune Hamidou.*

SLP 5   *Rythmes Africains. Conakry: Quinzaine artistique 1965.* Beyla, Dabola, Kissidougou, Gueckedou.

SLP 6   *Orchestre de la Garde Républicaine, 1ère et 2ème formation.*

SLP 7   *Ensemble Instrumental de la Radiodiffusion Nationale sous la direction de Kante Diely Mamoudou.*

SLP 8   *Guinée an X: Grand tierce musical.* Bembeya Jazz National, Balla et Ses Balladins, Keletigui et Ses Tambourinis.

SLP 9   *Guinée an X: Ensemble Instrumental de la Radiodiffusion Nationale.*

SLP 10   *Bembeya Jazz National: Regard sur le passé.* Reissued on SLP 64 and on CD as Bolibana/Mélodie 42064-2.

SLP 11   *Sons et rythmes de Guinée.*

SLP 12   *Kouyaté Sory Kandia.* Kouyaté Sory Kandia, Kouyate Dieli Sory, Ensemble National Djoliba, Orchestre Keletigui et Ses Tambourinis. Reissued on CD on Syllart/Mélodie.

SLP 13   *Sekou Toure: Poèmes militants.*

SLP 14   *Ballets Africains de la République de Guinée.*

SLP 15   *Guinée an XI: Keletigui et Ses Tambourinis, Balla et Ses Balladins, Bembeya Jazz National.*

SLP 16   *Guinée an XI: Ensemble Instrumental de la Radiodiffusion Nationale.*

SLP 17   *PDG* (Sory Kandia), *Boloba* (Horoya).

SLP 18   *Premier Festival National de la Guinée: Folklore de Guinée.*

SLP 19   *Premier Festival National Guinéen des Arts, de la Culture et des Sports de mars 1970.* Eight federal orchestras.

SLP 20   *Kouyate Sory Kandia: Tour d'Afrique de la chanson.* Keletigui et Ses Tambourinis. Reissued on CD as Syllart/Mélodie 38204-2.

SLP 21   *Guinée an XII: Balla et Ses Balladins.*

SLP 22   *Myriam Makeba: Concert public au Palais du Peuple de Conakry, "Appel à l'Afrique."* Reissued on CD on Syllart/Mélodie.

SLP 23   *Discotheque 70.* Bembeya Jazz National, Keletigui et Ses Tambourinis, Balla et Ses Balladins, Les Virtuoses Diabate, Demba Camara. Reissued on CD on Syllart/Mélodie 38208-2.

SLP 24   *Bembeya Jazz National: Dix ans de succès.* Reissued on CD as Bolibana/Mélodie 42024-2.

SLP 25   *Trio Fédéral de Pointe: Kebendo Jazz, Horoya Band, Niandan Jazz.*

SLP 26   *Édition speciale de la régie syliphone commémorant le 1ère anniversaire de la victoire du peuple de Guinée sur l'imperialisme international.* Sekou Toure.

SLP 27   *Concerts des orchestres nationaux: Bembeya Jazz National, Horoya Band.*

SLP 28   *Chorale fédérale.*

SLP 29   *L'Ensemble Instrumental et Choral de la "Voix de la Révolution," Ensemble Instrumental et Vocal de Kissidougou, Sory Kandia Kouyate.*

SLP 30   *Keletigui et Ses Tambourinis.*

SLP 31   *Pivi et les Balladins.*

SLP 32   *Super Boiro Band: Niassa et sa trompette.*

SLP 33   *Les rythmes et les chants sacrés des ballets "Djoliba National."*

SLP 34   *Bembeya Jazz: Regard sur le passé.*

SLP 35   *Discotheque 71.* Keletigui et Ses Tambourinis, Balla et Ses Balladins, Bembeya Jazz National, Virtuoses Diabate, Bafing Jazz Mamou, Myriam's Quintette. Reissued on CD as Syllart/Mélodie 38209-2.

SLP 36   *L'épopée du Mandingue, vol. 1: Sory Kandia Kouyate.* Reissued on CD as Bolibana/Mélodie 42037-2 and 42038-2.

SLP 37   *L'épopée du Mandingue, vol. 2: Sory Kandia Kouyate.* Reissued on CD as Bolibana/Mélodie 42037-2.

SLP 38   *L'épopée du Mandingue, vol. 3: Sory Kandia Kouyate.* Reissued on CD as Bolibana/Mélodie 42038-2.

SLP 39   *Authenticité 73, Bembeya Jazz: Parade Africain.*

SLP 40   *Discotheque 72.* Pivi et les Balladins, Bembeya Jazz National, Keletigui et Ses Tambourinis, Les Frères Diabate. Reissued on CD on Syllart/Mélodie.

SLP 41   *Horoya Band: Zoumana.*

SLP 42   *Neuvième Festival National des Arts et de la Culture.* Nimba Jazz, Kebali Jazz, Niandam Jazz, Kakande Jazz, Tele jazz, Kalum Star, 22 Novembre Band, Dirou Band, Palm Jazz.

SLP 43   *Folklore et ensembles instrumentaux.*

SLP 44   *Bembeya Jazz National: Mémoire de Aboubacar Demba Camara, 5 Avril 1973.*

SLP 45   *Discotheque 73.* Myriam Makeba, Bembeya Jazz National, Super Boiro band, Horoya Band National, Keletigui et Ses Tambourinis. 1975. Reissued on CD on Syllart/Mélodie.

SLP 46   *Super Boiro Band.*

SLP 47   *Balla et Ses Balladins.*

SLP 48   *Discotheque 74.* Reissued on CD on Syllart/Mélodie.

SLP 49   *Discotheque 75.* Sylli Authentique, Djoli Band, Horoya Band, Super Boiro Band, Camayenne Sofa. Reissued on CD on Syllart/Mélodie.

SLP 50   *Special Dixième Festival National.* Sombory Jazz, Bafing Jazz, Palm-Jazz, Camayenne Sofa, Niandan, Kolima, Sorsornet Rythm.

SLP 51   *22 Band-Kankan: Dans le vent.*

SLP 52   *Camayenne Sofa: Le Percée.*

SLP 53   *Les Virtuoses Diabate.*

SLP 54   *Musique sans paroles.* Sambory Jazz, Quintette Guinéenne, Ballets Africains, Momo Wandel, Trio Papa Kouyate.

SLP 55   *Le Retour: Keletigui.*

SLP 56   *Camayenne Sofa: A grands pas.*

SLP 57   *Syli authentic: Dans l'arène.*

SLP 58   *Super Boiro.*

SLP 59   *Bembeya Jazz National.* 1976.

SLP 61   *Bembeya Jazz: La continuité.*

SLP 62   *Kade Diawara: L'archange du Mandingue.*

SLP 63   *Pre-festival Lagos 77: Le rendez-vous des orchestres, special 11ème festival national.* Tele Jazz, Simandou Jazz, Sorsornet Rythme, Nimba Jazz.

SLP 64   *Bembeya Jazz: Regard sur le passé.* Reissue of SLP 10.

SLP 65   *Bembeya Jazz: Mémoire de Aboubacar Camara.* Reissue of SLP 44.

SLP 66   *Discotheque 76.* Super Lion, Bembeya Jazz . . . Reissued on CD on Syllart/ Mélodie.

SLP 67   *22 Band: Venez voir.* 1980.

SLP 68   *22 Band: Mankan.* 1980.

SLP 69   *Sombory de Fria: Minerai musical.* 1980.

SLP 71   *Les Nimba de Nzerekore.*

SLP 72   *Le Simandou de Beyla: La confiance.*

SLP 73   *Le Palm Jazz de Macenta.*

SLP 74   *Tele Jazz: Tele Mele.*

SLP 75   *Balla et Ses Balladins: Objectif perfection.* Reissued on CD as Popular African Music PAM ADC 302.

SLP 76   *Les Amazones de Guinée: Au coeur de Paris.* 1983.

SLP 77   *Sons de la Savanne: Sona Diabate.*

SLP 78   *La Rossignol de Guinée: M'Mah Sylla.*

GLOSSARY OF AFRICAN TERMS

Apollo.   A music and dance event using an amplified sound system, popular in Bamako in the 1960s.

ardin.   Ten- to fourteen-stringed harp played by female Moorish griots.

Ardin.   A tuning used by the lead koni player when two konis are played together.

baden.   Children of the same mother. See also *faden.*

bala (Md: *balo*).   Maninka heptatonic xylophone, usually having sixteen to twenty slats.

ba.   Big, great (when used as a suffix); otherwise a homonym meaning "mother" and "river."

badenya.   Family, community.

balafon.   Used by early European writers to refer to the bala; now used in European languages to refer to any West African xylophone. From *bala* (Maninka xylophone) *fo* (to play).

Bamana.   Known as Bambara in European writing, a predominant language in Mali used to refer to a diverse grouping of people associated with the kingdoms of Segu and Kaarta.

ben.   To meet or agree; to be in tune. Used by bala players to refer to the tuning of an instrument.

birimintingo.   Rolling, tumbling. Refers to quick downward melodic lines played on the kora. Often contrasted with *kumbengo.*

bolon.   Three- or four-stringed harp formerly used to incite warriors to battle.

buru (*budu*).   Animal horn or sculpted wood used as a trumpet.

Casamance.   The region of Senegal south of The Gambia.

dònkili (Md: *donkilo;* Bm: *dongili*).   Song. From *dòn* (dance) *kili* (call). To form the verb "sing" either the verb *da* (to create) in Bamana and Maninka or *laa* (to lay down) in Mandinka must be used (Mn: *dònkili da;* Md: *donkili laa*).

donso ngoni (*dunsu nguni*).   Hunter's harp (*donso:* hunter). A generic term referring to any of several varieties. Some of them have local names (see *simbi*).

dundun (*dunun*).   Large double-headed cylindrical drum played with a stick. Sometimes used to refer to any kind of drum.

faden.   Children of the same father but different mothers.

fadenya.   Competition with the father to distinguish oneself.

fasiya.   The lineage passed down from the father.

fina (Mn.)/*fino* (Md.).   Public speakers specializing in genealogies and knowledge of the Koran. Similar to jelis, but they do not sing or play musical instruments. Usually of the Camara lineage.

fle.   Flute or whistle.

fò.   To say, or to play an instrument (in Bamana and Maninka).

fodet.   Wolof term for accompaniment pattern played on the xalam or for a tuning.

Fulbe (Fula, Hal Pulaar, Peul, Pulaar, Tukolor).   A major West African ethnic group (or complex of groups) spread out through the sahel and savanna region who have been in close contact with Mande peoples for a long time. The different names for them reflect geographic and linguistic differences, though Mandenka refer to them in general as Fula.

fune (Bm.).   See *fina.*

furakaf.   Jola name for their hunter's harp. Sometimes called *simbingo.*

gambare.   A lute played by Soninke griots.

garanke.   Mande hereditary professional leatherworker.

gawlo (*gaulo*).   Fulbe professional hereditary musician.

gesere.   Soninka griot.

gewel.   Wolof hereditary professional musician.

gimbri (*guinbri, guimbri, ginbri, ginibri*).   Either of two kinds of North African semi-spike lutes: the rectangular box lute with leather tuning rings of the Gnawa or the teardrop-shaped lute with tuning pegs of Moroccan Arabs.

Gnawa (sing. Gnawi).   Black North African professional musicians of sub-Saharan origin.

griot.   West African professional hereditary musician–oral historian. Probably a frenchification of a local African term.

hardino.   One of four tunings used on the kora. It resembles a major scale. May be related to the term *ardin.*

hoddu.   Fulbe lute, essentially the same as the Maninka koni.

horon (Md: *foro*).   Mande freeborn or noble class.

iggiw (*iggio*).   Moor professional hereditary musicians. Female iggiw are the only griots in West Africa who play a melodic instrument (the ardin).

jamu (Bm.).   Family lineage as indicated by the surname. By extension, praise.

jaare.   Soninke hereditary professional musician-oral historian.

jeli (Md: *jali/jalo*).   Mandenka hereditary professional musician–oral historian.

jelike (Md: *jalike*).   Male jeli.

jelimuso (Md: *jalimuso*).   Female jeli.

jeliya (Md: *jaliya*).   What the jeli does, or the art of the jeli; *ya* is a suffix that translates as -ness or -hood.

jembe (*djembe*).   Single-headed drum shaped like a goblet and played with both hands. It is widespread in eastern Senegal, Mali, Guinea, Burkina Faso, and Côte d'Ivoire.

ji dunu.   Water drum. Half-calabash turned upside down in a basin of water, usually struck with a calabash spoon.

jinn (Ar.)   Genie.

Jola.   An ethnic group who may have been pushed toward the Atlantic Ocean to their present homeland in the Casamance by waves of migrating Mandinka. They do not have the degree of social stratification that marks the Mandinka, but the groups have been in close contact with each other for several centuries.

Judeus.   Early Portuguese term for griot.

kamalen ngoni.   Youth harp. Similar to *donso ngoni,* but used for lighter music.

kan.   Neck, voice, sound.

Kankurang.   Mandinka masked figure dressed in long strips of tree bark that is brought out during times of stress.

karignan, karinyan.   A narrow tubular iron chime twirled and struck by jelimusolu to accompany song and dance, or used as a scraper to accompany hunter's music. Perhaps from the French *carillon* (chimes, bells).

kasi. To cry, chirp. Used to describe the singing of birds and of nonjelis.

Kòmò (Kòma). Secret power society associated with Mande blacksmiths.

koni (nkoni, ngoni, kontingo). Four- or five-stringed lute used by Mande jelis.

Konkoba. A large masked figure associated with agricultural rites from upper Guinea.

kònò. Bird. Sometimes used to refer to nonjeli singers.

kontingo. See *koni.*

kontongo. Mandinka equivalent to *jamu,* but with an extended meaning of greeting rather than praising.

kora. Twenty-one-stringed bridge harp played by Mandinka jalis.

kosi. To beat, or to play an instrument (in Mandinka).

kuma. Speech.

kumbengo (Mn: *kumben*). From *kun* (head) and *ben* (to meet, agree). Has several related musical meanings depending on the context: tonic, octave, a tuning, rhythm, an accompaniment pattern.

kutiri/kutiro. Generic name for two of the three drums used in a Senegambian Mandinka drum ensemble.

kutiriba. Big *kutiro.*

kutirindingo. Small *kutiro.*

Mamaya. A bala-based music and dance event created in Kankan, Guinea, about the 1930s or 1940s.

Mande. A large West African language family and also a homeland.

Manden. A homeland situated along the Upper Niger River and west roughly between Bamako and Kouroussa.

Mandenka. A person who claims origins in the Manden homeland. In modern dialects Maninka is used by those in Guinea and Mali, and Mandinka or Mandinko by those in the Senegambia region.

mori. Muslim savants versed in religious science, primarily of Soninke origin.

naamu (Ar.). A sign of affirmation, often uttered after each phrase in a vocal performance.

naamu namina. *Naamu* answerer. Person who utters *naamu* during a performance.

naamu tigi. Owner of the *naamu.* Same as *naamu namina.*

ngana. Hero of action. Sometimes contrasted with *ngara.*

ngara (nwara). Master of speech or music. Sometimes contrasted with *ngana.*

numu. Mande hereditary professional blacksmith and sculptor.

numuya. What the numu does.

nyamakala (Md: *nyamaalo*). Mande hereditary professional artisan. Traditionally comprised four occupations: blacksmith (*numu*), jeli, leatherworker (*garanke*), and praiser-genealogist (*fune, fino*).

nyènajè. Entertainment.

sabaro. Long lead drum of the three-drum Mandinka Seruba ensemble.

sahel (Ar.). Shoreline, coastline. Name given by Arabic-speaking desert travelers to the transitional area at the southern border of the Sahara Desert eventually leading to the savanna.

Sauta. One of four tunings used on the kora. It resembles a major scale with a raised fourth degree.

Seruba. Senegambian Mandinka dance event. Sometimes used to name the three-drum ensemble that plays for it.

simbi (Md: *simbingo*). Seven-stringed Maninka hunter's harp.

simbon. Master hunter.

Sogonikun. Wasulu mask associated with agricultural fertility.

soron (seron). Bridge harp played by Guinean Maninka that is similar to the kora, but with a few less strings.

Sosso. *See* Susu.

su fle. Sorcerer's or hunter's whistle.

Susu. Ethnic group predominant in Guinea, associated with the rise of ancient Mali.

tabala. Wide, bowl-shaped drum often found outside mosques, used to summon the community for special events. Not used for dancing.

tama (ntama, tamani). Small double-headed hourglass-shaped tension drum played with a curved stick by griots. It is widespread in the sahel and savanna.

tangtango. Generic term for any of the three drums in the Mandinka three-drum ensemble. May have been used in the past to apply to a variety of drums.

tilibo. Sunrise, east. Used by Senegambian Mandinka to refer to Maninka culture from Mali.

tilijii. Sunset, west. Used by Senegambian Mandinka to refer to their own culture.

togo (Md: *too*). An individual's first name; a given name. Can also mean reputation.

Tomora mesengo (little *tomora*). One of four tunings used on the kora.

Tomoraba (big *tomora*). One of four tunings used on the kora.

tukul. Wolof equivalent of Mandinka *birimintingo.*

tulon. Play. Sometimes used to describe nonprofessional drumming.

Wasulu (Wassoulou, Wasolon). A region adjacent to the Manden in the east. Wasulunka (person from Wasulu) often have Fulbe names (Sidibe, Sangare, Diakite, Diallo) and are a mix of Maninka, Bamana, and Fulbe.

Wolof. Predominant ethnic group in Senegal.

wora. Sometimes used to describe descending lines on a bala. May be a variant of *wara,* "to come down in torrents" (Bailleul 1996:417), or *woro(n),* "to flow or glide" (Delafosse 1955:818–19).

xalam. Wolof lute, essentially the same as the koni.

Xasonka. Ethnic group that is a mixture of Soninke, Maninka, and Fulbe, whose homeland, called Xaso, is between Kayes and Bafoulabe in northwestern Mali.

BIBLIOGRAPHY

Eleventh Century to Nineteenth Century
(listed in chronological order)

al-Bakrī. 1068. *Kitāb al-masālik wa-'l-mamālik* (The book of routes and realms). In *Description de l'Afrique Septentrionale par Abou-Obeid-el-Bekri,* trans. Mac-Guckin de Slane. Paris: Adrien-Maisonneuve, 1911; new and corrected ed. 1965. In *Corpus of Early Arabic Sources for West African History,* trans. J. F. P. Hopkins, ed. N. Levtzion and J. F. P. Hopkins, 62–87. Cambridge: Cambridge University Press, 1981.

al-Idrīsī. 1154. *Nuzhat al-mushtāq fī ikhtirāq al-āfāq* (The pleasure of him who longs to cross the horizons). In *Description de l'Afrique et de l'Espagne par Edrisi,* trans. and ed. R. Dozy and M. J. de Goeje. Leiden: E. J. Brill, 1866. In *Corpus of Early Arabic Sources for West African History,* trans. J. F. P. Hopkins, ed. N. Levtzion and J. F. P. Hopkins, 104–31. Cambridge: Cambridge University Press, 1981.

al-ʿUmarī, Ibn Fadl Allāh. 1337–38. *Masālik al absār fī mamālik al amsār* (Pathways of vision in the realms of the metropolises). In *Masālik al absār fī mamālik al amsār* (Pathways of vision in the realms of the metropolises), trans. Gaudefroy-Demombynes. Paris: Librairie Orientliste Paul Geuthner, 1927. In *Corpus of Early Arabic Sources for West African History,* trans. J. F. P. Hopkins, ed. N. Levtzion and J. F. P. Hopkins, 252–78. Cambridge: Cambridge University Press, 1981. In *Routes toward Insight into the Capital Empires,* ed. Fuat Sezgin, book 4, series C, Facsimile Editions 46 (4). Frankfurt am Main: Institute for the History of Arabic-Islamic Science at the Johann Wolfgang Goethe University, 1988.

Battūta, Ibn. 1355. *Rihla* (Journey). In *Voyages d'Ibn Batoutah,* trans. C. Defrémery and B. R. Sanguinetti, vol. 4. Paris: Société Asiatique, 1858. In *Ibn Battuta in Black Africa,* trans. Said Hamdun and Noel King. London: Rex Collings, 1975. In *Recueil des sources arabes concernant l'Afrique Occidentale du VIIIe au XVIe siècle (Bilād al-Sūdān),* ed. and trans. Joseph M. Cuoq. Paris: Centre National de la Recherche Scientifique, 1975. In *Corpus of Early Arabic Sources for West African History,* trans. J. F. P. Hopkins, ed. N. Levtzion and J. F. P. Hopkins, 279–304. Cambridge: Cambridge University Press, 1981.

Ca da Mosto, Alvise. 1468. *The Voyages of Cadamosto.* Trans. and ed. G. R. Crone. Series 2, vol. 80. London: Hakluyt Society, 1937.

al-Lamtūnī. 1493. *As'ila wārida min al-Takrūr fī Shawwāl 898* (Questions arriving from al-Takrūr in Shawwāl 898/July–August 1493).

In al-Suyūtī, *Al-Hāwī li 'l-fatāwī*, 1:284–94. Cairo, 1933.

In "Notes on a Late Fifteenth-Century Document concerning 'al-Takrūr,'" trans. John Hunwick. In *African Perspectives: Papers in the History, Politics, and Economics of Africa Presented to Thomas Hodgkin*, ed. Christopher Allen and R. W. Johnson, 7–33. Cambridge: Cambridge University Press, 1970.

Gomes, Diogo. 15th c. "The Voyages of Diogo Gomes." In *The Voyages of Cadamosto*, trans and ed. G. R. Crone. London: Hakluyt Society, 1937.

Pereira, Duarte Pacheco. 1506–8. *Esmeraldo de situ orbis*. Trans. and ed. George H. T. Kimble. London: Hakluyt Society, 1937.

Fernandes, Valentim. 1506–10. *Description de la côte occidentale d'Afrique*. Trans. and ed. Th. Monod, A. Texeira Da Mota, and R. Mauny. Bissau: Centro de Estudios da Guine Portugesa, 1951.

Almada, André Álvares d'. 1594. *Tratado breve dos rios de Guiné do Cabo-Verde*. Ed. Luís Silveira. Lisbon, 1946.

In *An Interim and Makeshift Edition of André Álvares de Almada's "Brief Treatise on the Rivers of Guinea."* Trans. P. E. H. Hair. Liverpool: Department of History, University of Liverpool, 1984.

Jobson, Richard. 1623. *The Golden Trade*. London: N. Okes. Reprinted London: Dawsons of Pall Mall, 1968.

Donelha, André. 1625. *An Account of Sierra Leone and the Rivers of Guinea of Cape Verde*. Ed. Avelino Teixeira Da Mota, trans. P. E. H. Hair. Lisbon: Junta de Investigações Científicas do Ultramar, 1977.

Saint-Lô, Alexis de. 1637. *Relation du voyage du Cap-Verd*. Paris: François Targa.

Coelho, Francisco de Lemos. 1669. *Descrição da costa da Guiné desde o Cabo Verde athe Serra Leoa.* . . . An expanded version from 1684 is titled *Descrição da Costa da Guiné e Situação de todos os Portos e Rios della.* . . . Both versions published in *Duas descrições seiscentistas da Guiné*. Ed. Damião Peres. Lisbon: Academia Portuguesa de Història, 1953. In *Description of the Coast of Guinea (1684)*, trans. P. E. H. Hair. Liverpool: Department of History, University of Liverpool, 1985.

Dapper, Olfert. 1670. *Africa: Being an Accurate Description of the Regions.* . . . Trans. from Flemish by John Ogilby. London: T. Johnson.

Courbe, Sieur Michel Jajolet de la. 1685. *Premier voyage du Sieur de La Courbe fait a la coste d'Afrique en 1685*. Ed. P. Cultru. Paris: Edouard Champion, 1913.

Le Maire, Sieur Jacques-Joseph. 1695. *Les Voyages du Sieur Le Maire aux Iles Canaries, Cap-Verd, Senegal, et Gambie*. Paris: Jacques Collombat.

Froger, François. 1698a. *Relation d'un voyage fait en 1695, 1696, et 1697, aux côtes d'Afrique, détroit de Magellan, Brezil, Cayenne, et Isles Antilles, par une escadre des vaisseaux du roy, commandée par M. de Gennes*. Paris: M. Brunet.

Translated from the French as *A Relation of a Voyage Made in the Years 1695, 1696, 1697, on the Coasts of Africa, Streights of Magellan, Brasil, Cayenna, and the Antilles, by a Squadron of French Men of War, under the Command of M. de Gennes*. London: M. Gillyflower, 1698b.

Kâti, Mahmūd. 17th c. *Tarikh el-Fettach*. Trans. O. Houdas and M. Delafosse. 1913–14. Reprinted Paris: Librairie d'Amérique et d'Orient, Adrien-Maisonneuve, 1964.

Kikius, Everhard. 1701. "Drawings of American and African guitars, and of a mutilated bust, Add. 5234 artt. 72,73." Listed in *Index of Manuscripts in the British Library*, vol. 6. Cambridge, 1985. Published in Sloane 1707, facing 572.

Bosman, William [Willem]. 1705. *A New and Accurate Description of the Coast of*

Guinea. London: James Knapton. First published in Dutch, 1704. 4th English ed. New York: Barnes and Noble, 1967.

Sloane, Hans. 1707. *A Voyage to the Islands Madera, Barbados, Nieves, S. Christophers and Jamaica. . . .* 2 vols. London: British Museum.

Brue, André. 1715. "Voyages du Sieur André Brue au long des côtes occidentales d'Afrique." In Antoine François Prévost, *Histoire générale des voyages. . . ,* 3:267–456. La Haye, 1747.

Barbot, John [Jean]. 1732. "A Description of the Coast of North and South-Guinea; and of Ethiopia Inferior. . . . " In *A Collection of Voyages and Travels,* vol. 5, comp. John Churchill. London: Awnsham and Churchill.

A Description of the Coast of North and South Guinea, and of Ethiopia Inferior. 3d ed. London: Henry Linton and John Osborne, 1746.

French journal published as "Journal d'un voyage de traite en Guinée, à Cayenne et aux Antilles fait par Jean Barbot en 1678–79." Ed. Gabriel Debien, Marcel Delafosse, and Guy Thilmans. *Bulletin de l'Institut Français d'Afrique Noire,* ser. B, 40 (1978):235–395.

Compilation of unpublished French manuscript and expanded English version published in *Barbot on Guinea: The Writings of Jean Barbot on West Africa, 1678–1712.* Ed. P. E. H. Hair, Adam Jones, and Robin Law. 2 vols. London: Hakluyt Society, 1992.

Moore, Francis. 1738. *Travels into the Inland Parts of Africa.* London: E. Cave. 2d ed. London: D. Henry and R. Cave, 1740.

Smith, William. 1744. *A New Voyage to Guinea. . . .* London: John Nourse.

Astley, Thomas. 1745–47. *A New General Collection of Voyages and Travels.* 4 vols. London: T. Astley. Reprinted London: Frank Cass, 1968.

Adanson, Michel. 1757. *Histoire naturelle du Sénégal.* Paris: Claude-Jean-Baptiste Bauche.

Høst [Hoest], Georg. 1781. *Nachrichten von Marókos und Fes, im Lande selbst gesammlet, in den Jahren 1760 bis 1768.* Copenhagen: Christian Gottlob Proft. Selection reprinted in *Musikgeschichte in Bildern,* 1 (8), *NordAfrika,* ed. Paul Collaer and Jürgen Elsner, 168–70. Leipzig: VEB Deutscher Verlag für Musik Leipzig, 1983.

Matthews, John. 1788. *A Voyage to the River Sierra-Leone on the Coast of Africa.* London: B. White. Reprinted London: Frank Cass, 1966.

Lamiral, Dominique Harcourt. 1789. *L'Affrique et le peuple affriquain.* Paris: Dessenne.

Park, Mungo. 1799. *Travels in the Interior Districts of Africa.* Reprinted as *Travels into the Interior of Africa.* London: Eland Books, 1983.

Bright, Richard. 1802. "Richard Bright Journal, September and October 1802." In *Guinea Journals: Journeys into Guinea-Conakry during the Sierra Leone Phase, 1800–1821,* ed. Bruce L. Moser. Washington, D.C.: University Press of America, 1979.

Durand, Jean-Baptiste Leonard. 1802. *Voyage au Sénégal.* Paris: Henri Agasse.

Golberry, Silv. Meinrad Xavier. 1802. *Fragmens d'un voyage en Afrique, fait pendant les années 1785, 1786 et 1787. . . .* 2 vols. Paris: Treuttel et Würtz.

Winterbottom, Thomas. 1803. *An Account of the Native Africans in the Neighborhood of Sierra Leone.* 2 vols. London: C. Whittingham. 2d ed. London: Frank Cass, 1969.

Bowdich, T. Edward. 1819. *Mission from Cape Coast Castle to Ashantee.* London: John Murray. 3d ed. London: Frank Cass, 1966.

Bowdich, T. Edward. 1821. *An Essay on the Superstitions, Customs, and Arts, Common to the Ancient Egyptians, Abyssinians, and Ashantees.* Paris: J. Smith.

Mollien, Gaspard Théodore. 1822. *Voyage dans l'intérieur de l'Afrique, aux sources du Sénégal et de la Gambie.* 2d ed. Reprinted in *L'Afrique Occidentale en 1818 vue par un explorateur français.* Présentation de Hubert Deschamps. Paris: Calman-Lévy, 1967.

Gray, Major William, and Staff Surgeon Dochard. 1825. *Travels in Western Africa in the Years 1818, 19, 20, and 21, from the River Gambia, through Woolli, Bondoo, Galam, Kasson, Kaarta, and Foolidoo, to the River Niger.* London: John Murray.

Laing, Major Alexander Gordon. 1825. *Travels in the Timannee, Kooranko, and Soolima Countries, in Western Africa.* London: John Murray.

Caillié, Réné. 1830. *Travels through Central Africa to Timbuctoo; and across the Great Desert, to Morocco; Performed in the Years 1824–1828.* 2 vols. Trans. from French. London: Henry Colburn and Richard Bentley. Reprinted London: Frank Cass, 1968.

Beecham, John. 1841. *Ashantee and the Gold Coast.* London: John Mason.

Walckenaer, C. A. 1842. *Collection des relations de voyages par mer et par terre en différentes parties de l'Afrique. . . .* Paris: Chez l'éditeur.

Avezac, M. d', ed. 1845. "Vocabulaires Guiolof, Mandingue, Foule, Saracole, Séraire, Bagnon et Floupe, recueillis à la côte d'Afrique pour le service de l'ancienne compagnie royale du Sénégal, et publiés pour la première fois d'après un manuscrit de la Bibliothèque Royale." *Mémoires de la Sociéte Ethnologique* 2 (1): 205–67.

"African Curiosities." 1846. *Illustrated London News* 9 (239): 341.

Cruickshank, Brodie. 1853. *Eighteen Years on the Gold Coast of Africa.* 2 vols. London: Hurst and Blackett. 2d ed. London: Frank Cass, 1966.

Koelle, Sigismund Wilhelm. 1854. *Polyglotta Africana.* Reprinted Graz: Akademische Druck- u. Verlagsanstalt, 1963.

Hecquard, Hyacinte. 1855. *Voyage sur la côte et dans l'intérieur de l'Afrique Occidentale.* Paris: Bénard.

Mage, Eugene. 1868. *Voyage dans le Soudan Occidental (Sénégambie-Niger).* Paris: Librairie Hachette. 2d ed. 1872. Reprinted as *Voyage au Soudan Occidental (1863–66).* Paris: Karthala, 1980.

Engel, Carl. 1874. *A Descriptive Catalogue of the Musical Instruments in the South Kensington Museum.* 2d ed. London. Reprinted New York: Benjamin Blom, 1971.

Bayol, J. 1881. "Voyage au pays de Bamako." *Bulletin de la Société de Géographie,* ser. 7, 2:123–63.

Bérenger-Féraud, L. J. B. 1882. "Étude sur les griots des peuplades de la Sénégambie." *Revue d'Anthropologie,* ser. 2, 5:266–79.

Moloney, Governor. 1889. "On the Melodies of the Volof, Mandingo, Ewe, Yoruba, and Houssa People of West Africa." *Journal of the Manchester Geographical Society* 5:277–98.

Gallieni, Lieutenant-Colonel. 1891. *Deux campagnes au Soudan Français, 1886–1888.* Paris: Hachette.

Binger, Capitaine. 1892. *Du Niger au Golfe de Guinée.* 2 vols. Paris: Librairie Hachette.

Mahillon, Victor-Charles. 1893. *Catalogue descriptif et analytique du Musée Instrumental du Conservatoire Royal de Musique de Bruxelles.* vol. 1. 2d ed. Gand: Librairie Générale de Ad. Hoste.

Tellier, G. 1898. *Autour de Kita.* Paris: Henri Charles-Lavauzelle.

Twentieth Century
(arranged alphabetically)

Abspoel, Peter. n.d. *Chansons pour les masques Dogons.* Utrecht: Institut d'Anthropologie, Université d'Utrecht et Bamako: Musée National.

Afrique Élite. 1989. "Le phénomène Mory Kante," by François Bensignor, "Le griot électrique," by Jean-Michel Denis, and "Mory Kante Live," by Bernard Chenuaud. *Afrique Élite,* April 1989. Special Musique, iv–viii.

Ajayi, J. F. A. and Michael Crowder, eds. 1985–87. *History of West Africa.* Vol. 1, 3d ed., 1985. Vol. 2, 2d ed., 1987. Essex: Longman.

Akpabot, Samuel Ekpe. 1986. *Foundation of Nigerian Traditional Music.* Ibadan: Spectrum Books.

Alldridge, T. J. 1901. *The Sherbro and Its Hinterland.* New York: Macmillan.

"The All-Nigeria Festival of the Arts—1970." 1971. *Nigeria Magazine* 107–9 (December/August 1971): 18.

Ames, David A., and Anthony V. King. 1971. *Glossary of Hausa Music and Its Social Contexts.* Evanston, Ill.: Northwestern University Press.

Amselle, Jean-Loup. 1998. *Mestizo Logics: Anthropology of Identity in Africa and Elsewhere.* Trans. Claudia Royal. Stanford: Stanford University Press. Originally published as *Logiques métisses: Anthropologie de l'identité en Afrique et ailleurs.* Paris: Éditions Payot, 1990.

Anderson, Ian. 1988. "Blue Mali: Ian Anderson Unravels Some of the Ali Farka Toure Enigma." *Folk Roots* 56:30–31.

———. 1990. "The Great Diabates." *Folk Roots* 88:27–28.

Aning, Ben. 1982. "Tuning the *Kora:* A Case Study of the Norms of a Gambian Musician." *Journal of African Studies* 9 (3): 164–75.

———. 1989. "Kakaraba Lobi: Master Xylophonist of Ghana." In *African Musicology: Current Trends,* ed. Jacqueline Cogdell DjeDje and William G. Carter, 1:93–110. Atlanta: Crossroads Press.

Ankermann, B. 1901. *Die Afrikanischen Musikinstrumente.* Ethnologisches Notizblatt 3 (1). Berlin: A. Haack. Reprinted Leipzig: Zentralantiquariat der Deutschen Demokratischen Republik, 1976.

Arcin, André. 1907. *La Guinée Française.* Paris: Augustin Challamel.

Arnoldi, Mary Jo. 1995. *Playing with Time: Art and Performance in Central Mali.* Bloomington: Indiana University Press.

Arnott, D. W. 1980. "Fulani Music." In *The New Grove Dictionary of Music and Musicians,* ed. Stanley Sadie, 7:23–25. London: Macmillan.

Association SCOA. 1980. *Actes du colloque: Troisième colloque international de l'Association SCOA.* Niamey, November 30–December 6, 1977. Paris: Association SCOA.

Austen, Ralph A., ed. Forthcoming. *In Search of Sunjata: The Mande Epic as History, Literature and Performance.* Bloomington: Indiana University Press.

Baiko. 1979. "Entretien avec Banzoumana Sissoko." *Jeune Afrique* 985 (November 21): 54–55.

Bailleul, Charles. 1996. *Dictionnaire Bambara-Français.* 2d ed. Bamako: Éditions Donniya.

Ba Konaré, Adam. 1987. *L'épopée de Segu, Da Monzon: Un pouvoir guerrier.* Lausanne: Pierre-Marcel Favre.

———. 1993. *Dictionnaire des femmes célèbres du Mali.* Bamako: Éditions Jamana.

Balde, Adboulaye. 1980–81. *Lexique Mandenkakang (dit Mandinka) du Senegal*. Dakar: Centre de Linguistique Appliquée de Dakar.

Les Ballets Africains. 1959. Program for Tour of United States. Topic file, Africa. Newark, Institute for Jazz Study.

————. 1996. Collection of Programs, Articles, Reviews, and Interviews concerning Les Ballets Africains from the Mid-1950s to Mid-1990s. Collected and deposited by Louise Bedichek to accompany *Dance of Guinea* (see videography). Jerome Robbins Archive of the Recorded Moving Image, Dance Collection of the New York Public Library for the Performing Arts at Lincoln Center.

Bamba, Sorry, with Liliane Prévost. 1996. *De la tradition à la World Music*. Paris: Harmattan.

Barber, Karin, ed. 1997. *Readings in African Popular Culture*. Bloomington: Indiana University Press; Oxford: International African Institute and James Curry.

Barlow, Sean, and Banning Eyre with Jack Vartoogian. 1995. *Afropop! An Illustrated Guide to Contemporary African Music*. Edison, N.J.: Chartwell.

Barry, Boubacar. 1998. *Senegambia and the Atlantic Slave Trade*. Trans. Ayi Kwei Armah. Cambridge: Cambridge University Press. Originally published as *La Sénégambie du XVe au XIXe siècle*, 1988.

Bazin, Jean. 1985. "A chacun son Bambara." In *Au coeur de l'ethnie: Ethnies, tribalisme et état en Afrique*, ed. Jean-Loup Amselle and Elikia M'Bokolo, 87–127. Paris: Éditions la Découverte.

Béart, Ch. 1955. *Jeux et jouets de l'Ouest Africain*. Vol. 2. Mémoires de l'Institut Français d'Afrique Noire, no. 42. Dakar: IFAN.

Bebey, Francis. 1975. *African Music: A People's Art*. Trans. Josephine Bennett. Brooklyn: Lawrence Hill Books. Originally published as *Musique de l'Afrique*, 1969.

Bender, Wolfgang. 1991. *Sweet Mother: Modern African Music*. Trans. Wolfgang Freis. Chicago: University of Chicago Press. Originally published as *Sweet Mother: Moderne afrikanische Musik*, 1985.

Bendor-Samuel, John, ed. 1989. *The Niger-Congo Languages*. Lanham, Md.: University Press of America.

Berliner, Paul. 1978. *The Soul of Mbira: Music and Traditions of the Shona People of Zimbabwe*. Berkeley: University of California Press. Reprinted Chicago: University of Chicago Press, 1993.

Bhattacharya, Jotin. 1979. *Ustad Allauddin Khan and His Music*. Ahmedabad: B. S. Shah Prakashan.

Bird, Charles S. 1970. "The Development of Mandekan (Manding): A Study of the Role of Extra-linguistic Factors in Linguistic Change." In *Language and History in Africa*, ed. David Dalby, 146–59. New York: Africana.

————. 1971. "Oral Art in the Mande." In *Papers on the Manding*, ed. Carleton T. Hodge, 15–25. Bloomington: Indiana University.

————. 1972. "Heroic Songs of the Mande Hunters." In *African Folklore*, ed. Richard Dorson, 275–93, 441–77. Bloomington: Indiana University Press.

————. 1976. "Poetry in the Mande: Its Form and Meaning." *Poetics* 5:89–100.

————. Forthcoming. "The Production and Reproduction of Sunjata." In *In Search of Sunjata: The Mande Epic as History, Literature and Performance*, ed. Ralph A. Austen, 275–96. Bloomington: Indiana University Press.

————, ed. 1982. *The Dialects of Mandekan*. Bloomington: African Studies Program, Indiana University.

Bird, Charles S., John Hutchison, and Mamadou Kante. 1977. *An Ka Bamanankan Kalan: Introductory Bambara.* Bloomington: Indiana University Linguistics Club.

Bird, Charles S., and Mamadou Kante. 1976. *An Ka Bamanankan Kalan: Intermediate Bambara.* Bloomington: Indiana University Linguistics Club.

Bird, Charles S., and Martha B. Kendall. 1980. "The Mande Hero: Text and Context." In *Explorations in African Systems of Thought,* ed. Ivan Karp and Charles Bird, 13–26. Bloomington: Indiana University Press. Reprinted Washington, D.C.: Smithsonian Institution Press, 1987.

Bird, Charles S., Martha B. Kendall, and Kalilu Tera. 1995. "Etymologies of Nyamakala." In *Status and Identity in West Africa: Nyamakalaw of Mande,* ed. David C. Conrad and Barbara E. Frank, 27–35. Bloomington: Indiana University Press.

Bird, Charles S., Mamadou Koita, and Bourama Soumaoro. 1974. *The Songs of Seydou Camara,* Vol. 1. *Kambili.* English translation. Bloomington: African Studies Center, Indiana University.

Blanc, Serge. 1993. *Percussions africaines: Le tambour djembe.* Paris: Hexamusic. Published in English as *African Percussion: The Djembe.* Paris: Percudanse Association, 1997.

Blench, Roger. 1982. "Evidence for the Indonesian Origins of Certain Elements of African Culture: A Review, with Special Reference to the Arguments of A. M. Jones." *African Music* 6 (2): 81–93.

———. 1984. "The Morphology and Distribution of Sub-Saharan Musical Instruments of North African, Middle Eastern, and Asian, Origin." *Musica Asiatica* 4: 155–91.

———. 1997. "Language Studies in Africa." In *Encyclopedia of Precolonial Africa,* ed. Joseph O. Vogel, 90–100. Walnut Creek, Calif.: AltaMira.

Boulton, Laura. 1969. *The Music Hunter: The Autobiography of a Career.* Garden City, N.Y.: Doubleday.

Bouquiaux, Luc. 1969. "Les instruments de musique Birom (Nigeria septentrional)." *Africa Tervuren* 8 (4): 105–11.

Boyer, Gaston. 1953. *Un peuple de l'Ouest Soudanais: Les Diawara.* Mémoires de l'Institut Français d'Afrique Noire, no. 29. Dakar: IFAN.

Brandily, Monique. 1974. *Instruments de musique et musiciens instrumentistes chez les Teda du Tibesti.* Tervuren, Belgium: Musée Royale de l'Afrique Centrale.

———. 1984. "Gulom." In *The New Grove Dictionary of Musical Instruments,* ed. Stanley Sadie, 2:110. London: Macmillan.

Brett-Smith, Sarah C. 1994. *The Making of Bamana Sculpture: Creativity and Gender.* Cambridge: Cambridge University Press.

Brincard, Marie-Thérèse, ed. 1989. *Sounding Forms: African Musical Instruments.* New York: American Federation of Arts.

Brink, James. 1980. "Organizing Satirical Comedy in Kote-tlon: Drama as a Communication Strategy among the Bamana of Mali." Ph.D. diss., Indiana University.

Brooks, George E. 1986. "A Provisional Historical Schema for Western Africa Based on Seven Climate Periods (ca. 9000 B.C. to the 19th Century)." *Cahiers d'Études Africaines* 26 (1–2): 43–62.

———. 1993. *Landlords and Strangers: Ecology, Society, and Trade in Western Africa, 1000–1630.* Boulder, Colo.: Westview Press.

Broughton, Simon, Mark Ellingham, David Muddyman, and Richard Trillo, eds. 1994. *World Music: The Rough Guide.* London: Rough Guides.

Bühnen, Stephan. 1994. "In Quest of Susu." *History in Africa* 21: 1–47.

Bulman, Stephen. 1996. "The Image of the Young Hero in the Printed Corpus of the Sunjata Epic." In *The Younger Brother in Mande Kinship and Politics in West Africa,* ed. Jan Jansen and Clemens Zobel, 75–96. Leiden: Research School CNWS.

———. 1997. "A Checklist of Published Versions of the Sunjata Epic." *History in Africa* 24:71–94.

Camara, Laye [Camara Laye]. 1953. *L'enfant noir.* Librarie Plon.

———. 1954. *The Dark Child.* Trans. James Kirkup and Ernest Jones. New York: Farrar, Straus, and Giroux. New edition, 1994.

———. 1980. *The Guardian of the Word.* Trans. James Kirkup. London: Fontana. Originally published as *Le maître de la parole,* 1978.

Camara, Seydou. 1996. "La tradition orale en question." *Cahiers d'Études Africaines* 36 (4): 763–90.

Camara, Sory. 1976. *Gens de la parole: Essai sur la condition et le rôle des griots dans la société malinké.* Paris: Mouton. New edition Paris: ACCT/Karthala/SAEC, 1992.

Cashion, Gerald. 1984. "Hunters of the Mande: A Behavioral Code and Worldview Derived from the Study of their Folklore." Ph.D. diss., Indiana University.

Cathcart, Jenny. 1988. "Toucouleur Roots." *Folk Roots* 59:41.

Charry, Eric. 1994a. "The Grand Mande Guitar Tradition of the Western Sahel and Savannah." *World of Music* 36 (2): 21–61.

———. 1994b. "West African Harps." *Journal of the American Musical Instrument Society* 20:5–53.

———. 1996a. "A Guide to the Jembe." *Percussive Notes* 34 (2): 66–72.

———. 1996b. "Plucked Lutes in West Africa: An Historical Overview." *Galpin Society Journal* 49:3–37.

———. Forthcoming. "Islam and Music in Sub-Saharan Africa." In *The History of Islam in Africa,* ed. Nehemia Levtzion and Randall Pouwels. Ohio University Press.

Chauvet, Stephen. 1929. *Musique nègre.* Paris: Société d'Éditions Géographiques, Maritimes et Coloniales.

Chéron, Georges. 1931. "Le Dyidé." *Journal de la Société des Africainistes* 1(2): 285–89.

———. 1933. "La circoncision et l'excision chez les Malinké." *Journal de la Société des Africanistes* 3:297–303.

Church, R. J. Harrison. 1980. *West Africa: A Study of the Environment and of Man's Use of It.* 8th ed. London: Longman.

Cissé, Diango. 1970. *Structures des Malinké des Kita (Contribution à une Anthropologie Sociale et Politique du Mali).* Bamako: Éditions Populaires.

Cissé, Youssouf Tata. 1964. "Notes sur les sociétés de chasseurs malinké." *Journal de la Société des Africanistes* 34 (2): 175–226.

———. 1973. "Signes graphiques, représentations, concepts et tests relatifs à la personne chez les Malinké et les Bambara du Mali." In *La notion de personne en Afrique Noire,* ed. G. Dieterlen, 131–79. Paris: Centre National de la Recherche Scientifique.

———. 1994. *La confrérie des chasseurs malinké et bambara: Mythes, rites et récits initiatiques.* Paris: Éditions Nouvelles du Sud/Association ARSAN.

Cissé, Youssouf Tata, and Wa Kamissoko. 1975. *L'empire du Mali: Un récit de Wa Kamissoko de Krina, enregistré, transcrit, traduit et annoté par Youssouf Tata Cissé.* Paris: Fondation SCOA.

———. 1977. *L'empire du Mali (suite): Un récit de Wa Kamissoko de Krina, enregistré, transcrit, traduit et annoté par Youssouf Tata Cissé.* Paris: Fondation SCOA.

————. 1988. *La grande geste du Mali.* Vol. 1. *Des origines à la fondation de l'empire.* Paris: Karthala.

————. 1991. *La grande geste du Mali.* Vol. 2. *Soundjata, la gloire du Mali.* Paris: Karthatla.

Cissoko, Sékéné Mody. 1986. *Contribution à l'histoire politique du Khasso dans le Haut-Sénégal, des origines à 1854.* Paris: ACCT/Harmattan.

Clark, Andrew F., and Lucie Colvin Phillips. 1994. *Historical Dictionary of Senegal.* 2d ed. Metuchen, N.J.: Scarecrow Press.

Clark, J. Desmond. 1978. "The Legacy of Prehistory: An Essay on the Background to the Individuality of African Cultures." In *The Cambridge History of Africa,* ed. J. D. Fage, 2:11–86. Cambridge: Cambridge University Press.

————. 1982. "The Cultures of the Middle Paleolithic/Middle Stone Age." In *The Cambridge History of Africa,* ed. J. D. Clark, 1:248–341. Cambridge: Cambridge University Press.

Collaer, Paul, and Jürgen Elsner. 1983. *Musikgeschichte in Bildern.* 1 (8). *NordAfrika.* Leipzig: VEB Deutscher Verlag für Musik Leipzig.

Collins, John. 1985. *Musicmakers of West Africa.* Washington, D.C.: Three Continents Press.

————. 1992. *West African Pop Roots.* Philadelphia: Temple University Press.

————. 1996. *E. T. Mensah: King of Highlife.* Accra: Anansesem. First published London: Off the Record Press, 1986.

Conrad, David C. 1981. "The Role of Oral Artists in the History of Mali." Ph.D. diss., University of London, SOAS.

————. 1984. "Oral Sources on Links between Great States: Sumanguru, Servile Lineage, the Jariso, and Kaniaga." *History in Africa* 11:35–55.

————. 1985. "Islam in the Oral Traditions of Mali: Bilali and Surakata." *Journal of African History* 26 (1): 33–49.

————. 1990. *A State of Intrigue: The Epic of Bamana Segu according to Tayiru Banbera.* Ed. David C. Conrad, transcribed and translated with the assistance of Soumaila Diakité. London: Oxford University Press for the British Academy.

————. 1992. "Searching for History in the Sunjata Epic: The Case of Fakoli." *History in Africa* 19:147–200.

————. 1995. "Blind Man Meets Prophet: Oral Tradition, Islam, and Fune Identity." In *Status and Identity in West Africa: Nyamakalaw of Mande,* ed. David C. Conrad and Barbara E. Frank, 86–132. Bloomington: Indiana University Press.

————. 1999. *Epic Ancestors of the Sunjata Era: Oral Tradition from the Maninka of Guinea.* Madison: University of Wisconsin African Studies Program.

————. Forthcoming. *Almami Samori and Laye Umaru: Nineteenth-Century Muslim Heroes of Mande Epic Tradition.* Madison: University of Wisconsin African Studies Program.

Conrad, David C., and Barbara E. Frank, eds. 1995a. *Status and Identity in West Africa: Nyamakalaw of Mande.* Bloomington: Indiana University Press.

————. 1995b. "Introduction. Nyamakalaya: Contradiction and Ambiguity in Mande Society." In *Status and Identity in West Africa: Nyamakalaw of Mande,* ed. David C. Conrad and Barbara E. Frank, 1–23. Bloomington: Indiana University Press.

Coolen, Michael T. 1979. "Xalamkats: The Xalam Tradition of the Senegambia." Ph.D. diss., University of Washington.

————. 1982. "The Fodet: A Senegambian Origin for the Blues?" *Black Perspective in Music* 10 (1): 69–84.

————. 1983. "The Wolof Xalam Tradition of the Senegambia." *Ethnomusicology* 27 (3): 477–98.

Coulibaly, Dosseh Joseph. 1985. *Récits des chasseurs du Mali: Dingo Kanbili, une épopée des chasseurs malinké de Bala Jinba Jakite.* Paris: Conseil International de la Langue Française–EDICEF.

Couloubaly, Pascal Baba F. 1990. *Une société rurale bambara à travers des chants de femmes.* Dakar: IFAN.

Courlander, Harold. 1978. "Three Soninke Tales." *African Arts* 12 (1): 82–88, 108.

Crowder, Michael, and Donal Cruise O'Brien. 1987. "Politics of Decolonisation in French West Africa, 1945–1960." In *History of West Africa*, 2d ed., ed. J. F. A. Ajayi and Michael Crowder, 2:736–73. Essex: Longman.

Cuoq, Joseph M., trans. and notes. 1975. *Recueil des sources Arabes concernant l'Afrique Occidentale du VIIIe au XVIe siècle.* Paris: Éditions du Centre National de la Recherche Scientifique.

Cutter, Charles. 1968. "The Politics of Music in Mali." *African Arts* 1 (3): 38–39, 74–77.

el Dabh, Halim, with Frank Proschan. 1979. "Les traditions du masque et de la marionnette dans la République de la Guinée/Puppetry and Masked Dance Traditions of the Republic of Guinea." Typescript. Washington, D.C.: Smithsonian Institution.

Dahlhaus, Carl. 1983. *Foundations of Music History.* Trans. J. B. Robinson. Cambridge: Cambridge University Press. Originally published as *Grundlagen der Musikgeschichte,* 1977.

Dalby, Winifred. 1980. "Mali: 1–2." In *The New Grove Dictionary of Music and Musicians,* ed. Stanley Sadie, 12:573–77. London: Macmillan.

Darbo, Seni. 1972. "A Griot's Self-Portrait: The Origins and Role of the Griot in Mandinka Society as Seen from Stories Told by Gambian Griots." In *Conference on Manding Studies.* London: SOAS.

Darlington, Lois. 1994. "Date with Sylla—West Africa's Number One Producer." In *World Music: The Rough Guide,* ed. Simon Broughton, Mark Ellingham, David Muddyman, and Richard Trillo, 272–73. London: Rough Guides.

Delafosse, Maurice. 1912. *Haut-Senegal-Niger.* 3 vols. New ed. Paris: G. P. Maisonneuve et Larose, 1972.

————. 1955. *La langue mandingue et ses dialectes (Malinké, Bambara, Dioula).* Vol. 2. *Dictionnaire Mandingue-Français.* Paris: Librairie Orientaliste Paul Geuthner.

Dembski, Stephen, and Joseph N. Strauss, eds. 1987. *Milton Babbitt: Words about Music.* Madison: University of Wisconsin Press.

DeVale, Sue Carole. 1989. "African Harps: Construction, Decoration, and Sound." In *Sounding Forms: African Musical Instruments,* ed. Marie-Thérèse Brincard, 53–61. New York: American Federation of Arts.

Diabate, Massa Makan. 1970a. *Janjon, et autres chants populaires du Mali.* Paris: Présence Africaine.

————. 1970b. *Kala Jata.* Bamako: Éditions Populaires.

Diagne, Ahmadou Mapaté, and Hamet Sow Télémaque. 1916. "Origine des griots." *Bulletin de l'Enseignement de l'Afrique Occidentale Française* 25:275–78.

Diallo, Mamadou. 1972. *Essai sur la musique traditionnelle au Mali.* Paris: Agence de Cooperation Culturelle et Technique.

Diallo, Yaya, and Mitchell Hall. 1989. *The Healing Drum: African Wisdom Techniques.* Rochester, Vt.: Destiny Books.

Diawara, Mamadou. 1989. "Women, Servitude and History: The Oral Historical Traditions of Women of Servile Condition in the Kingdom of Jaara (Mali) from the Fifteenth to the Mid-Nineteenth Century." In *Discourse and Its Disguises: The Interpretation of African Oral Texts,* ed. Karin Barber and P. F. de Moraes Farias, 109–37. Birmingham: Center of West African Studies, University of Birmingham.

————. 1990. *La graine de la parole.* Stuttgart: Franz Steiner.

————. 1995. "Oral Sources and Social Differentiation in the Jaara Kingdom from the Sixteenth Century: A Methodological Approach." *History in Africa* 22:123–39.

————. 1996. "Le griot mande à l'heure de la globalisation." *Cahiers d'Études Africaines* 36 (4): 591–612.

————. 1997. "Mande Oral Popular Culture Revisited by the Electronic Media." In *Readings in African Popular Culture,* ed. Karin Barber, 40–48. Bloomington: Indiana University Press; Oxford: International African Institute and James Curry.

Diawara, Manthia. 1992. "Canonizing Soundiata in Mande Literature: Toward a Sociology of Narrative Elements." *Social Text* 31–32:154–68.

————. 1998. *In Search of Africa.* Cambridge: Harvard University Press.

Dieterlen, Germaine. 1951. *Essai sur la religion bambara.* Paris: Presses Universitaires de France.

————. 1955. "Mythe et organisation sociale au Soudan Français." *Journal de la Société des Africanistes* 25 (1): 39–76.

————. 1957. "The Mande Creation Myth." *Africa* 27 (2): 124–38.

————. 1959. "Mythe et organisation sociale en Afrique Occidentale (suite)." *Journal de la Société des Africanistes* 29 (1): 119–38.

Dieterlen, Germaine, and Youssouf Cissé. 1972. *Les fondements de la société d'initiation du Komo.* Paris: Mouton.

Dieterlen, Germaine, and Diarra Sylla. 1992. *L'empire de Ghana: Le Wagadou et les traditions de Yerere.* Paris: Karthala/Association ARSAN.

Diop, Abdoulaye-Bara. 1981. *La société wolof: Tradition et changement.* Paris: Karthala.

Diop, Birago. 1947. *Les contes d'Amadou-Koumba.* Paris: Fasquelle.

————. 1966. *Tales of Amadou Koumba.* Trans. Dorothy Blair. London: Oxford University Press.

Donner, E. 1940. "Kunst und Handwerk in No-Liberia." *Baessler-Archiv* 23 (2–3): 45–110.

Dozy, R. 1967. *Supplément aux dictionnaires arabes.* 2 vols. 3d ed. Paris: G. P. Maisonneuve et Larose. Originally published 1881.

Drame, Adama, and Arlette Senn-Borloz. 1992. *Jeliya: Être griot et musicien aujourd'hui.* Paris: Harmattan.

Durán, Lucy. 1978. "The Music." In *Kelefa Saane: His Career Recounted by Two Mandinka Bards,* ed. and trans. Gordon Innes, 16–26. London: SOAS.

————. 1981a. "Theme and Variation in Kora Music: A Preliminary Study of 'Tutu Jara' as Performed by Amadu Bansang Jobate." In *Music and Tradition: Essays on Asian and Other Musics Presented to Laurence Picken,* ed. D. R. Widdess and R. F. Wolpert, 183–96. Cambridge: Cambridge University Press.

————. 1981b. "A Preliminary Study of the Wolof Xalam (with a List of Recordings at the BIRS)." *Recorded Sound* 79:29–50.

————. 1984. "Simbing." In *The New Grove Dictionary of Musical Instruments,* ed. Stanley Sadie, 3:386–87. London: Macmillan.

———. 1989a. "Djely Mousso: Lucy Duran Describes Mali's Undisputed Stars, the Women Singers from Their Ancient Tradition." *Folk Roots* 75:34–39.

———. 1989b. "Key to N'Dour: Roots of the Senegalese Star." *Popular Music* 8 (3): 275–84.

———. 1991. "Kante Manfila." *Folk Roots* 100:20–26.

———. 1992a. "The Rail Sounds: Lucy Durán Hears about Griotism from Jalimadi Tounkara, a Rail Legend." *Folk Roots* 110:34–35, 63.

———. 1992b. "Ali Farka Toure: Djinnius of the River." *Folk Roots* 113:38–44.

———. 1994. "Music Created by God: The Manding Jalis of Mali, Guinea, and Senegambia." In *World Music: The Rough Guide,* ed. Simon Broughton, Mark Ellingham, David Muddyman, and Richard Trillo, 243–60. London: Rough Guides.

———. 1995a. "Birds of Wasulu: Freedom of Expression and Expressions of Freedom in the Popular Music of Southern Mali." *British Journal of Ethnomusicology* 4:101–34.

———. 1995b. "Jelimusow: The Superwomen of Malian Music." In *Power, Marginality and African Oral Literature,* ed. Graham Furniss and Liz Gunner, 197–207. Cambridge: Cambridge University Press.

———. 1995c. "Monsieur l'Ambassadeur: Lucy Duran Spent a Day in Paris with Salif Keita." *Folk Roots* 149:42–43, 45–47.

———. 1996. "The Songbird: Fanned, Fetished and Female: Lucy Duran Goes on the Road with Wassoulou Superstar Oumou Sangare." *Folk Roots* 154:40–41, 43, 45.

———. 1997. "Guinean Gold: In Praise of Sekouba 'Bambino.'" *Folk Roots* 168:41–45.

———. 1998. "Mory Kante." *Folk Roots* 175:40–47.

———. Forthcoming, a. "Stars and Songbirds: Mande Female Singers in Urban Music, Mali, 1980–99." Ph.D. diss., University of London.

———. Forthcoming, b. "Women, Music, and the 'Mystique' of Hunters in Mali." In *The African Diaspora: A Musical Perspective,* ed. Ingrid Monson. New York: Garland.

Eisenberg, Ronald. 1997. "Lyre, Lyre, Stamps Admire." *American Philatelist* 3 (7): 638–42.

Ellis, George W. 1914. *Negro Culture in West Africa.* New York: Neale. Reprinted New York: Johnson Reprint, 1970.

Enem, Edith. 1975. "Nigerian Dances." *Nigeria Magazine* 115–16:97.

Epstein, Dena J. 1975. "The Folk Banjo: A Documentary History," *Ethnomusicology* 19 (3): 347–71.

———. 1977. *Sinful Tunes and Spirituals: Black Folk Music to the Civil War.* Urbana: University of Illinois Press.

Erlmann, Veit. 1983. "Notes on Musical Instruments among the Fulani of Diamare (North Cameroon)." *African Music* 6 (3): 16–41.

———. 1986. *Music and the Islamic Reform in the Early Sokoto Empire.* Stuttgart: Franz Steiner.

Euba, Akin. 1990. *Yoruba Drumming: The Dundun Tradition.* Bayreuth: E. Breitinger; Bayreuth University.

Ewens, Graeme. 1991. *Africa O-Ye!* New York: Da Capo.

Eyre, Banning. 1994. "In Search of West African Guitar Genius." *Guitar Player* 28 (4): 97–104.

———. 1997a. "Mali Hatchet: In Search of West Africa's Master Axmen." *Guitar Player* 31 (8): 35–37, 39.

———. 1997b. "Pentatonic Passport: A Malian Phrase Book." *Guitar Player* 31 (8): 40, 42, 44.

———. Forthcoming. *In Griot Time: An American Guitarist in Mali.* Philadelphia: Temple University Press.

Fage, J. D. 1994. *A Guide to Original Sources for Precolonial Western Africa Published in European Languages.* Rev. ed. Madison: African Studies Program, University of Wisconsin–Madison.

Famechon, Lucien Marie François. 1900. *Notice sur la Guinée Française.* Paris: Exposition Universelle de 1900, Alcan-Levy.

Farmer, Henry George. 1924. "The Arab Influence on Music in the Western Soudan." *Musical Standard* 24 (448): 158–59.

———. 1928. "A North African Folk Instrument," *Journal of the Royal Asiatic Society* 1:25–34.

———. 1938. "Tunbūr." In *The Encyclopaedia of Islam,* supplement, ed. M. Th. Houtsma, A. J. Wensinck, H. A. R. Gibb, Willi Heffening, and Evariste Lévi-Provençal, 251–53. Leiden: E. J. Brill.

———. 1939. "Early References to Music in the Western Sūdān." *Journal of the Royal Asiatic Society* 4:569–79.

al-Faruqi, Lois Ibsen. 1978. "Ornamentation in Arabian Improvisational Music: A Study of Interrelatedness in the Arts." *World of Music* 20 (1): 17–28.

———. 1981. *An Annotated Glossary of Arabic Musical Terms.* Westport, Conn.: Greenwood Press.

———. 1983–84. "Factors of Continuity in the Musical Cultures of the Muslim World." *Progress Reports in Ethnomusicology* 1 (2): 1–18. Department of Music, University of Maryland Baltimore County.

———. 1985. "Structural Segments in the Islamic Arts: The Musical 'Translation' of a Characteristic of the Literary and Visual Arts." *Asian Music* 16 (1): 59–82.

Ferry, Marie-Paule. 1969. "Xylophones-sur-jambes chez les Bedi et les Bassari de Kédougou." *Objets et Mondes* 9 (3): 307–12.

Festival National. 1979. *Festival National des Arts et de la Culture.* Conakry, November 1979. 2d ed. Conakry: RDA, no. 149.

Fierro, Alfred. 1986. *Inventaire des photographies sur papier de la Société de Géographie.* Paris: Bibliothèque Nationale, Département des Cartes et Plans.

Fleming, Bruce. 1993. "A Conversation in Conakry: On Western Prejudices and Non-Western Dance." *DanceView* 11 (1): 59–60.

Fodeba, Keita. See Keita, Fodeba.

Folk Roots. 1998. "The Albums of '97." *Folk Roots* 175–76:37.

Fondation Léopold Sédar Senghor. 1981. "Actes du colloque international sur les traditions orales du Gabu, organisé, à Dakar, du 19 au 24 mai 1980 par la Fondation Léopold Sédar Senghor." Special issue of *Éthiopiques* 28, October 1981.

Frank, Barbara. 1988. "Mande Leatherworking: A Study of Style, Technology and Identity." Ph.D. diss., Indiana University.

———. 1995. "Soninke *garankéw* and Bamana-Malinke *jeliw:* Mande Leatherworkers, Identity, and the Diaspora." In *Status and Identity in West Africa: Nyamakalaw of Mande,* ed. David C. Conrad and Barbara E. Frank, 133–50. Bloomington: Indiana University Press.

———. 1998. *Mande Potters and Leatherworkers: Art and Heritage in West Africa.* Washington, D.C.: Smithsonian Institution Press.

Frobenius, Leo. 1921. *Spielsmannsgeschichten der Sahel.* Atlantis 6. Jena: Eugen Diederichs.

Frobenius, Leo, and Douglas C. Fox. 1937. *African Genesis.* Contains English translations of Frobenius 1921. Reprinted New York: Benjamin Blom, 1966.

Gaden, Henri. 1914. *Le poular: Dialecte peul du Fouta Sengalais.* Vol. 2. *Lexique poular-français.* Paris; Ernest Leroux. Reprinted Farnborough, Eng.: Gregg Press, 1967.

Gamble, David. 1967. *The Wolof of Senegambia, Together with Notes on the Lebu and Serer.* London: International African Institute.

————. 1987a. "Elementary Mandinka." San Francisco. Unpublished revision of *Elementary Mandinka Sentence Book.* London: Research Department of the Colonial Office, 1955.

————. 1987b. "Intermediate Gambian Mandinka-English Dictionary." San Francisco. Unpublished revision of *Mandinka-English Dictionary.* London: Research Department of the Colonial Office, 1955.

Ganay, Solange de. 1995. *Le sanctuaire kama blon de Kangaba: Histoires, mythes, peintures pariétales et cérémonies septennales.* Nouvelles du Sud.

Geertz, Clifford. 1983. "'From the Native's Point of View': On the Nature of Anthropological Understanding." In *Local Knowlededge: Further Essays in Interpretive Anthropology,* by Clifford Geertz, 55–70. New York: Basic Books. Originally published in *Bulletin of the American Academy of Arts and Sciences* 28, 1 (1974).

————. 1995. *After the Fact: Two Countries, Four Decades, One Anthropologist.* Cambridge: Harvard University Press.

Gesenius, William. 1952. *A Hebrew and English Lexicon of the Old Testament.* Trans. Edward Robinson, ed. Francis Brown. London: Oxford University Press. Originally published 1907.

Gibbal, Jean-Mari. 1982. *Tambours d'eau: Journal et enquête sur un culte de possession au Mali occidental.* 2d ed. Paris: Sycomore.

————. 1994. *Genii of the River Niger.* Trans. Beth G. Raps. Chicago: University of Chicago Press. Originally published as *Les génies du fleuve: Voyage sur le Niger,* 1988.

Glaze, Anita. 1981. *Art and Death in a Senufo Village.* Bloomington: Indiana University Press.

Godsey, Larry Dennis. 1980. "The Use of the Xylophone in the Funeral Ceremony of the Birifor of Northwest Ghana." Ph.D. diss., University of California, Los Angeles.

————. 1984. "The Use of Variation in Birifor Funeral Music." In *Selected Reports in Ethnomusicology,* vol. 5, *Studies in African Music,* ed. J. H. Kwabena Nketia and Jacqueline Cogdell DjeDje, 67–80. Los Angeles: Program in Ethnomusicology, Department of Music, University of California.

Gourlay, Ken A. 1976. "Letters to the Editor." *Ethnomusicology* 20 (2): 327–32.

————. 1984a. "Gurmi." In *The New Grove Dictionary of Musical Instruments,* ed. Stanley Sadie, 2:111. London: Macmillan.

————. 1984b. "Kuntigi." In *The New Grove Dictionary of Musical Instruments,* ed. Stanley Sadie, 2:487. London: Macmillan.

Gourlay, Ken A., and Lucy Durán. 1984a. "Balo." In *The New Grove Dictionary of Musical Instruments,* ed. Stanley Sadie, 1:117. London: Macmillan.

————. 1984b. "Bolon." In *The New Grove Dictionary of Musical Instruments,* Stanley Sadie, 1:246. London: Macmillan.

Graham, Ronnie. 1988. *The Da Capo Guide to Contemporary African Music.* New York: Da Capo.

———. 1992. *The World of African Music: Stern's Guide to Contemporary African Music.* Vol. 2. London: Pluto Press; Chicago: Research Associates.

Gravrand, Henry. 1983. *La civilisation sereer: Cosaan, les origines.* Dakar: Nouvelles Éditions Africaines.

———. 1990. *La civilisation sereer: Pangool, le génie religieux sereer.* Dakar: Nouvelles Éditions Africaines.

Gray, John. 1991. *African Music: A Bibliographical Guide to the Traditional, Popular, Art, and Liturgical Musics of Sub-Saharan Africa.* Westport, Conn.: Greenwood Press.

Gregoire, Cl. 1986. *Le Maninka de Kankan: Éléments de description phonologique.* Tervuren, Belgium: Musée Royal de l'Afrique Centrale.

Griaule, Marcel. 1954. "Nouvelles remarques sur la harpe-luth des Dogon." *Journal de la Société des Africanistes* 24 (2): 119–22.

Griaule, Marcel, and Germaine Dieterlen. 1950. "La harpe-luth des Dogon." *Journal de la Société des Africanistes* 20 (2): 209–27.

Guenneguez, André, and Afo Guenneguez. 1998. *Centenaire de la Côte-d'Ivoire 1887/1888–1988 en cartes postales.* Abidjan: Art et Édition/Édipresse.

Guignard, Michel. 1975. *Musique, honneur et plaisir au Sahara.* Paris: Librairie Orientaliste Paul Guethner.

Gwamna, Bitrus Paul. 1992. "Multi-cultural Programming as a Strategy in Public Diplomacy: Leo Sarkisian, and the Voice of America's Music Time in Africa." Ph.D. diss., Ohio University.

Hair, Paul E. H. 1966. "Collections of Vocabularies of Western Africa before the Polyglotta: A Key." *Journal of African Languages* 5 (3): 208–17.

———. 1967. "An Ethnolinguistic Inventory of the Upper Guinea Coast before 1700." *African Language Review* 6:32–70.

———. 1997. *Africa Encountered: European Contacts and Evidence, 1450–1700.* Brookfield, Vt.: Variorum.

Hale, Thomas A. 1998. *Griots and Griottes: Masters of Words and Music.* Bloomington: Indiana University Press.

Handelman, Don. 1977. "Play and Ritual: Complementary Frames of Metacommunication." In *It's a Funny Thing, Humour,* ed. A. Chapman and H. Fort, 185–92. Oxford: Pergamon Press.

Harrev, Flemming. 1992. "Francophone West Africa and the Jali Experience" In *West African Pop Roots,* ed. John Collins, 209–43. Philadelphia: Temple University Press.

Harris, Laura Arntson. 1992. "The Play of Ambiguity in Praise-Song Performance: A Definition of the Genre through an Examination of Its Practice in Northern Sierra Leone." Ph.D. diss., Indiana University.

Harris, P. G. 1932. "Notes on Drums and Musical Instruments Seen in Sokoto Province, Nigeria." *Journal of the Royal Anthropological Institute* 62:105–25.

Hause, H. E. 1948. "Terms for Musical Instruments in the Sudanic Languages." *Journal of the American Oriental Society,* supplement 7, issued with vol. 68, no. 1.

Henry, Joseph. 1910. *L'âme d'un peuple africain: Les Bambara.* Münster: Aschendorffschen.

Herdeck, Donald E. 1973. *African Authors: A Companion to Black African Writing.* Vol. 1. *1300–1973.* Washington, D.C.: Black Orpheus Press.

Herzog, George. 1949. "Canon in West African Xylophone Melodies." *Journal of the American Musicological Society* 2 (3): 196–97.

Hickmann, Hans. 1948. "Sur l'accordage des instruments à cordes (lyres, harpes, luths)." *Miscellanea Musicologica* 48 (2): 646–63. Reprinted in Hans Hickmann, *Vies et travaux*, ed. Diá Abou-Ghazi, 1:136–53. Cairo: Organization des Antiquities de l'Égypte, Service des Musées, 1980.

———. 1956. *Quarante-cinq siècles de musique dans l'Égypte ancienne, à travers la sculpture, la peinture, l'instrument.* Paris: Richard-Masse.

———. 1960. "Laute." In *Die Musik in Geschichte und Gegenwart*, ed. Friedrich Blume, 8:345–56. Basel: Barenreiter Kassel.

———. 1961. *Musikgeschichte in Bildern.* 2 (1). *Agypten.* Leipzig: VEB Deutscher Verlag für Musik Leipzig.

Hiskett, M. 1965. "The Historical Background to the Naturalization of Arabic Loan-Words in Hausa." *African Language Studies* 6:18–26.

Hoffman, Barbara G. 1990. "The Power of Speech: Language and Social Status among Mande Griots and Nobles." Ph.D. diss., Indiana University.

———. 1995. "Power, Structure, and Mande *Jeliw*." In *Status and Identity in West Africa: Nyamakalaw of Mande,* ed. David C. Conrad and Barbara E. Frank, 36–45. Bloomington: Indiana University Press.

———. 1998. "Secrets and Lies: Context, Meaning, and Agency in Mande." *Cahiers d'Études Africaines* 37 (1): 85–102.

Holl, Augustin. 1985a. "Subsistence Pattens of the Dhar Tichitt Neolithic, Mauritania." *African Archaeological Review* 3:151–62.

———. 1985b. "Background to the Ghana Empire: Archaeological Investigations on the Transition to Statehood in the Dhar Tichitt Region (Mauritania)." *Journal of Anthropological Archaeology* 4:73–115.

Hopkins, Nicholas S. 1971. "Maninka Social Organization." In *Papers on the Manding,* ed. Carleton T. Hodge, 99–128. Bloomington: Indiana University.

———. 1972. *Popular Government in an African Town: Kita, Mali.* Chicago: University of Chicago Press.

Hornbostel, Erich M. von. 1928. "African Negro Music." *Africa* 1:30–62.

Hornbostel, Erich M. von, and Curt Sachs. 1961. "Classification of Musical Instruments." Trans. Anthony Baines and Klaus P. Wachsmann. *Galpin Society Journal* 14:3–29. Originally published as "Systematik der Musikinstrumente: Ein Versuch," 1914.

Huet, Michel. 1978. *The Dance, Art and Ritual of Africa.* New York: Pantheon.

Huet, Michel, and Fodeba Keita [Keita Fodeba]. 1954. *Les hommes de la danse.* Lausanne: Éditions Clairefontaine.

———. 1996. *The Dances of Africa.* Text by Claude Savary. New York: Harry N. Abrams.

Humblot, P. 1921. "Kankan: Métropole de la Haute-Guinée." *Renseignements Coloniaux, Bulletin du Comité de l'Afrique Française* 6:129–40; 7:153–61.

Imperato, Pascal James. 1980. "Bambara and Malinke Ton Masquerades." *African Arts* 13 (4): 47–55, 82–85, 87.

———. 1981. "Sogoni Koun." *African Arts* 14 (2): 38–47, 72, 88.

———. 1983. *Buffoons, Queens and Wooden Horsemen: The Dyo and Gouan Societies of the Bambara of Mali.* New York: Kilima House.

———. 1996. *Historical Dictionary of Mali.* 3d ed. Lanham, Md.: Scarecrow Press.

Innes, Gordon. 1972. "Mandinka Circumcision Songs." *African Language Studies* 13: 88–112.

———. 1974. *Sunjata: Three Mandinka Versions.* London: SOAS.

———. 1976. *Kaabu and Fuladu: Historical Narratives of the Gambian Mandinka.* London: SOAS.

———. 1978. *Kelefa Saane: His Career Recounted by Two Mandinka Bards.* London: SOAS.

Irvine, Judith T., and J. David Sapir. 1976. "Musical Style and Social Change among the Kujamaat Diola." *Ethnomusicology* 20 (1): 67–86.

Ibn Ishaq. 1955. *The Life of Muhammad: A Translation of Ishāq's Sīrat Rasūl Allāh.* Trans. A. Guillaume. Reprinted Karachi: Oxford University Press, 1967.

Jackson, Michael. 1977. *The Kuranko: Dimensions of Social Reality in a West African Society.* New York: St. Martin's Press.

Jansen, Jan. 1991. *Siramuri Diabate et ses enfants: Une étude sur deux générations des griots malinké.* Trans. Cemako Kante. Utrecht: ISOR; Bamako: ISH.

———. 1996. "The Younger Brother and the Stranger: In Search of a Status Discourse for Mande." *Cahiers d'Études Africaines* 36 (4): 659–88.

Jansen, Jan, Esger Duintjer, and Boubacar Tamboura. 1995. *L'épopée de Sunjara, d'après Lansine Diabate de Kela.* Leiden: Research School CNWS, University of Leiden.

Jansen, Jan, and Clemens Zobel, eds. 1996. *The Younger Brother in Mande Kinship and Politics in West Africa.* Leiden: Research School CNWS.

Jatta, Sidia. 1985. "Born Musicians: Traditional Music from The Gambia." In *Repercussions: A Celebration of African-American Music,* ed. Geoffrey Haydon and Dennis Marks, 14–29. Author biography on p. 187. London: Century.

Jenkins, Jean. 1970. *Musical Instruments.* 2d ed. London: Horniman Museum.

———. 1983. *Man and Music.* Scotland: Royal Scottish Museum.

Jessup, Lynne. 1983. *The Mandinka Balafon: An Introduction with Notation for Teaching.* La Mesa, Calif.: Xylo.

Johnson, John William. 1986. *The Epic of Son-Jara: A West African Tradition.* Bloomington: Indiana University Press.

Johnson, John William, Cheick Omar Mara, Ibrahim Kalilou Tera, and Cheickna Mohamed Singare. 1979. *The Epic of Sunjata according to Magan Sisoko.* 2 vols. Bloomington: Folklore Institute.

Jones, A. M. 1964. *Africa and Indonesia: The Evidence of the Xylophone and Other Musical and Cultural Factors.* Leiden: E. J. Brill.

Joyeux, Charles. 1910. "Notes sur quelques manifestations musicales observées en Haute-Guinée." *Revue Musicale* 2:49–58.

———. 1924. "Étude sur quelques manifestations musicales observées en Haute-Guinée Française." *Revue d'Ethnographie* 18:170–212.

Ka, Abou Anta. 1959. "Les griots: Sont-ils condamnés à disparaître?" *Bingo* 83 (December): 30–32.

Kaba, Lansiné. 1976. "The Cultural Revolution, Artistic Creativity, and Freedom of Expression in Guinea." *Journal of Modern African Studies* 14 (2): 201–18.

———. 1990. *Le non de la Guinée à De Gaulle.* Paris: Éditions Chaka.

Kaba, Lansiné, and Eric Charry. Forthcoming. "Mamaya: Renewal and Tradition in the Maninnka Music of Kankan, Guinea (1935–45)." In *The African Diaspora: A Musical Perspective,* ed. Ingrid Monson. New York: Garland.

Kaba, Mamadi. 1995. *Anthologie de chants mandingues (Côte d'Ivoire, Guinée, Mali)*. Paris: Harmattan.

Kassis, Hanna E. 1983. *A Concordance of the Qur'an*. Berkeley: University of California Press.

Kauffman, Robert. 1980. "African Rhythm: A Reassessment." *Ethnomusicology* 24 (3): 393–415.

Kaye, Andrew. 1987. "The Problem of the *Ginbri*, or Internal-Spike Lute: Its Origins, Structure, Nomenclature, and Contemporary Usage." Paper read at the annual meeting of Society for Ethnomusicology, November 1987.

Keita, Boniface. 1988. *Kita dans les années 1910*. Bamako: Éditions Jamana.

Keita, Cheick M. Chérif. 1995a. *Massa Makan Diabaté: Un griot mandingue à la rencontre de l'écriture*. Paris: Harmattan.

———. 1995b. "Jaliya in the Modern World: A Tribute to Banzumana Sissoko and Massa Makan Diabate." In *Status and Identity in West Africa: Nyamakalaw of Mande*, ed. David C. Conrad and Barbara E. Frank, 182–96. Bloomington: Indiana University Press.

———. 1996. "A Praise Song for the Father: Family Identity in Salif Keita's Music." In *The Younger Brother in Mande Kinship and Politics in West Africa*, ed. Jan Jansen and Clemens Zobel, 97–104. Leiden: Research School CNWS.

Keita, Fodeba [Keita Fodeba]. 1948. "Chansons du Dioliba." *Présence Africaine* 4: 595–98.

———. 1950. *Poèmes africains*. Paris: Pierre Seghers. Reprinted with other material (including photos) as *Aube africaine et autres poèmes africains*. Paris: Présence Africaine, 1994.

———. 1958. "La danse africaine et la scène/African Dance and the Stage." *Le Théatre dans le Monde/World Theatre* 7 (3): 164–78.

King, Anthony. 1972. "The Construction and Tuning of the Kora." *African Language Studies* 13:113–36.

———. 1974. "Music: The Performance Modes." In *Sunjata: Three Mandinka Versions*, ed. Gordon Innes, 17–24. London: SOAS.

King, Anthony, and Lucy Durán. 1984. "Kora." In *The New Grove Dictionary of Musical Instruments*, ed. Stanley Sadie, 2:461–63. London: Macmillan.

Klobe, Marguerite. 1977. "A Dogon Figure of a Koro Player." *African Arts* 10 (4): 32–35, 87.

Knight, Roderic. 1968. "An Analytical Study of Music for the Kora, a West African Harp Lute." 2 vols. M.A. thesis, University of California, Los Angeles.

———. 1971. "Towards a Notation and Tablature for the Kora and Its Application to Other Instruments." *African Music* 5 (1): 23–36.

———. 1972a. "Letters to the Editor." *African Music* 5 (2): 112–13.

———. 1972b. Review of six LP discs from the Ministry of Information of Mali (1971-disc). *Ethnomusicology* 16 (2): 299–308.

———. 1973a. "Mandinka Jaliya: Professional Music of The Gambia." 2 vols. Ph.D. diss., University of California, Los Angeles.

———. 1973b. Review of Fanta Sacko (1972-disc) and Bazoumana Sissoko (1972a/b-disc). *Ethnomusicology* 17 (2): 378–81.

———. 1974. "Mandinka Drumming." *African Arts* 7 (4): 24–35.

———. 1983. "Manding/Fula Relations as Reflected in the Manding Song Repertoire." *African Music* 6 (2): 37–47.

————. 1984a. "Music in Africa: The Manding Contexts." In *Performance Practice: Ethnomusicological Perspectives,* ed. Gerard Béhague, 53–90. Westport, Conn.: Greenwood Press.

————. 1984b. "The Style of Mandinka Music: A Study in Extracting Theory from Practice." In *Selected Reports in Ethnomusicology,* vol. 5, *Studies in African Music,* ed. J. H. Kwabena Nketia and Jacqueline Cogdell Djedje, 3–66. Los Angeles: Program in Ethnomusicology, Department of Music, University of California.

————. 1989. "The Mande Sound: African Popular Music on Records." *Ethnomusicology* 33 (2): 371–76.

————. 1991a. "Vibrato Octaves: Tunings and Modes of the Mande Balo and Kora." *Progress Reports in Ethnomusicology* 3 (4): 1–49. Department of Music, University of Maryland Baltimore County.

————. 1991b. "Music out of Africa: Mande Jaliya in Paris." *World of Music* 33 (1): 52–69.

————. 1992. "Kora Music of the Mandinka: Source Material for World Musics." In *African Musicology: Current Trends,* ed. Jacqueline Cogdell DjeDje, 2:81–97. Los Angeles: African Studies Center, University of California.

Konate, Famoudou, and Thomas Ott. 1997. *Rhythmen und Lieder aus Guinea.* Oldershausen: Institut für Didaktik Populärer Musik. English translation forthcoming.

Kone, Kassim Gausu. 1995. *Bamanankan Dangegafe.* West Newbury, Mass.: Mother Tongue Editions.

————. 1997. "Bamana Verbal Art: An Ethnographic Study of Proverbs." Ph.D. diss., Indiana University.

Kone, Yaouaga Félix. 1990. "Hommage à Siramory Diabate." *Jamana* 25 (March): 19–20.

Kouyate, Namankoumba. 1970. "Recherches sur la tradition orale au Mali (pays Manding)." Diplôme d'études supérieures, Université d'Alger.

Krieger, Kurt. 1968. "Musikinstrumente der Hausa." *Baessler-Archiv,* n.s., 16 (2): 373–430.

Kubik, Gerhard. 1985. "African Tone-Systems: A Reassessment." *Yearbook for Traditional Music* 17:31–63.

————. 1989. *Musikgeschichte in Bildern 1 (11): Westafrika.* Leipzig: VEB Deutscher Verlag für Musik Leipzig.

Labouret, H. 1952. *La langue des Peuls ou Foulbé.* Mémoires de l'IFAN 16. Dakar: IFAN.

————. 1955. *La langue des Peuls ou Foulbé: Lexique français-peul.* Mémoires de l'IFAN 41. Dakar: IFAN.

————. 1959. "A propos du mot 'griot.'" *Notes Africaines* (IFAN) 50:56–57.

Lamm, Judith Ann. 1968. "Musical Instruments of Sierra Leone." M. Mus. thesis, University of Wisconsin.

Lamp, Frederick. 1996. *Art of the Baga: A Drama of Cultural Reinvention.* New York: Museum for African Art and Prestel Verlag.

Lane, Edward William. 1956. *Arabic-English Lexicon.* 8 vols. with supplement. New York: Frederick Ungar. Originally published 1893.

Law, Robin. 1980. *The Horse in West African History.* Oxford: Oxford University Press.

Laye, Camara. See Laye Camara.

Lee, Hélène. 1988. *Rockers d'Afrique: Stars et légendes du rock mandingue.* Paris: Albin Michel.

Lems-Dworkin, Carol. 1991. *African Music: A Pan-African Annotated Bibliography.* London: Hans Zell.

Levtzion, Nehemia. 1963. "The Thirteenth- and Fourteenth-Century Kings of Mali." *Journal of African History* 4 (3): 341–53.

———. 1980. *Ancient Ghana and Mali.* New York: Africana. Reprinted from 1973 edition with additions.

———. 1985. "The Early States of the Western Sudan to 1500." In *History of West Africa,* 3d ed., ed. J. F. A. Ajayi and Michael Crowder, 1:129–66. Essex: Longman.

Levtzion, N., and J. F. P. Hopkins, eds. 1981. *Corpus of Early Arabic Sources for West African History.* Trans. J. F. P. Hopkins. Cambridge: Cambridge University Press.

Leymarie-Ortiz, Isabelle. 1979. "The Griots of Senegal and Change." *Africa* (Italy) 34 (3): 183–97.

Leynaud, Emil, and Youssouf Cissé. 1978. *Paysans malinké du Haut Niger.* Tradition et Développement Rural en Afrique Soudanaise. Bamako: Edition Imprimerie Populaire du Mali.

Liberia, Department of Information and Cultural Affairs. 1971. *Musical Instruments of Liberia.* Monrovia: Department of Information and Cultural Affairs.

Lincoln, William A. 1986. *World Woods in Color.* New York: Macmillan.

Locke, David. 1979. "The Music of Atsiagbeko." 2 vols. Ph.D. diss., Wesleyan University.

———. 1982. "Principles of Offbeat Timing and Cross-Rhythm in Southern Eve Dance Drumming." *Ethnomusicology* 26 (2): 217–46.

———. 1990. *Drum Damba: Talking Drum Lessons.* With Abubakari Lunna. Crown Point, Ind.: White Cliffs Media.

Luneau, René. 1981. *Chants de femmes au Mali.* Paris: Luneau Ascot.

Ly-Tall, Madina, Seydou Camara, and Bouna Diouara. 1987. *L'histoire du Mande d'après Jeli Kanku Madi Jabaté de Kela.* Paris: Association SCOA.

MacGaffey, Wyatt. 1991. "Review Article: Who Owns Ancient Egypt?" *Journal of African History* 32 (3): 515–19.

Mahillon, Victor-Charles. 1909. *Catalogue descriptif et analytique du Musée Instrumental du Conservatoire Royal de Musique de Bruxelles.* Vol. 2. 2d ed. Gand: Librairie Générale de Ad. Hoste.

Mandel, Jean-Jacques. 1983. "Salif Keita, le crooner albinos." *Liberation,* June 14, 24–25.

Mané, Mamadou. 1978. "Contribution à l'histoire du Kaabu, des origines au XIXe siècle." *Bulletin de l'IFAN,* ser. B, 40 (1): 87–159.

Manniche, Lise. 1975. *Ancient Egyptian Musical Instruments.* Munich: Deutscher Kunstverlag.

Mark, Peter. 1985. *A Cultural, Economic, and Religious History of the Basse Casamance since 1500.* Stuttgart: Franz Steiner Verlag Wiesbaden.

———. 1992. *The Wild Bull and the Sacred Forest: Form, Meaning, and Change in Senegambian Initiation Masks.* Cambridge: Cambridge University Press.

Martin, John. 1959. "Dance: Africana. Lively and Handsome 'Ballet' Arrives from the Dark Continent." *New York Times,* February 22, sect. 2, p. 10.

Masonen, Pekka, and Humphrey J. Fisher. 1996. "Not Quite Venus from the Waves: The Almoravid Conquest of Ghana in the Modern Historiography of Western Africa." *History in Africa* 23: 197–231.

Mauny, R. 1952. *Glossaire des expressions et termes locaux employés dans l'Ouest Africain.* Dakar: IFAN.

———. 1954. "The Question of Ghana." *Africa* 24 (3): 200–213.

———. 1955. "Baobobs—cimetières à griots," *Notes Africaines* 67 (July): 72–75.

McDougall, E. Ann. 1985. "The View from Awdaghust: War, Trade and Social Change in the Southwestern Sahara, from the Eighth to the Fifteenth Century." *Journal of African History* 26 (1): 1–31.

McIntosh, Roderick J. 1989. "Middle Niger Terracottas before the Symplegades Gateway." *African Arts* 22 (2): 74–83, 103–4.

———. 1993. "The Pulse Model: Genesis and Accommodation of Specialization in the Middle Niger." *Journal of African History* 34 (2): 181–220.

———. 1997. "Agricultural Beginnings in Sub-Saharan Africa." In *Encyclopedia of Precolonial Africa*, ed. Joseph O. Vogel, 409–18. Walnut Creek, Calif.: AltaMira.

———. 1998. *The Peoples of the Middle Niger: The Island of Gold.* Malden, Mass.: Blackwell.

McIntosh, Roderick J., and Susan K. McIntosh. 1988. "From *Siècles Obscurs* to Revolutionary Centuries on the Middle Niger." *World Archaeology* 20 (1): 141–65.

McIntosh, Susan Keech. 1994. "Changing Perceptions of West Africa's Past: Archaeological Research since 1988." *Journal of Archaeological Research* 2 (2): 165–98.

———, ed. 1995. *Excavations at Jenné-Jeno, Hambarketolo, and Kaniana (Inland Niger Delta, Mali), the 1981 Season.* Berkeley: University of California Press.

McIntosh, Susan K., and Roderic J. McIntosh. 1983. "Current Directions in West African Prehistory." *Annual Review of Anthropology* 12:215–58.

———. 1988. "From Stone to Metal: New Perspectives on the Later Prehistory of West Africa." *Journal of World Prehistory* 2 (1): 89–133.

———. 1993. "Cities without Citadels: Understanding Urban Origins along the Middle Niger." In *The Archaeology of Africa: Foods, Metals and Towns*, ed. Thurston Shaw, Paul Sinclair, Bassey Andah, and Alex Okpoko, 622–41. New York: Routledge.

McLaughlin, Fiona. 1997. "Islam and Popular Music in Senegal: The Emergence of a 'New Tradition.'" *Africa* 67 (4): 560–81.

McNaughton, Patrick R. 1979. *Secret Sculptures of Komo: Art and Sculpture in Bamana (Bambara) Initiation Associations.* Philadelphia: Institute for the Study of Human Issues.

———. 1982. "The Shirts That Mande Hunters Wear." *African Arts* 15 (3): 54–58, 91.

———. 1988. *The Mande Blacksmiths: Knowledge, Power, and Art in West Africa.* Bloomington: Indiana University Press.

———. 1991. "Is There History in Horizontal Masks? A Preliminary Response to the Dilemma of Form." *African Arts* 24 (2): 40–53, 88–90.

———. 1992. "From Mande Komo to Jukun Akuma: Approaching the Difficult Question of History." *African Arts* 25 (2): 76–85, 99–100.

———. 1995. "The Semantics of Jugu: Blacksmiths, Lore, and 'Who's Bad' in Mande." In *Status and Identity in West Africa: Nyamakalaw of Mande*, ed. David C. Conrad and Barbara E. Frank, 46–57. Bloomington: Indiana University Press.

Meillassoux, Claude. 1968a. "Les cérémonies septennales du kamablõ de Kaaba (Mali) (5–12 avril 1968)." *Journal de la Société des Africanistes* 38 (2): 173–83.

———. 1968b. *Urbanization of an African Community: Voluntary Associations in Bamako.* Seattle: University of Washington Press.

Ménard, René. 1963. "Contribution à l'étude de quelques instruments de musique Baoule—region de Beoumi (Côte d'Ivoire)." *Jahrbuch für Musikalische Volks- und Völkerkunde* 1:48–99.

Mensah, Atta Annan. 1982. "Gyil: The Dagara-Lobi Xylophone." *Journal of African Studies* 9 (3): 139–54.

Merriam, Alan. 1970. *African Music on LP: An Annotated Discography*. Evanston, Ill.: Northwestern University Press.

———. 1982. "African Musical Rhythm and Concepts of Time-Reckoning." In *African Music in Perspective*, by Alan Merriam, 443–61. New York: Garland.

Metropolitan Museum of Art. 1907. *Catalogue of the Crosby Brown Collection of Musical Instruments of All Nations*. New York: Metropolitan Museum of Art.

———. n.d. *Metropolitan Museum of Art. Musical Instrument Collection*. New York.

Meyer, Andreas. 1997. *Afrikanische Trommeln: West- und Zentralafrika*. Berlin: Museum für Völkerkunde.

Meyer, Gérard, with Jean-Raphaël Camara and Fonsa Camara. 1985. *Proverbes malinké*. Paris: Conseil International de la Langue Française–EDICEF.

Ministère de la Culture, Senegal. 1986. *Carte d'identité des services du Ministère de la Culture à l'intention des jeunes*. Dakar.

Ministry of Education and Culture of Guinea. 1979. *Cultural Policy in the Revolutionary People's Republic of Guinea*. Paris: UNESCO.

Modic, Kate. 1993. "The Bamana Women Drummers." In *Drums: The Heartbeat of Africa*, ed. Esther A. Dagan, 78–79. Montreal: Galerie Amrad African Art Publications.

———. 1994. "Negotiating Power: A Study of the Ben Ka Di Women's Association in Bamako, Mali." *Africa Today* 41 (2): 25–37.

———. 1996. "Song, Performance and Power: The Bèn Ka Di Women's Association in Bamako, Mali." Ph.D. diss., Indiana University.

Monteil, Charles. 1915. *Les Khassonke: Monographie d'une peuplade du Soudan Français*. Reprinted Nendeln, Liechtenstein: Kraus Reprint, 1974.

———. 1924. *Les Bambara du Ségou et du Kaarta*. Reprinted Paris: G. P. Maisonneuve et Larose. 1977.

———. 1953. "La légende du Ouagadou et l'origine des Soninké." *Mémoires de l'Institut Français d'Afrique Noire (MIFAN)* 23 : 359–409.

Monteil, Vincent. 1968. "Un cas d'économie ostentatoire: Les griots d'Afrique Noire." *Economies et Sociétés* 2 (4): 773–91.

Monts, Lester P. 1982. "Music Clusteral Relationships in a Liberian–Sierra Leonean Region: A Preliminary Analysis." *Journal of African Studies* 9 (3): 101–15.

Moraes Farias, P. F. de. 1989. "Pilgrimages to 'Pagan' Mecca in Mandenka Stories of Origin Reported from Mali and Guinea-Conakry." In *Discourse and Its Disguises: The Interpretation of African Oral Texts*, ed. Karin Barber and P. F. de Moraes Farias, 152–70. Birmingham: Center of West African Studies, University of Birmingham.

Moser, Rex. 1974. "Foregrounding in the Sunjata: The Mande Epic." Ph.D. diss., Indiana University.

Munson, Patrick. 1971. "The Tichitt Tradition: A Late Prehistoric Occupation of the Southwestern Sahara." Ph.D. diss., University of Illinois at Urbana-Champaign.

———. 1976. "Archaeological Data on the Origins of Cultivation in the Southwestern Sahara and Their Implications for West Africa." In *Origins of African Plant Domestication*, ed. Jack R. Harlan, Jan M. J. de Wet, and Ann B. L. Stemler, 187–209. The Hague: Mouton.

———. 1980. "Archaeology and the Prehistoric Origins of the Ghana Empire." *Journal of African History* 21 (4): 457–66.

————. 1989. "About: 'Économie et société néolithique du Dhar Tichitt (Mauritanie).'" *Sahara* 2:106–8.

Musée de l'Homme. n.d. *Musée de l'Homme: Musical Instrument Collection.* Paris.

Musée National du Mali. 1996. *Sons et rythmes du Mali: Instruments et genres musicaux traditionnels.* Bamako: Musée National du Mali.

Muzzolini, A. 1989. "Essay Review: A Reappraisal of the 'Neolithic' of Tichitt (Mauritania)." *Journal of Arid Environments* 16 (1): 101–5.

————. 1993. "The Emergence of a Food-Producing Economy in the Sahara." In *The Archaeology of Africa: Food, Metals and Towns,* ed. Thurston Shaw, Paul Sinclair, Bassey Andah, and Alex Okpoko, 227–39. New York: Routledge.

————. 1997. "Saharan Rock Art." In *Encyclopedia of Precolonial Africa,* ed. Joseph O. Vogel, 347–52. Walnut Creek, Calif.: AltaMira.

Nakamura, Yusuke. 1992. "Hommes d'action et hommes de paroles: Sur l'art panégyrique cynégétique mande." In *Boucles du Niger: Approches multidisciplinaires,* ed. Junzo Kawada, 3:315–69. Tokyo: Institute for the Study of Languages and Cultures of Asia and Africa.

Newton, Robert. 1997. "The Epic Cassette: Technology, Tradition, and Imagination in Contemporary Bamana Segu." Ph.D. diss., University of Wisconsin.

Niane, Djibril Tamsir. 1965. *Sundiata, an Epic of Old Mali.* Trans. G. D. Pickett. Reprinted Essex: Longman, 1986. Originally published as *Soundjata, ou L'épopée mandingue,* 1960.

————. 1975a. *Recherches sur l'empire du Mali au moyen âge.* Paris: Présence Africaine.

————. 1975b. *Le Soudan Occidental au temps des grands empires XI-XVIe siècle.* Paris: Présence Africaine.

————. 1989. *Histoire des Mandingues de l'ouest: Le royaume du Gabou.* Paris: Karthala.

Nicklin, Keith. 1975. "Agiloh: The Giant Mbube Xylophone." *Nigerian Field* 40 (4): 148–58.

Nikiprowetzky, Tolia. 1966. *Trois aspects de la musique africaine: Mauritanie, Sénégal, Niger.* Paris: OCORA.

Nketia, J. H. Kwabena. 1963. *African Music in Ghana.* Evanston, Ill.: Northwestern University Press.

————. 1974. *The Music of Africa.* New York: W. W. Norton.

Norris, H. T. 1968. *Shinqīṭī Folk Literature and Song.* London: Oxford University Press.

Nourrit, Chantal, and Bill Pruitt. 1978. *Musique traditionelle de l'Afrique Noire: Discographie.* Vol. 1. *Mali.* Vol. 2. *Haute-Volta,* 2d ed. Vol. 3. *Mauritanie.* Paris: Centre de Documentation Africaine, Radio France International.

————. 1979. *Musique traditionelle de l'Afrique Noire: Discographie.* Vol. 4. *Sénégal et Gambie.* Paris: Centre de Documentation Africaine, Radio France International.

————. 1984. *Musique traditionelle de l'Afrique Noire: Discographie.* Vol. 5. *Niger.* Paris: Centre de Documentation Africaine, Radio France International.

Osborn, Donald W., David J. Dwyer, and Joseph I. Donohoe. 1993. *A Fulfulde (Maasina)-English-French Lexicon.* East Lansing: Michigan State University Press.

O'Toole, Thomas. 1995. *Historical Dictionary of Guinea.* 3d ed. Lanham, Md.: Scarecrow Press.

Panneton, Sylvain. 1987. "Le balafon *mandinka mori:* Compte-rendu et perspectives de recherches et d'études en Guinée-Bissau." Master's thesis, Université de Montréal.

Panzacchi, Cornelia. 1994. "The Livelihoods of Traditional Griots in Modern Senegal." *Africa* 64 (2): 190–210.

———. 1996. *Mbalax Mi: Musikszene Senegal*. Wuppertal, Ger.: Peter Hammer.

Paques, Viviana. 1954. *Les Bambara*. Paris: Presses Universitaires de France.

Perinbam, B. Marie. 1997. *Family Identity and the State in the Bamako Kafu, c. 1800– c. 1900*. Boulder, Colo: Westview Press.

Perron, Michel. 1930. "Chants populaires de la Sénégambie et du Niger." *Bulletin de l'Agence Générale des Colonies* 23:803–11.

Pevar, Susan Gunn. 1978. "The Construction of a Kora." *African Arts* 11 (4): 66–72.

Pfeiffer, Katrin, ed. 1997. *Mandinka Spoken Art: Folk-Tales, Griot Accounts and Songs*. Cologne: Rüdiger Köppe.

Picken, Laurence. 1955. "The Origin of the Short Lute." *Galpin Society Journal* 8:32– 42.

———. 1975. *Folk Musical Instruments of Turkey*. London: Oxford University Press.

Polak, Rainer. 1996a. "Das Spiel der Jenbe-Trommel: Musik- und Festkultur in Bamako (Mali)." Master's thesis, University of Bayreuth.

———. 1996b. "Zeit, Bewegung, und Pulsation: Theorierelevante Aspekte der Jenbe-Musik." *Jahrbuch für Musikalische Volks- und Völkerkunde* 17:59–69.

———. 1998. "*Jenbe* Music in Bamako: Microtiming as Formal Model and Performance Practice." *Iwalewa Forum* (Africa Centre, University of Bayreuth) 2:24–36.

———. Forthcoming. "A bèè kèra wòri ko ye—Alles wurde eine Frage des Geldes. Kommerzialisierung und Formenwandel: Die kulturelle Ökonomie der Bamakoer jenbe-Festmusik." Ph.D. diss. in progress (working title), University of Bayreuth.

Pollet, Eric, and Grace Winter. 1971. *La société soninké*. Brussels: Éditions de l'Institut de Sociologie de l'Université Libre de Bruxelles.

Powers, Harold. 1980a. "Classical Music, Cultural Roots, and Colonial Rule: An Indic Musicologist Looks at the Muslim World." *Asian Music* 12 (1): 5–39.

———. 1980b. "Language Models and Musical Analysis." *Ethnomusicology* 24 (1): 1–60.

Prince, Rob. 1989a. "The Kora Prince: Rob Prince Meets Innovative Plucker Toumani Diabate." *Folk Roots* 69:15–16.

———. 1989b. "Premier du Mali: Rob Prince Talks to Veteran Multi-instrumentalist Keletigui Diabate, a Key Figure in Mali's Modern Music." *Folk Roots* 74:17, 19.

———. 1990. "There's a Griot Going On! Rob Prince Has a Cosmic Time with Kasse Mady." *Folk Roots* 81:23, 25.

Prouteaux, M. 1929. "Premiers essais de théâtre chez les indigènes de la haute Côte d'Ivoire." *Bulletin du Comité d'Études Historiques et Scientifiques de l'A.O.F.* 12: 448–75.

Quinn, Charlotte A. 1972. *Mandingo Kingdoms of the Senegambia: Traditionalism, Islam, and European Expansion*. Evanston, Ill.: Northwestern University Press.

Qureshi, Regula Burckhardt. 1986. *Sufi Music of India and Pakistan: Sound, Context and Meaning in Qawwali*. Cambridge: Cambridge University Press.

Rashid, Subhi Anwar. 1984. *Musikgeschichte in Bildern*. Vol. 2, no.2: *Mesopotamien*. Leipzig: VEB Deutscher Verlag für Musik Leipzig.

Reeve, Henry Fenwick. 1912. *The Gambia*. London: Smith, Elder. Reprinted New York: Negro Universities Press, 1969.

Robinson, David. 1985. *The Holy War of Umar Tall: The Western Sudan in the Mid-Nineteenth Century*. Oxford: Oxford University Press.

Rouanet, Jules. 1922. "La musique arabe dans la Maghreb." In *Encyclopédie de la musique et dictionnaire du conservatoire*, Part 1, *Histoire de la musique*, ed. Albert Lavignac, 2813–2944. Paris: Librairie Delagrave.

Rouget, Gilbert. 1955. "Chroniques musicales." *Presence Africaine*, n.s., 1–2:153–58.

———. 1956. "Les Ballets Africains de Keita Fodeba." *Presence Africaine*, n.s., 7: 138–40.

———. 1980. "Guinea." In *The New Grove Dictionary of Music and Musicians*, ed. Stanley Sadie, 7:819–23. London: Macmillan.

Rouget, Gilbert, and Jean Schwarz. 1969. "Sur les xylophones equiheptaphoniques des Malinké." *Revue de Musicologie* 55 (1): 47–77.

Sachs, Curt. 1921. *Die Musikinstrumente des alten Ägyptens*. Berlin: Karl Curtius.

———. 1940. *The History of Musical Instruments*. New York: W. W. Norton.

Sadie, Stanley, ed. 1984. *The New Grove Dictionary of Musical Instruments*. 3 vols. London: Macmillan.

———. Forthcoming. *The New Grove Dictionary of Music and Musicians*. Rev. ed. London: Macmillan.

Salvador-Daniel, Francisco. 1986. *Musique et instruments de musique du Maghreb*. Paris: Boîte à Documents. Collection of writings from 1856 to 1867; cover drawing from 1863.

Schaeffner, André. 1936. *Origine des instruments de musique*. Reprinted Paris: Mouton, 1968; 2d ed. 1980.

———. 1946. "Les instruments de musique: Introduction, instruments à corps solide vibrant, instruments à air vibrant." In *La musique: Des origines à nos jours*, ed. Norbert Dufourcq, 13–45, 52. Paris: Librarie Larousse.

———. 1951. *Les Kissi: Une société noire et ses instruments de musique*. Paris: Hermann.

———. 1953. "Les rites de circoncision en pays Kissi." *Études Guinéennes* 3–56.

Schaffer, Matt, and Christine Cooper. 1987. *Mandinko: The Ethnography of a West African Holy Land*. Prospect Heights, Ill.: Waveland Press. Reissued with changes from the original 1980 edition.

Schulz, Dorothea. 1996. "Praise in Times of Disenchantment: Griots, Radios, and the Politics of Communication in Mali." Ph.D. diss., Yale University.

———. 1998. "Morals of Praise: Broadcast Media and the Commoditization of Jeli Praise Performances in Mali." *Research in Economic Anthropology* 19:117–32.

Schuyler, Philip. 1979. "A Repertory of Ideas: The Music of the Rwais, Berber Professional Musicians from Southwestern Morocco." Ph.D. diss., University of Washington.

———. 1981. "Music and Meaning among the Gnawa Religious Brotherhood of Morocco." *World of Music* 23 (1): 3–11.

Schwab, George. 1947. *Tribes of the Liberian Hinterland*. Papers of the Peabody Museum of American Archaeology and Ethnology, Harvard University, vol. 31. Cambridge: Peabody Museum.

Seavoy, Mary. 1982. "The Sisaala Xylophone Tradition." Ph.D. diss., University of California, Los Angeles.

Seck, Nago, and Sylvie Clerfeuille. 1986. *Musiciens africains des années 80*. Paris: Harmattan.

———. 1993. *Les musiciens du beat africaine*. Paris: Bordas.

Séminaire-atelier sur l'orthographe et le lexique. 1994. *Séminaire-atelier sur l'ortho-*

graphe et le lexique de base de la langue maninka (1994, Conakry). Conakry: Institut de Recherche Linguistique Apliquée et Agence de Cooperation Culturelle et Technique.

Senghor, Léopold. 1964. *Poèmes*. Reprinted Paris: Éditions du Seuil, 1973.

Shankar, Ravi. 1968. *My Music, My Life*. New York: Simon and Schuster.

Shiloah, Amnon. 1995. *Music in the World of Islam: A Socio-cultural Study*. Detroit: Wayne State University Press.

Sidibe, Mamby. 1930. "Nouvelles notes sur la chasse au Birgo (cercle de Kita, Soudan Français." *Bulletin du Comité d'Études Historiques et Scientifiques de l'A.O.F.* 13 (1): 48–67.

Simpson, J. A., and E. S. C. Weiner, preparers. 1989. *The Oxford English Dictionary*. 2d ed. Oxford: Clarendon Press.

Smend. 1908. "Negermusik und Musikinstrumente in Togo." *Globus* 93 (5): 71–75; 93 (6): 89–94.

Smith, Andrew B. 1992. *Pastoralism in Africa: Origins and Development Ecology*. London: Hurst; Athens: Ohio University Press.

Le Soleil. 1989. "Moi, journaliste de médiat d'état," by El Bachir Sow; "Sus aux inquisiteurs," by Mouhamadou M. Dia. *Le Soleil* (Dakar), January 28–29, 5.

Soma, Étienne Yarmon. 1988. "Les instruments de musique du pays Cerma (ou Goin), sud-ouest du Burkina Faso." *Anthropos* 83 (4–6): 469–83.

Sonko-Godwin, Patience. 1986. *Ethnic Groups of the Senegambia Region: Social and Political Structures. Pre-colonial Period*. Banjul, The Gambia: Government Printer.

Soumaoro, Bourama, Charles S. Bird, Gerald Cashion, and Mamadou Kante. 1976. *Seyidu Kamara ka Donkiliw: Kambili*. Bambara transcription. Bloomington: African Studies Center, Indiana University.

Spears, Richard A. 1973. *Elementary Maninka-kan*. Evanston, Ill.: Northwestern University.

Stapleton, Chris. 1988. "Golden Guinea: Chris Stapleton Speaks with the Superb Jali Musa Jawara." *Folk Roots* 61:27, 29.

———. 1989. "Paris, Africa." In *Rhythms of the World*, ed. Francis Hanly and Tim May, 10–23. London: BBC Books.

Stapleton, Chris, and Chris May. 1990. *African Rock: The Pop Music of a Continent*. New York: Obelisk/Dutton. Originally published as *African All-Stars*, 1987.

Staub, Jules. 1936. *Beiträge zur Kenntnis der materiellen Kultur der Mendi in der Sierra Leone*. Trans. from the German for the Human Relations Area Files by Cecil Wood, 1958. HRAF FC7 Mende 1: Staub. New Haven, Conn.

Stoller, Paul, and Cheryl Olkes. 1987. *In Sorcery's Shadow: A Memoir of Apprenticeship among the Songhay of Niger*. Chicago: University of Chicago Press.

Stone, Ruth. 1982. *Let the Inside Be Sweet: The Interpretation of Music Event among the Kpelle of Liberia*. Bloomington: Indiana University Press.

Stone, Ruth, and Frank Gillis. 1976. *African Music and Oral Data: A Catalog of Field Recordings, 1902–1975*. Bloomington: Indiana University Press.

Strumpf, Mitchel. 1970. "Ghanaian Xylophone Studies." *Review of Ethnology* 3 (6): 41–45.

Sunkett, Mark. 1995. *Mandiani Drum and Dance: Djimbe Performance and Black Aesthetics from Africa to the New World*. Tempe, Ariz.: White Cliffs Media.

Surugue, B. 1980. "Songhay Music." In *The New Grove Dictionary of Music and Musicians*, ed. Stanley Sadie, 17:523–24. London: Macmillan.

Sweeney, Philip. 1992. *The Virgin Directory of World Music.* New York: Henry Holt.

Tamari, Tal. 1991. "The Development of Caste Systems in West Africa." *Journal of African History* 32 (2): 221–50.

———. 1997. *Les castes de l'Afrique Occidentale: Artisans et musiciens endogames.* Nanterre: Société d'Ethnologie.

Tenaille, Frank. 1987. *Toure Kunda.* Paris: Seghers.

Thieme, Darius L. 1969. "A Descriptive Catalogue of Yoruba Musical Instruments." Studies in Music 37. Ph.D. diss., Catholic University.

Thompson, Robert Farris. 1973. "An Aesthetic of the Cool." *African Arts* 7 (1): 40–43, 64–67, 89–91.

———. 1974. *African Art in Motion: Icon and Act in the Collection of Katherine Coryton White.* Berkeley: University of California Press.

Thompson, Robert Lynn. 1993. "Mandinka Drum Patterns in The Gambia." In *Drums: The Heartbeat of Africa,* ed. Esther A. Dagan, 82–83. Montreal: Galerie Amrad African Art Publications.

———. 1994. Calloused Hands and a Drummer's Toolkit: Mandinka Drumming in The Gambia." Ph.D. diss., Indiana University.

Thoyer, Annik. 1995. *Récits épiques des chasseurs bamanan du Mali.* Paris: Harmattan.

Thoyer-Rozat, Annik. 1978a. *Chants de chasseurs du Mali par Mamadou Jara.* Vol. 1. Paris.

———. 1978b. *Chants de chasseurs du Mali par Ndugacé Samaké.* Vol. 3. Paris.

Thoyer-Rozat, Annik, and Lasana Dukure. 1978. *Kanbili: Chant de chasseurs du Mali par Mamadou Jara.* Vol. 2. Paris.

Toure, Sekou. 1963. *Guinean Revolution and Social Progress.* Conakry.

———. n.d. *L'action politique du parti démocratique de Guinée en faveur de l'émancipation de la jeunesse guinéenne.* Vol. 8. Conakry.

Tracey, Hugh. 1970. *Chopi Musicians: Their Music, Poetry, and Instruments.* London: Oxford University Press.

Traore, Mamadou. 1942. "Une danse curieuse: Le moribayasa." *Notes Africaines* 15: 5–6.

Travele, Moussa. 1929. "Le Komo ou Koma." *Outremer* 1 (2): 127–50.

"Triomphe à New York des Ballets Africains de Keita Fodeba." 1959. *Bingo* 77: 18–20.

Turnbull, Harvey. 1972. "The Origin of the Long-Necked Lute." *Galpin Society Journal* 25: 58–66.

Van Hoven, Ed. 1996. "Local Tradition or Islamic Precept? The Notion of *Zakāt* in Wuli (Eastern Senegal)." *Cahiers d'Études Africaines* 36 (4): 703–22.

Van Oven, Cootje. 1970. "Music of Sierra Leone." *African Arts* 3 (4): 20–27, 71.

Villalón, Leon. 1995. *Islamic Society and State Power in Senegal: Disciples and Citizens in Fatick.* Cambridge: Cambridge University Press.

Vogel, Joseph O., ed. 1997. *Encyclopedia of Precolonial Africa: Archaeology, History, Languages, Cultures, Environments.* Walnut Creek, Calif.: AltaMira Press.

Vydrine, Valentine. 1995–96. "Who Speaks 'Mandekan'? A Note on Current Use of Mande Ethnonyms and Linguonyms." *Mande Studies Association (Mansa) Newsletter* 29: 6–9.

Wachsmann, Klaus. 1964. "Human Migration and African Harps." *Journal of the International Folk Music Council* 16: 84–88.

———. 1973. "A 'Shiplike' String Instrument from West Africa." *Ethnos* 38 (1–4): 43–56.

————. 1984. "Lute: 1. The Generic Term" and "Lute: 2. Ancient Lutes." In *The New Grove Dictionary of Musical Instruments,* ed. Stanley Sadie, 2:549–53. London: Macmillan.

Wane, Yaya. 1969. *Les Toucouleur du Fouta Tooro* (Sénégal). Initiations et Études Africaines 25. Dakar: IFAN.

Ward, W. E. F. 1927. "Music in the Gold Coast." *Gold Coast Review* 3:199–223.

Waterman, Richard A. 1948. "'Hot' Rhythm in Negro Music." *Journal of the American Musicological Society* 1 (1): 24–37.

Wegner, Ulrich. 1984. *Afrikanische Saiteninstrumente.* Berlin: Staatliche Museen Preussischer Kulturbesitz.

Wehr, Hans. 1976. *A Dictionary of Modern Written Arabic.* Ed. J. M. Cowan. 3d ed. Ithaca, N.Y.: Spoken Language Services; Wiesbaden: Otto Harrassowitz.

Wilks, Ivor. Forthcoming. "The History of the Sunjata Epic: A Review of the Evidence." In *In Search of Sunjata: The Mande Epic as History, Literature and Performance,* ed. Ralph A. Austen, 25–57. Bloomington: Indiana University Press.

Willcox, A. R. 1984. *The Rock Art of Africa.* New York: Holmes and Meier.

Williams, B. Michael. 1997. "Mamady Keita's 'Kassa.'" *Percussive Notes* 35 (2): 36–43.

Williams, Jean Baptiste [Jeannot]. 1990. "Les merveilles du passé." Radio interview with Kanfory Sanoussy. Radio Guinée.

————. 1993. "Les merveilles du passé." Radio interview with Mory Camara. Radio Guinée.

Willis, John Ralph. 1978. "The Torodbe Clerisy: A Social View." *Journal of African History* 1–9 (2): 195–212.

Wright, Bonnie L. 1989. "The Power of Articulation." In *Creativity of Power: Cosmology and Action in African Societies,* ed. W. Arens and Ivan Karp, 39–57. Washington, D.C.: Smithsonian Institution Press.

Wright, Donald R. 1985. "Beyond Migration and Conquest: Oral Traditions and Mandinka Ethnicity in Senegambia." *History in Africa* 12:335–48.

————. 1997. *The World and a Very Small Place in Africa.* Armonk, N.Y.: M. E. Sharpe.

Zahan, Dominique. 1950. "Notes sur un luth dogon." *Journal de la Société des Africanistes* 20 (2): 193–207.

————. 1960. *Sociétés d'initiation bambara: Le N'domo, Le Korè.* Paris: Mouton.

————. 1963. *La dialectique du verbe chez les Bambara.* Paris: Mouton.

Zanetti, Vincent. 1993. "La nouvelle génération des griots: Entretien avec Bassi Kouyate." *Cahiers de Musiques Traditionnelles* 6:201–9.

————. 1996. "De la place du village aux scènes internationales: L'évolution de *jembe* et de son répertoire." *Cahiers de Musiques Traditionnelles* 9:167–87.

Zemp, Hugo. 1964. "Musiciens autochtones et griots malinké chez les Dan de Côte Ivoire." *Cahiers d'Études Africaines* 4 (3): 370–82.

————. 1966. "La légende des griots malinké." *Cahiers d'Études Africaines* 6 (4): 611–42.

————. 1967. "Comment on devient musicien: Quatre exemples de l'Ouest-Africain." In *La musique dans la vie,* ed. Tolia Nikiprowetzki, 1:79–103. Paris: OCORA.

————. 1971. *Musique dan: La musique dans la pensée et la vie sociale d'une société africaine.* Paris: Mouton.

————. 1980. "Ivory Coast." In *The New Grove Dictionary of Music and Musicians,* ed. Stanley Sadie, 8:431–34. London: Macmillan.

Zobel, Clemens. 1996a. "Les génies du Kòma: Identités locales, logiques religieuses et enjeux socio-politiques dan les monts manding du Mali." *Cahiers d'Études Africaines* 36 (4): 625–58.

————. 1996b. "The Noble Griot: The Construction of Mande Jeliw-Identities and Political Leadership as Interplay of Alternate Values." In *The Younger Brother in Mande Kinship and Politics in West Africa,* ed. Jan Jansen and Clemens Zobel, 35–47. Leiden: Research School CNWS.

————. 1997. *Das Gewicht der Rede: Kulturelle Reinterpretation, Geschichte und Vermittlung bei den Mande Westafrikas.* New York: Peter Lang.

DISCOGRAPHY

In compiling this discography and appendix B (which is keyed to the discography) I focused primarily on artists from the core traditions discussed in this book. Although I have tried to be comprehensive within this focus, I estimate that I have listed about 75 percent of the relevant CDs and LPs. Cassette listings are sporadic and not at all complete. The discography is current through 1997 with occasional listings from 1998 and 1999. Question marks after dates indicate either a general time frame (e.g., 198?) or an educated guess probably accurate within a year or two (e.g., 1997?). Although most of the dates without question marks come from the copyright notices on the recordings, some were estimates based on other recordings on that label or the artist's career. In general, dates can be unreliable (e.g., a CD recording may bear a later date than its initial release as a local cassette), so readers should be cautious. Further listings can be found in Graham (1988, 1992), Merriam (1970), Nourrit and Pruitt (1978, 1979, 1984), and Panzacchi (1996).

Burkina Faso
Balafons of Bobo Dioulasso. 1997. *Sababougnouma*. Playasound, 65172.
Best of Burkina. 1996. *Best of Burkina Compil'*. Vol. 1. Bolibana/AFIX, 150555.
Coulibaly, Lassina, and Yan Kadi Faso. 1998? *Lassina Coulibaly et Yan Kadi Faso: Musiques du Burkina Faso et du Mali*. Buda, 92693-2.
Dances of Burkina Faso. 1994. *Dances of Burkina Faso*. Buda, 82481.
Duvelle, Charles, prod. 1971. *Musique bisa de Haute-Volta*. OCORA, OCR 58.
Fà Kiyen Yiriwa. 1997. *Les Djembé de Bobo/The Djembe of Bobo*. Playasound, PS 65195.
La Famille Dembele. 1996. *Aira Yo, la danse des jeunes griots*. Amiata, ARNR 1596.
Farafina. 1992a. *Bolomakote*. Intuition, INT 2026-2.
——. 1992b. *Jon Hassell/Farafina: Flash of the Spirit*. Intuition, INT 3009-2.
——. 1993. *Faso Denou*. Realworld/Caroline, CAROL-2328-2.
——. 1997? *Nemako*. Intuition, INT 3241-2.
Les Frères Coulibaly. 1992. *Anka Dia*. Ethnic, B6775.
Kassama Percussions/Kassoum Diarra. 1996. *Kassama Percussions: Kassoum Diarra*. Playasound, PS 65170.
Kersalé, Patrick, prod. 1997. *L'art du balafon/The Art of the Balafon*. Arion, ARN 60403.
Koko du Burkina Faso. 1993. *Balafons et tambours d'Afrique*. Playasound, PS 65101.
Ouedraogo, Amidou, and Faso Tile. 1990. *Lamogoya Cole Bobo*. Koch International, 322415.

Côte d'Ivoire
Cissoko, Papa. 1986. *Papa Cissoko . . . rend hommage à Marietou Thiam*. Disques Esperance, ESP 7520.

Drame, Adama. 1979. *Rhythms of the Manding: Adama Drame (Jembe).* Recorded 1976–78. Phillips, UNESCO collection 6586 042. Also issued in 1984 as Grem, DSM 042.

———. 1980. *Percussions mandingues/Mandingo Drums.* Playasound, PS 33525. Reissued 1992 as PS 65085.

———. 1983. *Tambour djembe.* Auvidis, AV 4510.

———. 1986. *Djeli.* Auvidis, AV 4519.

———. 1987. *Grands maîtres de la percussion/Great Masters of Percussion.* Auvidis Ethnic, B 6126. Reissued as *Percussion: Tambour djembé/Djembé Drum,* 1996.

———. 1992. *Marc Vella et Adama Drame: Continents.* Label Bleu, LBLC 2504/Harmonia Mundi, HM 83.

———. 1994. *Percussions mandingues/Mandingo Drums.* vol. 2. *Foliba.* Playasound, PS 65122.

———. 1995. *Autres contacts.* With *Les Percussions de Strasbourg.* Harmonia Mundi/L'Empreinte Digitale, ED 13043.

———. 1996. *Thirty Years of Jembe.* Playasound, PS 65177.

Förster, Till, prod. 1987. *Musik der Senufo.* Museum für Völkerkunde Berlin, MC 4.

Les Go de Koteba. 1997. *Les Go de Koteba.* Juna, J2813CD.

The Ivorys. 1987. *Bala.* Wallbank Warwick Communications, WWCD 006.

Vuylsteke, Michel, prod. n.d. *Musique gouro de Côte d'Ivoire.* Ocora, OCR 48.

Zemp, Hugo, prod. n.d.a. *UNESCO Collection: An Anthology of African Music.* vol. 1. *The Music of the Dan.* Barenreiter Musicaphon, BM 30L 2301.

———. n.d.b. *UNESCO Collection: An Anthology of African Music.* vol. 8. *The Music of the Senufo.* Recorded 1962, 1965. Barenreiter Musicaphon, BM 30L 2308.

———. 1971. *Musique guéré: Côte Ivoire.* Vogue, LD764.

———. 1972. *Ivory Coast: Baule Vocal Music.* EMI-Odeon, 3CO64-17842.

The Gambia

Charters, Samuel, prod. 1975a. *African Journey: A Search for the Roots of the Blues.* Vanguard, SRV 73014/5.

———. 1975b. *The Griots: Ministers of the Spoken Word.* Folkways, FE 4178.

———. 1977. *Songs from The Gambia.* Sonet, SNTF 729.

Ifang Bondi. 1979. *Saraba.*

———. 1983. *Mantra.*

———. 1989. *Sanjo.* D&K.

———. 1994. *Daraja.* MW Records, MWCD 3009.

Jobarteh, Amadu Bansang. 1978. *Master of the Kora.* Eavadisc, EDM 101.

———. 1993. *Tabara.* Music of the World, CDT 129.

Jobarteh, Ebraima "Tata Dindin." 1994. *Salam.* World Network, WDR 56.981.

Jobarteh, Malamini. 1989. *Solo.* Proficiat Music. German cassette.

Jobarteh, Malamini, and Dembo Konte. n.d. *Jaliya.* 7081. Cassette.

Jobarteh, Pa Bobo. 1997. *Pa Bobo Jobarteh and Kaira Trio: Kaira Naata.* Real World/WOMAD, WSCD103.

Kabirr, Abdel. 1991. *Abdel Kabirr and The Soto Koto Band: Gumbay Dance!* Higher Octave Music, HOMCD 7044.

Knight, Roderic, prod. 1972. *Kora Manding: Mandinka Music of The Gambia.* Ethnodisc, ER 12102.

Konte, Alhaji Bai. 1973. *Alhaji Bai Konte*. Rounder, 5001.

———. 1989. *Alhaji Bai Konte*. Reissue of 1973 with previously unreleased material. Rounder, CD5001.

Konte, Alhaji Bai, Dembo Konte, and Ma Lamini Jobarteh. 1979. *Kora Duets by Alhaji Bai Konte and Dembo Konte and by Dembo Konte and Ma Lamini Jobate*. Folkways, FW 8514.

Konte, Dembo, and Kausu Kuyateh. 1987a. *Tanante*. Rogue, FSML 2009.

———. 1987b. *Simbomba*. Red House, RHR 27; Rogue, FSML 2011.

———. 1992. *Dembo Konte, Kausu Kuyateh and the Jali Roll Orchestra: Jali Roll*. Omnium, OMM 2004D.

———. 1998. *Kairaba Jabi*. Contains new material and selections from 1987a and 1987b. Rogue, WEBE 9032.

Konte, Dembo, Kausu Kuyateh, and Mawdo Suso. 1995. *Dembo Konte, Kausu Kuyateh and Mawdo Suso: Jaliology*. Xenophile, XENO 4036.

Kuyateh, Jaliba. n.d. *In Paris*. VSSF 001. Cassette.

Mangara, Abdou Rahman. 1993. *Griots of West Africa*. Vol. 2. World Music Institute, WMI 017. Cassette.

Pevar, Marc, prod. 1978. *Music from Gambia*. Vol. 1. Folkways, FE 4521.

Sacko, Sekou, and Ramata Kouyate. 1991. *Sekou and Ramata*. Mande/Island, 510713-4. Cassette.

Saho, Yan Kuba. 1998. *Yan Kuba: Kora Music from Gambia*. Lattitudes, 50611.

Super Eagles. 1969. *Viva Super Eagles*. Decca 258059.

Suso, Bamba. 1969? Recorded interview, with Jali Nyama Suso posing questions and Amadu Bansang Jobarteh playing kora.

Suso, Foday Musa. 1977. *Sounds of West Africa: The Kora and the Xylophone*. Lyrichord, LLST 7308.

———. 1978. *Kora Music from Gambia*. Folkways, FW 8510. Reissued in 1990. Smithsonian Folkways, 08510.

———. 1984a. *Hand Power*. Flying Fish, FF 70318.

———. 1984b. *Watto Sitta*. With Herbie Hancock. Celluloid, CEL 6103. Issued in 1988 as CEL N.Y. 5501.

———. 1986. *Mansa Bendung*. Flying Fish, FF 380.

———. 1987. *Jazz Africa*. With Herbie Hancock. Verve, 847 145-2.

———. 1990. *The Dreamtime*. CMP Records, CMP CD 3001.

———. 1994. *Music from The Screens*. With Philip Glass. Musical Heritage Society, 513781A.

Suso, Foday Musa, and Bill Laswell. 1990. *Ancient Heart: Mandinka and Fulani Music from The Gambia*. Axiom, 314-510148-2.

———. 1997. *Jali Kunda: Griots of West Africa and Beyond*. Ellipsis Arts, CD 3511.

Suso, Jali Nyama. 1972. *Mandinka kora par Jali Nyama Suso*. OCORA, OCR 70.

———. 1988. *Kora Master of The Gambia*. Swedish International Development Authority, BC 8970.

———. 1996. *Gambie: L'art de la kora*. Reissue of 1972 with other unreleased material. OCORA, C 580027.

Suso, Papa. 1993. *Griots of West Africa*. vol. 1. World Music Institute, WMI 016. Cassette.

Suso, Salieu. n.d. *Griot*. Lyrichord, LYRCD 7418.

Guinea

Africa Djole with Fode Youla. 1980. *Kaloum.* Free Music Production, FMP/SAJ 26.

————. n.d.a. *Live: The Concert in Berlin '78.* Reissue of FMP/SAJ 19 and 54. Free Music Production, FMP CD 1.

————. n.d.b. *Basikolo-Né-Né.* Recorded 1984. Reissue of FMP/SAJ 48 and 50. Free Music Production, FMP CD 44.

African Virtuoses (Sekou "Docteur" and Abdoulaye Diabate, Sekou Kouyate). 1983. *African Virtuoses.* JBZ.

Alberts, Arthur S., prod. 1949. *Field Recordings from West Africa.* Archive of Folk Culture, Library of Congress. Recordings from Guinea and Mali are also at Archives of Traditional Music, Indiana University, Accession no. 68-214-F, ATL 3564-3567, 3574-3577.

————. 1950. *Tribal, Folk and Cafe Music of West Africa.* Twelve ten-inch 78 rpm discs in 3 vols. Booklet notes by Melville Herskovits, Duncan Emrich, Richard Waterman, Marshall Stearns, and Arthur Alberts. Field Recordings, WA-1 to WA-24.

————. 1954a. *The Field Recordings of African Coast Rhythms: Tribal and Folk Music of West Africa.* Reissue of selections from 1950. Riverside, RLP 4001.

————. 1954b. *The Field Recordings of New Songs of the African Coast: Modern Cafe Music of Liberia and the Gold Coast.* Reissue of selections from 1950. Riverside, RLP 4003.

————. 1998. *The Arthur S. Alberts Collection: More Tribal, Folk, and Café Music of West Africa.* Previously unreleased material. Rykodisc, RCD 10401.

Les Amazones de Guinée. 1983. *Les Amazones de Guinée: Au coeur de Paris.* Syliphone, SLP 76. Reissued on Bolibana CD 42076-2.

Baga Guiné. 1995. *Guinée: Chants et percussions des femmes baga/Guinea: Songs and Drums of Baga Women.* Buda, 92627-2.

Balla et Ses Balladins. 1967. *Orchestre du Jardin de Guinée sous la direction de Onivogui Balla.* Syliphone, SLP 2.

————. 1972. *Pivi et les Balladins.* Syliphone, SLP 31.

————. 1975. *Balla et Ses Balladins.* Syliphone, SLP 47.

————. 1980. *Objectif perfection.* Syliphone, SLP 75.

————. 1993. *Reminiscin' in Tempo with Balla et Ses Balladins.* Popular African Music, PAM OA 302. Reissue of SLP 75, with selections from Guinea Compilations SLP 8, 15, 23, 35, and interviews.

Les Ballets Africains. 1991. *Les Ballets Africains.* Doundoumba, DDB 40001; Buda, 82513-2.

————. 1993. *Les Ballets Africains: Silo.* Buda, 92579-2.

————. 1995. *Les Ballets Africains: Heritage.* Doundoumba/Buda 92634-2.

Les Ballets Africains de Keita Fodeba. 1956? *Les Ballets Africains de Keita Fodeba.* Vogue, LDM-30040. Issued in 1969 as Vogue CLVLX 297. Also as Coral CRL-57280, and on seven-inch 45 rpm discs as Vogue EPL-7255, 7256, 7257.

————. 1959? *Les Ballets Africains de Keita Fodeba.,* vols. 4–6. Seven-inch 45 rpm discs. Vogue, EPL-7721, 7722, 7723.

————. 1960? *Les Ballets Africains de Keita Fodeba.* Vol. 2. Vogue, LDM-30082. Also issued as Vogue CLVLX 299.

————. 1981a. *Les Ballets Africains.* Vol. 1. Reissue of earlier Vogue and Facelli Kante Chant du Monde material. Bellot, MAG 129.

————. 1981b. *Les Ballets Africains.* Vol. 2. Reissue of earlier Vogue and Facelli Kante Chant du Monde material. Bellot, MAG 130.

Bembeya Jazz (National). 1963. *Sons nouveaux d'une nation nouvelle, la République de Guinée: Orchestre de Beyla.* Tempo, 7015.

————. 1967. *Bembeya Jazz sous la direction de Diaoune Hamidou.* Syliphone, SLP 4.

————. 1970. *Regard sur le passé.* Syliphone, SLP 10. Reissued as SLP 34, SLP 64.

————. 1972. *Dix ans de succès.* Syliphone, SLP 24. Reissued on Bolibana, 42024-2.

————. 1974. *Special recueil-souvenir du Bembeya Jazz National: Mémoire de Aboubacar Demba Camara décédé le 5 avril 1973 à Dakar.* Syliphone, SLP 44. Reissued as SLP 65.

————. 1975. *Le defi.* Syliphone, SLP 59.

————. 1976. *La continuité.* Syliphone, SLP 61.

————. 1985? *Telegramme.* Disques Esperance ESP 8418.

————. 1986? *Moussoukoro.* Disques Esperance ESP 8430.

————. 1986. *Bembeya Jazz National.* Disques Esperence ESP 8431.

————. 1988? *Sabou.* Disques Esperance ESP 8442.

————. 1989? *Wa kele.* Disques Esperance ESP 8460; Sonodisc 8460.

————. 1990. *Regard sur le passé.* Reissue of 1970, with selections from 1976. Bolibana, 42064-2.

————. 199? *Telegramme.* Contains ESP 8418 and selections from ESP 8430, 8431, and 8442. Sonodisc CD 8491.

————. n.d. Guinean cassette of live performance.

Camara, Aboubacar. 1994. *Telephone.* Celluloid/Mélodie, 66950-2.

————. 199? *Baba Moussa.* Bolibana, BIP 93.

————. 1996? *Couma.* T.A.T. Drame. DK 69. Cassette.

————. n.d. *Komi touma.* Camara CK7 008. Cassette.

Camara, Ladji. n.d.a. *Africa, New York.* Recorded 1975. Lyrichord, LYRCD 7345.

————. n.d.b. *Les ballets africains de Papa Ladji Camara.* Lyrichord, LYRCD 7419.

Camayenne Sofa. 1975. *La percée.* Syliphone, SLP 52.

————. 1976. *À grands pas.* Syliphone, SLP 56.

————. 1977. *Attaque.* Syliphone, SLP 60.

Diabate, Djanka. 1991. *Djanka.* Soundwave, 89006-2.

————. n.d. *Sabou sabou.* Sonima, SM1169.

Diabate, Djeli Sory, and Djessou Mory Kante. n.d. *Djeli Sory Diabate dit Papa et Djessou Mory Kante dit Foliba: Foudou.* Guinean cassette.

Diabate, "Djessou" Mama. 199? *La rossignol de la savane.* BGDA 2208.

Diabate, Ibro. 1993. *Allah nana.* Gris-Gris Productions, RB 001; Sonodisc CD 6817.

————. 1995? *Eh! Wotan.* Gris-Gris Productions, RB 003; Sonodisc CD 7018.

Diabate, Kerfala "Papa." 1999. *Grand Papa Diabate: Guitar, Extra Dry.* Popular African Music, PAM AG 703.

Diabate, Mama. 1995. *Koffi cola nâ yo.* Popular African Music, PAM OA 205.

————. 199? *La biche du Manding: Nambiyo.* Alpha Mamadou Cissé et frères, BGDA 9408. Cassette.

Diabate, Prince, and Amara Sanoh. 199? *Lamaranaa.* Buda 92578-2.

Diabate, Sekou "Bembeya." 1985. *Sekou Diabate Bembeya.* Disques Esperence, ESP 8419.

————. 1987. *Digné.* Disques Esperence, ESP 8443.

————. 1995. *Diamond Fingers.* Dakar Sound, DKS 008.

Diabate, Sekou "Bembeya," and Djanka Diabate. 1997. *Samba Gaye.* Dakar Sound, DKS 011.

Diabate, Sekouba "Bambino." 1992. *Le destin.* Popular African Music, OA 201.

————. 1994. *Homage au sylinational de Guinea.* Super Selection, SS 1270. Guinean cassettte.

————. 1996. *Bonya.* Syllart, SYL 83201. Cassette.

————. 1997. *Kassa.* Stern's Africa, STCD 1074.

Diabate, Sona. 1983. *Sons de la savanne: Sona Diabate des Amazones.* Production Enimas Conakry, SLP 77. Selections reissued on *Sona Diabate et M'Mah Sylla: Sahel,* 1988, Triple Earth, Terra 106.

————. 1990a. *Girls of Guinea.* Shanachie, SH 65007.

————. 1990b. *Kankele-ti.* Same as 1990a with two extra tracks. Popular African Music, PAM 401.

————. 1996. *Gare gare.* Popular African Music, PAM 404.

Diaby, Mohamed. 1997. *Karamba dinké.* Mohamed Diaby Productions, Somadisc 003.

Diallo, Alpha Yaya. 199? *Nene.* SA 93279CD.

Diawara, Djeli Moussa [Jawara, Jali Musa]. 1983. *Foté mogoban.* Tangent, LP 7002. Reissued in 1990 as *Yasimika,* Hannibal, HNCD 1355.

————. 1988. *Soubindoor.* Mango CCD9832.

————. 1992. *Cimadan.* Celluloid, 66910-2.

————. 1996. *Sobindo.* Celluloid, 66966-2.

————. 1997? *Flamenkora.* Mélodie, 66999-2.

Diawara, Kade. 1977? *L'archange du Mandingue.* Sylipone, SLP 62.

Dioubate Brothers of Kankan. 1949. Field recordings of Arthur S. Alberts featuring the Dioubate brothers Sidi Moussa, Sidi Mamadi, and Sidi Karamon playing balas along with female vocalists. Recorded 6 May 1949 in Kankan. ATL 3566-3567, Archives of Traditional Music, Indiana University. One selection issued on Alberts 1998.

Dioubate, Missia Saran. 1995? *Missia Saran: Petit piment.* Gris-Gris Productions/ Maestro Sound, RB 002. Cassette.

Dioubate, Oumou. 1992? *Fourou.* Gefraco 070.

————. 1993. *Lancey.* Stern's Africa, STCD 1046.

————. 1995? *Femmes d'Afrique.* Africando, DK 041; Mélodie 38147-2.

————. 1999. *Wambara.* Stern's Africa, STCD 1086.

Djoliba National. 1972. *Les rythmes et chants sacrés des ballets "Djoliba National."* Syliphone, SLP 33.

Ensemble Instrumental Africain de la Radiodiffusion Nationale. 1961a. *Sons nouveaux d'une nation nouvelle, la République de Guinée.* Special edition, series 1, October 2, 1961. Tempo, 7009.

————. 1961b. *Sons nouveaux d'une nation nouvelle, la République de Guinée.* Special edition, series 2, October 2, 1961. Tempo, 7010.

————. 1970. *Guinée an X: Ensemble Instrumental de la Radiodiffusion Nationale.* Syliphone, SLP 9.

Fatala. 1993. *Gongoma times.* Realworld/Caroline, CAROL-2331-2. Originally published 1988 by WOMAD.

Groupe Folklorique de Kankan. 1963. *Sons nouveaux d'une nation nouvelle, la République de Guinée: Groupe Folklorique de Kankan.* Tempo, 7017.

Guinea Compilations. 1961. *Sons nouveaux d'une nation nouvelle, la République de*

Guinée: Quatre enregistrements authentiques des régions de Dinguiraye, Faranah, Kankan et forestière. Tempo, 7008.

————. 1962a. *Sons nouveaux d'une nation nouvelle, la République de Guinée.* Tempo, 7011.

————. 1962b. *Sons nouveaux d'une nation nouvelle, la République de Guinée.* Tempo, 7012.

————. 196? *Boum à Conakry.* With orchestres Paillote, Jardin de Guinée, Bonne Auberge. Guitarists Diara [Kante?] and Sekou ["Docteur" Diabate?]. Electrola Ausland Sonderdienst, Editions Dyl 006.

————. 1967. *Kan ni mankan.* Featuring orchestres Kindia, Paillotta, Jardin de Guinée, Palm-Jazz, Tele-Jazz and Kissidougou. Syliphone, GUI-1.

————. 1970. *Guinée an X.* Featuring Balla et Ses Balladins, and others. Syliphone, SLP 8.

————. 1971. *Guinée an XI.* Featuring Bembeya Jazz National, Keletigui et Ses Tambourinis, Balla et Ses Balladins. Syliphone, SLP 15.

————. 1972a. *Discotheque 70.* Featuring Bembeya Jazz National, Keletigui et Ses Tambourinis, Balla et Ses Balladins, Les Virtuoses Diabate (Papa and Sekou "Docteur" Diabate), and Demba Camara. Syliphone, SLP 23.

————. 1972b. *Trio Federal de Pointe.* Featuring Kebendo Jazz, Horoya Band, Niandan Jazz. Syliphone, SLP 25.

————. 1972c. *Chemin du PDF.* Featuring Bembeya Jazz and Horoya Band. Syliphone, SLP 27.

————. 1973a. *Discotheque 71.* Featuring Balla et Ses Balladins and others. Syliphone, SLP 35.

————. 1973b. *Parade africain.* Featuring Bembeya Jazz and others. Syliphone, SLP 39.

————. 1974a. *Discotheque 72.* Featuring Pivi et les Balladins, Bembeya Jazz National, Keletigui et Ses Tambourinis, and Les Frères Diabate. Syliphone, SLP 40.

————. 1974b. *Neuvième Festival National des Arts et de la Culture.* Syliphone, SLP 42.

————. 1975. *Discotheque 73.* Featuring Bembeya Jazz National, Horoya Band National, Myriam Makeba, Keletigui et Ses Tambourinis, Super Boiro Band. Syliphone, SLP 45.

————. 1976. *Musique sans paroles.* Featuring Sambory Jazz, Quintette Guinéenne, Ballets Africains, Momo Wandel, Trio Papa Kouyate. Syliphone, SLP 54.

————. 1998. *Quarantième anniversaire syliphone.* 2 vols. Syllart/Mélodie 38201-2 and 38292-2.

Horoya Band. 1971. *Apollo, Hombressa.* 45 rpm. Syliphone, SYL 535.

————. 1974. *Savane profonde.* Syliphone, SLP 41.

————. 1997. *Paya-paya.* Reissue of selections from 1971, 1974, and other Syliphone 45 rpm discs. Dakar Sound, DKS 012.

————. n.d. *Horoya Band 74.* Unmarked Guinean cassette (live concert?).

Jawara (*see* Diawara)

Kaba, Baba Djan. n.d. *Feeling Mandingue.* African Music Production/Yaba Music.

————. 1992. *Kankan.* Sonodisc CD 5510.

————. 1993. *Les belles mélodies de la savane.* Sonodisc/EMI. Cassette.

————. 1995? *Sabou.* Mi Cora Son.

————. 1996? *Siguiri.* Mi Cora Son. Same as 1995? with added pieces. Cassette.

Kaloum Star. 1996. *Felenko.* Buda, 82933-2.

Kante, Djessou Mory. 1998. *Guitare sèche.* Popular African Music, PAM AG 701.

Kante, Facelli. 1954? *Chants et danses d'Afrique: Ensembles Keita Fodeba, Kante Facelli.* Chant du Monde, LDZ-S-4275. Also issued as *The Voices and Drums of Africa: Monitor Presents the Exciting Ensembles of Keita Fodeba, Mouangué, Kante Facelli,* Monitor, MF 373, and on seven-inch 45 rpm discs as *Chants et danses de Guinée: Ensemble Keita Fodeba,* LDY-4048, and *Chants et danses d'Afrique: Kante Facelli et son ensemble africain,* LDY-4049.

Kante, Kerfala. 1994. *L'oiseau du Sankara.* Sonodisc 6812.

———. 1995? *Farafina.* Super Selection, BGDA 96001. Cassette.

Kante, Manfila (ex-Ambassadeurs). 1969? Five seven-inch 45 rpm records. First songs on each: *Air Afrique, Mosso Gnouma, Super Bara Serah, Keleya, Confiance Africa.* Djima, DAD 801 to 805.

———. 1986. *Musicale mandingue.* Tangent, TAN 7016.

———. 1988. *Tradition.* Tangent, TAN 7017.

———. 1990. *Diniya.* Disques Esperance, ESP 8467.

———. 1991. *Kante Manfila and Ball Kalla: Kankan Blues.* Popular African Music, OA 201.

———. 1994. *N'na niwale: Kankan Blues II.* Popular African Music, PAM 402.

———. 1995. *Ni kanu.* EMI/Hemisphere 72438-32865-22.

———. 1998. *Back to Farabanah (Kankan Blues Verse III).* Popular African Music, PAM OA 207.

Kante, Manfila "Dabadou" (ex-Keletigui et Ses Tambourinis). 1989. *Momagni.* Guinean cassette, 7782.

Kante, Manfila ["Soba" Manfila] (ex-Balla et Ses Balladins). 1961? *Echos d'Afrique Noire,* vols. 1–3, 6–8: *Kante Manfila.* Seven-inch 45 rpm discs. Vogue EPL 7835 to 7837, 7985 to 7987.

Kante, Mory. 1982a. *Courougnegne.* Ledoux, ASL 7038.

———. 1982b. *N'Diarabi.* Same as 1982a plus one song. Mandingo Productions, MP 0000123.

———. 1984a. *A Paris.* Sacodis, LS 73.

———. 1984b. *A Paris.* Same as 1984a plus two songs. Barclay, BA 281.

———. 1986. *Ten Cola Nuts.* Barclay, 829 087-2.

———. 1987. *Akwaba Beach.* Barclay/Polydor, 833 119-2.

———. 1990. *Touma.* Barclay, 162 539 903-2.

———. 1993. *N'Diarabi.* Remix of 1982b. Celluloid, 66931-2.

———. 1994. *Nongo Village.* Barclay 521 267-2.

———. 1996. *Tatebola.* Misslin, DME 18.

Keita, Mama. 1995. *Paris bimo.* Mi Cora Son, MCS 001.

Keita, Mamady. 1989. *Wassolon.* Fonti Musicali, FMD 581159.

———. 1992. *Nankama.* Fonti Musicali, FMD 195.

———. 1995. *Mogobalu.* Fonti Musicali, FMD 205.

———. 1996. *Hamanah.* Fonti Musicali, FMD 211.

———. 1998, *Afö.* Fonti Musicali, FMO 215.

Keletigui et Ses Tambourinis. 1967a. *Orchestre Paillote sous la direction de Traore Keletigui.* Vol. 1. Syliphone, SLP 1.

———. 1967b. *Orchestre Paillote sous la direction de Traore Keletigui.* Vol. 2. Syliphone, SLP 3.

———. 1972. *Keletigui.* Syliphone, SLP 30.

———. 1975. *Le retour.* Syliphone, SLP 55.

Konate, Famoudou. 1991. *Rhythmen der Malinke*. Notes by Johannes Beer. Museum für Völkerkunde Berlin, CD 18.

———. 1997. *Hörbeispeile zu Rhythmen und Lieder aus Guinea*. Oldershausen: Institut für Didaktik Populärer Musik.

———. 1998. *Famoudou Konaté maître-djembé et l'Ensemble Hamana Dan Ba. Guinée: Percussions et chants malinké*. Buda, 92727-2.

Kouyate et Kouyate. 1990. *Faso*. Mélodie 38783-2.

Kouyate, (El Hadj) Djeli Sory. 1992. *Guinée: Anthologie du balafon mandingue*. 3 vols. Buda, 92520-2, 92534-2, 92535-2.

Kouyate, Famoro. 1992. *Famoro Kouyate and Kike: Assusu*. Popular African Music, PAM OA 204.

Kouyate, Kaniba Ouele. n.d. *Diya*. Camara, CK7 009. Cassette.

———. 1994. *Démocratie*. T.A.T. Audio-visuel Mr. Drame, DK 30. Cassette.

Kouyate, Kemo. 1994. *Kemo Kouyate et Aminata Kamissoko: La colombe de la paix*. Super Sound, SS 2166. Guinean cassette.

Kouyate, Lansana. 1996. *Mandeng djeli*. Lansana Kouyate Productions, LKP 002.

Kouyate, M'Bady, and Diaryatou Kouyate. 1996. *Guinée: Kora et chant du N'Gabu*. 2 vols. Buda, 92629-2 and 92648-2.

Kouyate, Mory Djeli Dienne. 1990. *Lamini Magassouba*. Super Selection, BGDA 9123. Cassette.

———. 1993. *La renaissance mandingue*. Sonia Store Production, BGDA 2091. Cassette.

Kouyate, Ousmane. n.d. *Ousmane Kouyate*. Recorded in Abidjan. Sacodis, LS 62.

———. 1990. *Domba*. Mango CD 539886-2.

Kouyate, Sekouba Kandia. 1990? *Sekouba Kandia Kouyate et les Heritiers*. Super Selection, SS 2822. Guinean cassette.

Kouyate, Sona Djely. 1993. *Hommage à Sona Mamady Conde*. Super Selection, SS 2165. Guinean cassette.

Kouyate, Sory Kandia [Kouyate Sory Kandia]. 1956? *Kouyaté Kandia des Ballets Africains de Keita Fodéba*. Seven-inch 45 rpm disc. Vogue EPL 7257. Also issued on Les Ballets Africains de Keita Fodeba 1956?.

———. 1970. *Kouyaté Sory Kandia*. With Ensemble National Djoliba, and Keletigui et Ses Tambourinis. Syliphone, SLP 12.

———. 1971. *Kouyate Sory Kandia: Tour d'Afrique de la chanson*. With Keletigui et Ses Tambourinis. Syliphone, SLP 20.

———. 1973. *L'epopée du Mandingue: Kouyate Sory Kandia et son trio de musique traditionnelle*. 3 vols. Syliphone, SLP 36, 37, and 38. Reissued 1990, as 2 vols. Syliphone/Bolibana, 42037-2 and 42038-2.

———. 1993. *Kouyate Sory Kandia*. 2 vols. Sonodisc CDS 6814 and 6815.

Orchestre Danse de Gueckedou. 1963a. *Sons nouveaux d'une nation nouvelle, la République de Guinée: Orchestre Danse de Gueckedou*. Tempo 7013.

———. 1963b. *Sons nouveaux d'une nation nouvelle, la République de Guinée: Orchestre Danse de Gueckedou*. Tempo 7014.

Orchestre de Beyla. See Bembeya Jazz.

Orchestre de Kissidougou. 1963. *Sons nouveaux d'une nation nouvelle, la République de Guinée: Orchestre Danse de Kissidougou*. Tempo 7016.

Orchestre de la Garde Republicaine. 1967. *Orchestre de la Garde Republicaine*. Syliphone, SLP 6.

Percussions de Guinée [Percussionists of Guinea]. 1989. *Percussions de Guinée.* Buda, 82501-2; Doundoumba, DDB 40002.

————. 1994. *Percussions de Guinée.* Vol. 2. Buda, 92586-2.

Peuls du Wassolon. 1987. *Guinée: Les Peuls du Wassolon. La danse des chasseurs.* Notes by Patricia Pailleaud, Daniela Langer, and Abdoulaye Diarra. OCORA, C558679.

Rouget, Gilbert, prod. 1954a. *Musique d'Afrique Occidentale: Musique des Malinke, musique des Baoule.* Vogue/Contrepoint MC-20045. Also issued as Counterpoint CPT-529, Esoteric ES-529 (1956), Vogue LDM-30116. Also see Merriam 1970, items 377–79. Reissued in 1993 on CD along with other material on Laserlight Digital, 12179. See Rouget 1999.

————. 1954b. *Dahomey: Musique du roi. Guinée: Musique malinké.* Contrepoint MC-20146. Malinke music also issued on Vogue LDM 30113 (1972). Also see Merriam 1970, items 377–79. See Rouget 1999.

————. 1972. *Musique malinké.* Recorded 1952. Contains selections from 1954b and others recorded at the same time but not released on 33 rpm LP. Vogue, LDM 30113. See Rouget 1999.

————, prod. 1999. *Guineé: Musique des Malinke/Guinea: Music of the Mandinka.* Le Chant du Monde/Harmonia Mundi, CNR 2741112. Reissue of all Guinean material from 1954a, 1954b, and 1972 with expanded notes.

Sano, Mohamed Kemoko. 1992. *Master of the Forest: Mystique d'Afrique.* African Percussion.

Seck, Mamadou, and Boubacar Diabate. 1977. *Africainement votre. . . . Deux authentiques griots Africaines: Mamadou Seck et Boubacar Diabate.* Songhor, Son 8208.

————. n.d. *Chansons africaines d'hier et d'aujourd'hui.* Barclay, 920-043.

Smith, Cheikh M. 1992. *Toubabou balafola.* Popular African Music, OA 203.

Sodia, Amadou. 1999? *Touma sera.* Syllart, SYLAF 96045.

Soumah, Momo "Wandel." 1991. *Matchowé.* Doundoumba, DDB 40004/Buda 82814-2.

Soumano, Sabre. 199? *Moussolou.* Bolibana, BIP 108.

Super Boiro Band. 1972. *Super Boiro Band: Niaissa et sa trompette.* Syliphone SLP 32.

Sylla, Macire. 1996. *Macire Sylla and Djembe Fare.* Misslin, DME 20.

Sylla, M'Mah. 1983. *Le rossignol de Guinée.* Production Enimas Conakry SLP 78. Selections reissued on *Sona Diabate and M'Mah Sylla: Sahel,* 1988, Triple Earth, Terra 106; and on *Les Amazones de Guinée: Au coeur de Paris et M'Mah Sylla,* 1983. Bolibana 42076-2.

Toureille, Pierre, prod. 1992. *Guinée: Récits et épopées.* Ocora, C 560009.

22 Band. 1975. *Dans le vent.* Syliphone, SLP 51.

————. 1980a. *Venez voir.* Syliphone, SLP 67.

————. 1980b. *Mankan.* Syliphone, SLP 68.

Virtuoses Diabate (Abdou, Sekou "Docteur," Siri). 1975. *Virtuoses Diabate: La nouvelle mariée.* Syliphone, SLP 53. Also see Syliphone SLP 23, 35, and 40.

Wassa. 1991. *Songs and Rhythms from the Coastal Region of Guinea.* Buda, 92518-2.

Wofa. 1995. *Rhythms and Songs from the Coastal Region of Guinea.* Buda, 92624-2.

Wofa-Tambou Bo Kannal. 1997? *Guinée-Martinique: Rencontre.* Buda, 92650-2.

Guinea Bissau

Kanoute, Sambala. 1995. *Baden Tonoma.* Sonodisc CDS 6845.

Tabanka Djaz. 1996. *Sperança.* Sonovox, Sono 11.342-2. Also see The Gambia: Suso and Laswell.

Mali

Les Ambassadeurs. 1975a. *Kante Manfila et les Ambassadeurs. Ambassadeur, Mana Mana.* 45 rpm single. Sonafric, SAF 1725.

—. 1975b. *Les Ambassadeurs du Motel. Super pitie, Bolola sanou.* 45 rpm single. Sonafric, SAF 1773.

—. 1976a. *Les Ambassadeurs du Motel. Saranfing, Sabar.* 45 rpm single. Sonafric, SAF 1786.

—. 1976b. *Les Ambassadeurs du Motel. Diandjon, Wara, Kibaru.* Sonafric, SAF 50014.

—. 1977a. *Les Ambassadeurs du Motel de Bamako.* Vol. 1. *Yassoumouka, Fatema, Super pitie, Bolola sanou, Mali denou, Sabar, Saranfing.* Sonafric, SAF 50030.

—. 1977b. *Les Ambassadeurs du Motel de Bamako.* Vol. 2. *N'Na, Nagana, M'Bouram mousso, Salimata, Ray m'bote, Djoula, Tiecolomba.* Sonafric, SAF 50031.

—. 1979a. *Kante Manfila et Salif Keita: Dans l'authenticité.* Vol. 1. *Djandjon, Finzamba, Toura makan, Wara mana.* Badmos, BLP 5031.

—. 1979b. *Kante Manfila et Salif Keita: Dans l'authenticité.* Vol. 2. *Tara, Dimbassin, Toubaka, Badougou.* Badmos, BLP 5032.

—. 1979c. *Ambassadeur International. Mandjou, Kandja, 4V, N'toman, Balla.* Badmos, BLP 5040.

—. 1980. *Ambassadeur International. Seydou Bathily, Saly, Jean ou Paul, Une larme d'amitié, Super coulou.* Badmos, BIR 002.

—. 1981a. *Les Ambassadeurs Internationaux. Tounkan, Wale, Sidiki, Kanlelenti.* Recorded in U.S.A. Sacko, SP 001.

—. 1981b. *Les Ambassadeurs Internationaux: Mana mani, Djata, Marfa, Primpin, Toubaka 81.* Recorded in U.S.A. Sacko, SP 002.

—. 1983a. *Les Ambassadeurs Internationaux: Djougouya, Wassolon foli, Bara wililé, Mandjougoulon.* Recorded in Abidjan. Celluloid, CEL 6635.

—. 1983b. *Best of Ambassadeurs: Mana mani, Sidiki, Marfa, Primpin, Wale.* Reissue of selections from 1981a and 1981b. Celluloid, CEL 6640. Reissued 1990.

—. 1984a. *Salif Keita, Kante Manfila et Les Ambassadeurs Internationaux: Tounkan, Djata, Kanlelenti, Toubaka 81.* Reissue of selections from 1981a and 1981b that are not on 1983b. Celluloid, CEL 6717.

—. 1984b. *Mandjou.* Reissue of 1979c. Celluloid, CEL 6721.

—. 1989. *Les Ambassadeurs Featuring Salif Keita and Kante Manfila. Primpin, Mana mani, Kanlelenti, Tounkan, Sidiki, Djata, Marfa.* Reissue of material from 1981a and 1981b. Tangent/Mélodie CD 47018-2.

—. 1990. *Dance Music from West Africa: Les Ambassadeurs, Featuring Salif Keita and Kante Manfila.* Reissue of 1983b. Rounder 5013.

—. 1992. *Les Ambassadeurs Internationales Featuring Salif Keita: Kolangoman, Seidou Bahkili, Mousso gnaleden, Super koulou, Sali.* Reissue of some material from 1980, along with other contemporaneous material. Rounder CD 5053.

—. 1994. *Salif Keita '69–'80.* Same as 1983b/1990 plus *Mandjou, N'toman,* and *4V.* Sonodisc, Sono 74646.

Bagayoko, Amadou, and Mariam Doumbia. 198? *Le couple aveugle du Mali.* 3 vols. Maikano. Cassettes.

—. 1999? *Amadou et Mariam: Se te djon ye.* Sonodisc, CDS 7044.

Bah-Sadio. 1977. *Folklore peulh chanté par Bah-Sadio.* Sonafric, SAF 50034.

Bajourou. 1993. *Big String Theory.* Green Linnet, GLCD 4008.

Bakayoko, Daouda. 199? *Daouda Bakayoko*. 2 vols. Cassette.

Bamba, Sorry. 1987. *La tonnerre dogon*. Bolibana, BP 15.

Benkadi International. 1997. *Djoulolou*. Djenné Music, DJCD 1004.

Boulton, Laura, prod. 1957. *African Music*. Folkways, FW 8852. Originally published 1939.

Brandes, Edda, Salia Male, and Josué Thierno, prods. 1998. *Mali: Musique bambara du Baninko/Bambara Music of Baninko*. Archives Internationales de Musique Populaire/Disques VDE-GALLO, VDE CD 980.

Camara, Mamadou "Kunkun." 1997. *Khassonka Dunun: Musique traditionnelle du Mali*. Playasound, PS 65187.

Camara, Seydou. 1968. *Kambili*. Recorded by Charles S. Bird in Mali. OT-2350, 71-259-F, Archives of Traditional Music, Indiana University.

Coulibaly, Soungalo. 1992. *Percussion and Songs from Mali*. Arion, ARN-64192/Mélodie, 09265.

Coumare, Koni. n.d. *Koni Coumare accompagnée à la guitare par Fotiqui Diabate*. Fiesta, 360.059.

Dagnon, Dogomani. 1993. *Domani: Wawamba*. Sonodisc, LPS 5513.

Damba, Dialou. n.d. *Boloka Traore*. Super Sound, SS 1. Cassette.

Damba, Fanta. 1971. *Première anthologie de la musique malienne*. Vol. 6. *Fanta Damba: La tradition épique*. Barenreiter Musicaphon, BM 30L 2506.

———. 1975a. *Fanta Damba*. (*Loterie nationale 1*.) Songhoi, SON 8201.

———. 1975b. *Fanta Damba accompagnée à la cora par Barourou Sekou Kouyate*. (*Hamet*.) Songhoi, SON 8202.

———. 1976. *Fanta Damba accompagnée à la cora par Barourou Sekou Kouyate* (*Ousmane Camara*). Songhoi, SON 8205.

———. 1983? *Fanta Damba*. (*Bahamadou Sylla*.) Celluloid, CEL 6637.

———. 1986? *Fanta Damba*. (*Mamadou magadji*.) Disques Esperence, ESP 7518.

Damba, Mah. n.d. *Bakaridjan*. Sweet Sound, S-016.

Damba, Walde. 1989a. *Balabolo*. Vol. 1. Sweet Sound, S-009.

———. 1989b. *Walde Damba et son ensemble: Blondaba*. Vol. 2. Sweet Sound, S-010.

Dembele, Daouda. n.d.a. *El Hadji Sekou Oumar*. Vol. 1. Beni Mariko, BM 5001. Cassette.

———. n.d.b. *Daouda Dembele et sa guitare dans l'histoire de Makan*. Vol. 1. Super Sound, SS-15. Cassette.

———. n.d.c. *Daouda Dembele et son épouse Hawa Dembele*. Vol. 2. Super Sound, SS-16. Cassette.

———. n.d.d. *Histoire de Bakaridjan*. Vol. 1. SSL 233. Cassette.

Diabate, Abdoulaye. 1995. *Djiriyo*. Stern's Africa, STCD 1066.

Diabate, Adama. 1995. *Jako Baye*. Stern's Africa, STCD 1062.

Diabate, Kasse Mady. 1989. *Fode*. Stern's Africa, STCD 1025.

———. 1990. *Kela Tradition*. Stern's Africa, STCD 1034.

———. 1997. *Yilli malo*. Elite Productions. IC0497. Cassette.

Diabate, Kele Monson. n.d. Rendition of Sunjata epic with guitar and koni accompaniment. Unmarked cassette obtained in Mali.

Diabate, Keletigui. 1996. *Keletigui Diabate*. Mission de Coopération Française au Mali, CF 9603. Cassette.

Diabate, Nainy. 1987. *RTM*. Cassette.

———. 1990. *Gna-Gna*. Cassette.

———. 1992. *Farafina mousso*. Camara, CK7 030. Cassette.

————. 1997. *Nafa.* Cassette.

————. 1998. *Nafa.* Reissue of 1992 and 1997. Stern's Africa, STCD 1083.

Diabate, Sidiki. 1987. *Sidiki Diabate and Ensemble: Ba togoma.* Rogue, FMS/NSA 001.

————. 1988. *L'histoire de Cora.* Concert performance at Feskora I, the First International Kora Festival in Conakry, Guinea. African market cassette, ENC 9027.

Diabate, Sira Mori. n.d. *Sira Mori.* Recorded at Radio Mali. Syllart, SYL 83106. Cassette.

Diabate, Toumani. 1988a. *Songhai.* Hannibal, HNCD 1323.

————. 1988b. *Kaira.* Hannibal, HNCD 1338.

————. 1993. *Shake Your World.* Cassette.

————. 1994. *Songhai 2.* Hannibal, HNCD 1383.

————. 1995. *Djelika.* Hannibal, HNCD 1380.

Diabate, Toumani, with "Ballake" Sissoko. 1999. *New Ancient Strings/Nouvelles cordes anciennes.* Hannibal, HNCD 1428.

Diabate, Zani. 1988. *Zani Diabate and the Super Djata Band.* First published 1985. Mango, CCD 9814.

Diabate Family of Kela. 1949. *Field Recordings of Arthur S. Alberts Featuring Vocalist Sira Mori Diabate and an Unidentified Balafon Player.* Recorded 2 May 1949 in Bamako. ATL 3564-3565, Archives of Traditional Music, Indiana University. Selection issued on Alberts 1954a (under Guinea).

————. 1994. *An bè kelen/We Are One: Griot Music from Mali.* PAN, 2015CD.

————. 1997. *Bonya/Respect: Griot Music from Mali #2.* PAN, 2059CD.

Diakite, Bala Djimba. n.d.a. Recordings housed at Institut des Sciences Humaines, Bamako, Mali.

————. n.d.b. Unlabeled Malian market cassette.

————. 1995. *Baala Guimba Diakite: Mande mori.* 3 vols. EMI/Sory Labita. Malian cassettes.

Diakite, Djeneba. 1992. *Djeneba Diakite.* Oubien. Reissued on Syllart/Mélodie 38108-2.

————. n.d. *Farafina lolo.* Samassa 83121. Cassette.

Diallo, Yoro. n.d. *Tiekorobani.* 2 vols. Cassette.

Diarra, Zoumana. 1997. *Ballad of Manding.* Djenné, DJCD 1003. Dist. By Stern's Africa.

Divas from Mali. 1997. *The Divas from Mali: Kandia Kouyate, Mah Damba, Sali Sidibe, Oumou Sangare.* World Network, WDR 28.301.

Divas of Mali. 1996. *Divas of Mali: Great Vocal Performances from a Fabled Land.* Shanachie, 64078.

Doumbia, Abdoul. 1995. *Abdoul Doumbia.* AKD 95.

Doumbia, Nahawa. 1988. *Didadi.* Syllart, SYL 8337.

————. 1990. *Nyama Toutou.* Also contains reissue of 1988. Stern's Africa, STCD 1033.

————. 1993. *Mangoni.* Stern's Africa, STCD 1041.

————. 1997. *Yankaw.* Cobalt, 09278-2.

Doumbia, Ousmane. 1997. *Ousmane Doumbia dit Samba Oussou.* Vol. 1. Cassette.

Drame, Assa. n.d. *Tata Bambo présente sa fille Assa Drame: Hommage aux griots.* Afrique Musique, AM 92002. cassette.

Dyer, Betty, and W. Gurnee Dyer, prods. 1966. *Music of Mali.* Folkways Records, FE 4338.

Electric and Acoustic Mali. 1994. *Electric and Acoustic Mali.* EMI Hemisphere, 7243 8 28186 2 5.

L'Ensemble Instrumental du Mali (National Instrumental Ensemble of Mali). 1971.

Première anthologie de la musique malienne. Vol. 4. *L'Ensemble Instrumental du Mali.* Barenreiter Musicaphon, BM 30L 2504.

————. 1977a. *Soundiata, l'épopée mandingue.* Mali Konkan, KO 770410.

————. 1977b. *Dah Monzon, ou L'épopée bambara.* Mali Konkan, KO 770411.

————. 1977c. *Zazuru.* Mali Konkan, KO 770412.

Kamissoko, Aminata. 1997. *Malamine.* Stern's Africa, STCD 1079.

Kanaga de Mopti. 1977. *Le Kanaga de Mopti: Gamnari.* Mali Kono, KO 770415.

Kanoute, Abdrahamane Gatta. 1992. *Le rossignol du Khasso.* Vol. 2. Samassa, SR 005. Cassette.

Kanoute, Santoutou. 1988. *Signaro.* Beni Mariko, BM 93. Cassette.

Kante, Mamadou. 1993. *Drums from Mali.* Playasound, PLS-65132.

Keita, Karamoko. n.d. *Karamoko Keita.* Super Sound, SS 36. Cassette.

Keita, Moussa ["Idaba" Moussa or Moussa "Segueledie"]. 1993? *Seguele Die.* Vol. 1. Maikano. Cassette.

————. 1997? *Seguele Moussa.* Sory Yattassaye. Cassette.

Keita, Salif. 1987. *Soro.* Mango, 162 539 808-2.

————. 1989. *Ko-yan.* Mango, CCD 9836.

————. 1991. *Amen.* Mango, 162 539 910-2.

————. 1993. *L'enfant lion.* With Steve Hillage. Soundtrack to the film *L'enfant lion.* Mango, 518 084-2. Selections issued on 1994a, and also on *Sirga,* African cassette, 121556.

————. 1994a. *The Mansa of Mali. . . . A Retrospective.* Includes a reissue of *Mandjou* from Les Ambassadeurs 1979c. Mango, 162 539 937-2.

————. 1994b. *Sosie.* Super Sound, SK 94. Cassette. Released 1998 on CD, Stern's Africa, DKMS 96001.

————. 1995. *"Folon" . . . The Past.* Mango, 162 531 022-2.

Kene Star de Sikasso. 1977. *Le Kene Star de Sikasso: Hodi hu yenyan.* Mali Konkan, KO 770416.

Kochyne, Serge, prod. n.d. *Musique du Mali.* Boite à Musique, BAM LD 5772.

Koita, Ami. n.d. *Hine Mansa.* Reissued in 1992 as *Pour collectioner.* Vol. 1. OCWAK 002.

————. 1986? *Ami Koita: Debe.* Disques Esperance, ESP 7517.

————. 1987. *Nakan.* Super Sound, SS 66. Recorded in Abidjan. Malian cassette.

————. 1988. *Tata Sira.* Bolibana, 42079-1.

————. 1989. *Mory Djo.* Oubien, OU 003. Malian cassette.

————. 1992. *Mamaya.* Mélodie, 38120-2.

————. 1993. *Songs of Praise.* Reissue of 1992 and 1987. Stern's Africa, STCD 1039.

————. 1995. *Carthage.* Sonodisc, CDS 6840.

Koita, Diaba. 199? *Khassonke.* Bolibana, BIP 91.

Koita, Moriba. 1997. *Sorotoumou.* Cobalt, 09279-2.

Koite, Habib, and Bamada. 1996. *Muso Ko.* Wotre Music, 612501.

————. 1999. *Ma Ya.* Putumayo, PUTU 146-2.

Kone, Babani. 1998. *Sanou Djala.* Stern's Africa, STCD1085.

Kone, Toumani. n.d. *Toumani Kone.* 4 vols. Cassettes.

Kouyate, Bassi. 1997? *Mali: Chants de griot bambara.* Buda, 92658-2.

Kouyate, Batourou Sekou. 1976. *Sekou Batourou Kouyate et sa cora.* Kouma, KLP 1041.

Kouyate, Fode. 1992. *Anka wili.* Syllart, 83147. Cassette.

————. 1994? *Salatou.* Super Selection, BGDA 95009. Cassette.

————. 1995? *Djelia.* Celluloid/Mélodie, 66947-2.

Kouyate, Kandia. 198? *Amary Daou présente Kandia Kouyate.* A.D. 001.

———. 1988. *Project Dabia.* 7333. Malian cassette.

———. 1993. *Griots of West Africa.* Vol. 3. World Music Institute, WMI 018. Cassette.

———. 1994. *Sa kunu sa.* Camara Production, CK7 094.

———. 1999. *Kita kan.* Stern's Africa, STCD 1088.

Kouyate, Mariam. n.d. *Tara.* Super Sound, SS 22.

Kouyate, Mariam, Mamadou Diabate, and Sidiki Diabate. 1995a. *Mamadou Djon Kounda.* Vol. 1. Samassa IC 1096. Cassette.

———. 1995b. *An ka sidjabou baro.* Vol. 2. Samassa IC 1096. Cassette.

Kouyate, Ramata. See Gambia: Sekou Sacko and Ramata Kouyate.

Kouyate, Sadio. n.d. *Sadio Kouyate et le Trio Mandingue du Mali: La nouvelle étoile.* Vol. 3. Disco Stock, DS 7920 (7220 on disc).

Kouyate, Sanougue. 1990. *Balendala Djibé.* Msimby, MS 001.

Kouyate, Tata Bambo. 1985. *À Paris 1985: Hommage à Baba Cissoko.* SA 300058. Reissued in 1989 as *Jatigui,* Globestyle, CD ORB 042.

———. 1988. *Djely mousso.* Syllart, SYL 8360. Reissued on *Hadja Soumano et Tata Bembo Kouyate,* Syllart/Mélodie 38110-2.

———. 1995. *Bambo.* Sory Labita 210. Malian cassette.

———. n.d. *Oury Sacko.* Samassa 077592-4. Malian cassette.

Maiga, Boncana. n.d. *Jingles, danses et musiques instrumentales.* Celluloid/Mélodie, 66877-2.

Mangala. 1993. *Complainte mandingue blues.* Badaban, BAD 5560.

Las Maravillas de Mali/Les Merveilles du Mali. 1967. *Maravillas de Mali/Les Merveilles du Mali.* EGREM, EGR 6112; Disco Stock, DS 8060. Reissued 1998 on Maestro Sound, MS004; Mélodie 08968-2.

Le Tanneur, Charles, prod. 1959. *Au coeur du Soudan.* Recorded 1956. Chant du Monde, LD-S-8246.

Ministry of Information of Mali/Ministère de l'information du Mali. 1971. *Première anthologie de la musique malienne.* 6 LPs. 1. *Le Mali des steppes et des savannes: Les Mandingues;* 2. *Le Mali du fleuve: Les Peuls;* 3. *Le Mali des sables: Les Songhoy;* 4. *L'Ensemble Instrumental du Mali;* 5. *Cordes anciennes;* 6. *Fanta Damba: La tradition épique.* Barenreiter Musicaphon, BM 30L 2501 to 2506. (See Knight 1972b.)

———. 1972. *Les meilleurs souvenirs de la Première Biennale Artistique et Culturelle de la Jeunesse (1970).* Five LPs. Barenreiter Musicaphon, BM 30L 2601 to 2604 and 2651.

Musiques du Mali. 1995a. *Musiques du Mali: Banzoumana.* Produced by Ibrahima Sylla. Reissue of selected material from Ministry of Information of Mali and other material. Syllart/Mélodie 38901-2.

———. 1995b. *Musiques du Mali: Sira Mory.* Produced by Ibrahima Sylla. Reissue of selected material from Ministry of Information of Mali and other material. Syllart/Mélodie 38902-2.

Mystère Jazz de Tombouctou. 1977. *Le Mystère Jazz de Tombouctou: Leli.* Mali Konkan, KO 770417.

National Badema. 1977. *L'Orchestre "Le National Badema": Soundiata, ou L'épopée mandingue.* Mali Konkan, KO 77.04.10.

———. 1983a. *National Badema.* Syllart, SYL 8355/Mélodie 38748-1. Also issued in 1977 on Mali Konkan, KO77.07.07.

———. 1983b. *National Badema: Kasse Mady.* Syllart, SYL 8390/Mélodie 38767-1.

Orchestre National "A" de la République du Mali. 1972. *L'Orchestre National "A" de la République du Mali*. Barenreiter Musicaphon, BM 30L 2605.

Orchestre Régional de Kayes. 1972. *Les meilleurs souvenirs de la Première Biennale Artistique et Culturelle de la Jeunesse (1970): Orchestre Régional de Kayes*. Barenreiter Musicaphon, BM 30L 2604.

Orchestre Régional de Mopti. 1972. *Les meilleurs souvenirs de la Première Biennale Artistique et Culturelle de la Jeunesse (1970): Orchestre Régional de Mopti*. Barenreiter Musicaphon, BM 30L 2602.

Orchestre Régional de Segou. 1972. *Les meilleurs souvenirs de la Première Biennale Artistique et Culturelle de la Jeunesse (1970): Orchestre Régional de Segou*. Barenreiter Musicaphon, BM 30L 2601.

Orchestre Régional de Sikasso. 1972. *Les meilleurs souvenirs de la Première Biennale Artistique et Culturelle de la Jeunesse (1970): Orchestre Régional de Sikasso*. Barenreiter Musicaphon, BM 30L 2603.

Polak, Rainer, prod. 1994. *Festmusik aus Mali*. Rainer Polak, Bayreuth. Cassette.

———. 1996. *The Mali Tradition: The Art of Jenbe Drumming*. Bandaloop, BLP 001.

———. 1997. *Dònkili/Call to Dance: Festival Music from Mali*. Pan Records, PAN 2060CD.

Radio France Internationale. 1958. *Mali*. 1978. Radio France Internationale, ARC 12, no. 728.

Radio Mali. 197? *Mali: Epic, Historical, Political and Propaganda Songs of the Socialist Government of Modibo Keita (1960–1968)*. Vol. 1. Recorded at Radio Mali 1960–64. Lyrichord, LLST 7325; Albatros, VPA 8326.

———. 1977. *Mali: Epic, Historical, Political and Propoganda Songs of the Socialist Government of Modibo Keita (1960–1968)*. Vol. 2. Recorded at Radio Mali 1960–64. Albatros, VPA 8327.

Rail Band. 1972. *Orchestre Rail-Band de Bamako*. Barenreiter Musicaphon, BM 30L 2606.

———. 1975. *Rail Band*. 5 vols. RCA/HMV, HNLX 5147 to 5151. HNLX 5151 contains *Soundiata*.

———. 1976a. *Melodias Rail Band du Mali*. With Salif Keita. Kouma, KLP 1040.

———. 1976b. *Concert Rail Band du Mali*. Kouma, KLP 1042.

———. 1976c. *Melodias Rail Band du Mali*. Reissue of part of 1972 with other material. With Salif Keita and Fanta Damba. Kouma. KLP 1043.

———. 1977. *Rail Band: Mory Kante*. Syllart SYL 8378/38757.

———. 1979. *Affair social: l'Orchestre Super Rail Band International*. Sacodis, LS 25.

———. 1982. *Super Rail Band: Buffet hôtel de la gare de Bamako*. 2 vols. Recorded in Togo. RCAM 3301 and 3302.

———. 1985. *New Dimensions in Rail Culture: The Super Rail Band of the Buffet Hôtel de la Gare de Bamako, Mali*. Reissue of selections from 1982. Globestyle, ORB 001.

———. 1992. *Super Rail Band de Bamako*. Label Bleu/Indigo LBLC 2500.

———. 1995. *Super Rail Band: Mansa*. Label Bleu/Indigo LBLC 2520.

———. n.d. *Rail Band: Salif Keita et Mory Kante*. Syllart/Mélodie, 38750-2. Reissue of 1972 and 1975 (HNLX 5151).

Rhythms of Mali. 1995. *Drums of Mali: Baco Djicorni*. Djenné, DJCD 1001. Distributed by Stern's Africa.

Sacko, Fanta. 1972. *Musique du Mali*. Vol. 1. *Fanta Sacko*. Barenreiter Musicaphon BM 30L 2551. (See Knight 1973b.)

Sacko, Ousmane. 1987. *La nuit des griots.* Recorded 1983. Ocora/Harmonia Mundi, HM CD83.

Sako, Mokontafe [Monkontafe]. 1960? *Echos du Mali: Sacko Monkontafé.* Vogue, EPL 7763.

———. 1976a. *Farafina mousow.* Sonafric, SAF 50012.

———. 1976b. *La grande vedette malienne.* Sonafric, SAF 50021.

———. 1977a. *Les aigles du Mali.* Sonafric, SAF 50033.

———. 1977b. *Monkontafe Sako et son Ensemble Traditionnel.* Sonafric, SAF 50059.

Samake, Sibiri. 1991. *Mali: Musique des chasseurs de Sebenikoro.* Buda 92523-2.

Sangare, Amadou. 199? *Amadou Sangare dit "Bari."* 2 vols. Cassette.

Sangare, Oumou. 1990. *Moussolou.* Syllart. Reissued 1991, World Circuit, WCD 021.

———. 1993. *Ko sira.* World Circuit, WCD 036.

———. 1996. *Worotan.* World Circuit, WCD 045.

Seck, Cheick Tidiane, and Hank Jones. 1995. *Hank Jones Meets Cheick-Tidiane Seck and the Mandinkas: Sarala.* Verve, 314 528 783-2.

Sidibe, Sali. 1993a. *Wassoulou Foli.* Stern's Africa, STCD 1047.

———. 1993b. *From Timbuktu to Gao.* Shanachie 65011.

Sissoko, Bazoumana. 1972a. *Musique du Mali.* Vol. 2. *Bazoumana Sissoko, le vieux lion I.* Barenreiter Musicaphon, BM 30L 2552. (See Knight 1973b.)

———. 1972b. *Musique du Mali.* Vol. 3. *Bazoumana Sissoko, le vieux lion II.* Barenreiter Musicaphon, BM 30L 2553. (See Knight 1973b.)

Sissoko, Djelimoussa "Ballake." 1998. *Djelimoussa Sissoko: Kora.* Cinq Planètes, CP 023012.

———. Forthcoming. *Jeli Moussa Sissoko: Kora Music from Mali.* Bandaloop.

Sissoko, Mama. n.d. *Nakana.* MKB, MS 4942. Cassette.

———. 1997. *Amours jarabi.* Buda, 82940-2.

Soumano, Hadja. 1988. *N teri diaba.* Reissued on *Hadja Soumano et Tata Bembo Kouyate.* Mélodie 38110-2.

Super Biton de Segou. 1977a. *Nyeleni.* Mali Konkan, KO 770413.

———. 1977b. *Nyaangaran foli.* Mali Konkan, KO 770414.

———. 1986. *Afro jazz du Mali.* Bolibana, BP 13.

Tounkara, Djeli Mady [Jalimadi]. n.d. *Seigneur Djali Madi Tounkara et le Rail Band du Mali.* 2 vols. See Sadio Kouysate for vol. 3. Disco Stock, DS 7918 and 7919.

Toure, Ali Farka. 1976a. *Ali Toure "Farka."* Sonafric, SAF 50016.

———. 1976b. *Ali Toure "Farka": Speciale biennale du Mali.* Sonafric, SAF 50020.

———. 1976c. *Ali Toure Farka.* Sonafric, SAF 50032.

———. 1977. *Ali Toure Farka.* Sonafric, SAF 50060.

———. 1979. *Ali Toure dit "Farka."* Sonafric, SAF 50085.

———. 1984. *Ali Farka Toure.* Disques Esperance, ESP 165558.

———. 1988a. *Ali Toure Farka.* Disques Esperance, ESP 8448.

———. 1988b. *Ali Farka Toure.* Mango CCD9826.

———. 1990. *African Blues.* Shanachie, SH 65002.

———. 1992. *The Source.* Hannibal, HNCD 1375.

———. 1994. *Ali Farka Toure with Ry Cooder: Talking Timbuktu.* Hannibal/World Circuit HNCD 1381.

———. 1996. *Radio Mali.* World Circuit, WCD 044.

Traore, Boubacar. 1992. *Kar Kar.* Stern's Africa, STCD 1037.

———. 199? *Mariama.* Stern's Africa, STCD 1032.

———. 1997? *Sa golo*. Indigo, 2534.

Traore, Djigui. 1999. *M'Bolon*. Cobalt, 09290-2.

Traore, Lobi. 199? *Bambara Blues*. Cobalt 82816-2.

Traore, Moussa. 1999. *Mali foli*. Talking Drum Records, TDCD 80108.

Traore, Zoumana. 1996. *Zoumana Traore*. Cassette.

Troupe Folklorique Malienne. n.d. *African Rhythms and Instruments*. Vol. 1. Recorded at the Première Festival Panafricaine, Algiers, 1969. Lyrichord, LYRCD 7328.

Troupes artistiques. 1972. *Les meilleurs souvenirs de la Première Biennale Artistique et Culturelle de la Jeunesse (1970): Troupes artistiques*. Barenreiter Musicaphon, BM 30L 2651.

Women of Mali. 1993. *The Wassoulou Sound: Women of Mali*. Stern's Africa, STCD 1035.

———. 1994. *The Wassoulou Sound: Women of Mali*. Vol. 2. Stern's Africa, STCD 1048.

Zobel, Clemens, prod. Forthcoming. *Hunter's Harp Music from Mali: The Siaka Sidibe Ensemble and Sidikiba Keita*. Bandaloop.

Senegal

Ames, David, prod. 1955. *Wolof Music of Senegal and The Gambia*. Folkways, P462. Reissued 1976, FE 4462.

Badjie, Saikuba. 1996. *Bougarabou: Solo Drumming of the Casamance*. Village Pulse, VPU 1005.

Baldeh, Amadu Bamba. 1996. *Amadu Bamba: Drums of the Firdu Fula*. Village Pulse, VPU 1004.

Cissoko, Sunjul. 1992. *Songs of the Griots (II): Sunjul Cissoko and Marhawa Kouyate*. JVC, VICG 5227.

Conde, Sekou. 1977. *Conde Sekou et le Koten' Diming Jazz: Sur les rives du fleuve Séné-gal*. Sonafric, SAF 50066.

———. n.d.a. *Sekou Conde et l'Orchestre Sinissiguy*. Ledoux, ASL 7013.

———. n.d.b. *Sekou Conde et son Orchestre le Sinin-Sigui Band*. Nassabou, SA 300042.

Diagne, Boubacar. 1992. *Tabala Wolof: Sufi Drumming of Senegal*. Village Pulse, VP-1002.

Diatta, Pascal. 1992. *Pascal Diatta and Sona Mane: Simnade + 4*. Rogue FMSD 5017.

Diop, Mapate. 1992. *Sabar Wolof: Dance Drumming of Senegal*. Village Pulse, VP-1003.

Drame, Lalo Keba. 1984. *Hommage à Lalo Keba Drame*. ABC, 1309. Cassette.

Koite, Sourakata. 1990. *Les griots: Sourakata Koite et Diombo Kouyate*. Koch International, 322 412.

———. n.d. *In Holland*. Tangent.

Konte, Lamine. 1974. *La kora du Sénégal: Les rythmes, les percussions et la voix de Lamine Konté*. Arion, ARN 33.179.

———. 1975. *La kora: Les rythmes, les percussions et la voix de Lamine Konté*. Vol. 2. Arion, ARN 33.313.

———. 1977. *Lamine Konte*. Sonafric, SAF 50049.

———. 198? *La kora du Sénégal*. Vol. 1. Arion, 64036.

———. 1989. *La kora du Sénégal*. Vol. 2. *Chant et poésie d'Afrique Noire*. Arion, ARN 64070. Contains selections recorded 1973, 1977, and 1983.

———. 1990. *Songs of the Griots*. JVC, VICG-5008.

Konte, Lamine, and Fode Drame. n.d. *Cora Funk*. Ebony, ER 5.

Kouyate, Diombo. See Sourakata Koite.

Kouyate, Djimo. 1992a. *Fa kae: Manding Kora Music*. Cassette.

———. 1992b. *Yankadi: Manding Drum Rhythms*. Cassette.

———. 1996. *Djimo Kouyate and Mamaya African Jazz: Gorée*. Mamaya, 71646.

Kouyate, Maa Hawa. n.d.a. *Maa Hawa Kouyate et Soundioulou Cissoko*. Vol. 1. 7578. Cassette.

———. n.d.b. *Le couple royal de la musique traditionnelle*. Vol. 2. 413. Cassette.

Kouyate, Morikeba. 1997. *Music of Senegal*. Traditional Crossroads, 4285.

Krémer, Gérard, prod. 1989. *Mass and Hymns from the Monastery of Keur Moussa, Senegal*. Recorded 1980. Arion 64095.

Lo, Ismael. 1985. *Xiif*. Syllart/Celluloid, SYL 8321/CEL 8725.

———. 1987. *Natt*. Syllart, SYL 8335.

———. 1989. *Diawar*. Stern's Africa, STC 1027.

———. 1990. *Ismael Lo*. Mango, 162 539 919-2.

Ly, Mamadou. 1992. *Mandinka Drum Master*. Village Pulse, VP-1001.

Maal, Baaba. 1988. *Wango*. Syllart, SYL 8348.

———. 1989. *Djam leelii*. Recorded 1984. Mango CCD 9840.

———. 1990. *Taara*. Syllart, SYL 8395.

———. 1991. *Baayo*. Mango, 162 539 907-2.

———. 1992. *Lam Toro*. Mango.

———. 1994. *Firin' in Fouta*. Mango, 162 539 944-2.

———. 1998. *Nomad Soul*. Palm Pictures, PLMCD 2002.

Mane, Malang. 1996. *Balanta Balo: Talking Wood of Casamance*. Village Pulse, VPU 1006.

Mbaye, Ousmane. 1959? *Echos d'Afrique Noire*. Vols. 4 and 5. *Ousmane Mbaye*. Seven-inch 45 rpm disc. Vogue EPL 7838 and 7839.

Ndour, Youssou. 1989. *The Lion*. Virgin, 91253-2.

———. 1990. *Set*. Virgin, 91426-2.

———. 1992. *Eyes Open*. Columbia, CK 48714.

———. 1994. *The Guide (Wommat)*. Chaos/Columbia, OK 53828.

Nikiprowetzky, Tolia, prod. 1965a. *La musique des griots: Sénégal*. Ocora, OCR 15.

Orchestre Africa Djembe. 1993. *Les tambours de Gorée/The Drums of Gorée*. Playa Sound, PS 65104.

Percussions d'Afrique. n.d. *Percussions d'Afrique/Percussions of Africa*. Playasound, PS 65004.

Rose, Doudou Ndiaye. 1994. *Djabote*. Realworld/Caroline, CAROL 2340-2.

Sapir, J. David, prod. 1965. *The Music of the Diola-Fogny of the Casamance, Senegal*. Folkways, FE 4323.

Seck, Mansour. 1994. *Nder Fouta Tooro*. Vol. 1. Stern's Africa, STCD 1061.

———. 1995. *Nder Fouta Tooro*. Vol. 2. Stern's Africa, STCD 1073.

Sedhiou Band. 1998. *Africa Kambeng*. Africassette, AC 9404.

Senegal. 1991. *Senegal: Kora, balafon, guitare, percussions et chants*. Arion ARN 64163. Reissued from 1981.

Sissoko, Bakary. 195? *Bakary Sissoko et Daouda Diabaté des Ballets Africains de Keita Fodéba*. Seven-inch 45 rpm disc. Vogue EPL 7256.

Super Diamono. 1984. *Mam*. Mélodie, 8011.

———. 1987. *People*. Encore, ENC 139.

———. 1989. *Cheikh Anta Diop*. Celluloid/Mélodie, 8530-2.

Sunkett, Mark, prod. 1994. *Mandiani Drum and Dance*. White Cliffs Media, WCM 9826.

Tama Walo. 1998. *Keepers of the Talking Drum*. Village Pulse, VPU-1008.

Thiam, Assane. n.d. *Mame*. Saprom. Senegalese cassette.

Tom-Tom Arabesque. 1990. *The Drums of Shell Island, Senegal*. JVC, VICG-5009-2.

Toure Kunda. 1980. *Les frères griots*. Celluloid, CEL 6549. Reissued on CD CEL 6779.

―――. 1982. *Turu*. Celluloid, CEL 6599. Reissued on CD CEL 6779.

―――. 1983. *Amadu tilo*. Celluloid, CEL 6646. Reissued on CD CEL 6781.

―――. 1984a. *Casamance au claire de lune*. Celluloid, CEL 6663. Reissued on CD CEL 6781.

―――. 1984b. *Paris-Ziguinchor (Live)*. Celluloid, CEL 6710/11.

―――. 1985. *Natalia*. Celluloid, CEL 6740. Reissued on CD CEL 6741.

―――. 1986. *Toubab-bi*. Trémal/RCA 310233.

―――. 1989? *Best of Toure Kunda*. Celluloid, CEL 66805-2.

Zanetti, Vincent, prod. 1997. *Senegal: The Saoruba from Casamance*. VDE-Gallo, VDE CD 926.

Miscellaneous

Africando. 1993. *Trovador*. Stern's Africa, STCD 1045.

―――. 1994. *Tierra Tradicional*. Stern's Africa, STCD1054.

―――. 1996. *Gombo Salsa*. Stern's Africa, STCD 1071.

―――. 1998. *Baloba!* Stern's Africa, STCD 1082.

Ames, David W., prod. n.d.a. *UNESCO Collection: An Anthology of African Music*. Vol. 6. *Nigeria: Hausa Music I*. Barenreiter Musicaphon, BM 30L 2306.

―――. n.d.b. *UNESCO Collection: An Anthology of African Music*. Vol. 7. *Nigeria: Hausa Music II*. Barenreiter Musicaphon, BM 30L 2307.

―――. n.d.c. *UNESCO Collection: An Anthology of African Music*. Vol. 11. *Nigeria III: Igbo Music*. Recorded in 1963–64, 1975. Barenreiter Musicaphon, BM 30L 2311.

Arom, Simha, prod. 1975. *Musical Atlas: The Peuls*. EMI-Odeon, 3C064-18121.

Blakey, Art. 1976. *Backgammon*. Roulette, SR-5003.

Brandily, Monique, prod. n.d. *UNESCO Collection: An Anthology of African Music*. Vol. 9. *Chad: Music of Kanem*. Barenreiter Musicaphon, BM 30L 2309.

―――. 1980. *Tchad: Musique du Tibesti*. CNRS/Le Chant du Monde, LDX 74722.

Duvelle, Charles, prod. 1966. *Musique maure*. Ocora, OCR 28.

Eide, Khalifa Ould, and Dimi Mint Abba. 1990. *Moorish Music from Mauritania*. World Circuit, WCD 019.

Gnaoua d'Essaouira. 1993. *Maroc: Hādra des Gnaoua d'Essaouira*. OCORA, C560006.

Hood, Mantle. 1969. *Africa East and West*. Institute of Ethnomusicology, UCLA, IER 6751.

Jay, Stephen, prod. 1976. *Africa: Drum, Chant and Instrumental Music, Recorded in Niger, Mali and Upper Volta by Stephen Jay*. Nonesuch, H-72073.

―――. 1979. *Africa: Ancient Ceremonies, Dance Music and Songs of Ghana*. Nonesuch, H-72082.

Jenkins, Jean, prod. 1979. *Sierra Leone: Musiques traditionnelles*. Ocora, 558549.

Mandeng Tunya. 1997. *M'Faké*. Mandinka Magic Music. U.S. cassette.

Mélodies nouvelles africaines. 1981. *Mélodies nouvelles africaines: Cora, balafon, guitar*. Sonafric, SAF 50 108.

Nikiprowetzky, Tolia, prod. 1965b. *Niger: La musique des griots*. OCORA, OCR 20.

————. 1966? *Nomades du Niger: Musique des Touareg, musique des Bororo.* Ocora, OCR 29.

————. 1990. *Anthologie de la musique du Niger.* OCORA, C 559056.

Nimba. 199? *Percussions et musiques d'Afrique de l'Ouest.* MPO 111001.

Oro, Catherine, and Albert Loudes, prods. 1976. *Assalam Aleikoum Africa: Traditional and Modern Folk Music of West Africa.* Vol. 2. Contains one track with Senegalese singer Fanta Sakho. Antilles, AN 7033.

Quersin, Benoit, prod. n.d. *Nigeria: Musiques du plateau.* OCORA, OCR 82.

Schuyler, Philip, prod. 1970. *UNESCO Collection: Musical Anthology of the Orient.* Vol. 27. *Morocco I: The Music of Islam and Sufism in Morocco.* Barenreiter Musicaphon, BM 30SL 2027.

————. 1971? *Moroccan Folk Music.* Lyrichord, LLST 7229.

————. 1972. *Music of Morocco: The Pan-Islamic Tradition.* Lyrichord, LLST 7240.

————. 1978. *The Rwais: Moroccan Berber Musicians from the High Atlas.* Lyrichord, LLST 7316.

Verdier, Raymond, and Anne-Marie de Lavilléon, prods. n.d. *Musique kabiye.* OCORA, OCR 76.

VIDEOGRAPHY

Burkina Faso
Kouyate, Dani. dir. 1995. *Keita: The Heritage of the Griot.* San Francisco: California Newsreel.

Côte d'Ivoire
Cadiou, Claude, dir. 1987. *La vie platinée.* Features L'Ensemble Koteba d'Abidjan with Souleymane Koly and Mamady Keita. Paris: La Cinématheque de la cooperation (AUDECAM).

Le Ballet National de Côte d'Ivoire. n.d. *The Best of African Ballet: Le Ballet National de Côte d'Ivoire, West Africa.* 3 vols.

The Gambia
Burns, Bonnie, prod., and Sandi F. Fulberton, dir. 1990. *Jazz Africa.* With Foday Musa Susa and Herbie Hancock. Polygram Video, 082-715-1.

Haydon, Geoffrey, and Dennis Marks, dirs. 1984. *Repercussions: A Celebration of African American Music.* Program 1. *Born Musicians: Traditional Music from The Gambia.* Chicago: Home Vision.

Knight, Roderic, dir. 1992. *Music of the Mande Parts I and II.* Original Music, OMV 006.

————. 1995. *Music of the Mande Part III: Mandinka Drumming.* Original Music, OMV 009.

————. 1997. *Music of the Mande Part IV: Balanta Balo.* Original Music.

Suso, Jali Nyama. 1992. *Jali Nyama Suso: Kora Player of The Gambia.* Produced by Roderic Knight. Original Music OMV 003.

Guinea
Achkar, David, dir. 1991. *Allah Tantou (God's Will).* San Francisco: California Newsreel.

Les Ballets Africains. 1967. *International Zone: Africa Dances.* Les Ballets Africains at the United Nations. Contemporary Films/McGraw-Hill.

————. 1991. *Les Ballets Africains, National Dance Company of Guinea.* A special one-hour performance recorded for Channel Four Television in the United Kingdom by After Image. Doundoumba, DDB 40001.

————. 1996. *Heritage.* A full two-hour performance recorded at Queensland Performing Arts Complex, Brisbane, Australia. Doundounba.

————. n.d. *Kalim International présent: Les Ballets Africains par Justin Morel.* Kalim International.

Chevalier, Laurent, dir. 1991. *Djembefola.* Interama Video Classics, 1994.

Dance of Guinea. 1991. Ten hours of video footage shot on a three-week tour of five regions of Guinea researching new material for Les Ballets Africains. With Kemoko

Sano, Hamidou Bangoura, and Lamine Camara (cameraman). MGZIC 9-5068 to 5072. Jerome Robbins Archive of the Recorded Moving Image, Dance Collection of the New York Public Library for the Performing Arts at Lincoln Center.

Diabate, Karamba. 1996. *Journey into Rhythm. The Comprehensive Learning Experience: The Rhythms of West Africa.* 2 vols. Third Ear Productions.

Diabate, Sayon Kane. n.d. *Sayon Kane.* Production T.A.T. Drame.

Sano, Mohamed Kemoko. 1991. *Kemoko Sano Teaches African Dance from the Republic of Guinea.* Sano Videos (P.O. Box 442, Scarsdale, N.Y. 10583).

———. 1994. *Les Merveilles d'Guinea: The Marvels of Guinea, West African Ballet Company.* African Percussion.

Mali

Austin, Chris, dir. 1991. *Salif Keita: Destiny of a Noble Outcast.* Island Visual Arts 440 083 125-3.

Les Ballets Maliens. 198? Festival International de la danse et de la musique à Kupio en Finland. Malian television emission.

Boulton, Laura, prod. 1934. Silent film shot in Mali and Guinea. Human Studies Film Archives, Smithsonian Institution, AF-87.9.26.

Cisse, Souleymane, dir. 1987. *Yeelen (Brightness).* San Francisco: California Newsreel.

Diabate, Kasse Mady. 1989. *Live Concerts: Kasse Mady Diabate.* Le Sabre/Celluloid/TF1.

Finch, Nigel, dir. 1989. *Salif Keita Live.* Polygram Video.

Kidel, Mark, prod. and dir. 1991. *Bamako Beat: Music from Mali.* BBC.

Kidel, Mark, prod., and Dennis Marks, exec. prod. 1990. *Under African Skies. Mali: The Music of Life.* BBC Education and Training. Dist. by Films for the Humanities and Sciences, 1997.

Kanoute, Abrahamane. 1991. *Le rossignol du Khasso.* Africassette, AFK 009. 45 rue Doudeauville 75018 Paris.

Ndao, Moustapha. n.d. *Le Mali en fête.* Camara Production CK7. Rue Marcadet 75018 Paris.

———. 199? *Ballet National du Mali.* Paris: T. A. T. Audio-visuel Drame.

Schiano, Jean-François, and Djingarey Maiga. n.d. *Musiques du Mali: I. Les gens de la parole.* Les films du village.

Sissoko, Cheick Oumar, dir. 1995. *Guimba the Tyrant.* San Francisco: California Newsreel.

Symphonie Mandingue. n.d. *La Symphonie Mandingue.* With Toumani Diabate, Keletigui Diabate, BaSekou Kouyate, Kasse Mady Diabate, and Kandia Kouyate. Production T.A.T. Drame. 50 rue Doudeauville, 75078 Paris, France. 42-23-86-00.

Senegal

Ba, Ndiouga Moctar, dir. 1993. *You, Africa! Youssou N'Dour and Super Étoile, the African Tour.* San Francisco: California Newsreel.

Le Ballet National de Senegal. n.d. *Le Ballet National du Senegal Presents: Pangols.* Columbia Artists Management.

Brice, Andy, prod. and dir. 1990. *Lions of Dakar.* New York: Gessler.

Kouyate, Djimo, prod. 1991. Personal videotape of *Feskora: Second International Kora Festival.* Sedhiou, Senegal, 1991.

Maal, Baaba. n.d. *Live concerts.*

Soulé, Béatrice, and Eric Millot, dirs. 1993. *Djabote: Doudou N'Diaye Rose.* Montpelier, Vt.: Multicultural Media.

Sunkett, Mark. 1998. *Mandiani Drum and Dance: A Journey to the Drum Culture of Senengal.* Gilsum, N.H.: White Cliffs Media.

Miscellaneous

Fujii, Tomoaki, ed. 1990. *The JVC Video Anthology of World Music and Dance.* Tokyo: Victor Company of Japan.

Hamm, Wolfgang, dir. 1993. *Die Kunst der Griots.* ZDF/ARTE.

Huraux, Marc, and François Migeat. 1988. *Batouka: First International Festival of Percussion.* With Djoliba National (Mali), and Adama Drame. Rhapsody Films.

Perry, Hart, dir. 1991. *Rhythms of the World Anthology.* Island Visual Arts, 440 083 873-3.

PERSONAL INTERVIEWS, LESSONS, AND RECORDINGS

Camara, Ladji. 1996. Personal unrecorded interview. September 1996. Bronx, N.Y.

Camara, Omar, and Babanding Sanyang. 1989. Personal recordings. 1988–89. Brikama, The Gambia.

Diabate, Djeli Mady, and Kemogo Diabate. 1990. Personal recordings. March 1990. Kita, Mali.

Diabate, Sidiki. 1990. Personal recordings. December 1989 to March 1990. Bamako.

Diabate Family. 1994. Personal recorded and unrecorded interviews with Sekou "Docteur," Kerfala "Papa," and Sire. August 1994. Conakry.

Diakite, Bala Djimba. 1990. Personal recording. Accompanied by Bakary Samake. July 1990. Bala, Mali.

Doumbia, Abdoul. 1995. Classes at the First Summer Jembe Institute, Greensboro, N.C. June 1995.

Doumbia, Fode (Kindia, Guinea). 1990. Personal recordings. July 1989 to May 1990. Brikama and Bakau, The Gambia.

Doumbia, Fode, and Mamadou Doumbia. 1990. Personal videorecordings. May 1990. Bakau, The Gambia.

Dounbouya, Bala (Norasoba, Guinea). 1989. Personal recordings. December 1988 to May 1989. Dakar.

Jiba, Abasi, and Ansumana Koli. 1990. Personal recordings. May 1990. Brikama, The Gambia.

Jobarteh, Amadou Bansang. 1990. Personal recordings. Portfolios A and B. November 1989 to July 1990. Kembujeh, The Gambia.

———. 1992. Personal unrecorded interviews. February to March 1992. Princeton, N.J.

Kante, Manfila (ex-Ambassadeurs). 1994. Personal unrecorded interviews. July 1994. Grigny, France.

Kante, "Soba" Manfila. 1994. Personal unrecorded interviews. August 1994. Conakry.

Kone, Drissa. 1990. Personal recordings. 1990. Bamako, Mali.

Konte, Dembo. 1989. Personal recordings. June and July 1989. Brikama, The Gambia.

Kouyate, Batrou Sekou. 1990. Personal unrecorded interview. July 1990. Bamako.

Kouyate, Mamadou. 1989. Personal unrecorded lessons and classes at the Conservatoire National. October 1988 to April 1989. Dakar, Senegal.

Kouyate, Moussa. 1990. Personal recordings. January to March 1990. Bamako.

Kouyate, Namankoumba (Niagassola, Guinea). 1994. Personal recordings. August 1994. Conakry.

Kouyate, "Salikene" Jemori. 1990. Personal recordings. July 1990. Niagassola, Guinea.

Kouyate, Siriman (Koundara, Guinea). 1989. Personal recordings. September to November 1989. Brikama, The Gambia.

Onivogui, Balla. 1994. Personal unrecorded interviews. August 1994. Conakry.

Souma, Momo "Wandel." 1994. Personal unrecorded interviews. August 1994. Conakry.

Tounkara, Solo, Fadiala Tounkara, and Toumani Diabate. 1990. Personal videorecording. Bamako.

Traore, Kabine "Tagus." 1995. Personal unrecorded interviews and publicity material for the band Sabari. March 1995. Leiden.

SUBJECT INDEX

The following abbreviations have been used with page numbers in all the indexes: f. = figure, n. = note, m. = map, pl. = plate, t. = table, tr. = transcription. For example, 86f. 2 means page 86, figure 2.

PERSONAL NAME INDEX

Includes authors, artists, and historical figures. For musical groups, see subject index.

Title Index

Includes titles of songs, albums, books, and films